# THE
# AMERICAN WOMAN
# IN SPORT

**ELLEN W. GERBER, Ph.D.**
*University of Massachusetts, Amherst*

**JAN FELSHIN, Ed.D.**
*East Stroudsburg (Pa.) State College*

**PEARL BERLIN, Ph.D.**
*University of North Carolina, Greensboro*

**WANEEN WYRICK, Ed.D.**
*University of Texas, Austin*

**ADDISON–WESLEY PUBLISHING COMPANY**
*Reading, Massachusetts • Menlo Park, California • London • Don Mills, Ontario*

This book is in the
ADDISON–WESLEY SERIES IN
THE SOCIAL SIGNIFICANCE OF SPORT

Consulting Editor
John W. Loy

ISBN 0-201-02353-9
ABCDEFGHIJ-MA-7987654

# Foreword

The purpose of the *Social Significance of Sport Series* is to provide an initial understanding of the manifold interrelationships among sport, culture, and society. This objective is to be achieved through the publication of several books whose authors examine the social phenomenon of sport from different theoretical and methodological perspectives. The focus of some authors will be on given subfields of sport studies, while the focus of other authors will be on substantive topics relevant to one or more general areas of sport studies.

Books representing three subfields of sport studies have been published to date. These are: Harold VanderZwaag, *Toward A Philosophy of Sport* (1972); John Betts, *America's Sporting Heritage: 1850-1950* (1974); and John Rooney, *The Geography of Sport* (1974). The present volume is the first text in the series whose content relates to a specific substantive topic: namely, women and sport.

*The American Woman in Sport,* by Professors Ellen W. Gerber, Jan Felshin, Pearl Berlin, and Waneen Wyrick, is a comprehensive, multidisciplinary analysis of the problems, patterns, and processes associated with the sport involvement of women in our culture. As the reader can readily surmise from the biographical sketches which follow, the four authors are eminently qualified to write on their chosen subject. They have actively engaged in athletics and are currently committed to research and writing concerning the causes and consequences of female sport participation.

Their analysis of the American woman in sport reflects their cognizance of the changing trends in both education and society at large, with particular attention to current feminist ideas. Special features of their topical book include: (1) a historical survey of women's

participation in sport, with special reference to intercollegiate and
Olympic competition; (2) a conceptual analysis of the institutional
nature of sport and its implications for sportswomen; (3) an explication
of the feminist movement today as related to sport involvement; (4)
social commentary on the stereotypes of sportswomen as revealed in
various modes of mass media; (5) presentation of a psychological profile and an original motivational analysis of the woman athlete; (6) a
thorough examination of the performance capacities of the sportswoman; and, (7) the compilation of excellent bibliographies for each
division of the book, including the citation of important dissertations
and theses related to women in sport.

   Perhaps the most noteworthy feature of the book is the fact that
although each author is clearly aware of the limited data on many
topics, each has attempted to set forth educated generalizations on
major issues, and has candidly professed her particular professional and
personal posture regarding women in sport.

   My reading of their work has led me to entertain the notion that
the critical test of sport's humanizing function in American society is
man's estimation of the sportswoman. Whether other readers will share
my observation is a moot matter, but I believe most will agree that
Drs. Gerber, Felshin, Berlin and Wyrick have provided an insightful
and provocative account of *The American Woman in Sport.*

*Amherst, Massachusetts*                                    John W. Loy
*April 1974*

# Preface

Why have we written a book on women in sport? First and foremost, to answer the need for information. Sport for American women has been a neglected phenomenon—both in terms of providing adequate opportunities for varied participation and in regard to the scholarly study of the sportswoman. Particularly in the last decade, sport has been recognized by several academic disciplines as an occurrence of sufficient importance to warrant careful investigation. Numerous research studies and the writing of journal and magazine articles and books have been undertaken and published. The result has been an increased—but distorted—understanding of athletes and sport in American society. The distortion has been the result of a nearly total focus on sports*men* and *men's* sport. Generalizations made as a result of research on males in sport are simply not universally applicable to females. The picture drawn of sport in the United States is therefore a half-truth.

Furthermore, sport for women in the United States is a fast-growing, fast-changing element of our culture. Decisions are being made by teachers, coaches, athletic directors, recreation leaders, athletic associations, and the courts, among others. Yet valid information on which to make good judgments is often lacking. Those who are now concerned with conducting and administering sport programs for women, as well as those who will be involved, have a responsibility to study and understand the uniqueness and similarities of sport for women and for men.

It seemed important to us, therefore, to undertake a comprehensive study of the American woman in sport. When we initially began to review the available literature, it was shocking to realize the sparsity

and inadequacy of data. Published histories of the American woman in
sport amounted to only a few pages in the histories of various sports.
Research about athletes almost always involved male subjects. Analyses
of the interaction of sport and society focused on the big-time male
sports of football and basketball. The knowledge of women's physical
capacities and performance was more a matter of opinion than the
result of investigation.

We set out to rectify the omission by a combination of two processes. First, insofar as time and funds permitted, we undertook new
research on women in sport. Second, we pulled together all the data we
could locate, synthesized it, and subjected it to rigorous scholarly analysis and interpretation. Granted the current state of knowledge about
the American woman in sport, we believe we have written a comprehensive and definitive text on the topic. It is our expectation that in
future years we and other researchers will undertake intense and prolonged study of the American sportswoman and her activities. New
information may radically affect or modify the interpretations of what
is now known. In the meantime, we have set forth our educated ideas
in the hope that they may contribute to the understanding of the
American woman in sport. Beyond that, it is our desire that this work
will stimulate future endeavors to study sportswomen.

A word about the delimitations of the content of this book. We
decided to focus our work on the American woman in sport. By this
we meant females of college age and beyond. Although it was occasionally necessary to discuss younger girls, no attempt was made to analyze
the high school girl or interscholastic sport. We chose to use the term
sport because we were interested in activities which involve: specific

administrative organization; a historical background of rules and customs which define the objective and limit the pattern of behavior; it involves competition toward a definite outcome, determined in part by physical skills. In other words, we have excluded physical recreation and leisure time entertainment from our primary analyses. Lastly, believing as we do that sport is embedded in the society in which it takes place, we excluded from consideration women's sport in other countries. However, the data from studies on the physical capacities of women, particularly that which has been gathered in Europe, were included because it did not seem as if major physical differences would exist among females in various countries throughout the world.

A work of this nature inevitably owes a debt of thanks to many people, including especially those whose research was available to analyze and build upon. These scholars have been properly acknowledged as their work was cited. We would also like to thank: C. Robert Paul, Jr., Assistant Director of Communications of the United States Olympic Committee, for his friendly assistance in tracking down information on female Olympians. Friends and colleagues, Virginia Evans, Merrie Fidler, and Betty Spears, for generously sharing the fruits of their labors; the "Chronicle of Participation" is enhanced by their permitting some of their original, unpublished research to be included in this book. Cathy Small, who generously contributed original theoretical integrations based upon her own research and to her and Edrie Ferdun for their gracious willingness to discuss and critically analyze the ideas within "The Social View." Linda Estes, for supplying material about the legal and political fight to increase women's sport programs. Various members of the women's movement, all of whom are unfailingly considerate and dedicated to the efforts of their sisters, and especially to Lynn Cole of the Project on the Status of Women of the Association of American Colleges and Deborah J. Glick, who were particularly concerned and helpful. Robert M. Malina, for his general guidance and helpfulness in editing the "Bio-Physical Perspectives" and making available scarce materials from his personal files. Betty Machella, Don Siegel, and Betty Schnabl for their assistance in preparing the manuscript.

*April 1974*                                                    E.W.G.
                                                               J.F.
                                                               P.B.
                                                               W.W.

# Contents

# Biographical Sketches

ELLEN W. GERBER obtained her Ph.D. from the University of Southern California in 1966 and is Associate Professor of Physical Education at the University of Massachusetts, Amherst. The author of *Innovators and Institutions of Physical Education* (Lea & Febiger, 1971) and editor of *Sport and the Body: A Philosophical Symposium* (Lea & Febiger, 1972), she is currently teaching, writing, and lecturing on American women in sport.

PEARL BERLIN, Research Professor of Physical Education at the University of North Carolina, Greensboro, received her Ph.D. from Pennsylvania State University in 1959. She is the author of several articles and papers on theoretical considerations of the acquisition of motor skill, and is currently engaged in research on the motivation of women athletes.

JAN FELSHIN, who holds an Ed.D. from the University of California, Los Angeles (1958), is Professor of Physical Education and Director of Graduate Studies at East Stroudsburg State College, Pa. The author of *Perspectives and Principles for Physical Education* (John Wiley and Sons, 1967) and *More Than Movement: An Introduction to Physical Education* (Lea & Febiger, 1972), she is currently engaged in teaching and writing in the social psychology of sport participation.

WANEEN WYRICK obtained her Ed.D. from the University of Texas in 1966 and is now an Associate Professor there. She is the author of *Foil Fencing* (W.B. Saunders, 1971) and co-author (with Lawrence F. Locke) of *How to Prepare a Research Proposal* (Teachers College Press, in press). Her current research and writing focuses on physiological aspects of women in sport.

Let her
swim, climb mountain peaks, pilot an airplane,
battle against the elements, take risks,
go out for adventure, and
she will not
feel before the world. . . timidity. . . .

Simone de Beauvoir

# Part 1

# CHRONICLE OF PARTICIPATION

Ellen W. Gerber

# Chapter 1
# Historical Survey

The history of the American woman in sport is more than a century old. Within that time frame it has encompassed activities ranging from simple recreational pastimes to high level international competition. The original few sports deemed appropriate for women's participation have expanded to an enormous variety of activities. In fact, there is hardly a single contemporary sport which remains outside the ken of female involvement. What was primarily a spontaneous, self-directed endeavor has now become a well-organized program replete with sponsors and promoters from educational institutions to cigarette companies. When sport for both men and women began to emerge as a viable cultural activity, only a handful of women gently played. At this time in history, literally millions of American women engage in organized sport, some of which is strenuous, adventurous, and highly competitive.

The pages which follow in this chapter present a broad, general view of the changing pattern of the American woman's participation in sport. An attempt is made to relate to the scope of sport for women: the concept of the Victorian ideal; political and social movements, such as the old and new feminism; and specific events, for example, wars and employment opportunities. An analysis of some particular aspects of women's sport from early physical recreation to the vagaries of sport costuming, and an overview of the sponsorship and promotion of women's sport, complete the survey and conclude the chapter.

In Chapters 2 to 4 the chronicle of a century of participation is detailed with explicit information about collegiate and Olympic competition and specific facts about the American woman's participation in eighteen different popular sports.

## GENERAL PATTERN OF PARTICIPATION

The emergent pattern of women's sport went through three distinct periods. The first, or early period is basically a nineteenth century phenomenon. The second period came to fruition in the "golden decade" of 1925-1935. The third period is the contemporary era, now flourishing in the 1970s.

Essentially, sport for women in nineteenth century America can be characterized as follows. Initially the acceptable activities were relatively few in number. Croquet, archery, bowling, tennis and golf were the primary sports, though a few women played baseball, rowed, and participated in track and field competitively. Vigorous activities were not developed for women, nor for most men. The clothing did not permit much movement and those who engaged in sport were typically gentlemen and gentlewomen who had no taste for hard effort and were content to engage in that which was readily available to them. Sports were chosen which could be performed without acquiring an indelicate sweat.

The primary purpose of sport or early physical recreation seemed to be the opportunity for a respectable social encounter. In an age of Puritanical sexual morality, it gave men and women something to do together. Therefore physical activities, including competitive sports, were most often conducted in a coeducational setting. Since the skill level and effort was not high for either sex, it was feasible for men and women to compete with one another individually or in couples.

The activities were chiefly of an outdoor nature, indoor facilities not having been constructed on any large scale. This of course placed further restrictions on the development of new activities and also affected the participation levels. Sport was essentially an activity of the upper classes, those who had leisure and the finances to belong to clubs which had facilities for playing. Municipal and federal governments had not yet developed facilities for the common people, though croquet and bicycling were two physical activities in which the masses could and did participate.

Activities were almost always of the individual sport type. Only when the colleges began to develop programs of physical activity for women did the team sports develop. However, that phenomenon did not occur until close to the end of the century. Prior to that time sports in the colleges were similar to those in the larger social environment. The colleges were also responsible for influencing a change from

Gentlewomen play croquet, 1866.

coeducational sport to separate sport for men and women. Probably this was due—at least in part—to the advent of physical education programs, which required dress and activities that the women teachers thought were best performed in female seclusion.

By the late twenties the nature of women's sport had undergone considerable change. The number of available activities had increased greatly. In addition to the earlier activities, large numbers of women played basketball, volleyball, and softball. Field hockey, lacrosse, polo, speedboat and sailboat racing, squash, badminton, fencing, swimming, diving, skiing, figure skating, speed skating, bobsledding, and aviation all had their adherents, though in limited numbers. The activities were far more vigorous than heretofore and sometimes dangerous.

Participants were no longer drawn primarily from the upper class, but a distinction still prevailed which saw the upper class taking part in the more expensive activities that required special facilities and the working class enjoying the basketball, bowling, and baseball sponsored by industries and municipal recreation departments and agencies. It is possible that the latter group made up the bulk of the competitors. Industries, municipalities, agencies such as the YMCA and YWCA, and educational institutions built large gymnasiums and pools to accommodate sports participants. In this era, the most popular activities, such as basketball and bowling, were indoor sports.

The growth of organized competition was the most prominent feature of the decade with national and international tournaments promoted for most sports. Related to the increased opportunities for high level competition was the growth of women's sport organizations. These were either separately established or formed as special women's committees within previously established groups.

One of the most far-reaching occurrences of this time period was the division that took place between sport in the larger social environment and sport in the schools and colleges. Precisely at the time when sport in society was extending in the ways just described, sport in the colleges was being circumscribed. The available activities were limited and the level of competition was lowered to the point of disappearing altogether.

Very little sport was coeducational by this time. The level of skill had grown too high to permit realistic competition between the sexes and there were other opportunities for social encounters in the jazz age.

Flag football, a new sport for college women. [Courtesy University Photo Center, University of Massachusetts.]

By the contemporary era sport for women again had undergone several changes. Bowling, softball, tennis, and golf still seem to have the greatest number of adult players. A few activities such as polo virtually disappeared for women. In their place are a number of new activities such as motorcycle racing, the martial arts, parachuting, non-tackle football, kayaking, cross-country running and skiing, marathon running, surfing, and water skiing. Most of the new activities are not only vigorous but are eustressing, that is, involve pleasurable stress that comes from controlling the danger involved. Several of the sports in which women now compete demand great endurance, a quality in sport not pursued by many women until the contemporary era.

The growth of organized competition continues to expand at a rapid rate with state, regional, national, and international competition available in an even greater variety of sports. Even women's collegiate teams are now taking part in competition through to the international level (e.g., the World University Games).

The division between college sport and sport in the larger social milieu is disappearing. A renewed emphasis on the club system in colleges has brought men and women together in activities which were previously not available on a college campus. Thus the return to more coed sport is taking place—and ways are being found for men and women to compete against each other in mixed teams such as are common in coed volleyball. Almost all national sport organizations now admit and encourage women members.

Though a class distinction still remains in sport, the generally greater funds available for leisure have helped to minimize this feature. Activities like water skiing which were once beyond the reach of most people are now more available.

One radical change in sport for women has been the growth of opportunities for professional play. Both the number of sports and the amounts of the purses are growing speedily.

A new interest in outdoor activities is evident, though the currently popular ones such as skiing, kayaking, cross-country running, sky diving, soaring, and mountain climbing are far more rugged than the croquet, archery, and tennis of the nineteenth century. Furthermore, they are of the natural sport variety in which elements of nature play a crucial role.

With all the changes, the biggest one is the growth of sport for women in comparison to men. Certainly, comparatively more women now take part in organized sport competition than at any other time in history.

## FACTORS AFFECTING PARTICIPATION

Every aspect of individual and social action is affected or influenced
by other individual acts and social forces. The precise extent of influence usually cannot be determined. In fact, cause and effect relationships are the hardest phenomena to document. The best that the
historian can do is to speculate, presenting evidence which reveals the
logical—or occasionally statistical—probability of relationship between
factors.

In Chapter 5 Felshin amply documents the concept that there is a
dialectic between society and women in sport. The factors discussed in
the following pages are considered by this author to be historically
major influencing forces. Obviously all were not present simultaneously,
nor is it necessary to claim that all of women's sport was the result of,
or was subject to, the effect of these factors. Individuals, whether in
their roles as sport participants or other roles, can and do resist even
strong social tides. In fact, it is because this occurs that society changes.
It can justly be claimed that the sportswoman herself was a strong force
in modifying society's picture of the weak, fragile woman into one
more consonant with reality. What *is* claimed is that these are *some* of
the factors which affected with varying intensity the general pattern of
sport for women through more than a century.

### Victorian Ideals

The latter half of the nineteenth century is known as the Victorian era
because Queen Victoria's reign over England was so long (1837-1901)
that the ideas and attitudes generated within it had a pervasive influence
throughout the world. Attitudes towards women, the family, and other
social institutions, including sport, had a distinctive character that was
fairly consistent throughout society.

In many ways the Victorian ideal of women was the antithesis of
Victoria the woman. She was a Queen, directly involved in the affairs of
a powerful state, making decisions of literally world-shaping importance.
She was physically strong, having borne nine healthy children. She knew
her own mind to the point of being considered stubborn. She proposed
to her husband and though she was a devoted wife, he was the Prince
Consort while she held the power of the throne. After Albert died, she
governed alone for forty years (Woodham-Smith, 1972).

In contrast, the ideal of woman that emerged during her reign was
of an ethereal person, on a pedestal, somewhere above the realities of life.

O'Neill (1971) hypothesizes that

> the Victorians had attempted . . . to compensate women for
> their increased domestic and pedagogic responsibilities by envelop-
> ing them in a mystique which asserted their higher status while at
> the same time guaranteeing their actual inferiority. . . . The
> Victorians taught women to think of themselves as a special
> class. . . . [They] believed they had accorded women a higher
> and more honorable estate than had any previous generation. . . .
> The Victorians had given the nuclear family a transcendent signi-
> ficance all out of proportion to its functional value. . . . While
> the Victorian conception of women as wan, ethereal, spiritualized
> creatures bore little relation to the real world where women
> operated machines, worked the fields, hand-washed clothing, and
> toiled over great kitchen stoves, it was endorsed by both science
> and religion. . . . Feminine delicacy was considered visible evidence
> of their superior sensibilities, the "finer clay" of which they were
> made. Women who were not delicate by nature became so by
> design.*

Once the ideal was accepted—promulgated in endless tracts and
pulpits—extreme pressure was brought to bear on women to behave in
accordance with its framework. To defy it was to be unwomanly. Thus
passiveness, obedience to husband, circumspectness of behavior, and
most of all, attractiveness, were necessary to maintain the Victorian
image of womanhood. A body could be made to appear delicate by
wearing a corset that pulled one's flesh into the shape of the fashionable wasp waist. By staying indoors, in the home, the world's evil was
unlikely to defile one and damage the image of purity. Furthermore,
one's full attention could be devoted to that most womanly of all
behaviors, motherhood. By avoiding exercise and cultivating a pale face
and an incapacity to do work, one gave the appearance of gentility—
always a desired image. Obviously, to have facial color and muscular
strength was a sign of having to work for a living.†

---

* From W. L. O'Neill, *Everyone Was Brave. A History of Feminism in America,*
Chicago: Quadrangle Books, pp. 4-8. Copyright © 1971 by Quadrangle Books and
reprinted by permission.

† It is interesting to note the reverse of that ideal. Today the poor appear pale
and/or weak; the jet set is known for the sunburned, vigorous appearance that
comes from skiing and yachting and other outdoor recreations.

Sport as a social encounter, 1880.

The Victorian ideal was antithetical to sport in many ways. Sport requires vigor; the ideal required delicacy. Sport takes one out of the home and into the tempting, defiling world. Sport places participants in positions where their flesh is exposed and their emotions are expressed; the ideal required modesty, propriety, and circumspectness. Furthermore, by exposing the face and reproductive organs to possible injury, sport endangers the ultimate Victorian goal: the twin functions of attracting a man and bearing a child.

When sport for women began to emerge as a viable possibility, numerous writers in popular journals and in the physical education literature encouraged it—but they were cognizant of public resistance based on the Victorian ideal. It is a significant indication of prevailing opinion that The *Review of Reviews* published in 1900 a symposium on women's sports. The first question asked of such eminent figures as Emile Zola, the great French author, was: "Are women ceasing to be women through their devotion to the physical exercises known under the general head of 'Sports'?" ("Women's Sports. . . ," 1900, p. 231).

A Vassar graduate reminiscing about playing baseball in the 1870s remembered that "the public, so far as it knew of our playing, was shocked, but in our retired grounds, and protected from observation even in these grounds by sheltering trees, we continued to play in spite of a censorious public" (Richardson, 1897, p. 517). Another popular magazine writer begging to "Give the Girls a Chance" remarked on the "absurd Puritanic notions prevailing in many households against vigorous romping. The girl-child is constantly being told that much a healthy girl would naturally do—like to do—is 'unladylike'; that to display her child legs, climbing a stone wall, for instance, is 'improper';. . ." (Canfield, 1910, p. 20).

As sport became more popularly accepted and even valued for its social and healthful qualities, the question arose as to the parameters of competition appropriate for women. Here the professionals—the physical educators—showed their adherence to the Victorian ideals in their writings. A woman "should always preserve her inborn sense of modesty and innocence; she must never be seen by the opposite sex when she is likely to forget herself"—i.e., when caught in the emotional excitement of an important contest (Perrin, 1924, p. 658). Publicity, especially that which championed a star athlete, violated the ideal that women should be unobtrusive. "The development of aggressive characteristics . . . added nothing of charm and usefulness, and were not in harmony with the best traditions of the sex" (J. Anna Norris, 1924 quoted in Lee, 1933, p. 468). Most important of all was the possibility that vigorous sport might cause the number, extent, and flow of menstruations to be reduced, in turn engendering a decrease in fertility, and a concomitant decrease in the size of the uterus (function makes the organ), which ultimately had a harmful effect on the all-important role of motherhood (Arnold, 1924). The notion of *limited* sport for women was accepted, provided that it took place under conditions which maximized what was thought to be good for women (as per the Victorian ideal), and minimized the threat to her womanliness.

The next issue caused by the nineteenth century standard was the identification of sports which were most likely to compromise the image of the woman.* Since the ideal embodied the concept of fragility, any sport which called for an overt display of strength was obviously inappropriate. When Vassar College held a field day in 1895, the first college ever to do so, they were immediately chastised. "We lament it as one of the outgrowths of a wrong appreciation of what physical training should do and be. To accomplish by education the full development of the feminine physique needs to some extent the choice of suitable material" (*Mind and Body* quoted by Ballintine, 1898, p. 40). The field events also were the chief target of anger in the later 1920s and are still only partially accepted today.

More positively, anything that emphasized the aesthetic appeal was most in keeping with the transcendent female image. This affected not only the choice of activities, but the style in which they were played. It became more important to look well than to win. In 1909 the Public School Physical Training Society heard Kellor stress:

> It is essential in playing games that women stand well, walk well, run well, throw well, and have a neat, attractive appearance. Disagreeable expressions, uncouth language, squalling and yelling, crying, lying about the floor, eating between halves of games, masculinity, boisterousness,—the absence of all these are the result of emphasizing the aesthetic feature of games . . . . I introduced the rule that form was one of the requirements for making the university class teams, and that no girl who persisted in careless dress and playing could play in any match game . . . (Kellor, 1906, p. 163).

---

* The reader is referred to Metheny (1965, pp. 43-56) for a full analysis of what sports are appropriate for women in keeping with historical ideals of feminity or womanliness.

These quotations, which are typical of the attitudes expressed in popular and physical education literature, demonstrate the influence of the Victorian ideal on women's sport. In sum, it must be concluded that it served to hamper and/or limit the development of sport for women.

## Medical Issues

Medical issues were closely related to the Victorian ideal and, in fact, were an outgrowth of it. The inferior health of Americans in the nineteenth century is amply documented by historians [see especially, Betts (1968)]. Several writers in the 1830s worried particularly about the health of females because they spent so much time confined to the house. A Boston surgeon, John Collins Warren, for example, wrote in 1830:

> The girl, when she goes home from school is, as we have before said, expected to go home and remain, at least a large part of the time, confined to the house. As soon as the boy is released, he begins to run and jump and frolic in the open air . . . The result is, that in him all organs get invigorated . . . while a defect exists in the other, proportionate to the want of physical education (quoted in Greene, 1950, p. 36).

Another reason for women's poor health was the practice of tight lacing. According to corset makers circa 1880:

> Fashionable ladies, and thousands who imitate them, purchase corsets which are from three to ten inches smaller than their waists, and then lace them so as to reduce their waists from two to eight inches (Lewis, 1882, p. 508).

The author comments that in an informal survey of physicians it was reported that more than half of their professional business came from displacement of pelvic viscera which results from the lacing (p. 509). *The Journal of Health* carried a little article entitled: "Fainting of Females during Public Worship." It appears that "it frequently happens, especially during the warm season, that females are seen fainting during divine service on the Lord's day, and at public meetings on other occasions. This is generally owing to a want of pure air, coupled with the murderous practice of tight lacing" (1831, p. 193).

The historian Page Smith hypothesized that the necessity for obedience to her "marital duty" at her husband's command left women with no other form of birth control than getting sick. Fainting, "sick headaches," and fatigue thus were necessary symptoms for women to acquire (Smith, 1970, pp. 138-139). That syndrome of course helped to contribute to their public image of weakness and possibly functioned as a form of self-fulfilling prophecy as well.

Coupled with these outcomes of the Victorian ideal were the generally unhealthy conditions of the times: polluted air and crowded, unsanitary conditions that accompanied the move to the cities caused by the industrial revolution; poor diet; poor medical treatment; the birth of numerous children and its attendant strain on the body—these factors all contributed to the lack of health and vigor of American women.

Thus, when women began to take up sport with any degree of seriousness, two reactions occurred. The first was positive; many were enthusiastic and wrote articles stressing the physical benefits to women of exercise. *Outing* magazine of the late 1880s and 1890s carried numerous articles urging women to take up cycling, fencing, rowing, tennis, and other sports. Most authors sought to convey the fact that the Victorian view of women's physical capacities was erroneous. A typical article entitled "A Medical View of Cycling for Ladies" noted that all agree that physical exercise benefits a man. "Prejudice alone has prevented this view being held with regard to women" (Fenton, 1896, p. 807). He recommended that "cycling is the ideal exercise to bring about a revolution in this respect" (p. 807).

One of the foremost and influential physical educators, Dudley Allen Sargent, wrote:

> It took educators and biologists some little time . . . to realize that girls, also, had within them this dynamic force seeking more normal and healthy outlets than had been universally accorded to them in the past. Women themselves had been slow to realize this tremendous power and had constantly overestimated their weakness, so that it needed many years of encouragement and of feeling their way through the stages of musical calisthenics and bean-bag drills to convince them that they would not fall to pieces in more violent exercise (1915, p. 831).

*But,* as it became apparent that women were *really* going to compete and make all-out efforts, the praise was qualified and the twentieth century is marked by countless articles expressing concern for the health of the woman athlete.

A major issue centered around physical activity during the menstrual period. Apparently the women of the nineteenth century had convinced doctors—and themselves—that it was tantamount to an illness. *The Journal of the American Medical Association* warned that "our young girls, in this age of feminine freedom, are also overdoing athletics. A girl should not be coddled because she is menstruating, but common sense . . . at such a period should be exercised. . . . The uterus is physiologically congested and temporarily abnormally heavy and hence, liable to displacement by the inexcusable strenuosity and roughness of this particular game [basketball] ("Extracts. . . ," 1925, p. 524). The physical educators worried that being on a team which was scheduled to compete would cause girls to be pressured into playing during their menstrual periods.

Mabel Lee typified the opinions of physical educators about vigorous sport for women with a phrase that later was often quoted: "They would be apt to get more 'physical straining than physical training'. . ." (Lee, 1924, p. 13). There seemed to be much concern, for instance, that "pelvic disturbances" could be brought on by overactivity and also the conviction that falls, collisions, violent contacts—all of which were a potential feature of highly competitive sport—were more dangerous for girls than for boys.

One person argued that "there should be no opportunities for punching or scratching as it has been found that many cases of neurosis in women have been caused by scratches, blemishes and disfigurements of the face" (Burdick, 1927, p. 367). "The emotional strain attendant upon competition would be injurious," said the women physical directors (Lee, 1924, p. 13).

Clelia Duel Mosher, a medical doctor, tried to counteract these ideas by warning physical educators that they

> must not think in terms of yesterday in dealing with the girl of today, who is the woman of tomorrow. . . . When we consider the woman of thirty years ago and the conditions which produced her, we can understand how this idea of her traditional weakness and incapacity hampers us even now in our work (Mosher, 1925, p. 535).

The attitudes toward women's physical capacity had their greatest effect on the level of competition available, as physical educators sought to convince the country—and largely succeeded—that it would be injurious to the health of women if they were permitted to engage in intense competition. The beliefs also affected the type of activities open to women. Events requiring endurance were deemed inappropriate and therefore competition in long distance running, for example, was not held. All events which involved physical contact were (and are) outlawed. Basketball was modified to minimize the possible danger of contact that would accidentally occur and rules penalized even accidental brushes. Sports which required some risk were omitted because of the possibility of physical disfigurement.

Originally the consensus about women's poor health led to considerable encouragement for them to take part in sport. Thus the medical issues influenced sport in a positive way during the nineteenth and early twentieth century. But as women passed the point of exercising for their health and started to compete with intensity, the effect of the medical issues became negative and inhibiting. The view that women are strong and capable of participating in most sports at a highly competitive level is contemporary and was accepted only after generations of sportswomen proved by their actions that no harm would befall them. Body-contact sports and those which require a landing jolt as in pole vaulting are still ruled out today, possibly because there is no opportunity to demonstrate gradually that they too can be safe for women.

## Social Changes

Social changes caused by great events such as World Wars I and II, the depression, the industrializing of the American economy, the growth of free public higher education, and the passage of important legislation, inevitably have a profound effect on the lives of the citizens. The outcome of these events will be different for each individual and special group. For women, some of this country's greatest tragedies have caused fuller participation in the rights and responsibilities of the nation. In times of stress and/or flux society cannot afford to ignore the talents of more than half its population. Thus a more liberal, more appreciative attitude toward women develops. Coupled with the occurrence of specific events, women's social roles then change markedly. The period from World War I through the depression is an era in which a combination of events helped to bring about a new position for women generally, and therefore also for women in sport specifically.

It is popular for historians to proclaim the decade of the 1920s as a period of great strides forward for women, particularly in the educational and economic spheres. The conclusions have been drawn because of the superficiality with which the mass statistical data was examined. Yes, there was an increase of about 26 percent of the female labor force during the twenties. Yes, proportionately more women than ever before entered college and earned baccalaureate and advanced degrees. But it is impossible to ignore the facts presented by Chafe (1972) which demonstrate that in "the period from 1920 to 1940 [women] witnessed very little progress toward the goal of economic equality" (p. 51). Women remained in low-paying jobs, studied for low-prestige and low-paying women's professions, and embraced marriage with no careers as a life's goal.

What *did* change, however, were the attitudes of the American public toward women. The Victorians were correct in believing that in order to preserve their ideal, women had to be kept hidden in the home. The increase in number of women workers and students, the increased incidence of women living alone or with friends in city apartments (the result of going where the work was) away from parental authority, the increased social freedom that came from the belief that suffrage symbolized equality of the sexes, and the model of the daring and successful women such as the suffragettes and the adventuresses like the aviatrixes, all served to alter the social milieu. The restrictiveness of the Victorian ideal gave way to the uninhibitedness of the jazz age.

> Magazines and novels portrayed the decade [of the 1920s] as a non-stop revel featuring jazz bands, risque dancers, and uninhibited sex. As much as anyone else, the "new woman" symbolized the era. Cigarette in mouth and cocktail in hand, she appeared to be both shocking and unshockable (Chafe, 1972, p. 49).

Freedom to do what one wishes, freedom to be physically active, to compete, and to perform acts of strength and courage are the necessary conditions which must exist in order that sport for women flourish. This circumstance developed in the 1920s. One cause was the exposure to the European continent caused by World War I, an entanglement which brought forth a significant change in American social attitudes. The major influence affecting women most directly was the ratification in 1920 of the Nineteenth Amendment to the Constitution, granting women suffrage. The right to vote ultimately did not bring with it the great equality that the women had expected, but for the immediate period the women felt and acted as if their lives were changing.

When the quest for the vote commenced with the Seneca Falls [New York] Declaration of Sentiments and Resolutions, passed at the convention in 1848, the women observed that:

> He [man] has endeavored, in every way that he could, to destroy her confidence in her own powers, to lessen her self-respect, and to make her willing to lead a dependent and abject life.
>
> Now, in view of this entire disfranchisement of one-half the people of this country, their social and religious degradation—in view of the unjust laws above mentioned, and because women do feel themselves aggrieved, oppressed, and fraudulently deprived of their most sacred rights, we insist that they have immediate admission to all the rights and privileges which belong to them as citizens of the United States (M. Schneir, 1972, p. 80).

For seventy-odd years women fought for the vote believing that it would revolutionize their lives, and when it came it brought a tremendous *social* release.

The effect of this release on women and sport was profound and interactive. With the increased numbers of women in industry and the colleges caused by the war, prosperity, and suffrage, there was an increased pool of sportswomen. The coincident rise of women in labor unions and labor legislation increased the amount of leisure time available. The social and industry restrictions which kept women confined to their quarters when not working had given way and women sought diversion. Many chose sport. The increased activity of the decade from 1925-1935 was discussed earlier (refer to p. 6).

That decade also produced genuine sport heroines such as Amelia Earhart, first woman to fly across the Atlantic Ocean in 1928. She vanished flying across the Pacific in 1937, leaving behind a note to her husband which read: "Please know I am quite aware of the hazards. . . Women must try to do things as men have tried. . ." (Jensen, 1971, p. 89). Gertrude Ederle, the first woman to swim the English Channel (1926), was another of the decade's sport heroines, as was Mildred "Babe" Didrikson, who covered herself and her country with glory in the 1932 Olympics.

If the attitudes of the times helped make it possible for women to attempt these feats, it was true also that their actions and those of countless lesser-known sportswomen made the times still freer. A statement by Anne O'Hogan, a golfer, made in 1901 remained valid thirty years later.

Amelia Earhart, ca. 1930.

To whomever the athletic woman owes her existence, to him or her the whole world of women owes a debt incomparably great. Absolutely no other social achievement in the behalf of women is so important and so far-reaching in its results. The winning of the Sacred Latchkey, from which such magnificent results were argued and the half winning of the ballot, are far less important, even in the minds of those who fought for them. With the single exception of the improvement in the legal status of women, their entrance into the realm of sports is the most cheering thing that has happened to them in the century past. . . . The woman who plays golf has made it possible for the woman who cannot distinguish between a cleek and a broom handle to go about her marketing in a short skirt; she has given the working girls who never saw a golf course freedom from the tyranny of braids and bindings. . .*

The effects of the Nineteenth Amendment and the war and the changes in labor practices were mitigated by the depression. The "crash" was social as well as economic because the two factors are related. Fewer women worked, went to college, or could afford to live away from home. The freedom that accompanied these activities was somewhat compromised. Though the post-depression years engendered a buildup of municipal and national recreation facilities, there is little evidence to show that increased numbers of women utilized them.

The further in time from the end of organized feminism—defined as the movement for women's political and social rights which began in Seneca Falls and culminated in suffrage—the greater was the increase in women's return to domesticity and dependence. O'Neill perceptively pointed out that the original feminist movement "was not a rebellion born of ancient slavery but part of a collective response to the sexual awareness deliberately inspired by Victorian society in an attempt to foster what the twentieth century would consider an oppressive domesticity" (1971, pp. 5-6). The new, post-depression domesticity was of a different and more tolerable sort. "Increasing mobility due to modern means of transportation, the persistent urbanization of American society, and the availability of birth control information had changed the sexual values of society" (Lerner, 1971, p. 144). The social restrictions were not as great; women did have legal rights and were no longer owned by their husbands; and many women continued to work. Therefore no organized "rebellion" took place.

---

* From M. E. Ford, *Little Women Grow Bold,* Boston: Bruce Humphries, pp. 15-16. Copyright © 1936 by Bruce Humphries and reprinted by permission.

During World War II it became essential for large numbers of women to return to work as replacements for the males in the armed forces. Again, women demonstrated their capacities to do tasks no one believed appropriate for them and to execute jobs with responsibility and authority. At war's end they returned home, but with a difference. "A Women's Bureau survey . . . showed that three out of four women who had taken jobs in the midst of the war wanted to continue working" (Chafe, 1972, p. 178). In fact, they did so in ever increasing numbers. "By 1970, 50% of American women 18-64 were in the labor force compared with 30% in 1940 and 20% in 1900" (Oppenheimer, 1973, p. 185). Perhaps more significantly, the traditional pattern of women working prior to marriage and then retiring to the home, changed. "Starting in the 1940s . . . the first great departure was the entry or reentry of women past 35 into the labor force. . . A second trend, starting in the 1950s but picking up momentum since then, has been the increased labor force participation of younger married women, including women with preschool children" (Oppenheimer, p. 185).

The buildup of women workers was probably a chief cause of the rise of the "new feminism." As the old feminism was a rebellion against conditions that had grown too oppressive to tolerate, the new feminism was a product of basic inequities that were too unjust to continue to tolerate. "Of the 31 million women in the labor force in March, 1970, nearly half were working because of pressing economic need. They were either single, widowed, divorced, or separated or had husbands whose incomes were less than $3,000 a year" (U.S. Dept. of Labor, 1971, p. 1). They simply could not afford to earn from one-half to two-thirds as much as their male peers. They were tired of inequality of pay and of career opportunities. They had enough of low-paying, low-status jobs. They rebelled against their exclusion from positions of authority where the decision-making process took place. Out of this economic inequity came the new feminism, a new organized movement for women's rights.

As with the old feminism, the original impetus soon expanded to a variety of women's causes related to their rights in every sphere: education, the family, medical practices, social customs—and sport. The new feminism, born in the 1960s, catalyzed by the publication of Betty Friedan's book *The Feminine Mystique* (1963), is a movement that is revolutionizing social attitudes. The changes that have taken place in sport for women during the 1960s and 1970s, as described earlier (refer

to p. 8) are in part a direct result of the social changes wrought by the
new attitudes of and toward women and their roles. It is no accident
that the National Organization for Women (NOW), the first group organized within the new feminism to campaign for women's rights, in
1973 devoted a workshop to women in sports and has organized a task
force on the subject. The emphasis on equality of opportunity in sport
is an extension of the call for equality in every sphere.

## ASPECTS OF WOMEN'S SPORT

The roots of modern day sport lie in the pre-sport era when physical
activity and recreation for women developed. Women's first acquaint-
ance with sport was as spectators. Later, sport participation became
socially sanctioned; eventually it became commonplace.

### Early Physical Recreation

Prior to 1870, play activities for women (and men) were recreational
rather than sport-like in nature. That is, they were noncompetitive,
informal, rule-less activities.

Horseback riding was considered the most salutary exercise for
women and it was widely practiced from the beginning of settlements
in America. Particularly in rural districts, everyone was expected to ride
and some women became "fearless" riders (Holliman, 1931, p. 169). In
the ante-bellum period fox hunting was added—largely in the south.
Prior to the 1830s, although hunts were held in honor of women,
"the actual participation was confined to blowing the horns before the
hunt" (Holliman, 1931, p. 166). In the early part of the nineteenth
century riding schools were established and days set aside for ladies
when no gentlemen were permitted. In 1854, the author of *The Lady's
Equestrian Manual,* "In which the Principles and Practices of Horsemanship for Ladies are Thoroughly Explained, To Enable Every Lady to
Ride with Comfort and Elegance," noted that it was a time "when riding
has become so eminently fashionable an exercise among the ladies and
when the road daily displays so many elegant women on horseback"
(Hazard, 1854, p. 1). At agricultural fairs equestrienne exhibitions took
place in which the ladies were judged not only on the speed of their
horses, but on the grace and elegance of their riding (Manchester, 1931,
p. 132).

Boating and bathing also were started during this early period. Few women knew how to swim and, in fact, the ladies bathing costume made it impossible anyway. They bathed—at first in bathing houses which were shared with men, taking turns in accord with a blast from a long tin horn. In the first half of the nineteenth century, sea bathing became popular and the use of bathing machines assured the privacy necessary for propriety. The machines were small wooded structures set on wheels, which were pulled into the water by horses. Bathers dressed within and then entered the sea via steps. Sometimes an awning was added to further conceal the bather (Kidwell, 1968, pp. 6-9). In the late 1860s articles began to appear urging women to learn to swim. In the next decade the construction of large bath houses in major cities, with alternate days for ladies, made this possible.

Although some writers urged women to exercise for their health, physical effort on the part of women was not encouraged. One of the most popular forms of physical recreation was sleigh or carriage riding, but the male usually did the actual driving. Similarly, when ice skating came into vogue around the middle of the nineteenth century, the woman who skated was encouraged "to take fast hold of the coat tails of her gentleman partner, for then, if he was a dextrous glider, and she maintained a firm position, a gay time she could have of it enjoying all the pleasure without incurring any of the fatigue of the exercise" (Dulles, 1963, pp. 96-97).

Recreation continued to develop in scope as technological inventions made new activities possible. The ball bearing skate made roller skating a fashionable amusement, ice skating rinks extended that sport to city dwellers, and the pneumatic tire made it possible for ladies to discard their tricycles and join the late-century craze on their new safety bikes. In 1896 there were an estimated four million riders.

The early physical recreation for women was important, not only because it engaged women in healthful, needed physical activity, but because it brought them outdoors. The physical recreation gave women a public social contact that was otherwise not available and helped to loosen some of the strangling ties of propriety which enveloped them.

## Women as Sport Spectators

Spectating was an important step in the transition for women from physical recreators to sports participants. By providing an opportunity to be present during competition, it established a connection to the activities. Furthermore, it made sport more familiar to the ladies which

"WE MET BY CHANCE; OR WAITING FOR THE SWELL."

The dangers of coed bathing, Currier & Ives, 1875.

perhaps helped to ease their discomfort when opportunities were presented to them to take an active part.

An early activity which attracted women spectators was ice skating. Since it was scandalous for a woman to skate, they contented themselves with watching, "giving signs of admiration and approval to some friend who happened to be excelling on the ice" (Holliman, 1931, p. 166).

The commercial value of women as spectators was recognized quickly by the promoters of horseracing—America's first large spectator sport. The presence of women gave racing a higher character. Thus in New Orleans when a course was erected in 1851, a ladies' stand was provided, complete with parlors and retiring rooms (Somers, 1972, p. 27). In the next decades ladies' stands became a common phenomenon.

They were also erected at ballparks and thus attracted hundreds of women to this fast-growing American pastime. The feminine seal of approval was a necessary adjunct and in 1867 at least one sportswriter argued for their presence at games:

> If there is any one thing calculated to serve the best interests of the game more than any thing else, it is the encouragement of the presence of the fair sex at baseball matches. It has hitherto been the greatest drawback to the popularity of sports and pastimes in this country that ladies have been prohibited, by the ridiculous custom of American society . . . from being spectators at any trial of skill. . . . Of late years a great change has been introduced here. . . . We therefore see the fair sex at the best classes of races on the turf, at cricket and baseball contests, on the skating ponds, and watching with eager interest the rowing and sailing matches, when, but a few years since, American ladies were not to be seen at such gatherings . . . experience has shown that nothing tends so much to elevate the game, to rid it of evil influences, to lead to proper decorum and to gentlemanly contests than the countenance and patronage of the ladies. . . .*

For similar reasons, it was the custom in the early days of the New York Athletic Club (NYAC) to ask members to bring ladies with them to club games, "in order that athletics might be made as respectable as they were in England" (Edwards, 1895, p. 14). Since the NYAC played a leading role in organizing the AAU, it is not surprising that "after the A.A.U. was organized [1888], meets were conducted on a plane which

---

* From J. R. Betts, "Organized Sport in Industrial America," Ph.D. dissertation, Columbia University, 1951, p. 165. Reprinted by permission.

would prove attractive to the ladies and it became a common occurrence for them to be seen at most of the events" (Korsgaard, 1952, p. 279).

Although spectating did have the virtue of bringing women out of the seclusion of the home into contact with sport, nevertheless it helped also to teach them the principle that their role in sport was chiefly to provide applause.

## Women's Athletic Clubs

It is customary to believe that athletic clubs were exclusively for male athletes. In a comprehensive account of "Life at the Athletic Clubs" (Edwards, 1895), the author only once mentions women and that, as quoted above, is in their role of spectators. Of course they were not necessarily the most commonplace phenomenon for women, nor were women part of the "pure" athletic clubs—those which sponsored only track and field events.

As women switched from physical recreation to sport, they first took up activities such as croquet. Though croquet was the first of the mass sports for both men and women—so popular that manufacturers had to put sockets for candles on the wickets enabling people to play at night—it was not an activity that demanded club organization. But as women began to take up archery, bowling, fencing, tennis, golf, and cycling, it became necessary to have clubs in order that facilities would be available and competitions organized.

One of the first, and certainly the most extensive of the women's athletic clubs was the Ladies' Club of the Staten Island Cricket and Baseball Club. Connected to the original men's club, the Ladies' Club for Outdoor Sports started in 1877 with about 30 women. Within ten years it had over 200 members. The chief activity was tennis and "arrangements were made for the use of the grounds so that there should be no clashing of interest" with the men. "The ladies were privileged to play on all the [tennis] courts during the morning; . . . the two or three nets nearest their [club] house [were] at all times their exclusive property; . . . during the afternoons they were at liberty to play at any other of the nets that were not required by the men; and every Friday the whole grounds were theirs exclusively, and the men could only occupy such nets as they did not want" (Clay, 1887, p. 108).

In the early years the men assisted with the conduct of tournaments and entertainments, but as the Ladies' Club prospered the women took over completely. Their Fridays and annual tournaments were well attended by a "large and fashionable gathering of members and their friends" (Clay, p. 108).

The ladies had their own clubhouse which was erected by the men's club to which they paid an annual rental of $150. It contained a reception room, complete with piano, and a locker room with some forty lockers (the men had 500 lockers in their clubhouse) and a bathroom with showers (Clay, p. 111). Although tennis was their big activity, they also played archery and other sports.

Many other clubs in the New York area admitted women as members. An 1889 article made special note of the fact that the New York Tennis Club admitted ladies on virtually the same terms and conditions as men. The writer also commented that "to enumerate and describe all of the clubs in the neighborhood of New York City which gladly welcome ladies to membership would be an almost endless task, for in the State of New Jersey alone there are quite too many to be described in one article" (Slocum, 1889, pp. 292-294).

Archery was the main sport of the Crescent City Female Archery Club, founded in the 1870s, and the Pearl Archery Club organized by women in 1880 (Somers, 1972, p. 210). Both were in New Orleans, a city which apparently had many potential sportswomen. The New Orleans tennis club permitted women to play on specified days and soon the Ladies' Days and Tennis Teas became regular practices. In a few years some women were admitted as associate members (Somers, pp. 211-212). Also in New Orleans, the Young Men's Gymnastic Club and the Southern Athletic Club both tried to introduce ladies' basketball during the 1890s. The Southern AC boasted that it was "the only club of any prominence in the world which unselfishly encourages the attendance of women at its gymnasium" (Somers, pp. 242, 284-285).

The Ladies' Tricycle Club of New York, organized in 1884, "is the only regular ladies' club [in the city], although a number of ladies belong to associations in which bicyclists have part" (Smith, 1885, p. 318). The club, organized with ten members, "adopted a costume consisting of a dark-blue flannel skirt, with a Jersey and cap of the same color; and their badge is a double star of gold on dark-blue enamel marked L.T.C., 1884" (Smith, p. 318).

The Nemo bicycle club which admitted only "sociable riders" had a rule that a lady and a gentleman were paired to vote jointly on club matters. "As *no one* member can vote, these words are taken as a free

translation of the word *nemo,* and give the club its name. This organization indicates and prophesies a millenial future of unity, when two
voices shall really speak as one thought, two votes shall count as one!"*
(Smith, 1885, p. 319)

An article on rowing for women reported that several women's
rowing clubs were organized in New York during the 1880s. On Staten
Island a women's crew was made up in the summer of 1884. "Having
no abiding place or necessary paraphernalia of their own, the men of
the Staten Island Rowing Club came to their assistance, offering the use
of their boat house and a barge three times a week. This was gladly
accepted, and for four seasons they have enjoyed and profited by the
exercise. . . . row[ing] the barge with the same form and length of
stroke as that used by the men, only pulling a bit slower" (Bisland,
1889, p. 424). Bisland also noted that in addition to the forty male
members of the Knickerbocker Canoe Club of New York, there were
sixteen honorary women members who took part in the canoe activities
(p. 425).

The Fencers' Club of New York had a large membership of some
of the city's best known and ultra-fashionable ladies. Three days a week
the club was devoted to the instruction of women. It was reported that
some regular devotees became quite adept at the sport (Barney, 1894,
p. 269).

New York seemed to be the seat of all sorts of activity, including
"innumerable and most prosperous bowling clubs for women" (Bisland,
1890, p. 34). The author reported that their meetings were well-attended
and the bowlers were apparently quite accomplished. For example,
"the ladies of the United Bowling Club in Brooklyn rolled some very
remarkable scores during the winter, and once something very near the
full three hundred was bowled by one of them" (Bisland, p. 35). The
most complete and well-furnished alley, exclusively for the women's
use, plus a gymnasium, made the Ladies' Berkeley Athletic Club (also
in New York), worthy of its description as "that temple of feminine
sport and gymnastics" (Bisland, p. 36).

---

* Their prophecies have come true! The Division for Girls and Women's Sports and
the Division for Men's Athletics of the American Association for Health, Physical
Education and Recreation share one seat on national sports councils, speak with one
voice, and have but one vote between them.

There were also parallel kinds of clubs in the colleges during this era. The major difference between the two groups of clubs was that those in the larger social environment frequently sponsored coed competition. In fact, the clubs provided the occasion for social gatherings. In the colleges, the competition was always for females only and even male spectators were generally not welcome.

In addition to the clubs described, ladies were members of bowling clubs, archery clubs, skating clubs, tennis clubs, and golf clubs all over the country. Sometimes they shared facilities with the men's clubs of which they were a part; sometimes they had their own clubs and facilities; occasionally their membership was "honorary" or "associate" rather than being accorded full status. Nevertheless, their presence in sport was organized and began to be recognized in periodicals of the time.

## Sport Costumes

Women in sport have been subject to dress codes, through both custom and law, since they began entering sport activities in obvious numbers. Consequently, magazines such as *Godey's Ladies Book* and organizations such as the Amateur Athletic Union, the United States Field Hockey Association, and the Women's Athletic Associations in innumerable colleges and universities, have all discussed at great length the "problem" of what to wear.

The exposure of arms and legs has been gradual—by inches, actually—and has gone from private to public very slowly and with great reluctance on society's part. The heavy, full-length, voluminous dress with numerous petticoats prescribed by the Victorians made activity almost impossible. It became essential, therefore, to develop a gymnastic dress for women as soon as some form of light exercise became fashionable. The early costumes consisted of a long-sleeved dress to the knees, under which were wide-cut pants, gathered at the ankles. The bloomer or some form of pantalette under a skirt remained in use for most of the century, though toward the end the skirt gave way to an overblouse and very full bloomers which utilized about four yards of material. Gradually the bloomer was trimmed and shortened to a below-the-knee knicker, though the legs were still covered by stockings and decency was therefore preserved.

Through all of these changes the press and "respectable people" reviled the degeneration of propriety presaged by change. Amelia Bloomer and her followers were severely chastised in the 1850s for daring to wear an outfit of skirt and long bloomers on the street. The famous feminist, Elizabeth Cady Stanton, promptly adopted the costume and reported: "What incredible freedom I enjoyed for two years! Like a captive set free from his ball and chain, I was always ready for a brisk walk through sleet and snow and rain, to climb a mountain, to jump over a fence, work in the garden, and, in fact, for any necessary locomotion" (Stanton, 1971, pp. 70-71). Sadly, though, even as independent a woman as Stanton gave way to the intense scorn and ridicule that the costume engendered. "The wearers . . . soon found that the physical freedom did not compensate for the persistent persecution and petty annoyances suffered at every turn. To be rudely gazed at in public and private, and to be followed by crowds of boys in the street, was exasperating" (Stanton, p. 71).

Nevertheless, the bloomer outfit became the standard gymnasium costume. It was, of course, adopted for college physical education programs. Therefore, when basketball became a popular sport, spectators were banned from the games, in part because physical educators did not wish women to be seen in their abbreviated dress. On at least one occasion, however, males at the University of Oregon circumvented this ban by dressing in women's clothes and veiling their faces (Spears, 1973, pp. 17-18).*

The flannel bloomers with the serge blouses were not always appreciated by the college students. In the manner of students everywhere, a humorous poem was written by an anonymous young woman from Goucher College, published in the student publication in 1892, and reprinted by Ainsworth (1930, pp. 95-96):

> I remember, I remember the gymnasium where we walked—
> Round and round the mystic circle
> With our shoes all nicely chalked
> In our pretty dark blue costumes
> Rather baggy round the knees
> And our yellow ties and slippers
> And our ankles on the freeze.

Like them or not, even in the nineteenth century the official costumes were required. As the 1891-1892 Mt. Holyoke Catalog stated: "For the

---

*Shades of Pherenike who disguised herself as a trainer in order to circumvent the ban on women's attendance at Olympic Games. Fortunately she was spared the prescribed punishment—death—when she was discovered, but thereafter trainers were required to attend without clothes. No such rule was passed at Oregon!

sake of uniformity the students are requested to secure their gymnasium suits through the department" (Ainsworth, 1930, p. 94).

Out-of-doors, in public, the gymnasium costume was not properly worn. Though tennis was a sport for women which really required vigorous activity, at the turn of the century one player noted:

> No girl would appear unless upholstered with a corset, a starched petticoat, a starched skirt, heavily button-trimmed blouse, a starched shirtwaist with long sleeves and cuff links, a high collar and four-in-hand necktie, a belt with silver buckle, and sneakers with large silk bows (USLTA, 1972, p. 26).

The golfers had a similar outfit. At the first tournament in 1895, the ladies

> All were attired in the golfing uniform of the day—hats, heavy leather boots, and layers of fabric. . . . Long cloth or tweed skirts reached from their waists to their ankles. Underneath was an assortment of petticoats, also touching the shoe tops. Blouses with full-length sleeves had starched collars around which ties were draped. Over the blouse it was fashionable to wear a bright-colored jacket carrying the club emblem on the breast pocket. On the ladies' feet were heavy shoes, some wore boots with metal tackets. On their heads were broad brimmed hats, held in place by hat pins or veils tucked under the chin. Around their waists were heavy leather belts with buckles.*

Field hockey players had a prescribed outfit which was published in their Spalding rule book:

> Skirts should be of light woolen material, made plainly, like a bicycling skirt. Petticoats should not be worn, for however short, they are awkward to run in; knickerbockers fastening at the knee should be substituted. The skirt or blouse, made of flannel to prevent risk of chills, must be loose (this does not necessitate untidyness), neat fitting and made after a uniform club pattern. The goalkeeper and fullbacks will find sweaters or coats made in the club colors useful on cold days. Keeping comfort and play in view the hair should be securely fixed; opportunities are so often

---

* From W. Grimsley, *Golf. Its History, People and Events,* Englewood Cliffs, N.J.: Prentice-Hall, p. 204. Copyright © 1966 by Prentice-Hall and reprinted by permission.

lost by a player who has to continuously attend to hairpins instead of the ball.*

The hockey players had a special problem with muddy fields. Thus it was stipulated in the rules that skirts should be four inches from the ground. But the backs of the skirts tended to trail anyway and a British player pleaded that "this drooping back quickly gets wet on a muddy ground and by the end of the game is often a foot deep in slush. This not only impedes running by adding greatly to the weight of the skirt, but is dangerous to health engendering many chills. . ." (*Well-Dressed,* 1929, p. 1). In answer to that problem, the rules were changed in 1901 to require that skirts be six inches off the ground. This created a new issue in that it was scandalous to appear in public with such a short skirt, so it was required that players travel to the games in a long skirt or wear a long coat over their "short" skirt.

The bicycle is said to have provided the big breakthrough for women's dress. It was so difficult—and dangerous—to ride with a long skirt that the divided skirt or knicker had to be adopted as the suitable costume or "rational dress." After a period of public antagonism with some women refused admittance to restaurants and other places, the riding outfit finally held sway. It marked the beginning of women's emancipation from restrictive clothing and therefore has been credited by historians as being one of the important hallmarks of the feminist movement. Many other factors probably helped to make the change acceptable at that moment in time (around the turn of the century), including the changing status of women that accompanied the industrial revolution. But the great numbers of bicycling women at the propitious moment provided the specific catalyst: a mass demonstration of proper women wearing the new dress in public.

Sports clothing grew increasingly sensible in the next two decades, but it was in the twenties and thirties that the major battles were fought. In 1919 Suzanne Lenglen (a famous French tennis player who in 1926 became the first woman to embark on a pro tour of the United States) revolutionized the tennis scene by appearing in a short-sleeved, one-piece pleated dress over shorts—with no petticoat. It was 1929 before a

---

* From Spalding, *Field Hockey for Women,* as quoted in J.P. Shillingford, "History of the United States Field Hockey Association 1922-1972," U.S. Field Hockey Association, 1972, pp. 12-13. Reprinted by permission.

The old dress to the new, *Cycle* Magazine, 1897.

woman dared to appear without stockings! Helen Jacobs was prohibited
by tournament officials from wearing shorts in a Wightman Cup match
in the early 1930s; it was 1937 before Alice Marble wore brief shorts on
the court, ushering in their use in that sport.

The biggest problem was on the public beaches of the country.
Swimmers—or, more accurately, bathers—had worn heavy dress-like
garments and later short-sleeved dresses over stockings and bloomers.
But as costumes became more and more abbreviated, public officials
felt called upon to pass dress regulations. In 1917 the American Association of Park Superintendents at New Orleans adopted bathing suit regulations for city beaches. For both men and women "No all-white or
flesh-colored suits are permitted or suits that expose the chest lower
than a line drawn on a level with the arm pits." For the ladies, the men
agreed that

> Blouse and bloomer suits may be worn with or without stockings,
> provided the blouse has quarter-arm sleeves or close-fitting arm
> holes, and provided the bloomers are full and not shorter than four
> inches above the knee. ("Bathing Regulations for City Beaches,"
> *American City,* 16 (May, 1917), 537 quoted in Kidwell, 1968,
> p. 29)

Olympic champ Ethelda Bleibtrey was given a citation for "nude"
swimming on a Manhattan (New York) Beach in 1919; she had removed
her stockings before going for a swim. In 1922, bathers in one-piece
knitted suits, with shoulder straps and short legs, were arrested on a
Chicago beach which was patrolled by policewomen who measured the
arm pits and necklines (Jensen, 1952, pp. 164-165).

The track stars, running in AAU-sanctioned events, of course wore
bloomer shorts. But in 1922, one of the first rules about women's track
which the AAU promulgated was that the girls' bloomers could not be
more than two inches above the knees.

In 1923 field hockey dress codes were abandoned. "Provisions
forbidding hat pins or the wearing of hard brimmed hats were omitted
and after 1921, no regulations of skirt length existed" (Shillingford,
1972b, p. 14).

The basketball players had their own revolution. In Dallas, Texas,
Colonel Melvorne J. McCombs contemplated starting a team for his
company, the Employers' Casualty Company.

> His first move was to climb into a balcony seat at a high school
> gymnasium and watch a couple of the girls' teams do combat.

The first thing that caught his eye was the superfluity of attire.
The misses were weaving around down there in baggy woolen
bloomers, long stockings and flapping middy blouses. . . (Cunningham, 1936, p. 61).

When the team, the Golden Cyclones, finally took the floor in 1928
they shattered tradition by appearing in blue shorts and a snappy white
jersey. Reportedly, the crowds assembled to see this display of female
flesh (or perhaps it was the team's star, "Babe" Didrikson, who attracted
the spectators). By the third year they shed the woolen shorts perma-
nently for panties of bright orange satin, causing a sensation but starting
a trend that still continues.

Thus by the time the All-American Girls Baseball League came on
the scene in the 1940s, the problem no longer centered on what was the
proper dress *on* the field. True, there was a league regulation which
stipulated that shorts could be no higher than six inches above the knee
(a net gain of four inches in twenty years). The new focus of the dress
codes was on clothing *off* the field—a new emphasis that plagues
athletes to this day, particularly in the colleges. The players were
required to:

Always appear in feminine attire when not actively engaging in
practice or playing the ball. . . . At no time may a player appear
in the stands in her uniform, or wear slacks or shorts in public.
(Rules of Conduct for League Players, reprinted by Riherd, 1953,
p. 86)

These restrictions typically are echoed in the following rules for
women intercollegiate competitors in a large American university, in
force in 1970:

Skirts must be worn at all times while boarding and debarking
[from the team bus] and except while actively participating in a
sport. . . . If you wish to wear shorts and slacks (no riveted jeans)
while riding the bus and are willing to change on the bus, this will
be permitted.

It is ironical that early dress codes were designed to prevent exposure
of flesh, particularly legs, while current ones are designed to prevent the
covering up of legs by wearing long pants.

Outside of the colleges, today's dress codes are more a matter of
custom than regulation. Most sport organizations do not legislate the
costume permitted in their tournaments. The belief that the style of

dress is important to sport continues, however. The 1972 edition of the USLTA's *Official Encyclopedia* reminds its readers that

> Traditionally, however, the basic principle of proper tennis dress is that *white is right.* . . . The woman's outfit should have as few frills as possible. The most highly recommended (and often required for tournament play) is the typical one-piece tennis dress with abbreviated pleated skirts (pp. 76-77).

Perhaps the best measure of how important the issue of dress may be, is the fact that contemporary players are known to pay as much as $225 for a tennis dress designed by Teddy Tinling.

## SPONSORSHIP AND PROMOTION

Women's sport, like men's sport, has been promoted by numerous institutions and organizations including schools and colleges, youth agencies, YM and YWCA's, municipal recreation agencies, industries, national sport organizations, religious groups, and various clubs and societies. Of these groups, the most important ones in the sense that their efforts account for the greatest numbers of participants, have been the national sport associations, industry, and the educational institutions. Since the collegiate sport organizations are discussed in detail in Chapter 2, this discussion will center around the other groups.

### Amateur Athletic Union

The AAU's first involvement in women's sport took place as a result of action during its annual meeting of 1914. Seward A. Simons of the Southern Pacific Association proposed amending the constitution to permit registration of women swimmers. He contended that he had "never seen in any contest any act of immodesty that would bring the blush of shame to any man, mother or child" (Minutes, 1914, quoted by Korsgaard, 1952, p. 280).

In the ensuing discussion, an interesting comment was made by one of the delegates who had attended an International Amateur Athletic Federation (IAAF) Congress where the issue of women's sport was discussed. He declared that "with the exception of France and the United States every member of the seventeen countries voted for the competition of women. I think the reason the United States voted against the proposal was due to the personal feeling of our late lamented secretary. . . ." (Korsgaard, pp. 279-280).

Simons' proposal was passed and the Registration article amended to include a statement that: "Nothing herein contained shall prevent the registration of women for swimming events confined exclusively to women" (Korsgaard, p. 280). A year later the Records Committee was authorized to consider and pass upon women's swimming records.

In 1921, Harry E. Stewart, a physical educator who had an interest in the athletic abilities of women, formed the National Women's Track Athletic Association, and later sent a team of women to compete in Paris. His action brought women's track and field into new prominence. The AAU appointed a committee to consider the advisability of controlling women's athletics and the Chairperson reported in 1922 that "the reason for the Committee being appointed arose because of the group of women being sent to France last summer" (Minutes, 1922, quoted by Korsgaard, 1952, p. 282). As a result of their study, the AAU concluded that:

> The time has come for properly regulating the girls' athletics. Numerous requests have come in from clubs in the AAU asking that girls' events be put on field day programs (*New York Herald*, April 9, 1922).

Therefore, it was

> Resolved that the Board of Governors of the AAU be requested to provide for competitions for women, and that they cooperate with women's athletics organizations, and consult with medical authorities, with a view to the standardization of events for women (*The New York Times*, April 9, 1922).

The motion carried unanimously and a year later the AAU began conducting National Indoor and Outdoor Championships for women.

Since their venture into women's swimming and track and field appeared successful, in January, 1923 the AAU approved registration for women in all the sports under their jurisdiction. For the next decade women's sport appeared to grow well under their aegis. But according to Korsgaard (1952), who researched the history of the AAU, the organization was disappointed as the years went by that the interest in women's competition did not reach the expected intensity (p. 291). The unremitting opposition of the women physical educators was certainly a factor which led to the absence of most school and college females in AAU meets. Thus in 1937 it was suggested that the AAU turn to industrial and recreation groups; the result of that action was considered successful (Minutes, 1937, quoted by Korsgaard, 1952, p. 289).

y that men enjoy. . ." (Brewer,
ariety existed, but it is doubtful
e available to more than a rela-
btful that most women had the

ustrial recreation for women, as
e conclusion that after the 1920s,
eir behalf until World War II. Although
he sponsorship of a champion team
ompany of Dallas' Golden Cyclones,
Connecticut), most companies con-
ing the women a team or two. Of
more than 10,000 companies sponsoring
ring the 1940s, that still represents a

equence in this country has its own national
generally have a board of officers, the larger
executive secretary and staff, an office or
ation, sometimes a hall of fame, and they spon-
cal (club) levels through international events.
t in which women have participated takes place
hese groups.
rveys (Riherd, 1953, and Fidler, 1973) were
urposes of assessing women's involvement in these
Where appropriate, the findings in relation to
iscussed under their respective headings in Chapter 3.
ound that almost every national sport organization
en members. However, as Table 1 indicates, this has
place at the time of their founding. Fidler found that
ided more often after 1920 (82.5%) than before (30%).
hat women were not prominent or influential in the
se sport groups and have only held leadership positions
rter of them (p. 39).
hese organizations have always had a greater membership.
mbership and involvement increases proportionally with
he organization and the longer it functions in time. About
organizations stated that they had problems recruiting and
omen members (p. 40).

cipating in almost every kind of activit
1944, p. 5). It is possible that such a
that most of the named activities wer
tively few people and even more dou
opportunity to experience them.

In sum, the scanty data on in
located by this author, leads to th
there was little effort made on
some companies went all out in
(e.g., The Employees Casualty C
and the Raybestos Brakettes of
tented themselves with permit
course, given that there were
industrial league recreation d
sizable population.

## National Sport Organizatio

Almost every sport of con
organization. These bodie
ones have a full-time paid
even a building, a public
sor competition from lo
A good deal of the spo
under the auspices of

Two extensive s
undertaken for the p
sport organizations.
specific sports are d

Both studies
has accepted wom
not always taken
these dates coin
She also found
founding of th
in about a qua

Men in t
Women's me
the size of t
half of the
retaining w

t
th.
the
eve.

He might
winners of
and bowling
In 1941
American Ind
*Journal* (ISJ).
reported on em
that the stepped
the amount of sp
a variety of sports
softball. One pictu
tioned: "A large pro
young, energetic. The
popularity in their rec
In some 1944-45 progr
1945, p. 33).

Another picture in
umpteen thousands of att
umpteen thousand banque
industrial bowling season" (
very few pictures of women
showing a woman archer. In t
numerous pictures of women's
casting equipment featured wor
Some companies seemed t
stance, in 1947 it was reported

The AAU currently sponsors competitive events in thirteen sports involving close to 5 million people. Though no breakdown by sex is available, it can be assumed that perhaps 800,000 to 1,500,000 of those involved are females.

## Industrial Sport

Promotion of sport by industry and recreation groups began as early as 1910 but began to be extensive during the 1920s. It is almost impossible to locate information about the actual amount of sport that was sponsored, particularly for women. Nevertheless, some inferences can be gleaned from reports of the U.S. Department of Labor, Bureau of Labor Statistics, which occasionally surveyed industry to see what provisions it was making for the "welfare" of the employees.

In 1913, they reported that about a third of the industries surveyed had gymnasiums, baseball diamonds, and a few mentioned tennis courts. Some rented gymnasiums at the YMCA. A few companies mentioned holding classes in physical culture for men and for women; one avowed that "once a week the gymnasium is reserved for the women clerks" (U.S. Dept. of Labor, 1913, p. 66). The most typical provision for the women was a "recreation room" which consisted of couches for resting and sometimes a piano or phonograph.

An extensive study was conducted in 1916-17 over 31 states. Information was secured for 431 establishments having an aggregate of 1,662,000 employees. About a third of the companies reported baseball grounds and club houses or rooms; close to a fifth had tennis courts and/or billiard or pool rooms; around a tenth had gymnasiums and/or swimming pools; 15 percent had bowling alleys. Most of the reports noted the use of these facilities by women workers, though generally at limited times. One club was open for the men every day from 9 A.M. till midnight; women employees and families were allotted one evening a month (U.S. Dept. of Labor, 1918, p. 78).

The survey performed in 1926 reported that "regularly organized [baseball] teams among women employees, while not common, were found in a number of instances. . . . Although baseball is the most popular game, diamond ball, hand ball, speed ball, kitten ball, and volley ball also enjoy considerable popularity. Several girls' diamond ball teams were reported . . . volleyball seems to have an increasing degree of popularity. . ." (U.S. Dept. of Labor, 1926, p. 47). Rifle teams and tennis were also mentioned as sports sponsored for women. One public service corporation reported several track teams among the employees of both sexes. A survey of community recreation cited basketball for women many times.

Writing in 1929, the sportswriter Tunis stated:

> Numerically, the college undergraduates form an inconsiderable proportion of the mass of girls all over the land who are interested in athletics to-day. Nearly all the big industrial concerns, the big banks, the big insurance companies, and large corporations conduct sporting activities for their employees. There are, it is true, some college women on the teams; but it is mainly from these girls—girls in factories, girls in offices, girls in shops—that the material comes which makes up our women's Olympic teams every four years (p. 213).

He might have added that it is also the industrial teams which were the winners of most of the national championships in basketball, softball, and bowling.

In 1941 industry started a new journal. Originally called *AIM* for American Industrial Manpower, in 1948 it became the *Industrial Sports Journal* (ISJ). Until 1962 this journal (then called *Employee Recreation*) reported on employee sport. During the later war years it was obvious that the stepped-up number of women workers had led to an increase in the amount of sport competition. Numerous pictures showed women in a variety of sports including basketball, tennis, bowling, bait-casting, and softball. One picture of the Beech Aircraft basketball team was captioned: "A large proportion of women employed today in industry are young, energetic. Thus the more vigorous sports have quickly acquired popularity in their recreation clubs. Basketball is particularly active here. In some 1944-45 programs women's teams exceed men's" (*ISJ*, April, 1945, p. 33).

Another picture in 1945 was captioned "In recent weeks some umpteen thousands of attractive young ladies such as these gathered in umpteen thousand banquets to celebrate the end of another successful industrial bowling season" (*ISJ*, June, 1945). After 1945 there were very few pictures of women athletes and only archery carried an ad showing a woman archer. In the early forties, not only were there numerous pictures of women's teams, but ads for softball, tennis, and casting equipment featured women.

Some companies seemed to support a great deal of activity. For instance, in 1947 it was reported that the Illinois Bell Telephone Company had approximately 1000 women in office teams playing volleyball. Fifty-eight teams formed into four skill classifications, with eight teams playing for the final title in each division. It was their 19th annual tourney! A study of fifteen automobile unions (March, 1949) found an effective recreation program but few women involved. One union reported one girls' basketball team in some years; one softball team, several bowling teams, some table tennis players, and eight golfers taking part in a municipal tournament were all the sport activities reported for women. The UAW-CIO Women's Committee, a group which still exists within the union to deal with special problems of women workers, observed a "lack of interest of women in recreation" and attempted to plan a camp weekend for them. "Sufficient interest could not be aroused in the project" (March, p. 14).

An informal perusal of the *ISJ* for all years that it was published, led this author to conclude that bowling, basketball, and softball were the only three sports that were played on any large scale. Occasional mention was made of volleyball and tennis; golf, when discussed, was usually for men although one or two companies reported sponsoring women's play; one company in Kentucky reported a nine team girls' field hockey league and included a picture to prove it (*ISJ*, July, 1949).

When Rosie the Riveter returned home, some of the sport leagues suffered casualties. The Industrial Recreation Federation of Greater New York sponsored a six-team girls' basketball league in 1945. In 1946 there were not enough teams to continue the league. In 1949 the league was revived and included softball and tennis with golf and swimming planned for the future (*ISJ*, December, 1949, p. 27).

From these accounts it is obvious that large numbers of women were probably involved in sport sponsored by industry, though the kind of activities was decidedly limited. In 1950 an *ISJ* writer commented:

> One [fact] is the enormous spread of activities, in variety, from what was little more than bowling before the war to more than 100 different sports and recreations today. . . . Bowling continues to hold the lead, percentagewise, in preference, the survey shows; but it is rapidly being approached by softball, basketball and golf; and other sports . . . particularly baseball, table-tennis, lawn tennis, fishing, shooting and archery . . . are not far behind (*ISJ*, March, 1950, p. 18).

A Field Representative of the National Recreation Association (NRA), writing on industrial recreation, observed that "women are now participating in almost every kind of activity that men enjoy. . ." (Brewer, 1944, p. 5). It is possible that such a variety existed, but it is doubtful that most of the named activities were available to more than a relatively few people and even more doubtful that most women had the opportunity to experience them.

In sum, the scanty data on industrial recreation for women, as located by this author, leads to the conclusion that after the 1920s, there was little effort made on their behalf until World War II. Although some companies went all out in the sponsorship of a champion team (e.g., The Employees Casualty Company of Dallas' Golden Cyclones, and the Raybestos Brakettes of Connecticut), most companies contented themselves with permitting the women a team or two. Of course, given that there were more than 10,000 companies sponsoring industrial league recreation during the 1940s, that still represents a sizable population.

## National Sport Organizations

Almost every sport of consequence in this country has its own national organization. These bodies generally have a board of officers, the larger ones have a full-time paid executive secretary and staff, an office or even a building, a publication, sometimes a hall of fame, and they sponsor competition from local (club) levels through international events. A good deal of the sport in which women have participated takes place under the auspices of these groups.

Two extensive surveys (Riherd, 1953, and Fidler, 1973) were undertaken for the purposes of assessing women's involvement in these sport organizations. Where appropriate, the findings in relation to specific sports are discussed under their respective headings in Chapter 3.

Both studies found that almost every national sport organization has accepted women members. However, as Table 1 indicates, this has not always taken place at the time of their founding. Fidler found that these dates coincided more often after 1920 (82.5%) than before (30%). She also found that women were not prominent or influential in the founding of these sport groups and have only held leadership positions in about a quarter of them (p. 39).

Men in these organizations have always had a greater membership. Women's membership and involvement increases proportionally with the size of the organization and the longer it functions in time. About half of the organizations stated that they had problems recruiting and retaining women members (p. 40).

Riherd found that a number of organizations provided opportunities for women to compete against men. These included: archery, equestrianism, revolver shooting, riflery, roque, skeet shooting, and trapshooting (p. 240).

Unfortunately, most of these national organizations do not keep extensive records, nor do they keep figures by sex. In Fidler's study only 12 organizations reported membership figures by sex. In 1972 these 12 organizations had a total of 371,772 women; the female-male ratio was 1:1.6. However, that does not include the largest groups such as the softball and tennis players and the bowlers. Taken as a whole, the national sport organizations probably accounted for the sponsorship of *organized sport competition for approximately 8-10 million women in 1972.*

## Coaches and Other Personnel

The coaches of high level competition for women have rarely been females. The logical reason for this is that with few exceptions, organized competition for women in a given sport was not developed until after it had been established for men. Therefore, when women in each sport decided to form teams and clubs for the purpose of playing against other like groups, there were few females with adequate experience in the activity. An early example was the formation of a women's crew in 1884. "Four young women with one of the men from the [Staten Island Rowing] Club acting as coxswain and coach" practiced their rowing (Bisland, 1889, p. 424). In recent decades, the change to the five person, full court basketball game has sent many women coaches to their male colleagues for assistance, since they have had little experience with this type of game.

Sponsoring organizations such as the AAU and the various sport federations were used to working with men; they almost always selected male coaches for teams which they were sending into international competition. Once the tradition was established it was difficult to break. Furthermore, the athletes preferred the males. In the mid-1930s, in an AAU questionnaire survey mailed to 850 competitors, half of whom had been in Olympic competition, the response favored men's coaches (Korsgaard, 1952, p. 287).

The women's Olympic teams have rarely had female coaches (five times in track and field, five times in gymnastics; in swimming, not since 1920 when the manager also coached). The track and field mana-

TABLE 1
Involvement of Women in National Sport Organizations, 1876–1972*

| Organization | Founded | First women members | First woman officer |
|---|---|---|---|
| National Rifle Association | 1871 | ——† | —— |
| Appalachian Mountain Club | 1876 | 1876 | —— |
| National Archery Association | 1879 | 1879 | 1947 |
| U.S. Lawn Tennis Association | 1881 | 1889 | 1957 |
| U.S. Golf Association | 1894 | 1894 | —— |
| North American Yacht Racing Union | 1897 | —— | none |
| American Canoe Association (White Water Division) | 1900 | 1900 | 1970 |
| U.S. Revolver Association | 1904 | —— | —— |
| U.S. Ski Association | 1904 | —— | 1964 |
| American Casting Association | 1906 | Unknown | 1970 |
| Amateur Fencer's League | 1891 | 1912 | —— |
| American Tennis Association | 1916 | —— | 1961 |
| Women's International Bowling Congress | 1916‡ | | |
| Amateur Trapshooting Association | 1900 | 1918 | —— |
| National Horseshoe Pitching Association | 1915 | 1919 | —— |
| U.S. Figure Skating Association | 1921 | —— | —— |
| U.S. Field Hockey Association | 1922‡ | | |
| American Motorcycle Association | 1924 | 1924 | 1972 |
| National Skeet Shooting Association | 1926 | 1926 | 1970 |
| National Duckpin Bowling Congress | 1927 | 1927 | —— |
| U.S. Women's Squash Racquets Association | 1928‡ | | |
| U.S. Volleyball Association | 1928 | —— | —— |
| Soaring Society of America | 1932 | 1932 | 1938 |
| National Muzzle Loading Rifle Association | 1933 | 1933 | 1940 |
| Amateur Softball Association | 1933 | 1933 | 1960 |
| U.S. Table Tennis Association | 1933 | 1933 | —— |

* From Merrie A. Fidler, "A Survey of the Nature and Extent of Women's Involvement in Selected National Sports Organizations." Presented at the Conference on Women in Sport, Macomb, Illinois, June 25-29, 1973. Reprinted by permission of the author.

ger's report in 1948 (a year in which the team had a woman coach) firmly recommended "that a man be named coach in order to insure team confidence and eliminate personalities entering affairs of administration" (Bushnell, 1948, p. 107). Since 1968 the women kayakers have also had a female coach.

The top level basketball and volleyball teams are almost invariably

**TABLE 1, continued**
**Involvement of Women in National Sport Organizations, 1876–1972**

| Organization | Founded | First women members | First woman officer |
|---|---|---|---|
| American Badminton Association | 1937 | 1937 | 1930s |
| Amateur Bicycle League, America | 1921 | 1938 | 1956 |
| American Water Ski Association | 1939 | 1939 | 1957 |
| National Field Archery Association | 1939 | —— | —— |
| American Jr. Bowling Congress | 1947 | 1947 | 1964 |
| U.S. Professional Tennis Association | 1947. | 1947 | —— |
| U.S. Women's Curling Association | 1947‡ | | |
| Eastern Tennis Patrons | 1950 | 1950 | —— |
| Ladies Professional Golf Association | 1950‡ | | |
| U.S. Handball Association | 1951 | —— | none |
| American Turners | 1850 | 1950s | 1969 |
| U.S. Judo Federation | 1952 | 1952 | none |
| International DN Ice Yacht Racing | 1953 | 1953 | 1960 |
| International Women's Fishing Association | 1955‡ | | |
| U.S. Parachute Association | 1957 | 1957 | none[1] |
| Underwater Society of America | 1959 | —— | 1964 |
| Professional Ski Instructors of America | 1960 | 1961 | none |
| Professional Archers Association | 1961 | 1961 | none |
| U.S. Track & Field Federation | 1961 | 1961 | —— |
| U.S. Gymnastics Federation | 1963 | 1963 | 1965 |
| Los Angeles Aikido | 1961 | 1963 | 1970 |
| Billiard Players of America | 1964 | —— | none |
| U.S. Duffers Association | 1965 | 1965 | 1968 |
| Billiard Congress of America | 1948 | 1967 | none |
| American Woman's Lawn Bowls Association | 1970‡ | | |
| American Platform Tennis Association | 1937 | 1971 | 1971 |
| U.S. Polo Association | 1890 | 1972 | none |

† No data reported

‡ All-women's organizations

[1] None have run for office

coached by men, though the American Softball Association reports that currently about half of the women's teams in its leagues are coached by women (Porter, 1973). Top level figure skaters have women coaches, but speed skaters do not. Almost all of the champion swimmers have been and are coached by men. About half of the intercollegiate gymnastic teams are coached by men.

The use of male coaches has always been a particularly antagonizing factor to the physical educators. In all of the published policy statements of the Women's Division of the NAAF and the Division for Girls and Women's Sports, it is stressed that competent or qualified women should direct, coach, and officiate women's sport. By 1957, however, the qualifying phrase "wherever and whenever possible" (DGWS, p. 58) was added—perhaps in recognition of the difficulties in securing sufficient numbers of able and willing women. In 1965 it was evident that the practice of using male coaches for collegiate teams was increasing and some of the women who were coaching were not members of the physical education department. Therefore, a new statement was added to the guidelines: "If a nonstaff member is teaching or coaching, a woman member of the physical education faculty should supervise and chaperone the participants" (DGWS, 1965, p. 36).

The use of chaperones was incorporated into the regulations of the national and international sport organizations. No matter how many male coaches there were, a female always accompanied the team in its travels. In 1915 the AAU provided the swimmers with an opportunity to request funds for a chaperone if they desired. But by 1923, their regulations required it and continued to provide assurances that the necessary funds would be made available. This was apparently meant to assuage some of the criticisms of the women physical educators who believed the male coaches were neither interested in nor knowledgeable about the special needs of women.

The AAU also found it necessary to prohibit the use of massagers or "men rubbers" for the women participants. More positively, in 1923 they made a mandatory rule that "women be members of all committees dealing with sports in which women take part." They also stipulated that "in all cases where clubs registered women to represent them in any sport, there had to be women officers or officials to deal directly with the women contestants" (Minutes, 1923, quoted in Korsgaard, 1952, pp. 76-77).

Olympic teams also have had women chaperones, though the team managers are most frequently men. Difficulties can be encountered on this point since the housing is separate. In such cases the chaperones often function as managers, but again difficulties may arise because they do not have the requisite authority. This problem was frequently noted in Olympic reports.

In sum, the only opportunity that women consistently have had in high level sport, besides direct participation as competitors, has been as chaperones. The administration, promotion, training, coaching, and managing of organized women's sport has been almost entirely in the hands of men with the exception of intercollegiate sport. The latter activities have been coached by women except sometimes when they have involved competition of high caliber.

# Chapter 2
# Collegiate Sport

Collegiate sport for women in the United States was and is an entity separate from sport in the larger social milieu. In this sense the pattern differs distinctly from that of the men whose activities were (and are) often inseparable. For example, most male Olympic athletes are (or were) on their high school or college varsity teams; most women have obtained their competitive experience through nonschool affiliations. Male track stars represent their colleges in meets with other colleges and also in AAU competition. With rare exception, mostly of recent vintage, women either play for college teams *or* for groups distinct from the colleges. In fact, colleges frequently had a rule which prohibited team membership to women who participated with other groups—especially during the same time period. As late as 1965, the official Division for Girls and Women's Sports (DGWS) "Statement on Competition for Girls and Women" declared that "a student may not participate as a member of an intercollegiate athletic team and at the same time be a member of a team in the same sport outside her institution" (1965, p. 37).

Collegiate sport developed in a relatively unified, controlled pattern across the country, governed as it was by the women physical educators with no external interference. There were three aspects of it: curricular, intramural, and extramural, which in the thinking of physical educators were built one on the other. This relationship was expressed in the familiar triangle (see Fig. 1) which had as its base, and most important part, the curricular program. It was assumed that programing each stage did not take place until the previous one was well established and adequately led and funded. Students were not permitted to ascend to varsity level competition without passing through intramural competition in that sport—a pattern that has changed in recent years.

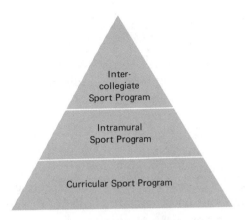

*Fig. 1    Pyramid illustrating the preferred relationship of the three aspects of the collegiate sports program*

## SPORT IN THE CURRICULUM

Recent research by Spears (1973) revealed that sport was introduced into the physical education curriculum in programs for women prior to 1890. During the next two decades a distinct shift away from gymnastic exercises and toward sport participation took place, so that "before 1910, sport had emerged as the dominant component in the physical education curriculum in many institutions" (p. 20). The purpose for including sport in the curriculum was instrumental. That is, it was seen primarily as a vehicle for healthful exercise. It was regarded as a substitute for gymnastics on the assumption that it would have the same beneficial aspects.

### Early Physical Education Programs

Exercise for women was considered essential by the founders and presidents of the early institutions of higher education for women because of the general suspicion that females did not have the physical stamina to endure the stresses and strains of the higher learning. In his inaugural address, the first president of Smith College did not fail to consider the problem:

> We admit it would be an insuperable objection to the higher education of women, if it seriously endangered her health . . . We understand that they need special safeguards . . . With gymnastic training wisely adapted to their peculiar organization, we see no reason

why young ladies cannot pursue study as safely as they do their ordinary employments (Addresses, 1875, pp. 27-28).

Consonant with his statement, the Course of Study included a section on "Physical Culture" which stated: "In addition to lectures on Physiology and Hygiene, regular exercises in the gymnasium and the open air will be prescribed under the direction of an educated physician. These exercises will be designed not merely to secure health, but also a graceful carriage, and well-formed bodies" (Addresses, 1875, p. 5). Seelye's statement and the Smith College approach were typical of the women's colleges and academies of that era. Also representative is the following scene, described in a journal in the late 1840s by a male friend of Emily Dickinson who visited her at Mt. Holyoke:

> Saw some of the young ladies exercise in Calisthenics a species of *orthodox dancing* in which they perambulate a smooth floor in various figures, with a sort of sliding, stage step; not unlike children's plays, all except the *kissing* part, which is probably omitted as not likely to prove interesting where all are of the same sex; the whole movement is accompanied by singing in which noise rather than tune or harmony seems to be the main object. By a species of delusion peculiar to the Seminary, they imagine that all this [is] very conducive to health, strength, gracefulness, etc.*

As sport began to be a viable form of activity for women in the larger social scene, it also was introduced to women in the colleges. Croquet, archery, tennis, bowling, and later track and field and even baseball were introduced at various colleges. Physical recreation in the form of walking, snowshoeing and horseback riding was a common occurrence. By 1890, fourteen sports, from walking to football, had been introduced to institutions as varied as private women's colleges, private coed colleges, state universities, and state normal schools (Spears, 1973, p. 8). Refer to Table 2.

Unlike the men's sport programs, which initially were organized and conducted by the students, sport for women was usually guided by the women physical educators. In fact, in some of the colleges, such as Vassar and Wellesley, it was deliberately provided for by the founders. Although it was originally extracurricular, in the form of spontaneous

---

* From M.D. Greene, "The Growth of Physical Education for Women in the United States in the Early Nineteenth Century," Ed.D. dissertation, University of California, Los Angeles, 1950, p. 94. Reprinted by permission.

**TABLE 2**
Introduction of Sport in 20 Selected Institutions of Higher Education in the United States, 1833–1910*

| Recreation | | | Club | | | Instruction | | |
|---|---|---|---|---|---|---|---|---|
| Sport | College | Year | Sport | College | Year | Sport | College | Year |
| Croquet | Mt. Holyoke | 1866 | Croquet | Vassar | 1866 | Walking | Mt. Holyoke | 1837 |
| Bowling | Vassar | 1866 | Baseball | Vassar | 1866 | Horseback riding | Mills | 1864 |
| Boating | Vassar | 1866 | Boating | Vassar | 1867 | Fencing | Brooklyn NSG (Arnold College) | 1886 |
| Ice skating | Vassar | 1866 | Crew | Wellesley | 1876 | Swimming | Brooklyn NSG | 1886 |
| Archery | Mills College | 1870 | Football | Berkeley | 1877 | Boating | Brooklyn NSG | 1886 |
| Tennis | Wellesley | 1875 | Tennis | Wellesley | 1885 | Track & field | Westchester | 1890 |
| Crew | Wellesley | 1876 | Swimming | Westchester | 1890 | Bowling | Wellesley | 1890 |
| Walking | Smith | 1878 | Walking | Nebraska | 1892 | Crew | Oregon | 1895 |
| Bicycling | Smith | 1878 | Skating | Nebraska | 1892 | Handball | Westchester | 1895 |
| Fencing | Nebraska | 1881 | Bicycling | Nebraska-Wisconsin | 1892 | Golf | Oberlin | 1896 |
| Swimming | Goucher | 1889 | Archery | Goucher | 1893 | Tennis | Mt. Holyoke | 1897 |
| Baseball | Mt. Holyoke | 1891 | Basketball | Oregon | 1894 | Volleyball | Oberlin | 1897 |
| Badminton | Oberlin | 1891 | Bowling | Wisconsin | 1894 | Bicycling | Oberlin | 1897 |
| Basketball | Smith-Holyoke | 1892 | Golf | Wellesley | 1895 | Roller skating | Wellesley | 1900 |
| Ice hockey | Mt. Holyoke | 1894 | Lacrosse | Wellesley | 1897 | Archery | Mt. Holyoke | 1902 |
| Roller skating | Oberlin | 1894 | Field hockey | Goucher | 1897 | Field hockey | Wisconsin | 1903 |
| Golf | Vassar | 1895 | Handball | Wellesley | 1901 | Ice hockey | Oberlin | 1903 |
| Track & field | Vassar | 1895 | Track & field | Westchester | 1901 | Ice skating | Wisconsin | 1906 |
| Skiing | Mt. Holyoke | 1896 | Volleyball | Winthrop | 1902 | Baseball | Smith | 1908 |
| Horseback riding | Mt. Holyoke | 1896 | Ping pong | Berkeley | 1906 | Cricket | | |
| Field hockey | Goucher | 1897 | Fencing | Berkeley | | | | |
| Volleyball | Wisconsin | 1897 | | | | | | |
| Cricket | Smith | 1900 | | | | | | |
| Canoeing | Smith | 1910 | | | | | | |

* Data extracted from B. Spears, "The Emergence of Sport in Physical Education." Presented at the American Association for Health, Physical Education, and Recreation 88th Anniversary National Convention, Minneapolis, Minn., April 16, 1973. Reprinted by permission of the author.

recreation or more formally organized clubs, its appeal was such that the teachers began to introduce it into the curriculum as a spur to improving the health of the women students. Some colleges, such as Oberlin, permitted students to substitute sports for exercises if certain required gymnastics had been completed. "During the student's first year, she could exercise out of doors one day a week, if her pulley weight examination had been passed" (Spears, 1973, p. 11). Exercising out-of-doors in some instances meant tending a garden or walking, but it also meant taking part in sports. Prior to the twentieth century, most sport for women was played out-of-doors, while gymnastics was invariably done in a small gymnasium. The health benefits of the open air were another reason for those in authority to substitute sport for exercise in the physical education program. Some far-sighted educators such as David Starr Jordan, the first president of Stanford, in 1909 reasoned that:

> Relatively few girls enter the University who are skilled enough in any outdoor sports to get recreation from them, and to bring about a wider participation, formal instruction by the University is necessary (Houston, 1939, p. 51).

The first sport in which instruction was given was horseback riding, at Mills College in 1864. Archery, fencing, swimming, rowing, crew, cycling, track and field athletics, and bowling were among the sports introduced into the curriculum during the nineteenth century (Spears, 1973, pp. 6-7). Gymnastics continued to be taught, but sport was substituted for part of the program.

The thinking of the women physical educators is revealed by an experiment conducted at Wellesley College in 1893 to determine if crew could be as beneficial to the physical improvement of the women as gymnastics was thought to be. The results indicated that "students could improve and maintain their physical vigor through sport" (Spears, 1973, p. 12). This finding helped to justify the increasing substitution of sport for gymnastics in the curriculum.

The purpose of sport in the curriculum for college women, prior to the twentieth century, is aptly expressed in the 1865 prospectus of Vassar College:

> [The Trustees] regard this branch of education [physical training], if not as first, intrinsicly considered, yet as fundamental to all the rest. Good health, is in the first place, essential to success in study. . . . In addition to the ordinary system of school calisthenics, which

Fencing class, Smith College, 1904.  [Courtesy the Sophia Smith Collection.]

will be thoroughly taught in its more approved and recent forms, the plan of the college embraces instruction in Swimming, Skating, Gardening with such variety of feminine sports and games as will tend to agreeably diversify the physical exercises, and make them in the highest degree attractive and beneficial to the students.

. . . A suitable portion of each day is set aside for physical exercise and every young lady is required to observe it as one of her college duties.*

## Twentieth Century Physical Education Programs

As the twentieth century progressed, the curriculum for women in physical education became increasingly dominated by sport. The original purposes, which centered on health, shifted in accord with the changing purposes of physical education. *In addition* to the notion of achieving physical vigor through sport, the colleges aimed to promote social values such as were thought to accrue to working in teams. Furthermore, it was hoped that the program of physical education could be designed to provide women and men with skills which could be utilized in the years after college. Consequently, a full program of sports *skills* were taught with the idea of fulfilling each of these purposes. Usually college students were required to learn one team sport (social values) and one individual sport (carry-over values). The health, grace, and posture aim was covered by a course in body mechanics and/or fundamental movement—which usually dealt with principles of diet and exercise as well—and later dance was added for all purposes. The college physical education program, then, generally required at least two semesters of sport instruction with an emphasis on acquiring the skills of the activity.

The kinds of sport offered were similar (if not identical) to those in the program at the turn of the century. In addition to those already named, the team sports of basketball, volleyball, field hockey, and sometimes soccer and lacrosse were taught from the century's first decade. Some activities, however, had lost their initial impetus. Golf, for example, was played in several colleges before the turn of the century. However, in a survey in 1916 only two colleges reported it as one of their activities (Jacobs, 1920, p. 49). Track and field, which received

---

* From H.I. Ballintine, *The History of Physical Training at Vassar College 1865-1915*, Poughkeepsie, N.Y.: Lansing & Bros., pp. 5-7. Reprinted by permission.

The golfers, Wellesley College, ca. 1900.

its start in this country primarily in the colleges, virtually disappeared from educational institutions beginning in the 1920s and continuing through the 1950s. The first report of the Sub-Committee on Track and Field Athletics of the Committee on Women's Athletics indicated that the committee found that schools and agencies had barred track and field because it was identified with intense training and competition (Sibley, 1924, p. 461). The exception to this "ban" took place in some black institutions, notably Tuskegee Institute in Alabama and Tennessee Agricultural and Industrial State University. The most popular college sport, a mainstay of every curriculum for at least the first half of the twentieth century, was basketball.

Not until the 1960s was the curriculum added to in any meaningful way. In that decade, curricular instruction in sport was expanded to include the martial arts (e.g., judo, karate), squash racquets, and occasionally mountain climbing or orienteering were plugged into the program. In this way sports in the contemporary curriculum, like sports in the nineteenth century curriculum, reflected the type of activities popular in the larger social scene. Only during the era of a heavy emphasis on team sports was this principle not in effect. Also in recent years, sports instruction for college women began typically to be given on a coeducational basis. This was a departure from a century of sex separation in sport programs.

## FORMS OF COMPETITION

Contrary to popular opinion, competitive sport has been an integral part of the college scene since the 1860s when baseball teams were organized at Vassar College and match games were played on Saturday afternoons (Ballintine, n.d., p. 9). Because most contests have taken place within the colleges, rather than between them, historians have generally dismissed collegiate sport for women as if it did not exist. This value judgment ignores the importance to the women of interclass competition, for example, and fails to recognize the validity and appropriateness of the various competitive forms developed to meet the needs of the college women. These include intramurals, in the form of clubs, interclass, interdorm or sorority matches, and extramurals, in the form of sports days, play days, interclass-interschool events, telegraphic meets, and, of course, varsity teams. Each had their purpose and their heyday.

An exciting game, Vassar College, 1905.  [Courtesy Vassar College Library.]

**Intramural Forms**

Intramurals were the first form of organized sport contests in the colleges for both men and for women. Some early examples include Vassar with its baseball matches (1870s), tennis tournament (1886), field day (1895), and croquet tournament (1909) (Ballintine, n.d., pp. 9-11). While Vassar had a tennis club in 1881, the University of California, Berkeley had "The Young Ladies Tennis Club," with a membership of thirty, organized in 1891. "In 1900 the Associated Women Students began to revive tennis, cross country, and basketball under the Sports and Pasttimes Association" (Houston, 1939, pp. 30-32). Mt. Holyoke had tennis tournaments and field days in the 1890s (Ainsworth, 1930, p. 86). Wellesley was famous for its crews as early as the 1880s, though at that time

> Wellesley crews were not picked for their oarsmanship, however, but for their singing voices, as . . . the rowing that was done, was a paddle down the lake a short distance to the cove where the college singing took place, and a paddle back to the boat house (Clifton, 1927, p. 10).

The competition, of course, was for the singing.

After the informality of the club era, with its sporadic competition, interclass sport became the chief form of intramurals. Sponsored by the newly organized athletic associations (refer to p. 77), they often reached elaborate levels of organization and sparked very intense emotions. One of the simpler examples was at Oberlin where the newly organized Gymnasium and Field Association instituted skating contests in 1904 with women competing first for their class honors and then for the interclass championships (Hanna, 1904, p. 56).

Smith College carried out an extensive interclass program in basketball which was typical of the most developed type of intramural programs. Senda Berenson, the "mother" of basketball for women and director of the physical education program at Smith, was firmly against competing with other colleges. But she fully sanctioned tournaments within the privacy of the Smith gymnasium. Teams were developed complete with class colors and mascots. Cheers were considered indecorous and consequently songs were written and sung by a class chorus. The words to one of the verses was typical. Written to the tune of "Give us a Drink Bartender" it ran as follows.

THE BOSTON SUNDAY GLOBE—SUNDAY, MARCH 18, 1894

# NO MAN IN IT.

## Smith College Gym Held 1000 Excited Girls.

## Basket Ball Roused Young Beauties' Spirits.

### Plucky Sophs Won After a Lively Game.

Their Captain Carried on Shapely Shoulders.

Songs Made a Noise, and Class Colors Were Everywhere.

*Fig. 2    Facsimile of a newspaper headline over article describing a basketball match between the freshmen and sophomores of Smith College.*

> So throw out the ball, we're ready, quite ready,
> Let the game be fair and clean.
> Play now your best, you grand ninety-niners,
> For the honor of the green.

The gymnasium balconies were decorated with buntings for the big games and it goes without saying that males were denied admittance as spectators. The *Boston Sunday Globe* carried a description of one of the contests held in 1894. Figure 2 is a facsimile of the headlines given to the article, which carried a picture of the winning team, a serious account of the game which was won by the Sophomores by a score of 13-7, and a description that pictured the excitement of the occasion nicely:

> The spectators, about 1000 girls, were seated in galleries. . . . One gallery was tastefully hung with violet, the sophomore team's color, and the other with yellow, the color of the freshmen. Hundreds of violet and yellow flags fluttered violently at the exciting periods of the game.

For weeks the two teams and their substitutes have been practicing under the direction of Miss Senda Berenson. . . .

The uniforms of both teams were the regulation gymnasium suits of navy blue consisting of loose blouses and bloomers. Around the sleeves of the sophomore players were bands of violet ribbon and the figures 96 in the same color were on the fronts of their suits. They wore neckties of the same color. . . .

At the close of the game amid a waving of handkerchiefs, flags and ribbons, Miss Dustin, the captain of the winning team, was hoisted on the shoulders of her victorious team. Thus proudly borne the girl captain was presented with the victors' banner. . . .

The gymnasium was the scene of wild enthusiasm, and everybody collectively and individually on the winning side and off congratulated and received congratulations.

Pres. Seelye wore a yellow ribbon in his coat, surmounted by a cluster of violets and thus honored both teams.

After the game the girls flocked into the city, and until supper time the streets presented a lively spectacle. . . . All were brilliant with their favorite color, and all were much excited (*Boston Sunday Globe,* March 18, 1894).

It is difficult to know the extent of intramural activities in the colleges because no published surveys are available before 1920. At that time Jacobs found that all 51 colleges responding to his survey conducted some form of interclass sport (p. 50).

Three more detailed surveys are available from 1937 to 1972 which give information on intramural programs in colleges throughout the nation. Table 3 summarizes the data by sport. Basketball has been the most consistently popular intramural activity, though in the latest survey it ranks behind volleyball. Although the demise of interest in the team sports, particularly on the college level, has been widely predicted and assumed, it is in the most recent survey (with the smallest sample) that the top three activities are team sports. Field hockey has disappeared as an intramural sport, with only one college in Fidler's survey indicating that it was still part of its program. Football has been added to the list; although only 54 percent of the colleges indicated this sport to be in their intramural program, this author believes that a study taken today, three years later, would show a marked increase. Archery and golf have steadily declined in popularity while bowling and badminton have increased. Baseball has been replaced by softball and its popularity has also grown over the years.

**TABLE 3**
Rank Order of Ten Most Popular Intramural Sports in Institutions of Higher
Education in the United States, 1936–1972*

| 1936 | 1943 | 1972 |
|------|------|------|
| Basketball | Basketball | Volleyball |
| Tennis | Tennis | [Basketball] † |
| Archery | Badminton | [Softball] |
| Swimming | Volleyball | Badminton |
| Baseball | Archery | Tennis |
| Field hockey | Softball | Bowling |
| Volleyball | Table tennis | Swimming |
| Table tennis | Field hockey | Table tennis |
| Badminton | Swimming | Archery |
| Golf | Bowling | Football |

* Sources of data:  Leavitt and Duncan (1937), Scott (1945), Fidler (1972b).
† Bracketed entries indicate equal popularity.

Almost all of the institutions surveyed over the years reported
sponsoring intramural programs (though it must be noted that the later
two surveys had respectively a 64 and 62 percent rate of return; colleges
not conducting programs may have simply ignored the questionnaires).
Only the earliest and latest studies report on the number of sports conducted in each institution. Leavitt and Duncan found that "the number
of activities offered in any one college or university ranges from four
to thirty, with the majority providing between eight and fifteen activities" (1937, p. 70). Fidler found a range of from four to seventeen
activities, with ten as the median (1972b, p. 3). Thus one can conclude
that the average number of activities offered has remained fairly stable
during the 35-year period.

Major changes noted in the studies relate to the administration of
the programs and the increasingly coeducational nature of the activities.
Fidler noted a new trend towards a centralized administrative structure
(e.g., through student unions or intramural offices) rather than through
women's athletic associations. She found 57 percent of her sample had
centralized administration, 85 percent of those having come into existence in the last ten years (Fidler, 1972b, p. 2). In 1937, only one out
of Leavitt and Duncan's entire sample reported central administration.
Those colleges with centrally administered programs tended to have
more coed activities with volleyball, badminton, bowling, tennis, and

softball the five most popular sports. Fidler found that 78 percent of the institutions responding to her survey had at least one coed sport (Fidler, 1972b, pp. 4-5).

Perhaps it is the trend to centralized administration which helped the National Intramural Association (NIA) realize that women's intramurals were within their purview. The NIA was organized in 1950; in 1971 it permitted the first women members.

## Extramural Forms

In 1894 Bryn Mawr challenged Vassar to a tennis tournament but the Vassar faculty refused the tennis club permission to enter such a competition (Litchfield and Mallon, 1915, p. 166). By this action, the two colleges were prevented from going down in history as participating in the first intercollegiate contest. Instead, that honor must be shared by the University of California, Berkeley vs. Stanford and the University of Washington vs. Ellensburg Normal School—both sets of competitors having had an intercollegiate basketball contest in 1896. It is recorded in *The Tyee,* the University of Washington's Class of 1901 Yearbook, that "Great interest was shown in the game, about six hundred people having been present, men being present for the first and last time" (Houston, 1939, p. 38).

Although other instances of intercollegiate competition took place in the next decade, it was by no means a common occurrence. The most popular sport—basketball—was handicapped by the numerous sets of rules then in effect. Since the men's game was considered too rough, women physical educators modified it, using many different variations. Furthermore, the women were opposed to extramural sport and preferred not to engage in it. The earliest survey found that

> most of the women's colleges in the East and many of the co-educational institutions do not play outside games but have interclass contests. Occasionally they play a game with their preparatory school or with a normal school. In the Middle West and West, intercollegiate contests are more common, but the percentage playing them there is less than one-half (Dudley and Kellor, 1909, p. 99).

About ten years later, Jacobs (1920) received answers from 61 colleges which indicated that 14 or 23 percent played interschool sport.

Those studies cannot show how great the variation was; some colleges really had full schedules while others played one or two games a year. By 1915 Radcliffe College had a schedule of 6 hockey and 8 basketball games and later added swimming and tennis (Ainsworth, 1930, p. 84). In the early 1900s the University of California, Berkeley had a seven-game basketball schedule, "but in 1903 these were discontinued for the time by those in authority. Class games then became prominent." However, intercollegiate competition was revived two years later and continued in basketball, tennis, and fencing through 1918 (Houston, 1939, pp. 32-33).

The University of Washington, after its promising beginning, played only 2 to 3 games a year in basketball. However, in 1906 they acquired a male coach, played a victorious seven-game schedule—and discontinued intercollegiate competition (Houston, 1939, p. 38). (The penalty for success?)

As interschool competition slowly became more commonplace, antagonism toward it also began to build. The immediate problem was one of accommodating larger numbers of women in competitive activities. This led to a search for more satisfactory forms of competition than varsity teams provided. The first solution engendered by the women physical educators was the interclass-interschool match. Under this system the popular interclass games were held, thus giving a full intramural schedule since, in the larger colleges, numerous teams first competed for their class championship. Then the interclass champions played their opposite numbers from other colleges. Sometimes, the class champions for each year met their peers. The latter system was tried between Berkeley and Stanford during the 1915-1916 season in both tennis and basketball and was extended to other sports the next season. The value of this approach was enthusiastically described by a Stanford instructor:

> At the close of the intramural interclass competitions, interest and enthusiasm culminate in the intercollegiate interclass matches. Each player who has won her numerals in her class team has, therefore, the additional joy of keen outside competition. No one team is responsible for the day; there are four teams to share the honors or losses and the nervous strain of responsibility for winning is decreased or is eliminated (Burrell, 1917, p. 18).

As indicated in Table 4, this form of competition was utilized by 10 percent of the colleges in Lee's 1923 study and by 18 percent in her 1936 study. It therefore was a substantial part of the intercollegiate scene through the 1930s.

TABLE 4
Extent of Extramural Competition for Women in Institutions of Higher Education in the United States, 1923-1951*

| Type | 1923 (N=50) | | 1930 (N=98) | | 1936 (N=77) | | 1943 (N=227) | | 1951 (N=230) | |
|---|---|---|---|---|---|---|---|---|---|---|
| | No. | % | No. | % | No. | % | No. | % | No. | % |
| Varsity | 6 | .12 | 11 | .11 | 13 | .17 | 36 | .16 | 64 | .28 |
| Interclass–Intercollegiate | 5 | .10 | 3 | .03 | 14 | .18 | – | – | – | – |
| Telegraphic | 5 | .10 | 39 | .40 | 57 | .74 | 108 | .48 | 46 | .48 |
| Play days | – | – | 53 | .54 | 54 | .70 | 110 | .49 | 36 | .49 |
| Sports days | – | – | – | | 32 | .41 | 112 | .49 | 77 | .49 |
| All extramural competition | 11 | .22 | Not reported | | 73 | .95 | 184 | .81 | 212 | .92 |

* Sources of data: Lee (1924 and 1931), Leavitt and Duncan (1937), Scott (1945), White (1954).

The telegraphic meet has consistently been one of the most popular sport forms, reaching its zenith in the 1936 study. In a telegraphic meet the contestants participate on their own campus in accordance with agreed-upon conditions. Results are then telegraphed to a designated official and later announced. Its advantages were obvious in that the expense and effort of traveling was obviated and therefore almost any number could conveniently take part. The feared emotions that could arise in face-to-face competition were negated. Sports such as archery, bowling, and riflery lent themselves to this form of competition, which in part accounts for the high popularity of those sports over the years.

When the negative attitudes toward intercollegiate competition were accepted by the great masses of women physical educators, almost all forms of competition virtually ceased. This created certain problems; the physical educators considered it part of their mission to provide physical activity for all women. Yet the years of Victorian ideals had left women with an antipathy to physical activity; a desire to play had to be instilled and competitive sport was an excellent motivator. Furthermore, both students and faculty enjoyed the social contact with women from other institutions.

The solution that emerged was the play day. At a play day women from several colleges were mixed together on color teams to play a variety of sports or recreational activities. There were more of the latter than the former, because of the obvious difficulty in playing a sport such as basketball with a group of people that has just been assembled. A description of the first known collegiate play day, which replaced the previous intercollegiate competition within the Triangle Conference of Mills, Stanford, and Berkeley, clarifies the scene:

> An enthusiastic group of girls gathered on the University of California campus. These girls were given tags upon which their names were written and were assigned to color squads. These squads met on the field, where time was given for choosing a name, yell, and captain. . . .
>
> The first two events were ones in which all members of the squads took part. These were shuttle relay and pass ball relay. The next events were ones in which selected members of squads participated, while the other members watched and cheered. These were net ball, hockey, tennis and swimming.
>
> A blue ribbon for first place, a red ribbon for second, was given to the squad winning these events, as well as promptness for

squad formation at the bugle sound which was given between each event.*

Though the first college play days were reported in 1926, the "movement" did not get underway till about 1929. In 1936 it was a form utilized by 70 percent of the colleges surveyed.

By that time a new sport form had been derived: the sports day. The sports day's important modification of the play day involved permitting representative teams. That is, competition was between women on teams representing their own institutions. In the early years numerous suggestions were made to be sure that this did not evolve into a type of varsity competition. Most colleges brought pickup teams and sometimes the players did not know beforehand in which sport they would participate. Winners were not announced for the day and even the scores of games were not given on occasion. Games were modified in length—sometimes to 10-15 minutes and rules were changed to play "running time" rather than with time outs for breaks in play such as foul shooting. This further distorted the contests. Finally, sports days were considered as providing good opportunities to rate officials—which meant that games often were officiated by students or others attempting to earn their rating, rather than by experienced officials. However, the sports day was a big improvement over the play day in that real sports were played and over the years, as colleges began to bring teams which had practiced a minimum number of times (as required by DGWS), the caliber of play improved.

The most controversial form of competition was the varsity program. The selection, training, and coaching of a single group of highly skilled players was inconsistent with the philosophy of women physical educators. (Refer to p. 71.) They did little to promote it and much to oppose it and the result is that as late as 1951 only 28 percent of the colleges surveyed reported having varsity teams. One interesting fact is that although in 1909 the west and midwest had the greatest number of varsity programs, from 1923-1972 the greatest percentage of varsity teams was in the east. However, the ratio has been steadily diminishing over the years. It is not known precisely how many colleges currently have varsity teams, but one indication of the extensiveness is that 278

* From M.M. Duncan, *Play Days for Girls and Women*, New York: A.S. Barnes, p. 80. Copyright © by A.S. Barnes and reprinted by permission.

TABLE 5
Rank Order of Ten Most Popular Varsity Sports in Institutions of Higher Education
in the United States, 1923–1971*

| 1923 | 1930 | 1951 | 1971 |
|------|------|------|------|
| Basketball | Tennis | Basketball | Basketball |
| Tennis | ⌈Basketball ⌉ | Field hockey | Tennis |
| Field hockey | ⌊Field hockey⌋ | Tennis | Volleyball |
| Swimming | Swimming | Softball | Field hockey |
| Baseball | Baseball | Swimming | Gymnastics |
| Archery | Archery | Archery | Swimming |
| ⌈Rowing ⌉ † | ——— | ⌈Volleyball⌉ | Softball |
| ⌊Handball⌋ | ——— | ⌊Badminton⌋ | Track and field |
| Fencing | ——— | ⌈Fencing ⌉ | Golf |
| | ——— | ⌊Skiing ⌋ | Badminton |

\* Sources of data:  Lee (1924 and 1931), White (1954), AIAW (1972).

† Bracketed entries indicate equal popularity.

institutions became charter members of the Association for Intercollegiate Athletics for Women (AIAW) in 1971–1972.

All of the data regarding extent of participation in extramural
sports must be viewed with caution. First, although the samples are
nationwide and a conscientious attempt was made to get a good cross-
section of the relevant population, it must be assumed that a higher
percentage of those institutions *not* returning the questionnaires did
not have any kind of extramural competition, than those who did.
Therefore, one cannot generalize that a figure of *x* percent of the colleges responding to the survey probably represents a similar percent of
the whole population. Second, while most of the surveys included
definitions of the different forms of competition, it still may have been
difficult for some colleges to place their programs in the appropriate
contexts. Some of the categories conceivably could overlap as, for
example, a varsity team that played primarily at sports days. Third, a
varsity program in one college might have meant a single team playing
a three-game schedule, while in another it could mean four teams each
playing ten or fifteen games a season. The latter situation is certainly
more common in 1972 and the former circumstance was highly likely
in 1923. Thus comparison across the years is limited in meaning.

The activities in which varsity programs have been conducted
reveal interesting changes over the years. As Table 5 reveals, basketball

and tennis have been the consistently most popular sports among the colleges responding to all the surveys. Field hockey has been replaced by volleyball as the second most popular team sport. Archery, which ranked sixth for almost thirty years, is now off the list of the top ten. Gymnastics and track and field have appeared for the first time. Softball or baseball and swimming rank near the middle of all lists.

One very interesting element, which was reported by White, was the incidence of participation of mixed (coeducational) teams. She found that "approximately one-fourth of the colleges report informal competition on mixed teams in individual sports, volleyball, and softball. Several colleges report basketball, hockey, and 'tail' football" (1954, p. 362). Even more surprising was her report that seven colleges reported having varsity teams composed of men and women. The sports in which this occurred were tennis, golf, sailing, badminton, and archery (p. 362). Unfortunately, no contemporary survey of coed teams in the colleges has been reported.

Changes in types of activities, like changes in sport forms, are natural. They reflect the new interests of the student population and different attitudes on the part of the physical educators. Perhaps the most striking revelation of the latest surveys of both intramurals and extramurals is the health of these programs. Sport for women in colleges appears to be in a boom phase. Shifts in the type of competition (toward more intercollegiate sport), and the organization of programs (toward a central, non-WAA administration) presage still greater changes in the future.

## CHANGING CONCEPTS OF COMPETITION

The concept of appropriate competition for women held by physical educators has changed over the years. In fact, three distinct periods can be discerned from the literature. The earliest era is characterized by informal and cautious disapproval for intercollegiate or interscholastic sport for women. The bulk of the literature against such competition spelled out the concern that it was not in keeping with the ideals of womanly behavior. It seemed to hold unnecessary risks for all concerned and furthermore was not necessarily appropriate to the goals of physical education. Nevertheless, some people spoke in favor of it.

The second period is marked by the presence of a formalized philosophy, stated by recognized organizations charged with responsibility for women's sport. The philosophy, bolstered by countless articles reiterating its main points—thus indicating widespread agreement—was a positive statement of the kind of sport which the physical educators deemed appropriate for women. It was specific in its recommendations, both for the things they wished to see implemented and those which should be discarded—including all forms of intercollegiate or varsity competition.

The third period is one in which a new appreciation for the values of intercollegiate sport at the highest levels of skill is demonstrated at official levels. The old purposes remain but are complemented by new goals which recognize the need of college women for opportunities to engage in high level competition.*

## The Early Era

Intercollegiate sport for women was not an issue until basketball was introduced at Smith College in 1892, soon after the game was invented. It quickly spread to other colleges and a student clamor arose for intercollegiate play (Evans, 1971). The opposition of the physical educators was equally immediate; they were not ready to sally forth in public with their teams, getting into situations over which they had no control.

The rationale which was typical of this early period of women's sport was expressed by Lucille Eaton Hill, Director of Physical Training at Wellesley College. After many pages of explanation about the value of sport for women, she warned that "fiercely competitive athletics have their dangers for men, but they develop manly strength. For women their dangers are greater, and the qualities they tend to develop are not womanly" (Hill, 1903, p. 6). She later added: "Where the conditions are favorable for the development of school games, matches between class teams in the school will inspire a larger number of entries in the sport and less danger from over-excitement than inter-scholastic matches, where a school furnishes but one team and more intense nervous strain accompanies the keener competition' (p. 12). In a nutshell, then, sport is good but it could be dangerous and anyway it's best to play within the school where the risks are fewer.

An interesting feature of the early attitudes was the belief that

---

* Detailed analyses of the changing concepts of competition were presented in dissertations by Bennett (1956), Leyhe (1955), Remley (1970), and Watts (1960). The rationale for the official position was detailed by Gerber (1973).

sport was not an ontogenetically appropriate activity for women, though it was for men. Darwinian evolution was a popular theory of the time, often cited by academics seeking to explain their ideas. Physical educators were particularly interested in its applications and even went so far as to develop games classifications in accord with the phylogenetic behaviors supposedly programed in humans. Thus there were games of chasing and fleeing, for example, reminiscent of the early hunters in the forests primeval. Luther Halsey Gulick, an eminent physical educator, applied Darwin's theory in a classical discussion of women's athletics delivered as his Presidential address before the Public School Physical Training Society in 1906. He said:

> Athletics are pretty largely built up of running, striking, and throwing. . . . The ability to run, to strike, and to throw is on the whole a masculine ability. That is, during the very early ages of man's history it was to a very considerable extent through his ability to run that he could escape from his enemies or attack his foes. So that there was a constant tendency for the best runners to survive and for the poorest runners to be eliminated. . . .
>
> The early man's ability as a hunter and fighter depended very largely upon his ability to run, to throw, to strike. . . . The man who could strike the hardest, the most swiftly and the most accurately, would be more apt to survive in those early, bitter days of struggle. . . .
>
> This process of selection going on for many years would produce not merely men who possessed great aptitudes in these matters, but would also produce a love of these exercises. . . .
>
> Thus ingrained deep in all of us is the love of athletic sports. . . .
>
> The case is very different with women. . . . They cared for the home. They carried on the industries. They wove the cloth, made the baskets, tilled the soil, cared for the domestic animals, reared the children, prepared the food, made the clothing, and performed the other numerous duties which centered about the home. It was not the women who could run, or strike, or throw best who survived. . . . The qualities of womanliness are less related to success in athletics than are the qualities of manhood.
>
> The important question is raised whether it may not be true that, in view of the wide competition into which women are coming in the modern world, it would not be wise for them to have the discipline that is afforded by athletic sports. . . . However much women may take work which at present is done chiefly by

men, their success will not be due to their ability to imitate the work and manner of men.

I believe . . . that athletics for women should for the present be restricted to sport within the school; that they should be used for recreation and pleasure; that the strenuous training of teams tends to be injurious to both body and mind; that public, general competition emphasizes qualities that are on the whole unnecessary and undesirable (Gulick, 1906, pp. 157-160).

"Unnecessary and undesirable"—an echo of Hill's words bolstered with a rationale ba      ~n currently respected theory. Such concepts combined with the              '·fficulties and risks attendant upon inter-collegiate competi                    ⁺ to ensure that for the next twenty years there would                    ''egiate sport, though by 1923 about a fifth                    ·ach other in some form.

### The Official Posit

In 1923 the foun                              the National Amateur Athletic Federati                        .unity for the women physical educatoi                        out competition for girls and women. Tow                        platform embodying six-teen resolutions                          onference on Athletics and Physical Recreat                        ,pril 6-7, 1923. The platform was endorsed *in*                        ested in or concerned with sponsoring girls'                        AAU being the most notable exception) inclu.

Committee on Women's Au.        , of the American Physical Education Association, 1923

The Association of Directors of Physical Education for Women in Colleges and Universities, 1924

American Association of University Women, 1925

National Association of Deans of Women, 1926

About a year later, the Executive Secretary of the Women's Division restated the original resolutions into a more concise "creed." Since this creed embodied the guiding principles for collegiate sport competition for several decades, it is reprinted here in its entirety:

The Women's Division believes in the spirit of play for its own sake and works for the promotion of physical activity for the largest possible proportion of persons in any given group, in forms suitable to individual needs and capacities, under leadership and environmental conditions that foster health, physical efficiency, and the development of good citizenship.

To accomplish this ideal for women and girls, it aims:

To promote programs of physical activities for all members of given social groups rather than for a limited number chosen for their physical prowess.

To protect athletics from exploitation for the enjoyment of the spectators or for the athletic reputation or commercial advantage of any institution or organization.

To stress enjoyment of the sport and the development of sportsmanship, and to minimize the emphasis placed on individual accomplishment and the winning of championships.

To restrict recognition for athletic accomplishment to awards which are symbolical and which have the least possible intrinsic value.

To discourage sensational publicity, to guide publicity along educational lines and to stress through it the sport rather than the individual or group competitors.

To put well-trained and properly qualified women in immediate charge of athletics and other physical education activities.

To work toward placing the administration as well as the immediate leadership of all physical education activities for girls and women in the hands of well-trained and properly qualified women.

To secure adequate medical examination and medical follow-up advice as a basis for participation in physical activities.

To provide sanitary and adequate environment and facilities for all physical activities.

To work for such adequate time allotment for a physical education program as shall meet the need of the various age groups for growth, development and maintenance of physical fitness.

To promote a reasonable and sane attitude toward certain physiological conditions which may occasion temporary unfitness for vigorous athletics, in order that effective safeguards should be maintained.

To avoid countenancing the sacrifice of an individual's health for the sake of her participation in athletic competition.

To promote the adoption of appropriate costumes for the various athletic activities.

To eliminate gate receipts.

To discourage athletic competition which involves travel.

To eliminate types and systems of competition which put the emphasis upon individual accomplishment and winning rather than upon stressing the enjoyment of the sport and the development of sportsmanship among the many.*

Although the creed did not call for an outright ban on intercollegiate competition, its stress on promoting programs in which all who desired to could take part, rather than those which focused on the specialized training of a few, certainly made varsity sport inherently inappropriate. In the main, the creed expressed the physical educators' beliefs that their role should be protective, guarding against situations which they deemed potentially injurious to women athletes. The under lying assumption throughout the creed was that athletic competition for girls and women *would* take place. That was why they set forth in considerable detail the conditions under which it should be conducted. Unfortunately, the creed and the resolutions upon which it was based were widely interpreted as embodying negative attitudes toward competition. Within a few years all forms of competitive sport for college women virtually disappeared (refer to Table 4).

Toward the end of the decade it became necessary, therefore, for the leaders of collegiate women's sport to clarify their position on competition. Agnes Wayman, one-time Chairperson of the Executive Committee of the Women's Division, forthrightly stated:

> The Women's Division does believe whole-heartedly in competition. . . . What it disapproves of is the *highly intensive specialized* competition such as exists when we have programs of interschool competition, intergroup open track meets, or open swimming meets, with important championships at stake (Wayman, 1929, p. 469).

* From L. Schoedler, "Report of Progress, Women's Division, National Amateur Athletic Federation of America," *APER*, 29 (June, 1924), pp. 308-309. Reprinted by permission.

Ethel Perrin, who chaired both the Executive Committee of the NAAF and the CWA wrote an article entitled "More Competitive Athletics for Girls—But of the Right Kinds" (1929) in which she wrote:

> The Women's Division . . . is more concerned about the promotion of a fine inclusive program for all girls, than it is with a destructive campaign based upon opinions of what may or may not happen to Olympic participants (p. 474).

Clearly though, varsity type competition was not a form appropriate to the aims of the women physical educators. Even mild forms of competition such as telegraphic meets still encouraged chosen groups and provided an incentive to win for alma mater. It was not until play days were developed as a sport form that a suitable extramural program met the criteria implied in the creed. Play days were available to all. No special skill was necessary and the need to practice, train, be coached, or evaluated was obviated; thus attention to a select few was unnecessary. All incentive for winning was eliminated and enjoyment was stressed. The activities were safe and all sports which might be too fatiguing or rough (including basketball) could easily be replaced by more recreational type activities.

This concept of competition prevailed until the middle of the twentieth century. The philosophy was implemented by substituting play days, sports days, and telegraphic meets for varsity programs (which were never entirely eliminated). The principles were reaffirmed by the Division for Girls and Women's Sports (DGWS) in a policy statement promulgated as late as 1957:

> DGWS believes participation in sports competition is the privilege of all, regardless of skills. . . . Limiting participation in competitive sports to the few highly skilled deprives others of the many different kinds of desirable experiences which are inherent in well-conducted sports programs. . . . The most desirable forms of extramural competition are *Sports Days . . . Play Days . . . Telegraphic Meets . . .* other *Invitations Events* (such as symposium, jamboree, game, or match). The extramural play also encompasses the supervised *Interscholastic* or *Intercollegiate* form of competitive activities. . . . It should be offered only when it does not interfere with the intramural and extramural programs (DGWS, 1957, p. 57).

## The Contemporary Era

The 1957 DGWS statement did contain one modification of the twenty-four-year-old official position. It acknowledged that intercollegiate programs *may* exist—provided they were at the top of the pyramid. In taking this stance, the policy setters were probably bowing to reality, because about a third of the colleges were then conducting varsity type programs.*

The 1963 "Statement of Policies. . ." went one small step further. It listed intercollegiate programs (varsity teams) as one of the four standard forms of extramural competition. Since it was also stated that "In *colleges and universities,* it is desirable that opportunities be provided for the highly skilled beyond the intramural program" (DGWS, p. 32), a virtual acquiescence was made to the desirability of varsity sports. Furthermore, all warnings about intramural programs taking precedence were removed from the statement.

One other interesting change in the DGWS' concept of competition should be noted. In 1957 it was noted that there was no opposition to a woman taking advantage of opportunities for competing in sport sponsored by nonschool agencies. In 1963 a sentence was added stating that students should be informed of such opportunities—which is tantamount to encouraging them. That is quite a change from days when high level competition was regarded as extremely suspect—especially if conducted by groups not under the control of the physical educators.

By 1966 a Commission on Intercollegiate Sports for Women had been organized and it reported a sanctioning plan "in order to encourage the holding of intercollegiate competitive events. . ." (DGWS, 1966, p. 10). Furthermore, the Commission took on the sponsoring of national championships for women—a tremendous departure from 1957 standards which still proclaimed that "extramural competition should not lead to county, state, district or national championships" (H. B. Lawrence, 1956, p. 109).

The greatest change in philosophy could be seen in the rationale for the national tournaments. It was stated that:

> Members of DGWS believe that creation of national championships will give talented young women something more to strive for and

---

* This is an extrapolation from the study of White (1954), which showed that 28 percent of the large number of colleges surveyed had varsity programs in 1951.

will give them greater incentive for continuing to develop their athletic skills. *The championships and the naming of national annual champions in the different sports should motivate less talented girls to learn sports skills* and to enjoy them on their own. In other words, sports activity will become more desirable as an area of endeavor for women (DGWS, 1968, pp. 24-25, italics added).

Thus after decades of believing that attention to high level competitors would take something *away* from the majority of women, the women leaders came to understand that high level sport brings something *to* the lesser skilled women. The once noxious publicity was turned into an important element in the sport participation of the masses.

It was inevitable once that understanding was reached, that after almost a half century of opposition to varsity teams, the DGWS Executive Council passed a resolution in 1971 which read:

The Division for Girls and Women's Sports subscribes to the belief that teams for girls and women should be provided for all girls and women who desire competitive athletic experiences (Thorpe, 1972, unpaged).

The ideals and principles of the earlier era are still unchanged in that the old overall standard, "the one purpose of sport for girls and women is the good of those who play it," is still a guiding concept. The belief that the welfare of the competitors is of overriding concern has not changed. The desire to provide for the needs of the college student still remains. What has changed are the beliefs of how to provide for these concerns within the context of competitive sport.

## COLLEGIATE SPORT ORGANIZATIONS

Collegiate sport for women was influenced and regulated by a number of organizations. Unlike the men's intercollegiate program, these organizations were all a part of the structure of education with the exception of the Women's Division of the NAAF which had physical educators as an integral part of its personnel. It also differed from men's regulatory bodies in that the various national groups had no power except that of moral suasion. Recently, with the advent of national championships for women, and vastly increased intercollegiate competition, some controls external to the institution have been developed. The important organizations affiliated with sport for college women include:

| | | |
|---|---|---|
| College Women in Sport (CWS) | formerly | Athletic Conference of American College Women (ACACW) |
| | | Athletic and Recreation Federation of College Women (ARFCW) |
| Division for Girls and Women's Sport (DGWS) | formerly | Committee on Women's Athletics (CWA) |
| | | National Section on Women's Athletics (NSWA) |
| | | National Section for Girls and Women's Sports (NSGWS) |
| (merged with NSWA) | | Women's Division of National Amateur Athletic Federation (NAAF) |
| Association for Inter-collegiate Athletics for Women (AIAW) | formerly | Commission on Intercollegiate Athletics for Women (CIAW) |

## Women's Athletic Associations

Although clubs, whose existence rose and fell according to the trends of the time, organized sporadic competition, they did not meet the needs attendant with the increased interest in sport manifest during the last decade of the century. Greater organization was warranted and thus the athletic associations came into existence. The first WAA was organized at Bryn Mawr in 1891 (Ainsworth, 1930, p. 76). By 1909 Dudley and Kellor reported that the WAAs existed in "more than 80 percent of the large colleges and exert a wide influence" (p. 103).

These associations were typically sponsored by and under the aegis of the physical education department. They were run by coalitions of students and faculty—usually elected student officers and a faculty advisor. Almost all sport of either an intramural or extramural nature was conducted by the WAAs. They appointed sport managers, set up boards and committees to run the competition, devised and administered awards using complicated point systems, set policies, made regulations ranging from dress codes to eligibility, and arranged social occasions such as end-of-the-year banquets.

The power of the WAAs lasted until the last decade when the direction of growth of both intercollegiate and intramural programs made it necessary for many colleges to move to centralized administration. Curricular and intramural activities became increasingly coeducational; the men's and women's buildings were no longer feasibly separated, nor were the equipment and relevant budgets easily attributable to one sex or the other. An increasing reliance on funding from student fees, budgeted through the student government or by the student union, provided still another reason, particularly in larger schools, for moving the locus of control to an office serving the entire student body rather than just the women. Expanded intercollegiate programs now require a faculty woman athletic director whose job is to supervise and make arrangements for the varsity teams—a function once handled by many WAAs. Nevertheless, WAAs continue to function in many colleges—particularly the smaller ones.

## College Women in Sport

During the years when the direct institutional control of women's sport rested with the WAAs and physical education departments, it became essential to establish an organization composed of representatives of these groups. Accordingly, in 1917 the Athletic Conference of American College Women was organized under the leadership of Blanche Trilling of the University of Wisconsin; 23 colleges were in the original group. Twenty years later a study reported that 75 percent of institutions surveyed were members (Leavitt and Duncan, 1937, p. 78). In 1966 Cheska reported that 350 WAA/WRAs were members of ARFCW (p. 13).

Originally the ACACW held a national conference every three years. Later that became a biennial event. In addition, meetings were held in states or regions. In 1961, ARFCW affiliated with the DGWS and became one of its standing committees (Cheska, 1966).

In its most productive years, the ACACW had an important role in shaping women's sport in the colleges. Reports of its conferences during the 1920s, for example, recorded the attempt to implement the philosophy of the NAAF and CWA. The ACACW grappled with the reduced motivation which they knew would result from the deemphasis on winning and the curtailment of interschool competition. Therefore it worked on developing a point system which could replace winning as a motivation for participation. The big problem "has been the standardization for the purpose of unification, and in order that the transference of athletic points from one school to another might be facilitated" (Swift, 1921, p. 306). The idea of transferring points, in the same manner as academic credits, is an indication of the seriousness with which the students were expected to work to accrue them. Equally illuminating is the next point: "That *standardized* points be given for athletic ability only" (p. 306). This was intended to prevent the use of points for serving on committees or as managers, for example.

The delegates to that conference—about 200 representing 54 schools—in no way meant for sport to be deemphasized, but rather that it be directed toward intramural activities. Thus in 1924 this was among the first groups to endorse the platform of the Women's Division of the NAAF when it was promulgated. It was also this group that forced the little Triangle Conference of Mills, Stanford, and the University of California, Berkeley, to cease holding intercollegiate contests by passing a resolution in 1924 requiring members to discontinue intercollegiate competition for at least three years (Rickaby, April, 1928).

With the formation of the AIAW, the ARFCW became redundant in its function of setting policies for the conduct of college women's sport. Consequently, in 1971 the delegates voted to eliminate the ARFCW constitution, and to change the name to College Women in Sport. The new purpose of the organization is: "To bring college women together in a biennial conference that would encourage leadership, promote an exchange of ideas, and further nationwide interest in sport for college women" (Flinchum, 1971).

## National Amateur Athletic Federation

The AAU's decision to take control of women's athletics aroused the ire of the physical educators. It was their firm belief that they were the proper group—the only group with the necessary professional expertise combined with interest in the welfare of women—to control women's sports.

At the same moment in history, concern over the low physical fitness of potential inductees in World War I had created a national interest in programs of physical activity for the country's youth. General dissatisfaction with the direction of boys' sport programs had led the War Department to take an active role in organizing the NAAF in the hope that it could promote desirable sport practices as a means to improving the general physical condition. The War Department itself wanted a women's division (partially in response to the expressed request of the women physical educators) and asked Lou Henry Hoover (Mrs. Herbert) to organize it.

An organizing conference was convened in Washington, D.C., April 6-7, 1923 attended by numerous physical educators from the CWA and representatives of various agencies. The delegates affirmed their belief:

> That we are in the early stages of a great advancement in athletics for girls and women . . . and we believe that the program of athletics for the welfare, health, and education of women depends upon the women experts on girls' and women's athletics organizing themselves as a deliberating and administrative body to deal with the special problems of athletics for girls and women. . . (Report, 1923, p. 284).

The conferees then decided to form the Women's Division of the NAAF. An Executive Committee was appointed consisting of seven women, all of whom were physical educators active in the CWA. Thus the policy of the two organizations working hand-in-glove was immediately established.

It was at this historic meeting that the famous Platform of the Women's Division—a set of sixteen resolutions embodying the basic beliefs about girls and women's sport to which the group subscribed—was adopted. (Refer to p. 72.) The remaining years of the organization's work were literally devoted to attempting to publicize and implement this platform and the specific recommendations which emanated from it.

The membership of the Women's Division was broad based and had a wide geographical distribution, enabling the Division to reach most groups concerned with women's sport. In 1938 the Division reached the high point of 768 members, about half of whom were individuals. The rest were WAAs, GAAs, colleges, public and private schools, YWCAs, and other organizations. Over the seventeen years of its existence, the Women's Division disbursed over $106,000, most of it for promotional and educational work (Sefton, 1941, p. 32). For example, over 100,000 copies of the Platform were printed and distributed (Sefton, 1941, p. vii).

In 1940 the NSWA and the Women's Division merged. As the last Chairman of the Executive Committee stated, it "was rather like moving from one home to another" (Waterman, 1941, p. 36). Although the two groups had worked well together for many years, the time demanded unification and consolidation of power in order to further the program. The Platform had been thoroughly disseminated and well-accepted. The NSWA was left to carry on the programs.

## Division for Girls and Women's Sport

In 1899 the confusion caused by the various sets of basketball rules used by the women (who insisted on modifying the men's game because it was too rough) led to the formation of a Women's Basketball Rules Committee. Under the leadership of Senda Berenson, this group instigated the publication of the first basketball guide. It became the National Women's Basketball Committee in 1905, continuing to function within the American Physical Education Association (APEA).

As the women's sport situation grew in complexity, in 1917 the Committee on Women's Athletics (CWA) of the APEA was formed and the basketball committee became its subcommittee. By 1922 there were five sport subcommittees including basketball, hockey, swimming, track and field, and soccer. The work of the sports committees was "concerned primarily with making, revising and interpreting rules" (von Borries, 1941, p. 8). The CWA was appointed because of the "insistent and increasing demands coming in from all parts of the country for assistance in solving problems in connection with the athletic activities for girls and women, which demonstrated the need for a set of standards which should be based on the limitations, abilities, and the needs of the sex" (*Athletic Handbook,* 1923 quoted in von Borries, 1941, p. 8).

When the AAU took control of women's athletics, it became apparent to the physical educators that they needed to develop greater status and power. Accordingly, they made arrangements to become a Section on Women's Athletics within the APEA. Such a position entitled them to membership on the Council, and gave them the right generally to manage their own affairs. In 1932, consonant with the reorganization of the APEA, they became the National Section on Women's Athletics (NSWA) whose aims, as stated in the constitution, were:

To promote a wholesome athletic program for all girls and women by

a. The stating of guiding principles and standards for the administrator, leader, official, and player.

b. The publication and interpretation of rules governing sports for girls and women.

c. The dissemination of accurate information in various types of periodicals and special publications and through convention programs.

d. The stimulation and evaluation of research in the field of women's athletics (von Borries, 1941, p. 13).

At this period of time the various sections of the APEA usually did little more than plan convention programs. The NSWA, however, functioned the year round and was particularly notable for its development of standards for girls' and women's athletics and its publications of these standards and rules guides for numerous sports which became widely accepted as the official rules to be used in schools, colleges, agencies, and even industries.

Because of the incompatibility of its philosophy of competition with other sport organizations, the NSWA chose to isolate itself from such groups. It was not until 1950 that the first liaison person was designated to a major sport organization, the Council for National Cooperation in Aquatics. Since then, joint committees of DGWS and several national and international sports groups have worked toward standardizing playing rules and official's ratings. The biggest achievement on this subject was the agreement with the AAU in 1964 on a common set of rules for basketball.

The NSWA became the National Section for Girls' and Women's Sport in 1953 and the Division for Girls' and Women's Sports (DGWS) in 1957. The former name change portrayed a more accurate picture of their functioning which included secondary school girls. The latter change was an improvement in status to one that was co-equal with Physical Education and other divisions of the AAHPER. This "separation" from physical education was a difficult choice because it gave the AAHPER control of their budget allotment since revenues from publications now went largely to the collective pot.

By this time the DGWS had an extensive network including a Legislative Board with District Chairmen, Chairmen of eleven Standing Committees, Members-at-Large, an Editor, Advisory personnel, Consultants, and Representatives of Allied Organizations (such as the Armed Forces and the National Congress of Parents and Teachers). There were State Representatives from each state who in turn presided over state committees. There were working committees for each of eighteen sports and Boards of Officials which were authorized to train and rate officials (since 1928) in these activities. There was a full-time paid Consultant (since 1951) functioning out of AAHPER headquarters.

All in all it was (and indeed remains) a vast network that provided not only standards and rules for each sport, but an extensive in-service training program. Sports guides included helpful articles and bibliographies. Through the state representatives clinics were held which presented advanced techniques of teaching and coaching. Special officiating sessions not only trained officials but provided information on rules changes. Films, filmstrips, games books, conference reports were (and are) all published and sold by the Section and Division. No other Division of the AAHPER has had so much direct influence on the actual day-to-day functioning of its members as has the DGWS over the last forty-five years.

## Association for Intercollegiate Athletics for Women

By the late 1950s the growth of intercollegiate sport for women indicated that new attention would have to be turned toward its organization and regulation. The particular situation which brought matters to a head was the problem of what to do with the intercollegiate golf tournament. Since 1941 (except for a few of the war years) a national intercollegiate golf tournament had been held annually at the Ohio State University. Since national championships were not in accord with the principles of the NSWA, many physical education leaders did not approve of the tournament. Nevertheless, when Ohio State was ready to give up its sponsorship, there was sufficient interest in extending competitive opportunities for women for a group to be created to sponsor this tournament and other potential competitions.

Thus in 1957 the National Joint Committee on Extramural Sports for College Women (NJCESCW) was formed by the ARFCW, NAPECW, and DGWS. The major project of the NJCESCW involved the sanctioning of intercollegiate events. However, the process was unwieldly and the Joint Committee really had no power to enforce its policies. In 1965 it agreed to disband and remand its functions to the DGWS.

In 1966 the DGWS appointed a Commission on Intercollegiate Sports for Women (CISW) which, in addition to absorbing the functions of the NJCESCW, was designed to assist in the conduct of intercollegiate competitions. One purpose of the Commission was:

> To provide a framework and organization pattern which will be appropriate for the conduct of intercollegiate athletic opportunities for college women. . . . The Commission also propose[d] to develop and publish guidelines and standards for the conduct of intercollegiate events. . . . In order to encourage the holding of intercollegiate competitive events and to assist those who are currently conducting such events, the Commission will provide the service of a sanctioning procedure (Scott and Ulrich, 1966, p. 10).

In order to give weight to their intent to deal with high level competition, the CISW was renamed in 1967, the Commission on Intercollegiate Athletics for Women (CIAW).

The Commission also took on the task of sponsoring DGWS national collegiate championships, not only in golf and tennis (in cooperation with the USLTA College Championships) which already existed, but in other sports in which there seemed to be an interest. The schedule of championships which was announced for 1969 included national competition in gymnastics, and track and field. In 1970, swimming, badminton, and volleyball were added, and basketball followed in 1972. It soon became apparent that a membership organization for women's intercollegiate competition was needed. This led to the decision to replace CIAW with AIAW—the Association for Intercollegiate Athletics for Women.

The AIAW was established in 1972 and counts 278 different colleges as charter members. It sponsors seven national championships including regional qualifying tournaments. For the first time in the history of collegiate women's sport, a governing organization with the power to enforce its policies was established. Member colleges *must* adhere to the AIAW's policies in order to retain their membership. Participation in regional and national tournaments is open to member colleges only. Since colleges and not teams or individuals obtain membership, all teams in a college must abide by the regulations. Consequently, if any team in a college desires to compete on a regional or national level, the entire college is bound by the AIAW's policies.

The AIAW establishes membership criteria, sets policies, sanctions

events, and sponsors regional and national tournaments in seven sports.
It also sanctions tournaments such as the Women's College World Series
of Softball. Another important function is its cooperative work with,
and voting rights in,* important national and international sport-
governing bodies such as the United States Collegiate Sports Council. It
is another historical "first" that through AIAW and its parent organization the DGWS, school and college sport is firmly connected to national
and international sport in the larger social environment. Such affiliation,
unheard of in earlier decades, appears eminently appropriate to the
needs and desires of collegiate women athletes who seek even more
extensive opportunities in competitive sport.

---

* The AAHPER holds the membership in these organizations. The Division for
Men's Athletics and the AIAW share the representation and the *single* vote.

# Chapter 3

# Sport in Society

In the pages which follow, the reader can discover the detailed history of women's organized participation in most of the major sports taking place in the social environment outside of schools and colleges. From their early beginnings to the development of international and even professional competition, the chronicle of events, organization, and stars is set down as far as it is known. Unfortunately, some of this information is impossible to locate—especially for less popular sports. Sport organizations, institutions, and sponsors often do not keep records. When records have been kept, they frequently are not separated by sex. It is therefore difficult to assess the level of women's participation with complete accuracy. Furthermore, though some organizations or institutions are able to give precise figures on their own membership, this does not account for the millions of players who enjoy competing in informal circumstances or under the auspices of local organizations or institutions which sponsor meets and tournaments for their members or residents.

Thus the information presented in these pages is sometimes incomplete. Nevertheless, it is accurate insofar as diligent research was able to uncover the data presented. The chapter is also incomplete in that several sports have been omitted, including some of those activities which are newly popular. Space does not permit, nor are data available to discuss, exciting activities such as sky diving, soaring, the martial arts, surfing, and water skiing—all of which are beginning to gather numbers of adherents. The sports presented were all established as competitive activities for women in the United States by the 1930s.

Ladies' archery tournament, 1908.

## ARCHERY

A series of articles appearing in *Harper's Magazine* in 1877 and 1878 is said to have caused the sudden popularity of archery in the 1870s. Since the only other "lawn sport" available at that time was croquet, archery quickly became a universal pastime. "There were literally hundreds of clubs and almost every gentleman's lawn had its target" (Elmer, 1925, p. 3). One of its attractions as a sport was that a gentleman could participate with his lady friends. However, according to a contemporary writer, the women caused a problem with regard to the selection of bows:

> It did not matter to them what the weight of the bow was, or the kind of wood it was made of, or its general usefulness, or its price, so long as the color of the plush on the handle matched the costume of the owner [each lady had a special color for her archery outfit], and it really did bother us to find the necessary shades of color in plush handles (Maumee, 1884, pp. 34-35).

By 1879 there were more than 25 clubs from New York to Illinois including archers of both sexes. The next five years or so archery continued to grow in popularity, but then suffered a considerable decline. Some archers attribute that to the growth of a rival sport: tennis. Even protestations that tennis was too vigorous for women failed to prevent the new sport from taking over.

In the 1920s, during a general sport boom, archery began again to draw adherents. Prior to that time the National Archery Association (NAA), founded in 1879, and the Eastern Archery Association were the only evidence of organized archery. Beginning in 1925 several regional associations were formed. Another indicator of the ups and downs of archery's popularity is the extent of female participation in the national tournaments. In the first one in 1879 there were 20 ladies entered. In 2 of the years between 1895-1902 there were only 5 women. In 1951 there were 127 women and 30 girls.

Although there does not appear to have been an abundance of archery sponsored by industry, equipment manufacturers advertised in the *Industrial Sports Journal.* During the 1940s, Ben Pearson advertisements consistently were illustrated with a woman archer—the only sport in the *ISJ* to do so. Apparently women were viewed as a potentially good participant source. When Springfield, Massachusetts became the first city to institute archery in programs for the industrial workers of the city, *The Sportswoman* commented: "This represents a step forward

toward providing opportunities for athletics for women in Springfield. . ." (Cummins, 1926, p. 25).

The major archery organizations, the NAA, the National Field
Archery Association, and the Professional Archer's Association, all admit
women members though the latter group has none at present. In fact,
since competitive archery's inception in this country women have been
an integral part. The sexes rarely compete against each other except in
indoor flights where the lighter bows used by women are not a handicap. There is, however, nothing in the rules prohibiting women from
entering men's events, though the reverse is not allowed. Women's
rounds are different from the men's, generally requiring fewer arrows
at shorter distances.

Besides the local and national championships, the International
Federation of Target Archers (FITA) sponsors a World Championship
tournament every two years, including men's and ladies' divisions. Since
1952 the American women have won almost every tournament. In 1972
archery became an Olympic sport and an American woman and man
each won the single gold medal available.

Using longevity of supremacy as a measure, one of America's
greatest sportswomen must be Lydia Scott Howell who won her first of
*seventeen* national championships in 1882 and her last one in 1907.
She also led her team to victory in the St. Louis Olympics in 1904,
capturing the three gold medals available for the Double National Round,
the Double Columbia Round, and the Women's Team Championship.
This remarkable record is often unrecognized because archery in 1904
was an unofficial Olympic event.

## BADMINTON

Although badminton racquets were advertised in this country as early
as 1766, the sport did not become really popular until the late 1920s.
Prior to that time, participation was limited almost exclusively to the
Badminton Club of New York whose members included both men and
women. In 1948 in an unsuccessful attempt to encourage industrial
leagues to adopt badminton, an article in the *ISJ* noted that "it is as
much of a woman's game as a man's game" (p. 26).

The American Badminton Association was formed in 1937 with a
membership of about 65 clubs. In two years there were 400 member
clubs, but in the 1960s the membership had stabilized at around 250

clubs. Women were admitted to membership from the beginning and were soon elected as association officers.

The first national tournament was held immediately with singles and doubles events for men and for women, as well as mixed doubles events. By 1951 that tournament drew 60-80 women players (Riherd, 1953, p. 43). Although the game is played all over the country, the greatest area of participation is in the southwest (Fidler, 1973, p. 27).

The chief international opportunity for women is the Uber Cup Competition. Started in 1957, it is a team championship held every three years. In 1969 17 different countries entered. The United States won the championship for the first three matches but has since been unable to regain the world title. Individual international championships for both women and men have been sponsored by the International Badminton Federation since 1939.

This country's greatest badminton star was Judy Devlin Hashman. No one, male or female, has matched her record of 25 United States Championships (9 singles, 10 doubles, 6 mixed doubles) from 1954 through 1963. It was the playing of Devlin and her doubles partner, sister Sue Devlin Peard, that enabled the United States to dominate Uber Cup play in its early years.

## BASKETBALL

It is difficult to talk about the game of basketball for women because there have been several different games simultaneously played by various groups in this country, all with legitimate claim to the name. In addition, the men's game in this country and the women's game as it is played internationally have been quite different from the women's game in the United States. Volleyball and lacrosse are the only other sports in which the men's and women's games differ so radically.

Basketball was invented in 1891 and early in 1892 the women began to play the game. Initially its development for women was through the schools and colleges; therefore the physical educators could and did control its structure, modifying it so that it was less vigorous and rough than the men's game. Through an accident in which the dotted lines on a diagram intending to show the desirable guarding, maneuvering, and offensive areas were mistaken as official divisions of the court, the game became a three-court game in 1899. In 1914 the rules permitted the court to be divided in half rather than thirds if the size of the court was less than 2,500 square feet. The two-court game for all courts was officially adopted in 1938. After about 70 years of use, the court divisions were abolished and all players again were permitted to run the full length of the court.

The size of the courts was often small. The first rules specified a *maximum* space of 3,500 square feet (about 70 x 50 feet) which was increased to 6,000 square feet. Provisions for courts under 50 feet long and less than 1,600 square feet were in the rules as late as 1917 and in 1922 it was specified that high school playing space should not exceed 1,600 feet (per division). In such tiny areas it was difficult to prevent body contact among fast-moving players. Consequently, numerous rules were invented to limit movement in order to minimize the possibility of contact. The game became highly restrictive as a result.

Although most places adhered to the official rules, as promulgated by the Women's Basketball Committee of the American Physical Education Association (APEA) and published by Spalding, some geographical areas played their own version. To this date, Iowa High School Girls have their own playing rules, for example.

In 1926 the AAU decided to promote woman's basketball. Although the first national championships were played under boys' rules, later ones used the rules of the APEA. Korsgaard notes that this was intended to placate the physical educators whose implacable opposition was hurting the AAU programs (1952, p. 289). However, there was a great difference of opinion as to what constituted an exciting game and in 1937 the AAU made official its own set of rules for women. The game it structured was quite different in that the rules were less inhibiting. The AAU rules and the APEA Basketball Committee rules did not again become identical until 1964, after six years of work by liaison personnel determined to effect an articulation between the two groups.

Despite the differing rules, basketball has been one of the most popular sports for women since its invention. Organized play has been sponsored by the AAU, industry, municipalities, agencies, churches, and, of course, schools and colleges. Hinton reported a study in the 1930s which found 1,700 women playing basketball in 14 leagues located in 8 states of the central district (Hinton, 1941, p. 518). Although AAU rules generally prevailed in the industrial leagues, the differing possibilities did cause special problems. The Eastern States Industrial Recreation Association had a "Boys' Rules Division" and a "Girls' Rules

Basketball then (1895) . . .

... and now (1960s).  [Courtesy Mullarky Photo Shop.]

Division" for its 1949 championships. "Time did not permit a combination game between these girls' teams [the winners in each division] to
decide the 'MILADY' title" (*ISJ*, May, 1949). Interestingly enough,
both divisions had three teams competing including Westinghouse of
Pittsburgh which entered—and came in last—in *both* divisions!

In 1926 the AAU sponsored the first Women's National Basketball
Tournament with an entry of 6 teams. In a chapter entitled "Queens
of the Court," Alexander Weyand (1960) gives a year-by-year account
of the national tournaments. One striking fact to emerge is the relative
lack of eastern players; most teams seem to have come from the midwest and southwest. Through 1939 the tournament was most often
played at Wichita, Kansas and after that generally in St. Joseph, Missouri—a town which often supports the contest with sell-out houses.

By 1933 there was an entry of 45 teams (in later years it was
limited to 32) sponsored by businesses, wealthy individuals, and civic
organizations, though a few bore the names of business or church colleges. One of the teams in contention for the championship for several
years was the Golden Cyclones, made up of women from the Employers
Casualty Company of Dallas. This was the team of the great athlete
Mildred "Babe" Didrikson; in 1931 she scored 106 points in 5 tournament games to help her team to the championship. Although she was
not on the first All-America team selected in 1929, her name appears
on the lists for 1930-1932. In the 1950s, the Flying Queens from Wayland Baptist College in Texas and Nashville Business College were two
of the chief contenders. The Queens had their 131 game, 5-year winning streak broken in 1958.

Although women's basketball is not yet an Olympic sport (it is
definitely scheduled for 1976), it has been one of the popular Pan-
American Games events since 1955; the United States women have
usually won. The winner of the AAU National Championships is the
team which represents the United States. The Wayland College Queens
had this honor in the first two Pan-American women's basketball
competitions.

Women's basketball does have its pros. The longest-lived team is
the Red Heads, first playing as the All-American World's Champion
Girls' Basket Ball Club in 1936. In 1947, after having had a 5-year
break during the war, it was reported that "over two million basketball fans in forty-six states have paid to watch the girls kid America's
biggest winter sport" (Lagemann, 1947, p. 65). The Red Heads—who

wear red wigs as a gimmick—are highly accomplished players who function somewhat as do the Harlem Globetrotters, using their skill to entertain the crowds in matches against local men's teams. In 1947 they traveled some 30,000 miles and played 180 games. In 1971 they won 169 games against all-male teams playing men's rules.

Unfortunately, there are few other professional opportunities for top women players as Iowa's famous star Denise Long discovered. Long, who once scored 93 points in a tournament game, averaged 69 points, and had a high school career total of 6,250, was drafted by the San Francisco Warriors of the National Basketball Association. Prohibited from playing in the NBA, she was relegated to a women's team which the Warriors sponsor, but found it a limiting experience.

## BOWLING

Bowling, one of the earliest sports in which women competed, is today the most popular sport for women. No other activity can match its figure of 3.4 million women members of a single sport organization, the Women's International Bowling Congress, bowling regularly in 125,000 weekly leagues.

In 1875 when the National Bowling League was founded, bowling was an amusement for upper-class women and men. By 1892 it had reached fad proportions; in 1900 there were more than 100 bowling clubs in New York City alone. Despite its original connections with the upper class, a big boost to bowling came from industry which began to sponsor leagues for both men and women early in the century. Prior to World War II, bowling was the largest—and often the only—industrial sport. Even in 1946, of the 800 women participants reported by Allis-Chalmers, 500 were bowlers (*ISJ*, February, 1946, pp. 8-12).

The first indication of organized women's bowling in the United States was in 1907 when a league was organized in St. Louis, Missouri. That year the American Bowling Congress conducted a women's tournament in connection with the men's contest. By 1916 the women were ready to strike out on their own; the Women's International Bowling Congress (WIBC), then called the Women's National Bowling Association, was founded in St. Louis with a roster of 40 women. Within a decade the membership had grown to almost 5,000. In 1958 it topped 1,000,000, doubled that in 3 years, and added another 1,000,000 in the next 4 years. One explanation advanced for the phenomenal increase

U. S. players cheer a strike, 1971 World Bowling Championships.  [Courtesy WIBC.]

in membership was the invention of automatic pinspotters. No longer tied to the free time of young boy pinsetters, housewives could bowl during the day. Bowling became "a popular pastime to relieve the household routine—after children are in school and chores done, of course." Furthermore, "the lovely bowling apparel and equipment now available no doubt played their part in popularizing bowling among women" (WIBC, *History,* 1967, p. 54).

This influx of women to the sport ultimately had an effect on it. The women engaged in a deliberate campaign to refine its atmosphere. In a 1957 meeting, the President of the WIBC announced that " 'alleys were no more' and anyone using the term 'alley' would be assessed a small token fine. . . . It was the official beginning of the campaign by women bowlers to improve bowling terminology" (WIBC, 1967, pp. 30-31).

The midwest was the center of women's bowling. From 1916 through 1961 all Five-Woman Championship Teams came from a midwestern city and in that same time period only seven Singles Champions came from outside the midwest. However, since 1961 only four midwesterners have won the singles championship and four California teams have won the team championships. It is obvious that the vastly increased membership has diluted the concentration of skilled players.

Approximately 400,000 women have bowled in the WIBC Championship Tournaments since their official inception in 1916 and the total prize money is about $3,000,000. The tournaments are open to all members without qualification and therefore draw large numbers of women. In 1973 the field encompassed 9,644 five-women teams—48,220 bowlers competing for a prize kitty of $706,431, which is double the 1972 fund. The tournament was 107 days long. The championship teams in all years have been sponsored by an interested business.

A more selective tournament—the Queens Tournament—was added in 1961 and is limited to high-average bowlers. The first tournament attracted 122 entrants and since 1963 has always achieved its maximum of 403. The first-place prize in 1973 was $2,000. The highest average in match games in the Queens Tournament is 216, hit in 1970. The high qualifying score in the 12 years of the tournament has gone from 1,597 to 1,728, an 8 percent increase.

Women may also earn money in tournaments sponsored by the Professional Women Bowlers Association (PWBA) which currently sponsors about eleven tournaments a year. The prize money is not good—a fraction of that available to male bowlers. The 1972 winner of five tournaments—Peggy Costello—averaging 205 a game, earned only $14,000 ("Super Bowler. . .," 1973, p. 14). However, the first tournament of 1974 had $85,000 in prize money and received national television coverage.

The major international amateur bowling tournament has been sponsored since 1954 by the Fédération Internationale des Quilleurs (FIQ); American membership is held by the American Bowling Congress (ABC) which invites the WIBC to field a team. Women have participated in the World Tournament only since 1963; like the Olympics, it is held every four years. The U.S. women are chosen at team trials which bring together the 12 women amateurs with the highest all-events scores in the WIBC Championship Tournaments. In 1963 and 1971 the American women performed exceptionally well and currently hold the records for the six-game, four- and five-player team events.

Another international opportunity for American women is the Tournament of the Americas, staged annually in Miami, Florida since 1963. Entrants come from North, South, and Central America.

Since 1963 about 70 women have had a chance to experience international competition in bowling. With the extensiveness of competition available in this country, international matches are of less importance to this sport than to activities such as track and field where it is necessary to expand the opportunities to compete against the best athletes.

Inevitably, with such numbers of bowlers, the stars are almost too numerous to single out. There are currently 40 women in the WIBC Hall of Fame, officially created in 1965. One outstanding star is Marion Ladewig of Grand Rapids, Michigan. She was selected Woman Bowler of the Year by the Bowling Writers Association of America *ten* times between 1950 and 1963. In 1964, she was the first person chosen in the Superior Performance Category—now part of the Hall of Fame. In her heyday she earned about $50,000 a year and amassed eight All-Star and three World's Invitational titles.

A "Star of Yesteryear" was Floretta McCutcheon who bowled in the 1930s and managed to record 10 perfect games and 9 games of 299, though she was 35 years old when she started to bowl. Her ten-year average was 201 for more than 8,000 games and she once had a three-game high of 832. By contrast, the current WIBC record for a three-game series is only 818.

## FENCING

Fencing is a sport with little mass popularity in America though it certainly has its cognoscenti. In the 1880s and 90s it was a fashionable fad for women to take fencing classes. Interest in fencing was centered in the east, particularly in New York and Philadelphia. During the 1920s a strong women's membership began to build along the west coast.

The Amateur Fencers League of America was organized in 1891 and began to conduct national championships the next year. It was not until 1912 that there was sufficient interest among women to hold a National Women's Championship. In the years through 1925, the winner's honors were shared by women from New York or Philadelphia. The need to improve women's fencing performances, especially in Olympic competition, spurred the AFLA to organize a Women's Committee in 1927 "to stimulate interest and help train an Olympic Team of Women Fencers" ("1928 Fencing," 1928, p. 239). Within 25 years approximately 700 women members of AFLA were competing in the only women's event, the foil, on sectional and national levels (Riherd, 1953, pp. 101-102). "Women fencers in general will tell you that they simply haven't the strength to play the rougher game [sabre or epée], though friendly and exhibitional bouts between men and women are sometimes held" (Rich, 1926, p. 34).

Although fencing was not a sport generally sponsored by industry, the Brooklyn Edison Company employed a master for its workers and entered a women's team in the 1926 national championships (Rich, 1926, p. 34).

Women began fencing in the Olympics in 1924. Only one American woman has ever reached the semi-finals twice in Olympic competition (1928 and 1936): Marion Lloyd, the National Foils Champion in 1928 and 1931. The first woman to carry the American flag in the opening Olympic ceremonies was a fencer, Janice Lee York Romary, 10 times National Champion, and member of every Olympic team from 1948-1968, a record in itself. Her best performance, however, was a fourth place, which is one indication of the comparatively poor quality of American women's fencing.

## FIELD HOCKEY

In 1901 Constance M.K. Applebee argued with colleagues at the
Harvard Summer School about the relative abilities of English and
American women athletes. It led to her discovery that Americans knew
nothing about field hockey; a demonstration was arranged.

> So on a hot August afternoon a group of men and women, Har-
> vard Summer School teachers and students [including the director,
> Dudley Allen Sargent], were initiated into the game of Field
> Hockey. Although the pitch was a small concrete yard at the back
> of the Harvard gymnasium, and the available equipment primitive
> jumping stands for goals, an indoor baseball, and shinny or ice
> hockey sticks, and the players, though willing and eager, were
> wild and unskillful, this crude attempt at hockey aroused much
> interest and enthusiasm (Applebee, 1955, p. 10).

An invitation to spend a week at Vassar College, initiating students
to the game, resulted from the exhibition. It was followed by similar
experiences at five of the other "sister schools."

Although hockey had its initial beginning on the college circuit,
its development in this country was primarily through the clubs.
Originally, this meant that players were graduates and friends of those
who attended posh women's colleges, making hockey an upper-class
sport at that time. However, as it became a more common school sport,
its membership became less limited. In fact, in 1949, at least one league
of nine teams was reported in the *Industrial Sports Journal* (July, 1949),
though it was definitely not a common sport in industrial leagues.
Similarly, from its beginnings in the northeast (for decades the Philadelphia area was the bastion of field hockey), the sport's popularity
spread to all parts of the country; but even today the USFHA membership of approximately 20,000 is still concentrated in the northeast.

The first club was founded in 1901 in Poughkeepsie, New York.
Later that year another club was formed at the Merion Cricket Club in
Philadelphia and in 1907 the "Inter-city Hockey League of Philadelphia
and Vicinity" was formed with at least five clubs contending for a
championship cup (Applebee, 1955, p. 11). By 1922, the year that the
United States Field Hockey Association (USFHA) was founded, there
were 24 clubs combined in 4 associations. Fifty years later there were
273 clubs/colleges affiliated with the USFHA and 40 associations—a
tenfold increase. One of the most important functions of the new
USFHA was to conduct the first national tournament. Held during the

Field hockey, 1901.  [Courtesy the Sophia Smith Collection.]

Thanksgiving holiday of 1922 (and almost every Thanksgiving thereafter), games took place between the five member associations of New
York, Boston, Richmond, Chicago, and Philadelphia (Shillingford,
1972).

In an unusual reversal of development, national competition came
*after* international play was established in field hockey. In 1920 a Philadelphia player tried to persuade the Olympic Committee to permit a
team of Philadelphia women to enter the Olympics to be held that year
in London. Although they were refused, the letter did bring forth an
invitation from England for an American team (Applebee, 1955, p. 12).
Thus the All-Philadelphia team sailed for England in October, 1920—
the first American team of women in any sport to engage in international
competition.* Since then numerous hockey teams have gone on tour
and foreign teams have visited this country. The USFHA was a charter
member of the International Federation of Women's Hockey Associations when it was organized in 1927 with a membership of 8 countries.

In 1963 an International Field Hockey Conference was held in the
United States and 18 foreign teams came here to play. The United
States has never done particularly well in international matches. The
first English touring team which visited in 1921 scored 252 goals to 10
for the Americans. It was not until 1970 that a United States team
defeated the English team. This is probably due to the fact that in
places like England the game is almost a national sport, while here its
popularity is limited. Some indication of the way the sport is viewed
abroad is the fact that as many as 45,000 people have filled Wembly
Stadium in England to view a match.

The "star" of field hockey in this country will always be Constance
M.K. Applebee (who celebrated her 100th birthday in 1973). In addition to introducing the game, she instructed and coached, founded the
first hockey camp in the Poconos (still flourishing), standardized the
rules, helped form the USFHA, and in general remained the guiding
spirit of the game for at least six decades.

A candidate for laurels as one of this country's best players is
Anne B. Townsend. She captained the United States team from 1923
through 1936 except for one year. Demonstrating an incredible versa-

---

* In 1904 American women archers competed as a team in the St. Louis Olympics,
but no foreign competitors were entered. Also in 1920, a number of American
women swimmers and some figure skaters joined the United States team in the
Antwerp Olympics.

tility, she played variously on the forward line, at center halfback and at left fullback position.

## FIGURE SKATING

Skating was introduced to the United States about the middle of the eighteenth century. However, for almost the next century, it was not a permissible sport for women. Considered scandalous—probably because of the danger of revealing one's ankles or legs in a fall—a teacher in Salem, Massachusetts in 1801 aroused the ire of the whole town when it was thought that she had instructed her female pupils in the art of skating (Holliman, 1931, p. 166).

The Philadelphia Skating Club was the first of its kind when it was organized in 1849. In 1859 the Central Park Commissioners fixed the New York City ponds for skating and it suddenly became a fashionable sport for both women and men. Crowds as large as 50,000 packed the park and special excursion trains left Boston for outlying ponds with as many as 1,500 skaters aboard (Stephenson, 1970, p. 9).

The first evidence of mass enthusiasm for watching figure skaters was in 1914 when a large ice-skating show of Germans opened at the Hippodrome in New York City. Over 2 million people attended the show and skating became front page news. It was further popularized by Sonja Henie, the Norwegian figure skating champion. Beginning in the late thirties, Henie's Hollywood Ice Revue played to 15 to 20 million fans during the next fifteen years (Menke, 1969, pp. 650-651). Her performances are said to be one of the major factors behind the popularization of the sport.

The United States Figure Skating Association (USFSA) was organized in 1921 with 7 Charter Member Clubs. Two years later, when it was accepted as a member of the International Skating Union, there were 15 clubs. In 1927 the Women's Committee of the USFSA was formed to promote figure skating for girls and women. Today there are more than 200 member clubs of the Association with more than 27,000 registered figure skaters of whom probably at least half are females. Any person wishing to compete in USFSA-sanctioned events must be a member, either personally or through a club.

In a pattern different from most sport groups, the organization came after the first national championship which was held in 1914. The standard events include: singles for women and for men; pairs, in which a man and woman skate together; and ice dance. All events have both compulsory and free skating programs.

Figure skating became an Olympic sport in 1908, but Americans did not participate until 1920; at that time the event was still part of the summer Olympic program. Only two skaters, Theresa Weld and her partner, Nathaniel W. Niles, made the trip, unaccompanied by a coach or manager. Weld won a bronze medal in the singles. A similar time lapse occurred between the beginning of the World Championships in 1906 and the first competitors sent by the USFSA in 1924. Since that time, two or three women have been sent every year to each of the major international events. A total of between 75 and 90 women have participated in international competition since 1920.

Prior to World War II, the women were able to place in the top ten out of 15-25 skaters but never captured the World Championship. During the time from 1939-1946 when the world championships were not held, the American skaters developed a new style. "Into a sport of grace and moderate athletic feats, [Dick] Button brought the concept that figure skating was a physically demanding *sport* which could be performed with an emphasis on athleticism. He introduced jumps with double and triple revolutions and with height exceeding the rink barriers" (Boucher, 1973).

The American women followed Dick Button's successful lead and since then have won several world championships, beginning with Tenley Albright's wins in 1953 and 1955 and following with Carol Heiss' string of world championships from 1956 through 1960. They were also the Olympic champions in 1956 and 1960, respectively. Peggy Fleming carried on the tradition by winning the World Ladies Championship three times starting in 1966 and an Olympic gold medal in 1968.

Some of the famous figure skaters of earlier days include Theresa Weld Blanchard, winner of six U.S. singles and nine pairs titles from 1914 to 1927 and Maribel Y. Vinson who won nine singles and six pairs titles from 1928 to 1937. Vinson raised two figure skating daughters, both of whom were on the 1960 Olympic team. Tragedy struck the family when all three were killed in the plane crash which claimed the lives of all 18 members of the U.S. team on their way to the 1961 World Championships.

The latest star of the ice is Janet Lynn, U.S. Ladies Champion 1969-1973. Recently she signed a three-year, $1,445,000 contract with an ice follies group, making her the highest-paid woman athlete in the world.

## GOLF

It was said that the early male golfers preferred women to decorate the clubhouse instead of the links. Nevertheless, the ladies insisted on playing. The first record of women's participation was in a mixed foursome on March 30, 1889 at St. Andrews, the first club in the United States which had been founded only two years earlier (Grimsley, 1966, p. 144). The first clubs to encourage women players were the Shinnecock Hills Golf Club in Southampton, N.Y. (1891) and the Chicago Golf Club (1892), followed by several others in the New York-Philadelphia area. In 1895, according to one writer (Tunis, 1929, p. 211), there were probably not more than 100 women golfers in the whole country. Two years later the Women's Golf Association of Philadelphia was founded; for three years it remained the only organization of its kind in the country. In 1900 the Women's Metropolitan Golf Association was formed, embracing 22 of the more important clubs suburban to New York.

There has been a steady growth in women's participation in the sport. In 1916 women purchased about 15 percent of the golf equipment, according to A.G. Spalding and Brother (Jacobs, 1920, p. 48). By 1947, the year that the National Golf Foundation began keeping records, there were 478,142 women golfers; by 1972 the number had risen to 2,228,000 women (compared to 6,956,000 men—about a 1:3 ratio). Interestingly, although golf originated as an upper-class club sport, the largest number of golfers now play on municipal courses and the fewest number at private clubs.

In a 1956 study, golf was the most popular sport of women over 18 years old, 7.6 percent of surveyed women with a college education reporting participation, while only 1.0 percent of non-college women did (de Grazia, 1964, appendix). As in tennis, this probably relates to the sport's origin as an upper-class activity. In the 1940s some industries began to sponsor golf for the recreation of their women employees (men's golf had started at least a decade earlier). For example, B.F. Goodrich in Akron, Ohio started an annual women's tournament in 1944 (men's in 1931). In 1948 there were 20 men's and 4 women's leagues with over 100 women players (*ISJ*, February, 1949, p. 6). Allis-Chalmers in Milwaukee in 1946 had over 100 women playing golf (*ISJ*, February, 1946, pp. 8-12). There is little evidence of much industry-sponsored golf for women in areas outside of the midwest.

Morris County Golf Club Team, 1900.  Subs stood in back row.

Golf tournaments for women have been held since 1895 when the first championship was played at the Meadowbrook Hunt Club under the auspices of the United States Golf Association (USGA). The tournament was simple medal play of 18 holes and the winner was Mrs. Charles B. Brown with the fine score of 132! Brown was both surprised and dismayed to learn that she was the first national golf champion. Socially prominent and hardly the sportswoman type, she treated the episode as lucky and rather a joke (Ford, 1936, p. 150). In the next national tournament the eight best scores in the qualifying round ranged from 95 to 111, indicating a marked improvement in women's play. In addition, the entry list had more than doubled from 13 to 29! The entries rose steadily and the scores dropped equally consistently. In 1923 the medalist had an 84 and the field had 196 entries. One year later it was down to 98—due no doubt to the imposition of a handicap of not more than 10 strokes imposed by the USGA. It was 1939 before the field surpassed the former mark with 201 entries; the winner also posted a record with a qualifying score of 74. In 1973 the maximum entry for the Women's Amateur Championship was limited to 150 and players may not have a handicap of more than 5 strokes (*USGA*, 1973).

In the meantime, golf tournaments continued to multiply. In 1928 a commentator noted that the Women's Metropolitan Golf Association had 34 events scheduled in 52 days and complained that "I am beginning to wonder if competition play may not crowd mere practice entirely out of the picture" (Rickaby, June, 1928, p. 246).

International play was formalized in 1932 with the inauguration of the Curtis Cup matches between women of Great Britain and America. Donated by the Curtis sisters of Boston—who are credited with being "largely responsible for developing women's technique from a mild form of croquet to strenuous and healthy exercise. . ." (Rickaby, June, 1929, p. 14)—it was intended to provide a tournament similar to the men's Walker Cup. The United States team of not more than 8 players and a Captain is selected by the USGA. They have been quite successful, winning 13 times and losing and tying twice.

Since 1964, women from at least 55 different countries which belong to the World Amateur Golf Council have been able to compete in the Women's World Amateur Team Championship. Held biennially, the United States has won each year except the first, when the team lost the 72 holes stroke play by one stroke. The winning team is awarded custody of the Espirito Santo Trophy for two years.

Professional golf had its inception in the 1940s when Mildred (Babe) Didrikson Zaharias excited the public so much that a cross-country women's tour was organized with the backing of Handmacher, a clothing manufacturer. The ladies modeled Handmacher suits and played golf from coast to coast, originating the ladies tour. The group then organized the National Women's Open Championship in 1946, but it wasn't until 1950 that the Ladies Professional Golf Association (LPGA) was formed with 11 charter members; by 1964 the organization had 125 members and currently has more than 200. In 1960 it staged its first golf school. The prize money for pro women golfers has grown steadily from the $3,400 earned by the top money winner in 1948 to the $65,063 earned by 1972's top winner, Kathy Whitworth. Still, it was a long way from the comparable men's figure of $320,542—or even from the more than $119,000 earned by tennis' top women. Attendance at matches has risen also, the record being 9,787 for 3 days in 1961 (*USGA*, 1973, p. 31). According to the Executive Director of the USGA, the promotion of golf by these women professionals is a major reason for the growth of women's golf (Dennis, 1972, p. 32).

Some of America's greatest athletes have been golfers, including Babe Zaharias, chosen by sportswriters in an Associated Press poll as the greatest woman athlete of the half century. (She also was a track star, played on a championship basketball team, and competed in other sports as well.) The Babe, as she was called, was U.S. Women's Amateur Champion in 1946 and Open Champion in 1948, 1950, and 1954. In the latter tournament she set a USGA record (men's and women's) for winning by the largest margin: 12 strokes.

Mickey Wright holds the record for the lowest woman's score, a 62, shot at a course of over 6,000 yards. She also holds the record for the longest drive recorded by a woman golfer: 272 yards. The first hole-in-one during championship play was hit by Patty Berg in 1959 on a 170-yard 7th hole. Probably the finest woman golfer was Glenna Collett Vare, *six* times (from 1922 to 1935) winner of the U.S. Women's Amateur Championship. The Vare Trophy awarded annually since 1953 to the player with the lowest average score in official LPGA tournaments is awarded in her name. A current star is Kathy Whitworth, who for seven years (1966-1973) was named Player-of-the-Year and has won the Vare Trophy seven times. She was winner of the LPGA Championship in 1967 and 1971.

Glenna Collett, ca. 1930. [Courtesy United Press International.]

## GYMNASTICS

The term "gymnastics," meaning "to exercise naked," has been used since the time of the ancient Greeks to mean a form of physical training. During the nineteenth century several different systems of exercise were developed and usually termed gymnastic systems (i.e., Swedish gymnastics). One such activity, German gymnastics, involved the use of heavy apparatus such as parallel bars. It is from this system that the events currently used for world gymnastic competition are derived.

In the middle of the nineteenth century, a large number of Germans, many of whom were *turners* (gymnasts), emigrated to the United States and formed *turnvereine* (gymnastic societies). It was through these societies that gymnastics was carried on in this country. However, throughout the nineteenth century usually only German-Americans belonged to the *turnvereine*. Although women were permitted to take part in the activities, as late as 1904 they were not admitted to full membership. The *turners* popularized gymnastics, introduced it into the schools, and held exhibitions and competitions. However, gymnastics never did become a standard part of the curriculum. With the advent of the "new physical education," starting in 1910, the formal gymnastics systems were discarded in favor of sport-type activities which were thought to be more natural. After World War I, it virtually disappeared from the educational curriculums. In the meantime, the AAU had assumed control of the sport in 1897. It continued to flourish through *turner* societies and other private clubs with competitions sponsored by the AAU.

In 1931 the AAU held the first national championships for women. Twenty years later there were approximately 1,000 girls and women competing in AAU championships at the district and national levels. The events included balance beam, flying rings, calisthenics, side horse vaulting, and even or uneven parallel bars. Each contestant did both a compulsory and optional routine in each event, competing for an All-Around title (Riherd, 1953, p. 95). The balance beam had been developed by the great Swedish teacher Maja Carlquist, in the later 1930s; the unevens were the creation of a Czechoslovakian man who sought, circa 1920, to find an event especially for women. In 1936, when Olympic gymnastics with heavy apparatus became a reality for women, the events included the horse, unevens, and balance beam. With the addition of the floor exercises (the old calisthenics), the four events

Cathy Rigby, 1968.  [Courtesy Wide World Photos, Inc.]

have since been the standard international program (though the rings were used instead of the bars in 1948).

The International Gymnastic Federation (FIG) governs all international competition. Women's rules are set by the Women's Technical Committee. Until 1962 the AAU governed gymnastics in this country. However, the United States Gymnastics Federation was formed in 1963 in a break-away from the AAU. At that time it had 200 women and 4,000 men members. By 1972 there was a *tenfold* increase to 2,000 and 40,000 members respectively (Fidler, 1973, p. 19). Both groups continue to hold national championships, but the USGF's are considered the "true nationals" and it is that group which is responsible for the American Olympic entry.

In 1963 the USOC and DGWS chose gymnastics as one of the two Olympic sports most in need of developing. Since that time it has become a popular school and college competitive sport for women. The activity experienced a special surge of public interest as the result of the Russian gymnast Olga Korbut who captured the world's attention during the 1972 Olympics.

American women gymnasts have been patently unsuccessful in international competition against Europeans, possibly because of the short history and small pool of women in the sport in this country. Since the educational institutions were devoid of gymnastic competition until very recently, a competitor in women's gymnastics, unlike virtually every other sport, could compete *only* through private sources and funding. However, Americans have always come in first in the All-Around team score in Pan-American competition since it was introduced in 1959 for women.

One of the best American performers was Linda Metheny, five times winner of the AAU All-Around (total of 4 events) championship. In the 1967 Pan-American Games she took gold medals in three events plus the All-Around and came in second in the fourth event, the bars—a remarkable achievement. She was on the Olympic team in 1960 and 1964, but her best performance was a fourth on the bars.

## LACROSSE

Lacrosse is a sport originally played by the American Indians which was later transported via Canada to England where it was modified and played by women, and brought by English women coaches and players to the schools and colleges of the United States. Thus the modified

English game is the basis for the American women's game, while the American Indian game is the basis for the American men's game. The differences are considerable, the chief one being a dependence on skill and agility (women) rather than body contact power (men).

Like field hockey, the game developed through clubs which relied on colleges and their graduates for the primary membership source. The first club, however, was composed of working girls over 17 years old. In 1926 the "athletic director" at the Bryn Mawr School in Baltimore, an Englishwoman, organized the club and obtained permission to play on the school's grounds (Weyand and Roberts, 1965, p. 272). In the early 1940s a survey of teams at the national tournament showed that about half of the players had learned to play in hockey camps or through their clubs (Richey, 1944, p. 98).

The United States Women's Lacrosse Association (USWLA) was formed in 1932 with five local associations: Baltimore, Boston, New York, Philadelphia, and Westchester. The founding women planned the association during a session at Constance M.K. Applebee's Pocono hockey camp, where instruction in lacrosse was also given. The game became popular, particularly among the hockey players who sought a spring sport to keep in shape. However, the general decline in participation in many sports during the war years hit the relatively small lacrosse group especially hard. In 1948 the President of the USWLA announced an "expansion program," designed to bring the game to more people (Richey, 1948, p. 135). At that time there were six local associations (North Jersey had been added to the original group) and 23 schools and colleges listed as allied members, primarily in the Philadelphia area where the strength of the association was centered. Since then, the game has spread to other parts of the country, though the current membership of 13 associations is still in the northeast with the exception of the Midwest Colleges Association.

The first national tournament was held in 1933 and has continued on an annual basis ever since. A United States and a Reserve team is selected at the tournaments. Beginning in 1935, these teams have occasionally toured the British Isles and several return visits have been made. For the Americans, the chief purpose of such interchange was to improve play by observing and studying the English techniques. By 1951 the improved skill made real competition possible as well and an American team touring the British Isles won twenty of twenty-seven games.

The Americans contest the English, 1934.

The most outstanding women's lacrosse player is probably Betty Richey of Vassar College. She was selected for the United States team 21 times, beginning with the first team in 1933, generally in the 3rd Home position. Richey also served as President of the USWLA and was awarded honorary membership by that organization.

## SKIING

The beginning of competitive skiing in the United States is generally credited to the Scandinavian gold miners in the California Sierras. Reportedly, the first tournament was held in 1867; it included races for men, boys, women, and girls under 12 (Peterson, 1967, p. 13). Nevertheless, ski racing did not become a popular activity for women in America until the 1920s. At that time the colleges began to offer winter sports in the curricular and recreational programs and the Lake Placid Club organized special winter sports events for college women.

The National Skiing Association (NSA) was founded in 1904 and became the United States Ski Association in 1962. Since 1911 when the International Ski Federation (FIS) was organized, the USSA has been the governing body for skiing in this country. When women's skiing became a serious activity, a Ladies Committee was organized to help promote women's skiing. From its original five clubs in 1904, the USSA reported 10,000 classified ski racers in 1966, approximately 1,000 of whom were females (Peterson, 1967, pp. 141-143).

At Lake Placid the ski events for women included a 3-mile cross country race (later shortened to 2 miles) and a slalom and downhill event. No ski jumping contests were held but apparently some women tried the event on their own ("Women Have a Large Share...," 1930, p. 11). Around 1930-31, women raced in divisional and NSA-sanctioned events as representatives of the Dartmouth Outing Club. The Woodstock Ski Runners Club of Vermont held the first sanctioned downhill race for women in 1932 (Peterson, 1967, p. 16).

Although cross country skiing was done by women in the 1920s, it was considered too strenuous and consequently dropped from competition. Not until 1970 did the United States send a team to compete in all the events at the FIS World Nordic Championships. The last Olympics in 1972 was the first in which American women entered skiers in the Nordic events. Ski jumping is, however, still not available to women.

Trials for the 1972 Olympic Nordic team.

The first American women's FIS team was organized in 1934 with the backing of the Amateur Ski Club of New York (Wolfe, 1937, p. 194). The team was only in its second winter of competition when it entered the 1936 Olympics, much less experienced in Alpine skiing than the European women. It was 1948 before Gretchen Fraser won the first Olympic gold medal for the American women. In 1952 Andrea Mead Lawrence won two gold medals in the Olympics in slalom and giant slalom. Ski competition for women in the United States had arrived!

In January, 1973 the first professional ski events for women were held. The Hang Ten Cup consisted of a giant slalom and a slalom race, with $4,400 in prize money at stake.

## SOFTBALL

Softball, devised as an indoor baseball game, was invented in 1887. The name was officially adopted in 1932 at the organization meeting of the Amateur Softball Association (ASA). From the beginning, women were an integral part of the game, playing on teams sponsored by schools, colleges, agencies, municipalities, and, above all, industries. The number of women participating in organized softball competition is phenomenal, second only to bowling. In 1938 in a study of softball's growth in southern California, 1,000 women's teams were listed, the majority sponsored by various industries. During World War II there were 40,000 semiprofessional women's teams (Garmen, 1969, pp. 27-28). According to the Executive Director of the ASA, reliable statistical organizations have estimated that there are currently 18 million participants annually, 5 million of whom are women. Within the association there are about 6,000 women's teams—which means about 85,000 women are now in ASA organized amateur play (Porter, 1973). During the 1960s, slow-pitch softball became popular and now accounts for about 70 percent of the play in the United States. The ASA holds both a slow-pitch and a fast-pitch national championship for women each year.

Women's softball has also been popular as a spectator sport. In 1948 the All-American Girls Baseball League (AAGBL)—which used the underhand softball pitch—drew close to a million paid admissions. In 1965 the National Women's Softball Tournament drew 12,000 people per game. In 1973, nearly 80,000 spectators watched the championship games.

Commentators agree that it is the quality and excitement of the women's play that draws the spectators. In a popular magazine article the point was succinctly made:

> From the start, girls' softball games have outpulled men's games as boxoffice attractions. Naturally, a lot of citizens jumped to the conclusions that it was the male spectators' lively interest in girls cavorting about in shorts that filled the stands. This notion blew up with a bang as soon as certain teams outclassed others. When the headliners met, the stands were jammed. When the cellar nines played, they were next to empty, although the girls were just as easy on the eyes as those in the major games (Taylor, 1938, p. 38).

Ever conscious of their image, the choice of clothing was an important consideration as demonstrated by an article in the *Industrial Sports Journal* about the "new look" in softball.

> The Queens [Arizona Brewing Company Queens of Phoenix] are the most popular and best-looking aggregation in the world today and annually are voted the best-dressed. This year . . . they again drew down the trophy for that snap in dress, blossoming out in new uniforms which were designed by one of their own pitchers. . . . A very short skirt over brief tights gives the effect of a chorus line when the girls go into action—the "New Look in Softball" ("New Look. . . ," 1949, pp. 18, 28).

Along the same lines, it should be noted that the professional players were required to attend charm school during their spring training camp session! "They learned posture and etiquette, how to choose and wear clothes, how to apply cosmetics, and how to take a called third strike like a lady" ("Baseball: Babette Ruths," 1946, p. 68).

The first national championships (then called the world championships) were held for both men and women in 1933. They have been held annually ever since. Most teams either were represented or were sponsored by industries. To get to the national tournament, teams play through a series of city, state, district, and regional tournaments. The winners of the sixteen regional tournaments come together for the championship event. Some teams also have gone on tour. For instance, in 1948 the Arizona Brewing Company Queens traveled 9,000 miles, playing before 175,000 spectators on the road and another 105,000 in their home park in Phoenix ("New Look. . . ," 1949, p. 28). Clubs such as the Brakettes commonly play between 65 and 80 games per season.

Professional women's softball or baseball had its heyday in the
1940s though the first Female Base Ball Club was a product of the
1880s. At that time a gentleman of the press wrote that "the female
has no place in baseball, except to the degradation of the game. For
two seasons . . . [people] have been nauseated with the spectacle of
these tramps, who have been repeatedly stranded and the objects of
public charity" (Voigt, 1966, p. 211). The All-American Girls Baseball
League did much better as it was organized by Phil Wrigley, owner of
the Chicago Cubs, in 1943; it folded in 1954. During its existence it
expanded to 10 clubs, all in the midwest. They had spring training
camps and tours, a 126-game schedule, post-season playoffs, and all-star
appearances. The players' salaries ranged from $50-$85 a week plus
expenses, but stars sometimes earned up to $125. The players were
chosen for playing ability, appearance and character ("Baseball: Babette
Ruths," 1946, p. 68). Each team had a chaperone who strictly supervised
the behavior and appearance of the players. Shorts, slacks, smoking, and
drinking in public were prohibited; living quarters and eating places
were subject to approval of the chaperone (Riherd, 1953, p. 86).

In recent years international competition has become a facet of
the women's game. Teams from the United States occasionally go on
international tours playing exhibition matches with women in other
countries. In 1965 the first Women's World Championship took place
in Melbourne. Six countries participated and the United States women
(the Raybestos Brakettes) lost a final 1-0 game to Australia for the
championship. In 1970, in the only other world tournament, American
women lost to the Japanese team in the final game. The team that won
the national championship the previous year is the team which competes in the world events.

Lately the Raybestos Brakettes of Stratford, Connecticut have
been the top women's team. Since 1958, they have usually won or been
runner-up in the national championships, most often the former. In
1965 they made a 42,000-mile goodwill tour of the world, raising more
than one-quarter of a million dollars for charity. The club has never had
a losing season and, as of 1971, its record was 1,101-155. It was the
first women's team ever to make such an extensive trip though they had
toured the Caribbean area 5 years earlier. On that trip they played
men's teams from armed forces bases, winning 9 of the 17 games played.

One of the Brakettes' and softball's greatest players was Bertha
Ragan Tickey. Tickey, wooed away from the champion Orange Lionettes

# BASEBALL FANS
## *ATTENTION!!*

### TONIGHT - JULY 1st

#### AT PLAYLAND PARK

The AMERICAN GIRLS'
BASEBALL LEAGUE

WILL USE THE REGULATION
MAJOR LEAGUE 9" BASEBALL
FOR THE FIRST TIME
• IN HISTORY •

# A DOUBLE HEADER
# PACKED WITH THRILLS
## STARTING AT 7:00 O'CLOCK
### GRAND RAPIDS vs. SOUTH BEND
### FORT WAYNE vs. SOUTH BEND

## *HOME RUNS and POWER PLAYS*
### THE MOST DARING REVISION EVER
### MADE IN GIRLS PRO BASEBALL

*Can the Girls*
*HANDLE THIS SMALL BALL?*

Admission
25c to $1.50
PLENTY OF PARKING

## COME OUT AND SEE TONIGHT
### THIS ADVERTISEMENT BY COURTESY OF

# SWANSON CONSTRUCTION CO.

Advertisement in an Indiana newspaper.

of California, was the star behind the Brakettes rise to power. She pitched 787 victories during a 23-year career, 100 of which were no-hitters, including her final three national tournament games. She struck out more than 4,500 batters. In 1972 Tickey became the 13th woman (along with 29 men) to be named to the National Softball Hall of Fame (Ondek, 1971, pp. 9-14, 17).

## SPEED SKATING

There is some evidence that women were competing in speed skating as early as 1856—the year of the first International Skating Competition held by the North American Ski Association. Although the event was intended for men only, some women took part, competing against the men (Brown, 1959, pp. 148 150).

Officially, the North American speed skating championships including American women began in 1921 under the auspices of the International Skating Union. National championships for women have been conducted since 1926 by the Amateur Skating Union of the United States.

In 1932 women's speed skating was included in the Olympics at Lake Placid, New York as a demonstration sport. The six Americans did quite well, taking a gold medal at 1,000 meters in 2:04 and another gold in the 1,500-m race at 3:00.6. They earned a silver medal in the 500 meters, the only other event.

It was not until 1960 that speed skating for women became an official part of the winter Olympics, which is a good measure of its relative lack of popularity in the intervening years. A 3,000-meter race was added to the original 3 events. The best the American women did that year was to win a bronze medal in the 500-m race. It was 1972 before they could return to their winning ways; Dianne Holum earned a gold medal in the 1,500-m with a time of 2:20.85—22 percent better than the 1932 time. Annie Henning won the 500-m sprint race in 43.33 seconds.

One peculiarity about speed skating in the United States is that it seems currently to be centered around the single location of Northbrook, Illinois. No less than 5 skaters (3 women and 2 men) from Northbrook were on the 1972 Olympic team of 17 skaters. Both Holum and Henning are from Northbrook.

## SQUASH RACQUETS

Although squash is a sport played by both men and women, unlike the other racquet sports of tennis and badminton, the women's game developed in a segregated fashion and somewhat later than the men's play. This may have been the result of a need for special, expensive courts, usually located in men's athletic clubs. When women first began to play squash, in the late 1920s, their first problem was to locate courts which they could use. In 1928, the Harvard Club of Boston and the Boston Athletic Association both opened their courts and showers for women to use in the morning (Rickaby, February, 1928, p. 146).

With such assistance, it is no wonder that Boston was the site of the first national tournament held in 1929. This was just two years after inter-city squash play between Greenwich, Connecticut and Philadelphia took place. Boston, Philadelphia, and New York seem to have been the primary locations for women's squash at that time. Still, there was sufficient interest to warrant the founding of the United States Women's Squash Racquets Association in 1928. The organization had approximately 250 members in 1972, still concentrated in the northeast. Since they had 218 members in 1952 (Riherd, 1953, p. 231), the sport's rate of growth for women is very slow. The association reports that finding courts available to women is still their greatest problem in attracting new members (Fidler, 1973, p. 35). The association sponsors an annual tournament including singles, doubles, and veteran's singles events. The Wolfe-Noel Cup Matches, held annually, represent the chief international event for women in squash.

The person given most credit for popularizing the sport for women is the super-athlete, Eleanora Sears, the winner of the first national tournament at age 46. This is the same Sears who walked from Newport, R.I. to Boston, covering the 74 miles in 16 hours and 50 minutes, creating quite a sensation in the process. An outstanding athlete, she won a total of more than 240 trophies in squash, tennis, and riding.

## SWIMMING

It is said that women gained their real interest in swimming during World War I when pools were forced to hire women as lifeguards. Another possible factor in the great increase in women swimmers in the early 1920s was the phenomenally successful entry of American women swimmers into the 1920 Olympics. Probably the major single catalyst was the excitement surrounding Gertrude Ederle's well-publicized channel swim. Whatever the cause, in the 8 years beginning with 1920, more than 60,000 girls and women earned their American Red Cross life saver's certificates and sportswriters began to refer to swimming as a woman's sport (Ford, 1936, p. 196).

Since that time, every survey of the leisure time habits of American women lists swimming at or near the top. Of course, participation is primarily noncompetitive, physical recreation, though by 1952 girls' and women's participation in AAU meets from the local to the national level was estimated at around 25,000 competitors (Riherd, 1953, p. 94). In 1972 there were 429 women (and 334 men) representing 145 clubs in the AAU national championships.

Competitive swimming for women began in the early part of the century under the auspices of organizations such as the YWCA. In 1914 its popularity had increased sufficiently to entice the AAU into making its first venture into women's sport by registering female competitive swimmers. This action was well-received by the women involved who perceived the need for organization and promotion. Just a few years later the famous and influential Women's Swimming Association of New York was formed:

> What started the stampeding for pools and competitive honors was a meeting which took place at a New York pool one day during the early part of the war when several friends had gathered for a little surcease from the knitting of socks for the boys over there. "You know," said one . . . "I wish we had some sort of a club where we could hold meets and things." "I do, too," said another. . . . Right then was planted the seed which grew into the Women's Swimming Association of New York, formed in 1917 as strictly an amateur club. . . . The club grew from a handful to its present total of nearly two thousand members. . . . The ages of the members from the first ranged from about eight to nearly eighty.*

In 1929 the WSA opened its own clubhouse, boasting a 75-foot pool as its main feature (Rickaby, April, 1929, p. 15).

One measure of the popularity of women's competitive swimming during this period is the fact that in 1924 *The New York Times* devoted

---

* From M.E. Ford, *Little Women Grow Bold,* Boston: Bruce Humphries, p. 200. Copyright © 1936 by Bruce Humphries and reprinted by permission.

over 70 articles to women's swimming events (Evans, 1973, p. 11). Five years later an article in the *Delineator* noted that "seldom was a swimming meet held anywhere in the country without events for women" (Kidwell, 1968, p. 13).

Since the 1920s marked the first period during which American women seriously competed in swimming, it was a time of record breaking. In 1922 Sybil Bauer broke the world's record for both men and women in the 440-yard backstroke. In 1924 she broke 21 records for women. In 1927 Martha Norelius set 29 world swimming records for women. That same year the AAU received applications to certify 128 swimming records, 71 by women and 57 by men (Rickaby, 1928, p. 120). Until the early 1940s, swimmers from the east coast—particularly the WSA of New York and the Washington Athletic Club—dominated the competitions. In recent years the west coast—particularly Santa Clara in California—has been the area to beat.

In 1916, the year that the AAU held the first national championships for women—both indoor and outdoor—the events included all of the freestyle events now standard for women: 100, 220, 440, 880 yards, and 1 mile. (These are now measured in corresponding meters as 200, 400, 800, and 1500—with the exception of 100 meters which is longer than the old 100 yards.) The 100-yard backstroke and breaststroke were added in 1920, the 220-yard backstroke in 1924, and the 200-yard breaststroke in 1917. The 100-yard butterfly was not on the program until 1954 with the 220 added two years later. The 300-yard individual medley was introduced as early as 1922 but the 400-meter medley did not appear until 1954, when the medley relay was also introduced at that distance. The 400-yard freestyle relay was added to the program in 1920 and the 880 in 1923. The longest distance event is the 3-mile race introduced as early as 1916. The 3-mile team event was added in 1927.

The women swimmers have numerous opportunities for international competition, including the Olympic and Pan-American Games and various world tours. In fact, the United States National Championships are now international.

Professional swimming for women began with the swimming and marathon events in the 1920s. The big news, of course, was Gertrude Ederle's Channel swim in 1926. Not only was she the first woman to accomplish that feat, but her time was the fastest then recorded for that

---

* In the summer of 1973 Lynne Cox swam from England to France in a time of 9:36 hours, bettering the standing men's record by 8 minutes.

20-mile swim from France to England.* She was honored with a ticker-
tape parade in New York City and the famous suffragette, Carrie Champ-
man Catt hailed the accomplishment as a feminist victory ("How a
Girl. . . ," 1926, p. 66).

Because of the sensationalism which accrued to women swimming
great distances, various people and industries were willing to put up
sums of money as prizes for these endurance contests. One example was
the annual Wrigley 10-mile swim with a $10,000 prize for the winner.

Besides the distance swimming, the best opportunity for women to
earn money by swimming was through exhibitions. Ultimately, these
evolved into great commercial ventures such as the Aquacades, started
in the late thirties starring Eleanor Holm, the backstroke champion.

There have been so many individual swimming stars that it is
difficult to single out one or two. Many of the most famous swimmers
have been mentioned in the preceding paragraphs and the accomplishments of Helene Madison should be added to them. In her 3-year career,
1930-32, she won all available Olympic freestyle events, all available
National Championship freestyle events, and in 1932, all 17 official
world freestyle records. She was also the first woman to swim the 100-
yard freestyle in 1 minute flat. Such a plethora of championships has
never since been equaled by another swimmer—man or woman (International Swimming Hall of Fame, 1971, p. 74). It is also noteworthy
that in 1944 the first woman to receive the Sullivan Award, given
annually by the AAU to the outstanding athlete of the year, was a
swimmer, Ann Curtis, holder of 18 American records. When a second
swimmer, Debbie Meyer, received the same award in 1968 she was only
the fourth woman to be so honored.

## TENNIS

The sport of tennis was introduced to the United States in 1874 by a
woman, Mary Outerbridge. The first record of American women's participation is a picture taken in 1876 on the grounds of the Staten Island
Cricket and Baseball Club where she established the first court. The
game's popularity was rapid and by 1889 *Outing* magazine was able to
assure its readers that "there are numerous clubs in the vicinity of New
York city which offer facilities for the practice of lawn tennis to ladies.
. . . In whatever direction she turns she will assuredly find some organization of young women who are enthusiastically devoted to lawn
tennis. . ." (Slocum, 1889, pp. 290, 294).

Ladies' tennis tournament, Staten Island Cricket Club, 1883.

The abundance of opportunities for women marked quite a change from the early part of that decade when ladies were generally not admitted to membership in clubs with open tournaments. A contemporary writer objected to the exclusion and argued that:

> Not alone the nature of the game, but also its popularity among the ladies, has proved that it is a ladies game, and in every locality where tennis is in vogue there are ladies who play as well as the gentlemen, considering the disadvantages under which they lie. It has been objected that American ladies would not like the publicity that would attach to their appearance as contestants in an open tournament. This objection, it may safely be assumed, does not come from the ladies themselves, but it is a gratuitous plea put in by some person . . . who is ignorant of the fact that American ladies, now, and for several years passed, do and have taken part in open competition in archery. . . (Starey, 1883, pp. 463-464).

But in 1889 the game had grown to be a serious sport for women, as signified by the support of the United States National Lawn Tennis Association which, in that year, "moved and seconded that the Association extend its protective wing to the Lady Lawn Tennis Players of the country.—Carried" (USLTA, 1972, p. 23). A decade later, at the annual meeting, a profound interest in women's tennis was noted and accounted for as a "natural result of increasing tendency on the part of women to enter athletics" (USLTA, 1972, p. 27).

In 1920 *The New York Times* reported three million players in the country. In 1924 the same paper carried over 120 articles on women's tennis—a measure of its great popularity (Evans, 1973, pp. 11-12). Tennis and golf were the most popular sports for women (though in organized competition there were probably more players in other sports). In fact, a columnist noting the marriage of a golf champion and tennis ace commented that it "symbolizes the linking of the two most popular recreations of the modern world" (Darmstadt, November, 1929, p. 19).

In a study of the leisure time habits of 5,000 people, the National Recreation Association in 1934 listed tennis as the competitive activity which had the greatest number of participants (National Recreation Association, 1934). In 1956 a study of almost 2,000 women over 18 years of age revealed that 4 percent of those with a college education played tennis, though only .5 percent without a college education did so, a factor in keeping with the class origins of the sport (deGrazia,

1964, appendix). Recently, television commentators have remarked
that tennis is today one of the fastest growing sports in the country.

The east coast in general and the Philadelphia area specifically,
dominated women's tennis until the late 1920s. In 1927, two out of the
top ten ranked players were from California and four from Massachusetts. New York, Virginia, and New Jersey were also represented in the
rankings. No woman from the far south or midwest had been on the list
for many years. Only two years later, California held six of ten places
including three of the first four. Since that time, that state has supplied
a large number of the top women players.

The first national singles championship was held in 1887 and
doubles in 1890. A group of women at the Philadelphia Cricket Club
organized the first national tournament and sent out the invitations to
play. One organizer, Ellen F. Hensell, won and was awarded the trophy
—a silver tennis girl bearing aloft a silver platter. However, it was not
until two years later when the USNLTA took over sponsorship of the
tournaments, that Hensell's victory was recognized as official (much to
the anger of her chief rival at the Staten Island Cricket Club). This
prestigious championship was won three successive times by only one
player, Maureen Connolly, from 1951 through 1953. Another highlight
of the national tournament was its racial integration by Althea Gibson,
a black woman player who won in 1957 and 1958.

International play for American women began in 1923 with the
inauguration of the Wightman Cup series as an annual contest between
the ladies of England and America. The United States won that first
year and in most of the years that followed. It is not surprising, then,
that in the World Ranking established for women in 1925, a woman
from the United States has been at the top about two-thirds of the time.
The International Lawn Tennis Federation launched in 1963 the Federation Cup as a worldwide competition for women similar to the Davis
Cup. The United States won the first Cup and compiled a 4-5 record
through 1971, though they won 27 matches and lost only 5 in those
years.

The first professional tennis tour—including both men and women
—took place in 1926. But it was not until the early 1940s, when Alice
Marble and Mary Hardwick played pro matches all over the country,
that the idea really caught on. Under the auspices of the USLTA, professional tennis for women did not become a lucrative endeavor; this
changed with the formation of the independent Women's Pro Tour in

Helen Wills, 1938.  [Courtesy Wide World Photos, Inc.]

1970. In that year, women earned as little as $800 winning a champion-
ship title. In 1973 the prize money for the United States National
Singles Championship was $25,000—equal to the men's prize. Thanks
to the remunerative Virginia Slims Circuit, in 1971 Billie Jean King
became the first woman athlete to earn over $100,000; her accom-
plishment was acknowledged by a congratulatory telephone call from
the President.* Tennis today is the highest-paid activity for women
in sport.

Heroines of women's tennis were recognized by the papers as early
as 1878 when the play of the reigning queen at the Staten Island Cricket
Club was described as "quite masculine in its aggressiveness and determination" (USLTA, 1972, p. 23). It was May Sutton, though, who in
the early 1900s introduced the net game for women and caused a sensation with her vigorous play and hard overhead smashes. A decade later,
Mary K. Browne set the pace with the most varied game yet played by
women. When women began to get official ranking in 1913, Browne
was first on the list.

The real queen of the courts was Helen Wills Moody who was
ranked number one for seven years. She was three times winner of the
U.S. Singles Championship, four times of the U.S. Doubles, and *eight*
times winner at Wimbledon (1927-1938)—generally acknowledged as
the most prestigious tournament in the world. From 1927 to 1932 she
did not lose a set in singles play! In 1950, the Associated Press polled
sports writers to determine the greatest athletes of the half century;
Helen Wills Moody was chosen second in the women's division.

The current top woman is Billie Jean King whose earnings in five
years exceeded $350,000 and who has won the Wimbledon crown five
times and three U.S. Championships. King's off-the-court battle for
equal treatment for women players has contributed immeasurably to
the women's game. Under her leadership, women players have learned
to use the power of the boycott and thus have made their financial
position the most favored of all sportswomen. King's decisive win over
Bobby Riggs (1973), in response to his challenge to the ability of
women players, brought the game much publicity and was considered
a victory for feminists.

---

* However, that same year Rod Laver earned $292,717 and the number two and
three men's winners both exceeded $120,000.

## TRACK AND FIELD ATHLETICS

The first known athletic events for women in the United States were held at the Boston YWCA in 1882 (Betts, 1951, p. 100). In 1895 Vassar College held the first collegiate field day. Although little is known about the extent of track and field competition in those early years, a 1905 publication by Spalding carried a list of "Women's Athletic Records" (p. 132). Half of the 14 records listed were held by Vassar College students, three others were listed from Poughkeepsie, N.Y. (where Vassar is located), and the rest came from Montclair, New Jersey; Elmira, New York; Boston; and Washington, D.C. Obviously track and field had spread along the east coast by 1905. A later British publication, surveying the growth of women's track and field, commented that "America is the pioneer of women's athletics* in modern times" (Webster, 1930, p. 10).

For a few years track and field for women remained primarily an eastern sport. But by 1929 the winners of the national meets came from all over the country. Some were sponsored by industry, most notably the Prudential Assurance Athletic Association of Boston which had many medalists. Also in that year the Central Association Championships drew 887 competitors and was described by one observer as "the largest women's athletic meeting the world has yet witnessed" (Webster, 1930, p. 17). The sport then declined and in 1956 there were only 200 women at the AAU championships. In the early 1970s there was an unusual interest in women's track and AAU registration figures jumped from 9,832 to 18,157. Track clubs now number in the hundreds and as a result qualifying standards have had to be adopted for national championships (Amdur, 1972, p. D1).

During the years of its relative unpopularity, one of the important bastions of women's track and field was Tuskegee Institute in Alabama. Sponsor of the AAU-sanctioned Tuskegee Relays which included events for women from 1929, the college developed fine athletic talent. Between 1936 and 1951 Tuskegee Institute won 13 outdoor and 4 indoor AAU championships. When Tuskegee's program declined, another black college, Tennessee State University, came to the fore. Beginning in 1955, Tennessee State won 25 AAU championships (Thaxton, 1970).

---

* In most of the world the term "athletics" is synonymous with track and field.

In 1923 the running events consisted of 50- and 100-yd dashes, 60-yd hurdles, and a 440-yd relay. Field events included the broad and high jump, 8 lb shot put, discus, javelin, and baseball throw. The 220-yd dash was added in 1926 and the 60-yd hurdles were lengthened to 80-m in 1929; thereafter the program remained stable until 1958 when the 440- and 880-yd runs were listed. The first national pentathalon championship was in 1959, though in 1929 it was on the program of at least one AAU-sanctioned meet (Darmstadt, October, 1929, p. 19). The 880-yd medley relay was added in 1960 and the difficult 200-m hurdles in 1963. The triathlon is the newest event.

In general the AAU avoided long-distance events for women. The controversial 800-m race was omitted from the Olympics after 1928 and not restored until 1960. The 1,500-m run was not put on the program until 1965; recently it was followed by the two-mile run. Most controversial of all have been the cross-country and marathon races. The first National Cross-Country Championships were held in 1963. Forty women entered the second one and 700 females competed in 1973, indicating a great growth in interest in ten years. The marathon was even more difficult to gain entry to, and it was not until 1970 that the AAU's first sanctioned women's entry—in the Atlantic City AAU-Road Runners Club marathon—occurred. It took still two more years before the prestigious Boston marathon permitted official women entrants. The winner of the Women's Division (which runs with the men but is scored separately) came in ahead of 600 men.

The first international athletics in which American women participated were the Paris games of 1922. They were sponsored by the Fédération Sportive Féminine Internationale (FSFI)* and titled the First Women's Modern Olympic Games. The United States sent 15 competitors for the 11 events and won gold medals in 4 (100-yd hurdles, high jump [tied with Great Britain], long jump, and shot put); they came in second to Great Britain in overall points. Despite this auspicious beginning, the United States did not participate in any of the other Women's

---

* The FSFI sponsored international women's track and field meets until 1936 when, after several years of negotiating, they reached an agreement with the International Amateur Athletic Federation (IAAF) on appropriate representation and an increase in the number of women's events in the Olympics. With an assurance that their records would be accepted officially, they disbanded and discontinued the Women's World Games, of which four had been held (1922, 1926, 1930, and 1934). Refer to p. 140 for an account of their role in getting women's track and field into the Olympics.

World Games* or in the increasingly frequent international matches held in Europe and Great Britain/ Undoubtedly this was due to the fact that the AAU assumed control of women's track in this country and would only send teams to events sponsored by the rival IAAF with whom it was (and is) affiliated. Of course a team was sent to the Olympics in 1928—the first time track and field events for women were included. They earned one gold and three silver medals in the five events, performing creditably. Since that time American women have participated in all Olympic and Pan-American athletic events and in numerous international tours. The overall performance has been spotty; except in Pan-American competition the women have usually won few medals. Occasionally, as in 1972 when they beat the Russians 52-42 in a dual meet, they have turned in stellar performances.

In part this has been due to a few stars—especially those developed at Tuskegee and Tennessee State. Tuskegee placed six members or former members of its teams on Olympic teams. The Tennessee State Tigerbelles have had 29 women on Olympic teams. The Tigerbelles accounted for 11 gold medals, 4 silvers, and 4 bronzes. Among the best known Tigerbelle stars are Wilma Rudolph and Wyomia Tyus (refer to p. 300). Rudolph won 3 gold medals in the 1960 Olympics, was the first female winner of the United Press International Athlete-of-the-Year European Poll, and in 1961 was the third woman recipient of the Sullivan Trophy award for amateur athlete of the year. Tyus is the only person—man or woman—to win a gold medal in the 100-m race in two successive Olympiads, 1964 and 1968; she also broke several world sprint records.

The most famous American track star of earlier years was Mildred (Babe) Didrikson who in 1932 won the National AAU Outdoor Championships in *five* events (80-m hurdles, high jump, shot put, javelin, and basketball throws) and also won two gold and one silver medal in the Olympics. That year the Associated Press Poll designated her woman athlete of the year.

The greatest woman track athlete of all time is probably Stella Walsh (Walasiewicz) of Poland who made her home in the United States. In the years between 1930 and 1951 she won 35 national champion-

---

* The name Women's Olympic Games was changed after strenuous objection by the International Olympic Committee, to International Ladies' Games and later to Women's World Games.

"Babe" Didrikson (right) about to win the 80-m hurdle in the 1932 Olympics.

ships in events as diverse as sprints, broad jump, discus, and basketball throw.

## VOLLEYBALL

It was not long after volleyball was invented in 1895 in a YMCA that women in schools and colleges began to play the game. However, outside of the educational scene, there seems to have been little organized participation by women prior to the 1940s. Perhaps this was due to the fact that volleyball was supervised by the YMCA until 1928 when the United States Volleyball Association (USVBA) was formed. Women did not join the USVBA until 1949, but today 2,646 women members are approximately 40% of the total membership (Fidler, 1973, p. 19). This of course does not account for the estimated millions who enjoy informal play.

The first U.S. Open Championship for Women was not held until 1949, over two decades after the USVBA began to sponsor men's championships. The lateness of this opportunity for women is inconsistent with the pattern which prevailed in other sports, most of which developed national and international competition for women during the 1920s. In 1951 only 6 teams were entered in the national tournament. The AAU also conducts a national championship for women, having begun in 1953 (1925 for men). The oldest national tournament for women was conducted by the American Turners Association who began to sponsor the event in 1936. The strongest women's teams are located in southern California.

International play for women began in 1955 when volleyball was added to the Pan-American Games program. In 1967 the U.S. women's team won its first Pan-American championship. However, they have never come close to an Olympic medal and, in fact, in 1972 failed to qualify for the competition. Volleyball has been on the Olympic program since 1964—the first and only team sport for women.

# Chapter 4

# Olympic Competition

The opportunity to participate in Olympic events provided the American woman's first chance for international competition. The publicity given these occasions has made the Olympics one of the few long-term, consistent sources of advertisement for women's accomplishments. The athletic forum has been able to demonstrate to the world that women have the physical and psychological capacity to engage in strenuous activity and to perform exciting feats of skill. Although the publicity hasn't always been supportive of the endeavor, particularly during the late 1920s, in the main it has been very positive. Sportswriters and others have demonstrated a great pride in the performance of American women and this has had a good effect on sport for women. Particularly in recent years, the American public has seemed to change its attitudes about the virtues of high level competition for women. (Refer to p. 359). Television viewing of the female Olympic performers—of whom there have been approximately 8,500 from 1900 to 1972—has probably contributed in large measure to this change in attitude, which, in turn, has probably been an important factor in the increased participation of women at all levels of sport.

## ENTRY INTO OLYMPICS

When the Olympics was reestablished in 1896, a woman named Melpomene requested entry in the marathon race. The Olympic Committee refused and was reprimanded by a Greek newspaper for its discourtesy in refusing a lady's request. It assured "those concerned that none of the participants would have had any objections" (Földes, 1964, pp. 108-113).

*Perhaps* the participants would have approved, but certainly the founder of the modern Olympics, Baron Pierre de Coubertin, was

vehemently opposed to women competing in the Olympics.* His conception of women was completely Victorian and therefore typical of
his age. For example, of the phenomenon of women in aviation he said:

> Respect of individual liberty requires that one should not interfere
> in private acts . . . but in public competitions, their [women's]
> participation [particularly in aviation, but also in horse racing,
> polo or football championships] must be absolutely prohibited.
> It is indecent that the spectators should be exposed to the risk of
> seeing the body of a woman being smashed before their eyes.
> Besides, no matter how toughened a sportswoman may be, her
> organism is not cut out to sustain certain shocks. Her nerves rule
> her muscles, nature wanted it that way. Finally, the egalitarian
> *discipline* that is brought to bear on the male contenders for the
> good order and good appearance of the meeting risks being affected
> and rendered inapplicable by female participation. For all these
> practical reasons as well as sentimental ones, it is extremely·desir-
> able that a drastic rule be established very soon (1910, pp. 109-110).

In terms of the Olympics, he fought a losing battle to retain it as a male
preserve, strongly reflecting a kind of modern version of the territorial
imperative:

> We feel that the Olympic Games must be reserved for men. . . . As
> the saying goes: a door must be open or closed. Can women be
> given access to *all* the Olympic events? No? . . . Then why permit
> them some and bar them from others? And especially, on what
> basis does one establish the line between events permitted and
> events prohibited? There are not just tennis players and swimmers
> [both events already in the Olympics for women]. There are also
> fencers, horsewomen, and in America there have also been rowers.
> Tomorrow, perhaps, there will be women runners or even soccer
> players. Would such sports practiced by women constitute an
> edifying sight before crowds assembled for an Olympiad? We do
> not think that such a claim can be made.
>      . . . Such is not our idea of the Olympic Games in which we
> feel [that] we have tried and that we must continue to try to
> achieve the following definition: the solemn and periodic exalta-
> tion of male athleticism with internationalism as a base, loyalty as

---

* The location and translation of all materials relating to Coubertin's opposition to
women in sport and the Olympics, contained in this chapter, is credited to Mary
Leigh (1974).

a means, art for its setting, *and female applause as reward* (1912, pp. 109-111, italics added).

## Earliest Events

The Baron was overruled, and to add insult to injury, the first women competed in the 1900 Olympics held in Paris—his own country. Held in conjunction with an international exposition, the second Olympiad was a badly organized, haphazard affair in which the French government had little interest. Many athletes did not know they were taking part in an Olympiad. No proper facilities were prepared and as a result, events were held in diverse places, sometimes quite removed from Paris. There seemed to be little control over what events were included in the program. The exposition was held for several months and many organized sporting events held in the vicinity during that time period ultimately came to be considered part of the Olympics.

That is probably the explanation for the fact that the first *official* American woman to win an Olympic gold medal was a golfer named Margaret Abbot of the Chicago Golf Club. Abbot was the winner of the Ladies Division of an International Tournament held at the Société de Sport de Compiegne, October 2-9, 1900, held in connection with the Paris Exposition. Although golf was a short-lived Olympic event (surviving only through 1904), her record stands as achieved and her name is duly inscribed on a plaque along with those of other American gold medalists, hung on a wall in Olympic House in New York City.

Tennis events for women were also included in the Paris Olympics, but no American competitors were entered. In fact, American women did not participate in Olympic tennis until the last year it was held, in 1924. This was undoubtedly due to the conservatism of the United States Lawn Tennis Association (USLTA) rather than the Olympic Committee since American women were part of the delegation before that year and American men had competed in tennis since 1900.

In 1904 the Olympics were held in St. Louis, also in conjunction with a world fair. Almost every sport event that took place at the fair was billed as an Olympic event and consequently the Olympic records list seven different activities in the record books as "unofficial." Included in that category is archery for women (and also for men). Lydia Scott Howell was the winner of both individual events, the Double National and Double Columbia Rounds, and was also a member of the Cincinnati Archery Club which captured the Team Round. She stands, therefore, as the first American female to win three gold medals in an Olympic competition. Archery events for men were made official in 1908, but the women's events were not so honored and American women did not enter them. Archery then was discontinued until 1972 when events for both sexes were officially made part of the summer Olympic program.

In 1908 figure skating was added to the competitive opportunities for women and demonstrations classified as noncompetitive were staged in gymnastics, swimming, and diving. American women did not enter any of these events because the American Olympic Committee was opposed to the idea:

> The American Olympic Committee at its meeting at the New York Athletic Club last night went on record against women competing in the Olympic games except in class work of gymnastic exhibitions [calisthenic type exercises]. In other words, the committee was opposed to women taking part in any event in which they could not wear long skirts (*New York Times,* March 31, 1914, p. 9).

Destiny prevailed however, probably coming in the form of pressure from the Amateur Athletic Union (AAU) which in late 1914 had taken over the promotion of women's swimming. In 1920 the United States team went to Antwerp, Belgium with a full team of 15 women swimmers and two figure skaters. Charlotte Epstein, a prominent figure in women's swimming, was designated the manager of the women's swimming team and was also listed in one place (p. 352) in the Official Report as coach for the women. Six of the fifteen members of the team were from the Women's Swimming Association of New York and the other members came from all over the country including California, Oregon, Detroit, Minneapolis, Philadelphia, and Hawaii. The entry of the women swimmers can be said to mark the first time that American women achieved full status on an Olympic team.

## Building the Women's Programs

The battle for women's events in Olympic competition was not yet over. In fact, it still continues! The next sport that received serious consideration was track and field athletics. Coubertin, of course, remained opposed to the idea:

> The Olympic Games, let us not forget, are not parades of physical exercises, but aim at breaking or at least maintaining existing records. *Citius, altius, fortius.* Faster, higher, stronger, this is the motto of the International Committee and the *raison d'être* of all

Olympism. No matter what the ambitions of female athletes may be, they cannot be high enough to pretend to win over men in running, in fencing, in equitation. . . (1912, pp. 9-11).

Undaunted by such attitudes, the women pressed for inclusion. By staging numerous international competitions—particularly the one they dared to call the First Women's Olympiad (refer to p. 132)—and founding in 1921 a Fédération Sportive Féminine Internationale (FSFI)—they demonstrated to the world the efficacy of women's athletics. Perhaps more important, they succeeded in arousing the interest of the International Amateur Athletic Federation (IAAF), the ruling body for track. The IAAF set up a Special Committee to negotiate with the FSFI. The FSFI traded control of women's athletics by agreeing to conduct them by delegation from the Council of the IAAF, complying with its rules and decisions. In return, the IAAF agreed to recommend to the International Olympic Committee (IOC) that women's athletic events be included in the Ninth and subsequent Olympiads, though the "and subsequent" was deleted later. Thus:

> The President of the Council, Mr. Sigfrid Edström (Sweden), presented the report of the Special Committee to the Eighth Congress of the I.A.A.F. during its deliberations at The Hague from August 5 to 8, 1926, and warned the Congress that it had now before it a matter of the greatest moment, and pointed out that refusal to permit women to compete at the Olympic Games would mean that the I.A.A.F. refused also to control athletics for women.
>
> Mr. Pikhala, Finland, at once opposed the whole idea of women's athletics, which he considered contrary to the classical Olympic ideal, and suggested that women's participation in Olympic Games would only serve to bring ridicule upon them (Webster, 1930, p. 99).

Ultimately, a motion to support five women's track and field events for the 1928 Olympics—as an experiment—passed the Congress by a 12-5 vote.* The United States supported the idea for by then the AAU had taken charge of women's athletics in America (refer to p. 38) and therefore was interested in promoting the activity.

Although it was only to be an experiment, the success of the

---

* The reader is referred to Webster (1930) for a detailed account of the intriguing "Fight for Inclusion in the Olympiads."

events won new adherents and following the Amsterdam Olympics the Congress voted 16-6 to retain track and field. However, the 800-m race included in 1928 was deleted and only six events were approved for 1932—one more than in 1928. (In 1928 the events were the 100-m, 400-m relay, 800-m, high jump, and discus. In 1932 the 80-m hurdles and javelin throw were added.)

In the meantime other sports were being proposed for entry and those already included wanted to enlarge the number of events. Simultaneously, the pressure for reducing the Olympiads in size, in order to make it a more manageable occasion, kept increasing. It is interesting to note the squibs in *The New York Times* relating to women's events which have appeared over the years. Some choice examples follow:

*1939*
The Committee decided against including field hockey, basketball, and handball and women's gymnastics in the program for next year's meeting at Helsingfore (*The New York Times,* June 19, 1939, p. 22).

*1946*
Hockey for women was also ruled out at the London games, but probably will be permitted in 1952. Committee members said "the idea is to get the Olympics started again, but not to make the first post-war games too heavy with events" (*The New York Times,* September 7, 1946, p. 10).

*1949*
Brundage is chairman of a committee which will recommend drastic reductions in such sports as women's track and field, rowing, walking, gymnastics and basketball. He fully realizes that spokesmen for the affected sports are going to the Rome meeting with blood in their eyes. If Brundage's recommendations are accepted, women's track and field at Helsinki would be reduced to little more than the 100-meter dash, the 80-meter hurdles and the high and broad jump (*The New York Times,* April 15, 1949, p. 35).

The I.O.C. decided against eliminating any events from the schedule of the 1952 summer games at Helsinki, Finland (*The New York Times,* April 27, 1949, p. 35).

*1953*
Erik von Frenckell of Finland presided over the "axing" committee session (which wanted to drop 1,000 participants from the

Games). "We have not taken revolutionary steps, such as suppress-
ing the team sports or eliminating the women," von Frenckell
said. ". . . We all agreed to keep the women in the games, but cut
off two events discus and shot-put." The committee's proposals
were scheduled to be taken up at Lausanne, Switzerland in April
[where they were rejected] (*The New York Times,* November 11,
1953, p. 38).

*1954*
The I.O.C. refused to add an 800-meter foot race for women, a
pet British request (*The New York Times,* May 13, 1954, p. 39).

*1960*
The first time this race (800 meter run) was tried at Amsterdam
in 1928, the gals dropped in swooning heaps as if riddled by
machine-gun fire. This year the event was restored. Why? The
weaker sex did better in surviving than it had thirty-two years
ago . . . (*The New York Times,* September 9, 1960, p. 20).

*1964*
The United States has agreed to replace Brazil in the women's
volleyball event at the Tokyo Olympics in October, the Japan
Volleyball Association reported today. The substitution was made
at the recommendation of the International Volleyball Federation
after Brazil had reported that she would not compete because of
a lack of funds (*The New York Times,* May 7, 1964, p. 48).

It is evident from these reports that not only have the women had
to fight hard for the inclusion of new events, but events once included
have been constantly threatened with being cut out. In the earlier years
a kind of Victorian ideal of femininity was primarily responsible for
limiting or excluding women's events. To many of the leaders of world
sport, women's competition was at best insignificant and at worst
indecent and unfeminine. In more recent years, however, the problem
is largely one of practicality rather than ideals. The IOC gives to each
of the International Federations the power to recommend their own
programs within specified limitations, while retaining the final authority
to approve or veto the inclusion of sports or events on the Olympic
program. Therefore, an international sport body which decides to introduce women's events must use part of its time and facility allotment to
do so. For example, if basketball were to respond to the terrific pressure
being put on it to include women's games, it must work the tournament into its maximum allotment of 16 entries. A compromise has

now been reached and the women will have six basketball teams in the 1976 Olympics.

The latest sport for women (and men) on the Olympic program was archery, added in 1972. Following the 1972 Games in Munich, the IOC met (*USOC Newsletter,* 1973, p. 10) and

—rejected the international Shooting Union's request to include separate competition for women

—agreed to a separate tournament for women in team handball

—established women's rowing events, including singles and doubles sculls, coxless pair, coxed four, quadruple and eight

—rejected a proposal to include modern rhythmic gymnastics.

Therefore there are three new sports for women scheduled for the Montreal Games: basketball, crew and team handball. The new President of the IOC, Lord Killanin, is generally in favor of limiting the number of competitors in each event, rather than eliminating events (*USOC Newsletter,* 1973, p. 10). This principle will be helpful to the women's events.

### The Program and American Women

Table 6 summarizes the entry of events in women's Olympic competition. It can be seen that there was often a discrepancy between the time women first entered the Olympics in a particular sport and the time that American women took part in the competition. The explanation for the figure skating, swimming and diving, and tennis events has already been given. It rests squarely with the beliefs of various sports leaders as to the appropriateness of women in Olympic competition— and perhaps their estimate of the abilities of American women at that point in time. In 1928 the gymnastic events were a team exercise, making use of balls or hoops or clubs, of the sort that American women did not do. It was not until 1936 that the gymnastic events such as the uneven bars and vaulting were introduced and the Americans were able to participate. Kayaking and Nordic skiing (cross-country) are sports which require either great endurance or the taking of high risks. Neither type of activity had been sanctioned in America—socially or by sport organizations—until quite recently. Consequently, there was no organized competition in which the American women could train for these sports.

**TABLE 6**
**Olympic Competition for Women**

| Sport | First year in Olympics | American entry year |
|---|---|---|
| | Summer Olympics | |
| Golf | 1900 | 1900 |
| Archery* | 1904 | 1904 |
| Figure skating | 1908 | 1920 |
| Swimming and diving | 1912 | 1920 |
| Tennis | 1900 | 1924 |
| Fencing | 1924 | 1924 |
| Track and field | 1928 | 1928 |
| Yachting | 1936 † | 1936 |
| Gymnastics | 1928 | 1936 |
| Equestrian | 1952 † | 1952 |
| Canoeing and kayaking | 1948 | 1960 |
| Volleyball | 1964 | 1964 |
| Shooting | 1968 † | ——— |
| | Winter Olympics | |
| Figure skating | 1924 | 1924 |
| Alpine skiing | 1936 | 1936 |
| Speed skating ‡ | 1960 | 1960 |
| Tobogganing | 1964 | 1964 |
| Nordic skiing | 1952 | 1972 |

* Listed as unofficial event.
† Women competed as members of essentially men's teams. Teams without women had been in the Olympics since 1900.
‡ Included in the 1932 Winter Olympics as an exhibition sport.

The shooting involved a woman on the single team representing a country—as in the yachting and equestrian events. Presumably, should a woman qualify for the U.S. team by virtue of her performance in Olympic trials, she would (and will) be accepted on the team. In fact, the first alternate for the 1968 rifle team was a woman. The first year that the American equestrian team was not a U.S. Army riding team was in 1952. The new civilian group chose ten men and one woman for the equestrian team. The yachting crews and their boats are chosen as a unit and in 1936 several women were either crew or reserve members of some of the units.

A summary of the participation of American women throughout the history of their participation in the Olympics is provided in Table 7.

**TABLE 7**
Participation of American Women in the Olympic Games:  Entries by Sports*

| Sport | Total entries | Individual entries | Multiple entries† |
|---|---|---|---|
| Summer Olympics | | | |
| Swimming | 193 | 172 | 21 |
| Track and field | 190 | 147 | 36 |
| Diving | 63 | 43 ‡ | 15 |
| Gymnastics | 58 | 44 | 5 |
| Fencing | 37 | 23 | 4 |
| Volleyball | 24 | 19 | 5 |
| Equestrian | 20 | 15 | 4 |
| Canoeing and kayaking | 17 | 11 | 3 |
| Archery | 10 | 10 | — |
| Yachting | 8 | 8 | — |
| Tennis | 5 | 5 | — |
| Golf | 1 | 1 | — |
| Totals | 626 | 498 | 93 |
| Winter Olympics | | | |
| Alpine skiing | 58 | 50 | 7 |
| Figure skating | 54 | 39 | 13 |
| Speed skating | 25 | 19 | 4 |
| Luge | 8 | 7 | 1 |
| Nordic skiing | 6 | 6 | — |
| Totals | 151 | 121 | 25 |

\* Data supplied by the courtesy of C. Robert Paul, Public Information Director, United States Olympic Committee.

† Athletes who competed in more than one set of Games.

‡ Includes two divers who doubled in swimming.

From the table it can be seen that the largest increase in participation took place in 1964—a 42 percent increase from 1960. A number of factors might have been responsible for this occurrence, including the increased interest in the Olympics as a symbol of cold war status resulting in better financial support from the public. The biggest boost to the women, however, probably came from the exciting performance given by the track team, as well as the swimmers in 1960. Wilma Rudolph was an American sensation who stimulated tremendous interest in women's track and field. This may be one more example of the old axiom that success begets support which begets success. . .

## Carrying the Flag

It has been shown that as early as 1900 American women competed in the Olympics for the United States and that by 1920 it could be said that they had achieved full status as team members. Generally they traveled across the ocean with the full delegation, though till this day the men and women train separately. In some sports (e.g., track and field) the Olympic trials to choose the team members are held separately. In other sports (e.g., swimming) they are held at the same time.

But the *real* mark of status—of having been totally accepted—was the choice of a woman to carry the flag in the opening ceremonies. In 1968 Janice Lee York Romary of San Mateo, California, a forty-year-old fencer with 10 national championships to her credit, became the first woman chosen for this honor.

In 1972 a woman speed skater—the only person who also had been on the 1968 team—carried the flag in the Winter Olympics. The Summer Olympic delegation marched in behind Olga Fiktova Connolly, entering her fifth Olympics. She commented:

> I carried it as high as I could. . . . I caught a glimpse of the Soviet flag bearer, who was a very large man, a heavy weight wrestler, and I saw some other flag bearers who were large men. I thought that in order to make the flag of the United States as beautiful as I wanted to see it, we needed not only strong men but also strong women. So I gripped the flag in one hand, just like the men. . .
> (*The New York Times*, August 27, 1972, p. V1).

## THE OLYMPIC PROTEST

Although women's events were officially accepted as permanent parts of the Olympic Games, and the participation of American women had begun in earnest by 1920, opposition did not fade away. In fact, it built up during the 1920s and a strong movement took place to ban American women participants from the United States team. The physical educators, both men and women, were the leaders of this protest movement and their actions make an interesting episode in the history of Olympic competition for American women.

### Professional Opinion

The idea of American women competing in Amsterdam in 1928 in the new track and field events in the Olympics was in direct conflict with the philosophy of American physical educators. It obviously involved intense and prolonged training of a few highly skilled women rather than attention to the very many unskilled girls and women whom the physical educators believed should have priority. The title of an article by Blanche Trilling, an influential woman physical educator, sums up their view of the issue succinctly: "The Playtime of a Million Girls or an Olympic Victory—Which?" Within it the question was asked, "Shall the spirit of wholesome play for all girls be sacrificed to developing the superior prowess of a few?" (Trilling, 1929, p. 51).

Furthermore, the physical educators were not sure that women had the physical or emotional stamina to compete in such high level competition:

> Girls are not suited for the same athletic programs as boys. The biological difference between them cannot be ignored unless we are willing to sacrifice our school girls on the altar of an Olympic spectacle. Under prolonged and intense strain a girl goes to pieces nervously (Perrin, 1928, p. 10).

A prominent male physical educator also voiced the common concern that Olympic participation would have adverse effects on the femininity of the participant. Writing in an article titled "Olympics for Girls?" he said:

> Life should be a process whereby the unique prepotencies of each individual are protected, developed and finally brought to blossom and fruition. For girls and women this means the development of all those traits which are necessary to attract the most worthy fathers for their children, provide the most healthful physiques for child-bearing and build the most maternal emotional and social behavior patterns. Intense forms of physical and psychic conflicts, of which athletics provide the best example in modern life, and of which Olympic games provide the extreme type, tend to destroy girls' physical and psychic charm and adaptability for motherhood. . . . Olympic games are large-muscle skill and endurance contests which involve highly competitive psychic conflicts. They are essentially masculine in nature and develop wholly masculine physiques and behavior traits. Attempts to induce girls to enter them should be condemned without reservations, for the welfare of the girls as well as society (Rogers, 1929, p. 194).

The running of the 800-m race in the 1928 Olympics seemed to bear out the worst fears of all who opposed Olympic competition for women. As reported by the eminent sportswriter John R. Tunis (and recently verified by eyewitnesses connected with the American Olympic movement), it was a debacle of the worst sort. Tunis described what he saw:

> Below us on the cinder path were eleven wretched women, five of whom dropped out before the finish, while five collapsed after reaching the tape. I was informed later that the remaining starter fainted in the dressing room shortly afterward (Tunis, 1929, p. 213).

Tunis' description of the conditions on the boat to Amsterdam also supported the strong concern that the circumstances accruing to Olympic sport for women were not in accord with the best interests of women:

> The whole voyage was the worst possible thing for the women on board. It was all entirely animalistic; the competitors, both men and women, ate, slept, and worked daily like animals rather than human beings. Not once during the entire trip of six weeks was any appeal made to the morals of these young people, any suggestion of the Olympic ideal, or of what the Olympic oath meant, any hint that in the eyes of the world at Amsterdam these young people represented their country. Nothing in fact but a strenuous effort to develop winners for every event. In fact there was little difference between the management of the last Olympic team and the management of a kennel! (Tunis, 1929, p. 215).

The occasion was interpreted quite differently by the commentator for the magazine *The Sportswoman,** who said:

> Track is often a very secretive sport and its luminaries sometimes never shine outside the pale of their individual sport circle, be it school, college or club. This year, however, the Olympic games have brought track stars to the fore and the winners enjoy worldwide recognition. . . .
>
> In my opinion, the 1928 Olympics have proven just once more that women have earned a permanent place in sport. The discussion as to whether women's events should be part of the next Olympics was a pathetic anachronism. Even the stupidest mortal must by this time realize that a few women are capable of

* *The Sportswoman* was a monthly magazine published from 1924-1936. Supported by the United States Field Hockey Association and later by the United States Lacrosse Association, it contained news of any kind of sport for women from all over the world. The magazine was distinctly feminist in its pride of women's accomplishments.

developing into such experts in particular lines of sport that to
watch them is a great pleasure. And it does not take any great
astuteness to realize that the feats of these few increase the interest
of the vast feminine public, spurring them to further their own
efforts.*

These few samples of opinion were typical of the time. Many popular magazines throughout the 1920s carried articles in support of the
idea of women competing in sports. Nevertheless, the authors rarely
sanctioned Olympic competition directly. It seems as if women could
compete within some vague limits that were being breached by the
Olympics. The Olympics were (are) a highly public forum; the athletes
were (are) on display for all the world to observe; the emotion accruing
to the responsibility of representing one's country added to the natural
desire to win was (is) very intense. All of these inherent characteristics
of Olympic competition violated ancient taboos against women entering
into overtly aggressive behaviors on a large public scale.

### Formal Reaction

Lack of enthusiasm for sport competition for girls and women was not
a new idea to American physical educators. Articles against interschool
competition had appeared as early as the turn of the century. Nevertheless, there was no *formal* movement against it and when the women
swimmers and figure skater participated in the 1920 Olympics, little
opposition was raised. It was the assumption of control of women's
track and field athletics by the AAU in 1922, which served to galvanize
the women into action. The resultant founding of the Women's Division
of the National Amateur Athletic Federation (NAAF) in 1923 gave the
women a locus of control and enabled them to develop and promote a
coherent national platform for girls' and women's sports.

Furthermore, by 1927 the old Committee on Women's Athletics
had become a Section on Women's Athletics (SWA) within the American
Physical Education Association (APEA), giving it greater status and
power. Both groups, which worked hand-in-glove and shared many of
the same personnel, had adequate financial support and a consistent
network of communication through the *American Physical Education
Review,* national conferences, and assorted bulletins. The groups had
already achieved major changes in women's sports through their work.

---

* From R.D. Rickaby, "Circumspice!," *The Sportswoman* (October, 1928), p. 19.
Reprinted by permission.

Therefore, when they were confronted with the participation of women in the Olympics—which was a total affront to the philosophy they had been vigorously promoting over the previous five years—they believed they could prevent its recurrence. Their particular goal was 1932 when the Olympics were to be held in Los Angeles.

In 1929 at the annual meeting of the Women's Division, the members put their opposition on record in the form of resolutions:*

> I. *Whereas,* Competition in the Olympic Games would, among other things, (1) entail the specialized training of a few, (2) offer opportunity for the exploitation of girls and women, and (3) offer opportunity for possible overstrain in preparation for and during the Games themselves, be it
> *Resolved,* That the Women's Division of the National Amateur Athletic Federation go on record as disapproving of competition for girls and women in the Olympic Games.

Then, recognizing that their power did not extend beyond the United States, and not wanting to appear inhospitable, they added a second resolution:

> II. *Whereas,* The United States will be acting in the capacity of host to the other nations participating in the games of 1932, in order that we may not seem to be inhospitable to the girls and women who may take part in the Games, especially those from foreign countries, be it
> *Resolved,* That the Women's Division send a letter to the proper committee or authority offering to assist in every way possible in the entertainment of the women participants in the Games in 1932.

As good pedagogues more interested in the positive promotion of girls' and women's sport than in reaction against it, they offered an alternative in a third resolution:

> III. *Whereas,* The Women's Division is interested in promoting the ideal of Play for Play's sake, of Play on a large scale, of Play and recreation properly safeguarded,
> *Whereas,* It is interested in promoting types and programs of activities suitable to girls as girls, be it
> *Resolved,* That the Women's Division or whomever it shall

---

* From A. A. Sefton, *The Women's Division National Athletic Federation,* Palo Alto, Calif.: Stanford University Press, pp. 82-83. Copyright © 1941 by Stanford University Press and reprinted by permission.

designate shall ask for the opportunity of putting on in Los Angeles during the Games (not as a part of the Olympic program) a festival which might include singing, dancing, music, mass sports and games, luncheons, conferences, banquets, demonstrations, exhibitions, etc.

They concluded with a ringing resolution to go back and spread the principles advocated by the Division.

Certainly these resolutions were in tune with the thinking of the time, for they were endorsed by numerous groups including the National Board of the YWCA, and similar ones were adopted by all of the organizations connected with sport for college women.

In 1930 they forwarded their resolutions of protest, along with a petition,* to M. le comte de Baillet-Latour, President of the IOC, and to all 67 national Olympic committees[†] (Sefton, 1941, pp. 83-84). Their petition began with an affirmation of their belief in competition:

The Women's Division, National Amateur Athletic Federation, believes wholeheartedly in competition and believes that competition is the soul of athletics and of sports and games, and that without it they could not exist; . . .

That statement was absolutely necessary if their petition was not to be dismissed as written by cranks who were against all sport for women. In fact, that aspect of the Women's Division philosophy was widely misunderstood. The petition continued from there with a seven point list of what types of sport programs they desired to promote. Then they objected to the Olympic track and field events as being precisely the opposite kind of activity:

Participation in the Olympic Games, particularly participation in Track and Field Events,
(1)   Entails the specialized training of the few,
(2)   Offers opportunity for exploitation and commercialization,
(3)   Stresses individual accomplishment and winning of championships,
(4)   Places men in immediate charge of athletic activities for girls and women,

---

* The following excerpts from the petition are taken from A.A. Sefton, *The Women's Division National Amateur Athletic Federation*, Palo Alto, Calif.: Stanford University Press, pp. 83-84. Copyright © 1941 by Stanford University Press and reprinted by permission.

[†] In 1973 there were 131 National Olympic Committees.

(5)   Offers opportunity for possible overstrain in preparation for or during the Games themselves; . . .

The petition next reminded the IOC that its founder had also objected to women in the Olympics:

> Pierre de Coubertin, founder of the modern Olympic Games, said to the Athletes and all taking part at Amsterdam in the XI [*sic;* it was the IX] Olympic Games, "As to the admission of women to the Games, I remain strongly against it. It was against my will that they were admitted to a growing number of competitions: . . ."

Finally, they declared that it was within the power of the IOC to vote on the participation of women in track and field events and they finished with the request that

> The Women's Division, National Amateur Athletic Federation, petitions this International Olympic Congress to vote to omit track and field events for women from the 1932 program.

Many of the criticisms raised about track and field could have been made about swimming, but somehow that sport never provoked the negative reaction that track and field did. Probably the distinction had to do with notions of femininity. Events such as the high jump and throwing the discus called for an overt display of strength and muscle-power, while swimming and diving called for more aesthetically pleasing movement. As late as 1966, a woman physical educator and Chairman of the Women's Board of the United States Olympic Development Committee, wrote:

> To most of the women in the United States and to many women of other nations, the shot put and discus throw are forms of competition that are generally unacceptable to the feminine image. They are men's sports, requiring tremendous explosive strength and a large physique for a superior performance. Generally speaking, women do these very badly, poor mimics of men, and these sports have a limited appeal to the female sex. It is a known fact [!] that chiefly the hefty, masculine woman gains sufficient satisfaction from performance of these two athletic activities. There are many men and women around the world who would be delighted if the International Olympic Committee would eliminate the shot put and discus from the field events for women in the Olympic Games because often the feminine self-image is badly mutilated when women perform in these two sports (Jernigan, 1966, p. 73).

A second reason may lie in the fact that track and field athletes were usually from lower economic classes while the swimmers and divers were at least middle class. The working girl who competed in track was often sponsored by industry which was known for its exploitation, while the swimmer generally had the means to belong to the private swimming club. For whatever the reasons, it was definitely the track and field athletics which received the brunt of everyone's displeasure.

## Outcome

As everyone knows, the petition of the Women's Division was rejected and track and field events continued to be an integral part of the Olympic Games. After they lost their plea, the physical educators ceased formal agitation against the Olympic participation of women. Instead they turned their attention to promoting the kind of sport they desired in places where they had some influence: the schools, colleges, and agencies such as the YWCA.

However, they refused to condone Olympic sport for women by assisting in any way with the various committees and groups which promoted it. Therefore, unlike men's sport, most women Olympic athletes received their training in organizations that had no connection with schools or colleges (the major exception until recently were the athletes from Tennessee State University). Because of this, women Olympic athletes usually have not received the benefit of public financing as it is available in educational institutions in the form of free training and coaching, use of expensive equipment and facilities, and supported competition against others of their own level. The major result of the Olympic protest was to require that prospective female Olympians find a private source of financing their preparation—either through their families or other private individuals or through industry-sponsored sport groups. This of course made participation more difficult and limited the potential pool of female Olympic talent.

## PERFORMANCE COMPARED

Despite the barriers to women's participation in the Olympics, their performance has, on the whole, been good. The Olympic Games are supposed to be international championships where individuals perform as representatives of their country. Counting up a country's total medals is considered inimical to the spirit of the games. Nevertheless, such counting almost always takes place for people are always curious about how well the citizens of their country can compare to those of another nation.

Since men and women do not compete against each other, it would be pointless to compare their performances in any given event. However, it is interesting to compare the relative performances of the American men and women in competition with men and women in the rest of the world.

## Other Women

As Fig. 3 indicates, American women competed in the Summer Olympics for a total of 272 gold medals (not including equestrian and yachting events). In winning 92 medals, they captured one-third of all the events which they entered. Most, though not all countries (123 in 1972) which enter the Olympics send women competitors. In general, the observation made by Jokl about the 1952 games still holds true. He noted that "on the whole, the United States, Europe, Russia and the British Dominions displayed by far the greatest interest in the women's events at the Olympic Games" (Jokl, 1964, p. 75). Given the number of countries that do have women competitors, the American women's performance is quite good.

The sports in which women from the United States have been most successful are diving, swimming, and track and field, in that order (not including sports in which they officially competed in only one Olympiad). In diving, the American women captured 76 percent of all the

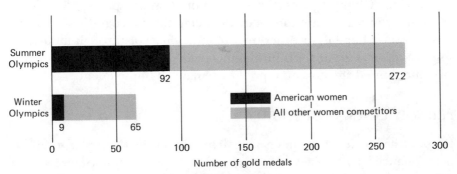

*Fig. 3    Comparison of the Olympic championship performances of American women with all other women competitors in all sports entered, 1900–1972.*

American women sweep springboard diving in the 1948 Olympics.  [Courtesy USOC.]

events; in swimming they won 57 percent and in track and field, 21 percent. In the Winter Olympics, they have won 19 percent of all Alpine skiing events, 13 percent of the speed skating contests and 13 percent of the figure skating championships.

Swimming and diving are sports in which American women have had the longest history of competitive participation: national championships were held as early as 1916. It was the first women's sport organized by the AAU, another evidence of long-term support. Finally, the national excitement engendered by Gertrude Ederle's famous channel swim in 1926 and subsequent spectator exposure to women swimming in aquacades and movies with stars such as Eleanor Holm and Esther Williams also helped to bring about acceptance and support for women's swimming and diving events.

Track and field, on the other hand, has been more of an orphan sport for women. As noted previously, physical educators launched a campaign against its inclusion in the Olympics and virtually ignored the sport in schools and colleges. Women have received little support for their endeavors and track and field athletes have recently begun to complain about the inequality of treatment on the national level.*

Winter sports have never been an American forte primarily because there is limited opportunity to participate in most of the country. Furthermore, although they are popular recreational activities, they are not in great demand as competitive sports. Support for the ski program has been so limited, for example, that a few years ago an American team embarked upon a European tour without being issued uniforms. Figure skating has had a long history of competition in America, for both men and women. However, the sport is a judged sport and very political in its application. European standards and styles appear to differ from American ones sufficiently enough to hamper American success in international competition.

The sports in which American women have had least success are fencing, gymnastics, kayaking, and volleyball in the Summer Olympics and nordic skiing and tobogganing (luge) in the Winter Olympics. No woman from the United States has ever won a gold medal in any of those sports. Reasons for this failure vary. Fencing and gymnastics are not popular sports in the United States. Although the men have occasionally won medals in gymnastics, they have had no success in winning

---

* See Franks (1973) and Dosti (1972) for descriptions of the problems women face in track and field competition, particularly with regard to the 1972 Olympics.

fencing championships either. Support for these activities is extremely limited and therefore the talent pool is not developed. Volleyball is a sport which is just beginning to become popular in America. For women, it was the last of the major sports in which a national championship was staged and that did not happen until 1949. The fact that the style of international play is different from American play is a further barrier to success—though that is also changing.

Kayaking, nordic skiing, and tobogganing are all high endurance/ high risk sports. Until very recently American women did not take part in activities which were so characterized. Consequently, the development of high caliber talent has been severely limited.

## American Men

While it is obvious that American women and men as groups have both been successful in Olympic competition, it is interesting to see their success relative to each other. There are several difficulties in making such comparisons. The fact that many more American men than women are on the team is a factor which affects the overall performance. This situation is improving though—in 1972 there was a low 4:1 ratio compared with the 21:1 ratio in 1920! Obviously, it is not fair to compare absolute records in any given event such as the 100-m dash. In most sports the physical advantage is definitely with the males and the women's best score will therefore be lower. (Refer to p. 412 for a discussion on sex differences in performance.) Women have not had the opportunity to participate in many of the events in which the men compete, nor have their activities been held in as many Olympiads.

Their performance was compared, therefore, in terms of percent of success in the light of potential for success in identical years. The number of potential championships and the number of medals actually won were totaled for both men and women. The performances in Fig. 4 are only for years in which both sexes competed in the six selected activities.

The sports selected were the major sports in which both sexes competed in the Winter and Summer Olympics. These were the common activities in which both men and women from the United States achieved their greatest successes. A cursory glance at Fig. 4 reveals that in terms of winning potential gold medals, the American men's and women's performances do not differ greatly. The women's record in two sports is better than the men's, in two sports almost identical, and in two sports is poorer.

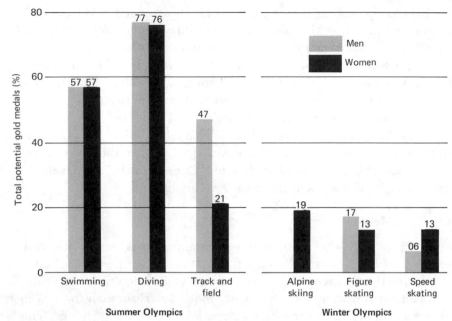

*Fig. 4    Comparison of American women's and men's Olympics championship performances in years both sexes competed in the six selected sports.*

Factors already have been offered in explanation for the women's strong showing in swimming and diving. The comparability of male-female performances may be explained further by the fact that competitions are frequently held simultaneously and teams often train together, which means that women in swimming and diving are more likely than women in some other sports to receive equal coaching, training, and use of adequate facilities. Note also that since 1924 men have had only one more swimming event and generally the identical number of diving events as the women. This near equality of Olympic competitive opportunity is another factor which tends to increase similarity in the performance records.

The exact opposite phenomenon prevails in track and field. The ratio of men's to women's events in the Olympics has ranged from 4.4:1 to 1.7:1 in 1972—the lowest ratio in history. Support for the two groups differs markedly in this country. Currently the AAU puts only about 20 percent of its gate receipt income into women's track and field, with men getting the other 80 percent (Dosti, 1972, p. 23). Opportunities for international competition are not equivalent and

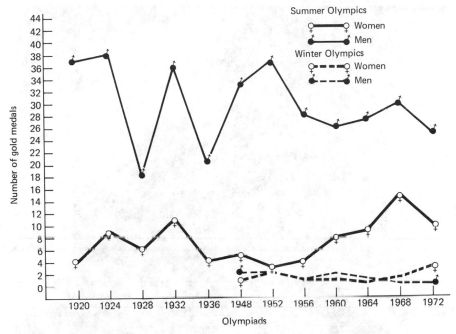

*Fig. 5    United States Olympic Championship performances: Summer Olympics, 1920–1972; Winter Olympics, 1948–1972.*

consequently the women track and field Olympians are less experienced than their male counterparts.

The winter sports provide a most interesting phenomenon. In two of the three activities the performance of American women is better than that of the men. In the third activity, figure skating, the difference is 4 percentage points or one gold medal. The largest variation is in Alpine skiing, a sport in which American men have never won a gold medal in the Olympics. One probable explanation for the matching performances in the Winter Olympics is that the talent pool is so limited by geography and financing that it is equally small for women and men. Since training and opportunities for men and women are roughly comparable, it is therefore not unreasonable that performances are also roughly comparable. The difference in skiing, while large percentagewise (19 percent) is only a matter of four medals. Nevertheless, in Alpine skiing the American women have clearly performed better than the men.

In Fig. 5 the total number of gold medals won by each sex is compared for every Olympiad since 1920, the year women achieved

Andrea Mead Lawrence, winner of two gold medals in the 1952 Olympics.
[Courtesy Wide World Photos, Inc.]

full team status. Since the differences in total number of medals is not a meaningful statistic for reasons explained at the beginning of this section, this graph is included to compare the pattern of accomplishment.

In the twelve Summer Olympics surveyed there is a remarkable similarity in the two patterns; only in the years 1952-1960 is there a difference in the trends. The Winter Olympics show a similar tendency to match, with the exception of 1968 and 1972. There are probably several possible explanations for this phenomenon but the most likely one seems to be that both the men and women were affected by the entry of strong teams from other national powers—particularly Germany and Russia. American supremacy in the Olympics took a sharp dip in 1928. For men the decrease in championships was 53 percent; for women it was 33 percent. It was the year that Germany first returned to Olympic competition after World War I; they were immediately successful, tying with Finland for the second largest number of gold medals. Also in that year, one-third more countries than in 1924 won at least one gold medal, indicating that the competition was definitely growing keener.

The American performance curve might have stayed depressed for the next few Olympiads, but in 1932 the Games were held in the United States, which gave the home team a decided advantage. In 1936 they returned to Europe (Germany) and the ever stronger Europeans continued their winning ways. The Netherlands proved particularly hard for the women to beat—perhaps because, as Jokl remarked, it was a country governed by a succession of queens (1964, p. 75).

When the Olympics were resumed after World War II, Europe was decimated and the Americans were again the strongest competitors; Germany was out of the picture. By the end of the forties, however, the status of women in America had shifted drastically. No longer needed in the factories, women returned to their roles as housewives and interest in competitive sport fell sharply. Much of their industry-sponsored competition was disbanded. Nowhere is the evidence of lack of national support as clearly indicated as in the makeup of the American women's track and field team. It was reduced to 10 athletes and a manager-coach. There were no discus throwers or high jumpers and only one shot putter, javelin thrower, broad jumper, and hurdler. This happened at a time when the total number of women athletes in the Olympics was jumping to 518 from the 385 in 1948. Thus the women's showing in 1952 was poorer than in 1948, while the American men were the best in the world. The dip in 1956 for the men and low performance for the women reflected the growing strength of Russia in the Olympics. The USSR was the overwhelming winner of championships.

The steady increase in swimming races, a sport traditionally dominated by American women, has been the major reason that their performance improved throughout the sixties. Another factor may have been the general increase in interest in women's sport in this era when women began to make their strength felt throughout American society. This undoubtedly led to increased support for their endeavors.

Although the overall pattern of performance is similar, there are two marked differences between the women's and men's gold medal curve. First, the women show greater variation from Olympiad to Olympiad, averaging a 56 percent difference vis-à-vis 33 percent for the men. This probably indicates that historically the women have lacked stability in sport competition. Since their events are fewer, a difference of just two or three medals reflects a greater shift in overall performance. Without the depth which comes with years of solid accomplishment in sport, the presence or absence of one or two star performers can strongly affect the American women's performance in a given Olympiad. For just the opposite reasons, the men are more likely to have less variation in any given time period.

The second and last difference in the patterns is that the women have grown increasingly successful. In 1968 they earned the most gold medals they had ever won in Olympic competition. The men's performance has declined relative to the earlier years; they have never won as many medals as they did in 1924. This phenomenon can probably be accounted for by the fact that American men developed a great interest and skill in sport long before their European peers. When Europe developed a like enthusiasm, and found means to implement its interest through sport clubs and state support of athletes, competition for the American men grew tougher. These factors also affect the competition for the American women, but support for female sport in America came relatively late. Not until the 1920s was there any real interest in it. Consequently, the American women could and did become increasingly successful during the period under discussion.

## OLYMPIC DEVELOPMENT

The amount of attention to and development of female Olympic talent varied over the years with a particular increase during the 1960s. Raising money to send participants to the Olympics was an ongoing problem,

particularly for the women. As an aid to financing the women, famous
figures were asked to serve as chairmen or honorary chairmen of various
committees. Thus Eleanor Roosevelt agreed to be honorary chairman
of the 1940 Women's Track and Field Committee of the American
Olympic Committee (*The New York Times,* November 3, 1938, p. 30)
and Doris Duke Cromwell (heiress of the Duke tobacco fortune) agreed
to serve as honorary chairman of the Women's Swimming Committee.
Cromwell also agreed to head a committee of 100 women to organize a
financing campaign for the women swimmers (*The New York Times,*
December 13, 1938, p. 34).

A new and different effort on behalf of the women was begun in
the 1960s.

## Women's Board

In 1960, the same Doris Duke Cromwell decided to donate half a
million dollars to the USOC to help in the development of women's
Olympic sport. This gesture ultimately resulted in the formulation of
a Women's Advisory Board under the aegis of the United States
Olympic Development Committee (USODC). The USODC was organ-
ized in 1958 to "expand, improve, and coordinate programs involving
Olympic activities, in order to build up our nation's athletic potential"
(Jernigan, 1962, p. 25f).

About a year earlier, the AAHPER, which holds one seat on the
USOC, requested the Executive Committee to consider placing repre-
sentatives from the Division for Girls and Women's Sports (DGWS) on
Sports Committees concerned with women's activities. The Executive
Committee unanimously approved the motion (Jernigan, 1962, p. 26).
Thus, when the Cromwell money became available, it was logical to
create a Women's Advisory Board (the term "advisory" was later
dropped from the name), and to place on it representatives from
DGWS who were desirous of serving the Olympic organization.

> The general purposes [of the Women's Board] are to help increase
> opportunities for girls and women to participate in sports; to aid
> the skilled girl to reach her potential in sports; to help women
> physical education teachers, coaches, and recreation leaders to
> become more competent in teaching and coaching specific sports;
> and to provide opportunities for women to become more com-
> petent in officiating and judging Olympic sports (*Proceedings of
> Fifth National Institute on Girls Sports,* 1969, p. 121).

## Institutes of Girls Sports

The involvement of the DGWS on the Women's Board was something of a phenomenon. As discussed earlier in this chapter, the attitude of the women physical educators towards women in the Olympics was extremely negative. They refused to serve on the committees of any organizations which promoted high level sport for women because that would have been tantamount to condoning them. By 1947 their attitude had softened somewhat. Faced with plans for the post-war revival of the Olympic Games, the women appointed a committee to study the problem. The Olympic Study Committee report, which was adopted by the NSWA and approved by the AAHPER, neither endorsed nor condemned the idea of women in Olympic competition, but rather recommended certain standards:

> The [Olympic Study] committee believes that the National Section on Women's Athletics should suggest certain standards for competition of women in the Olympic Games rather than to endorse or condemn such competition.
>
> In view of the fact that the Olympic Games will be revived in the summer of 1948, the National Section on Women's Athletics suggests the following standards for competition:
>
> 1. The participants have a doctor's certificate of approval for competition in the Olympics.
>
> 2. The participants are at least 16 years of age.*
>
> 3. The participants are coached by women trained in physical education from the time the preliminary preparation begins, through the competition, and where it is possible, the participants are under the direct supervision of trained women physical educators.
>
> 4. The participants are adequately housed enroute and at the Olympics in areas entirely separated from the men.
>
> 5. The health of the individual is considered of paramount importance at all times.
>
> It is further recommended that:
>
> 1. The Olympic Games Committee seek the advice of leaders in the physical education profession in regard to policies concerning women in the Olympics.

---

* One American Olympic diver, Marjorie Gestring, won a gold medal in the 1936 Olympics at age 13.

2.  Publicity be directed toward achievement in the sport
rather than exploitation of the individual.*

Thus in one statement the women reasserted all their old concerns
and still took a tentative step toward involvement. They stopped short
of agreeing to associate with *directing or organizing* Olympic participation for women in any way, but insisted on having responsibility for the
competitors themselves. It was nine more years before the National
Section for Girls and Women's Sports (NSGWS—the old NSWA) Board
"approve[d] the recommendation that NSGWS request representation
on the Olympic Sports Committees which involve women participants"
(Jernigan, 1962, p. 25).

Once that decision was made, the DGWS (NSGWS with a new
name) was ready to make an all-out effort. Not only did it approve of
appointing people to the Women's Board, but it also cooperated as an
organization in the Board's major project: the national institutes on
girls' sports.

All the years of turning their backs on high-level competition for
women had left most physical educators without sufficient expertise
to coach or officiate high level competitors. Furthermore, they had little
or no knowledge of two major Olympic sports: track and field and
gymnastics. Neither activities were included in the physical education
programs at that time. A basic assumption of the Olympic development
program is that the schools have an important role in the teaching and
locating of young people at a sufficiently early age to help them eventually to become world class competitors. Thus the institutes were
designed to assist the women physical educators in acquiring the
knowledge necessary to carry out good programs in the schools in the
Olympic sports.

Cosponsored by the Women's Board and the DGWS, five institutes
were held, each with a different focus: (1) 1963, gymnastics and track
and field; (2) 1965, gymnastics, track and field, kayaking, fencing,
diving; (3) 1966, skiing and figure skating; (4) 1966, coaching basketball and volleyball; and (5) 1969, coaching and officiating basketball
and gymnastics and track and field. Unfortunately, the Cromwell money
has been used up and it is doubtful that future institutes can be held.

---

* From "Editorial: Participation in Games by Women," *Sports Bulletin*, **II** (December, 1947), p. 2. Reprinted by permission.

It is difficult to assess the effect of these institutes in regard to the development of Olympic talent. However, certain outcomes are distinctly visible. Gymnastics and track and field (particularly the former) have now become an important part of the girls' and women's sport scene in schools and colleges. The introduction of these activities, both into the curriculum and as competitive sports, has been in many cases directly attributed to instruction of the teacher in connection with the institutes or the clinics later held by those who attended the institutes (see, for example, Bayless, 1966).

The second, and equally important, outcome has been a distinct change in attitudes towards women's Olympic competition. Women competitors are now encouraged by physical educators, rather than discouraged. This may have a strong influence on the number of girls who aspire to Olympic participation—which is sure to prove an asset to the goals of the Olympic Development Committee.

Increased experience with Olympic sports, combined with a positive attitude toward the idea of American women competing in the Olympics, should eventually affect the performance potential of women from the United States.

# Bibliography

*Addresses at the Inauguration of Rev. L. Clark Seelye as President of Smith College, July 14, 1875*, Springfield, Mass.: Clark W. Bryan, 1875.

Adkins, V.B.E., "The Development of Negro Female Olympic Talent," P.E.D. dissertation, Indiana University, Bloomington, 1967.

Ainsworth, D.S., *The History of Physical Education in Colleges for Women*, New York: A.S. Barnes, 1930.

Amdur, N., "Track Acquiring Sex Appeal," *The New York Times*, February 27, 1972, D1, 3.

Applebee, C.M.K., "Early Landmarks of American Hockey," *Selected Hockey-Lacrosse Articles*, Ed. by C.M. Newhof, Washington, D.C.: National Section on Girls and Women's Sports, 1955.

Arnold, E.H., "Athletics for Women," *APER*, 29 (October, 1924), 452-457.

Association for Intercollegiate Athletics for Women, *Directory Charter Member Institutions 1971-1972*, Washington, D.C.: Division for Girls and Women's Sports, 1972.

Ballintine, H.I., "Out-of-Door Sports for College Women," *APER*, 3 (March, 1898), 38-43.

_____ , *The History of Physical Training At Vassar College 1865-1915*, Poughkeepsie, N.Y.: Lansing & Bros., n.d.

Barney, E.C., "The American Sportswoman," *Fortnightly Review*, LVI (1894), 263–277.

_____ , "Baseball: Babette Ruths," *Newsweek* 28 (July 29, 1946), 68–69.

Bayless, M.A., "The Minnesota Story," *Mademoiselle Gymnast*, 1 (Spring, 1966), 6-9.

Bennett, P., "The History and Objectives of the National Section for Girls and Women's Sports," Ed.D. dissertation, Mills College, Oakland, Calif., 1956.

Betts, J.R., "Organized Sport in Industrial America," Ph.D. dissertation, Columbia University, New York, N.Y., 1951.

_____ , "Mind and Body in Early American Thought," *Journal of American History*, **LIV** (March, 1968), 787-805.

Bisland, M., "Rowing as a Recreation for Women," *Outing*, **XIV** (September, 1889), 422-425.

_____ , "Bowling for Women," *Outing*, **XVI** (April, 1890), 33-36.

Boucher, B.R., Editor of *Skating*, personal letter, June 15, 1973.

Brewer, C.E., "Industrial Recreation," reprinted from *Recreation* (March, 1944), 3-8.

Brown, N., *Ice Skating. A History*, New York: A.S. Barnes, 1959.

Burdick, W., "Safeguarding the Athletic Competition of Girls and Women," *APER*, 32 (May, 1927), 367.

Burrell, F.C., "Intercollegiate Athletics for Women in Coeducational Institutions," *APER*, 22 (January, 1917), 17-19.

Bushnell, A.S., Ed., *Report of the United States Olympic Committee. 1948 Games, XIV Olympiad*, New York: United States Olympic Association, 1948.

Canfield, F.E., "Give the Girls a Chance," *Collier's Outdoor America*, **XLIV** (May 12, 1910), 20-21.

Chafe, W.H., *The American Woman. Her Changing Social, Economic and Political Roles, 1920-1970*, New York: Oxford University Press, 1972.

Cheatum, B.A., "A History of Selected Golf Tournaments for Women with Special Emphasis Upon the Growth and Development of the Ladies Professional Golf Association," Ph.D. dissertation, Texas Women's University, Denton, 1967.

Cheska, A., "Historical Development and Present Practices of Women's Athletic/ Recreation Association," manuscript compiled for delegates to WAA/WRA Study Conference, Washington, D.C., October, 1966.

Chester, D., *The Olympic Games Handbook*, New York: Charles Scribner's Sons, 1971.

Clay, C.E., "The Staten Island Cricket and Baseball Club," *Outing*, **XI** (November, 1887), 99-112.

Clifton, E., "The Training of a College Crew," *The Sportswoman*, 4 (September, 1927), 10-12.

Coubertin, P. de, "Chronique du Mois," trans. by M. Leigh, *La Revue Olympique*, (July, 1910), 109-110.

_____ , "Les Femmes aux Jeux Olympiques," trans. by M. Leigh, *La Revue Olympique*, (July, 1912), 109-111.

Cummins, L., "News and Views," *The Sportswoman*, 2 (September, 1926), 15, 25.

Cunningham, B., "The Colonel's Ladies," *Collier's*, (May 23, 1936), 28, 60-62.

Darmstadt, R.R., "Circumspice," *The Sportswoman*, various issues from 1929-1930.

Dennis, L., "Who Are All Those Women and What are They Doing on my Golf Course?," *Golf Digest,* 23 (July, 1972), 30-33, 90.

Division for Girls and Women's Sports, "Statement of Policies and Procedures for Competition in Girls and Women's Sports," *JOHPER,* 28 (September, 1957), 57-58.

——————— , "Statement of Policies for Competition in Girls and Women's Sports," *JOHPER,* 34 (September, 1963), 31-33.

——————— , "Statement on Competition for Girls and Women," *JOHPER,* 36 (September, 1965), 34-37.

——————— , "National Intercollegiate Championships for Women," *JOHPER,* 39 (February, 1968), 24-27.

Dosti, R., "The Girls of Summer," *Los Angeles Times West Magazine,* (August 13, 1972), 20-23.

Downing, M.R., "Women's Basketball: An Historical Review of Selected Organizations Which Influenced its Ascension toward Advanced Competition in the United States," Doctoral dissertation, Texas Women's University, Denton, 1973.

Dudley, G., and Kellor, F.A., *Athletic Games in the Education of Women,* New York: Holt, 1909.

Dulles, F.R., *America Learns to Play,* Gloucester, Mass.: Peter Smith, 1963.

Duncan, M.M., *Play Days for Girls and Women,* New York: A.S. Barnes, 1929.

"Editorial: Participation in Games by Women," *Sports Bulletin,* II (July, 1895), 4-23.

Edwards, D., "Life at the Athletic Clubs," *Scribner's Magazine,* 18 (July, 1895), 4-23.

Elmer, R.P., "Organized Archery in America," *The Sportswoman,* 1 (May 15, 1925), 3, 6.

Evans, V.L., "The Formative Years of Women's College Basketball in Five Selected Colleges, 1880-1917," M.A. thesis, University of Maryland, College Park, 1971.

——————— , "Women's Sport in the 1920 Era," presented at the First Annual Convention of the North American Society for Sport History, Columbus, Ohio, May 25-27, 1973.

"Extracts, Abstracts and Notice of Magazine Articles," *APER,* 30 (November, 1925), 523-528.

"Fainting of Females During Public Worship," *Journal of Health,* II (February 23, 1831), 190-194.

"1928 Fencing," *The Sportswoman,* IV (June, 1928), 239.

Fenton, W.H., "A Medical View of Cycling for Ladies," *Living Age,* CCIX (June, 1896), 806-810.

Fidler, M.A., "Women's Intramurals in Relation to Women's Extramurals: An Historical Viewpoint," presented at the 23rd National Intramural Conference, University of Illinois, Champaign, April 14, 1972a.

——————— , "Survey of the Organization and Administration of Women's Intramural Programs," unpublished study, 1972b (mimeographed).

_____ , "A Survey of the Nature and Extent of Women's Involvement in Selected National Sports Organizations," presented at a Conference on Women and Sport, Western Illinois University, Macomb, June 25-29, 1973.

Flinchum, B., Consultant for Student Services, AAHPER, mimeographed communication to all ARFCW/CWS members, September, 1971.

Földes, E., "Women at the Olympics," *Report of the Fourth Summer Session of the International Olympic Academy,* Olympia, Greece, 1964.

Ford, M.E., *Little Women Grow Bold,* Boston: Bruce Humphries, 1936.

Franks, L., "See Jane Run: Women in the 1972 Olympics," *Ms.,* 1 (January, 1973), 98-100, 104.

Friedan, B., *The Feminine Mystique,* New York: Dell, 1963.

Garmen, J.F., "A Study of Attitudes toward Softball Competition for Women," M.S. thesis, University of California, Santa Barbara, 1969.

Gerber, E.W., "The Changing Female Image: A Brief Commentary on Sport Competition for Women," *JOHPER,* 42 (October, 1971), 59-61.

_____ , "The American Woman's Sport Experience: An Analysis of Historical Trends," *Proceedings of the Second Canadian Symposium on the History of Sport and Physical Education,* Windsor, Ontario, Canada, May 1-3, 1972.

_____ , "The Controlled Development of Collegiate Sport for Women, 1923-1936," presented at First Annual Convention of the North American Society for Sport History, Columbus, Ohio, May 25-27, 1973a.

_____ , "Contemporary Issues in Historical Perspective," presented at a Conference on Woman and Sport, Western Illinois University, Macomb, June 25-29, 1973b.

Grazia, S. de, *Of Time, Work, and Leisure,* New York: Anchor Books, 1964.

Greene, M.D., "The Growth of Physical Education for Women in the United States in the Early Nineteenth Century," Ed.D. dissertation, University of California, Los Angeles, 1950.

Grimsley, W., *Golf. Its History, People and Events,* Englewood Cliffs, N.J.: Prentice-Hall, 1966.

Gulick, L.H., "Athletics Do Not Test Womanliness," *APER,* XI (September, 1906), 157-160.

Hanna, D., "Championship Skating as One of the Events of a Woman's Athletic Association," *Mind and Body,* 11 (April, 1904), 56.

Hazard, W.P., *The Lady's Equestrian Manual,* Philadelphia: by the author, 1854.

Hickok, R., *Who Was Who in American Sports,* New York: Hawthorne Books, 1971.

Hill, L.E., *Athletics and Out-door Sports for American Women,* New York: Macmillan, 1903.

Hinton, E.A., "Basketball for the Employed Girl," *Recreation,* 35 (November, 1941), 518, 525-526.

Holliman, J., "Women's and Children's Sports" in *American Sports (1785-1835)*, Durham, N.C.: Seeman Press, 1931.

Houston, R.E., "Development of Physical Education Departments" in *Modern Trends in Physical Education Facilities for College Women*, New York: A.S. Barnes, 1939.

"How a Girl Beat Leander at the Hero Game," *Literary Digest*, 90 (August 21, 1926), 52-67.

Hull, M.F., "A Critical View of the Men and Women Athletes of the Year, 1931-1956," M.S. thesis, The Ohio State University, Columbus, 1957.

*Industrial Sports Journal*, various issues from 1945-1950 (also published under the title *AIM*).

Jacobs, E.E., *A Study of the Physical Vigor of American Women*, Boston: Marshall Jones, 1920.

Jenson, J.L., "The History and Development of Volleyball for Girls and Women," M.S. thesis, The Ohio State University, Columbus, 1959.

_____ , "The Development of Standards for Women's Athletics and their Influence on Basketball Competition in the State of New York," Ph.D. dissertation, The Ohio State University, Columbus, 1972.

Jensen, O., *The Revolt of American Women*, New York: Harcourt Brace Jovanovich, 1971 (originally published: 1952).

Jernigan, S.S., "Women and the Olympics," *JOHPER*, 33 (April, 1962), 25-26.

_____ , "The Challenge—Womanhood in Sport," *Report of the Sixth Summer Session of the International Olympic Academy*, Olympia, Greece, 1966.

Jokl, E., "Olympic Competitions for Women" in *Medical Sociology and Cultural Anthropology of Sport and Physical Education*, Springfield, Ill.: Charles C Thomas, 1964.

Kellor, F.A., "Ethical Value of Sports for Women," *APER*, XI (September, 1906), 160-171.

Kidwell, C.B., *Women's Bathing and Swimming Costume in the United States*, United States National Museum Bulletin 250, Washington, D.C.: Smithsonian Institution Press, 1968.

Korsgaard, R., "A History of the Amateur Athletic Union of the United States," Ed.D. dissertation, Teachers College, Columbia University, New York, N.Y., 1952.

Krout, J.A., *Annals of American Sport*, New York: United States Publishers Association, 1929.

Lagemann, J.K., "Red Heads You Kill Me," *Colliers*, (February 8, 1947), 64-66.

Lawrence, H.B., Ed., "Basketball Standards for Girls and Women," *Official Basketball Guide for September 1956-1957*, Washington, D.C.: National Section for Girls and Women's Sports.

Leavitt, N.M., and Duncan, M.M., "The Status of Intramural Programs for Women," *Research Quarterly*, VIII (March, 1937), 68-69.

Lee, M., "The Case For and Against Intercollegiate Athletics for Women and the Situation as it Stands To-Day," *APER*, 29 (January, 1924), 13-19.

_____ , "The Case For and Against Intercollegiate Athletics for Women and the Situation Since 1923," *Research Quarterly*, 2 (May, 1931), 93-127.

_____ , "A Consideration of the Fundamental Differences between Boys and Girls as They Affect the Girls' Program of Physical Education," *Education*, 53 (April, 1933), 467-471.

Leigh, M., "The Evolution of Women's Participation in the Summer Olympic Games, 1900-1948," Ph.D. dissertation, The Ohio State University, Columbus, 1974.

Lerner, G., *The Woman in American History*, Reading, Mass.: Addison-Wesley, 1971.

Lewis, D., Stanton, E.C., Chadwick, J.R., "The Health of American Women," *North American Review*, CCCXIII (December, 1882), 503-524.

Leyhe, N.L., "Attitudes of Women Members of the American Association for Health, Physical Education, and Recreation toward Competition in Sports for Girls and Women," D.P.E. dissertation, Indiana University, Bloomington, 1955.

Manchester, H., *Four Centuries of Sport in America 1490-1890*, New York: Benjamin Blom, 1931.

March, R., "A Study of the International Recreation Department United Automobile Workers CIO and a Comparative Study of the Recreation Program in Fifteen Local Unions," Master's thesis, Wayne State University, Detroit, Mich., 1949.

Maumee, "Modern Archery in America," *Outing and The Wheelman*, IV (April, 1884), 34-35.

Menke, F.G., *The Encyclopedia of Sports*, 4th Rev. Ed., New York: A.S. Barnes, 1969.

Metheney, E., "Symbolic Forms of Movement: The Feminine Image in Sports," *Connotations of Movement in Sport and Dance*, Dubuque, Iowa: Wm. C. Brown, 1965.

Mosher, C.D., "The Means to the End," *APER*, 30 (December, 1925), 535-540.

Murray, M.C., "A Study of Documented Changes in Women's Gymnastics from 1940 through 1965," Master's thesis, Springfield College, Springfield, Mass., 1967.

National Recreation Association, New York, *The Leisure Hours of 5,000 People: A Report of a Study of Leisure Time Activities and Desires*, 1934.

*The New York Times*, various editions from 1914-1972.

"New Look in Softball," *ISJ*, 8 (February, 1949), 18, 28.

Nicolusi, G.F., "The Development of Competitive Track and Field for Women in the United States," M.A. thesis, Ball State University, Muncie, Indiana, 1966.

Ondek, D., "The Incredible Brakettes," *ASA Softball*, (December, 1971), 9-14, 17.

O'Neill, W.L., *Everyone Was Brave, A History of Feminism in America*, Chicago: Quadrangle Books, 1971.

Oppenheim, F., *The History of Swimming*, No. Hollywood, Calif.: Swimming World, 1970.

Oppenheimer, V.K., "Demographic Influence on Female Employment and the Status of Women," *Changing Women in a Changing Society*, ed. by J. Huber, Chicago: University of Chicago Press, 1973.

Perrin, E., "Athletics for Women and Girls," *Playground*, 17 (March, 1924), 658-661.

_____ , "More Competitive Athletics for Girls—But of the Right Kind," *APER*, 34 (October, 1929), 473-474.

Peterson, P.M., "History of Olympic Skiing for Women in the United States: A Cultural Interpretation," Ph.D. dissertation, University of Southern California, Los Angeles, 1967.

Philbeck, E., "The Development of Women's Golf in the United States," Master's thesis, University of North Carolina, Chapel Hill, 1950.

Porter, D.E., Executive Director, American Softball Association, personal letter, June 13, 1973.

Price, M.A., "The Role of the United States Women's Participation in the Modern Olympic Games," Ed.D. dissertation, Teachers College, Columbia University, New York, N.Y., 1953.

*Proceedings of the Fifth National Institute on Girls' Sports*, "Sponsoring Organizations," University of Illinois, Champaign, January 21-25, 1969.

Remley, M.L., "Twentieth Century Concepts of Sports Competition for Women," Ph.D. dissertation, University of Southern California, Los Angeles, 1970.

Rich, W.L., "Playing With Steel," *Woman Citizen*, LIV (Old Style), X (New Style), (February, 1926), 19, 34.

Richardson, S.F., "Tendencies in Athletics for Women in Colleges and Universities," *Popular Science Monthly*, L (February, 1897), 517-526.

Richey, B., "It's Never Too Late," *Official Field Hockey-Lacrosse Guide 1944-1945*, ed. by B.H. Rudd and G.E. Felker, New York: A.S. Barnes, 1944.

_____ , "The USWLA Expansion Program," *Official Field Hockey-Lacrosse Guide 1948-1950*, ed. by A.L. Delano and B. Richey, New York: A.S. Barnes, 1948.

Rickaby, R.D., "Circumspice!," *The Sportswoman*, various issues from 1924-1929.

Riherd, F., "A Study of Sports Opportunities for Girls and Women in the United States as Offered by National Organizations," M.A. thesis, The Ohio State University, Columbus, 1953.

Rogers, A., *Women Are Here to Stay*, New York: Harper & Brothers, 1949.

Rogers, F.R., "Olympics for Girls?" *School and Society* XXX (August, 1929), 190-194.

Sargent, D.A., "Interest in Sport and Physical Education as a Phase of Woman's Development," *Mind and Body*, 22 (November, 1915), 830-833.

Schneir, M., Ed., "Declaration of Sentiments and Resolutions, Seneca Falls," *Feminism: The Essential Historical Writings*, New York: Vintage Books, 1972.

Schoedler, L., "Report of Progress, Women's Division, National Amateur Athletic Federation of America," *APER*, 29 (June, 1924), 305-310.

Scott, A.F\, *The American Woman: Who Was She?*, Englewood Cliffs, N.J.: Prentice-Hall, 1971.

Scott, M.G., "Competition for Women in American Colleges and Universities," *Research Quarterly*, 16 (March, 1945), 49-71.

Scott, P., and Crafts, V., "The History of Track and Field for Girls and Women" in *Track and Field for Girls and Women*, New York: Appleton-Century-Crofts, 1964.

Scott, P., and Ulrich, C., "Commission on Intercollegiate Sports for Women," *JOHPER*, 37 (October, 1966), 10, 76.

Sefton, A.A., *The Women's Division National Amateur Athletic Federation*, Palo Alto, Calif.: Stanford University Press, 1941.

Sheahan, M.M., "The Story of Lacrosse," *Official Field Hockey-Lacrosse Guide 1944-1945*, ed. by B.H. Rudd and G.E. Felker, New York: A.S. Barnes, 1944.

Shillingford, J.P., "The United States Field Hockey Association 1922-1972 Golden Anniversary," *Field Hockey-Lacrosse Guide June 1972-June 1974*, ed. by M.L. Thornburg and J. Pitts, Washington, D.C.: Division for Girls and Women's Sports, 1972a.

_____ , "History of the United States Field Hockey Association 1922-1972," by the Association, 1972b.

Sibley, K., "First Report of the Sub-Committee on Track and Field Athletics, April 15, 1924," *APER*, 29 (October, 1924), 461-462.

Slocum, H.W., "Lawn Tennis as a Game for Women," *Outing*, XIV (July, 1889), 289-300.

Smith, M.C., "Women as Cyclers," *Outing*, VI (June, 1885), 317-321.

Smith, P., *Daughters of the Promised Land*, Boston: Little Brown, 1970.

Smith, R.A., "The Rise of Basketball for Women in Colleges," *Canadian Journal of History of Sport and Physical Education*, 1 (December, 1970), 18-36.

Somers, D.A., *The Rise of Sports in New Orleans*, Baton Rouge, La.: Louisiana State University Press, 1972.

*Spalding's Official Athletic Almanac for 1905*, Special Olympic Number, New York: American Sports, 1905.

Spears, B., "The Emergence of Sport in Physical Education," presented at the American Association for Health, Physical Education, and Recreation 88th Anniversary National Convention, Minneapolis, Minnesota, April 16, 1973.

Stanton, E., "Excerpts from her Autobiography," *Growing Up Female in America: Ten Lives*, ed. by E. Merriam, New York: Dell, 1971.

Starey, A.B., "Lawn Tennis in America," *Wheelman*, II (September, 1883), 463-468.

Stephenson, L., and R., *A History and Annotated Bibliography of Skating Costume*, Meriden, Conn.: Bayberry Hills Press, 1970.

Stroeker, M.L., "The Origin and Development of Synchronized Swimming in the United States," Master's thesis, University of Wisconsin, Madison, 1956.

"Super Bowler Patty Costello," *The Sportswoman,* 1 (September–October, 1973), 14-15.

Swift, M.J., Report of the National Athletic Conference of American College Women," *APER,* XXVI (June, 1921), 305-306.

Taylor, F.J., "Fast and Pretty," *Colliers,* 102 (August 20, 1938), 22-23, 28.

Thaxton, N.A., "A Documentary Analysis of Competitive Track and Field for Women at Tuskegee Institute and Tennessee State University," D.P.E. dissertation, Springfield College, Springfield, Mass., 1970.

Thorpe, J., Speech to the National Collegiate Athletic Association, January, 1972 (mimeographed).

Tunis, J.R., "Women and the Sport Business," *Harper's Monthly Magazine,* CLIX (July, 1929), 211-221.

Underhill, "Golf—The Women," *The Book of Sport,* ed. by W. Patten, New York: J.F. Taylor, 1901.

U.S. Department of Labor, Bureau of Labor Statistics, *Employers' Welfare Work,* Whole Number 123, Washington, D.C.: Government Printing Press, 1913.

——————— , *Welfare Work for Employees in Industrial Establishments in the United States,* Bulletin No. 250, Washington, D.C.: U.S. Government Printing Office, 1919.

——————— , *Health and Recreation Activities in Industrial Establishments, 1926,* Bulletin No. 458, Washington, D.C.: U.S. Government Printing Office, 1928.

——————— , Women's Bureau, *The Myth and the Reality,* Washington, D.C.: U.S. Government Printing Office, 1971.

United States Golf Association, Far Hills, N.J., *Competitors of the United States Golf Association,* Information for News Media, 1973.

United States Lawn Tennis Association, *Official Encyclopedia of Tennis,* New York: Harper & Row, 1972.

*United States Olympic Committee Newsletter,* "I.O.C. Actions," 7 (January, 1973), 10.

——————— , "Lord Killanin, IOC President, Speaks Out Freely. . . ,"7 (January, 1973), 10-11.

Voigt, D.Q., *American Baseball,* Norman, Okla.: University of Oklahoma Press, 1966.

von Borries, E., *The History and Functions of the National Section on Women's Athletics,* Washington, D.C.: National Section on Women's Athletics, 1941.

Waterman, E.F., "A Message from the Women's Division," *JOHPER,* 12 (January, 1941), 36-37.

Watts, D.P., "Changing Conceptions of Competitive Sports for Girls and Women in the United States from 1880 to 1960," Ph.D. dissertation, University of California, Los Angeles, 1960.

Wayman, A.R., "Competition," *APER*, 34 (October, 1929), 469-471.

Webster, F.A.M., *Athletics of To-Day for Women. History, Development and Training*, London and New York: Frederick Warne, 1930.

"The Well-Dressed Hockey Player," *The Sportswoman*, V (June, 1929), 1-2.

Weyand, A.M., "Queens of the Court," in *The Cavalcade of Basketball*, New York: Macmillan, 1960.

——————— , and Roberts, M.R., *The Lacrosse Story*, Baltimore, Md.: H.&A. Herman, 1965.

White, C., "Extramural Competition and Physical Education Activities for College Women," *Research Quarterly*, 25 (October, 1954), 344-363.

Wind, H.W., *The Story of American Golf*, New York: Simon and Schuster, 1956.

Wolfe, A.D., "American Skiers at the Olympics—The Women. Red Stockings in the Alps," *American Ski Annual*, ed. by the U.S. Eastern Amateur Ski Association, Brattleboro, Vt.: Stephen Daye Press, 1936.

——————— , "Ten Years of Ski Racing for Women," *Skiing. The International Sport*, ed. by R. Palmedo, New York: Derrydale Press, 1937.

Woman's International Bowling Congress, *WIBC History*, by the Association, 1967.

"Women Have a Large Share in Winter Sports Events. . .," *The Sportswoman*, VII (December, 1930), 11, 13-14.

"Women's Sports: A Symposium," *Review of Reviews*, XXII (August, 1900), 231-232.

Woodham-Smith, C., *Queen Victoria*, New York: Alfred A. Knopf, 1972.

Part 2

# THE SOCIAL VIEW

Jan Felshin

# Chapter 5

# The Dialectic of Woman and Sport

A social perspective of woman in sport presumes that neither "woman" nor "sport" can be understood fully or in juxtaposition except with reference to the society that uses the concepts. Social conceptions imply a host of meanings derived from both societal heritage and contemporary function. They express culture and serve to influence experience by providing a standard for evaluating social processes and behavior in the sense that such conceptions involve "desirable," as well as actual, dimensions of social life. As social definitions, both "woman" and "sport" represent more than the identifiable, observable entities of biological organism or rules-bounded contest. Social constructs serve to summarize and explain the pervasive connotations of common agreement, and include the normative data of collective experience.

Many contemporary approaches to study rest on cognizance of the existence of sport as a social phenomenon and situation. Clearly, sport functions as an institution of some magnitude in American society. Any consideration of sport must include an analysis of its role as a social institution. Similarly, "woman" as a construct refers to a social role that represents a host of attitudes as well as biological referents. Insofar as social conceptions imply prescriptions for behavior, an analysis of the socialized understanding of the role of woman is basic to any consideration of woman.

The social view of woman *in* sport is a dialectic of woman *and* sport. Both sport and woman must be understood in relation to society, and the clarification of each concept contributes to understanding the relationship between them. In the largest sense, however, it is an analysis of the dynamics of the woman-sport-society relationship that permits full comprehension of the social view.

179

## SPORT AS A SOCIAL PHENOMENON

Because sport exists at once as symbolic and actual experience, its
abstract connotations necessarily attend to participation in any singular contest or involvement in any particular athletic pursuit. As a social
phenomenon, sport represents its own importance in society and
encompasses both the associated values that are used to account for its
role and the structure of human interactions that comprises its substance and defines its goals. Like most human activities, sport expresses
the context of culture in its existence and modifies the culture by its
existence. The symbolic content of sport is institutionalized as its
conduct and structures are formalized. The institution functions in
society, but it depends upon an abstraction of sport that provides a
crystallized view of social relations and behavior. This means that sport
is always a recognizable version of its own characteristic essence or
symbolic content. Institutions are particularly vulnerable to social
influence, however, and sport is also recognizable as an aspect of the
life of society.

 Although Kenyon has suggested that for the sociologist the single
reference "sport" is sufficient (1972, p. 33), others have chosen to
consider sport from various perspectives. Loy has discussed sport as
". . . a *game occurrence,* as an *institutionalized game,* as a *social institution,* and as a *social situation* or social system" (1969, p. 56). Keating
differentiated between play and athletics (1972), and has described
sport in essence as "a kind of diversion" with ends of "fun, pleasure,
and delight" and athletics as an agonistic activity whose end is victory
and which is characterized by "a spirit of dedication, sacrifice, and
intensity" (1964, p. 265). Perhaps it is sufficient to suggest as Schmitz
did that sport emphasizes good performance and contains the element
of contest, and that although based on play, sport can be carried out
with a lack of the spirit of play (1972, p. 30). In other words, the abstraction of sport, when dealt with as a social phenomenon, refers to
what Ingham and Loy have called "an institutionalized form of social
behavior" (1973, p. 3). Within the framework of the dialectic of
woman and sport, the focus is the institutionalization of contexts,
roles, expectations, and attitudes in sport as these affect the perception
and participation of women.

## Sport and Society

It is a truism that sport and society are related. Kenyon, for instance, said that sport was "in concert" with society in some ways, and concluded "It must be since it *is* society" (1972, p. 41). He also suggested, however, that sport is "at odds" with society, and accounted for the dichotomy by postulating a sport "reality" responsive to society and a sport "ideology" reflective of a different era (1972, p. 41). The point is that the relationship of sport to society is a multifaceted one. Full understanding of the ways that sport functions in social experience and societal life can be gained only by a careful analysis of that relationship.

**Sport is a symbolic formulation of ideal values.** As such, particular sports serve as symbols of social interaction, organization, values, and goals, and sport itself represents an attractive domain. Societies, like individuals, seem driven to enhance their own images, and a certain amount of flattering mythology surrounds all social institutions. The domain of sport, however, is idealized consistently and occasionally absurdly, and there appears to be a widespread social conspiracy to maintain belief in sport as an expression of the finest human values. Most of these values are directly related to the characteristics of sport as a contest and as a challenge to exhibit excellence of physical prowess and skill; they are viewed as part of what Schmitz has called the "distinctive order" of sport and its prerequisite "suspension of the ordinary" (1972). Ashworth suggested that sport is a "symbolic dialogue" that includes requirements as to *"how* a dialogue should be conducted." He said that modern man insists on equality in sport because he *"defines* himself as equal" and must ensure that "natural" differences not be confused "with the accidentality of social life" (1971, p. 45). In his novel *End Zone,* Don DeLillo's hero said, "The exemplary spectator is the person who understands that sport is a benign illusion, the illusion that order is possible . . . that tends always to move toward perfection" (1973, p. 89). Harry Edwards commented that "Sport thus is strongly marked by nonutilitarian loyalties and commitments . . . In sum, sport is essentially a secular, quasi-religious institution" (1973, p. 90).

Eleanor Metheny offered an heroic description of the Olympic Games and said that their sports "may well symbolize man's conception of himself as a consequential force within the grand design of the universe, as well as each man's conception of his own ability to perform those functions that identify him as a man among men" (1965, p. 42). With reference to the fact that women were excluded from the "sacred precincts of Olympia," Metheny commented: "At the time of the early Olympic Festivals, which date back beyond the first recorded games of 776 B.C., the images of masculinity and femininity within the emerging culture of ancient Greece were clearly delineated" (1965, p. 45). Given, then, that sport has come to represent ideal values and to symbolize the whole dramatic process of human actualization, it is clear that in contemporary society sport is identified as heroic activity and is conceived as masculine activity.

The bounded order of sport wherein excellence of performing and contesting are emphasized in relation to values of "the good strife" and enthusiastic voluntarism would seem to connote *human* qualities as its "conception of the desirable." Sport as an abstraction, however, still contains masculine assumptions. In its social definition it is obvious that sport in the United States serves as a masculine rite of passage. It could not be a vehicle for socialization into manhood except that the idealized values invested in sport symbolically and socially have important masculine connotations. This may be so because men played more important roles in establishing both society and sport, or because men are simply more important in a social view; in any case, the assumption of sport as masculine is a basic aspect of it as a symbolic formulation of ideal values.

**Sport is institutionalized in American society.** Its importance and centrality in individual and social life is indisputable. Furthermore, the significant functions of sport remain largely unaccounted for despite the serious efforts of scholars and theologians. Huizinga simply accepted the importance of the play element in culture and said that, "In culture, we find play as a given magnitude existing before culture itself existed, accompanying it and pervading it from the earliest beginnings right up to the phase of civilization we are now living in" (1950, p. 4). The relationship of play and sport seems always obscure, but it may be helpful to consider the explanation suggested by Ferdun:

> Play, then, functions in such a way as to enhance and extend the various capacities and abilities of man in relation to his ever-increasing cultural interdependence. The modes of play are both experiential and experimental, and these are correlatives, or

complementary and reciprocal aspects, to the basic human processes that have been described as perceptual and effectual . . .
    There are, however, institutionalized forms of play and
creativity that provide for the continuous actualization of these
phenomena and their resultant positive functions for both the
individual and the culture. Both sport and art are such forms . . .
(1972, p. 80).

It is also interesting to note that Huizinga recognized that play seemed
to include an aspect of display. He suggested that it could function "as
a contest *for* something or a representation *of* something," and went on
to comment that "These two functions can unite in such a way that the
game 'represents' a contest, or else becomes a contest for the best representation of something" (1950, p. 13).
    The notion of the institutionalization of human activity has to do
with culture as a contextual design. As has been pointed out by many
theorists, culture can be viewed as the means to human actualization
insofar as it provides a structure, or it can be seen as a restrictive force
in relation to a social order. This writer has commented that in either
view, "it is the notion of pre designed structure which is compelling,"
and has stated further that although human motivations are surely
sources of meaning, "only the culturally shaped modes of expressing,
fulfilling, or gratifying them . . . may be explored or understood"
(1969, p. 43).
    As an institutionalized form, sport is a structured reality; that is,
behavior is both prescribed and evaluated according to agreed-upon
values. This implies that the abstraction of sport and institutionalized
values or proscriptions do not apply to every manifestation of sport,
but do obtain generally and serve as socialized goals and effects. Structure is both the basis of institutionalization and the process by which
the institution is maintained. This means that the way sport is conducted, in the larger sense of its regulation and the specific aspect of
its rules, represents its function as social vision and reality. It must be
remembered, however, that the idea of sport as a symbolic formulation
of ideal values may coexist with actual sport as a reflection of socially
operant values. It is vision, in the sense of significant needs and values,
that provides the impetus for the creation of social institutions, but the
emergent creation is always an expression of what the society is. Social
institutions are also particularly amenable to mutual influence, and

sport functions in society as part of the fabric of politics, business, education, and spectacle.

Sport as social reflection is well-documented. Cozens and Stumpf said that "Sports and games provide a touchstone for understanding how people live, work, think and may also serve as a barometer of a nation's progress in civilization" (1953, p. 2). Boyle entitled his work, *Sport—Mirror of American Life* (1963), and Miller and Russell said, "In America, sport seems to symbolize the American way almost as much as a hamburger or the Statue of Liberty" (1971, p. vii). The implication of this view is that sport may serve at once as an expression and an example of a social ethic. It helps explain the perspective of sport *as* life or as preparation for social participation. Within this view, sport in both social experience and societal life reveals and reinforces a desirable system of values and behavior. The system is institutionalized to the extent that values and behavior are socially understood, accepted, and manifest in all of the rules, rituals, and reactions to sport as both ethos and reality.

Sport is a social documentary of aggression toward both excellence and achievement. Sport institutionalizes a behavioral mode that is understood to conform to an image of masculinity no less strong in contemporary America than in ancient Greece. Sport represents: the American tendency toward association, characteristically reserved for men; the opportunities to aggress and prove self, believed to be inherent male instincts; and the demand for perseverance and comparison, elements of male assertiveness. In addition, sport provides a public arena in which to compete openly or to pay tribute to those who do. Frederickson said of stadiums:

> They are monuments to the pride of individuals, institutions, and nations in the skill and prowess of their youth. They are an affirmation of a philosophy of life that insists man's life is better and fuller for having such moments of excitement and splendor, and that fitting homage should be paid the heroes who bring such color and emotion into the life of the average citizen (1960, p. 642).

Surely, it is understood that "youth" refers to young man, and that "man" is used specifically rather than generically. The institutionalized nature of sport defines the goals and modes of socialization within sport.

## Socialization

Sport itself can be said to be socialized when the values and modes institutionalized within it conform to those evidenced or emphasized in the larger society. Sport is a socializing agent when its own structures demand conformity to certain normative values and behaviors. One can, therefore, become socialized into the culture of sport or one can become socialized within a culture in general through sport.

Socialization refers to the internalizing of values, and it presumes the existence of norms that define values, of collectivities that function in relation to values, and of roles that establish individual behavior in the social system to implement the values. Ingham and Loy presented one view of socialization into the social institution of sport according to "the frames, forms, and fronts of sport" when they said:

> Through socialization, sport as an entity imposes itself upon the individual, since in its transmission it assumes ontological status. The reality of sport appears immutable. Individuals learn and internalize the frame of values legitimating sport; they learn and internalize the constitutive rules which guide interaction and which give sport its form; and, they identify with idealized stereotypes exemplifying the necessary behavioral and attitudinal requirements for preferred role performance (1973, p. 6).

Although these authors rejected the deterministic view in which the individual is at the mercy of socialization as the only alternative, it does seem the most viable empirical conception.

Obviously, socialization is never a completely smooth and integrated process. As Talcott Parsons has pointed out, "Since social systems, cultural systems, and personality systems are independently variable, there will never be complete correspondence between them; some degree of discrepancy is inevitable." Parsons applied the concept of "structured strain" to those situations in which the discrepancies appear to be built into the social system (1967, p. 156). Malintegration can occur with reference to any aspect of the socialization process. Parsons, however, suggested that ideology always has a cultural reference and that values are related to social structure through institutionalization; therefore, deviance and strain are likely to "focus on the relation between empirical conceptions of the society and its subsystems, and societal values and their subspecifications" (1967, p. 156). Harry Edwards, in *Sociology of Sport,* devotes a great deal of attention to the concept of strain in terms of what he calls "the dominant American sports creed, the humanitarian counter-creed, and the equalitarian counter-creed." Although Edwards suggested that all these creeds can "co rectly claim legitimacy in the American cultural heritage," he concluded:

The overriding value orientation salient throughout the institution of sport and the dominant sports creed is that of the 'individual achievement through competition.' This orientation gives sport in America a demeanor of practicality and gives cohesion to the specific values, activities, and role relationships of the institution.*

**Sport as a social system is at once a socializing agent and a vehicle for reinforcing the socialization goals of society.** As Edwards pointed out:

> Sports are seen as primary vehicles for enculturating the youth who will 'be the future custodians of the republic,' in the words of the late General MacArthur. In America, roles involving the establishment and maintenance of security, leadership, control, and other instrumental functions are typically reserved for males. Therefore, given the claimed relation between sport and the greater society, it is to be expected that the focus will be upon males, with females being more or less ignored and excluded from the claimed benefits of sport.†

This is an important assumption in the consideration of sport and socialization. Neither the norms, collectivities, nor roles within the "dominant sports creed" in American society have much, if any, reference to woman. The resultant dynamics of that is treated in the final section of this chapter, but the discussion here is in the perspective of a masculine socialization model.

Within sport, socialization refers to both ideology and reality. Because sport is a symbolic formulation of ideal values and a functioning social institution, the characteristics and values attributed to it are occasionally dichotomous. This is not the same thing as Kenyon's explanation of the sport ideology as emanating from a different era (1972, p. 41), but it does concur with the conclusion that there is a difference between "sport ideology" and "sport reality."

As far as socialization is concerned, sport ideology, which may even be mythology, is a powerful agent that serves as a rationale for the norms and collectivities of sport and attracts the commitment of individuals to the roles of sport. The socialization theme related to sport ideology is an heroic model of superlative effort and sacrifice that assumes the ecstasy of victory and the agony of defeat. The regulatory bodies of sport exploit idealized versions of play sources whenever

---

*From Harry Edwards, *Sociology of Sport*, Homewood, Ill.: The Dorsey Press, p. 334. Copyright © 1973 by The Dorsey Press and reprinted by permission.

† *Ibid.*, p. 100. Copyright © 1973 by The Dorsey Press and reprinted by permission.

it is expedient to do so within the social system of sport. Thus, players are "amateur" or "professional"; "eligible" or "ineligible"; "sanctioned," "suspended," and otherwise controlled in ways that would not be tenable without the belief in sport as a mythic mode. In no other social system is it quite so crucial to succeed; for in sport, success and manhood are equated, and the athlete, even in contemporary society, can accept his own obedience and compliance to authority in his heroic quest. The socialization goals in sport are twofold: (1) individuals must internalize appropriate mores and beliefs, and this process also has implications for personality development, and (2) individuals must identify with the collectivities, represented by the various contexts within which sport functions. This latter goal implies a social integration of individuals as a result of the identification process. As it says on many locker room walls, "There is no 'I' in TEAM."

Because society invests sport with ideal values, even social experience acts as a socializing agent for sport. Perhaps, in the 1970s, sport is not entirely treated as being "sacred" or heroic, but, on the other hand, its detractors are not really given much credence either. In *The New York Times Book Review* (of paperbacks) section of Sunday, February 11, 1973, Jonathan Yardley said:

> Sport and sport figures do for the American male what the glamorous figures of show business do for his sister. In front of his TV set he can carry on his love affair with a fantasy world evenings and weekends; when the little screen offers no game, he can curl up with a paperback that makes him feel close to his heroes (*The New York Times,* p. 4).

Commenting that nearly two million copies of books about Brian Piccolo, the professional football player who died young, had been sold the previous year, Yardley added that, "for all our voyeuristic interest in the seamier sides of sport, some of the old 1950s sentimentality and hero-worship linger on." Both the conventional and media image of sport is largely an idyllic one that expresses almost complete faith in positive and beneficial outcomes of sport participation.

Society also affirms pervasive values *about* sport, and there is widespread belief that sport contributes to potential economic gain, upward social mobility, status, and generalized interpersonal attraction. Bernie Parrish, one of football's angry critics, suggested that a young athlete had to possess extraordinary "desire" and that this made him vulnerable to exploitation. "Naive and vain, the player has been tricked . . ." he said (1972, p. x). Yet, he concluded his own desperate indictment of professional football with the statement:

> Public awareness of the sport is acute. Warlike, unusual, exciting, elaborate, and important—such are the characteristics that become bigger than life on the day of the game. The aura is intoxicating; for players, it is absolutely stupefying. They will endure practically anything to be part of the team, part of what they call the game of pro football (1972, pp. 278-279).

There is confusion, then, about socialization and sport. Competition and achievement are obvious sport characteristics. In the ideology of sport, they suggest, as Metheny stated:

> . . . every man who would submit his own excellence to the test of sport competition must 'stand naked before his gods' and reveal himself as he is in the fullness of his own human powers. Stripped of all self-justifying excuses by the rules of sport, he must demonstrate his own ability to perform one human action of his own choosing; and naked of all pretense, he must use himself as he is, in all the wholeness of his being as a man (1970, p. 66).

On the other hand, the reality of sport, and especially football, implies a terrible kind of socialization model described by Bianchi as follows:

> Through these autumnal rites of passage, we avidly introduce our young to the saving knowledge of adult life: brutality, aggressive competition, profit-greed, male chauvinism, and the discipline of dull conformity to the status quo (1972, p. 31).

Sport is a structured and ordered domain; the roles within it are clear and do reflect all of the qualities of any social system. Most Americans are enculturated early to accept the values of sport unquestioningly; therefore, socialization into and through sport is a crucial social process that probably affects most men, at least. Sport norms are so ingrained in this society that the language of sport most clearly expresses American values. Presidents refer to "game plans" and citizens to "rundowns" between bases rather than to "Scylla and Charybdis." Sport ideology may refer to fantasy and illusion, but, if so, it provides a significant vision of human goals. In part, the "wonderful world of sport" is an elaborate symbolic society sometimes confused with America. Athletes, coaches, spectators, fans, sponsors, and citizens are socialized to the extent that they recognize the domain.

## THE SOCIAL CONSTRUCT OF WOMAN

In *Changing Women in a Changing Society*, Joan Huber concluded the editor's introduction with the statement, "The ideology of equal opportunity is ill served when half our citizens are either kept on the sidelines or are allowed to play only part of the time" (1973, p. 4). That a sociologist chose a sport metaphor to symbolize the social situation of women is understandable. The social construct of woman has restricted the opportunities, aspirations, expectations, and social behavior sanctioned for women, and this has been seriously applied in the masculinized social conception of sport.

As long as men and women are socialized successfully to accept the stereotypic norms for their sexual identity, they can be expected to accept and exhibit appropriate role behavior in fulfilling them. Certainly, this has never been true for all the members of a society, but it has been more or less true in various periods, and role definitions have been more or less rigid. Contemporary social strain arises in relation to an ideology of equality. For whatever reasons, the United States and much of the rest of the world has been in the throes of an "equality revolution" in recent decades. The prevailing social construct of woman (like that of other racial and age or status groups) becomes dissonant or discrepant in relation to changing social values based on the importance of equality. Objection to the minority and oppressed status of women emerges as a social theme. In the midst of social change it is difficult to assess the relative weight of themes and counterthemes.

Consideration of the social construct of woman must take traditional and emerging views into account. The prevailing construct of woman is based on "femininity" with roles for women perceived in accord with the norms and values ascribed to being or becoming feminine. The alternative construct emerges from "feminism" with roles for women conceived in relation to the attitudes and values of the feminist position.

Because the concern here is with the dialectic of woman and sport, the discussion of these constructs is based on those aspects that are central to sport. This does not, however, yield a simple model because each view of woman depends upon a host of interrelated assumptions about what women are, can be, or should be. Social constructs presuppose a theory of identity based on a social self-fulfilling prophecy. This means that there is a tremendous effort by adherents to both views of woman to promote their view in every conceivable public way. Feminist literature abounds and is no longer limited to identification with the Women's Liberation Movement. At the same time, traditional views are consistently manifest in the media and other forms of social dialogue.

## The Feminine Construct

In the *American Heritage Dictionary of the English Language,* three-quarters of an inch of type is used to define "woman" while it takes three and a half inches of type to define "man." Women, generally, are defined in relation to men; usually, the male qualities are presumed to be the normative ones and females adjudged to be more or less in relation to them. The concept of masculinity-femininity suggests the existence of a continuum of traits, with the most desirable men being those who are most masculine and the most desirable women those who are most feminine. Weisstein, in her brilliant indictment of psychology, identified the failure of psychology as due to the fact that it "looked for inner traits when it should have been looking for social context," and added, "the theoreticians of personality have generally been clinicians and psychiatrists, and they have never considered it necessary to have evidence in support of their theories" (1970, p. 2).

Florence Howe, in a discussion of the studies done by Broverman and others at Worcester State Hospital in Massachusetts, pointed out that clinical psychologists equated the clinically healthy male and the clinically healthy adult. These male and female psychologists viewed the clinically healthy female as quite divergent (1971, p. 80). The "male valued items" used in these investigations were such things as: very aggressive, very independent, not at all emotional, very logical, very direct, very adventurous, very self-confident, very ambitious; the "female valued items" included: very talkative, very tactful, very gentle, very aware of feelings of others, very religious, very quiet, very strong need for security. In a study of college students using the same instruments, the findings led the investigators to conclude that:

> Despite historical changes in the legal status of women and despite the changes in permissible behaviors accorded men and women, the sex-role stereotypes continue to be clearly defined and held in agreement by both college men and college women (Broverman, et al., 1968, p. 293).

The socialization process depends upon individuals internalizing the norms and roles that society expresses and requires. Women come to see themselves as they are assumed to be in society, and then they fulfill the prophetic roles suggested by the image. McClelland found that "the female image is characterized as small, weak, soft and light. In the United States it is also dull, peaceful, relaxed, cold, rounded, passive and slow" (1965, p. 173). Many studies have documented that the qualities women and girls attribute to themselves are those generally considered "feminine" and are those that are also considered less valuable than so-called "masculine" qualities. Philip Goldberg concluded that women considered their own sex to be so inferior that they became generally prejudiced against other women. His classic study of college women used articles with arbitrary assignment of author by sex; the same set of articles in one booklet, for instance, bore a male name as author, and in another, a female name. Thus each booklet contained three articles by "men" and three by "women"; the same article might appear in one booklet as authored by "John T. McKay" and in the other as by "Joan T. McKay." Women were found to judge women inferior not only in masculine fields, but in feminine ones as well, and the articles presumably authored by men were found to be judged superior on every criterion (1968, p. 28).

Obviously, if intellectual competence is considered "masculine," a problem develops for the individual with reference to socialized goals of being "feminine." Maccoby posited that women develop a great deal of anxiety about social pressures and role-expectations; she said:

> It would appear that even when a woman is suitably endowed intellectually and develops the right temperament and habits of thought to make use of her endowment, she must be fleet of foot indeed to scale the hurdles society has erected for her and to remain a whole and happy person while continuing to follow her intellectual bent (1963, p. 37).

Matina Horner summarized this view with reference to the socially pervasive values of femininity when she suggested:

> Thus consciously or unconsciously the girl equates intellectual achievement with loss of femininity. A bright woman is caught in a double bind. In testing and other achievement-oriented situations she worries not only about failure, but also about success. If she fails, she is not living up to her own standards of performance; if

she succeeds she is not living up to societal expectations (1969, pp. 36-38).

Societal expectations require women to express the feminine virtues which are the polar opposites of masculine activity, aggression, and achievement. Since, as Janeway suggested, "weakness and power are opposite sides of the same coin in more situations than the myths which sustain and explain woman's place in the world," the effect is the subordination of women. She concludes that "To the extent that an individual agrees that he is subordinate and barred from the highest ambitions of the society in which he lives, he will project this attitude into the roles he plays and build it into the internal structure of his own psychology" (1971, pp. 107-108).

Sex differences, roles, and stereotyping are pernicious elements of the socialization process. Appropriately different concepts of masculinity and femininity are justified in diverse ways and the Bible, ethology, anatomy, genetics, psychology, and even society are invoked as supportive sources. Galbraith offered an economic explanation in relation to what he called the "Convenient Social Virtue," which ascribes merit "to any pattern of behavior, however uncomfortable or unnatural for the individual involved, that serves the comfort or well-being of the more powerful members of the community." Galbraith suggested that the conversion of women into a "crypto-servant class" was an important economic accomplishment, and it required that the value of the services of housewives, estimated at one-fourth the total of the Gross National Product, be masked by the concept of the "household" representing the family (1973, pp. 76-79). The feminine mystique described by Betty Friedan in the early 1960s represented the concept of "self-fulfillment-femininity" of women in roles that revolved around the home and family. The norm for women is marriage, and feminine roles have to do with supportive and subordinate services in relation to home and family; these assumptions persist within a construct of femininity without reference to the social reality of women's lives.

United States Department of Labor statistics for 1970 suggested that thirty-one million women work comprising over one-third of the labor force. Furthermore, more than half of the women in the labor force are married and living with their husbands. Mothers work, and affluent women work, although the Women's Bureau of the U.S. Department of Labor pointed out that of the thirty-one million women in the labor force in March, 1970, nearly half were working because of pressing economic need (1971). Bem and Bem clarified the kinds of occupations women hold, and suggested that these are always inferior ones compared to men (1971, p. 2). The Commission on the Status of Women concluded that "Most women work in 'women's' jobs which ordinarily pay less than 'men's' jobs" (1973, p. 1), and a lengthy treatment in *Psychology Today* analyzed salary differentials between men and women and stated "to be exact, she earns only 58 percent of what an equally qualified man would make" (Levitin, et al., 1973, p. 89).

The notion of femininity as a social construct and powerful socialization model is not a clear one. The treatment here suggests the ways in which this image seems to function in society and for the individual without presenting an unmitigated view of the lovely, passive, submissive, nurturant female as a pervasive ideal that becomes an internalized norm for all women. At the same time, elements of this view, and the attendant roles of woman as helpmeet, homemaker, devoted wife and mother, and generalized complement to everything male and masculine, do persist as important societal constructs. More pointedly, women are evaluated according to ideas about what it means to be feminine, and the extent to which individuals internalize and are able to fulfill the values ascribed to femininity is frequently equated with self-worth as well.

## The Feminist Position

In June, 1959, *Cosmopolitan* published a special issue, and the cover articles were listed as: "Psychiatry and Beauty," "How We All Betray Our Age," " 'I Was Afraid to Be A Woman,' " and "Princess of the Beauty Business." *The Ladies Home Journal* cover of June, 1964 advertised a special issue which heralded, "A Daring New Concept to Expand Your Life—Woman the Fourth Dimension—by the Editors and Betty Friedan—Author of *The Feminine Mystique.*" *Time Magazine* presented a special issue, "The American Woman," on March 20, 1972, and introduced it with the statement:

> The women's issue could involve an epic change in the way we see ourselves, not only sexually but historically, sociologically, psychologically and in the deeper, almost inaccessible closets of daily habit. Its appearance has startled men and women into self-perception (p. 25).

In July, 1973, the magazine cover said *"Esquire—The Magazine for Men"* and the cover stated only, "This Issue is About Women," and referred to the women's liberation movement as "probably the most significant movement in the country today." Also in its issue of July, 1973, *Ms.* celebrated its first birthday, and reported 200,000 subscribers and a newsstand sale of 200,000. In congratulating its success, *Ms.* asked, "whoever heard of a popular magazine concerned with changing lives, not just offering escape from them?" Another special issue of *The Ladies Home Journal* was the one of August, 1970, which was turned over to women after some two hundred feminists invaded the office of the editor, John Mack Carter, on March 18, 1970. In an introduction to the special issue, Carter said, "We seemed to catch a rising note of angry self-expression among today's American women, a desire for representation, for recognition, for a broadening range of alternatives in a rapidly changing society." Shaffer, in her analysis of the status of women at the time of the fiftieth anniversary of suffrage in 1970, commented that the women's movement was "mounting an assault on an entrenched pattern of relations between the sexes that . . . demeans and restricts one-half the human race" (1970, p. 566).

Perhaps, the feminist view was stated best in relation to the women's movement in the preview issue of *Ms.* by Gloria Steinem, who said:

> Women are human beings first, with minor differences from men that apply largely to the act of reproduction. We share the dreams, capabilities, and weaknesses of all human beings, but our occasional pregnancies and other visible differences have been used— even more pervasively, if less brutally, than racial differences have been used—to mark us for an elaborate division of labor that may once have been practical but has since become cruel and false. The division is continued for clear reason, consciously or not: the economic and social profit of men as a group.*

In the same issue, Jane O'Reilly's "The Housewife's Moment of Truth" introduced the concept of the "click" as the consciousness raising recognition of all the stereotypic and actual ways that women are oppressed on the basis of assumed sex norms and roles.

Both the concepts and events of the women's liberation movement are fascinating; the gains that have been made in a changed awareness of what it means to be a woman are indisputable, and no one living in contemporary America could avoid the ramifications of women's efforts to change the stereotypic assumptions of femininity. There is a body of

---

* From Gloria Steinem, "Sisterhood," *Ms.* preview issue (Spring, 1972), p. 48. Reprinted by permission.

literature, and an organized movement, and a feminist attitude toward rights that must be considered in any approach to women. Both attitudes and behavior have changed in significant ways in response to feminist challenges and demands. In 1971, when it struck down an Idaho statute that said that when a man and woman of the same degree of kinship to a deceased person file competing petitions to administer the estate, the man must be chosen, the Supreme Court declared a law unconstitutional because it discriminated against women *(The New York Times,* November 28, 1971). As reported in *The New York Times* of May 20, 1973, the Supreme Court not only ruled for women in a similar case, but also judged that all laws involving classification by sex would be regarded in the future as "inherently suspect," a decision that had been sought in vain in the 1971 case. Only two years had passed between these two decisions, and the *Times* was led to conclude that this reflected "Lightning-like progress when you consider that women did not get the vote until 50 years after black men did." This is only one example of the literally thousands of ways in which women have altered society and its perceptions as an outgrowth of the feminist position. Although chronicling these, which range from employment rights to the presentation of women in textbooks and children's literature, is beyond the scope of this work, feminist literature is readily available, and *Ms.* included a listing of sources in its Gazette section, "Hot Off the Feminist Presses" in July, 1973.

It is important to keep in mind that both femininity and feminism are the socialization themes for women in contemporary society. Bardwick has suggested that "Evolutionary change in sex roles is inevitable —but radical change is unlikely" (1973, p. 26). She seems to reject the social possibility of an androgynous society, fostered by some feminists, by endorsing the importance of sexual identity and the fact that "the ways in which the sexes interact are basic to our ideas of normality." Bardwick pointed out that men who are "sexists" and women who want to be "sex objects" are "both . . . playing out learned roles that allow them to feel attractive and sexual" (1973, p. 30). As Howe indicated, "sexual stereotypes start early"; many studies have documented them in preschool children. For this reason, even changed consciousness is not sufficient impetus to an easily changed sex role, but it does initiate a process that may lead to more choice for both sexes. This is a little easier for women, perhaps, because the stereotypes of femininity have been dissonant with what is socially valued. That is, the values and qualities that are valued in American society are those traditionally associated with masculinity. The deviant woman does suffer, frequently expressing the quandary Horner identified as "the double bind," and *may* come to avoid success in her life, but if she doesn't, she still has the comfort of competitive success as it is socially valued. Successful women are not considered very "desirable" in the social ways that express femininity as a value, and in the past such women have not become role models for other women because of that fact. Even if child rearing is not revolutionized, however, changing attitudes toward women are going to ensure more esteem for the achieving woman, and, ultimately, the social construct of woman will be drastically altered.

### The Social Perception of Physicality

Both the social construct of femininity and the social position of feminism emphasize the importance of the body and physicality. Since they influence determination of sexual identity and appropriate roles, attitudes toward the body are crucial to the establishment of values and must be considered as forming a central concept with reference to woman in sport.

**Femininity has always implied attention to personal appearance.** Primarily, femininity has represented an externalized view in which women are evaluated according to their appearance and attractiveness, and it has implied heavy responsibility to the grooming and care of the body. The billions of dollars spent each year on both cosmetics and cosmetic surgery in America has been well documented and, of course, men as well as women accept the value of a youthful and attractive appearance. For women, however, the assumptions underlying the importance of their appearance are much more crucial and all-consuming than they are for men.

Fleming's article on "Psychiatry and Beauty" in *Cosmopolitan* (June, 1959), for instance, suggested that "Often, psychiatrists and psychologists will prescribe beauty treatments for a female patient before therapy or analysis begins, in the hope that the beauticians can help the woman reestablish some of the self-respect her neurosis has nibbled away" (p. 32). It goes on to characterize a woman's making herself attractive as saying, "I have done my best to please you, and I expect you will treat me with equal kindness and respect" (p. 35). Perhaps, the quintessential statement of this view is: "The deliberately

unbeautiful, the women who neglect their looks, are rarely enjoying
the best of mental health" (p. 35).

Marge Piercy, in a review of Phyllis Chesler's *Women and Madness*
that appeared in *The Village Voice* on November 30, 1972 affirmed
that this 1959 assumption still obtained. She said:

> I was struck how psychiatrists and therapists in the course of the
> book were quoted as judging a female patient by looks, by whether
> she's been combing her hair and is therefore improving, or refusing
> to take care of herself, to make an effort. Are male patients
> judged by their attractiveness to nurses? Several of the women
> remembered learning to use make-up or submitting to having their
> hair done as a way to get out (p. 26).

Although presented in a way that "sounds" more scientific, these same
assumptions underlie the view stated by Seymour Fisher:

> Girls and women invest much more open interest in the body than
> do their male counterparts. They feel free to study their own
> appearance and to experiment with techniques for altering it by
> means of clothing and cosmetics. . . .
>     A woman apparently sees a clearer and more meaningful
> relationship between her body and her life role than a man.
> Despite the influence of Women's Liberation, the chief goals of
> most women still revolve around being attractive, entering into
> marriage, and producing children. Such aims readily permit the
> female to see her body as a vehicle for her life career (1972, p. 32).

Fisher, as he has evidenced in other writings, seems to accept socialized
values as though they are innate, and to refer to the "interest" of
women in their bodies and the "life goals" of women as inherent norms.
This same subject can, however, be approached quite differently.

In a brilliant statement about the concept of aging and its effects
on women, Susan Sontag said:

> From early childhood on, girls are trained to care in a pathologi-
> cally exaggerated way about their appearance and are profoundly
> mutilated (to the extent of being unfitted for first-class adulthood)
> by the extent of the stress put on presenting themselves as physi-
> cally attractive objects. Women look in the mirror more frequently
> than men do. It is, virtually, their duty to look at themselves—to
> look often. Indeed, a woman who is not narcissistic is considered
> unfeminine. And a woman who spends literally *most* of her time
> caring for, and making purchases to flatter, her physical appear-
> ance is not regarded in this society as what she is: a kind of moral

idiot. She is thought to be quite normal and is envied by other women . . . .*

The norms for femininity in terms of the importance of appearance also imply specific values with reference to the body and appearance. In a general way, the feminine role requires that one appear "feminine"; this means always being well-groomed and seeming to have invested a great deal of attention in how one looks. In addition, it implies conformance to certain standards of style in dress, hairdo, use of personal accessories and accoutrements, and the like. Fashions change, of course, but the social construct of femininity at any time can be analyzed according to the role demands implied for its fulfillment. Although woman and the female body particularly are conceived as "objects" almost exclusively in an extreme conception of femininity, there are implications for physical behavior. Woman is expected to be passive, of course, but not to the point of being inert; rather, she is encouraged to use her body in wholesome but decorous ways, and to be sexually attractive but not overly suggestive. In other words, role behavior in relation to physicality emanates from the feminine construct. Since it is unacceptable for women to be "masculine," the despised behaviors relate to the use of strength, activity, aggression, and too much bodily competence.

**Feminism seeks to establish a concept of woman as strong, physical, and bodily competent.** One of the strongest attacks of the women's movement has been on the stereotype of woman as weak, passive, unable, and a decorative "sex object." Magazines, newspapers, television, commercials, books, and every other image-making source have all been chastised unmercifully and with some result for the presentation of women in terms of their mindlessness and physical attractiveness. *Ms.* (July, 1973) reported that women were "womancotting their local Schlitz beer distributor" in protest of the ad that says, "Rugby and Women . . . The Great Contact Sport" (p. 20). Women have pinched men on Wall Street, and have whistled at hardhats. Even the stewardesses were reported gleeful when the first male steward was assaulted suggestively by an aggressive woman passenger. Fishel, in "This Ad Insults Women," stated the case against the image-makers as follows.

---

* From Susan Sontag, "The Double Standard of Aging," *Saturday Review of the Society* (September, 1972), p. 34. Reprinted by permission.

Never have the admen even come close to showing a flesh-and-blood female, a woman with a good head and a heart. For in the advertisers' last analysis, it's really not necessary for a woman to have a personality, to live and breathe. In the Madison Avenue scheme of things, a woman exists only to be man's chief accessory: functional, passive and, with a little bit of luck (or help), good-looking (1970, p. 11w).

The feminist position also deals specifically with programs and guidelines for changes in women's role behavior. The women's movement has consistently endorsed self-defense activities for women, and there has been a corresponding proliferation of opportunities for women to learn judo and karate, particularly in the cities. Rape has received a great deal of attention, and most women's groups have organized counseling programs to assist women in discouraging the development of sexist attitudes that may assume the woman guilty of attracting assault. In fact, feminism encourages women to attend to their bodies as part of themselves, and to avoid externalized attitudes that permit the body to be viewed as decorative and nonfunctional. The new body therapies, the whole range of eastern body-centered experience systems, the Esalen approach to sport and movement as self-expressive, as well as the martial arts, are promoted within a feminist view that recognizes that women are enhanced as persons when they can be competent and able.

## THE SOCIAL DYNAMICS OF WOMAN IN SPORT

Woman in sport is both social reality and anomaly. Within a social view, the participation of women in sport generally, and in certain sports in particular, can be seen as either rational and desirable or as a fairly ubiquitous social problem. Although the reality cannot be ignored, it can either be recognized and encouraged, or considered a minor sort of social data. Various social perspectives can be confirmed or denied as rationales, and apologetics are conceived and accepted. Woman in sport as an issue can serve as polemical thrust or political stance; and it can do so with reference to men, or to women, or to sport.

The status of woman in sport in the United States is exceedingly interesting, and will be discussed in the next chapter. It is, however, also confusing insofar as the roles and perceptions of woman in sport and about woman in sport do not present a clear and cohesive image of either the norms associated with the phenomenon or the roles within it. For this reason, the woman-sport relationship must be considered in terms of its social dynamics. As alternative social assumptions are clarified, the possibility of explaining social reality is increased.

## The Social Anomaly

If masculinity and femininity are viewed as appropriate social conceptions of the polar differences in the qualities and behavior of men and women, and if sport is logically deduced as a desirable masculine domain, then the role of woman in sport is a social anomaly. As a pervasive assumption, in fact, this view is the basis for most of the conceptions of sport norms and collectivities that exclude women. In the face of the impossibility of excluding women completely, a view of female sport participation as an anomaly accommodates versions of limited, separate, and vastly less important athletic opportunities for women. This view exists in relation to several social hypotheses about sport as well as about men and women.

**Conceptions of masculinity and femininity are important both because they reflect some truth and because they are socially necessary.** Lionel Tiger, who also expressed the concept of "male bonding" as a masculine and not a feminine characteristic, is one exponent for the ethological view of the "truth" of male-female differences in behavior. He uses the argument that anything that exists over a long time and is found in various cultures "suggests conformity to nature rather than to male conspiracy," and he refers to the difficulty of the feminist attempt "to change a primate who is very old genetically and who seems stubbornly committed to relatively little variation in basic sexual structures" (1970, p. 136). Despite the way in which the differences between men and women are conceived as truth, a corollary assumption is that the differences are necessary in order for both men and women to develop appropriately and for the functioning of the social order. Gilder, for instance, adumbrated the social practices that expressed the oppression of women, but concluded that "they make possible a society in which women can love and respect men and sustain durable families. They make possible a society in which men can love and respect women and treat them humanely" (1973, p. 49). Within this view, then, not only are "The differences between the sexes . . . the single most important fact of human society" (Gilder, 1973, p. 54), but the maintenance of differences depends upon a contrast in behavior between men and women.

It is, of course, easy to document sport as a masculine mode. If socialization goals are perceived in relation to maintaining socially defined sex roles, then it is logical to defend sport as a masculine preserve, and to decry the anomaly of women's participation. A. Craig Fisher presented this point very clearly in *The Physical Educator* (October, 1972). He suggested that *although* "it may be correct to speak of the merging of the sex roles, it must be made clear that this may be due to the female's encroachment upon traditional male activities" (p. 120). After citing several authorities in support of the masculine hypotheses and effects of sport, Fisher concluded:

> How much longer can the aforementioned claims be made in light of the fact that there is a decreasing number of sports and games that differentiate the sexes? The clear male identity is beclouded by feminine participation in traditional male activities. The claims could perhaps be better substantiated if certain sports were reserved for males and feminine participation in them was restricted (1972, p. 122).

This same point of view was expressed succinctly by Wally Florence, the 235-pound linebacker who smeared Pat Barczi Palinkas of the Orlando Panthers football team when she fumbled the snap from center, in his comment, "I'm out here trying to make a living and she's trying to make a folly of a man's game" (*Sports Illustrated*, September 7, 1970). In one of the suits against Little League baseball's refusal to allow girls to participate, Pamela Magill's parents alleged discrimination. In ruling that the Avonworth Baseball Conference had every right to bar a ten-year-old girl from playing Little League baseball, Federal Judge Barron P. McCune supported the contention of the board of directors of the Conference who said:

> . . . the 45-pound girl's admission to Little League play would downgrade the team she joined talent-wise, inhibit the play, complicate the task of getting fathers to volunteer for coaching and managing duties, and greatly embarrass the boys who had to sit on the bench while a girl was on the playing field (*Lehighton Times-News,* July 6, 1973).

It is apparent that there are two considerations basic to the defense of sport as a masculine preserve. Somehow, masculine socialization is deemed to encompass both assertiveness, especially as that is manifest in sport, and also importance. Insofar as women have less importance and status in society, their participation in sport is seen to denigrate sport and, therefore, mitigate its function as a source of desirable masculinization. This is extremely important because it helps to explain the exclusion of women from sport as well as the ways in which their participation, when it does occur, is limited or derided. Because concepts of masculinity and femininity are relational, the assumption that it is desirable to maintain socially defined sex roles includes the belief that women must strive to fulfill the norms of femininity. In some way, however, it must be remembered that the concept of femininity refers not only to what woman is and should be, but to the effect of that on man. Clifford Fagan, executive director of the National Federation of State High School Athletic Associations, was cited in *Good Housekeeping* as being open-minded about girls playing on boys' teams, but also suggested that it is not socially acceptable for a girl to defeat a boy in athletic competition, and that, therefore, the federation felt that both boys and girls could be affected adversely psychologically and such competition should not be encouraged (October, 1969, p. 215). Another girl, Robby Brunhuber, was barred from Little League competition in Westport, Connecticut, and the chairman, Mrs. George McCarthy, was quoted as commenting:

> I wouldn't be against having a Little League for girls, but I think they should be segregated. I've been in Little League for 19 years and I think the most important thing is the relationship between the boys and their managers. Girls would tend to minimize that relationship (*Sports Illustrated,* April 30, 1973).

In "Desegregating Sexist Sport," Edwards suggested that sport functions as a "prime perpetuator of female subjugation," and commented that "In America a female's athletic competence is seen to detract from her womanliness" (1972, p. 82). Bianchi characterized big-time football as "the ideal of masculine identity in the United States" and explicated the role of woman as follows:

> In the football spectacle, the role of woman in our society is clearly defined against the masculine criteria. The important action is male-dominated: women can share only from a distance in a man's world. They can shout and squeal from afar, but their roles are accessory to the male event. They can show their thighs at half time in the various pageants or leap about as cheerleaders in

emotional dependence on men. For ultimately they are his 'bunnies,' his possessions for pleasure and service (1972, p. 32).

## The Dialectic

The dialectic of woman and sport emerges from the social dynamics of conceptions of sport and of woman. It consists of rationales for both women's exclusion from sport and women's participation in sport; it revolves around the ways in which women's athletic pursuits are justified and denigrated. Within this dialectic, which is both dialogue and babel of scholars, athletes, social commentators, sportswriters, and anyone else of either sex, argument and apologetic become confused. The two major thrusts of discussion emerge, first, from the assumptions that define woman and sport as a social anomaly and, second, from an application of the social conceptions of feminism to sport. In both cases, the important focus is the interactive dimension of the concepts of woman and sport. The social view of woman in sport rests on the dialectic of woman and sport in relation to social constructs.

**If woman in sport is accepted as a social anomaly, then it is logical for women to develop an apologetic for their participation in sport.** Because femininity is the most pervasive standard for woman's social acceptability, it is also the most obvious basis on which woman's athleticism must be defended. As Harris pointed out:

> Nevertheless, the young woman who participates in physical activities risks her feminine image. The stereotype frequently associated with females who enjoy vigorous activity poses such a threat that participants bend over backwards to counteract it. Examples can be seen in numerous situations: the blond, bouffant, sprayed hairdos of female track teams, the ruffles on the tennis outfits, the mod apparel worn by many women golfers; the ski togs that flatter the feminine figure, the fancy swim caps and suits, etc. All of these artifacts of femininity assist in reducing the threat of sports participation to the revered feminine image.*

The necessity and importance of confirming femininity on the part of woman athletes is so accepted, that there almost seems to be a conspiracy on the part of everyone concerned to advance arguments for it.

---

* From Dorothy V. Harris, "The Social Self and the Competitive Self in the Female Athlete," unpublished paper (August, 1971), p. 1. Reprinted by permission of the author.

Thus when the chief sex tester at the Mexico City Olympics, Dr. Ludwig Prokop, commented that after testing 911 girl athletes he was convinced that sports made them ugly and that they had hard, stringy bodies, and, in some cases, hair on their chests, *Sports Illustrated* printed the comments, but added:

> Ann Wilson, the staunchly British pentathlon star, says the doctor must have been thinking of Russian girls. Miss Wilson, 22 and shapely, says she has been putting the shot in competition for six years and insists she has no hair on her chest. She adds, as a clincher, that British sports girls do not lack for boyfriends (*Sports Illustrated,* October 4, 1971, p. 18).

In an article about Julia Barash, who played as a member of a boys' high school varsity tennis team, Bob Sales quoted her as saying, "I hate the word 'jock' and I'm not an amazon. I had to defend my image: I *had* to look feminine" (April, 1971, p. 21).

The apologetic for the maintenance of femininity by female athletes is so widespread that examples of it are apparent throughout the culture. It is manifest in social conventions as well as social discussion. It forms the basis for many of the social practices surrounding women's participation from standards of dress to conduct to such things as serving tea. Basically the apologetic suggests that the woman athlete: can *appear* feminine, which is why so many descriptions of women's sports include reference to the attractiveness and physical attributes of the athletes; *is* feminine, which has to do with sexual normality and attractiveness as well as so-called "lady-like" behavior; and *wants* to be feminine, which means that social roles are valued more than sport roles, and life goals include marriage and motherhood rather than being a champion athlete. It is also necessary to deal with feminine biological functioning as part of this apologetic, and evidence is continually invoked that supports the position that not only does athletic participation not interfere with female physiology, but that, in fact, athletic women have more success and less difficulty in bearing children. It is possible that female athletes really are, as some evidence suggests, as aggressive, achievement-oriented, dominant, and committed to sport as male athletes, but the importance of femininity as a social assumption for women requires that those athletes who value social acceptance deny it and affirm that they are real women with feminine goals and interests. This apologetic, then, affirms the feminine mystique and legitimates the woman's role in sport by minimizing the anomaly.

Perhaps, as usual, the best summary of the social dilemma appeared in a newspaper advice column. Jean Adams, the columnist who handles teen-age problems, received a letter from a thirteen-year-old girl who wanted boys both to like her and to play football and baseball with her. The reply was as follows:

> A girl who wants boys to like her, and almost every girl does, usually learns as she grows older to be more like a girl and less like a boy. She tries to look like a girl, smell like a girl, and act like a girl.
>
> She doesn't have to give up football or baseball, but she does a lot better if she lets the boys do the playing while she watches and admires them.
>
> If actually playing is very important to you, keep at it. Many girls are doing it these more relaxed days. But the ones who want to attract boys are following the rules faithfully. They look, feel, smell and act like girls. It takes quite a girl to play rough and still do that. Good luck.*

A second important apologetic for the involvement of woman in sport relates to the importance of maintaining femininity, but suggests specifically that sport is pursued less as achievement than socialization, is always under control, is never taken too seriously, and is sensibly limited. Margaret A. Coffey described this justification with reference to the socialization of woman in sport during the period 1930-1943. She suggested that the sportswoman heard a great deal about "a game for every girl and every girl in a game," and learned "to act with moderation, to play for play's sake, and to be a lady at all times" (1965, p. 41). Leona Holbrook took a view of sport specific to woman when she said:

> Sport for girls and women is activity which is suited to their ways. . . . Sport is a way of life for girls and women. The selected and directed action of girls and women will enhance the way of life for all girls and women. Their sport will be increasingly creditable. . . . We have our women's ways (1972, p. 58).

The most important manifestation of this approach to athletic pursuit is in the choice of so-called "feminine" sports. Hart cited a study that recommended that women participate in such sports as tennis, swimming, ice skating, diving, and so forth, and commented "all of which

---

* From Jean Adams, "Teen Forum," in *Pocono Record.* Reprinted by permission.

have esthetic social and fashion aspects" (1971, p. 64). As Edwards said, "So while males are participating in football, basketball, baseball . . . women are propelling themselves gracefully over the ice or through the water . . . (1973, p. 232).

Weiss pointed out that women can participate in "foreshortened versions" of men's sports and in this sense "the performance of males can be treated as a norm, with the women given handicaps in the shape of smaller and sometimes less dangerous or difficult tasks" (1969, p. 215). Weiss, of course, in his one chapter on "women athletes" devoted as much attention to men as to women; for he, like many scholars, seems to accept the premise that women are understood by comparing them to men. VanderZwaag credits Weiss with being "one of the few if not the only writer who speculates on *why* women have participated in sport in a limited manner," and calls it an "extreme hypothesis" (1972, p. 47). It is an hypothesis particularly consonant with the apologetic that suggests that sport is not so serious nor central to woman; for Weiss suggested that women live their bodies naturally and men must be trained to do so. He said:

> A woman, therefore, will typically interest herself in sport only when she sees that it will enable her to polish what she had previously acquired without thought or effort.
> . . .By competing in games, she can learn where she stands. . . . Usually, though, it is easier for her to judge herself by her attractiveness, and measure this in terms of its social effects. Where a man might be proud of his body, she is proud in her body; where he uses it, she lives it as a lure (1969, p. 218).

Whether controlled by men or women, the contexts for athletic participation by women have generally limited the female athletic model and mode. Intense competition, serious training, attitudes of cruciality, and many other characteristics of men's sport have been negated in women's sport. The apologetic advancing the nonseriousness of woman's pursuit of sport has been well served by such concepts as: the playday and sportsday, the importance of intramural rather than extramural sport in education, the abandonment of athletic pursuits by females in late adolescence, and the avoidance of exhibition and expenditure. Women have seemed to "know their place" in sport and have advanced an ideology that justified and maintained it.

Despite the existence of apologetics, there is social conflict with reference to women in sport. As indicated, the social anomaly of woman and sport derives from ideas about femininity in terms of idealized norms which hold the female and her concerns as subservient to the importance of men, and from ideas about the importance of sport. Hence the emergence of a whole syndrome of attitudes about women in sport that are characterized in contemporary society as sexist; that is, there are a number of rationales for why women should not participate in sport at all, or why they should participate in very limited ways that seem to emanate only from the assumed inferiority of women. In a sexist social view, the very participation of women tends to downgrade an activity, and sport is much too important and stands for far too many valuable social norms for that to be permitted. Sexist arguments are fairly well known; they assume that women are not good enough to be worthy of time and money being devoted to them in sport; that women do not really care about sport anyway; and, most pernicious of all, that women in sport are so adversely affected that they are no longer real women. Some of the arguments involved in the latter consideration revolve around physiological and biological functioning, but they have to do with sexuality as well.

Hart suggested that "we seem to see sport as a field for men, and female homosexuals" (1971, p. 64). With reference to female athletes, Edwards said that "Most are forced by cultural definitions to choose between being an athlete (thereby facing barely hidden suspicions as to the degree of their heterosexuality) and their womanhood" (1973, p. 232). In Part 2 of its series on women in sport in 1973, *Sports Illustrated* suggested that "Behind the myth that participation in sports will masculinize a woman's appearance, there is the even darker insinuation that athletics will masculinize a woman's sexual behavior" (June 4, 1973, p. 47). Interestingly enough, that same comment was extended by Gilbert and Williamson into the familiar apologetic and they cited Dr. Christine Packard, "a London consultant on birth-control and sex problems," as suggesting "just the opposite. Girl athletes tend to make better lovers and are much sexier than less active women" (June 4, 1973, p. 47). In the first article on sport in *Ms.* (January, 1973), Franks referred to the sex tests required of all female Olympic entrants as "humiliating" as well as painful (p. 98). In July, 1973, Fasteau spoke of the discouragements to women's sport participation in terms of "the unenlightened suspicion that a woman's interest in athletics violates the docile female stereotype and indicates lesbianism (remember the rumors about gym teachers?) . . ." (p. 57). In the same issue, Loggia said:

> The historical choice has been simple: woman or athlete? To choose the latter meant risking censure—the pejorative "tomboy" for the child, "dyke" for the woman—plus suffering the paradox that the better a woman became, the worse became her self doubts (July, 1973, p. 63).

**The feminist position reflects an important perspective of woman in sport.** Obviously, the dynamics of the relationship of woman, sport, and society have never been static. On the other hand, the important assumptions about what an athlete is and what a woman is have been fairly consistent and have maintained a prevailing social anomaly in terms of woman and sport. It seems that it is the introduction of feminist points of view that provides the impetus for a discontinuity of attitudes in contemporary society. Feminism, however, must be viewed in relation to a broad spectrum of social and ideological change of which it is part. It is only one aspect of a revolution for equality and individual humanity, but it is that fact that seems to suggest that contemporary women's movements are likely to be more far-reaching than some of the abortive efforts of the past. The feminist position simply changes the rules; it suggests that woman does not need an apologetic for her behavior because the normative stereotypes for women are oppressive and antithetical to the development of human actualization. With reference to the charge of lesbianism within the women's movement, for instance, the Radicalesbians said:

> For in this sexist society, for a woman to be independent means she *can't be* a woman she must be a dyke. That in itself should tell us where women are at. It says as clearly as can be said: woman and person are contradictory terms (1970, p. 2).

The women's movement, like women athletes, is vulnerable to charges that those in the forefront are not "real women." *Time Magazine* (March 20, 1972) suggested that the "issue of lesbianism, for example, has hurt the movement" (p. 30), but the National Organization for Women has, nevertheless, supported "freedom of sexual orientation" as a humanist concern. Although it is possible to dismiss the women's movement as unimportant, because relatively few women are involved in its organized contexts, or as foolish, because it sometimes reflects unrealistic social goals, the changed social realities and attitudes for which it is already responsible cannot be dismissed. The Equal Rights Amendment is only the symbol of the efforts of women to litigate their equal rights and options, and their success has been inordinate and, as will be shown, has influenced woman in sport in serious ways.

There are many unresolved issues about woman's role in sport, and it is clear that the shape of women's sport has not been defined. Jill Johnston, writing in *The Village Voice,* said:

> . . . may the lord be truly thankful concerning the fitness of women for sports there can be no question even in their curlers. I urge all women not to worry about your demons but to teach your angels karate for the new future sexually, politically, intellectually creative woman will also be an athlete a whole person trained in body and mind and not necessarily a terrified competitor modeled on the male idea . . . (September 23, 1971, p. 37).

Fasteau also commented:

> I don't mean to suggest that sports should become for women what they have been for men: a display of aggression, a proof of toughness, and a kind of primitive communication that replaces emotional intimacy. Sweating, swearing, and grunting together as they play, men manage to create a fellowship which they find hard to sustain elsewhere. And sports provide men with yet another vehicle to test domination and preeminence. ("Let the best man win.") (*Ms.,* July, 1973, p. 57).

The most important assumptions that emerge from the feminist position are those expressed by Cathy Small, writing in the *Journal of Health, Physical Education and Recreation,* who said:

> What a *woman* does *is* feminine. By addressing the question of femininity in sport, we are professionally recognizing that this is not so, and that physical activity might, in some way, affect one's sexual identity. To further support sport on the basis of its positive effect or lack of effect on sanctioned feminine mores is to affirm the worth of traditional sex-role values. At a time when feminine role attitudes are undergoing scrutiny and revision, the implications of our arguments may well be objectionable (January, 1973, p. 27).

The achievements on behalf of changing opportunities for women are significant. Billie Jean King said, "Sure, I made $119,000 last year . . . and we still have to fight twice as hard as the men do to get fair treatment. We haven't made it yet" (*Ms.*, July, 1973, p. 40). The entry of feminist attitudes in the dialectic of woman and sport is clearly responsible for a new dimension in the relationship and, hence, in the realities of sport for woman.

# Chapter 6

# The Status of Women and Sport

The status of women and sport is related to the dialectic between changing social conceptions and definitions of both woman and sport. A focus on status includes consideration of women in sport (in terms of the particular individuals who participate) and women's sport (as the collective representation of women's participation) since both of these are vulnerable to social views. Furthermore, because there is societal dissonance about woman and sport, there are discrepant indications of the status of women in sport.

It seems pointless to try to deal with singular views of the status of women and sport. There is a great deal of evidence that social conceptions, at least, are in a state of extreme flux and stress. If the normative data about women's actual participation in sport does not yet reflect the same degree of change, there is every reason to believe that it soon will. At the same time, the most important hope is that increasing attention to woman as a social issue, and to her role in sport as social evidence will result in more attention and more data about women in sport.

The framework of the dialectic of woman and sport provided a perspective for specific attention to the status of women and sport. The consideration of status proceeds here in relation to the social context, the institution of education, and women *in* sport. Previous chapters have clearly indicated the status of women's actual participation in sport with reference to society, collegiate sport, and Olympic competition. The focus of this chapter is on the status of women and sport as part of the social view.

## THE SOCIAL CONTEXT

One of the concerns of status is the legal character or condition. This becomes a central aspect when people actively pursue social change through legal means. The whole concept of an activist approach as part of the equality revolution in the United States has been tied to legal frameworks. Even the sound and fury of protest and civil disobedience revolved around legal inequities or failures, and as these faded with the end of the 1960s, legal action has become synonymous with militance.

It is too late to ask whether or not the ancient Greeks had the "right" to bar women from Olympia, but it is not too late to insist that a woman has the "right" to enter the press box in the stadium of Yale University, even during a football game. Insistence on rights, however, even when "fairness" or "humanity" is invoked has not proved to be socially effective. Legal recourse has. Interestingly enough, the institution of sport has proved less vulnerable to legal action than any other. The confusion of Supreme Court decisions relative to the application of federal antitrust laws to professional sport is the most obvious testimony to the fact that sport in American society occupies a special place as a social conception.

Somehow, the whole tradition of sport includes a host of quasi-legalistic assumptions and attendant rules and policies that affect not only how contests shall be conducted, but who shall play, and how players shall conduct themselves. The weight of tradition and the idealized social vision of sport have been substantive support for the organized groups that regulate sport. It seems apparent that if Curt Flood could challenge the "reserve clause" in baseball, and Wimbledon could be boycotted as it was by the men's players association in 1973, that times are changing. Men's sport will undoubtedly be modified as a result of legal and political action; women's sport may be revolutionized.

### Politics and Law

The Citizen's Advisory Council on the Status of Women reported that "Unprecedented political, legal, and economic advances made 1972 an historic year for women" (May, 1973, p. 1). Cited as evidence were such things as political power; election to public office; passage of the Equal Rights Amendment in the Senate on March 22, 1972 and the ratification process; as well as the passage of other Federal and State legislation improving the legal and economic status of women.

The ERA is the most symbolic legislative act. Writing in *The New York Times Magazine,* Thimmesch presented "three simple sections" and then commented, "If the sentences are simple, they are rich with far-reaching legal and ultimately social implications . . ." (June 24, 1973, p. 9). The ERA has until March 22, 1979 to be ratified. At the time that Thimmesch was reporting, twenty-nine states had voted final ratification, thirteen states had rejected the ERA, it was stopped before it reached the floor of the legislature in six states, and one state, Nebraska, had responded to a growing counter-offensive of public opinion and voted to rescind its ratification. Although Congress may have to decide upon the legality of voting to rescind ratification, the Counsel to the Constitutional Amendments Subcommittee of the U.S. Senate concurred with the Attorney General of Idaho in declaring such action null and void. In addition, six states ratified Equal Rights Amendments to their State Constitutions in November, 1972—Colorado, Hawaii, Maryland, New Mexico, Texas and Washington, thus joining Illinois, Pennsylvania, and Virginia who had done so previously, and Connecticut projected such consideration for 1974 (p. 69). Pat Goltz, international president of the Feminists for Life, commented that even if the ERA is never ratified it has accomplished its purpose (July, 1973, single page).

Amendment 11375 revised Executive Order 11246, which was geared toward affirmative action in employment, to include sex. This Amendment and the Equal Employment Opportunity Act of 1972, giving the Equal Employment Opportunity Commission authority to enforce Title VII of the Civil Rights Act of 1964, affirm a changed social view. Because of Title VII, the EEOC can file complaints in court in relation to discrimination in employment because of race, color, religion, sex, or national origin. On March 31, 1972, the EEOC issued revised guidelines on discrimination because of sex, and established the relationship of Title VII to the Equal Pay Act.

Government has limitations with reference to social change, but in the present society political action is seen as the most viable means to legitimizing both social conditions and ideology. The prevailing status of women (as well as other groups with minority characteristics) became socially intolerable and dissonant with the realities of industrialization and affluence. Because there was, in fact, some consensus in the society that inequities existed, the incipient move toward social revolutions, rebellions, and civil strife as avenues toward change proved defeating. Social change is resisted, most often, because the members of a society have been socialized to accept certain elements that are congruent with the *status quo.* It is important to remember that socialization implies attitudes, customs, moral sentiments, and even personal feelings. All of these are most strongly affected specifically in terms of such a pervasive and personalized aspect of life as one's sex, and generally in terms of the appropriate roles and behaviors of the sexes.

In the present society, then, there seems to be some general agreement that an inequitable and "unfair" situation does exist. The principle of equality of opportunity is an important one in American society, and takes on the proportion of a moral sentiment for most people, so it is fairly well accepted that women should have equal pay for equal work, and should not be denied *all* professional opportunities on the basis of sex alone. Beyond that level, however, a great deal of political effort is required to change either existing perceptions of women and their appropriate status in society or the social mechanisms that would enable change. The focus of political efforts is a dual one and includes demands for: (1) equality as permitted by social structures, but denied by sexist attitudes and practices, and (2) change in both existing attitudes and structures.

Although one of the arguments for maintaining the social *status quo* for women is that they themselves are satisfied, this is obviously not the case. The legal activity on behalf of women as a result of changing legislation has been phenomenal and successful. In a multitude of cases, most of them brought by the EEOC, the courts have ordered employers and unions to stop discriminatory practices and policies, and have enjoined them to set up improved hiring, transfer, classification, and promotion practices and affirmative action programs. Furthermore, in most cases, the large amounts of money involved discourage employers from continuing discrimination. A recent suit against the General Electric Company, for instance, was settled with an agreement that would cost the company $300,000 in back pay and an additional $250,000 annually in higher wages (*The Spokeswoman,* August 15, 1973, p. 2).

## Political Action in Sport

The legal and political action in sport in society is less impressive than that occurring generally on behalf of women. The Women's Liberation

Movement was slow to recognize the importance of sport as a symbolic domain for women's advances. Of course, the infinitely greater visibility of men's sport led to its early recognition as a target for political action, and the Black Power salute at the Mexico City Olympics received world-wide attention. There is also still a vaguely embarrassed attitude on the part of most women toward athletic involvement, so that Nora Ephron's piece in *Esquire* about Bernice Gera, the first woman umpire in professional baseball, is satiric. Ephron commented that "I should say, at this point, that I am utterly baffled as to why any woman would want to get into professional baseball, much less work as an umpire in it" (January, 1973, p. 36).

**Bernice Gera's experience provided some insight into the kinds of difficulties inherent in the issue of women in sport and, ultimately, reflected the changing political scene.** For whatever reasons, this woman was an avid devotee of baseball. In the early 1960s she sought employment in baseball in any capacity, and met with consistent rejection. In 1967, she filed an application to the Al Summers Baseball Umpires School in Florida, was accepted, and then rejected when Summers discovered she was a woman. Bernice Gera did enroll in the National Sports Academy in West Palm Beach, Florida in June, 1967, and graduated with honors. Lawsuits began in 1968 when Gera could not obtain employment, and in 1969, she was given a contract by the New York-Pennsylvania Class A League. When the president of the National Association of Professional Baseball Leagues invalidated the contract by refusing to sign it, Mario Biaggi, her attorney, filed a complaint with the New York State Human Rights Commission. The Commission ruled in November, 1970 that the National League discriminated not only against women, but against men belonging to short ethnic groups as well (the League had used Gera's height of 5'2" as unacceptable qualification for being an umpire). There was an appeal and further litigation, but the State Court of Appeals upheld the Human Rights Commission ruling and on July 25, 1972, Bernice Gera signed a contract with the New York-Pennsylvania League.

The happy ending, of course, did not occur. In the opener of the New York-Pennsylvania League season in Geneva, New York, Gera was both harrassed and not very effective; she announced "I've just resigned from baseball" at the end of the game, and burst into tears. The National Organization for Women was not involved in any of Bernice Gera's efforts, but she was contacted by them afterward. It is fairly clear that this woman was acting in terms of her own motivations and not as a political symbol, but the successful legal maneuvers involved did establish both precedent and encouragement with reference to women in sport. In some ways, then, the case of Bernice Gera is a landmark example, and does, in fact, represent the extent of the time period involved in the use of legal action to change women's roles in sport.

**Women jockeys provided the first significant breakthrough in terms of new sport roles for women in professional sport.** The triumph of women in horse racing incorporated all the elements of drama, self-assertion, and ultimate vindication of the underdog so dear to American mythology. Although the greatest resistance to women riders came from male jockeys, and many men were generally amused or upset, public sentiment seemed to be with the women. Perhaps because horsemanship has always been considered an appropriate feminine and upper-class activity, the idea of women racing was not quite so upsetting. In fact, it was Kathy Kusner, the Olympic equestrienne, who paved the way by winning a court order forcing the Maryland Racing Commission to license her.

There were several women fighting for the right to ride at the same time, and all of them were attractive and feminine according to prevailing social standards. At the same time, it is possible that the fact that male jockeys are obviously considered somewhat less desirable men because of their size contributed to the view that their objections could be discounted. Both Penny Ann Early and Barbara Jo Rubin were boycotted by male jockeys following their successful campaigns to be licensed by the Racing Commission. The boycotts ended, however, when the Florida State Racing Commission upheld the Tropical Park stewards who had fined thirteen jockeys a hundred dollars each for the part they took in the demonstration against Barbara Jo Rubin. These efforts on the part of women jockeys began in 1968, and in February, 1969, Tuesdee Testa became the first woman rider ever to compete in a regular race at Santa Anita, although she did finish last.

Perhaps, the fact that racing is more a contest between horses than humans also contributed to the acceptance of women jockeys. In any case, despite the social furor, the proliferation of jokes, and other attempts to ridicule them, the woman jockey seems to be a permanent part of the sport. It also became quickly apparent that women had, in fact, been part of the horseracing scene for some time. They had served as hot-walkers, who walk the horses after a race or workout to cool them, pony persons (pony boys), grooms, and exercise persons. The existence of women jockeys served both to legitimize these auxiliary roles and to attract more girls and women to them, and the participation of women in the world of horseracing seems to be established.

**Once established, the procedure of bringing suit against discriminatory practices in sport was manifest in diverse ways.** Elinor Kaine, the sports-writer who was refused the right to sit in the press box of the Yale Bowl, won an out-of-court settlement when she brought suit. Legal action was threatened by Stephanie Salter, a writer for *Sports Illustrated*, who was refused admission to the annual banquet of the New York chapter of the Baseball Writers Association of America [*The Sportswoman* (Spring, 1972), p. 5]. Debbie Seldon sued the American Motorcycle Association for refusing to license her as a professional and when Kerry Kleid brought similar action, she became the first professional woman rider.

After several suits were initiated on behalf of girls who wanted to play in Little League baseball, and several contradictory rulings, the strongest suit was filed in May, 1973 by Carolyn King, the Ypsilanti American Little League, and the city of Ypsilanti against the National Little Leagues organization over its "no girls allowed" rule. In this case, Carolyn King won her position as a centerfielder on the basis of her ability over a hundred competing boy players. The Ypsilanti City Council ordered the local league either to let her play or lose the use of city facilities, staff, and financial aid, and when they complied, the National Little League office revoked their charter [*The Spokeswoman* (August 15, 1973), p. 2]. On June 20, 1973 Representative Martha W. Griffiths introduced bill H.R. 8854 into the United States House of Representatives to amend the Little League Baseball Federal Charter to include girls as well as boys. On August 25, 1973, the Little League World Series in Williamsport, Pennsylvania was picketed by members of the National Organization for Women. In November, 1973 the New Jersey Civil Rights Division ruled that the league should let girls play, and Sylvia Pressler of the Division said, "The institution of Little League is as American as the hot dog and apple pie. There is no reason why that part of Americana should be withheld from girls." On February 27, 1974, a three-judge panel of the appellate division of Superior Court responded to a request by Little League, Inc. for a stay of the order issued by the State Division on Civil Rights. The League had argued that girls were not physically fit to play, but the judges ordered that girls must be allowed to play in New Jersey and should be allowed to register immediately (*The New York Times,* February 28, 1974).

**In addition to legal efforts, other kinds of pressures have served to change women's sport.** As Myron Stuart wrote, "Women's lib in golf and tennis has finally come of age. Girls who used to play for silver trophies topped off, perhaps, by a kiss on the cheek from the tournament's chairman, finally are playing for gold—big chunks of it" (June, 1973, p. 44). Earnings and the inequities between what men and women earned, frequently for the same job, were obvious targets in a society where women, in fact, were paid fifty-eight percent of what men were paid. Although sport is a separate case when it comes to the "value" of work or the "worth" of athletes, it was logical that the differentials of money in men's and women's sports would be an issue.

Sports Illustrated reported that although Billie Jean King became the first woman athlete to win $100,000 (the congratulatory phone call from President Nixon let the nation know that even if women's sport wasn't important, money always was) in 1971, Rod Laver's earnings that year were $290,000. When King won $10,000 for winning the U.S. Open at Forest Hills in 1972, her male counterpart, Ilie Nastase, collected $25,000, and while golf's leading woman money winner, Kathy Whitworth, collected $65,063 in 1972, in 29 tournaments, Jack Nicklaus won $320,542 in 19 (May 28, 1973, p. 92).

At the time that Billie Jean King and other women tennis players protested the disparity in purses for men's and women's events in 1970, the ratio in most tournaments approached ten to one. The support of Gladys Heldman, the formation of the Women's International Tennis Federation, the suspension of the dissenting players by the USLTA, and the successful Virginia Slims Tour was an appropriate drama for the women's movement in sport. The drama was heightened by the challenges of Bobby Riggs who billed himself as "the greatest women's tennis player in the world." On September 20, 1973, Billie Jean King, at twenty-nine, and Bobby Riggs, at fifty-five, played a $100,000 winner-take-all singles match on the floor of the Astrodome before a crowd of 30,492 and a national television audience, "that turned the event into a one-of-a-kind 3-million-dollar spectacular filled with circus trimmings" (*The New York Times,* December 23, 1973). Riggs had staged a similar match against Margaret Court the previous Mother's Day and had won that $10,000 event handily. Billie Jean King became an important heroine of the women's movement when she beat Riggs 6-4, 6-3, 6-3. Although the Riggs-King match was less sport than entertainment in its social connotations, the contest itself did ultimately become the drama, and women and tennis were well served by King's victory. A kind of backlash effect was the fury directed toward Rosie Casals who assisted in reporting the event and adopted a fiercely partisan and feminist stance.

Tennis became the symbolic testimony that is exploding the myth that people neither care about women athletes nor will watch them. The United States Open Tennis Championships at Forest Hills in 1973 became the first tournament of any consequence to give men and women financial parity through equal prize monies. The World Team Tennis League is not only sexually integrated, but the player drafts clearly indicated that women stars were the most desirable drawing cards. Prize money for women has continued to increase, and in 1973, Margaret Court became the first woman to exceed earnings of $200,-000. In the richest tournaments for women, Rosemary Casals won $30,000 in the Family Circle tournament at Sea Pines, South Carolina, and Chris Evert, who earned $123,000 in 1973, collected $25,000 of it beating Nancy Gunter at Boca Raton, Florida. It seems impossible that between August, 1972 and September, 1973, NBC televised 366 hours of "live" sport with *one hour* of it, the finals at Wimbledon, devoted to women (*Sports Illustrated,* May 28, 1973, p. 96). Surely, that will never happen again.

## Women's Status in Sport

Both sport and women's status are changed by women serving in prestigious or unique roles in sport. There is, of course, a danger of "tokenism" insofar as a single woman may be permitted to advance or to do something as a way of quieting criticism. In terms of social change, however, it seems more often that even a single woman fulfilling a heretofore "masculine" role becomes a substantial aspect of a changed consciousness as social conception.

When NOW challenged Roone Arledge about the insufficient network treatment of women's sports, he commented that he would "hire any woman as competent as Ellie Riger." She has since been named a full producer for ABC and says, "At ABC sports, we keep working to promote women all the time" (*Ms.,* September, 1973, p. 20). In January, 1974 Ellie Riger produced a Special on Woman Athletes.

New York City named its first woman golf pro in 1971, after more than eighty years of municipal golf. In May, 1973, Bobbie Montgomery of Anderson, South Carolina became the general manager of a baseball team in the Western Carolina League. In February, 1971, a story about Idaho State University rejecting the application of Nila Gilcrest to be an assistant football coach, without pay, was distributed by UPI. In the same week in August, 1973, both *The New York Times* and *Sports Illustrated* reported that Lee Corso, head football coach at Indiana University, was looking for a woman to fill the position of assistant varsity coach in charge of academics and counseling, and had received fifty applications.

In the Colgate-Dinah Shore Winners Circle golf tournament in the spring of 1973, the $139,000 in prizes was impressive, but so was the fact that ninety women were involved in the conduct of the tournament, from caddying to running the press scoreboard.

Jan Magee became Michigan's only registered woman football official in the fall of 1972. Maxine Shields, who became the third woman to hold a professional motorcycle racing license, came in second in the Internationals race in Valley Hermosa in Mexico in 1972; the only woman in flat track racing at the time (*The Sportswoman,* Summer, 1973, p. 22).

In contemporary society, women are prizefighting and running in distance events (as well as in the Boston Marathon, at last). They are playing the same excellent hockey and lacrosse they have throughout the century, as well as taking part in all the traditionally feminine and social activities like swimming, tennis, and golf, but softball, basketball, soccer, and football are popular too. *The Sportswoman* reports professional women's football teams in Los Angeles, Toledo, Dallas, Detroit and "supposedly Cleveland, New York, and Buffalo" (Summer, 1973, p. 19). And international soccer for women is thriving.

There is no end to the contemporary chronicle of change in both the individual participation of women in sport and the collective phenomenon of women's sport, but there is a question as to the real social significance of these examples. It's true that *Sports Illustrated* reported that two women, Donna Buckley and Truda Gilbert, *finished* the AuSable Canoe Marathon, a 240-mile race [(August 27, 1973),

p. 36]. And women drag racers and ice hockey players consistently make the news. Women in professional track seem to be doing as well as the men are, but Denise Long, the Iowa basketball superstar who was drafted by the Golden Warriors in San Francisco, has had to give up her sport in frustration.

Questions about the importance of sport opportunities for women or of the significance of the phenomenon of women's sport simply cannot be answered in contemporary terms. There have been few attempts to study sport in relation to women in social views, and the ones that exist are clearly obsolete. It is apparent that some inroads have been made on the assumption that the word "sport" itself refers only to male behavior, and women in sport are more visible in the media.

Because the institution of education is somewhat less amorphous as a social construct than is the broad society, some of the issues about women in sport have been clarified within it.

## THE INSTITUTION OF EDUCATION

The women's movement has made phenomenal progress on many fronts in a few short years. Any individual has only to recall the stereotypes and conditions that both pervaded society and seemed either natural or necessary. At the same time that strong efforts for change have been directed toward such social issues as abortion, day care centers, equal employment, and a multitude of sexist attitudes and practices, the institution of education has also been a primary target.

In education, three major concerns have seemed primary. The first of these rests on recognition of the fact that sexual stereotyping persists in relation to socialization. Since young girls and women are exposed to information and experiences containing the vivid message that women are less able and inferior human beings, they internalize those norms and blindly accept the accompanying subservient social roles. The fact that boys and men are similarly socialized compounds the existing social reality of women's lack not only of power and status, but also of full human dignity and worth. Although not at issue here, interesting and substantive investigations and challenges have been made in terms of: the way women are portrayed in literature, including textbooks; how women are tested and counseled in relation to vocations and life goals; the role models that are provided for women; and when and how females are segregated from males.

Not unrelated to socialization, the second concern has focused on the actual equality of educational opportunities and experiences for girls and women. The assumed lesser importance and status of women has fostered a pattern of education in which boys and men are encouraged to have high aspirations and the resources of education are used to facilitate their pursuit of them. The Citizen's Advisory Council on the Status of Women identified the areas in which discrimination was most likely to exist and stated:

> *Physical education, sports, and other extracurricular activities.* This is an area where discrimination is most pervasive and most readily apparent. Per capita expenditures on these activities by sex are an objective measure of the discrimination. Principals and teachers sometimes discourage an interest in participation in sports by girls. Facilities as swimming pools, tennis and basketball courts are generally far less available, measured on a dollar per capita basis of interested participants, to girls than boys. In addition, coaches of girls' sports are rarely supplied and if available are often not included in policymaking committees. . . . The opportunity for achievement in sports, scholarships and other recognition for ability in sports and for developing a competitive spirit within a framework of team cooperation should be available to girls.*

Related to the concerns for socialization and equality, the third major thrust in education has had to do with the status of women as that concept relates to significance. *The New York Times* reported that the State Board of Regents (which consists of fourteen men and one woman) charged that the educational system was "clearly responsible for perpetuating discriminatory attitudes towards women," and had ordered an end to abuses. Although women "made up 58.7 per cent of the professional staff of the public schools, only 21 per cent of all elementary school principals and about 3 per cent of the senior high school principals were women" (May 14, 1972). The national figures vary slightly; women, for instance, constitute 84.7 percent of elementary school teachers but only 19.4 percent of supervisory principals (Citizen's Advisory Council on the Status of Women, 1972). The situation in higher education is not very different. *The New York Times*

---

* From Citizen's Advisory Council on the Status of Women, *Women in 1972*, p. 3. Washington, D.C.: U.S. Government Printing Office, May, 1973.

reported that on college and university faculties, males are two and a half times more likely to become full professors and two and a half times more likely to earn more than $10,000 (October 8, 1972).

## Litigation and Education

*The New York Times* credited Bernice Sandler of the Project on the Status and Education of Women of the Association of American Colleges with initiating the counterattack to the status of women in higher education by writing a single letter of complaint (January 10, 1972). Some hundreds of complaints have since been filed, either by individuals, or by WEAL (Women's Equity Action League). Most of the complaints of discrimination in education are filed as class actions, which means they are complaints by groups, rather than individuals. The advantage of class actions is that the decisions resulting from them apply to all the members of a group. Furthermore, a showing of a pattern of discrimination can be brought in as evidence in support of a class action.

Initially, existing civil rights legislation was simply applied in education. Amendment 11375 of Executive Order 11246 expressly barred discrimination against women by all federal contractors and specified the requirement for affirmative action plans. The Equal Employment Opportunity Act of 1972 extended coverage of Title VII of the Civil Rights Act of 1964 to educational institutions, and empowered individuals and the EEOC to file suit to compel a school to increase its numbers of women whether or not the school receives federal funds. Under the EEOA, individuals can file complaints against any institution, and if a finding of discrimination is made by the EEOC, either the Commission or individuals may file suit in a Federal District Court on behalf of either the individual or a class of individuals.

One of the most significant legislative advances for women was the passage of Title IX of the Education Amendments of 1972, which states:

> No person in the United States shall, on the basis of sex, be excluded from participation in, be denied the benefits of, or be subjected to discrimination under any education program or activity receiving Federal financial assistance.

J. Stanley Pottinger, Director of the Office for Civil Rights of the Department of Health, Education, and Welfare pointed out that "These laws, Regulations, and Guidelines underscore the growing recognition

in our society that discrimination still exists and must be remedied."
He also pledged that when the Guidelines for Title IX were available,
HEW would both help those in education fulfill their responsibilities
and enforce the law when they didn't (DHEW, December, 1972).

Perhaps, the series of events that transpired in Pennsylvania best
illustrates the effect on education of the legal context. The equal rights
amendment to the Pennsylvania Constitution was approved in May,
1971. In the same month, a coalition of women's and feminist groups
formed an organization known as Pennsylvanians for Women's Rights
(PWR). Having gathered broad support, this group met with the Governor on May 21, 1971, and by June he distributed Executive Order No.
13, which stated that a "major effort will be exerted to end discrimination against women . . ." On June 15, 1971, the PWR met with the
Pennsylvania Department of Education (PDE) and the Pennsylvania
Human Relations Commission (PHRC), and a Joint Task Force on
Sexism in Education was set up. In August, 1972, the new Secretary
of Education published and distributed the report of the Joint Task
Force, *Sexism in Education,* and on August 30, 1972, sent the following letter:

Subject:   Sexism in Education

To:        University and College Presidents and Deans
           State-owned and State-related

From:      John C. Pittenger
           Secretary of Education

I have committed the Department of Education to making the
elimination of sexism in education a priority. This is in accordance
with the amendment to Article I of the Constitution of the Commonwealth and in keeping with the policy of Governor Milton J.
Shapp, as set forth in Executive Directive 13, which states, "A
major effort will be exerted to end discrimination against all
minority groups and women. . . ."

In order to meet this commitment, I hereby request that you
make plans immediately to carry out the policies embodied in the
Constitutional Amendment and in Executive Directive 13 as
follows:

1.    Eliminate sex-segregated classes, programs, activities
      and courses of study.

2.  Eliminate special rules for women or men (housing, hours, athletics, jobs, etc.)

3.  Establish the same admission qualifications for women and men except where these are shown to discriminate against women or men.

4.  Library and course materials should include information on women, presentation of women role-models and feminist perspectives of history, psychology, sociology, politics, economics and law.

5.  Annual goals be set for hiring, training and promoting women of all races and all ages at every level of employment.

6.  Develop women's studies as an integral part of the curriculum.

I recommend that you develop programs such as the following to implement these policies:

1.  Child Care/Development Programs for children of staff, faculty and students, with costs according to ability to pay.

2.  Staff and faculty should reflect the same balance by sex and race in each job class at all employment levels (including administration) as the Commonwealth's general labor force.

A similar letter was sent to all Chief School Administrators and Intermediate Unit Executive Directors on September 5, 1972. Although this procedure would seem to be an exemplary one, it was facilitated by the passage of the State equal rights amendment, and the organizing of women on the state level in response to that. In the late fall of 1973, the Attorney General of Pennsylvania, acting on behalf of the Commonwealth, brought suit against the Pennsylvania Interscholastic Athletic Association with reference to its rule barring girls from practicing or competing with boys. This was the first suit filed under a state equal rights amendment.

A similar chain of events occurred in Michigan, specifically in relation to the Ann Arbor Public Schools, as a result of the efforts of a group of women in the city who formed The Committee to Eliminate Sexual Discrimination in the Public Schools, and submitted a report, *Let Them Aspire! A Plea and Proposal for Equality of Opportunity For Males and Females in the Ann Arbor Public Schools* (Federbush, 1973).

Originally submitted in May, 1971, the third edition of this report summarizes a number of significant gains that were made in response to it. Of the forty-seven specific aspects of discrimination covered by the Ann Arbor study, thirteen are intrinsic to physical education and athletics. These women documented such things as: high school coaching for men accounts for 608% above salary, an equivalent of six salaries, while even when all women's extracurricular activities are lumped together, the total is 88% of *one* salary; that athletic financing, not including coaching, includes a budget of $68,025 for boys, and one of $6,296 for girls in high school, with the same inequity appearing in the junior high schools; and that a host of other inequities are apparent in terms of awarding credit, faculty load, scheduling, use of facilities, and so on. The gains reported in the third edition of this report (1973) did not refer to physical education or sport, but it was pointed out that the regulations of the Michigan High School Athletic Association had been listed as "recommendations" in the 1972-73 Handbook as a result of legislation and court action.

## Litigation and Sport

As the status of women and sport is examined in education, and especially with reference to the legal frameworks for change, it becomes evident that if such consideration were restricted to the collegiate level, there would be very little to consider. Generally, the area of women in sport has been neglected because of the lack of social emphasis on both of these concerns. As the demand for equality for women reaches a crescendo, however, it becomes apparent that the lack of attention to women's sport must relate to a dearth of advocates. Women in higher education in general have been the most articulate group with reference to discrimination, and a most aggressive group in pursuing equality. Women in sociology documented the discrimination against them in an issue of *American Journal of Sociology* (January, 1973), later published as the book, *Changing Women in a Changing Society*. Such statements were also issued by the American Historical Association (1971) and the American Political Science Association (1969-71). The Association for Women Psychologists demonstrated at the 1969 APA Convention and forced placement booths that were discriminating against women to close. They issued a statement, "Psychology and the New Woman" in 1970. It seems incredible that the women in higher education in sport and physical education have not been the most effective of all women activists in combating sexism and discrimination. Perhaps the discrimination was not even recognized in these fields since so much professional effort had been expended in keeping activities separate and different from the programs for men.

Most of the litigation that initiated change has occurred at the high school level. Collegiate sport, however, has been responsive to change, and in some cases, changed conditions have preceded legal challenges.

**One of the first questions raised through litigation was whether or not girls could compete as members of boys' teams.** Obviously, the legal petition is in terms of equality of opportunity; the extension of constitutional rights to women. The litigants in cases involving the right to play on boys' teams have usually been girls interested in a particular sport for which no girls' team existed. When The New York State Education Department instituted a sixteen-month experiment permitting girls to compete as members of boys' teams in noncontact sports in which no comparable opportunity for girls existed as of 1969, a law that had been in existence since 1916 prohibiting girls from interscholastic competition was thereby invalidated. On March 27, 1971 the experimental procedure became law and permitted coed competition in archery, badminton, bowling, fencing, golf, gymnastics, riflery, shuffleboard, skiing, diving, table tennis, tennis, track and field, and rowing—but only as coxswain because it was said rowing was too strenuous for girls (*New York Daily News*, March 27, 1971).

In a ruling that became effective on July 1, 1973, the California Interscholastic Federation allowed all high school sports teams to be coeducational, and stated that "coaches will still make the decisions on who is most skilled and who should play" (*Philadelphia Inquirer*, April 23, 1973). During the 1973 season, at least two girls played on a football team in California.

Between the New York and California rulings, there was a lot of discussion, some changed legislation, several court cases, and more athletic opportunities for women. California, Connecticut, Florida, Indiana, Iowa, Michigan, Minnesota, Nebraska, New Jersey, New Mexico, New York, and Nevada have all changed their regulations to permit girls to play as members of coeducational teams. One suit on behalf of the right of a girl to play on boys' teams was lost in Illinois, and it is generally believed that the deciding evidence was the testimony of a woman physical educator to the effect that such a ruling would be detrimental to athletics for girls.

**Lawsuits have also been won with reference to other specific rights of women in sport.** The Iowa Girls High School Athletic Union had a rule barring girls associated with marriage or motherhood from playing in union-sanctioned events. A former girls all-state basketball player, Jane Rubel, mother of an 11-month-old girl (and married) filed suit and the rule was repealed (*The New York Times,* November 21, 1971). The Citizen's Advisory Council on the Status of Women reported two related cases. In *Davis* v. *Meek,* Ohio, preliminary injunction was granted to a married student who was denied participation in extra-curricular activities on the grounds that the rule was an invasion of privacy. The Council commented, "While this is not a sex discrimination case, some of the language in the opinion might be useful in sex discrimination cases involving sports." In *Holt* v. *Shelton,* Tennessee, the school board rule prohibiting married high school students from extracurricular participation was held to be unconstitutional (September, 1972). Brenda Feigen Fasteau, an attorney, referred to a ruling in New Jersey that "makes clear that outstanding female athletes receive opportunities for training and competition at their ability level." She stated further that lawsuits have been won in Louisiana and Oklahoma (*Ms.,* July, 1973, p. 58).

**Other litigation, though not directed at women in sport, affects programs in both sport and physical education.** Though not properly "litigation," legislation is obviously a related aspect of the problem, and frequently is a concomitant to the positions expressed in lawsuits. The Women's Educational Equity Act, for instance, introduced in the House by Patsy T. Mink, would provide funds specifically for nonsexist curriculums and materials, including sports education and other programs designed to achieve educational equality for all students, regardless of sex.

Court actions in several states have challenged the constitutionality of programs that are either sex segregated, available only to one sex, or unequal for the two sexes. Although there are similar bases for the litigation that evolved with reference to girls playing as members of boys' teams, these cases are slightly different in that the rulings affect existing programs and the regulations surrounding them. Obviously, successful litigation in this aspect of school programs will facilitate the development of athletic and physical education programs for girls and women.

## Change at the College Level

As indicated, most of the change that has occurred in collegiate programs has seemed to be a result of the legal and legislative gains won by high school athletes. It is difficult to assess the seriousness of some aspects of change. Differences between men and women in athletic ability are more pronounced at the college level, and, therefore, perhaps women are more likely to be satisfied with their own programs and perhaps men are more willing to admit them to theirs, knowing that not more than one or two outstanding women athletes could ever be involved. In the context of women competing as members of men's teams, there have been some apparently successful coeducational efforts, and a few situations that were probably designed to be more humorous than serious. There are other evidences of change, however, in the new roles that women are playing in men's sport, and in a few new visions for women's sport. Finally, there is the unalterable change in the structure of women's sport that is symbolized by the change in policy with reference to athletic scholarships. Each of these aspects of change at the collegiate level is discussed in terms of some of the examples that clarify and document it.

**Women have assumed roles in what were previously "men's" sports as both players and administrative personnel.** The Seton Hall University football club elected a woman president in 1971. Ellen O'Kane handled all of the administration of the club efficiently as well as its public relations; in fact, Howard Cosell devoted a radio show to Seton Hall football and its club president (*Star-Ledger*, November 11, 1971, p. 41). While Harvard was debating whether or not to award a letter to the woman manager of its ski team in 1971, Bucknell University did award one to Valerie J. Kiernan, the first woman manager of a Bucknell varsity team (*The New York Times*, April 18, 1971). Another track team was also managed by a woman, Joyce Aschenbrenner of Drew University (*The New York Times*, April 23, 1973). These women all fulfilled duties in relation to the sport itself as well as its administration. Alice Casimiro, who managed the varsity baseball team at Drew University in 1972, was also in charge of keeping computerized statistics for both the baseball and the basketball teams (*The New York Times*, April 2, 1972, p. 6).

The Eastern College Athletic Conference ruled that women could play on men's teams in the fall of 1972. Hunter College endorsed that possibility, and Marina Cohen, who had been the manager of the swimming team, and Kim Piker, a freshman, both made the squad (*The New York Times,* January 28, 1973, p. 6). Presently, there are numerous examples of women competing on swimming and tennis teams.

Debbie Lee played number one for the Yale University junior varsity polo team (*Sports Illustrated,* February 7, 1972), and Cornell University fielded a woman's ice hockey team (*Philadelphia Inquirer,* February 27, 1972, p. 10-D), while at Lehman College, Janet Goodman played as the only woman on the varsity ice hockey team (*The New York Times,* January 28, 1973, p. 6).

Because they are popular men's sports, perhaps, the greatest uproar seems to attend women playing on varsity baseball and basketball teams. When Ray Blake put a woman into the lineup of the San Bernardino Valley College basketball team early in 1973, it received widespread attention in the media. The incident was rendered especially noteworthy because the San Diego team, behind 114-85, elected to leave the court rather than play a team with a woman on it. Ray Blake was quoted as saying, "I'll stoop to anything to win" (*Pocono Record,* February 9, 1973). Although women have not seemed to endure very long on baseball and basketball teams, coed touch football clubs and intramural programs seem to be thriving in many institutions.

Women may begin to serve as faculty members in administrative posts in athletics. Women have, of course, been chairpersons of combined physical education departments, but somehow Joni Barnett's appointment as Yale University's Director of Physical Education was hailed as a breakthrough for women. She commented, "There really isn't a more masculine job. I am honored" (*Sunday Record,* February 18, 1973, p. 99). Columbia University hired Libby Keefer as the first woman assistant in the athletic department, and assigned her as director of the tennis club at Baker Field (*The New York Times,* January 9, 1972). Massachusetts Institute of Technology appointed Mary-Lou Sayles as assistant professor of athletics with a top priority of increasing the number of women's sports (*The New York Times,* August 26, 1973, p. 15). In the fall of 1973, women were appointed to similar posts in many institutions.

**Women's sport has also changed somewhat in the colleges.** Most obviously, the changing perceptions of women's possibilities has broadened. Cornell women were able to request an ice hockey team. Williams College and the University of Oregon had female coxswains for their crews, which was the first departure from a completely masculine norm for that intercollegiate sport in more than a hundred years, except for the fairly protected version of crew at Wellesley. Women's intercollegiate crew developed quickly and women's crew was scheduled as an Olympic event for 1976. There are a number of colleges with women's crews, and some clubs and high schools as well; fifteen colleges were represented at the New England women's championship in 1973, including Wellesley.

Women are competing more and being more casual about the nature of the competition. Although not usually under the direct auspices of collegiate sport, college-age women are entering open competitions in many sports, and frequently in competition with men. Canoe racing, distance running, riflery and skeet shooting, as well as a varied array of hiking and climbing activities, are among those in which women are represented. In addition, college women are taking part in skiing, surfing, soccer, and other sports available in competitive structures outside the colleges.

It is very difficult to know the extent to which programs have really been influenced or altered by women with changed perceptions of themselves and of the possibilities or freedoms they should have. As early as January 9, 1970, *The New York Times* reported that women demonstrated against an all-male karate class at the University of California, Berkeley. They were identified as "militant feminist Women's Liberation" members, and it is likely that they were. In *The New York Times* of January 28, 1973, however, it was simply reported that "ten Cornell University coeds staged a protest in the nude over regulations at the University swimming pool." It seems apparent that this was newsworthy only because the girls took off their swimming suits, but they did win the right to nude swimming. In a serious protest by women at Boston State College in February, 1973, they took over central offices for fifty-two hours until administrators promised that their demands would be given every consideration. These demands included "space for a women's center and a day care facility, elimination of alleged salary discrepancies between men and women . . . equalization of athletic expenditures between physical education programs for men and women . . ." (*The New York Times,* February 18, 1973).

**Some of the changes in collegiate sport have implications for rather drastic change in the structure of programs and/or patterns of participation.** The American Association of State Colleges and Universities surveyed its membership in August, 1971, and received 130 returns.

The results generally indicated that there was some sentiment toward limiting athletic programs, abolishing athletic grants, and controlling athletic policies, but the greatest agreement was evidenced as follows:

> Students at some of the AASCU institutions are requesting intercollegiate programs for women. If student fees are used to support men's intercollegiate athletics, they ought to be used to support women's intercollegiate athletics as well.

| | |
|---|---|
| Agree | 103 |
| Disagree | 18 |
| Not Sure | 9 |
| Total | 130 |

At the convention of the American Association for Health, Physical Education and Recreation in Minneapolis, April 13 through 17, 1973, the subject of "women in sport" was an extremely significant and controversial one. Several speakers on the topic, however, did suggest that equality of opportunity and expenditure in women's athletics was a viable goal. DGWS published many of these papers in a booklet, "Women's Athletics—Coping with Controversy."

Many issues about both education and women and sport converge around the questions of intercollegiate programs of competition for women. In the December, 1972 issue of AAHPER's *Update,* it was stated:

> Men coaches and athletic directors who have been questioned by *Update* on the subject of girls athletics all indicate a desire to be helpful. They say, and we believe them, that their concern is to help the women to avoid the mistakes they made which sometimes caused grief and a lot of work to correct (December, 1972, p. 7).

*Sports Illustrated* quoted Mary Rekstad, "AIAW's lone executive," to a similar effect in the first of their articles on women in sport, but then commented:

> On the surface the concern of the admittedly corrupt men for the purity of their female counterparts seems more hilarious than touching—something like a confirmed alcoholic guzzling all the booze at a party to protect the other guests from the evils of drink (May 28, 1973, p. 92).

The actual changes in program are discussed in the final section of this chapter, "Women *in* Sport," but the consideration with the most far-reaching implications is the change in the policy toward athletic scholarships. The long-standing position of the Division for Girls and Women's Sports was stated clearly in a discussion of the formation of the Association for Intercollegiate Athletics for Women in the publication of the National Association for Physical Education of College Women as follows:

> AAHPER's Division for Girls and Women's Sports is on record against the awarding of athletic scholarships, financial awards, or financial assistance designated for women participants in intercollegiate sports competition. Such awards impose undesirable pressures and have been a means of control by those who can offer the greatest financial inducement, leaders believe (*Spectrum*, November, 1971).

It must be pointed out that not all physical educators have subscribed to the policies of DGWS or those of the various committees and commissions that regulated collegiate competition before the AIAW was formed. In many states, high school personnel have chosen to adopt the policies of the state high school athletic associations rather than those of DGWS, and this has meant playing under different rules. In the current atmosphere of change, colleges, too, have sought other alternatives, and there has been the suggestion that given some of the attitudes expressed by DGWS and AIAW, women's sport would be better off under the regulation of the NCAA and the NAIA. The most unkind comment that some women have fostered is that "DGWS has always stood for 'Don't Give Women Sports'." There is also no clarity about what the scholarship situation for women has really been throughout the past decades. It is quite apparent that there have been athletic scholarships for women, and these were proliferating. It was the advent and success of AIAW national championships, however, that made this a real issue; for AIAW policies prevented the participation of women from institutions that granted athletic scholarships.

The facts of the legal challenge to the existing policies of DGWS and AIAW have been well documented in many publications. The suit was filed in United States District Court for the Southern District of Florida by a number of students who were recipients of athletic scholarships in tennis at Marymount College as well as the director of physical education and the school's tennis coach. The case was referred to as *Kellmeyer* v. *NEA,* though Kellmeyer was only one of the litigants, and the defendants named were actually the NEA, AAHPER, DGWS,

AIAW, NAPECW, FAPECW, Florida Commission of Intercollegiate Athletics for Women, and Southern Association for Physical Education of College Women. The leaders of the organizations involved, members of the AAHPER staff, and members of the NEA legal staff met in Washington, D.C. as a committee on February 6, 1973, by which time the NEA legal counsel had investigated the situation. In a one-hour conference call on February 13, 1973, including Carl Troester, Mary Rekstad, Joel Gewirtz (NEA Counsel), Barbara Forker, Betty Hartman, and Carole Oglesby, it was decided to accept the recommendations of the NEA legal counsel, and procedures for disseminating information were established. The position stated by Joel Gewirtz (1973) was concluded with the following statement:

> . . . The legal climate is ripe for such litigation, and now is the time when your organizations must face the practical consequences of their rules. However noble the purpose of the DGWS scholarship statement, I believe that a court, when properly confronted with the question, would find that it operates discriminatorily and illegally. I therefore urge you to begin whatever procedures are necessary for changing your rule so that when defendants must finally file their answer in the *Kellmeyer* litigation they can declare that no discrimination exists under the rule which will then be in effect.

In the May, 1973 issue of *Update,* a revised philosophical statement and new interim regulations were printed in full. A statement, which appeared unsigned in *Update,* and as a letter signed "AIAW" in the Summer, 1973 issue of *The Sportswoman,* suggested that:

> . . . the consciousness of women as to their rights and privileges has been raised, and the whole theory of protecting women from exploitation, of paternalistic action "for their own good" has been a casualty of the student movement and the women's rights movement (p. 30).

The documentary of changing status for women and women's sport is an ongoing one. It is clear that all of the elements of women's present status are undergoing transition. At the same time, the contemporary situation does foreshadow the trend of future developments. The shape of the future is not clear, but it is appropriate to examine contemporary status in terms of women *in* sport as a possible clue to the effects that change will have.

# WOMEN IN SPORT

The conventional wisdom about women in sport abounds, and there are counterthemes about girls and women who are athletes as well. Insofar as ideas or images of the American woman in sport are part of a social commentary, they are included in Chapter 7. The focus here is on the intrasport status of women and the realities of sport in the context of social milieu and social situation for women. The major thrust of consideration revolves around the institution of education, and there has been no attempt to delineate concern with sport in relation to society separately. In fact, as the institutions of both education and sport are increasingly vulnerable to broad social effects, a conception of synchronous social change seems to characterize the interactive relationship of sport, society, and education. This precludes traditional sociological analysis based on a concept of "lag." It also mitigates the importance of the results of formalized sociological study. Contemporary analysis concerned with the social views and status of women *in* sport suggests that each year of the 1970s may constitute an historical period wherein specific events or data are either potential confirmation of the past or evidence of incipient social *dis*continuity.

## The Sport Context

It is tempting to adopt a linear view of the changes that are occurring and have occurred within the context of sport for women. To do that, however, assumes that each aspect of the context is affected singularly, and this is obviously not the case. All of the issues and controversies and modifications in sport for women are related to each other, and to social views of both woman and sport as well. In fact, much of the existing literature that treats women in sport is misleading in that it fails to take cognizance of all the aspects of change represented in the interactive syndrome of events and views. For whatever reasons, the professional ideology espoused by DGWS and the various Commissions that preceded it, as well as the AIAW, did retain a conservative attitude toward sports programs. The trend toward liberalizing this point of view is apparent in its historical chronology, but the successful challenge of the scholarship policies made it clear that change in events had outdistanced changes in philosophy to the point where litigation became the impetus for changing attitudes, or, at least, legitimized attitudes that may have been prevailing ones.

As reported in the May, 1973 issue of *Update* and in *The Sportswoman,* in a poll on whether the existing DGWS statement on scholarships for women students should be changed, eighty percent of the member institutions of AIAW voted "yes." This datum is confounded by the fact that litigation had already been instituted and people may have been expressing an acceptance of a "changing world" rather than the "consciousness" referred to by *Update.* The statement, too, managed to incorporate a whole commitment to the fact that "the prevention of possible abuses in the awarding of athletic scholarships to women can be accomplished more appropriately by the strict regulation of such programs than by the outright prohibition of such forms of financial assistance." In a letter published in *The Sportswoman* (September-October, 1973), Fran Koenig, Chairman [*sic*] DGWS stated that member schools had voted to accept the modification of the scholarship policy, "*only* because they realized it was not *legally* tenable . . ."

**The situation that developed in New Mexico is a good example of the complex aspects of change in women's sport contexts.** The ingredients of the situation were: a paucity of sport opportunities for girls in high school; the enrollment of Cathy Carr, winner of two gold medals in the Munich Olympics, in the University of New Mexico; the award of the Bell Scholarship to Cathy Carr by the University for its own public relations purposes; the Albuquerque American Civil Liberties Union; and the fact that Linda Estes was the Director of Women's Intercollegiate Athletics at the University of New Mexico. New Mexico also passed an equal rights amendment to the state constitution that took effect in July, 1973.

As early as November, 1971, an article appeared in the *Albuquerque Journal* citing the American Association of State Colleges and Universities poll, and stating that, "With nearly unanimous agreement, the presidents felt that women should be permitted to take a greater part in the overall college athletic program" (November 14, 1971). If Ferrel Heady was one of those who agreed, he fulfilled his commitment. Beginning in the spring of 1972, Linda Estes, Director of Women's Intercollegiate Athletics, and the first woman member of the Athletic Council, began bombarding Heady, President of the University of New Mexico, with the evidence of inequities in the men's and woman's programs and with increased budget requests. The Athletic Council proposed a substantial increase in the budget for women's intercollegiate sports for the year, 1973-74, after the budget requests for 1972-73 were not honored. The budgets for men's and women's sports at the University of New Mexico reflect the differentials that exist in most of the country in expenditures, and certainly were among those that give women favorable consideration. The women's program was budgeted $9,150 for 1970-71 and $9,350 for 1971-72. The men's program received student fee allocations and state appropriations totaling $527,000 in 1970-71 and $200,000 in state appropriations alone in 1972-73.

In December, 1972, President Heady made national headlines by stating that he had set as a top priority the expansion of women's athletic programs, "even if it means a cutback in some areas of men's athletics." *Sports Illustrated,* commenting on these events and the fact that the budget for women's sports had increased from $9,300 to $35,000 for 1973-74, also quoted three men from the University of New Mexico. The athletic director was quoted as saying, "I think it's fine, but I'm going to battle anything that will take money away from our own program." The football coach said, "I'm all for supporting women's athletics, but there must be someplace to draw the line on fiscal responsibility," and the basketball coach referred to women "dipping into my pocket ever since I learned about them on a farm in Indiana" (December 25, 1972). Since it also referred to doing "everything we can to keep them happy," *The Sportswoman* deemed this last a "heartwarming statement" (Spring, 1973, p. 5).

In the meantime, Linda Estes was active in a matter being handled by ACLU cooperating attorneys, Roberta Ramo and Robert P. Tinnin, concerning a female golfer and a female tennis player who had asked the NMAA to change their rule so that they might compete on varsity teams. The State Board of Education heard testimony and, confronted with the threat of litigation, ruled on January 4, 1973 that where there was no "comparable competitive opportunity" for girls, high school girls could compete with boys on interscholastic teams in noncontact sports. Some twenty girls did participate on coeducational varsity teams by May, 1973, but interscholastic tournaments for girls were also held for the first time in four sports—basketball, track, golf, and tennis (with the exception of basketball, all sports in which girls had successfully played on boys' teams). In addition, the NMAA decided to hire a woman staff member. In Hobbs, New Mexico, the high school had interscholastic competition in gymnastics for girls. For the year 1973-74, competition in tennis, softball, basketball, gymnastics, volleyball, and track was scheduled for girls in Hobbs and the Athletic Director, Gene Wells, stated that the program was the result of "legal action brought by female athletes . . . who had sought to compete on boys' interscholastic teams." Three female coaches were hired by August, 1973, and some 125 girls were pre-enrolled in the program (*Albuquerque Journal,* August, 1973).

In November, 1972, Linda Estes wrote to Carole Oglesby, President of AIAW, asking for a ruling on the legality of Cathy Carr's scholarship. She pointed out that no woman faculty member nor anyone representing women's athletics at the University of New Mexico had ever discussed attendance at the University or competing with Cathy Carr, and the scholarship itself carried no restrictions or stipulations whatever. Lou Jean Moyer, Chairperson of the Ethics Committee of AIAW, responded on January 3, 1973 that Cathy Carr would be ineligible to compete in AIAW tournaments, but indicated that apparently because "ignorance is an excuse" the fact that no one knew the scholarship was being awarded meant that the University's membership in AIAW was not jeopardized (Letter, January 3, 1973).

Cathy Carr, the first athlete from New Mexico to win Olympic gold medals, withdrew her acceptance of the Bell Scholarship indicating that she did wish to compete in college, and the action of AIAW made headlines in New Mexico. Linda Estes responded to Lou Jean Moyer with the statement that, although it was her responsibility to see that the University of New Mexico did not violate AIAW policies, "I, personally, have no interest in promoting the AIAW standard which prohibits athletic scholarships for women. I think that particular standard amounts to blatant discrimination against women and I am opposed to anything that discriminates against women, no matter how well intentioned" (Estes, *Letter,* January 29, 1973). Estes made similar statements to the press, and with the cooperation of people in the University of New Mexico Law School was prepared to join the personnel of Marymount College in filing suit.

**Athletic scholarships for women became a reality immediately following the Kellmeyer case.** As might be expected, the University of New Mexico was mobilized to act, and in June, 1973, the *Albuquerque Journal* announced the awards to six high school graduates and two University of New Mexico students in a variety of sports and on a yearly basis. *The New York Times* reported on May 23, 1973, that the

University of Miami in Coral Gables, Florida had awarded five athletic scholarships to women during the past two weeks and had ten more to award to members of the incoming freshman class. The *Times* said:

> It is considered to be the first time a college with such a bigtime athletic stature has given an athletic grant to a woman. Certainly no other bigtime sports college has offered 15 women's athletic scholarships in one year (May 23, 1973).

The University of Hawaii is also approaching both the problems of budgets and scholarships under the leadership of Donnis Thompson, Chairwoman of the AAU Women's Track and Field Committee, a member of the United States Olympic Committee, and the Women's Athletic Director of the new Women's Athletic Department. According to *The Sportswoman,* campus channels were insufficient (the Athletic Director did not want to "weaken the men's program"), and the Women's Athletic Department was created by legislative action. Thompson decries the discrimination inherent in the men's program receiving $242,000 of state funds and $68,000 of student fees and women receiving none of these monies. She projects an incremental budget for women over the next five years to include, ultimately, sixty tuition waivers and several thousands of dollars in athletic scholarships (*The Sportswoman,* Summer, 1973, p. 26).

One of the most interesting scholarships was that announced by the University of Chicago. According to Mary Jean Mulvaney, Chairperson of the Women's Division of the Department of Physical Education, "With the increased emphasis on equality for women, the University administration thought that the athletic scholarships should, in turn, be equalized. Therefore, the scholarship was established for the 1973-74 school year." Three academic-athletic scholarships given in memory of Amos Alonzo Stagg were already available to entering male students; the Gertrude Dudley Scholarship for women was established according to similar criteria. In neither the case of the men nor the women is there any stipulation that the scholarship winners compete. The University of Chicago has a ratio of 3:2 of men to women, and two scholarships have been awarded to women. The two women, a swimmer from California and a volleyball, basketball, and softball player from Ohio, received full tuition, $2,825. There were forty-five scholarship applicants although the University of Chicago has no major program in physical education. The scholarships are renewable for three subsequent years, given good academic progress (*Letters,* August 1 and 15, 1973).

**The sport context is also affected with reference to the patterns of competition and participation that are emerging.** Audax Minor, who writes the column, "The Race Track" for *The New Yorker* made an interesting comment. He was describing the success of a filly named Desert Vixen, whose earnings for the season were already $167,048, and he said:

> As I was watching the Alabama, on television, the thought came to me . . . how much closer female horses are to "equal pay, equal rights" than their human counterparts. The stakes and handicaps have always been open to them, and they also have their own events, many as rich and important as you could ask, from which males are barred. What price women's lib? (August 20, 1973, p. 83).

Obviously, women in sport do not trust that this ideal situation can emerge for human females from the current controversies and problems.

In discussing the suit in Illinois in the fall of 1971 where several exceptional girls wanted to be permitted to play on boys' teams, *Update* commented, "Again, the responsible educators pointed out that the answer is better programs for girls," and went on to report that the secretary of the Illinois High School Association said "that opening up boys' teams to girls could result in no program at all for most of the girls" (December, 1972, p. 6).

Both men and women in sport are frequently disturbed by the issue of women playing on men's teams. On the one hand, feminism suggests that prohibiting such participation is illegal and sexist and that it is important to fight for the right of women to take part in any sport contexts. The alternative view is based on the recognition of the lesser athletic abilities of women and on the fear that programs for women will be hampered as long as sponsoring agencies can testify that they do not discriminate in offering opportunities, whether or not many women are actually able to compete. Since women and girls have been competing on male teams for a short time, it is difficult to assess the implications. Generally, however, programs for girls and women have improved quickly once coeducational varsity teams have been established.

In an editorial about the problem, *The Sportswoman* suggested that neither insistence on not distinguishing between the sexes nor commitment to total separation of the sexes was sufficient at this time. The editorial supported aggressive efforts toward equality in programs for men and women and concluded:

> By basing our demands for women to compete on men's teams as a temporary reparation until women's programs are comparable, we will not run the risk of having men taking over women's teams. We will also give those schools where the men's athletic director blanches at the thought of women on his teams a good incentive to make sure that school's women's program is built up quickly. Most important, we will be building up our women's programs to the quality they need and deserve without sacrificing our top female athletes (*The Sportswoman,* September-October, 1973, p. 6).

It has become apparent that there are more and more cases of men and women competing together, either as members of one team, or on separate teams in a kind of joint competition. The Spring Newsletter of the Department of Physical Education of the University of California, Berkeley reports that the men's and women's swimming teams held a coed meet in which there were men's and women's regular events and also two special eight-person relays, and that it was highly successful. Many institutions have found that running men's and women's gymnastic meets at the same time not only makes for a more interesting meet, but contributes to a more varied view of that sport. In fact, although usually restricted to the so-called "minor" sports, joint competitions are in evidence more and more, and seem to have increased spectatorship for both men's and women's events in the particular sports.

The "joint" approach may be a prelude to acceptance of the idea proposed by Marcia Federbush and endorsed by Brenda Fasteau in which an Olympic-style approach is used and men's and women's varsity teams *together* constitute the school's varsity team. This precedent has been established in international competition, though the United States has not always liked it. It seems clear that if men's teams were dependent on women's teams in terms of winning and losing, women would receive more encouragement.

Whether the actual scoring for teams is combined or not, establishing closer ties between men's and women's teams has obvious advantages in terms of travel, facilities, coaching, and so on. It isn't a simple issue, of course, but in the past, "separate" has meant inferior

for both women and blacks; on the other hand, equality is not ensured
by association, and women's programs may develop better on the basis
of affirmative action principles. In a humane view, it is appealing to see
U.S. men and women gymnasts competing with the Red Chinese
together, for instance, and it has not seemed to affect the sport adversely.

As women in sport seem less of a social anomaly there is also a
burgeoning of competitive structures for women's sport. Their participation with men, whether in terms of joint scheduling or combined
teams, has become commonplace and has been spurred on by such
important structures as the Olympics and World University Games. The
concept of the World Team Tennis League and the professional track
context serve to underscore these principles in professional sport. At
the same time, interscholastic, intercollegiate, and amateur competition
for women alone is also increasing. In some sports, there is presently a
choice for collegiate institutions between AIAW national tournaments
and AAU-sponsored tournaments, and further opportunities for
women to pursue sport may pertain to either structure. The women's
basketball team in the World University Games had players from AAU
and AIAW, and women's basketball will be in the 1976 Olympics.

Although the prevailing feminist view is that sport must be integrated, there are some subgroups that endorse the principle that women's
sport should be separate from men's and from men. A group of New
York feminists involved in the martial arts (karate, judo, aikido, and
other fighting systems) has formed the Women's Martial Arts Union.
It is believed that the organization will promote communications
among women in the martial arts throughout the country. This group
states that it hopes its members can "aid each other in finding ways to
fight the sexism found in most martial arts schools" (WMAU, *Statement*, Spring, 1973). The Lesbian Feminist Lib of New York sponsored
the first annual Women's Olympics on September 16, 1973. It was
initiated by LFL in conjunction with sports-minded feminists "to
demonstrate that an active interest in sports is not solely a 'masculine
pursuit,' " (*Lesbian Feminist*, August 25, 1973, p. 3) and it began with
several hundred women carrying a symbolic torch and wending their
way through the streets of New York to Riverside Park. Olympic events
included softball, volleyball, track and field, and other individual
events, all of which "utilize strength, grace and skill" (*Lesbian Feminist*,
p. 3). Actually, the events seemed a demonstration of *lack* of skill.

In contrast, perhaps, there is Miss Rodeo America, a professional contest that includes both beauty and horsemanship, and that held its fourth contest in Las Vegas in late 1972, with nineteen states and Canada represented (*Sports Illustrated,* December 11, 1972, p. 86). There is also an annual Miss Softball America contest held for the first time in August, 1972. Only eight states were represented, but the Foundation is operative in twenty-two states involving girls nine to fifteen years of age (*The Sportswoman,* Spring, 1973, p. 25).

## The Sportswomen

One of the most striking aspects of a changing view of women in sport is the numbers of women interested in sport and anxious to pursue it in all of its various contexts. Of the hosts of new programs developing on all levels in both social and educational contexts, only a small number have not experienced an overwhelming and unexpected response. A few years ago, the "sports camps" all over the country began considering the possibility of a one- or two-week session for girls, and found then and continue to find that the number of girls as well as scholastic teams that are interested in summer sport seems inexhaustible. The camps now offer a wide range of opportunities, and seem to have no effect on the numerous summer experiences available in hockey and lacrosse, which are also growing. Furthermore, many of the sponsors of these camps have commented that the girls are even more hard-working and dedicated athletes than boys.

**Although whatever personality studies of women athletes there are have suggested that women are serious competitors, the social view has generally discounted their dedication.** In a perspective that posits femininity as a social goal, this is a logical but undocumented view. The unfortunate social corollary of it is that if a woman is a dedicated athlete, she is probably unfeminine. In general, there is an unstated social assumption that for the good of girls and women, they must be restrained from devoting themselves to athletics and be encouraged to devote attention to social concerns. In a study of heterosexuality of women in physical education (1970), Locke and Jensen found little evidence that such women were not heterosexual; they did find that a time pressure existed for women physical education majors, especially since they were expected to participate in sport. The authors commented that "Conforming to such a substantial and pervasive time press undoubtedly affects the amount of time available for all avocational pursuits—men included." Landers (1970) found that physical education majors had significantly lower and less feminine scores than education majors on the MMPI and Gough Scale of Psychological Femininity, but further analysis indicated that the differences were on only two categories; i.e., Restrained and Cautious vs. Brag and Exaggerate, and Religious Beliefs. These kinds of data continue to be available, but they are usually reported only to the effect that athletes are "more masculine" than other groups. As Bardwick has pointed out, masculinity and femininity are social constructs primarily, and the instruments that measure them as traits are derived from sex-role stereotypes (1971).

The social situation is difficult for the woman athlete. Denise Long, whose lifetime average in basketball in Iowa was 69.6 points per game, with a high of 111 points, couldn't stand the semisocial, intramural aspect of the professional women's league in San Francisco. She stopped playing and commented:

> In our state finals, we had over 15,000 people screaming and jumping around in their seats. It was televised in nine states. Then I go to San Francisco where the only audience for the entire tournament is a handful of parents. I can't play basketball that way—I have too much respect for myself and the game. A team sport needs the support and the emotion of the crowd to make it exciting. Without that there is very little (*The Sportswoman*, Spring, 1973, p. 9).

Denise Long returned to Iowa where she is a student at the University.

The recent events that have been reported about Shane Gould, the Australian swimmer who won three gold medals at the 1972 Olympics, seem to explicate the social ambivalence that may accompany the sport involvement of women. In July, 1973, the sixteen-year-old swimmer announced her retirement saying that the necessary arduous training for swimming left her little time for studies or a social life. In August, her 100-meter freestyle record was broken by Kornelia Ender, a fifteen-year-old from East Germany. *The New York Times* reported on August 26, 1973 that Shane Gould had announced she would enter a meet in Sydney, held from August 31 to September 2 (p. 13). In December, 1973, she turned professional.

The social conflict between the desire to participate and achieve in sport and to fulfill appropriate feminine sex roles is believed to characterize the experience of women athletes. There are a host of assumptions implied by this belief, and many of the studies that provide the social data about women in sport are related to them. Much of the existing research is reviewed in the seven papers contained in the section, "Sociological Considerations" of *Women and Sport: A National Research Conference* (Harris, ed., 1972). There are a few hypotheses that seem most relevant to this view and should be considered in relation to the sportswoman.

In 1971, Harris reported on the differences between the social self and competitive self of the female athlete. Since the athletes did not differ from the average population in terms of "social self" and did present a significantly different view of themselves in competitive situations, Harris concluded:

> It appears that the athletic female must assume the role of the chameleon; she must be feminine or assume the socially acceptable role for the female in social situations. At the same time, if she desires to be successful in athletic competition, she must become more aggressive, dominant, achievement oriented and demonstrate more tough mindedness and endurance and be less afraid to take risks (1971).

Berlin found no relationship between "the ideal woman" and "the woman athlete" as perceived by female athletes (1973). Small found no differences in perceptions of the feminine role for self between female collegiate varsity athletes and nonathletes, but the groups did differ in perceptions of the feminine role for "the average woman" (1973).

Sportswomen are confronted with a variety of conceptions of sex-role standards, assumed social attitudes, and the fact of their own participation. Kratz (1958) reported that middle-class adult women, selected on the basis of their participation, generally viewed sports participation within their identity and status as women, and generally believed that women athletes did not deviate greatly from their ideas of American womanhood. They also believed, however, that men encourage and at the same time discourage women in sports participation and that women's participation was related to society's determination of the appropriateness of the sport. For both themselves and their daughters, these women identified the least acceptable sports as track, motorcycling, wrestling, softball, football, and billiards. Burris, Faust, and Felshin (1971) in a study of high school female varsity athletes found that these girls held more positive attitudes toward female athletes than did either female nonparticipants or boys; the athletes, however, projected the attitudes held by female nonparticipants and by boys to be both lower than their own and lower than they actually were.

In his discussion of sex-role standards, Cheffers (1973) reported case studies of women succeeding in certain masculine activities in track. His conclusions were that sex-role standards could be changed, although with reference to the experiences of Jean Roberts in weight training, he added that "it showed that sex role standards could be changed without loss of either femininity or dignity." Since Cheffers reported that it was the male weight lifters who had tried to embarrass the women by working out nude in the weight room, it isn't certain whose "dignity" needed to be retained.

The questions raised by these particular studies are confounding ones. Since research has not dealt with background factors nor with the adoption and classification of perceived sex roles with reference to women athletes, there are few clues to interpreting the data. It seems that women athletes do not differ from other populations in terms of views of themselves or of their own feminine roles. Although evidenced in personality research findings, studies that utilize social data have not found differences between athletes engaged in individual sports and those active in team sports. While athletes tend to assume that perceptions about them may not be positive, their own attitudes *are* usually positive.

On a commonsense level, it seems clear that women are familiar with the normative values associated with sex role. It also seems obvious that "appropriateness" as a behavioral construct is both specific and situational. It would not appear that the problem for the female athlete is how to maintain consistent attitudes and behavior in and out of sport; rather, the problem may be in the attractiveness of sport as a social phenomenon in relation to the desirability of a feminine view of the social construct of woman. It is probably safe to hypothesize that female athletes do most closely resemble successful women in terms of the kinds of background factors that have been identified in relation to so-called *contemporary* (as opposed to traditional) sex roles. If this be so, then a dichotomy between feminine goals and sports participation cannot be assumed for the athlete. In other words, the social anomaly of woman in sport may not be a pertinent hypothesis to apply in the case of the sportswoman, and may even suggest a social conflict that does not, in fact, exist.

## The Sport Situation

The social anomaly of woman in sport can be documented as part of the social commentary; it is a questionable hypothesis with reference to the sportswoman, and it is most likely irrelevant in the sport situation. Although not their focus, the studies cited show uniformity of results in their application to the sport situation. It seems that in sport the values and modes appropriate to the contest prevail. There is, of course, a dearth of research that pertains to women athletes in the sport situation, but as more findings emerge, they are likely to confirm the importance of values associated with the athletic subculture and situation.

This is not to suggest that male and female athletes necessarily express the same sociometric values, or that there may not be differences in interactive modes, but sport structures provide a compelling source of socialization themselves. The discriminating variable may be the choice of whether or not to *be* an athlete. A recent study of male and female collegiate athletes with reference to the variables concerned with becoming "psyched up" and "psyched out" found that both men and women identified indications of success, many times in the form of a teammate's performance, as the most important variable in becoming psyched up. Women differed from men, however, in becoming psyched out when subjected to "unfairness and slights." And whereas men were most affected overall by sources in self, women tended to give the greatest credence to others (Felshin, 1973).

Van Housen (1973) found no difference in collegiate men's and women's varsity basketball teams with reference to the relationships among perceived skill, sociometric standing, and passing interaction in games. Only the most successful men's and women's teams and the least successful women's teams had significant correlations between perceived skill and sociometric standing. It was found that the positions of players were an important variable affecting passing interaction for both men and women, which lends weight to the importance of the structure of the game as a social variable. Some factors of interest that were found incidentally by Van Housen were that women tended to give higher ratings than men, both on skill and sociometric ratings, and they also tended to receive more passes per minute. As men's and women's sports become more alike, these kinds of comparative studies can be pursued and may yield similar data.

If the prevailing social model for sport, which is male, is assumed to be the norm, the idea of an athletic role model may not be an appealing one. At the same time, if society is presumed to be the source for the socialization of sport, it is, perhaps, even less appealing. The role of women *in* sport, however, has yet to be really defined. In part, it is the social commentary that will affect the shape and direction of that definition.

Chapter 7

# Social Commentary

The social commentary about woman in sport derives from a variety of sources and reflects social views on a continuum from affirmation to denial of the social anomaly of woman and sport. All commentary refers to the social conceptions presented as part of the dialectic of woman and sport. Although the participation of women *in* sport is also a social comment, the focus here is on the amount and kind of attention given woman and sport, the kinds of images of woman and sport that are portrayed, and on the diverse attitudes and perceptions that are held and projected about woman and sport.

## COVERAGE AND ATTENTION

Sport is recognized in American society as a compelling aspect of behavior and social concern. The attention to sport evidenced in private lives, public domains, and the media suggests that sport is, indeed, one of the most significant social phenomena in the United States. Every aspect of sport is attended to in both outline and detail. The anomaly of sports coverage and attention is that the participation of women can serve to offset the importance of sport effectively. It would seem that the involvement of women renders sport completely uninteresting; if not, there seems to be a conspiracy to maintain the mythology of sport as an exclusively masculine domain. There are, obviously, some recent countertrends, but generally it is still true that if the evidence of coverage and attention to women's sport was used as the criterion, the conclusion would be that either only one or two outstanding women compete in sport at all, or that women do compete, but when they do, it is always in a nonserious and trivial way.

## Sportswriting

Sportswriting is a specialized focus within the field of journalism. As an approach to an analysis of the kind and extent of coverage of women in sportswriting, a basic text in the field, *Modern Sportswriting,* was analyzed. Published in 1969, this book was written by Louis J. Gelfand, a newspaperman and public relations specialist, and Harry E. Heath, director of the school of journalism at Oklahoma State University. Not only is the work in question the most comprehensive attention to sportswriting available, but Heath, particularly, must be assumed to influence the field, and to represent an educated viewpoint since he holds a Ph.D. degree from Iowa State University. He was also co-author of *A Guide to Radio-TV Writing,* and has written in the professional literature of journalism.

Gelfand and Heath devote no specific attention to women, nor is that a category in the index. This is a well-researched book, but of 268 bibliographical references, five were written by women, and seven co-authored by women. It is possible that some authors identified by initials were women, but it is doubtful. In the additional seventy-three listings of Sports Desk Reference Materials and General Journalistic Sources, women were not represented either as a focus or as authors (pp. 606-628).

There are thirteen human interest elements identified in the first chapter, and women are mentioned specifically only in the description of "sex." The paragraph includes the following comments:

> Some news pictures of female tennis players are chosen by desk-men primarily because they have more sex appeal than other pictures available. A press agent's staged photo of a busty movie queen in a low-cut dress giving an athlete a congratulatory kiss may provide sports page sex appeal (p. 13).

The format of this book rests on the presentation of some descriptive matter followed by numerous examples, all of which are drawn from actual published sportswriting. The first four and the last three chapters treat general concerns in sportswriting, and there are fifteen chapters devoted to the consideration of particular sports. The attention to women is consistent throughout.

Out of eighty-five examples of "leads" to news stories, there is one reference to a woman; John "Ox" DaGrosa was reported to be "bowing to his wife's wishes" in resigning as the Holy Cross Head Football Coach (p. 31). In a lengthy treatment of various kinds of "advance" stories, there were no references to women; nor were there any in the discussion and examples related to press relations (pp. 38-52).

Out of forty-five examples of "features," a humorous reference to a woman was included which involved a story about a woman with a cello entering a team's locker room by mistake, and saying, "EEEK! This isn't the right place," which had something to do with relieving a team's tension (p. 79). There was also a picture of a female bowler in this section, but no reference to women in the accompanying article (p. 101).

The twenty-two examples of "columns" included three references to women. One had to do with the use of detail, and involved a complicated story about a dinner party. There were such descriptions as: "O'Malley took a seat next to a lovely blonde in the company of Leo Durocher"; "Leo . . . kissed Mrs. Walter Alston . . . then, he kissed Mrs. O'Malley"; "Frank's wife, Carol, is a quiet, well-mannered lady who stands 5-feet-2 and weighs about 100 pounds" (p. 120). The second reference was simply a story included in a column that stated "A tactical victory is when your wife lets you go to the ball game; a strategic defeat is when she decides to go with you" (p. 131). The final reference involved the romantic interest described by a tennis player toward a female tennis player (p. 132).

In the treatment of the specific sports there were no references to women included for auto racing, baseball, boxing, football, gymnastics (except that an athlete was described as "married"), hockey (except that the Lady Byng trophy was mentioned), horseracing (except female horses), soccer, or wrestling. Of forty-one examples in the chapter on golf, there was one reference to a woman's tournament and one woman included in a score listing. There were four references to women in tennis, out of sixteen examples; two from *Sport's Golden Age* that referred to Helen Moody and Helen Jacobs, and the names of Althea Gibson and Sally Moore appeared in a statistical summary. One example out of fourteen in track and field included women; two out of nine in bowling; three out of twenty-one in swimming; three out of ten in skiing; one out of twelve in hunting and fishing, and a single paragraph out of seventeen related to women in softball (specific chapters, pp. 138-498).

In the final chapters of this book, eighty-eight examples were presented of news coverage in the treatment of "the desk job" and none of them mentioned women (pp. 499-540). The chapter that dealt with typography included thirty-five examples of complete sports pages (primarily from 1964-65). Perusal with a magnifying glass disclosed that these contained seven references to women, or approximately two percent of the coverage. Four of these were pictures, including one of a cheerleader and one of George Wilson with his wife and daughters, captioned, "Wilson and His Girls" (pp. 541-592).

In the final chapter, "Ethics," these authors state that the sportswriter should "be guided by fact and fairness, showing no prejudice because of race, religion, or personal emotional involvement" (p. 593). Later they conclude, "Fortunately, most sports reporters' sins are those of omission rather than commission" (p. 605).

This analysis has been reported at length because recent empirical data suggest that the situation has not really changed significantly in terms of the extent of coverage. Whether or not it is a sin, the omission of women from sports coverage in newspapers is impressive. A resolution passed by the House on August 2, and the Senate on August 3, 1973, designated August 26 as Women's Equality Day (*Women Today,* August 20, 1973). Although *The New York Times* did mention the feminist rally held in Battery Park on August 25, it did not mention Women's Equality Day in its edition of Sunday, August 26, 1973. Interestingly enough, extensive treatment, beginning on page one, was given to the first of a series of ten articles on black America, and to the signing of "Humanist Manifesto II."

In the sport section of the *Times* on Women's Equality Day, five percent of the articles and columns did treat women, but none of the reporting of scores did, so that the coverage amounted to 3.5 percent of the column space (*Sports,* August 26, 1973). The largest single article included pictures and testimony to Hazel Wightman, since tennis competition in the Wightman Cup tournament was in progress.

Although the extent of newspaper coverage of women's sport remains minimal, empirical data reveal that the presentation of women as "sex objects" inherent in the few references in *Modern Sportswriting* is no longer pervasive. This change is accounted for, partly, in the discussion of the images portrayed of women later in this chapter.

## Magazines

Miller and Russell reported that in the years 1954-67, *Sports Illustrated* estimated that it had included more than 200 stories and articles on women athletes and had featured them on forty-four covers (1971, p. 124). It remains for assiduous graduate students to apply the rigors of content analysis to *Sports Illustrated* and other magazines. Obviously, there is almost no attention to women in sport in magazines in general. The most significant coverage given women by *Sports Illustrated* was the three-part series that began on May 28, 1973 in an issue whose cover showed a female runner and the banner, "Women are Getting a Raw Deal." This excellent and comprehensive treatment of a great many aspects of women's sport by Nancy Williamson and Bil Gilbert seemed to crystallize a shift in attitude on the part of *Sports Illustrated.* It does not seem accidental that since these articles began, no issue has presented an all-male cast of "Faces in the Crowd" although that was not unusual in the past. The message to *Sports Illustrated* is exemplified by a letter that appeared in the June 11 issue that suggested the following considerations:

> In that same May 28 issue you lived up to the painful truths presented in the story of the raw deal women are getting in sports. To wit:
> 1) No other articles on women; 2) no women in FACES IN THE CROWD; 3) a picture of only one woman—not even an American—offered in your poster sale; and 4) unidentified photographs of the women athletes included in the article—not to mention the girl on the cover.
> Schools, universities, and television stations consider women athletes as "unsalable" and uninteresting to watch. Must you, too, only underscore their attitudes?
> Jan Nikolaides (1973, p. 128)

Actually, the coverage in *Sports Illustrated,* however minimal, has been about the best coverage of women available. Neither *Sports* nor *Black Sports* devotes much attention to women, and the particular sport publications all seem to follow a common policy in covering women once in a while in some kind of "special issue" or relegating their concerns to a separate section of coverage. This is not universally so, but occurs sufficiently to confirm the impression that women in sport are not quite the "normal" subjects. *Golf Digest,* for instance, followed this pattern in devoting a special twelve-page section to "The Liberation of the Woman Golfer" in July, 1972. The editorial statement confirmed the approach in reporting that The Simmons Audience Research Company had informed *Golf Digest* that twenty percent of their readers, some 360,000 per issue, were women. The conclusion to the editorial suggests that *Golf Digest* is committed to women golfers, and states:

> ... we not only have dedicated an important part of this issue to woman golfers, but also have proclaimed 'Woman Golfers Week.' ... hundreds of golf professionals and retailers across the country will join in the salute to the gender that has helped bring a broader vitality to the game (p. 6).

It is clearly assumed that the professionals and retailers are men, and, furthermore, it affirms only that some and specific attention need be directed to this "gender." A study by Kennard reported that *World Tennis* was the only magazine studied that had equal male-female representation and seemed to deal with women as athletes (1973).

Although Marie Hart did analyze the content of sport magazines for the period 1889-1965, she did not attend specifically to women in sport (1972, pp. 369-377). Two unpublished studies did focus on women, but with severe limitations in the scope of the consideration. McKenna (1972) analyzed the treatment of women in sport in *Time Magazine* for the years 1928, 1938, 1948, 1958, and 1968. He found that the largest number of articles appeared in 1948 and then declined, but that 1928 included more articles than did 1968. Women's coverage in the sport section of *Time Magazine* did not reach six percent in any of the years studied. Corrigan (1972) studied the coverage of women in *Sports Illustrated* in the years 1960, 1965, and 1970. Her findings (Corrigan, p. 9) were as follows:

| Year | Number | Number on Women | Percentage on Women |
|------|--------|-----------------|---------------------|
| | | Article pages | |
| 1960 | 1268 | 62 | 4.9 |
| 1965 | 1235 | 21 | 1.7 |
| 1970 | 1273 | 17 | 1.4 |
| | | Photographs | |
| 1960 | 2609 | 394 | 15.1 |
| 1965 | 1215 | 181 | 14.9 |
| 1970 | 1317 | 109 | 8.2 |

In keeping with a trend toward special interest magazines, the inaugural issue of the *Women's Sports Reporter* was published in February, 1970, and billed itself as "Women's First Sports Magazine." It did not survive, but a similar publication, *The Sportswoman,* was published first in Spring, 1973, and is still in existence. And Billie Jean

King initiated a magazine, *WomenSports,* in Spring, 1974. In addition, there are particular sport magazines for women, such as *The Eagle,* published by the USFHA, and *Crosse Checks,* published by the United States Women's Lacrosse Association, and others such as *The Woman Bowler* and *The Lady Golfer.* These, and professional publications in physical education, have organizational support, but their circulation is usually also limited to the membership, and their coverage tends to be specific.

## Television

The coverage and attention to women's sports by the television media has been widely decried. The analyses that have been done suggest that women do not receive even one percent of the sport coverage. The kind of attention that women in sport do receive is frequently in the context of news of the "dog bites man" variety. Apart from minimal coverage of women in the Olympic Games and the World University Games, the only programing of actual women's events has been a few scattered tournaments in tennis and golf. There has been some special attention to gymnastics and figure skating, but it is almost impossible to watch an entire competition involving women on television and almost impossible to avoid watching one involving men. One notable exception was a woman's football game shown locally in the New York City area in the fall of 1973.

## WORDS AND IMAGES

The process of socialization is a self-fulfilling prophecy for the individual. Merton, who originated the phrase, at least, suggests that, "The self-fulfilling prophecy is, in the beginning, a *false* definition of the situation evoking a new behavior which makes the originally false conception come *true*" (1968, p. 477). He has also said:

> The self-fulfilling prophecy, whereby fears are translated into reality, operates only in the absence of deliberate institutional controls. And it is only with the rejection of social fatalism implied in the notion of unchangeable human nature that the tragic circle of fear, social disaster, and reinforced fear can be broken (p. 490).

As long as the "unchangeable human nature" of women as passive, weak, unable, and subservient to men is accepted, social fatalism is defined in terms of their roles in serving men. The destiny of the woman, then, is seen in motherhood and homemaking; her worth depends upon the quality with which she performs these services, and her contribution to the social situation lies in being nice to look at and facilitating to the comfort of others.

In the absence of "deliberate social controls," the process whereby girls internalize the normative values associated with being "feminine" and prophesy their lives in relation to such values becomes a never-ending cycle. Cultural stereotypes begin to seem like unchangeable human nature, and it is logical, therefore, that all of the images projected as public and private definitions reflect them. Sex-role stereotypes don't have to relate to reality; as long as woman's role is idealized within the home, the fact that since 1971 more than half of even married women have worked can be discounted. And the "discounting" includes serious attention to the rights and equality of those women who do work.

The women's movement has been a significant force in combating sex-role stereotyping. For women, stereotyping has meant being inferior, and sexist images and practices have restricted the dignity and opportunity for women to pursue goals in relation to themselves. The contemporary thrust is toward fashioning "deliberate institutional controls" that would break the cycle of self-fulfilling prophecies. Toward this end, there have been a variety of attacks on the images of women projected by advertising, curriculum planning, legal restriction, common practice, or normal communication. Litigation, protest, institutional threat, consumer boycott, and the projection of antithetical images of women have also served to confuse the consciousness about sex role. The problem, however, is that there is ambivalence in both reality and attitudes. Bardwick and Douvan suggested that, "The socialization model is no longer clear; in its pure form it exists primarily in the media, less in life" (1972, p. 237). But in life, too, some women work and some women don't; some women resent being considered subservient to men, and some women believe that is their finest fulfillment. *The Ladies Home Journal,* in an article about Cristina Ford, described her as "the unpretentious individualist who has been married to one of the world's richest and most important men for eight years" (September, 1973, p. 80). In reply to the question, *"What do you think is the major problem of women today?"* Ford responded:

> The whole question of competing with men. A feminine woman *collaborates* with her man, tries to help him and be comfortable

with him, to relax him and to do all the things that a man needs (p. 8).

Cristina Ford also indicated that she bicycled every day, and skiied, and believed that women should flirt because "You feel feminine and pretty, and we women can flirt until we die" (p. 8).

## The Image of Woman

The social view recognizes the importance of individual socialization within the family and in relation to personality and other psychological variables, but its primary focus is on the social data as a source of norms and role orientations.

The women's movement, as an impetus for social change, has focused on the social experience. As the study of the institution of education indicated clearly, the effect of sexist attitudes in educational practice does not only serve to discriminate against women in terms of opportunities, but in terms of images as well. In other words, in both society and its particular institutions, it is important to oppose the biases that exist as restrictions to women's actual behavior and limitations on women's perceptions of possible behavior.

**Education has been an important focus for changing the image of women both because it is an important element in the socialization of youth and because it is vulnerable to attack as an institution responsible to ideal social values.** Although children's readers have provided one model for consciousness of sex stereotyping, they have not been the only focus for change. Women on Words and Images, a committee affiliated with NOW, studied 134 elementary school readers, and published the results of their study in a pamphlet, *Dick and Jane as Victims: Sex Stereotyping in Children's Readers* (1972). The study showed the presentation of boys as active and competent and girls as passive, docile, and dependent. Boys, in fact, were simply the subjects of stories five times as often as girls.

Similar studies of textbooks in all fields, the kinds of examples they use, the kind of history they purvey, the kinds of suggestions they present for life alternatives or bodily health or leisure time pursuits, all suggest an image of woman as unimportant and unable. In fact, in New York, the men's committee of NOW has taken on responsibility for working to change the prevailing images. If woman as "sex object" is objectionable and damaging as an attitude toward self and one's worth, so is the image of man as "success object."

The kind of bias against women and men in education that has been a focus for attention includes: single sex classes of all kinds, especially in areas where only one sex is permitted access to that aspect of the curriculum; counseling of students in terms of vocational or career choices; program areas that are obviously unequally developed for one sex or the other; textbooks and literature, and any rules and procedures that are applied differently because of sex.

In the colleges, there has been a great deal of attention to women's studies programs; two programs in 1970 became seventy-two in 1973, while 100 courses on sixty campuses became 2000 on 500 campuses (Howe, 1973, p. 46). The 108 items in the bibliography of Lora H. Robinson's research report for ERIC (1973) attest to the growing attention to women's studies.

**The media and advertising have been the primary targets in terms of the images of women that are portrayed.** The most direct attack on the media was for women to gain some control of information sources. Two major feminist presses have been exceedingly successful: The Feminist Press, and KNOW, Inc. As KNOW sometimes advertises, "Freedom of the press belongs to those who own the press." Together, these presses produce and reproduce a host of feminist materials, many of which are used in relation to women's studies courses. There is also a Women's Video Project, located in New York City, that produces programs of interest to women and disseminates them on the public access channels and in closed-circuit presentations both in New York and throughout the country. A seeming multitude of women's groups now produces publications in one form or another devoted to the concerns of their organizations and of women in general, and, of course, there is *Ms.,* a national magazine that has experienced considerable commercial success. *Women & Film* is a magazine published by a group of women in California dedicated to changes in woman's image in film. Jill Johnston quoted Sharon Smith in *Women & Film* to the effect:

> Try thinking 'in female' for a moment. Imagine: That everything you have ever read uses only female pronouns, she, her, meaning both men and women. Recall that most of the voices on radio and faces on TV are female, especially when important events are in the news . . . Imagine that films show men as simple-minded little sex objects, and you despair of finding a strong role-model for

your little boy (for whom you see other futures than slut, bitch or househusband). Imagine that the women in charge of the film industry use their power to ridicule the men's liberation movement . . . Then imagine that if you complain you are given the biological explanation: by design a female's genitals are compact and internal, protected by her body. A man's genitals are exposed and must be protected from attack. His vulnerability requires sheltering . . . Men are passive, and must be shown the way in films, to reflect and protect reality. Anatomy is destiny.*

In the New York NOW study of 1241 commercials, almost all of them showed women inside the home. In 42.6 percent, they were involved in household tasks; in 37.5 percent, they were domestic adjuncts to men, and in 16.7 percent, they were sex objects. In reporting the results of this study, Hennessee and Nicholson went on to comment:

> . . . women are the stars. Above and beyond their consumer function . . . , they play two stock roles—the housewife-mother or the sex object. In both, they are viewed solely in their relation to men (May 28, 1972, p. 12).

In an analysis of the roles of women portrayed in magazine advertising, Courtney and Lockeretz studied seven national magazines and showed that whereas forty-five percent of the men were shown in working roles, only nine percent of the women were. They also found evidence to support the stereotypes of women as sexual objects, dependent upon men, and not able to do important things or make important decisions (1971). The "This Ad Insults Women" campaign of the women's movement was a very effective one. After a two-and-a-half-year struggle, NOW's Legal Defense and Education Fund has officially launched a Public Service Advertising Campaign on the theme of equal rights for women, and it has been accepted by the advertising council (*The Spokeswoman*, June 15, 1973, p. 6).

Advertising has been a likely target for feminist activities because there are products associated with it, and the consumerism of women is well known. Portrayal in films and television in general is not so easy to deal with. Kinzer pointed out that:

> The soap-opera heroines are always acted *upon*. They are raped, divorced, abandoned, misunderstood, given drugs, and attacked by

---

* From Jill Johnston, "Women & Film," *The Village Voice* (July 12, 1973), pp. 30, 36. Reprinted by permission.

mysterious diseases. More females than males go mad, have brain tumors, and die (1973, p. 48).

Kinzer also commented that "Sudsville heroines give rise to a birthrate on afternoon TV that is eight times as high as the U.S. birthrate as a whole, and higher than the birthrate of any underdeveloped nation in the world" (p. 48).

## Women in Sport

The image of woman generally portrayed by the media affirms a dichotomy between stereotypic "femininity" as an ideal and the roles of women in sport. The juxtaposition of woman and sport confuses the stereotypes of each, and their mutual accommodation implies several alternative perspectives.

**Women in sport are rarely the subjects of films.** Generally, there is a lack of attention to sport in film, except, perhaps, as an incidental activity for the hero. When sport is the subject, the athletes are men, and the women tend to be portrayed as sex objects; it is true, though, that where there are male athletes, sometimes there are also female athletes shown, especially in skiing, tennis, and golf. There are some exceptions. Katharine Hepburn was a successful and dedicated (at least to Spencer Tracy's aspirations) athlete in *Pat and Mike,* and actually performed athletic feats on camera. Raquel Welch was a beautiful Roller Derby skater, at least.

The most recent exception was the segment on women in the David Wolper film of the 1972 Olympics, *Visions of Eight.* The eight directors from different countries were given free rein to choose an aspect of the Games that intrigued them and to shoot a minifilm. Mai Zetterling, the only woman, said that she was tempted to treat women, but chose weight lifters instead. Michael Pfleghar of Germany did choose the topic of women, and George Plimpton commented on his segment:

> In his vision a gentler and more joyous spirit exists, with little of the grim demeanor that typifies the world of the male athlete. The women athletes talk to each other; they wear love beads, bandannas; the losers sob briefly, smile, and congratulate the winners. Their beauty stuns . . . (*Sports Illustrated,* August 27, 1973, p. 34).

Many women, however, feel that the treatment did confirm the stereotypic approach to women's sport as less serious.

**Although advertising is one area in which "coverage" is accorded women generally, there is little inclusion of sport.** Slatton analyzed the data relevant to advertisements showing women in sport for five magazines for the period 1900-1968, but she reported results only for the *Ladies Home Journal* in relation to the total advertisements. In that magazine, in no year did the number of advertisements showing women in sport exceed twenty, while the total number of advertisements in a single year approached 1400 (1970, p. 33). All these magazines combined (*Life, Look, Saturday Evening Post, Ladies Home Journal, Good Housekeeping*) contained a maximum number of advertisements showing women in sport in 1940: fifty-three (p. 36). It is clear, although there is no way to establish it from this study, that the percentage of

*"I think you just missed something. The ball went up in the air and somebody caught it and the crowd's yelling like mad."*

Drawing by Saxon; copyright © 1969 *The New Yorker* Magazine, Inc.

*"There, but for the fact that I shot a 74 to his 79, go I."*

advertising devoted to women in sport could not have exceeded one percent in all probability.

Slatton also presented her data according to the twenty-one sports represented in the study and categories for products. These data were not presented in terms of years, so that they represent the period 1900-1968, but further analysis of the data reveal that sixty percent of all the references to women in sport in these magazines were in relation to household or sex-object roles. Dominick and Rauch in a study of 986 prime-time television commercials found similar results in that seventy-five percent of all ads using females were for kitchen and bathroom products (*Journal of Broadcasting*, 16, Summer, 1972).

Recent empirical investigation of women and sport in advertising, with reference to both magazines and television, indicates that there has been some change in the images being portrayed of women, and that sport is much more in evidence than ever before. The use of male athletes' identification with products has long been accepted, but it is only recently that successful women golfers, tennis players, skiiers, skaters, and gymnasts have been presented as symbols of desirability for product identity. Although the female association with sport is usually presented in a more "wholesome" healthful way than that of men, when known competitors, such as Billie Jean King, are depicted in commercials actually playing, it is obvious that their involvement is serious. Colgate, in its extensive campaign before the Colgate-Dinah Shore golf tournament chose to show the women golfers in the home, but many women are shown being active. Cathy Rigby performs on the unevens before she discusses grapefruit juice.

**Descriptions of women and contexts for women in the media generally confirm sex-role stereotypes, even in sport.** This is obviously true, and just as obviously changing. Corrigan (1972) in her study of *Sports Illustrated* also considered the presentation of the female athlete. She found every article surveyed (1960, 1965, 1970) contained one or more descriptions of physical appearance, with the greatest number of adjectives directed toward hair color, eye color, height, and weight (p. 14). Examples of stereotyping women according to their roles as sex

## FUNKY WINKERBEAN

"Funky Winkerbean" by Tom Batiuk.  Courtesy Publishers-Hall Syndicate.

objects or as less important than men are everywhere, and can be confirmed in the media. *Sports Illustrated* is criticized frequently for its treatment of women in sport, but, at the same time, it is one of the only sources for such coverage. It has been suggested that *Sports Illustrated* raised its own consciousness through its series of articles on women in sport that began on May 28, 1973. Actually, two articles preceded that which exemplify excellent consideration for women in sport: Jane Gross wrote about Theresa Shank, the superb player for Immaculata College in an article, "She's the Center of Attention" (April 9, 1973), and Bil Gilbert described the first AIAW track and field championships in "The Second Sex Engages in a First" (May 21, 1973).

**There are other examples of progress in terms of the changing image of women in sport and sport for women.** Although sport has not been well represented in women's studies programs, the ERIC Research Report (Robinson, 1973) does refer to one course, *The Sportswoman in American Society* at Towson State College (p. 21), and Ellen W. Gerber has taught *The American Woman in Sport* at both the University of Massachusetts and East Stroudsburg State College. Pat DelRey taught an honors course, *Sport and the American Woman* at Queens College in the fall semester, 1973, as did Judith Zoble at Cornell University. The literature related to this kind of focus is also proliferating in magazines, journals, and books, and additional course and workshop opportunities are developing.

Although the battle to change the image of girls and women *through* changing sports programs and opportunities in education may have originated in the feminist movement, the concern with sport has become an important focus. The *Minnesota Law Review* considered sex discrimination in high school athletics and all of the related litigation in great detail in its issue of December, 1972. It concluded that the doctrine of "separate but equal" programs for girls and women had to be rejected. According to the Review, "separation of the sexes in athletics does not only imply inferiority for women, it is perceived as it" (p. 369). In their view, separate can never be equal. Especially if the defenders of separate programs are correct in saying that girls are physiologically different, less skilled, and so on, the prestige factor will always accrue to men's sport, and the programs will be separate but not equal (p. 369). In the judgment of the Review, girls' programs do not need to be hampered by this inequality; it could act as a catalyst by stimulating thought and demonstrating the inequities of the present system. Most importantly, however, the Review concludes that women's rights are not served by "grouping" girls and women in categories, and that under the law, people have the right to be treated as individuals (p. 371). Litigation is presently focused in the colleges across the United States, and many of the principles that have come to attention in terms of high school girls will soon be considered for college women.

The sportswoman may provide a central focus for the changing words and images that reveal our attitudes toward woman and sport. Somehow, the women's movement did not focus on sport until recently, and the effects of changing consciousness are not yet directly evident nor available for study, but all of the evidence indicates that they soon will be.

## PERCEPTIONS AND PROBLEMS

Ken Foreman said it very well: "For while the male athlete has been scrutinized from psoas to psyche, the female athlete has received so little attention it is as if she were yet unborn" (1972, p. 3-1). Interestingly, the amount of research about the female athlete is matched by the amount about what *others* think about the female athlete. The female athlete is confronted with the double bind of having an association with a domain generally considered not worth bothering with, while at the same time having to consider what others think of this association. Foreman himself conducted a survey of seventy-five sports, and found that while two (field hockey and ballet) were classified as essentially feminine, fifteen were designated exclusively masculine, and a majority of the remaining fifty-five as primarily masculine. He commented:

> While these findings are shocking enough, it was even more revealing to consider . . . the men who responded to the opinion-naire virtually relegated women to the home, where housework, child bearing and sewing were said to be her primary modes of bio-physical expression (1972, p. 3-1, 2).

### Perceptions

These findings are not really shocking; they are usual and predictable, and it is not so clear what they mean. The studies of attitudes toward women athletes and intensive competition for women have been summarized well in such publications as *DGWS Research Reports: Women in Sports* and *Women and Sport: A National Research Conference*. Generally, both the studies that have been done and available empirical data suggest that women's athletic competition is fairly well accepted, and that there is some ambivalence about the appellation "female athlete." Griffin suggested that both the woman athlete and the woman professor were perceived to be active and potent, "which is inconsistent with the accepted behavioral norms for women; as a result, theirs are non-preferred roles" (1973, p. 98). But this hypothesis rests on assumptions that the "ideal woman" is the ultimate preferred role for women and that, therefore, the semantic distance is a pejorative statement about the athlete and professor roles.

Perhaps, Griffin should have included "woman politician" as a category. Surely, this role also involves activity and potency, and yet when the Gallup Poll raised the question, "What woman that you have heard or read about living today in any part of the world, do you admire most?" Golda Meir headed the list, and along with wives of politicians, Indira Gandhi, Margaret Chase Smith, and Shirley Chisholm were also on this list of ten (1972, p. 2338). In fact, a poll of persons listed in the *International Who's Who* in the same year (1971) yielded Indira Gandhi as the person—man or woman—most admired; when the question was directed to "all of history," no women were mentioned (1972, p. 2305).

If it is true that people are socialized according to images and social self-fulfilling prophecies, then all of the attitude studies must be viewed as "suspect by virtue of their classification." It is analogous to the situation that prevailed in terms of racism; the north was believed to be liberal and tolerant in its attitudes until it was confronted with the realities of both racial problems and consciousness. For most populations, responding to questions about "women athletes" probably presumes a stereotypic abstraction; how could it be otherwise in a society that has denied that women are athletes?

The attitudes toward women athletes that are of most concern to them are probably the ones affecting their participation. The fight for equality in terms of facilities, budget, time, and space is frequently a confrontation with the assumptions that women are not as important as men and that women's sport, in addition, is not very important. Perhaps, in the next attitude survey, there should be a question at the end that asks, "Do you believe there really are serious women athletes?"

Francine Sichting seems to be a serious competitor in track; at least she has broken the American women's record twice. In neither case did it count, however, because once the meet officials forgot to provide a wind gauge and once they had her run in an illegal ninth lane. In addition, her husband has forbidden her to compete next year (*Sports Illustrated,* July 2, 1973, p. 53). Since none of these things is likely to have happened to a male athlete, they must be related to attitudes about women in sport.

**Attitudes toward female black athletes may provide another perspective on perceptions of women in sport.** Cynthia Fuchs Epstein, in a study of black professional women, suggested that these women have much less ambivalence about their roles, and that double discrimination can work in reverse (*Psychology Today,* August, 1973, p. 57). It is probably not an accident that the first woman superagent in films, one who uses karate, is 6-feet-2-inches tall, and works out at a gym every day, is black. Tamara Dobson, who plays "Cleopatra Jones" in a film outdoing both "Shaft" and "Super Fly" at the boxoffice, says that being a woman is no problem; "The stigma placed on you because you're black gives you enough *kill* to get you through the woman thing" (*The New York Times,* August 19, 1973, p. 11).

Marie Hart, after discussing the plight of the woman in sport, commented:

> In startling contrast is the black woman athlete. In the black community, it seems, a woman can be strong and competent in sport and still not deny her womanliness. She can even win respect and status; Wilma Rudolph is an example (1971, pp. 64, 66).

Wilma Rudolph's young daughter Yolanda has already declared herself as an Olympic hopeful (*The New York Times,* April 18, 1973), and Althea Gibson, at forty-five, announced that she was returning to professional competition in tennis (*The New York Times,* May 6, 1973). Apparently, age doesn't affect the willingness of black female athletes, either.

The Women's Intercollegiate Director at UCLA is a black former Olympian, Shirley Johnson, who considers her budget of $34,000 vastly insufficient, and who decries the national policies in women's sport against charging admission and recruiting; in other words, "a woman who is going to try to make UCLA as formidable in women's sports as it is in men's" (*UCLA Monthly,* May-June, 1973, p. 5). On

September 1, 1973, Nell Jackson was named assistant director of athletics for women's athletics at Michigan State University.

There is no doubt that affirmative action principles make it very inviting to institutions to put black women in leadership positions and, thus, satisfy two pressures at once. Since sport is an area in which black women have participated and excelled, notably in collegiate institutions like Tennessee State, this may be the logical place to begin recruiting women for administrative positions.

Any hypotheses derived on the basis of these few pieces of evidence must be tentative. There is no evidence that Hart's assumptions about the black community are correct; in fact, recent analysis has tended to dispel some of the myths about women in relation to roles in the black community. A more probable explanation is that black women, like Tamara Dobson, are aware of oppression and tend to value success more than vague approval of femininity. In addition, the white community, which effectively controls sport, is primarily masculine and is less threatened by a black woman. It has been suggested by Ferdun that, "it is easiest to be a black female athlete and most difficult to be a white male dancer" (1973, p. 2). In any case, it is possible that the model for the woman athlete might be patterned after the black woman, since she does seem more socially acceptable. Furthermore, if black women do actively pursue leadership positions in sport as well, attitudinal changes may occur more quickly than they would otherwise.

## Problems

The *Pocono Record,* a small, semirural area newspaper, headed its editorial page with larger-than-usual type that said, "Sex Goes out of Want Ads." The editorial reported that the paper would try to accede to the Supreme Court ruling that separated male and female want-ad columns are discriminatory, and also that it would try to eliminate "offensive references to sex as in brakeman, salesman, carrier boy, waitress, or girl friday." The editorial concluded by stating:

> Agitation from what have been described as militant female groups has made newspapers aware of this cause for over a decade but we resisted on the simple premise that the old system was the best service to people looking for jobs and jobs looking for people. Wrong again (*Pocono Record,* August 27, 1973, p. 4).

This is as significant an evidence of change as the fact that in 1971 twelve percent more people, in fact, a total of sixty-six percent of them, responded affirmatively to the question of whether they would vote for a qualified woman presidential candidate nominated by their party than had in 1969 (*Gallup Poll,* 1972, pp. 2189, 2319).

Within the changing dialectic of woman and sport, there are also many who must admit that they resist change on the simple premise that the old systems are working. It is to be hoped that ultimately they, too, will be able to say, "wrong again" and approach the task of building new structures that will dispel the myth of woman and sport as a social anomaly once and for all.

**There is general support for the participation of women in sport, the expansion of opportunities for them, and an increase in the significance attached to their efforts.** Many diverse groups have issued statements, passed resolutions, created task forces, and otherwise committed them selves to sport for women. Hopefully, it may become an ideological bandwagon wherein it becomes *anti*social to oppose women's participation. As feminine and feminist conceptions of "woman" move closer to broader definitions, it is apparent that sport for women is already accommodated within an ethic of well-being, vigor, wholesomeness, and health. The feminine conception endorses exercise as weight control and a source of improved attractiveness. The feminist construct gives high priority to a strong and competent body and the attendant skills of self-defense. As sports, themselves, are viewed as varying structures for movement, even the notion of "femininity" permits participation in a few more activities than swimming, tennis, golf, gymnastics, and bowling.

**On the other hand, there are a great many problems based on conceptions of both sport and woman, and these are compounded by the issue of sexism.** The feminist has learned that in a power structure, the powerless do only inferior things. Every bias, every segregation, every subjugation works only in the direction of enhancing men and denigrating women. Therefore, on one hand, the feminist position demands that the inequality of women in sport be perceived as a political issue and be confronted as sexism, without reference to evaluations of the outcome. In this view, one fights for immediate *rights* and for power rather than for longer-range goals that are truly perceived as desirable. On the other hand, the women's movement tends to work toward feminist/humanist goals and to reject masculine standards as the norms; on this basis, a new conception of sport for women is required.

Contemporary women who have not quite been radicalized (insofar as they are not willing to see society as really sexist) are committed to avoiding the adoption of a male model for sport, and they reject efforts which might lead in that direction. For them, there is an element of femininity as a desirable goal, and they are unwilling to assert that women have the right to participate in *any* sport they want to.

Because the conventional wisdom has suggested for so long and so absolutely that women are less able than men, the self-fulfilling prophecy assures that they are. Whether or not this is significant in relation to such matters as strength, endurance, and physical prowess is simply not known. The anatomical and physiological differences that have been found between men and women may not support the *social* conclusion that women can never compete with men. The feminists point out that at some time in history the difference in size between male and female brains was used as an argument against women being permitted to attend college, or to learn mathematics, and that present arguments about the deeper breathing capacities of men, or their greater muscle mass may be just as spurious. Because there are so few trained women athletes, and they are never trained as long or as well as are men, the evidence remains inconclusive but does suggest that the differences between men and women diminish with training.

The conservative or nonfeminist position continues to express paternalistic (more often maternalistic) attitudes toward women. The DGWS "Position Paper on Sports Programs for Girls and Women," dated June 27, 1973, and circulated with an accompanying letter signed by Fran Koenig, "Chairman [*sic*] DGWS," states the belief that girls should have "*equal* but *separate*" programs. DGWS suggests that few girls can qualify with boys, and implies that integration would result in limited opportunities for girls. AIAW has taken a similar stance, and has proposed barring those women who compete as members of men's teams from participation in national championships.

Clearly, the issue of separate or integrated teams is the divisive one for women's sport. State athletic associations, school districts, and similar groups have no problem enlisting the aid of women physical educators as witnesses against those who seek to enjoin their policies that exclude women from certain athletic activities or teams. There is, of course, the pervasive fear of a takeover of women's activities by men, and the history of social oppression of women attests to the possibility. On the other hand, contemporary efforts in the sociolegal context are based on the recognition of sexism and the principle of affirmative action, so that the implications of that fear are expressed in inequitable protection of women. Affirmative action implies that girls and women could have both separate and integrated teams, or, at least, as stipulated in the proposed Guidelines for Title IX, would have the right to *choose* the kind of athletic activities and structures they wished to have. Continued insistence on separate and exclusive programs based on classification by sex seems irrational in the face of some girls' athletic success on boys' varsity teams and current understanding of rights and equality.

A third position confounds the problems of what is necessary and desirable for women in sport even further. The Lesbian Feminist Liberation group in New York City has evidenced a great deal of concern with sport for women. One of the members of this group stated her own position as follows:

> I also object to women playing on men's teams—the exceptional woman is always welcomed once it is recognized that she cannot be dissuaded. Then, her energy and talent is drained off for the benefit of men—who then take the credit. Women need the strength, power, drive, determination, and energy of all women— especially their strongest sisters (*Letter,* August 15, 1973).

In a previous letter, this woman had suggested that women had to develop both training techniques and actual skills apart from men because there was every likelihood that they would emerge differently from those imposed by men. She had also used women's gymnastics as an example of a sport in which a "weak, femme image" was incorporated into the rules. Finally, she had said, "Any woman who is totally independent of men is considered a lesbian (dyke), because lesbians need nothing from men—not even sexual encounters" (*Letter,* July 17, 1973).

**The problems of woman and sport can be resolved by the perceptions of woman and sport.** Many of the people who have considered women in sport have concluded that an outgrowth of the current confusion may be a new vision of sport. If one adopts the humanistic perspective without reference to dimensions of masculinity and femininity, some altered positions emerge with reference to sport. Football, for instance, is objectionable for women on the same grounds of brutality that render it objectionable for any human. In describing an incident that occurred in women's sport, Stuart Miller said:

> But the incident also indicates a collective resistance to the psycho-

technologizing of games, the total rationalization of the human beings involved and the introduction of mind-control techniques into something that is supposed to be play (September, 1973, p. 48).

The Esalen Sports Center Newsletter discusses their goal to:

. . . broaden the existing dimensions of sport, physical education and recreation. . . . many people feel that a reconceptualization is needed . . . (August/September, 1973, p. 1).

If there are no differences between the sexes that matter and if the ones that do exist are the result of socialization only, then it is creditable to believe that women's sport will become just like men's sport if the restraints of protective practices and insufficient funding are removed. The mitigating factor in that logic, even if you accept the premises, is that by sharing the existing budgets and facilities equally, men's programs too will be drastically altered.

Another point, however, is that, whether as a result of socialization or not, women are different from men, and many women value those differences. The feminist/humanist perspective addresses sisterhood and brotherhood and a more humane value system. It has already become evident that the pervasive social models have not worked so well for American society; the alternatives suggested by the present movements for social change may be more attractive ones.

As the events of the "equality revolution" have amply demonstrated, social trends tend to be more discontinuous than progressive in contemporary society. There is always the urgent likelihood of some specific event negating all the assumptions of the conventional attitudes and realities that prevail. The Amateur Athletic Act, for instance, could be such an event. Introduced in the Senate by John Tunney of California, this bill gives a lot of control of sport to the federal government, and creates a national foundation with as much as $50 million a year for sports development. Given the existing legislation that prescribes equality as an affirmative action goal on behalf of women, there is no doubt that a great deal of the development would have to be in women's sport. Perhaps, it is not surprising that this bill is opposed by the AAU, NCAA, NRA, USLTA, and USOC. The social assumptions must rest on openness and options; hopefulness inheres in the right to choose.

# Bibliography

American Institute of Public Opinion, *The Gallup Poll, Public Opinion 1935-1971,* New York: Random House, 1972.

American Association for Health, Physical Education and Recreation, *Update,* December, 1972; April, May, June, 1973.

American Association of State Colleges and Universities, "Questionnaire on Intercollegiate Athletics," unpublished document, August, 1971.

Ashworth, C.E., "Sport as Symbolic Dialogue," *Sport: Readings from a Sociological Perspective,* Ed. by Eric Dunning, Toronto: University of Toronto Press, 1971.

Association for Women Psychologists, "Psychology and the New Woman," Pittsburgh: KNOW, Inc., September, 1970.

Bardwick, J.M., *Psychology of Women,* New York: Harper and Row, Publishers, 1971.

——————— , "Women's Liberation: Nice idea, but it won't be easy," *Psychology Today* (May, 1973), 26, 30-33, 110-111.

——————— , and Douvan, E., "Ambivalence: The Socialization of Women," *Women in Sexist Society,* Ed. by Vivian Gornick and Barbara E. Moran, New York: A Signet Book from New American Library, 1971.

Bem, S.L., and Bem, D.J., "Training the Woman to Know Her Place: The Social Antecedents of Women in the World of Work," unpublished paper, Stanford University, 1971.

Berlin, P., "Perceptions of 'The Ideal Woman' and 'The Woman Athlete' by Selected College Students," unpublished paper presented at the First Canadian Congress for the Multi-Disciplinary Study of Sport and Physical Activity, Montreal, Quebec, October 12-14, 1973.

Bianchi, E., "Pigskin Piety," *Christianity and Crisis* (February 21, 1972), 31-34.

Boyle, R.H., *Sport—Mirror of American Life,* Boston: Little, Brown and Company, 1963.

Broverman, I., Broverman, D.M., Bee, H., Rosenkrantz, P., and Vogel, S., "Sex Role Stereotypes and Self-Concepts in College Students," *Journal of Consulting and Clinical Psychology* 32:5 (1968), 287-295.

Burris, B., Faust, D., and Felshin, J., "A Study of Actual and Projected Attitudes toward High School Girl Participants in Varsity Team Sports Held by Urban and Rural Students," unpublished paper, 1971.

Cheffers, J.T.F., "The Influence of Sex Role Standards in Shaping Adolescent Behavior Examined in the Context of Sports Participation. Real or Imaginary?", *Sport Sociology Bulletin*, Ed. by Benjamin Lowe (Spring, 1973).

Citizen's Advisory Council on the Status of Women, *Women in 1972*, Washington, D.C.: U.S. Government Printing Office, May, 1973.

Coffey, M.A., "The Sportswoman Then & Now," *JOHPER*, 36:2 (February, 1965), 38-41, 50.

Collins, B., "Billie Jean Evens The Score," *Ms.* (July, 1973), 39-43, 101-102.

Commission on the Status of Women, *Improving the Status of Women in the Labor Force*, Washington, D.C.: Government of the District of Columbia, February, 1973.

Corrigan, M., "Societal Acceptance of the Female Athlete as Seen through the Analysis of Content of a Sports Magazine," unpublished paper, May 11, 1972.

Courtney, A.E., and Lockeretz, S.W., "A Woman's Place: An Analysis of the Roles Portrayed by Women in Magazine Advertisements," reprinted by KNOW, Inc. (published originally, 1971).

Cozens, F.W., and Stumpf, F.S., *Sports in American Life*, Chicago: The University of Chicago Press, 1953.

De Lillo, D., *End Zone*, New York: Pocket Books, 1973.

Dominick, J.R., and Rauch, G.E., "The Image of Women in Network TV Commercials," *Journal of Broadcasting* 16 (Summer, 1972), 259-265.

Edwards, H., "Desegregating Sexist Sport," *Intellectual Digest* (November, 1972), 82-83.

——————, *Sociology of Sport*, Homewood, Ill.: The Dorsey Press, 1973.

Ephron, N., "Women," *Esquire* (January, 1973), 36-40.

Epstein, C.F., "Black and Female: The Double Whammy," *Psychology Today* (August, 1973), 57-61, 89.

*Esalen Sports Center News*, 1:1 (August/September), 1973.

Estes, L., *Letter to Jan Felshin*, August 19, 1973.

——————, *Letter to Lou Jean Moyer*, January 29, 1973.

Fasteau, B.F., "Giving Women a Sporting Chance," *Ms.* (July, 1973), 56-58, 103.

Felshin, J., "Variables Reported by Varsity Athletes in Critical Incidents Related to Becoming 'Psyched Up' and 'Psyched Out'," unpublished paper, 1973.

——————, "Sport and Modes of Meaning," *JOHPER* 40:5 (May, 1969), 43, 44. Also in *Anthology of Contemporary Readings: An Introduction to Physical Education*, Second Ed., Ed. by Howard S. Slusher and Aileene S. Lockhart, Dubuque, Iowa: Wm. C. Brown Company, 1970.

Ferdun, E., "Dance: . . ." unpublished paper, 1973.

——————————— , "Experience and Meaning," in Jan Felshin, *More Than Movement: An Introduction to Physical Education,* Philadelphia: Lea & Febiger, 1972.

Fishel, E., "This Ad Insults Women," *Newsday* (July 18, 1970), 8-11.

Fisher, A.C., "Sports as an Agent of Masculine Orientation," *The Physical Educator* (October, 1972), **29,** 3, 120-122.

Fisher, S., "Experiencing Your Body: You Are What You Feel," *Saturday Review of Science* (July 8, 1972), 27-32.

Fleming, E.D., "Psychiatry and Beauty," *Cosmopolitan* (June, 1959), 31-36.

Foreman, K., "What Research Says About the Female Athlete," unpublished paper, March 19, 1972.

Franks, L., "See Jane Run!," *Ms.* (January, 1973), 99-100, 104.

Frederickson, F.S., "Sports and the Cultures of Man," *Science and Medicine of Exercise and Sports,* Ed. by Warren R. Johnson, New York: Harper and Brothers Publishers, 1960.

Freeman, J., "The Social Construction of the Second Sex," Pittsburgh: KNOW, Inc., 1970.

Galbraith, J.K., "The Economics of the American Housewife," *The Atlantic Monthly* (August, 1973), 78-83.

Gardner, J., "Women's Athletics: The Hurdle is Cash," *UCLA Monthly* 3:7 (May-June, 1973), 5.

Gelfand, L.J., and Heath, H.E., *Modern Sportswriting,* Ames, Iowa: The Iowa State University Press, 1969.

Gewirtz, J., *Memorandum to Carl Troester,* copy of letter, February 21, 1973.

Gilbert, B., "The Second Sex Engages in a First," *Sports Illustrated* (May 21, 1973), 96-98.

——————————— , and Williamson, N., "Women in Sport: Part 1, Sport is Unfair to Women; Part 2, Are You Being Two-Faced?; Part 3, Programmed to be Losers," *Sports Illustrated* (May 28, June 4, June 11, 1973).

Gilder, G., "The Suicide of the Sexes," *Harper's Magazine* (July, 1973), 42-54.

Goldberg, P., "Are Women Prejudiced Against Women?" *Transaction* (April, 1968), 28, reprinted in *The Philadelphia Bulletin* (May 26, 1968).

Goltz, P., "Equal Rights," unpublished paper: Feminists for Life, July, 1973.

Gornick V., and Moran, B.E., Eds., *Woman in Sexist Society,* New York: A Signet Book from New American Library, 1971.

Griffin, P.S., "What's a Nice Girl Like You Doing in a Profession Like This?", *Quest XIX* (January, 1973), 96-101.

Gross, J., "She's the Center of Attention," *Sports Illustrated* (April 9, 1973), 30-31.

Harris, D.V., "The Social Self and Competitive Self of the Female Athlete," unpublished paper presented at the Third International Symposium on the Sociology of Sport, University of Waterloo, Waterloo, Ontario, August 22-28, 1971.

——————— , "The Sportswoman in our Society," *DGWS Research Reports: Women in Sports*, Ed. by Dorothy V. Harris, Washington, D.C.: American Association for Health, Physical Education and Recreation, 1971.

——————— , Ed., *Women and Sport: A National Research Conference*, Penn State HPER Series No. 2, College of Health, Physical Education and Recreation, The Pennsylvania State University, 1972.

Hart, M.M., Ed., *Sport in the Socio-Cultural Process*, Dubuque, Iowa: Wm. C. Brown Company, 1972.

——————— , "Sport Women sit in the back of the bus," *Psychology Today* (October, 1971), 64-66.

Hennessee, J.A., and Nicholson, J., "NOW Says TV Commercials Insult Women," *The New York Times Magazine* (May 28, 1972), 12-13, 48-51.

Holbrook, L., "Women's Participation in American Sport," *Athletics in America*, Ed. by Arnold Flath, Corvallis, Oregon: Oregon State University Press, 1972.

Horner, M., "Fail: Bright Women," *Psychology Today* (November, 1969), 36-38, 62.

Howe, F., "Sexual Stereotypes Start Early," *Saturday Review* (October 16, 1971), 76-82, 92-94.

——————— , "Women's Studies: No Ivory Towers Need Apply," *Ms.* (September, 1973), 46-48.

Huber, J., Ed., *Changing Women in a Changing Society*, Chicago: The University of Chicago Press, 1973.

Huizinga, J., *Homo Ludens: A Study of the Play-Element in Culture*, Boston: The Beacon Press, 1950.

Janeway, E., *Man's World, Woman's Place: A Study in Social Mythology*, New York: Dell Publishing Company, Inc., 1971.

Johnston, J., "Teach Your Angels Karate," *The Village Voice* (September 23, 1971), 37-38, 44-45.

——————— , "Women & Film," *The Village Voice* (July 12, 1973), 29-30, 36.

Keating, J.W., "Paradoxes in American Athletics," *Athletics in America*, Ed. by Arnold Flath, Corvallis, Oregon: Oregon State University Press, 1972.

——————— , "Sportsmanship as a Moral Category," *Ethics* **LXXV** (October, 1964), 25-35. Also in *Sport and the Body: A Philosophical Symposium*, Ed. by Ellen W. Gerber, Philadelphia: Lea & Febiger, 1972.

Kenyon, G.S., "Sport and Society: At Odds or in Concert?," *Athletics in America*, Ed. by Arnold Flath, Corvallis, Oregon: Oregon State University Press, 1972.

Kennard, J.A., "The Woman Athlete in Magazines," unpublished paper, February, 1973.

Kinzer, N.S., "Soapy Sin in the Afternoon," *Psychology Today* (August, 1973), 46-48.

Klafs, C.E., and Lyons, J.M., *The Female Athlete: Conditioning, Competition, and Culture*, St. Louis: The C.V. Mosby Company, 1973.

Kratz, L.E., "A Study of Sports and the Implications of Women's Participation in them in Modern Society," unpublished Ph.D. dissertation, The Ohio State University, Columbus, 1958.

Landers, D.M., "Psychological Femininity and the Prospective Physical Educator," *Research Quarterly*, 41 (May, 1970), 164-170.

Lesbian Feminist Liberation, *The Lesbian Feminist*, I:1 (August 25, 1973).

LFL Member, *Letters to Jan Felshin*, July 17, 1973, August 15, 1973.

Levitan, T.E., Quinn, R.P., and Steines, G.L., "A Woman is 58% of a Man . . .," *Psychology Today* (March, 1973), 89-91.

Locke, L.F., and Jensen, M., "Heterosexuality of Women in Physical Education," *The Foil* (Fall, 1970), 31-35.

Loggia, M., "On the Playing Fields of History," *Ms.* (July, 1973), 62-64.

Loy, J.W., Jr., "The Nature of Sport: A Definitional Effort," *Quest* X (May, 1968), 1-15, in *Sport, Culture and Society*, Ed. by John W. Loy, Jr., and Gerald S. Kenyon, New York: The Macmillan Company, 1969.

_____ , and Ingham, A.G., "The Social System of Sport: A Humanistic Perspective," *Quest* XIV (January, 1973), 3-23.

Lüschen, G., Ed., *The Cross-Cultural Analysis of Sport and Games*, Champaign, Ill.: Stipes Publishing Company, 1967.

Maccoby, E. E., "Woman's Intellect," *The Potential of Women*, Ed. by Seymour M. Farber and Roger H.S. Wilson, New York: McGraw-Hill Book Co., 1963.

McClelland, D., "Wanted: A New Self-Image for Women," *The Women in America*, Ed. by Robert J. Lifton, Boston: Beacon Press, 1965.

McKenna, J.R., "Content Analysis of Women in Sport: *Time Magazine* 1928-1968 —Every Ten Years," unpublished paper, December, 1972.

Merton, R.K., *Social Theory and Social Structure*, 1968 Enlarged Edition, New York: The Free Press, 1968.

Metheny, E., *Connotations of Movement in Sport and Dance*, Dubuque, Iowa: Wm. C. Brown Company, 1965.

_____ , "The Excellence of Patroclus," *Anthology of Contemporary Readings: An Introduction to Physical Education*, Second Edition, Ed. by Howard S. Slusher and Aileene S. Lockhart, Dubuque, Iowa: Wm. C. Brown Company, 1970.

Miller, D.M., and Russell, K.R.E., *Sport: A Contemporary View*, Philadelphia: Lea & Febiger, 1971.

Miller, S., "New Directions in Sport," *Intellectual Digest* (September, 1973), 48-50.

Minor, A., "The Race Track," *The New Yorker* (August 20, 1973), 83.

Morgan, R., Ed., *Sisterhood is Powerful: An Anthology of Writings from the Women's Liberation Movement*, New York: Vintage Books, 1970.

Moyer, L.J., *Letter to Linda Estes*, January 3, 1973.

Mulvaney, M.J., *Letter to Jan Felshin*, August 1, 15, 1973.

National Association for Physical Education of College Women, *Spectrum*, November, 1971.

Parrish, B., *They Call it a Game*, New York: A Signet Book of New American Library, 1972.

Parsons, T., *Sociological Theory and Modern Society*, New York: The Free Press, 1967.

Plimpton, G., "Olympic Visions of Eight," *Sports Illustrated* (August 27, 1973), 30-35.

Radicalesbians, "The Woman Identified Woman," Pittsburgh: KNOW, Inc., 1970.

Robinson, L.H., "Women's Studies: Courses and Programs for Higher Education," *ERIC/Higher Education Research Reports No. 1*, Washington, D.C.: American Association for Higher Education, 1973.

Sales, B., "She's Just One of the Guys," *Today's Health* (April, 1971), 19-22, 71.

Schmitz, K.L., "Sport and Play: Suspension of the Ordinary," *Sport and the Body: A Philosophical Symposium*, Ed. by Ellen W. Gerber, Philadelphia: Lea & Febiger, 1972.

Scott, J., *The Athletic Revolution*, New York: The Free Press, 1971.

"Sex Discrimination in High School Athletics," *Minnesota Law Review*, **57**:2 (December, 1972), 339-371.

Shaffer, H.B., "Status of Women," *Editorial Research Reports 11*, Washington, D.C.: Congressional Quarterly, Inc., August, 1970.

"Should Girls Play on Boy's Teams?", *Good Housekeeping* (October, 1969), 215.

Slatton, Y.LaB., *The Role of Women in Sport as Depicted Through Advertising in Selected Magazines, 1900-1968*, unpublished Ph.D. dissertation, The University of Iowa, Iowa City, 1970.

Slusher, H.S., *Man, Sport and Existence: A Critical Analysis*, Philadelphia: Lea & Febiger, 1967.

Small, C., "A Comparison of Feminine Role Perceptions of Selected College Female Team and Individual Sport Varsity Athletes and Non-Athletes for Themselves and 'The Average Woman'," unpublished Master's thesis, East Stroudsburg State College, East Stroudsburg, Pa., 1973.

————— , "Requiem for an Issue," *JOHPER* **44**:1 (January, 1973), 27-28.

Sontag, S., "The Double Standard of Aging," *Saturday Review of the Society* (September 23, 1972), 29-38.

Steinem, G., "Sisterhood," *Ms.* preview issue (Spring, 1972), 46-49.

Stuart, M., "Now the Girls are Playing for Pay," *Ticketron Entertainment* (June, 1973), 44.

Thimmesch, N., "Will Nine More States Approve? The Sexual Equality Amendment," *The New York Times Magazine* (June 24, 1973), 8-9, 53-57, 61.

Tiger, L., "Male Dominance? Yes, Alas. A Sexist Plot? No," *The New York Times Magazine* (October 25, 1970), 35-37, 124-127, 132-136.

**U.S. Department of Health, Education, and Welfare,** "Education and Women's Rights: What the Law Now Says," Washington, D.C.: U.S. Government Printing Office, 1972.

**VanderZwaag, H. J.,** *Toward a Philosophy of Sport,* Reading, Mass.: Addison-Wesley Publishing Company, 1972.

**Van Housen, C.,** "A Comparative Study of Passing Interaction in Relation to Sociometric Standing and Perceived Skill between Male and Female Collegiate Varsity Basketball Players," unpublished Master's thesis, East Stroudsburg State College, East Stroudsburg, Pa., 1973.

**Weisstein, N.,** "Psychology Constructs the Female, or The Fantasy Life of the Male Psychologist," Boston: New England Free Press, 1970.

**White, W., Jr., Ed.,** *North American Reference Encyclopedia of Women's Liberation: The New Woman,* Philadelphia, Pa.: North American Publishing Company, 1972.

**Women on Words and Images,** *Dick and Jane as Victims: Sex Stereotyping in Children's Readers,* ERIC, 1972.

**Women's Bureau, U.S. Dept. of Labor,** "The Myth and the Reality," Washington, D.C.: U.S. Government Printing Office, 1971.

**Women's Martial Arts Union,** "Self-Defense for Women," unpublished paper, March, 1973.

——————————, *Statement,* Spring, 1973.

# Part 3
# THE WOMAN ATHLETE

Pearl Berlin

# Chapter 8
# Descriptive Characteristics

Mention the word *tomboy* and more likely than not one conjures up
an image of a lithe but sturdy-looking little girl clad in jeans and sneakers
with pig-tails or pony-tail flying. Also associated with the idea of a
tomboy is an active outgoing or bold youngster who uses her body
capably. Some people would probably say that a tomboy is athletically
inclined. Regardless of identifying traits, we generally tend to think of
a tomboy as being cute. But what about the adult woman athlete? What
features distinguish her? Do quarter-century-old notions about some
sort of Amazon-like creature accurately depict today's female sportswoman? How can one describe the collegiate woman athlete if, in fact,
the large majority of undergraduate students enrolled in institutions of
higher education, males and females alike, wear bluejeans or some other
pant-type garment with sweatshirt or t-shirt as regular garb? Even many
accessories worn by college students today, e.g., beads, headbands,
bracelets, and in a few cases, earrings, are unisex items.

The following discussion attempts to characterize the females of
the species who, in spite of its customary acceptance as a bastion of
maleness, have invaded arenas of competitive sport. Data are presented
first about collegiate women athletes who have made a serious commitment to at least one varsity sport. This has been established by their
trying out and being selected as members of a bonafide squad and their
engagement in at least one full season of competition. Personal information was obtained from young women attending schools in north-
eastern states—Connecticut, Massachusetts, New Hampshire, New York,
and Pennsylvania. Whether or not they may be considered to be typical
of all college women athletes is probable but neither proven nor herewith asserted. Sports represented by the collegians surveyed include

basketball, crew, field hockey, gymnastics, lacrosse, skiing, swimming, tennis, and volleyball. Types of schools polled ranged from privately endowed prestige institutions to state universities and state colleges. Next some general facts and figures about champion performers, women who have engaged in national champion competition and Olympic events, are presented in the form of mini-biographical sketches. These derive primarily from the literature. Finally, a few of the descriptive traits of professionals, women who currently participate in the Virginia Slims Women's Tennis Circuit, are offered. Collectively, this information is intended to provide a general picture of *The American Woman in Sport*.

## COLLEGIATE PERFORMERS

### Personal Factors

Clearly, the majority of college women athletes are young WASPS. Fifty-two percent of the group of 200 sampled are either 19 or 20 years of age. Another 32% fall in the 17 and 18 year age bracket. Only about 15% of those engaging in competitive intercollegiate sports are 21 years or older. Ninety-nine of the women, 49.5%, indicated that they are members of the Protestant faith. About 30% are members of the Catholic church. Only 2.5% are Jews. In response to the optional request to indicate religious affiliation, it is interesting to note that 10% of the athletes elected to check *none* as being indicative of their religious preference; 3.5% chose not to answer the question at all.

Table 8 depicts some of the physical features of college women athletes. These figures seem to explode the myth that female sportswomen are gross. Examination of normative height and weight statistics of American women reported in the *World Almanac* reveal that collegiate women athletes are rather typical. Generalizing from the statistics in the table, the mean age of varsity female performers is 19.13 years. She is 64.09 inches tall and weighs 131.07 pounds. It might be inferred that extremes on the short-tall and light-heavy continuums are primarily accounted for by gymnasts and basketball players respectively. (Refer to Fig. 20.) Forty-seven gymnasts and 51 basketball players were included in the sample. The dress size of female collegiate sportswomen is represented by an 11 or 12. Distribution of the dress size data is obviously skewed toward the smaller end of the scale.

Another characteristic that may be regarded as personal is color

**TABLE 8**
Height, Weight, Dress Size of 200 College Women Athletes

| Variable | | *f* | % |
|---|---|---|---|
| *Height* | Shorter than 60 in. | 2 | 1.0 |
| | 60 – 62 | 26 | 13.0 |
| | 63 – 65 | 68 | 34.0 |
| | 66 – 68 | 78 | 39.0 |
| | 69 – 71 | 19 | 9.5 |
| | 72 – 74 | 3 | 1.5 |
| | Taller than 74 in. | 1 | .5 |
| | Missing information | 3 | 1.5 |
| | | | |
| *Weight* | Less than 100 lb | 5 | 2.5 |
| | 100 – 109 | 9 | 4.5 |
| | 110 – 119 | 29 | 14.5 |
| | 120   129 | 56 | 28.0 |
| | 130 – 139 | 45 | 22.5 |
| | 140 – 149 | 31 | 15.5 |
| | 150 – 159 | 10 | 5.0 |
| | 160 – 169 | 8 | 4.0 |
| | More than 169 lb | 2 | 1.0 |
| | Missing information | 5 | 2.5 |
| | | | |
| *Dress size* | Smaller than 8 | 32 | 16.0 |
| | 8 –  9 | 28 | 14.0 |
| | 10 – 11 | 38 | 19.0 |
| | 12 – 13 | 60 | 30.0 |
| | 14 – 15 | 23 | 11.5 |
| | 16 – 17 | 11 | 5.5 |
| | Missing information | 8 | 4.0 |

preference. It would probably be no surprise at all to the noted psychologist David C. McClelland that the favorite color of women athletes is blue. Two-thirds of the women sampled stated a strong preference for blue and green, two "soft" colors. Red and yellow, two more primary colors, account for another 16% (4.5% and 11.5% respectively) of favorite colors. The remaining 18% are distributed among pink, lavender, orange, brown, and black. Pink, sometimes considered to be a "ladies' color," was preferred by only 4% of those sampled. Additional comments follow in the discussion of athletes' motivations that bear upon the personal choice of blues and greens.

## Home and Family Background

More than half of the college women studied who engage in sport competition indicated that as children they lived in communities that would be considered as small. Only 7% of the group can be regarded as city-bred, that is, residing in a city of one million or larger. Fifty-six percent reported that they attended a high school ranging in size between 1,000 and 2,500 pupils; 35% graduated from smaller high schools. Only 6% were educated in a secondary school larger than 2,500.

In a sense, these athletes are all-American. Ninety percent of the parents reported the United States as their place of origin. A comparatively small percentage of parents, 6%, were European-born. The remaining few parents of these New England athletes come from Latin America and the Far East.

As might be expected, the father was designated as head of household by 91.5% of the group surveyed. Fifty-three percent of the household heads held a college or university degree; 41.5% were high school graduates; 4.5% completed junior high school. Only 1% had less than a junior high school education. Job types of heads of household were broadly classified as follows: 32% professional; 35% manager, official, proprietor; 13% sales, clerical, white collar; 5% skilled craftsmen, kindred workers; 10% semiskilled or unskilled services; and 5% in other various types of work.

Consideration of family size and birth order does not turn up any unique factors that may be associated with collegiate sportswomen. Table 9 provides a composite picture of birth order and the sibling status of students studied. Although the data take into account the sex factor of siblings, there is no consideration of spacing between siblings as a variable. Sutton-Smith and Rosenberg (1970) would consider this a factor to be reckoned in studying athletes' family background. There is, however, a considerably larger percentage of athletes, 56.5%, reporting no older brothers in contrast to Malumphy's (1970) accounting of golfers and tennis players studied in the late 1960s. She reported that about one-third of the women collegians did not have an older brother. Rosen's (1961) assertion that first-borns tend to be more competitive than their siblings is reasonably supported. Forty-two and a half percent of the athletes reported having no younger brothers and 51% no younger sisters. Just less than half, then, might be regarded as first-born.

**TABLE 9**
Siblings and Birth Order of 200 Collegiate Women Athletes

| Variable | f | % | Variable | f | % |
|---|---|---|---|---|---|
| **Siblings** | | | | | |
| *Brothers* | | | *Sisters* | | |
| None | 37 | 18.5 | None | 63 | 31.5 |
| One | 91 | 45.5 | One | 64 | 32.0 |
| Two | 46 | 23.0 | Two | 47 | 23.5 |
| Three | 17 | 8.5 | Three | 16 | 8.0 |
| Four | 4 | 2.0 | Four | 8 | 4.0 |
| Five | 1 | .5 | Five | 1 | .5 |
| Six | 3 | 1.5 | Six | 1 | .5 |
| Missing information | 1 | .5 | | | |
| **Sibling order** | | | | | |
| *Older brothers* | | | *Older sisters* | | |
| None | 113 | 56.5 | None | 115 | 57.5 |
| One | 69 | 34.5 | One | 65 | 32.5 |
| Two | 10 | 5.0 | Two | 17 | 8.5 |
| Three | 5 | 2.5 | Three | 1 | .5 |
| Four | | | | | |
| Five | 1 | .5 | | | |
| Twin | 1 | .5 | Twin | 1 | .5 |
| Missing information | 1 | .5 | Missing information | 1 | .5 |
| *Younger brothers* | | | *Younger sisters* | | |
| None | 85 | 42.5 | None | 102 | 51.0 |
| One | 85 | 42.5 | One | 68 | 34.0 |
| Two | 18 | 9.0 | Two | 21 | 10.5 |
| Three | 8 | 4.0 | Three | 5 | 2.5 |
| Four | 1 | .5 | Four | 2 | 1.0 |
| Five | 1 | .5 | Five | 1 | .5 |
| Six | 1 | .5 | | | |
| Missing information | 1 | .5 | Missing information | 1 | .5 |

## Academic Status

About two-thirds of the athletes studied were underclasswomen; 31.5%
of these were in their initial year at college and 34% were pursuing
sophomore studies. Juniors comprised 19% of the sample, and the
remaining 15.5% were members of the senior class. Scholastic performance, as represented by grade or honor point average, is an index that
should be interpreted with caution. Standards vary among the institu-

tions surveyed. Furthermore, scholarship demands are not consistent across fields of study nor is there equivalency among credit-hour loads carried from year to year. Sanford (1962) addresses the inadequacy of the measure and cites nine specific limitations (p. 816, 817). The following data may explain, nonetheless, why women athletes can be "lost" in the total college or university population when academic records are reviewed. Grade point averages ranged from 4.0 to 1.7. In general, the varsity woman competitor can be described as a B student. Mean grade point average for those studied is 2.92; median and modal grades fall in the 3.0 to 3.4 category. These figures are slightly higher than the records of tennis players and golfers reported by Malumphy (1970).

A large majority of these young women, 58%, are enrolled in physical education curriculums. Another 7.5% are committed to a career in education. Next largest popular field among women athletes is the humanities; 10% reported majoring in subjects classified as the humanities. Five and a half percent are studying physical/natural sciences; 6.5% are focusing their work in the social/behavioral sciences. One of the 200 athletes polled is looking forward to a career as a performing artist, another as a physician. Only 2% of the group had not declared any field of academic specialization.

## Sport Preferences

College women athletes were asked to designate their first, second, and third sport preferences on an open response form. They were directed to specify any activity regardless of immediate team affiliation or competitive interest. In situations where these individuals had dual commitments, e.g., hockey in the fall and tennis in the spring, it was necessary for them to indicate a priority. Table 10 summarizes the stated sport preferences of the athletes. Basketball, field hockey, lacrosse, softball, and volleyball, combined in a general classification of team sports, are most preferred. Individual and/or dual activities including gymnastics and track and field combine to rank second in popularity. Undoubtedly, these data reflect the specific program opportunities of the schools included in the survey as well as the particular varsity teams that made up the sample. Gymnastics, for example, is obviously a first choice of team members, but few other athletes selected gymnastics as a second or third preference. Swimming, on the other hand, is more or less consistently selected in all three ranks. Only field hockey has similar across-the-board preference. (Refer to Tables 3 and 5.)

**TABLE 10**
Sport Preferences of 200 College Women Athletes

| Activity | First | | Second | | Third | |
|---|---|---|---|---|---|---|
| | $f$ | % | $f$ | % | $f$ | % |
| Aquatic art | 2 | 1.0 | 1 | .5 | | |
| Badminton | | | 3 | 1.5 | | |
| Baseball | | | 1 | .5 | 1 | .5 |
| Basketball | 51 | 25.5 | 30 | 15.0 | 12 | 6.0 |
| Bowling | | | 3 | 1.5 | 6 | 3.0 |
| Crew/kayak/rowing | 2 | 1.0 | 2 | 1.0 | 2 | 1.0 |
| Diving | | | 1 | .5 | 1 | .5 |
| Fencing | | | | | 1 | .5 |
| Field hockey | 20 | 10.0 | 24 | 12.0 | 25 | 12.5 |
| Figure skating | | | 1 | .5 | | |
| Golf | 4 | 2.0 | 12 | 6.0 | 15 | 7.5 |
| Gymnastics | 47 | 23.5 | 2 | 1.0 | 2 | 1.0 |
| Horseback riding | | | 4 | 2.0 | 5 | 2.5 |
| Lacrosse | 3 | 1.5 | 11 | 5.5 | 5 | 2.5 |
| Sailing | 2 | 1.0 | 2 | 1.0 | 2 | 1.0 |
| Skating | | | | | 1 | .5 |
| Skiing | 14 | 7.0 | 21 | 10.5 | 11 | 5.5 |
| Soccer/speedball | | | | | 4 | 2.0 |
| Softball | 9 | 4.5 | 16 | 8.0 | 11 | 5.5 |
| Squash | | | 1 | .5 | 1 | .5 |
| Swimming | 25 | 12.5 | 17 | 8.5 | 28 | 14.0 |
| Tennis | 17 | 8.5 | 25 | 12.5 | 25 | 12.5 |
| Track and field | | | 5 | 2.5 | 12 | 6.0 |
| Volleyball | 3 | 1.5 | 8 | 4.0 | 7 | 3.5 |
| Other | 1 | .5 | 10 | 5.0 | 16 | 13.0 |
| Missing information | | | | | 7 | 3.5 |

The drop-off in popularity of basketball from first to second to third choice is opposite to the increase in popularity of golf from first to third choice. Activities not identified at all among first choices but acknowledged as later preferences include: badminton, baseball, bowling, diving, fencing, horseback riding, skating, soccer/speedball, squash, track and field. One can only speculate as to whether or not sports not mentioned at all by these athletes, e.g., archery, casting, scuba, surfing, to name but a few, would have been included among responses of athletes from the west coast or some other geographical area.

Comparing the sport preferences of this group of athletes with those of a group of general women students ($N = 319$) enrolled at

Michigan State University and reported by Petrie (1970) yields some similarities as well as distinctions. Female general students at MSU ranked sports for popularity in the following order: swimming, tennis, bowling, baseball, badminton, volleyball, softball, basketball. Athletes' preferences, considered collectively, would place activities in the following ranking: basketball, swimming, hockey, tennis, skiing, softball, and golf, with volleyball and track and field "tied" for eighth place. Bowling, obviously popular among midwest undergraduate women enrolled at MSU, does not qualify in the top eight listing of athletes' preferred sports, nor does baseball or badminton. Athletes, however, select hockey, skiing, and golf among their favorites, whereas general students do not. Swimming and tennis are almost equally rated by both the general student and the athlete groups. Basketball is markedly more popular among the athletes. These distinctions should be considered in the light of differences in geographic area, academic class differences, and the method of obtaining athletes' composite ranking. It would appear likely, as well, that commitment to varsity sport also contributes considerably to distinctions among sport preferences.

## CHAMPIONS

### Champion Diver: Micki King

According to an account in the *Women's Sports Reporter* ("Micki King," 1970), Micki King of industrial Pontiac, Michigan, did not dive competitively until the age of 15 when she successfully represented her local "Y." Previously, she taught herself swimming and diving and became proficient in the latter by playing the role of leader in a challenge dive type of game. She has not stopped training and competing and winning since that time.

Ms. King began the pursuit of the championship during her undergraduate career at the University of Michigan where she majored in physical education. While attending the famous Big 10 institution, she came under the tutelage of Dick Kimball, celebrated diving champion and coach. Micki also competed in water polo; on two occasions, she was selected as All American goalie while a member of the Ann Arbor Swim Club.

Interspersed with hard training that continuously demanded Micki's time and powers of self-discipline, she did manage to engage in some other types of sport activities. To keep in shape during the fall and spring, for instance, she participates in both tennis and paddleball. On the waters, Micki takes to sailing, a pastime in which she reportedly finds tremendous enjoyment; she also aspires to becoming a surfer. A bit out of the physical activity realm but closely allied to it is Micki's hobby of photography. She has a growing collection of her own pictures of athletes in action—a King specialty.

One of the bonuses for Micki that she has enjoyed along with competition has been the opportunity to travel. She takes as much pleasure from this aspect of being a champion as she does from the competition itself. On AAU goodwill tours, she has performed in England, Wales, Monaco, Portugal, Spain, and Japan. She holds a national title in Spain as well as in Canada. Internationally, she has competed in Mexico and Germany.

Although she is referred to as an officer in the Air Force who flies without wings, she has hopes of some day obtaining a pilot's license. For the present, this ambition has been set aside. Becoming a private pilot will have to await her retirement from diving.

A soft-spoken individual, Micki King did bare some of her thoughts about the nightmare of ". . . Death stalking the Olympic Games (James, 1973, p. 11)." Her commitment to the idea and ideals of the Olympics is strong. In explaining the conduct of the awards ceremony at the 1967 World Student Games in which she participated, Micki described the non-nationalistic "controls." There was no flag-raising and anthem for each country: ". . . if it were going to save the Olympic Movement, I would opt for an Olympic anthem rather than the national ones" (James, 1973, p. 12), she stated.

This winner of 6 national AAU titles and the Olympic Gold urges hopeful young divers not to become discouraged and give way to the grueling practices and heart-breaking disappointments of the kind that she experienced over a span of many years. "A good diver is a consistent diver and only repetition develops consistency. So, the longer you dive and the more mature, your moves become, the better you get" ("Micki King," 1970, p. 30). She offers assurance to all potential champions that all the toil and tribulation is more than worth the effort.

Two traits distinguish Micki King from other champions. She is one of the very few prominent athletes, including males, to pursue a career in the military. Micki is a captain in the U.S. Air Force and has been strongly supported in her competitive athletic pursuits. The Air Force has made assignments that permit her to train, and has given her necessary time off to become the national champion that she is. Also, for those who tend to think of female athletic greats as being youthful, "Micki's age of 28 is over the hill for an athlete" (James, 1973, p. 12). But Capt. King is of the opinion that divers do not peak until their mid-twenties. This explains her advice to developing divers above.

One achievement that makes Micki King unique is her comeback ability. She returned from the 1968 Mexico City Olympics with a cast on her left arm that bore the autographs of world-renowned Olympic athletes. Her subsequent gold medal in Munich, four years later, is a tribute to her courage and tenacity as well as her skill.

### Tennis Champion: Althea Gibson

"From 143rd Street in Harlem to the center court at Wimbledon is about as far as one can travel" (Orr, 1970, p. 175). Earlier in her life, though, Althea Gibson did some traveling of another nature. At age 3, she moved from her place of birth, Silver, South Carolina, with an aunt, to New York to be later joined by her parents. While in her teens, she made one of the most important journeys of her life, via night rail coach, from New York to Wilmington, North Carolina, to take up residency in the home of one of her two major sponsors who saw in Althea Gibson a black athlete who could make the tennis big time.

Althea spent her childhood on the streets of Harlem during the difficult days of the Depression. Home was on 143rd Street with her parents, three sisters, and one brother. She acknowledges that she was "the wildest tomboy you ever saw" (Gibson, 1958, p. 5). She was ambitious, arrogant, and tough and got into mischief running away from home frequently. Stickball, basketball, baseball, paddle tennis, and football were street games she played during the daytime. A favorite night occupation was hanging around bowling alleys. Sugar Ray Robinson was someone she idolized; he was a tremendous inspiration to her.

While in New York, Althea quit high school and worked as a counter girl at Chock Full O'Nuts, and as a messenger for a blueprint company. She was also employed at a button factory, at a dress factory, and at a department store. She operated an elevator; she cleaned chickens at a butcher shop; but during that restless time of her life the job that most appealed to her was being a mail clerk at the New York School of Social Work.

She broke into tennis circles via Police Athletic League paddle ball competition. One-hundred forty-third street was designated as a play street. Althea won the block championship. Spotted while playing paddle ball by Buddy Walker, a musician, he provided Althea with used tennis rackets and balls and started her working against the concrete handball court backboards at Morris Park. From there, it was to the Harlem River Tennis Courts and then The Cosmopolitan Tennis Club which was referred to by Althea as "the ritzy tennis club in Harlem. All the Sugar Hill society people belonged to it" (Gibson, 1958, p. 28).

In 1941, Althea Gibson entered her first tennis tournament, a state level competition, and won. Later in the same year she was unsuccessful in her first national event losing in the finals. Then came her life in Wilmington and with it completion of high school, hard training, the American Tennis Association's women's singles championship and the decision to move on. She was recommended for a scholarship to Florida A & M by the tennis coach and was 22 years old when she started her college career in Tallahassee. At 25 she graduated. It was Alice Marble who engineered Althea's membership into the USLTA in 1950; seven years later, Gibson was victorious at Wimbledon and Forest Hills. She repeated her successes in 1958.

Daly (1973) reports that in the early 1960s Althea gave the professional golf tour a try and stayed with pro golf for ten years. Now, married to William Darben, she is a tennis pro at a new club near her East Orange, New Jersey, home. Althea Gibson, black *and* female, made sport history: she integrated the playing courts at Wimbledon and Forest Hills. And she was a winner.

## Speed Skating Champion: Annie Henning

Winner of the 500-meter sprint in the XI Winter Olympiad at Sapporo, Japan, Annie Henning, 16, started skating at the age of 4 with the assistance (physical) of her mother. At 10 she began to participate in the organized speed skating program in her home community of Northbrook, a Chicago suburb. In addition to being a hay and soybean center of the midwest, Northbrook is populated by some 27,000 white-collar residents and has contributed 5 skaters to the 17-member United States speed-skating team. Ed Rudolph, Annie's coach, reportedly saw "gold medals dancing" (Johnson, 1972a, p. 33) before his eyes when he first observed the young, happy, relaxed athlete. He has trained her ever since.

Described as having "elfin features," Annie is strong and still referred to as a tomboy. Among her other sport pursuits are swimming, skiing, sailing, and baseball. Olympic obligations forced her to give up participation in intramural Powder Puff football. In the 1970 Powder Puff Super Bowl, as star halfback, Annie Henning scored 5 touchdowns. Jogging and bicycling are activities she has engaged in as a part of her Olympic training regimen.

Mr. and Mrs. Henning, a hospital consultant and nursery-school teacher respectively, have supported Annie in her skating endeavors but have not pressed her to strive for champion level performance. Her father indicated, "If she needs our support, we're here to give it. This is sport—not a lifetime career" (Johnson, 1972a, p. 33). Annie has made the statement that "Everything I am today I owe to Snoopy and peanut butter" (Johnson, 1972a, p. 33). She travels with several jars of peanut butter in her suitcase and a worn-out old Snoopy doll. She skates with her brother's faded knit cap atop her blonde curly hair. Another part of her regulation uniform is a small Snoopy pin.

Olympic style speed skating is hardly popular in the United States. For example, there is only one standard competition racing rink in the country. It is located in West Allis, Wisconsin, just outside of Milwaukee. Any American who participates in international speed skating competition has to perform quite differently than what might be called "the American way." Instead of charging from a bunch, European racing style which is practiced in all world events, pits the performer against a stopwatch. There are no special rewards or endorsements for success in speed skating in this country either. Annie Henning's achievement, therefore, is particularly significant. When one considers also that the median age of women Olympic speed skaters is 20, Annie's gold medal at 16 is good reason for her coach to speculate that she can sweep all four golds in 1976.

An unusual incident adds to Annie Henning's distinction as a champion. Because she was fouled on her initial, but winning, sprint at Sapporo, the judges allowed her a second sprint—a solo trial after all other competitors had skated. Annie beat her own winning time by 4/10ths of a second (Johnson, 1972b, p. 13). So, she clocked two gold medals in the same event.

## Champion Swimmer: Donna deVarona

Born in the city of San Francisco, Donna moved to Lafayette, a small community in the hills east of San Francisco Bay, with her parents at age 3. As a young child, Donna would have much preferred to play on her brother's Little League baseball team than to engage in the regular diving lessons and practice in which she was enrolled. Her father, a former professional football player, aspired to a diving championship for his youngest daughter; her first coach thought she had the potential. But the idea of swimming appealed much more to Donna.

Without formal training and proceeding merely on some tips from her father, she entered her first AAU swimming meet and finished tenth among 10 competitors. Donna did not even know how to take her mark and was embarrassed by making several false starts. But she was determined and the initial competitive experience led to regular coaching and practice at the Berkeley YMCA. The next formulative years were marked by hard work. At age 11, all 58 inches and 88 pounds of Donna deVarona entered the nationals. She swam in the mile swim, 100-yard butterfly and 220-yard butterfly. "The competition in all of them was too tough. She didn't make the finals" (Thomas, 1968, p. 71).

Following the close of the school year in 1960, Donna engaged in all-out training for the Olympics. It was at that time that she joined other famous aquatic athletes at the Santa Clara Swimming Club, "champion factory." In 1960, at the outdoor nationals in Indianapolis, she broke her first world record. She was 13 years old. Then came the 1960 Olympic Games in Rome. Donna was the youngest member of the United States team.

The *International Swimming Hall of Fame Fifth Anniversary Yearbook* summarizes this champion's achievements as follows:

Miss deVarona won 37 individual national championship medals, including 18 golds and three national high point awards. She held world records in 8 long course events and American records in 10 short course events, which would have been world records if FINA still recognized 25 yard pool times as they did in 1957. Most of Donna's world and American records were broken and rebroken numerous times by Donna herself, so she actually held many times more records than the 18 events she held them in.

Her versatility is reflected in her absolute dominance of the tough four stroke Individual Medley often thought of in track terms as "the decathlon of swimming." She further won national titles and set world fastest times in 3 of the 4 strokes in individual events (backstroke, butterfly, and freestyle), establishing herself at various times as the world's fastest as well as the world's best all around swimmer of her day.*

* From *Fifth Anniversary Yearbook 1965-1970*, Ft. Lauderdale, Fla.: International Swimming Hall of Fame, Inc., p. 35. Copyright 1971 by International Swimming Hall of Fame, Inc. and reprinted by permission.

Donna deVarona's competitive swimming career ended early, as it began, for she believed that she should quit while on top. She participated in only one competition, in 1965, in Germany, after the Tokyo Olympics.

Upon entering UCLA in 1965 Donna became interested in many campus activities. Among other things, she coached the UCLA women's swimming team. She also began to model swim suits for a popular manufacturer, promote pool and chemical sales, and announce swimming events on "Wide World of Sports" for ABC television. One of the most photographed athletes of her era, Donna was cover girl on *Life, Time, Saturday Evening Post,* and twice on *Sports Illustrated.* Among her awards in 1964, a heavy award year, were: America's Outstanding Woman Athlete, Outstanding American Female Swimmer, San Francisco's Outstanding Woman of the Year. In addition she was honored by *Mademoiselle* and by the National Academy of Sports.

Diminutive Donna deVarona was a distinguished champion; her petiteness and the young age at which she represented this country in the Olympic Games differentiated her. The relative shortness of her championship career was also unusual. Finally, her service to the Antipoverty Program in the summer of 1966, conducted under the auspices of the President's Council on Physical Fitness, took her to slums in Baltimore, Chicago, Detroit, St. Louis, and New York and provided a sharp contrast to the international journeys and glory she knew as a great woman athlete.

### Champion Figure Skater: Peggy Fleming

Peggy Fleming, born in San Jose, California, moved to Cleveland with her family when she was ten years old. That was when she tried on her first pair of skates. Among the immediate effects was loss of interest in other activities such as baseball and tree-climbing. Within one year she was winning juvenile championships. It was not until the age of 13, however, that Peggy began serious training. She worked with former English champion, John Nicks, and later with Carlo Fassi, famous Italian skater. Peggy discovered ". . . to skate well takes more than a love of the sport. . . . It means practicing the same figures over and over and over, six to eight hours a day, six days a week" (McFadden et al., 1968, p. 2). At 15 Peggy became the youngest Senior Ladies Champion in the history of skating, her first national championship. At the Innsbruck Olympics that year, 1964, she finished sixth in her first attempt in the international arena.

Peggy Fleming, 1960. [Courtesy Wide World Photos, Inc.]

The Fleming family, father, mother and three sisters, moved to Colorado Springs when Peggy was 16. Thereafter, she became successful in world-wide competition winning her first championship in 1966 at Davos. She was overwhelmingly victorious, by more than 60 points, over the reigning Canadian champion. Success was all too soon followed by sadness. Her father died of a heart attack after visiting her during an exhibition.

Peggy's interests include a special love for the cartoon "Peanuts" and music. In her early teens she learned the violin and has felt that music has been an important factor in her life. Peggy has a strong attachment to her family. One of her favorite foods is macaroni, which she frequently enjoyed as a pre-performance meal. While in Colorado Springs, she attended high school and then graduated from Hollywood Professional School. A career at Colorado College and aspirations to complete degree requirements and earn a certificate to be an elementary school teacher had to be abandoned. Skating and studying simultaneously were too demanding.

Peggy Fleming, United States figure skating champion 5 times and World Ladies Champion 3 times, was the only United States gold medal winner in the 1968 Grenoble Olympics. And she won "big," outscoring the nearest of her 31 opponents by an amazing 88.2 points. She has been described as "flawless" and "incomparable." But one of the highest tributes was expressed by Gabrielle Seyfert of East Germany, the opponent she defeated at Grenoble. "Peggy has no weaknesses," she said, "on the ice she is pure ballerina" (McFadden et al., 1968, p. 2). Peggy Fleming was a great champion, one who was never defeated in competition.

### Champion Golfer: Kathy Whitworth

Referred to in the *LPGA 1972 Guide* as "the tall, talented Texan (p. 96)" Kathrynne Ann Whitworth has been acclaimed by many as one of the greatest all-time women golfers. A native of Jal, New Mexico, Kathy now considers Richardson, Texas, her home. The all-time money winner on the LPGA circuit was born in 1939 and started to play golf at the age of 15. Kathy attended Jal High School and then Odessa Junior College.

She comes by descriptions of being tall quite naturally. Whitworth is 5 feet 9 inches and now tips the scales at a trim 140 pounds. This is 85 pounds less than she carried with her when she first joined the women's pro tour in 1959. During the first few months of pro-

fessional competition, she had a hard time. She was winless and discouraged to the point of wanting to quit. It was her family's persistence
that purportedly kept her going (Mulvoy, 1967). And she has been at
it ever since.

A highly personable individual, off the course Kathy is said to be
as likely to join the younger group of tour players for a movie as she is
to play hearts with the older set. But there is only one consideration
when she is on the course—her game. And that seems to be at the root
of the Whitworth success story. No one, no special event or magical
formula warrants acknowledgment in Kathy's rise to championship
status. The credit goes to Kathy Whitworth herself—her enormous
powers of concentration and the remarkable attitude she has expressed
about the pressure that builds up from being on top and trying to stay
there. "You're never allowed to have a bad round," she says, "and
you're supposed to win all the time. You try, sure, but you can't do it
every week. There has to be a value placed on pleasure, not just winning . . ." (Mulvoy, 1967, p. 63). Kathy tries to deal with pressure by
paying attention to her own game instead of worrying who is one or
two or three strokes ahead of her.

In a published question-and-answer report with Ann Jameison,
Kathy acknowledged that she does not necessarily pursue any exercise
regimen to keep in shape when she's not on tour. But she allowed that
she possibly should. Concerning the issue of how old a woman golfer
could be and remain a contender, the $331,738.26 tour earner, over
the years, wisely speculates that it is a totally individual matter. The
more critical factors influencing play and forcing it downhill would
be ". . . nerves . . . and . . . concentration" (Jameison, 1973, p. 29).

Kathy Whitworth served as President of the LPGA. She, like many
of her tour colleagues, was involved in the struggle to raise the purse for
women pros. Under her leadership some important gains were made. A
bit of "the stuff" of Kathy Whitworth is revealed by the story of her
reaction to a PGA putdown. When plans for a series of elimination
matches, mixed Scotch foursomes of 12 men and 12 women, were
rejected by the PGA, Kathy said, "Now we know where we stand with
the men. We know we're not going to get any help from them, and
we'll have to do it on our own. Well, that's fine." And so the die was
cast.

What does a person like Kathy Whitworth do to relax? In a recent
*Golf Digest* feature on the subject, it was explained that she takes her
metal-detector out for a walk when she is home on the Gulf ("How the

Lady Pros Relax," 1971, p. 44). She scours the area, according to the report for—well, anything. "I'm hoping to find a Spanish coin, or an old gun—something like that," Kathy indicated. Though the article suggested a real goal was to find a buried treasure, it was candidly pointed out that Kathy Whitworth has "mined" pro golf for sufficient loot to support her hobby for many years to come.

An abundance of awards have been bestowed upon this great champion. Since 1959, she has won some 64 tournaments, 59 individual titles, and last year (1972) earned a record $65,000. LPGA "Player of the Year" for six successive years, Associated Press "Woman of the Year" in 1965 and 1966, *Golf Digest* Performance Average Champion year in and year out, Kathy Whitworth has demonstrated what it means to be a top-level female athlete with a consistency that can be associated with few others.

### Track Champion: Wyomia Tyus

Born in 1945 in Griffin, Georgia, Wyomia was the fourth child in the Tyus family. Her three older siblings were brothers. Only one was an athlete; he played tackle on the high school football team. Willie Tyus, father, was a dairy worker. Mrs. Tyus (Marie) worked in a laundry. Wyomia's father died when she was 15.

As a high school student, Wyomia Tyus' favorite sport was basketball. But when the season was over and there was no other activity in which she could participate, she went out for track and field. At first, her efforts were directed toward high jumping. But she realized the event was not for her and so switched to running.

Well-known Tennessee State University at Nashville coach, Ed Temple, was on a recruiting trip in the summer of 1961 that took him to high school competitions. He spotted Wyomia and was impressed by her potential. She entered his summer training program. At the end of one month of training, she went to the AAU girls' national championships where she continued to learn but did not win.

One year later she was successful at the girls' nationals in Los Angeles in three events: 50, 75, and 100 yard races. In winning, she broke two American records. In 1963, Wyomia competed in both the girls' AAU meet and just one month later, the women's meet, the latter for the first time. A win in her 100-yd heat allowed her to enter the finals in which she finished second. The achievement was important because it led to a trip to Moscow for a United States-Soviet Union

Wyomia Tyus (right) wins gold medal in the 100-m race in the 1964 Olympics.
[Courtesy USOC.]

competition. Her fourth-place finish in the 100-m dash against a field of three others, including a U.S. teammate and two Russians, was a very unhappy experience for Wyomia. Two years later when she returned to Russia she said, "I wanted to win so bad there . . . . All I could remember was finishing last in 1963" (Henderson, 1968, p. 265). And win she did. She equaled the world record in the 100; ran second in the 200; and proved that she was the world's fastest in the 400-m relay making up a 4-yard deficit and crossing the tape 5 yards ahead of her opposition. Her success was viewed on TV by many Americans.

In September 1963, Wyomia Tyus entered Tennessee State University and was awarded a track scholarship. She became one of the famous "Tigerbelles," 29 of whom represented the United States in Olympic Games from 1956 through 1972 and 3 more who ran as representatives of their own countries (foreign) during the same period. Wyomia thrived under expert daily coaching and practice in a setting that produced female track stars. She won the 100-m dash in the 1964 AAU women's nationals and two weeks later earned a place on the 1964 Olympic team. It was a close call at the Olympic trials for Wyomia's aspirations to go to Tokyo were so great that it made her nervous and all she could manage was a third—by inches—in her event. But it was good enough for squad selection.

In Tokyo in 1964 she won her heat of the 100-m dash in 11.3 seconds; the quarter finals in 11.2; the semi-finals in 11.3. Then she won the finals "by two yards in 11.4 seconds and became the world's fastest female (Henderson, 1968, p. 265). National honors were again hers in subsequent years and in the 1968 Olympics in Mexico City, she once more captured a gold medal in the 100-m dash becoming the only person, male or female, to win the gold in the 100-m event in two successive Olympiads. It was obvious that the Black Power issue at the 19th Olympic Games stirred Wyomia. As one of the four members of the winning 400-m relay team, Wyomia said in a news conference, ". . . we dedicate our relay win to John Carlos and Tommie Smith" ("US Women Dedicate Victory to Smith, Carlos," _The New York Times,_ October 21, 1968, p. 60). The two Black star runners had just been suspended and ordered to leave Olympic Village.

There is a lot of champion in Wyomia Tyus—134 pounds on a 67-inch frame. She is reportedly quiet and somewhat shy. Upon being compared to Wilma Rudolph, something which occurred very frequently, Wyomia acknowledged being flattered but retorted, "I can't be her. I'm just Wyomia" (Henderson, 1968, p. 263).

**TABLE 11**
United States Softball Team, Osaka World Championship 1970*

| Player | Position | Age | Height (in.) | Occupation |
|---|---|---|---|---|
| Adams, M.S. | Outfield | 22 | 63.5 | Computer assembler |
| Adams, R.M. | 2nd Base | 18 | 62.0 | College student |
| Bredeen, S.M. | Outfield; Catcher | 27 | 61.5 | PE teacher |
| Davis, M. | Outfield | 28 | 67.5 | PE teacher |
| Graham, K. | Catcher; Outfield | 20 | 67.0 | College student |
| Rice, J.L. | Pitcher | 29 | 67.5 | PE teacher |
| Y. Ito, N. | Catcher | 36 | 67.0 | Computer programmer |
| Ponce, C.A. | Outfield | 22 | 62.0 | College student |
| Schnell, P.J. | Utility | 21 | 62.5 | College student |
| Sims, S.K. | 3rd Base | 21 | 64.0 | College student |
| Spanks, C.A. | Shortstop | 33 | 66.5 | PE teacher |
| Topley, S.A. | 1st Base | 35 | 67.8 | Cost accountant |
| Welborn, N. | Pitcher | 25 | 71.0 | PE teacher |
| Zavala, R.M. | Outfield; Pitcher | 17 | 67.5 | High school student |
| Combined average | | 25.29 | 65.52 | |

\* Roster copied in order presented in the official program, *Women's World Softball Championship, Osaka, '70.*

## U.S. Team:  1970 World Softball Championship Tournament

Nine softball teams engaged in the 2nd Women's World Championship at Osaka, Japan, August 22 through 30, 1970. In the finals the United States team lost to Japan. Nonetheless, players on the squad warrant recognition as champions. To supplement descriptive data offered above about performers of individual sports who have participated in international competitions, a few statistics taken from the official program, *Women's World Softball Championship Osaka '70,* are listed in Table 11. Mean height is just slightly more than collegians reported earlier in the chapter; softball players average 1.43 inches taller. No weight data were available. And in spite of the six students on the Osaka team, women softball champions are significantly older; 25.29 mean years old in comparison to the collegians 19.19. Occupational information seems to suggest that the women are well educated. Remarks about each player lead one to conclude that most of them have been playing softball for a number of years on teams in their home areas.

**TABLE 12**
**Virginia Slims Players according to Country and Age**

| Country | Number of competitors | Age/ mean age |
|---------|-----------------------|---------------|
| Australia | 8 | 23 |
| Canada | 1 | 28 |
| France | 1 | 31 |
| Great Britain | 3 | 23 |
| Indonesia | 2 | 25.5 |
| Netherlands | 1 | 28 |
| South Africa | 1 | 26 |
| Sweden | 1 | 26 |
| United States | 31 | 23 |
| Combined average | | 24.25 |
| Total | 49 | |

## THE "NEW" PROS

It is not surprising that the first commercial product associated with the women's lib movement, women's most popular cigarette, Virginia Slims, provided key support to the organization and growth of the current Women's Professional Tennis Tour. Pushing the million dollar mark as a business venture and claiming a total of 68 outstanding female players on its roster, the Virginia Slims Circuit is still gaining popularity in spite of USLTA attempts to control female players. Heldman (1973) points out that of the original nine tennis starts in the initial Pro Tourney, ". . . two have retired from competition . . . and the others are still going strong, bloody but unbowed, wiser and richer, and still stubborn as hell" (p. 44).

Examination of some of the statistics about the pros who joined the Circuit offers a general idea of some of their characteristics. Player profiles presented in *Lob* (1973), official publication of the Virginia Slims Women's Tennis Circuit and Women's International Tennis Federation, provided the following information.

### Personal Factors

The mean, median, and modal age of 48 pro tennis players on the Circuit profiled in *Lob* is 24. The oldest player claims France as her native land and is 31; the youngest, an American, is 18. Table 12 permits

**TABLE 13**
**Height, Weight, Dress Size of 49 Virginia Slims Pros**

| Variable | United States players | | Foreign players | |
|---|---|---|---|---|
| | $f$ | % | $f$ | % |
| *Height* | | | | |
| Shorter than 60 in. | 0 | | 0 | |
| 60 – 62 | 2 | 6.0 | 0 | |
| 63 – 65 | 9 | 30.0 | 5 | 26.0 |
| 66 – 68 | 14 | 47.0 | 10 | 52.0 |
| 69 – 71 | 4 | 14.0 | 2 | 11.0 |
| 72 – 74 | 1 | 3.0 | 2 | 11.0 |
| *Weight* | | | | |
| Less than 100 lb. | 1 | 3.0 | | |
| 100 – 109 | 2 | 6.0 | 0 | |
| 110 – 119 | 8 | 27.0 | 1 | 6.0 |
| 120 – 129 | 4 | 14.0 | 5 | 26.0 |
| 130 – 139 | 9 | 30.0 | 8 | 42.0 |
| 140 – 149 | 4 | 14.0 | 2 | 11.0 |
| 150 – 159 | 2 | 6.0 | 2 | 11.0 |
| 160 – 169 | | | | |
| More than 169 lb. | | | 1 | 6.0 |
| *Dress size* | | | | |
| Smaller than 8 | 4 | 14.0 | 0 | |
| 8 – 9 | 6 | 20.0 | 4 | 22.0 |
| 10 – 11 | 10 | 33.5 | 2 | 11.0 |
| 12 – 13 | 7 | 23.5 | 10 | 52.0 |
| 14 – 15 | 2 | 6.0 | 3 | 15.0 |
| 16 – 17 | 1 | 3.0 | | |
| $N$ | 30 | | 19 | |

comparisons between the Americans who make up the large majority of tour players and those from other countries. Foreign players, except for the English, are slightly older than their American colleagues. Within the United States distribution, the number of women in the youngest age bracket, 18-19, exceeds those in the oldest, 30-31, by one.

Mean weights are 124.50 for the Americans and 127.36 for the foreigners. United States tennis pros average 66.23 inches, their other-land associates average 67.16 inches. Karen Krantzcke of Australia is the tallest and heaviest player on the tour. She is 73 inches tall and carries 170 pounds. Little Sue Vinton, who calls Sarasota, Florida, her hometown, is the smallest. She is 62 inches tall but weighs only 97 pounds. Dress sizes run about even-up. But one should bear in mind that garments manufactured outside of the United States may not necessarily be the same as those cut to American standards.

Table 13 summarizes the height, weight, and dress size data. Categories were set up to complement those of the collegiate athletes presented earlier in the chapter. Percentages of the pro statistics must be interpreted with caution because of the very small sample involved.

## Other Traits

Review of some of the additional information reported in *Lob* (1973) under player profiles reveals that only five of these athletes are lefties. Lita Sugiarto-Liem of Djkarta, Indonesia, is listed as being both right- and left-handed. Twenty-three of the players have a nickname; the remaining 26 indicate that they do not. More than half of the women have brown hair, 20 reporting brown and 8 more specifying light brown. There are 11 blondes on the Circuit; 8 players with black hair; one reddish-brown; and one redhead. Twenty of the women are also brown-eyed; 19 have blue eyes; 2 are identified as having blue-green eyes, 4 green, and 1 gray-brown.

For those who might wonder if the "new" breed of woman professional athlete might be uniquely described by a particular symbolism —specifically, the Zodiac signs—an analysis of the pro's 49 signs turns up what might be regarded as a somewhat "normal distribution." More of the Virginia Slims stars come under the sign of Taurus than any other; 1 each is a Libra and a Capricorn. The Zodiac data is compiled in Table 14. Thirty-four of the 49 Circuiters' signs are Bull, Crab, Lion, Ram, Twins and Virgin. The meanings Senard (Cirlot, 1962) designates for each of these signs respectively: undifferentiated magnetism, gestation and birth, individuation and will, urge to create and transform, creative synthesis and imagination, and intelligence (which seems highly appropriate for a group who excluded men, for the first time in 90 years, from the locker room of the wealthy Newport Casino). Dember's (1972) account of the effects of bringing the Virginia Slims Invitational to Newport for Tennis Week in 1972 provides a factual, amusing, and realistic account of the phenomenal success of these highly skilled performers who, together, have changed the realm of one pro sport.

The simple descriptive information about 270 athletes organized and presented in this chapter does not turn up special features that would set off women who take their sport involvement very seriously

Zodiac Signs of Virginia Slims Athletes

| Dates | Symbol | f | Meaning |
| --- | --- | --- | --- |
| March 21 – April 20 | The Ram (Aries) ♈ | 5 | The exuberance of spring; pioneering, progressive, ambitious |
| April 21 – May 21 | The Bull (Taurus) ♉ | 7 | Use of earthy things; strength |
| May 22 – June 21 | The Twins (Gemini) ♊ | 5 | Dualism, alternation; open to ideas, continuous self-education |
| June 22 – July 23 | The Crab (Cancer) ♋ | 6 | Carrying-forward-force; quality of touch, selectivity |
| July 24 – August 23 | The Lion (Leo) ♌ | 6 | Sense of life; vitality, power, will |
| August 24 – September 23 | The Virgin (Virgo) ♍ | 5 | Correction and adjustment; methodical, orderly, efficient |
| September 24 – October 23 | The Balance (Libra) ♎ | 1 | Wholeness, association; keen perception and judgment |
| October 24 – November 22 | Scorpion & Eagle (Scorpio) ♏ | 2 | Secretiveness; outspoken, emphatic, strong, unyielding |
| November 23 – December 21 | The Archer (Sagittarius) ♐ | 3 | Seer of goals; love for the out-of-doors, adventure |
| December 22 – January 20 | The Goat (Capricorn) ♑ | 1 | Ambition; strong-minded, grave and serious |
| January 21 – February 19 | The Water Bearer (Aquarius) ♒ | 4 | Love of human beings; new ideas—beyond the staid, corrective action of wisdom and love |
| February 20 – March 20 | The Fishes (Pisces) ♓ | 4 | Destiny and divinity; hospitality, generosity, good will |
| N | | 49 | |

from those who comprise the general population. Perhaps the comment purportedly made about Peggy Fleming (McFadden et al., 1968, p. 4), "remarkably typical," would apply to most American sportswomen. Facts about physical features, educational background, interests, and their families serve as testimony that female athletes are not gross or dumb creatures. Rather, they may be characterized as having a particular aptness for using their physical endowments to the fullest. They are developing or have already acquired high-level skills. In so doing they obviously place involvement in sport competition with its challenges and demands above other endeavors.

# Chapter 9
# Personality Traits

Personality theorists, sport psychologists, and, in fact, most students of human behavior have been unable to provide a single meaning for the word *personality*. Hall and Lindzey (1957) state that ". . . no substantive definition of personality can be applied with any generality" (p. 9). They suggest defining the term according to a particular personality theory and its specific constructs. But while it seems relatively simple to discuss various aspects of personality in regard to Freudian or Neo-Freudian theory or Goldstein's organismic theory or Murphy's biosocial theory, to cite but a few of the several dozen major theoretical frames of reference that are accepted as part of the body of knowledge of psychology, the issue is much more complicated. For example, problems are encountered in operationalizing definitions according to assessment techniques and the interpretations of such measurements. Also, translating meanings from the contexts in which they were formulated to that which is related to sport makes for further complexities. The study of personality is, at best, a difficult undertaking. Methodological and research strategies into athletes' personalities have been previously discussed by Berlin (1970), Kane (1972), Kroll (1969), Rushall (1972) and Smith (1969). These works partially explain the rather limited status of our knowledge of the subject.

There are additional reasons for the sparsity of information about the personalities of sportswomen. Psychologists have tended to have little or no concern about athletes. Those who specialize in the study of personality inquired into determinants and explanations of deviant behaviors. Then, normative data about personality were amassed. Physical educators, on the other hand, with their enormous interest in sport and physical activity, have lacked the expertise in personality and its

measurement to produce meaningful research. Until a comparatively
short time ago, there was no such thing as a sport psychologist. But,
obviously the most restrictive factor in the collection of descriptive
personality data about women athletes has simply been the almost
complete focus of research on males. Summaries of these works have
been written by Cooper (1969), Husman (1968), and Morgan (1972).
It was in 1934 that Flemming first sought to ascertain whether
emphasis on athletics might spoil the modern girl. Only recently, since
the development and refinement of multivariate research designs along
with the availability of the computer for analyses, has the quest for
insight in sportswomen's personalities begun to be fruitful. A summary
of selected studies utilizing female athletes as subjects is set forth in the
following pages. What these investigations tell us is also discussed.

## SELECTED STUDIES INVOLVING
## FEMALE ATHLETES

The earliest published report of a personality study with specific interest
in female athletes, known to the writer, appeared in *School & Society*
in 1934. The methodology pursued in the investigation depicts the
status of personality research of the time. In the fifties and sixties
inquiries took on a more formal style. Three master's theses represent
the growing sophistication of graduate student research associated with
the era. Studies undertaken in 1967 and more recently provide better
sources for comparison. Synopses of selected studies are presented in
Table 15.

The reported investigations identify six different assessment techniques. Subjects' ages span from juniors and seniors in high school
through mature adults. Experiences in competition are accounted for
which, at a lower level, acknowledge interclass high school competition
and, at a higher level, include international meets, tournaments, games
—Pan Am, United States Women's Lacrosse Association, and Olympic
events.

## ANALYSIS OF FINDINGS

Four of the studies reported above utilized assessment tools that do not
lend themselves to cross-study comparison. Flemming's checklist, for
example, is a rather unique instrument; the data generated by its use
can only be viewed in isolation. Hisey's findings, derived from the

Guilford-Zimmerman Temperament Survey, and Ibrahim's scores on GAMIN factors of the Guilford-Martin Inventory lack comparable responses from other studies of women athletes. And, although Jackson's rationale for selection of the California Psychological Inventory in her research sets forth valid points of view, her data cannot be interpreted specifically with other findings unless one generalizes meanings/definitions of terms as well as scoring standards and systems.

### Research Employing the Edwards Personal Preference Schedule

Five of the tabled studies report results in terms of the Edwards Personal Preference Schedule, EPPS. This well-established standardized test provides scores on 15 traits. It is difficult, however, to determine consistencies, inconsistencies, and trends in relation to these traits when the specific research question underlying each study is understood. In the account that follows, no attempt was made to interpret Ramsey's findings with those of Bird, Dayries and Grimm, Neal, and Williams et al. Sport differences, time spans between data collection (almost ten years at the extreme), age distinctions and competitive level differences all suggest that Ramsey's data do not warrant comparison with the other four works.

**Overview.** In examining the data trait by trait, both differences and similarities are evident in the comparison of athletes' scores with either the scores of nonathletes or with norms, as well as in the comparison among groups of sportswomen. On only four traits are no distinctions at all discernible: *deference, succorance, change,* and *endurance.* On the whole, Canadian ice hockey players' personality as assessed by Bird with the EPPS tended to be closest to average. The highest score she reported was in the 67th percentile for *autonomy;* the lowest scoring trait of the ice hockey group was in the 37th percentile, *dominance.* The highest measurement on all four studies was the fencers' need for *achievement,* which was in the 85th percentile; the lowest score, 30th percentile, in *nurturance,* was also registered in Williams' et al. athletes. A more critical view of these data, i.e., beyond the interquartile range or in terms of statistically tested significances of difference, provides a slightly better description of athletes' personality.

**Comparison with norms/nonathletes.** In all four studies, athletes scored higher than the norms with which they were compared on the traits *autonomy* and desire for *achievement.* Except for Canadian ice

**TABLE 15**
Selected Personality Studies of Female Athletes

| Date reported | Principal investigator | Instruments | Sample size/ geographical area | Level of competition |
|---|---|---|---|---|
| 1972 | P.A. Johnson | California Psychological Inventory | 190; various areas | Regionals/sectionals for basketball and hockey players and bowlers; national level golfers |
| 1971 | L.K. Shofar | Cattell 16 PF Questionnaire | 179 athletes; 92 nonathletes; California | Interscholastic (high school) |
| 1970 | J.M. Williams, B.J. Hoepner, D.L. Moody, and B.C. Ogilvie | Cattell 16 PF Questionnaire, Edwards Personal Preference Schedule | 30; various areas | National Championship |
| 1970 | C.L. Mushier | High School Personality Questionnaire and Cattell 16 PF Questionnaire | 308; various areas | All levels—scholastic through USWLA; US and reserve players |
| 1970 | J.L. Dayries R.I. Grim | Edwards Personal Preference Schedule | 21; Montana area | Intercollegiate |

| Sports represented | Summary of major findings |
|---|---|
| Basketball, field hockey, bowling, golf | Significant differences on 12 of 18 variables among the four groups. Basketball players lower on dominance, capacity for status, sociability, social presence, self-acceptance, responsibility, self-control, achievement via conformity, achievement via independence, intellectual efficiency and psychological mindedness. Bowlers, hockey players and golfers more alike. Basketball group inhibited, shy and awkward behavior, immature intellectual and social behavior. No differences in socialization, sense of well being, good impression, communality, flexibility, femininity. (*Research Quarterly*, 1972, 43:409–415.) |
| Basketball, field hockey and volleyball; tennis, badminton, track and field; also nonathletes | Differences ascertained between athletes and nonathletes; team sportswomen more trusting, practical, and group dependent. Individual sport team members more intelligent than nonathletes. Nonathletes more sophisticated and self-sufficient than either group of athletes. (Unpublished master's thesis, Long Beach State College, California, 1971.) |
| Fencing | Competitive fencer is very reserved, self-sufficient, autonomous with a below-average desire for affiliation and nurturance. Has a need to be the very best. Is intelligent, creative, experimenting, and imaginative. Tends to be assertive and aggressive. Top competitors are more dominating than low level competitors. (*Research Quarterly*, 1970, 41:446–453.) |
| Lacrosse players representing various ages | Jr.-high sample differed from norms on 4 factors, senior-high on 11, college on 8, association on 9—top players on 3 and national level players on 6 factors. At all levels, women lacrosse players are more reserved, intelligent, assertive, happy-go-lucky, toughminded and experimenting than norms. (*International Journal of Sport Psychology*, 1972, 3:25–31.) |
| Basketball, tennis, track and field, volleyball | As a group, athletes were higher than norms on achievement, exhibition, autonomy, affiliation, intraception, dominance, nurturance, heterosexuality, and aggression. Lower than norms on the factors of deference, order, succorance, abasement, change, and endurance. Athletes desire to be independent, unconventional, and the center of attention. They want to be successful and to accomplish tasks requiring great skill and effort. They express aggression with no guilt feeling, have need to indicate interest in others' problems, have low need for neatness and organization. Athletes could not be well differentiated from general (normal) college women. (*Perceptual & Motor Skills*, 1970, 30:229–230.) |

(*Cont.*)

**TABLE 15, continued**
**Selected Personality Studies of Female Athletes**

| Date reported | Principal investigator | Instruments | Sample size/ geographical area | Level of competition |
|---|---|---|---|---|
| 1970 | E.I. Bird | Ogilvie-Tutko Battery | 54; Eastern Canada | Intercollegiate |
| 1968 | T.M. Malumphy | Cattell 16 PF | 77 athletes, 42 nonathletes; state of Ohio | Intercollegiate |
| 1967 | S.L. Peterson, J.C. Weber, W.W. Trousdale | Cattell 16 PF | 156; various areas | AAU and Olympic caliber |

| Sports represented | Summary of major findings |
|---|---|
| Ice hockey | On the Cattell 16 PF, athletes were very high in general ability, somewhat reserved, self-sufficient, and liberal in thought, average in independence and creativity. Tendency toward assertiveness and tough poise in addition to shyness and introversion. On the Jackson Form B, players show very high autonomy, high in endurance and abasement. Aggression score is comparatively high. Dominance and achievement score at 56th and 55th percentiles. Players are below average in affiliation, social approval, and harm avoidance. On the EPPS, athletes score highest in autonomy above the 50th percentile in heterosexuality, abasement, nurturance, aggression, and achievement. Endurance score close to average. Dominance score was lowest. The winning intercollegiate team compared to aggregate profile shows champions to be more conscientious, anxious, dependent, introverted and conservative than others. (G.S. Kenyon, Ed., *Contemporary Psychology of Sport*, Chicago: The Athletic Institute, 1970.) |
| Individual sports—tennis, golf, fencing, swimming, archery; subjectively-judged sports—synchronized swimming, gymnastics; team sports—basketball, field hockey, softball; combination group—individual sports above plus volleyball, badminton, and bowling | Groups were similar on 14 dimensions of personality and significantly different on 9. Individual sport and subjectively-judged sports participants were more alike and also more similar to nonparticipants than to the other two groups. Team and team-individual groups tended to be alike and dissimilar to the other three groups. Team players high on group dependence and anxiety; low on leadership and extraversion in comparison to individual sportswomen and nonathletes. Combination group more toughminded than nonathletes. (*Research Quarterly*, 1968, 39:610–620.) |
| Individual—Olympic swimming, diving, riding, fencing, canoeing, gymnastics, and track and field; Team—Olympic volleyball, AAU top ten basketball teams | Women athletes who compete in individual sports rated higher on factors of dominance, adventurousness, sensitivity, introversion, radicalism, and self-sufficiency. These women were lower on sophistication than team sport competitors. No differences were found in regard to sociability, intelligence, stability, surgency, conscientiousness, suspecting, guilt-proneness, high self-sentiment or high ergic tension. (*Research Quarterly*, 1967, 38:686–690.) |

*(Cont.)*

| Date reported | Principal investigator | Instruments | Sample size/ geographical area | Level of competition |
|---|---|---|---|---|
| 1967 | H. Ibrahim | Guilford-Martin Gamin Inventory | 40 females, (96 males); California | College |
| 1963 | P. Neal | Edwards Personal Preference Schedule | 42; various areas | Pan-American Games competitors |
| 1962 | L.M. Ramsey | Edwards Personal Preference Schedule | 106 varsity athletes from Iowa and Texas; 130 intramural athletes from Illinois high school | High school |
| 1957 | C. Hisey | Guilford-Zimmerman Temperament Survey | 29; state of North Carolina | College |
| 1934 | E.G. Flemming | (Adjective) Trait check-list— unpublished | 303—84 athletes, 219 nonathletes; New York City | High school athletes as identified by teachers |

| Sports represented | Summary of major findings |
| --- | --- |
| Females—athletes, dancers, physical education majors; (Males—basketball, baseball, football players and physical education majors) | Dancers surpassed athletes in their tendency towards general activity. Physical education majors scored lowest. All groups combined were above average in this factor. On ascendency-submission, athletes scored in the 44th percentile, dancers 42nd and physical education majors 30th. Dancers scored highest in femininity. Athletes were found to be the group with least feeling of inferiority, dancers next. Physical education majority indicated a feeling of inadequacy and lack of confidence. In regard to nervousness, athletes were calmest and most relaxed among the three groups. Dancers and majors were average on this factor. (*Research Quarterly*, 1967, 38:615–622.) |
| Equestrian, fencing, gymnastics, tennis, swimming and diving, basketball, track and field, volleyball | Higher on achievement, autonomy, and aggression; lower in affiliation, order, and nurturance than norms. |
| Basketball—varsity and intramural | Data showed similarity among varsity and intramural athletes. Significant differences were found between players at representative levels on five of the fifteen EPPS variables: deference, exhibition, dominance, nurturance, and affiliation. Deference, nurturance, and affiliation scores for varsity were higher; exhibition and dominance scores for intramural players were higher. Differences between two varsity groups, from Iowa and Texas, were greatest. |
| Subjects had either played interscholastic basketball for four years or played with interscholastic teams and had been selected to participate in district competition | Raw scores converted to T scores yielded the following on the four traits for the four-year players: general activity, 50.33; ascendance, 50.33; emotional stability, 54.33; personal relations, 50.66. For players selected for district competition, T scores were 55.35 on general activity; 51.42 on ascendance; 51.07 on emotional stability; 47.14 on personal relations. None of these differences in traits were statistically significant. (Unpublished master's thesis, Woman's College, University of North Carolina, 1957.) |
| Interclass competition in hockey, basketball, swimming, and tennis. Other experience in badminton, archery, baseball, golf, and horseback riding for some of the subjects. | The athletic type of girl is not strikingly different from the nonathletic type except in her interest in sports. *If* there is a difference (as perceived by teachers) it is that the athletic type is more of a "good sport," fairer, livelier, has a more pleasant voice, has wider interests, is more beautiful or pretty, is more interesting in conversation, is more honest or truthful and more helpful than average. The athletic type of girl also tends to have more personality, to be more pleasing to other girls than the average and to be found in more numerous or significant positions of leadership. (*School and Society*, 1934, 39(998): 166–169.) |

hockey players, high scores were also found on the trait referred to as *exhibition*. Dayries and Grimm report significantly lower scores on *order* and high scores on *intraception* for their subjects. Neal's subjects, Pan Am competitors, were lower than norms in *order*, need for *affiliation*, and need for *nurturance*. There is some consistency in the findings on the latter two traits with Williams' et al. fencers.

**Comparisons among athletic groups.**  Viewing the data from study to study, three (i.e., Dayries and Grimm, Neal, and Williams et al.) obtained identical percentile scores, 63, in *exhibition* for their respective groups of subjects. On that same trait, Bird's hockey players scored in the high 40s. Dayries and Grimm and Neal also report identical percentile scores on *achievement*, 72. On *achievement*, fencers scored 85; Canadian ice hockey players were in the 55th percentile. Dayries and Grimm stated that Montana collegiate athletes were significantly lower than Neal's athletes on the trait designated as *order*. This was generally in agreement with Bird's as well as Williams' et al. scores on *order* which were in the 40s. The trait for which the most confused scores were obtained is *affiliation*. Dayries and Grimm data on *affiliation* is significantly higher than that of the Pan Am athletes. Ice hockey players tend to be nearer average in their *affiliation* score, 55th percentile; Williams' et al. fencers' scores were in the 32nd percentile. Neal's athletes were significantly lower, at .01, than norms.

Above-average *abasement* scores, 57th percentile, and *heterosexuality* scores, 61st percentile, were indicated by Bird for ice hockey collegiate female athletes. *Aggression* scores for the same group were in the 56th percentile. By contrast, fencers' aggression scores were in the 71st percentile.

**Likenesses to other athletic profiles.**  Similarities between Neal's findings and those of Williams et al. were considered by the latter researchers to be so striking that they speculated that there might possibly be a "sport type." The profile identified by Williams et al. to which their data most closely related was that of male and female race car drivers rather than of more common sportspersons. Without specifying a particular profile, Bird also generalized about a possible sport type of personality. Interestingly, the researchers who offered this speculation also utilized more than one personality scale in carrying out their studies.

## Research Employing the Cattell
## Sixteen Personality Factor Questionnaire

Six of the studies in Table 15 described personality traits as obtained
from scores on the Cattell Sixteen Personality Factor Questionnaire,
16PF. This reputable and highly popular paper and pencil test yields
data on sixteen primary source traits, specific personality factors, and
seven second-order traits which Cattell, Eber and Tatsuoka (1970) point
out are broader factors which derive from correlations that exist among
primary factors. Only three studies reported findings of second-order
traits. All 16PF factors are interpretable at two levels: descriptions of
the traits are available in either popular or professional nomenclature.
Simple descriptive labels, for which there are several per factor, were
used in most of the studies reported above. To avoid confusion in the
analysis of findings, particularly in instances where several terms may
refer to the same factor, Cattell's letter symbol is specified in the discussion that follows.

For purposes of interpretation, studies concerned with reasonably
similar samples and having a similar research purpose were examined
separately. Thus, high school students who play lacrosse and were in
cluded in Mushier's sample were compared, in Cattell traits, with Shofar's
subjects. Comparisons of female athletes who participate in team sports
and those who engage in individual sports were made in research
reported by Malumphy, Peterson et al., and Shofar. Because data were
presented in relation to norms by Bird, Malumphy, Mushier, and
Williams et al., their reported findings permitted cross-study analysis.

Overview. Not one of Cattell's 16 factors was found to be distinguishing
in all of the studies employing the instrument. The Factor labeled Q2 and
described by the bipolar terms group-dependent–self-sufficient was
accounted for in 6 of the studies. Only Malumphy did not report differences between Q2 and any of her athletes or nonparticipants. Bird,
Mushier, Peterson et al., and Williams et al. reported high scores on the
trait. Shofar, whose subjects were young high school athletes, indicated
lower Q2 scores for athletes than nonathletes.

Experimenting as contrasted to conservative, Factor Q1, turned up
as significant in four of the investigations: Bird, Mushier, Peterson et al.,
and Williams et al. These same inquiries reported similar findings for
Factor E, which recognizes athletes as being more assertive. Four differ-

ent studies revealed high scores in Factor M, practical as contrasted to imaginative. Shofar's reported differences between athletes were of an intrasport nature rather than in relation to norms. She found that high school team sport players are more practical than those engaging in individual sports. Factor H, shyness–adventurousness; Factor I, tough-minded–tender-minded; and Factor A, reserved–outgoing were principal differences on at least three of the studies.

Examination of traits that were not distinctive on any of the six investigations excluding high school subjects identifies C, Q3, and Q4: emotional stability, self-sentiment, and ergic tension. Factor G, expedient-conscientious and Factor B, low-high intelligence were found to yield significant differences on only two of the investigations.

**Comparison of high school subsamples.** Mushier reported significant differences on eleven primary source traits between senior high school respondents and norms. Lacrosse players were more reserved (A), intelligent (B), assertive (E), happy-go-lucky (F), expedient (G), tough-minded (I), suspicious (L), forthright (N), experimenting (Q1), undisciplined (Q3), and tense (Q4). Shofar, on the other hand, found differences between athletes and nonathletes on only two traits: N and Q2. She stated that nonathletes were more sophisticated and self-sufficient than were her team or individual sport samples. There is, then, distinct contradiction between Mushier's and Shofar's findings on Factor N.

**Comparisons between team sports players and individual sport athletes.** Three of the tabled studies, works by Malumphy, Peterson et al. and Shofar, investigated differences in personality factors according to sport type—individual or team. In examining these data, only a segment of Malumphy's findings were considered; her combination groups of team and individual sport athletes and those who were affiliated with subjectively judged sports (as she referred to them) were excluded from the following comparison.

No trait distinguished team sportswomen from those who engage in so-called individual types of activities in all three studies. Peterson et al. and Malumphy reported individual sports athletes as scoring higher on Factor H, more venturesome than shy. On Factor M, practical–imaginative, AAU and Olympic-level individual sports athletes studied by Peterson et al. are more practical than team sports players representing the same level of competition. Just the opposite finding was reported by Shofar for high school athletes. High school team sports players are more imaginative (Factor M) than individual sport performers. The same differences were observed in Factor Q2, self-sufficiency. Mature individual sportswomen score high on Q2 whereas high school age team sports players score high on the same trait.

All other findings of differences between those who participate in team events as compared to individual sports are unique to each study. Peterson et al. reported individual sport athletes as being more dominant (E), tender-minded or more sensitive (I), and more experimenting (Q1) than the team sports athletes they studied. On one trait, Factor N, shrewdness, individual sport participants scored lower than basketball and volleyball team members. In accord with obtained scores on Factor L, Shofar reported team sports players of high school age to be more trusting than their individual sport counterparts.

**Differences between athletes and norms/nonathletes.** Data reported by Bird, Malumphy, Mushier, and Williams et al. are compared in the following discussion. On Factor A, athletes in Mushier's high-level association group were found to be more reserved than norms. Williams' et al. data on fencers offered the same distinction. Three investigations, Bird, Mushier, and Williams et al., reported higher scores on intelligence, (Factor B) than norms for their athletes. The same three investigations were in agreement on Factors E and Q1. That is to say, athletes may be described as more assertive and more experimenting. Mushier's lacrosse subjects, specifically the lower-level association players, were alone in producing high scores than norms on Factor E, happy-go-lucky. College level lacrosse players were the only athletes compared to norms who scored higher on Factor L, more suspicious. Only Malumphy reported differences in Factor G with norms. Those she grouped as engaging in subjectively judged sports are more conscientious and persistent than norms. Such a finding is not in the least surprising when one considers the nature of gymnastic and synchronized swimming involvement. Mushier and Malumphy reported greater shyness, Factor H, among their respective sample than are considered normative.

Factor I is described as tough-minded or tender-minded. Malumphy found athletes more tough-minded than nonathlete participants in her research. Among Mushier's association lacrosse players, those who participated on less successful teams were the only segment of her sample who could be described as more tough-minded than norms. On Factor M, practical–imaginative, Malumphy, Mushier, and Williams et al. had similar observations. Their athletes' scores all indicated more practicality than did the data for the average individual. Mushier also reported her college lacrosse players to be more forthright (Factor M) and one group, lower-level association players, more self-assured (Factor O).

**Differences among second-order traits.**  Bird, Malumphy, and Williams et al. investigated second-order traits. It should be noted that the *1970 16 PF Handbook* cautions that the definition of secondary factors "is not yet good enough to allow identification or extensive use" (p. 17). Nonetheless, findings pertaining to women athletes reported in the above studies are summarized to add completeness to the personality picture.

Bird offered her data in comparison with norms. Canadian ice hockey players score above the 50th percentile on anxiety. Factors referred to as introversion–extraversion and emotionality yield still higher scores. Her highest scoring second-order trait is creativity.

Comparisons in terms of statistically significant differences among the five groups that comprised her sample were reported by Malumphy. Athletes in the team sports subsample were significantly more anxious than either individual sports performers or those engaged in subjectively judged sports. In the trait described as introversion–extraversion, the following differences were revealed: all groups were more extraverted than team sports players; those participating in subjectively-judged sports and individual sports were more extraverted than the combination individual and team sport group; and, nonparticipants in sport were more extraverted than two of the sport groups with which they were compared—team sportswomen and combination team and individual sportswomen. Malumphy also found that individual sports athletes and subjectively-judged sports athletes were more tough poised than nonparticipants. This would suggest that sportswomen are more emotionally sensitive or tend to feel rather than think. Leadership, still another second-order factor, revealed differences between subjectively-judged and individual sports group and other athletes in Malumphy's study. In all instances, leadership scores were significantly higher for these two sport types.

## SEX DIFFERENCES

Prior to pointing out the meager information that is available relative to sex differences among athletes' measured personality traits, the issue of distinctions between male and female personality in the population at large warrants a few words. Cattell, Eber and Tatsuoka (1970) state that "the difference between men and women, in our own culture and others, shows up very clearly on the 16PF" (p. 69). In their explanation of these differences, they identify only four of the 16 factors, corrected for age, that are the same for both sexes: Factor B, intelligence; Factor C, ego strength; Factor F, surgency; and Q2, self-sufficiency. According to Cattell and his colleagues, sex differences are of magnitude in comparison to age differences. Although the latter are identified, they are regarded as less influential. Barry, Bacon, and Child (1964) generalize age differences in relation to sex insofar as socialization is concerned. Their comment seems to bear especially on the athlete. According to these researchers, sex differences in personality are unimportant in infancy. "But . . . in childhood there is . . . a widespread pattern of greater pressure toward nurturance, obedience, and responsibility in girls, and toward self-reliance and achievement striving in boys" (p. 606).

In regard to specific sex differences among athletes, Ogilvie (1968) reported a somewhat unclear relationship between personality and competition when separating athletes by sex and age grouping. However, when controlling for sex differences and level of competition among Santa Clara Swim Club team members, Ogilvie stated that ". . . we find that boys and girls become much more similar between the ages of ten and fourteen years of age" (p. 781). Females shift toward being more outgoing, but do not achieve the level of youthful males in Factor A, reserved-outgoing. Differences, as well as similarities, were also found by Ogilvie for the same age group of male and female swimmers from Indiana. In his summary of the study of these traits he stated that ". . . these data suggest that there is a movement toward extraversion with age for males but less so for females" (p. 781).

With college-age competitors, swimmers, that is, comparison of personality trait scores yielded quite similar profiles. Among differences that were noted, however, were that ". . . Indiana males were slightly brighter and more outgoing. The college women [San Jose State] were much more venturesome-bold, more experimental, lower in resting level of anxiety and less tense" (p. 782). Klafs and Lyon (1973) discuss these findings in more detail.

Kane (1972), in comparing female personality data of athletes with that of males, reported that his findings for women subjects tended to fit social expectations. Women were described as measuring lower on Factor E, dominance, and Q2, self-sufficiency. On the other hand, they were higher on Factors I, M, Q1 and A; Kane explains these traits as more emotionally sensitive, anxious, conservative, and socially warm (p. 28). Relative to sex differences, Kane poses a critical question in wondering whether differences in personality between sportsmen and sportswomen are less than those of the so-called average nonparticipating men and women.

In conjunction with a long-range inquiry into collegiate women's athletic motivation, the writer amassed data relative to achievement needs of selected athletes as measured by the Lynn Questionnaire (Lynn, 1969). Responses were obtained from men and women tennis players, squad members attending the same institution as well as other colleges, who served as subjects. No statistically significant difference was found in the achievement need scores of men and women college competitors (Berlin, 1973).

## STATUS OF KNOWLEDGE

One of the best-known sport psychologists, a man whose study of the athletic personality and motivation has been in the vanguard of thinking on the subject, made the following statement:

> There is insufficient evidence to conclude that high-level competition makes a positive contribution to personality. We can state with some degree of certitude that those who retain their motivation for competition will have most of the following personality traits: ambition, organization, deference, dominance, endurance and aggression. There will be fewer introverted types by adult-level competition. Emotional maturity will range from average to high average and be complemented by self-control, self-confidence, tough-mindedness, trustfulness, intelligence, high conscience development and low levels of tension. Such traits as autonomy, exhibitionism and affiliation prove to be less general."*

Ogilvie set forth the above views based on in-depth study of male and female athletes' responses to several personality tests. Since publication in 1968, considerable new evidence has been collected. Studies reported earlier in this chapter, concerned only with females, both support and contradict portions of the Ogilvie summary.

---

* From B.C. Ogilvie, "Psychological Consistencies within the Personality of High-level Competitors," *Journal of the American Medical Association*, 205 (September 9, 1968), p. 786. Reprinted by permission.

John Kane, recognized British scholar and physical educator, has also been extensively involved in the study of athletes' personality in recent years. In a paper in which he specifically addressed the subject of female competitors, Kane (1972) acknowledged the difficulties of making generalizations but nonetheless stated:

1. There is some support for the general description of the woman athlete as "extraverted and somewhat anxious" especially at lower levels of performance. . . . There are, of course, many exceptions.

2. Low personality variation within a particular activity is reported in the studies on ice-hockey players, track athletes, swimmers and lacrosse. There is good support here for the notion of specific 'sport types.'

3. There seems to be some indication of a cultural difference . . . other studies undertaken on U.S.A. subjects demonstrate (admittedly over a variety of sports) somewhat more varied profiles and less clear extraversion and anxiety.

4. When comparisons with males were included, the findings for women subjects were in accord with social expectation showing the women to be lower on dominance (and therefore perhaps on achievement orientation) and confidence and higher on impulsiveness, tension and general anxiety . . .

5. The personality supports for achievement in competitive sports that are indicated . . . as necessary for women show a great deal of similarity with those that have been linked with sporting achievement among men (Husman's 1969 review). The similarities are mainly in the need for a relatively tough, dominant, self-sufficient approach. Competitive sport, however, needs in addition, an ability to handle stress. Here the researches on women tend to show that rather too much anxiety and emotionality is present which might be a pointer to the necessity for the careful preparation of women in these unaccustomed roles of achievement oriented competitors. The general impression remains, however, and it would seem to have a lot of face validity that success in competitive sport may need certain personality supports and that these are more similar than dissimilar for men and women.*

---

* From J.E. Kane, "Psychology of Sport with Special Reference to the Female Athlete," *Women and Sport: A National Research Conference,* Ed. by D.V. Harris, University Park, Pa.: The Pennsylvania State University, pp. 27-28. Copyright © 1972 by The Pennsylvania State University and reprinted by permission.

While it would be fitting to offer a summarizing statement about women athletes' personalities that might parallel the above quotation, a less popular but allegedly more realistic point of view is herewith expressed. The sum and substance of the above data and their analyses fails to render conclusive evidence of relationships, differences, and/or effects of competitive sport involvement on the psychological phenomenon referred to as personality. Adding the conclusions reported in another dozen or so master's level inquiries to the information presented in the above table merely confounds the picture of what standardized personality tests do, in fact, tell us about aspects of personality variously described as traits, factors, attributes. (See bibliography for specific identification of additional reported research.)

Regardless of sport type, specific activity, level of competition, somatotype, fitness level, geographical region, educational level, and/or innumerable other variables, there is just not sufficient consistency from study to study or within studies to have confidence in more than superficial descriptive-level information. And even then, such findings more often than not pertain to only *some* of the traits included in assessment instruments. To carry the writer's contentions just a step further, Rushall's (1970a) expressed dubiousness about whether personality is a significant factor at all in sport performance seems to be one of the most cogent comments yet to appear on the subject in the literature. His doubts emanate from highly sophisticated research, using male subjects, which held constant the environment, was designed in such a way as to repeat measures, and looked at subjects in various subsample groupings. His statistical manipulations, multiple analyses, included t-tests, chi square, canonical correlations, and step-by-step multiple discriminant function analysis.

That is not to say, however, that there are no appropriate applications to be made from personality trait test data. Rushall (1970b) calls attention to the potential assistance individual information might render to coaches in selection and in the management of athletes. In their comprehensive accounting entitled "Personality Psychology," Baitsch et al. (1971) laud the contributions of Ogilvie and Tutko in forming a "scientific and effective basis for the individual coaching of athletes" (p. 200). Most assuredly, there seems to be a clinical-type of use to which personality tests scores could be put.

To seek some unique factor(s) that would permit typifying sportswomen with any reasonable degree of confidence or predicting athletic success is like searching for a pot of gold at the end of a rainbow. Personality traits, defined by Cattell or Edwards or Gordon or the California Psychological Inventory, seem to have no more utility toward such ends than color of eyes, father's income, family size, height, or the like. In place of a summarizing statement, then, which would, of necessity, include a precautionary notice about exceptions, limitations, and tentativeness of the data, as is customary in statements of conclusions about personality research, the following comments are offered. Hopefully, they will influence the rationale and the strategies employed in future studies of female athletes' personalities.

First, the idea that personality is a set of static traits each one of which has meaning when extracted from the total structure of the personality sphere is untenable. The inference of a personality type from 6, 7, 8, or even 9 or more distinct traits that make up a segment of some 15 or 16 factor scales without regard for the "nonidentified" factors is a case of reasoning by omission. Utilization of only a portion of the data obtained from trait assessment constitutes the acceptance of a definition of personality which denies some very fundamental notions of totality, integration, and organization as being germane to an individual's behavior. Cattell, Eber, and Tatsuoka (1970) advise that one take cognizance of the *total* personality. They say that "Despite his personal interest in one concept . . . the investigator would be wise, in his first attack in a field, to enter with 'a wide net' and discover what is happening on other personality dimensions at the same time" (p. 6).

Second, the study of the athletic personality, even at the level of explanation, that fails to take into account specific values, goals, orientations, and standards that are inherent in the sport context is inadequate. Sherif (1971) and Lenk and Lueschen (1973) offer most convincing arguments pertaining to the importance of social situational variables and processes as basic considerations in social psychological research. In other words, the appropriateness of general personality inventories and assessment techniques for discriminating behaviors that are specifically related to the processes and situations occurring in sport is highly questionable. What kinds of insights, after all, can *general factors* provide about the female athlete? Maccoby (1970) pointed out that qualities of independence, initiative, and assertiveness relate highly to the development of the ability to think analytically. Obviously, competitive sportswomen do not hold a "corner on the market" for these traits. Maccoby cited the advice offered by a Fels Institute of Research

worker concerning the background essential to the development of a
girl into an intellectual person. "The simplest way to put it is that she
must be a tomboy at some point in her childhood" (Maccoby, 1970,
p. 22). One wonders about the suggestion of this learned individual if
she were asked advice about making a girl into a competitive athlete. As
stated by Kroll (1969), "It seems very unlikely that the measurement
instruments designed for the study of general personality structure and
dynamics will ever offer more than guideposts for the kind of definitive
work demanded by the goals of athletic personality research" (p. 364).

Third, complete disregard in the majority of the athletic personality
research for multiple sport and/or competitive sport experiences makes
much of the data fallible and the seeking of any cause-effect relationships between sport and personality an absurdity. Werner and Gottheil
(1966), whose inquiry into the personality of cadets at the United States
Military Academy was carried on over a four-year time span and had
the advantage of certain environmental "controls" that other investigations rarely enjoy, concluded:

> Despite regular participation in athletics over a four-year period at
> the Academy, the nonparticipants were found to have not changed
> in personality structure, as measured by the Cattell 16 P-F Test,
> to a greater extent than the athletes. Their pattern of personality
> structure change did not differ from the athletes, nor did they
> become more like the athletes (p. 130).

In spite of precise sample selection and some statistical manipulations of
data that would, hopefully, decontaminate some of the personality
research data, Layman's comment should be kept in mind. She said that
". . . the difficulty, if not the impossibility of controlling for . . . intervening variables that do not always lend themselves to quantitative
measurement doubtless obscures some of the real relationships which
exist between personality trends and performance in physical activities"
(1969, p. 367).

Fourth, some consideration must be given to the "universe" of
female athletes from which samples studied to date have been drawn.
This raises a critical question, namely, "When is an athlete an athlete?"
Given that competitive programs of sports for girls and women are
just developing into well-supported and organized endeavors, it must
be admitted that comparatively few women have had opportunity for
long-term and intensive involvement in sport. Until quite recently, a
"varsity" basketball player on the women's squad of a state-university

team may have practiced as little as 60 hours per season and participated in as few scheduled games as 5 or 6 in a given year. Surely, the definition of *a woman athlete* and the criteria which will, in the future, admit females to such a category for research purposes may cause us to alter our ideas about the sportswoman's personality.

Lastly, one can hardly be accepting of a considerable amount of the data reported about female athletes' personality when some of the conditions surrounding the data collection generate biases. Cattell, Eber, and Tatsuoka (1970), for example, discuss differences in the 16PF between volunteer and nonvolunteer subjects. Rosenthal and Rosnow (1969) also discuss this particular procedural issue in relation to personality research along with the problem of response sets. In the studies included in Table 15, only two of the investigations offer data from more than one test: Bird (1970) and Williams et al. (1970). These offer a far richer source of information than the "one shot" studies that comprise most of the research literature. And in terms of the expertise of researchers, only Ogilvie and some of his colleagues and Kane have demonstrated a commitment to the persistent study of athletes' personality—structure, dynamics, and trait descriptions—over a period of years. Regrettably the majority of their efforts have been devoted to male athletes, but at least they have not completely ignored females. Hopefully, the current expansion of competitive sport programs for women will encourage others to contribute, creatively and generously, to our knowledge of the subject.

As an alternative, then, to the continued study of female sportswomen's personality as it has been carried on to date, the writer suggests that future endeavors be directed toward in-depth study of female athletes carried on longitudinally and controlling for numerous variables, that instruments be developed which take into consideration the unique aspects of the sport setting, and that known information be adapted to more useful purposes, e.g., understanding and guiding individual performers.

In the preface to the 1970 edition of the *16PF Handbook,* Cattell reminds those who would be critics of his test that "one cannot make an omelet without breaking eggs" (xxiv). This writer agrees. But perhaps it is time for some variety. Should we consider poaching, coddling, scrambling, or perhaps even creating a lovely souffle?

# Chapter 10

# Motivational Factors

Human motivation is an exceedingly complex phenomenon. The scholarly investigation of the energizing, directing, sustaining and, in part, regulating aspects of behavior is a relatively new subfield of specialization within psychology. Yet there has been notable progress toward the establishment of sound theoretical frames of reference for understanding numerous causes and determinants of some human activities. Sport involvement, however, cannot necessarily be included in the latter category. For the most part, an individual's endeavors in competitive athletics have only been explained by a variety of simple effects, e.g., reward, incentive, thrill, satisfaction, challenge, etc. Such explanations are appropriate for only a segment of the sporting population, or for certain specific sports, or for rather limited levels of competition. Clearly, it is no easy task to discern why a woman, for example, would invade the masculine preserve known as sport. To understand why females choose to engage in sports, one must consider at least the following: (1) certain environmental circumstances which, in a sense, "prime" athletic involvement, (2) a conglomerate of highly personal factors, unique to each athlete, e.g., her feelings, needs, aspirations, plans, and wishes, and (3) the objectives of the sportswoman relative to her participation, her beliefs, her values, and the like (Cofer and Appley, 1964).

Fabun (1968) contends that one cannot simply ask *why?* To do so, he claims, ". . . is infinitely regressive—behind every 'why?' lurks another 'why?' " (p. 3). Like the scientific study of personality dynamics, research in human motivation must cope with the pervasive problem of measuring motives. At the heart of the issue is the question of whether an individual's motives are conscious and inferable from some form of self-report or unconscious and, therefore, more accurately identified from fantasy. Some notable researchers have pursued still other approaches to the assessment of motives, e.g., the inference of motive from demonstrated physical persistence, from effects of arousal manipulations, from bodily conditions. The study of sport motivation has not been immune to this problem of measurement.

The present status of our knowledge of the subject may be a consequence of research strategies involved to date, of factors inherent in the very nature of the sport experience itself which do not readily lend to identification, explanation, or analysis, or of some other logical reason. Whatever the case, the fact of the matter is that the sport literature is devoid of motivation information that adequately acknowledges antecedents to sport entry and athletes' sustained commitment to the competitive sport scene. Some information could be collated about initial and early attraction to competition by superstars from their best-selling paperback narratives; but for the most part, the study of sport motivation is in the stages of infancy.

Published works and papers which discuss athletes' motives to compete generally offer speculations about males only and are based primarily on empirical data (Bouet, 1969; Cogan, 1968; Coutts, 1966; Epuran and Horghidan, 1970; Frost, 1970; Lawther, 1972). The most notable publication, one devoted exclusively to why man plays, is a collection of writings edited by Slovenko and Knight (1967). Not only are its contents predominantly male-oriented, there is also a clinical cast to a large number of the essays. Others lend to popular "human interest" reading. The majority of the concentrated research into athletic motivation carried on by Ogilvie (1968) and by Ogilvie and Tutko (1966) over a period of years may also be described as male-focused and of a clinical nature. Currently, the work of Ogilvie and his associates is prescriptive; it has a much needed practical purpose to it. The same therapeutic tone, referred to in the Slovenko and Knight selections, is fundamental to Beisser's (1967) highly popular book.

Research per se, studies designed to contribute to specific aspects of understanding competitive athletes' motives, has been reported by Gorsuch (1968), Plummer (1969), Webber (1970), and Willis (1968). All four of these investigations were concerned with achievement motivation, a model postulated by McClelland (1953) and refined over a number of years by his very able colleagues. All four of the projects were devoted exclusively to male collegiate athletes.

In effect, then, there is meager substantive data that can render even superficial appraisal of female athletic motivation. An attempt is made, nonetheless, on the following pages, to review known works about women who engage in sport as well as to present some new information about background factors that may possibly come to be regarded one day as predeterminants of adult female athletic participation. The conclusion of the section deals with the writer's own research, a long-term project which seeks to describe a hypothetical structure of collegiate women's sport motivations.

## GENERAL EXPLANATIONS OF WOMEN'S SPORT MOTIVATIONS

### Theoretical

Several of the essays contained in *Connotations of Movement in Sport and Dance* by Metheny (1965) allude to some reasons why females pursue sports. "The Feminine Image in Sports" (p. 43-56) elucidates some of the historical events and social thinking that explain the environmental circumstances that precipitate women's sport participation. Other selections also capture relevant points of view that bear on the subject. But it is in "The 'Woman's Look' in Sport," that answers to the question, "Why sport?" are offered by Metheny. She stated:

> All sports offer diversion—a change of activity—an involvement in something different from our daily occupations and preoccupations . . .
>
> But the real fascination of sports is not found in idle diversion. We are drawn to sports because they provide a testing ground on which we determine our own abilities by attempting to overcome the resistance offered by another person, group of persons, or a defined set of circumstances. Competition, itself, is inherent in many life situations; but seldom do we have an opportunity to compete openly, freely, fully, in situations where the purpose of the moment is defined as competition . . . In that test, we find out what we can do, and how we react to success, failure, and uncertainty; and this self-testing forces upon us a kind of self-evaluation in specific terms not often provided by other life situations.*

* From E. Metheny, *Connotations of Movement in Sport and Dance,* Dubuque, Iowa: William C. Brown, Publishers. Copyright © 1965 by William C. Brown and reprinted by permission.

Further in her text, Metheny considers the matter of what determines the involvement in specific sports. Her comments cite not only individual abilities; she also calls attention to the availability of activities and facilities, social significances associated with certain sports, and socioeconomic factors.

Huelster (1966) proposed that the expression of the humanism of the body could be fulfilled through sports. At the conclusion of an address to an assembled group of women sport leaders, she referred, in her customary tactful manner, to the conflict of women at the time with respect to rights and privileges. Within this context, Huelster spoke of the role of sports in contributing to the potential of selfhood and self-mastery—for females as well as males.

In explaining her views about women's sport involvement, Zoble (1972) discussed antecedents of individual differences, factors pertaining to temperament, play, and sex, and role models. She culminated her paper, though, with the idea that sport involvement of women is related to need to achieve. Zoble reasoned that in spite of the dilemma she faces in behaving in a way that is untypically feminine, the sportswoman with her sense of self-esteem makes her choice of sport and enjoys her freedom to do so.

Small (1970) attempted to derive a hypothetical model of achievement motivation, appropriate for women athletes, through a highly creative process. Following the development of a word checklist which represented, for Small, various facets of sport participation, collegiate varsity team members from several sports responded to words on the list which were either attractive in sport or which had particularly attracted them to sport. Words were categorized in three descriptive structures: cognitive, emotional, and physical. An arbitrary numerical value was assigned to each of them. Furthermore, they were judged in terms of semantic similarity, word objects, and word potency. The tentative model, conceptualized from words to which athletes related, recognized two major dimensions of women's sport motivation: ego involvement and esteem. For Small, belongingness and both active and passive dynamic involvements serve ego involvement motives. Mastery, prestige, and self-regard comprise segments of the esteem motive associated with sport.

What do the above explanations reveal to us about female athletic motivation? Metheny focused on self-fulfilling and self-revealing aspects of sport. Huelster considered contributions to personhood that might accrue from athletic involvement. Zoble emphasized achievement. Small's two-category model acknowledging ego involvement and esteem seems to place these two larger concepts in a more definitive unit—for understanding and interpreting. While it is difficult, for example, to determine exactly how or why sport competition enhances one's sense of self, the notion of esteem can readily be allied to the adequacy, capability, and appreciation that success in sport is believed to yield. All four points of view make a case for sport motivation being a deeply personal phenomenon.

A well-trained behavioral scientist and highly experienced sport competitor herself, Butt (1971) proposed three models for the study of sport motivation: (1) aggression, (2) neuroticism, and (3) competence. Developing a background vignette for each theoretical model in the form of three case studies of female athletes who participated in the same sport, Butt offered the very strong argument that "sports behavior and organization should be studied within its social context, that is in terms of its effects upon and relationship to the development of individuals and of groups" (p. 1).

The aggression model is allied to Lorenz' position. Butt hypothesized a psychohydraulic model in which the person with the greatest fund of energy will have most motivation to channel it and use it for athletic activity (p. 5). She explains ". . . because aggression no longer serves evolutionary function in the human animal and has become perpetrated [sic] , due to selective breeding and the development of weapons and so on, Lorenz suggests that sports activity and competition as [sic] one major outlet for the unwanted destructive impulses that plague mankind" (p. 5, 6).

Freud is credited with the basic notions incorporated in the neuroticism model. Butt used illustrations from Beisser to translate Freudian ideas into the sport situation. The neuroticism model is based on the assumption that ". . . all sports motivation arises out of personal conflict between opposing forces of personality" (p. 6).

It is Butt's hypothetical competence model toward which the writer feels most friendly. "The ability to manipulate and deal effectively with the environment is the essence of the theory" (p. 9). Butt alleges that athletes display competence motivation in their desires and efforts to engage in sport contests, that they take pleasure from their experiences, and also that they become masterful in the athletic environment.

Butt discussed the lack of instrumentation with which to test the three models but urges the pursuit of research to make these ideas about motivation, and others, progress beyond the level of speculation. Her scholarly consideration of the topic does not take into account her own experiences in high-level competition. At least she makes no direct reference to her own sport involvement. In concluding, Butt does suggest that the competence model seems to offer the most promise for human self-fulfillment.

## Prescriptive

The Institute for the Study of Athletic Motivation came into being through the efforts of Ogilvie, his long-term associate, Tutko, and several other students of athletes' behaviors. Based on intensive research of thousands of athletes, mostly male, the Institute today offers a service of identifying a motivational profile for individual athletes. By interpreting responses to a self-administered paper and pencil test, the ISAM scores the results and provides an analysis of 11 motivational traits (ISAM, n.d.). These include: drive, aggressiveness, determination, guilt proneness, leadership, self-confidence, emotional control, mental toughness, coachability, conscientiousness, and trust. In addition to the analysis, the service provides very tangible suggestions for handling the athlete. A sample of the ISAM treatment of one trait and recommendations for the coach follows:

> Trust: This is an extremely trusting competitor who accepts everyone at face value and rarely suspects the motives of others. He places a great deal of faith in his coach and his fellow team members and thus will be an important contributor to team unity. He has a great capacity to communicate openly with others and feels that almost everyone in his life has treated him in a direct and honest manner. He also feels that people are dependable and can be relied upon. *Handling:* In the area of trust, no problems are anticipated between this player and the coach. Should he be high on "coachability" and "conscientiousness," you can depend upon him to be a loyal and dedicated player. Individuals who have an extremely trusting nature may be gullible at times, and more sophisticated teammates could take advantage of them. Therefore, he should be made aware of this possibility.*

---

* From Institute for the Study of Athletic Motivation, Publicity communication, p. 4. Reprinted by permission.

Bird (1972) reported private conversation with Ogilvie pointing out that four traits need to be added to the Athletic Motivation Inventory before it can be used for female athletes. Siedentop (1973) proposed an applied behavior approach to motivation problems allied with the coaching of girls or women. Addressing an initial joint Sports Institute of the Division for Girls' and Women's Sport and the Ohio High School Athletic Association, Siedentop told his audience that motivation is inferred from observing performance. He also reminded his listeners that concern for motivation derives, most all of the time, from *not* coming up to expectations and from aspects of performance that do not take into consideration skill, capability, or opportunity. From a behavior modification frame of reference, Siedentop focused on the importance of reinforcers (i.e., specific consequences of specific behaviors) and the effects of these as motivators.

Classes of reinforcers, competing reinforcers, and some of the processes of reinforcement that are relevant to the female athletic scene were elaborated by Siedentop (1973). If one were to follow his prescription, positive reinforcers used by coaches would include: (1) maximization of the positive and minimization of the adverse, (2) promotion of opportunities for success, (3) the rewarding of competitive effort, (4) creation of an atmosphere that is social, (5) development of a form of group belongingness or team association, and (6) the minimization of failure.

Committed to concepts of behavior modification, Siedentop urged coaches to analyze their situations in terms of behaviors and consequences in order to achieve greater motivation. He argued that this can be done in the reality of competitive sport, but offered the reminder that there is no easy road nor magical formula that will bring about drastic changes in behaviors, sport or other, of young female athletes engaged in school competition.

### Survey-derived

One of the early reports of survey research into female sport participation was offered by Heuser (1965). Although the study pertains to young German women between the ages of 14 and 28, the technique utilized by Heuser is somewhat unique and the findings provide interesting comparative data. Eighty girls, from a given high school, wrote anonymous essays concerning why they liked to engage in sports and why they did not like to participate in physical activity. Heuser culled the responses and explained that she found an overwhelmingly positive attitude toward physical exercise. The reasons she offered for this include:

1. The simple joy of physical movement.
2. A special enjoyment of a particular type of favored sport.
3. Productive effort, combined with the satisfaction of competition. .
4. Delight of exercising in the open air, including the pleasure of nature.
5. Contact possibilities with sport-minded people.
6. Health benefits of physical exercise and recreation.
7. The reduction of body weight and the objective to reach good poise and posture (p. 55).

According to Heuser, "between the lines" of the essays she discerned a group of motives that would prevent devotion to sport in spite of subjects' general affirmation of physical exercise. Possibly the following reasons for nonparticipation would relate to a similar representative American group of females:

1. Lack of time . . .
2. Distance from sport facilities.
3. Unattractive sport facilities.
4. Expense of the desired types of sport.
5. Unwillingness to comply with club obligations.
6. Lack of qualified instructors.
7. Too narrow sport program in school (p. 57).

Given their interest in the structure of the family as contributing to the development of certain personality and behavioral patterns, Landers and Lüschen (1970) investigated sibling sex-status and ordinal position in relation to female sport participation. Findings of ordinal position differences among male athletes who engage in dangerous sports, but not nondangerous sports, seem to have influenced their research. Data were gathered from a large population of college women students during the 1967-68 academic year. From the responses, 56 women majoring in physical education and 146 education majors were identified as having met complete family criteria (one- and two-child); information provided by these women was compared in further analysis. In addition to the background and family data collected, measures of psychological femininity (Gough Scale and MMPI-Fm Scale) and sport participation were utilized in the study. In regard to the latter, researcher-derived categories, nine in all, were specified: games of physical skill, physical skill plus strategy, physical skill performance, outdoor skills, games of chance, games of strategy, chance plus strategy, high masculine, and high feminine recreational activities.

Results of the study were incongruous. Landers and Lüschen found no meaningful sex-status or ordinal position relationships to sport participation. Significant differences were found between the physical education major students and education majors on measures of femininity and in participation in four of the sport categories. The investigators proposed logical explanations for the outcomes of the research. Sampling error, the nature of self-report data, and the possibility that peer group, for example, may be just as relevant in determining the sport pursuits of college women as family are cited by Landers and Lüschen. The writer proposes that other considerations be made. Are the categories of sport participation not overlapping and biased? Are psychological measures of masculinity and femininity viable in this era of changing sex standards? Furthermore, the validity of these measures has been challenged. According to Bott (1970) the Gough scale is representative of the thinking of the 1920s, the 1930s, and the 1940s. One can agree with Landers and Lüschen, however, in their recommendation that longitudinal case studies would contribute more to our understanding of sport motivation and its antecedents than *ex post facto* types of inquiries.

Loy's (1968) investigation of sociopsychological attributes that might be related to the early adoption of a sport innovation included a small subsample ($N$=17) of women among the British swimming coaches who served as subjects of the inquiry. In his research, Loy utilized two questionnaires specially devised for the study, the Cattell 16PF (Form A) and the operational indicators of early adoption, which include educational status, occupational status, professional status, cosmopoliteness, venturesomeness, and creativity. Both the degree and relationship between early adoption of the "controlled interval method" (CIM) of training and selected characteristics were considered.

For women, Loy reported:

> A multiple correlation of 0.93 was found between the dependent variables. . . . The independent variables taken into account and their partial correlation coefficients with the dependent variable were: perseverence (G) (0.91), dominance (E) (0.89), self-sufficiency (Q2) (-0.83), venturesomeness (H) (0.81), intelligence (B) (0.79), and sociability (A) (-0.47) (p. 146).

One of the researcher's concluding comments was of particular interest to the writer. Loy stated that ". . . innovative female coaches have typically masculine characteristics. In addition the personality factors found to be associated with the early adoption of a sport innovation are those related to the prediction of creativity" (p. 146). In regard to the latter, an exception among the women is cited, the -0.83 correlation of CIM and self-sufficiency. Loy also pointed out the possibility of sampling error contaminating the women's data because of the small number of subjects. Yet the findings add grist to the mill of those who would argue that within the sport context, there are many more similarities among men and women who make a commitment to compete than there are differences. In view of Loy's findings, a "right on" women's libber might state that innovative male coaches tend to display the same character-istics of a sociopsychological nature as those found in innovative women coaches.

The hypothesis that family factors influence choice of sport mode was investigated by Birrell (1973). She classified sport into five modes but in the analysis of her data consolidated the categorization into two: competitive group sports involving a winner/loser, and natural sport participation in which an individual competes with some natural force such as mountains, snow, water. . . . She also looked into background factors and was unable to produce conclusive findings relative to fac-tors of birth order, socioeconomic status, family size, family moves, and physical disabilities within the family. The 139 undergraduate college women who completed her questionnaire did generate some data which suggests attitudinal effects of considerable import to sport motives. In general, Birrell found:

1.  Parents' attitudes seem to have greater influence on choice of sport by females than parents' actual sport participation.

2.  Fathers' high participation and high regard for sport seems related to daughters' choices to pursue the natural sport mode; mothers' high regard for sport is related to daughters' involvement in com-petitive sports.

3.  Brothers and sisters seem to exert greater influence on the pur-suit of competitive games and sports than they relate to partici-pation in natural types of sport.

4.  Influence of male members of the family—fathers and brothers—is unclear. However, both mothers and sisters relate to the choice of the competitive sport mode by females. This particular finding is

somewhat contradictory to data collected about high-level collegiate women athletes. (Refer to Table 19.)

Wright and Tuska's (1966) study of 2650 middle-class college and university women gives some insight into the complexity of the problem. They divided their sample into a masculine and feminine group based on responses to a twenty-six word-pair semantic differential. In regard to the influence of opposite-sex parent, their findings indicate the father's role is quite clear. For so-called masculine women, he seems to have related more favorably; for the feminine segment of Wright and Tuska's sample, he provided a more favorable image. Specifically, the researchers stated:

> . . . the role of the mother is very important in the development of feminine feelings. But what about the father? He plays a significant role, too. It is not only an emotionally satisfying mother, *but* the image of a successful father that make for a 'feminine' woman; not only a frustrating, unsympathetic mother *but* an emotionally satisfying father that make for a 'masculine' woman (pp. 147-148).

It might be well to bear in mind that the above has meaning for the sportswoman only if one accepts her as being more masculine than feminine. Loy (1968) and Landers (1970a) do; Small, referred to by Felshin (see p. 212), does not.

Petrie's (1970) investigation of motivations for participation in physical activity among college students included males in his sample and turned up some notable sex differences. Women students at Michigan State University ranked participation for social interaction, fun, and aesthetic expression as significantly higher than other motivational statements. Males, on the other hand, identified the pursuit of risk, demonstration of skill with a weapon, competition on the basis of skill, competition on the basis of combat, and competition against the natural environment as more motivating (pp. 111-112). No differences between the sexes were discerned for motivational statements representing participation for health and fitness and for involvement against chance (p. 112).

Motivation for risk-taking as a function of marital status was considered by Petrie. He found no difference between married and unmarried males nor for married and unmarried females in regard to risk-taking (p. 113). Neither males nor females were found to show differences in their preferences for activities when sex was introduced as a control variable in the analysis of socioeconomic status and preference for risk-taking (p. 113). Petrie's data, gathered from general university students, lends support to the idea that the achievement needs of so-called typical college women students are not gratified by means of sport involvement. At the same time, however, this raises question about the collegiate female athlete, the student who does commit herself to competitive athletics. In sport, does she satisfy her need to achieve?

In her own investigation of some of the background factors that precede collegiate sport involvement of females, the writer collected data relative to two age factors: (1) age at which the college performer was first introduced to the sport(s) in which she elects to compete during her college years, and (2) the age at which she made the decision to pursue competition seriously in the activity. The modal age at which these young women were introduced to the sport was in the early teen years. However, more than half of the athletes, 55.5%, had their intro-ductory experience earlier. Serious pursuit of the sport was also deter-mined during the early adolescent years of 12 to 14. Thirty-five and a half percent of the subjects indicated a later decision to compete and only 10.5% revealed making a commitment to their sport during the childhood years before age 11. Table 16 reports the responses to ques-tionnaire data concerned with age variables.

The nature of prior sport experience and level of aspiration might be taken to be indicative of sport motivation. In quest of information that might reveal some trends pertaining to these variables, college women athletes were asked to specify the highest level of competition experienced and their goals for further experiences. Table 17 indicates that prior to her collegiate involvement, the large majority of the ath-letes had been exposed to only a relatively "local" level of competition. Only 17% competed in national events; 1%, or 2, college women had been involved in international sport. Levels of aspiration suggest that one athlete in ten aspires to international competition and three in ten strive to engage in competition at the national level.

The reader should bear in mind that the athletes surveyed come from a relatively restricted geographical region of the country—the northeast. Also, they represent nine different varsity sports and three types of institutions of higher education. (Refer to p. 288.)

Inasmuch as role models are thought to be important behavioral influences, the following questions were put to Ss comprising the Berlin sample. "Who do you strive most to emulate in your sport accomplish-

**TABLE 16**
**The Collegiate Woman Athlete: Age Variables**

| Variable | f | % |
|---|---|---|
| *Age* introduced to current competitive sport | | |
| Before 6 years | 16 | 8.0 |
| 6 – 8 | 42 | 21.0 |
| 9 – 11 | 47 | 23.5 |
| 12 – 14 | 58 | 29.0 |
| 15 – 17 | 25 | 12.5 |
| 18 – 20 | 8 | 4.0 |
| Over 20 | 1 | .5 |
| Missing information | 3 | 1.5 |
| | | |
| *Age* of decision to pursue competitively | | |
| Before 6 years | 1 | .5 |
| 6 – 8 | 8 | 4.0 |
| 9 – 11 | 12 | 6.0 |
| 12 – 14 | 82 | 41.0 |
| 15 – 17 | 71 | 35.5 |
| 18 – 20 | 22 | 11.0 |
| Over 20 | 1 | .5 |
| Missing information | 3 | 1.5 |

$N = 200$

ment? What, if any, is your relationship to this individual?" An open response was provided for. This posed some difficulties in interpretation of answers. For example, some of the athletes indicated that they strived to emulate their teacher, but did not designate which specific teacher. Others identified the physical education teacher as the person emulated. When one considers that the answer "coach" could also refer to the same individual as the teacher and/or physical educator, the true meaning of the answers cannot be discerned. See Table 18 for a tabulation of answers.

That 118 of the athletes, or 59% of the sample, did not designate any person might be interpreted in a number of ways. Possibly, the athletes have no specific role model of which they are aware. Or, female athletes might not wish to acknowledge whom it is they strive to emulate—especially if their sport hero is a male. That more of the athletes

TABLE 17
The Collegiate Woman Athlete:
Level of Experience and Level of Aspiration

| Variable | f | % |
|---|---|---|
| *Highest level of competition experienced* | | |
| Local (club) | 15 | 7.0 |
| Collegiate (varsity) | 86 | 43.0 |
| State | 24 | 12.0 |
| Regional | 29 | 14.5 |
| National | 32 | 16.0 |
| International | 2 | 1.0 |
| Missing information | 13 | 6.5 |
| *Highest level of competition aspired to* | | |
| Local (club) | 3 | 1.5 |
| Collegiate (varsity) | 64 | 32.0 |
| State | 13 | 6.5 |
| Regional | 25 | 12.5 |
| National | 66 | 33.0 |
| International | 22 | 11.0 |
| Other | 3 | 1.5 |
| Missing information | 4 | 2.0 |

$N = 200$

identified friends and teammates than members of the family certainly lends credence to Landers' and Lüschen's (1970) speculation that peers may be just as relevant in influencing sport pursuit as members of the family. Finally, although the category including national champions, superstars, etc. appears to have been designated by few numbers of responses, in relation to athletes who did respond to the question, 18% of those emulated fall in this category.

Pursuing the influence of the coach a bit further, an attempt was made to discern whether or not female collegiate athletes had been coached primarily by women or men in their sport experiences. Survey responses revealed that 52% of the 200 women athletes questioned had been coached by a male at some time; 45% had worked only under female coaches. Two and one-half percent of the sample did not answer the question. These associations did not necessarily stem from school-

**TABLE 18**
**The Collegiate Woman Athlete: Person Emulated**

| Variable | f | % |
|---|---|---|
| *Person emulated* | | |
| Father | 4 | 2.0 |
| Mother | 2 | 1.0 |
| Parent | 1 | .5 |
| Brother | 3 | 1.5 |
| Sister | 3 | 1.5 |
| Friend | 12 | 6.0 |
| Teammate | 9 | 4.5 |
| Coach | 20 | 10.0 |
| Teacher—physical education | 2 | 1.0 |
| Teacher—other | 1 | .5 |
| National champion | 5 | 2.5 |
| Professional superstar | 8 | 4.0 |
| Other heros (heroines) | 2 | 1.0 |
| Myself | 4 | 2.0 |
| Other | 5 | 2.5 |
| [No response | 118 | 59.0] |
| $N = 200$ | | |

sponsored programs. Half of the respondents reported that they did have nonschool sport affiliations. Most notable among these were the YWCA, municipal sponsored programs, private clubs, AAU, USFHA, and church- and business-sponsored clubs.

Role model notwithstanding, athletes were asked, directly, to identify the three individuals, in rank order, who most influenced them to pursue competitive sport. Responses are presented in Table 19.

Again, the responses of teacher, physical education teacher, and coach warrant consideration in combination as well as separately. Also notable is the greater recognition given to family members than to friends in terms of direct influence to participate in competition. Because an open response was used, there is some confounding of data. Some athletes specifically designated the father or mother. Others indicated parent.

The influence of the father was no surprise at all to the writer. Both achievement and sport are commonly regarded as the domain of the male. The logic that the father is capable of exerting a stronger

**TABLE 19**
**The Collegiate Woman Athlete:  Persons Influencing Competitive Participation**

| Variable | First | | Second | | Third | |
|---|---|---|---|---|---|---|
| | $f$ | % | $f$ | % | $f$ | % |
| *Person exerting influence to compete* | | | | | | |
| Father | 38 | 19.0 | 31 | 15.5 | 23 | 11.5 |
| Mother | 14 | 7.0 | 24 | 12.0 | 16 | 8.0 |
| Parent | 7 | 3.5 | 6 | 3.0 | 6 | 3.0 |
| Brother | 9 | 4.5 | 9 | 4.5 | 2 | 1.0 |
| Sister | 2 | 1.0 | 3 | 1.5 | 4 | 2.0 |
| Friend | 16 | 8.0 | 29 | 14.5 | 20 | 10.0 |
| Boyfriend | 1 | .5 | | | 1 | .5 |
| Teammate | 1 | .5 | | | 3 | 1.5 |
| Coach | 21 | 10.5 | 17 | 8.5 | 12 | 6.5 |
| Teacher—physical education | 14 | 7.0 | 6 | 3.0 | 4 | 2.0 |
| Teacher—other | 33 | 16.5 | 26 | 13.0 | 22 | 11.0 |
| Myself | 25 | 12.5 | 8 | 4.0 | 7 | 3.5 |
| Other | 9 | 4.5 | 6 | 3.0 | 11 | 5.5 |
| [No response | 10 | 5.0 | 35 | 17.5 | 68 | 34.0] |
| $N = 200$ | | | | | | |

influence on his daughter to engage in sport and more interested in doing so than the mother is clearly supported by these data. Grebow (1973) tested a similar hypothesis in relation to intellectual values and academic achievement. She found that girls influenced by their fathers tend to be less conventional in woman's role terms (p. 208). Surely, this could be said of the female collegiate athlete. And so Berlin and Grebow support the findings of Wright and Tuska discussed above.

Table 19 provokes several other comments. For example, the number of respondents who designated "myself" as the most influential person in the competitive sport pursuit should not be disregarded. In this era of self-psychology theories and individualizing educational experiences and doing one's own thing, it is not surprising that a college woman who somewhat defies social standards and values and commits herself to sport is most responsible to herself for such action.

Some of the persons cited by athletes were consistently identified across the ranks, e.g., father, coach, friend, teacher. This would tend to strengthen one's respect for the importance of these individuals in affecting sport commitment.

And, finally, the increased inability on the part of subjects to identify more than one or two persons of influence, demonstrated by the greater number of "no response" returns for third rank than for second and for second rank than for first, suggests several explanations. Possibly there are few individuals perceived as being responsible for encouraging young women's sport involvement. But for those who would argue that the subject of motivation encompasses a considerable realm of unconsciousness, i.e., identifying persons of influence in one's choices to select behavioral modes, the data render support for their views.

Collectively, surveys by Landers and Lüschen, Birrell, Petrie, and Berlin indicate no clear evidence concerning the antecedents of female adult competitive sport involvement. What the research does propose, however, are numerous tentative hypotheses that warrant further investigation. Consider, if you would, what would be revealed by testing the following hypotheses:

1.  There is no relationship, over a period of years, between participation patterns in sport and theoretical values held for physical activity.

2.  Concepts of masculinity and femininity, as formulated by general psychological test criteria, do not "hold" in the context of sport competition.

3.  The categorization of sports by mode (types) does not accommodate situational and personal variables.

4.  Individuals perceived to influence female athletes' commitment to competitive sport are unaware of their role as motivators.

5.  Socioeconomic status and family size are less of an influence on sport motivation than factors associated with geography and climate.

6.  School-sponsored physical education class experiences do not favorably influence female sport participation.

Two final research-oriented reports that deal with female sport motivation are next cited. The brief reference to the Institute for Motivational Research survey represents the efforts of a commercial concern to explain sport involvement. As Kane (1971) pointed out, the Institute is generally concerned with notifying car manufacturers and makers of candy bars how to put sex appeal into their products. There-after, Burton's investigation, one of the few published reports that treats the achievement motivation construct, is intended to pave the way for the material presented in the last portion of the chapter.

A study of the psychological factors that make skiing attractive to so many individuals was reported in *Sports Illustrated.* According to Dichter of the Institute for Motivational Research:

> Women, as well as men, often have a feeling of potency, virility.
> The apres-ski sense of companionship and sociability is no accident . . . it is caused by the shared experience . . . the freedom of complete, satisfying accomplishment away from an alienating and mechanized world (Kane, 1971, p. 8).

Dichter's quote calls attention to several motivation-related ideas. First, he is one of the rare persons to directly associate virility with women who engage in sport. Secondly, within the short commentary, he re-iterated a motive for sport participation cited earlier by Huelster (refer to p. 333) when she referred to the humanizing experience of sport. In the third place, Dichter's statement strongly supports the categorization of sports by Birrell and Petrie into activities which take into account the natural environment. And lastly, reference to satisfying accomplishment introduces the psychological concept referred to as achievement motiva-tion that is discussed in the following studies.

In her investigation of the interaction between selected personality attributes of women beginners in two sports, riflery and bowling, and situational influences in the learning environment, Burton worked with 212 college women. She treated achievement motivation as two disposi-tions: (1) the need to do a job well, and (2) the need to be a success, which results in emulation of the successful rather than in hard work. Measures of these dispositions were obtained by use of Costello's (1967) scales. The STAI was administered to subjects in order to obtain scores of state and trait anxiety.

Burton found some relationship between anxiety measures and skill attainment and also between trait anxiety and need to achieve through one's own efforts (p. 143). However, no relationship was found to exist between the two motivational dispositions. Nor did either of the Costello scales yield a positive relationship to skill acquisition in either sport—riflery or bowling. At the present time, Burton seems to stand alone as the only researcher who has utilized Costello scales in sport motivation research. Also, her indices of skill, i.e., actual obtained performance scores, are highly realistic measures not always obtainable in other types of sports.

## A HYPOTHETICAL MODEL OF COLLEGIATE WOMEN'S SPORT MOTIVATIONS

For the past four years, the writer has been involved in a series of studies designed to formulate a hypothetical structure of the motives of college women athletes. This amalgam of certain accepted ideas in psychological theory and sport situational elements as they are perceived by female college athletes was derived from research strategy based on the following: (1) Allport's (1953) support for self-rating types of measures in the development of motivational theory; (2) Stephenson's (1953) Q-methodology; (3) the basic tenets of McClelland et al. (1953) and Atkinson's (1958) conceptualization of the need to achieve; and (4) factor analysis as a technique that makes possible the explication of constructs. Still in the process of being statistically validated, the model, nevertheless, provides some clear-cut understandings about college women's commitment to sport competition.

To date, approximately 1000 college women have been involved in the derivation of the hypothetical structure. Five hundred of these individuals were athletes, women whose sport involvement was affirmed by at least one season of intercollegiate competitive experience on a bonafide college or university team employing a designated coach and participating in a full season's schedule of games/matches/meets. The other 500 subjects were general college students who provided important comparative data. Private institutions, state colleges, and large state universities were represented in the sample. The athletes whose sorting of Q-statements provided the basic data for the research include west coast (California and Oregon) sportswomen and east coast students extending from New Hampshire to the south as far as North Carolina. The rationale invoked in identifying the sport sample was to establish homogeneity by applying a standard of admission to, and experience in, varsity competition to all subjects. To avoid confusion from different types of sport and/or multiple involvements as team members, no consideration was made of specific sport participants. The discussion that follows, then, pertains to female college athletes in general, women who engage in institution-sponsored competitions in various activities.

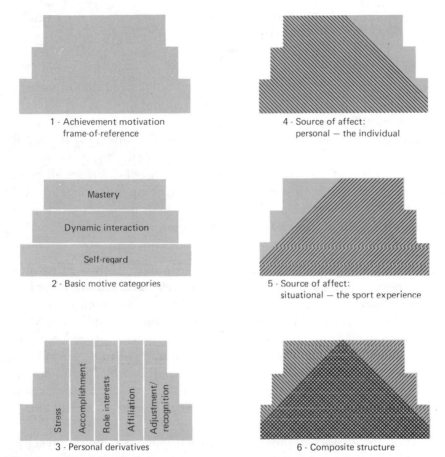

*Fig. 6    Analog model:  the collegiate woman's sport motivation.*

## Development of the Structure

The basic unit of structure of the model is a statement pertaining specifically to some belief, feeling, attitude, behavior that occurs in sport.
Thus, the sport context was duly acknowledged rather than used
to infer a value about sport from some general behavioral measure. In
all, sixty such statements, each representing a particular part of the
structure, comprise the model.* Figure 6 presents the model and the
sequence through which it evolved.

* Details pertaining to research procedures, i.e., identification and evaluation of
the statements, statistical analyses supporting the distinctiveness of motive categories, reliability of statements, etc. have been reported by Berlin (1971, 1972,
1973a).

**Achievement motivation frame of reference.** As a point of departure, McClelland's (1955) idea that motivation can be conceived of not only as a drive but also in terms of striving behavior was accepted as an underlying assumption. Figure 6(a) shows the representation of this broad referent. The development of statements acknowledged the following: (1) motives to participate in sport are learned and grow out of affective experiences, (2) standards of excellence and competition with these standards are fundamental to sport achievement motives, (3) desire for success and desire to avoid failure, expectancy of success, incentive for success, and fear of success as identified by Horner (1970) are all operative in disposing the college woman to pursue competitive sport experiences. Support for the adaptation of achievement need to sport was obtained from the works of Maehr and Sjogren (1971) and Maehr (1953).

**Basic motive categories.** The broad classification of motives, horizontal structures of the model, interpret the ideas of several noted psychologists as a function of sport participation. These are represented in Figure 6(b). At the very foundation of the college woman's motivation is her concept of self-regard, a designation which attempts to encompass self-esteem needs of Maslow (1970), notions inherent in Rogers' (1961) self-theory, Mead's (1934) concept of the socially formed self, and Allport's (1937, 1961) uniqueness of the individual, to cite but a few conceptualizations acknowledging the primacy of the person as being responsible for her own destiny.

The top category in the structure, that which is imposed on self, reiterates the concept of competence as it was set forth by White (1954). For interpretation in the model, it was labeled as mastery and is distinguished from self in that all mastery statements were skill related or performance related. Self-regard statements, on the other hand, were person oriented in meaning.

Making possible some form of reciprocity between motives pertaining to mastery in the sport situation and motives associated with one's sense of self-regard is the middle horizontal area of the model designated as dynamic interaction. Purportedly acknowledged within this group of statements are mediating processes and effects in which the individual "comes to terms" (Goldstein, 1939) with the environment. Goal setting and the integration of elements of sport and values of self as they have been explained by Bühler (Bühler and Massarik, 1968) are accommodated in the basic motive category called dynamic

interactions. Angyal's (1941) self-expansion principle, the acknowledgment that the person is an open system with two phases—input and
output—suggested this coordinating type of function for the middle
horizontal category of motives.

**Personal derivatives.** The five vertical columns of the model were
identified by factor analysis of sort responses. Athletes sorted self-
reference statements along a forced-choice "most like me" to "least
like me" continuum. Numerical values were assigned to each statement
according to placement within the sort, ranging from 10 to 0. Five
factors, extracted from the first principal components analysis, were
labeled according to the substantive meanings of the statements
loading on the factors. The results of this procedure revealed that,
included among motivating effects of competitive sport involvement as
perceived by collegiate women athletes, are: (1) the experience of
stress, (2) maneuvering for accomplishment, (3) the gratification of
certain role interests, (4) the consequences of affiliation, and (5) the
satisfaction of adjustment and recognition. Figure 6(c) recognizes these
factors.

**Sources of affect: person and situational.** Parts (d) and (e) of Fig. 6 seek
to take into account, within the model, ideas pertaining to one's
personal responsibility for the outcome of an event and the sources of
affect associated with the experience. It was Feather (1968) who called
attention to the fact that research in achievement motivation tended
to neglect this consideration. Further, he proposed that Rotter's (1966)
distinction between skill and chance might well be an oversimplification.
Certainly, within the sport context, one cannot ignore how the athlete
perceives her own responsibility in her ultimate evaluation of a game
or contest. However, the skill-chance dichotomy has been an exceedingly
difficult treatment to work into the statements. It can be noted that
only small areas of the model are alleged to stand either as personal *or*
situational sources of affect. Actually, 52 of the 60 statements allow
for either or both perceptions of sources of affect.

**The composite model.** Putting it all together, Fig. 6 depicts the total
schema. Viewed as contributing to the total structure, not as mutually
exclusive, fifteen cells are specified; within each cell, four self-reference
statements stand for one of three basic motive categories. The same
statements also represent personal or situational sources of affect, or,
in the case of mastery-stress and mastery-adjustment statements, affect

**TABLE 20**
Sample Motivation Statements:  Most Like Me and Least Like Me—
1972–1973 Data

| Number | Mean* | Model cell[†] | | | Statement |
|--------|-------|------|-----|-----|-----------|
| *Most like me* | | | | | |
| 6 | 7.589 | R | III | p&s | I take pride in being an athlete. |
| 57 | 7.201 | D | III | p&s | There are special kinds of excitement and thrills that go along with participating in competitive sport. |
| 48 | 6.987 | R | IV | p&s | I feel proud when I engage in sport. |
| 7 | 6.795 | M | IV | p&s | I have been able to cultivate many friendships as part of my sport involvement. |
| 34 | 6.745 | D | II | p&s | Playing and/or practicing provides a "release" that makes me feel good. |
| *Least like me* | | | | | |
| 32 | 1.509 | D | IV | p&s | A difficult thing for an athlete to do is maintain friends. |
| 55 | 1.781 | D | I | p&s | Sometimes I think that as an athlete I am a social outcast. |
| 49 | 2.527 | M | I | (p) | The idea of losing "hangs" over me all season long. |
| 19 | 2.710 | D | IV | p&s | The loneliness of being an athlete cannot be shared with others. |
| 20 | 3.094 | R | I | p&s | The build-up of pressure just prior to competition interferes with my desire to perform. |

$N = 224$

* Mean range = 10–0

[†] Symbols representing the cell model: R = self-regard; D = dynamic interaction; M = mastery; I = stress; II = maneuver for accomplishment; III = gratification of role interests; IV = consequences of affiliation; V = adjustment/recognition; p&s = personal & situational affect; (p) = personal affect; (s) = situational affect.

that emanates from one or the other source within the sport context. In the most recent principal components analysis undertaken of sort responses of 225 athletes that were collected during the 1972-73 academic year (Smith, n.d.), 15 factors were extracted which accounted for 54.5% of the total variance and acknowledged 51 of the 60 statements. To date, these cell labels have not been determined.

   To add to the understanding of the model and the process described above by which it was developed, Table 20 presents examples of sort statements. The five statements which were judged by athletes to be "most like me" and five evaluated as "least like me" in the sort analysis cited above by Smith are included in the table. Representative motive category, personal derivative, and source of affect are identified.

## Establishing Isomorphism

The critical question about the above endeavor is, of course, "is the structure isomorphic?" That is, does it correspond to the reality of college women's sport motivation? Intuitively and logically, and also in the light of theoretical speculations of known behavioral scientists, the elements of the model and placement of particular segments appear to be tenable. The actual testing for isomorphism, through a series of procedures currently under way, will, hopefully, provide grounds for even more confidence in the proposed structure.

To date, the Lynn (1969) Achievement Motivation Questionnaire has been used to ascertain subjects' need to achieve. Scores obtained are higher than those of general college students but significance at .05 has only been established for some championship level teams. In comparing Lynn scores of males and females participating in a like activity, tennis, Berlin (1973b) found no statistically significant difference.

McClelland (1961) discusses the color preference of high achievement-need individuals. As a means of garnering support for the achievement-need frame of reference, athletes were asked to designate their color preference. As reported earlier (refer to p. 285), two out of three female collegiate competitors specify a distinct preference for blue or green. Thus they conform to McClelland's declaration of the partiality of high-need-to-achieve individuals to somber colors.

Findings reported by Kaatz (1973) give cause to be accepting of the personal derivative labeled as stress *if* one is willing to accept stress represented in the sort statements as signifying a kind of psychological anxiety. Using the STAI, Kaatz found women athletes significantly higher in state anxiety scores than female undergraduate norms. M. R. Griffin's (1972) study of state and trait anxiety also supports the motive referred to in the model as "to experience stress." Griffin did not compare her results with norms. But she did examine differences in state and trait means across sport types and age groups. Among her findings were: (1) differences in state anxiety among age groups—most anxious subjects were the 12- and 13-year-olds and the least anxious the 19 and older group; (2) significant differences among sport groups in state scores—individual sports were higher than team sports; and (3) differences in trait anxiety scores among age levels and sports. Griffin comments that there is always the possibility that anxiety may have an unfavorable effect on performance. She urges more research into the phenomenon.

Numerous other paper and pencil instruments warrant consideration in the determination of the model's isomorphism. Obtaining measures from projective tests, e.g., those used by McClelland's associates, would yield further validating evidence. One question, however, tends to suggest that caution be exercised in using additional psychological measures to test the model. Considering that such constructs as need to affiliate, power motive, level of aspiration, and the like are contrivances of the human mind, can we be certain that these conceptualizations themselves are isomorphic with reality?

Alternative strategies need to be invoked to test the model. For example, the use of an unstructured Q-sort would reveal how much, if anything at all, is distorted by the forced-choice arrangement of statements that is presently used. Also, sort responses to statements by athletes who do not compete under the sponsorship of an institution of higher education, but who are capable of interpreting meanings because of their experiences in another athletic situation, might provide some important comparative data. Furthermore, if male college athletes, especially those who attend institutions having incentives and rewards (e.g., scholarships), comparable to the athletic opportunities for women, would evaluate these statements that purportedly make up the unit of structure of the model, then sex differences and/or similarities might be ascertained. For the present, no more is claimed for the model than the definitive direction it has provided for the ongoing study of why college women engage in competitive sport. Obviously, much work remains to be done.

Having contemplated theoretical speculations, prescriptive notions, survey results and an exercise in model building all concerned with why females engage in competitive sports, a few comments are in order about the meanings that are discernible from these ideas and research reports. For although no specific causal events or energizing human processes can be delineated as either precipitating or sustaining women's sport commitment, the foregoing discussion does provide a basis for summarizing the status of knowledge and research into female sport motivation.

Considering what we do and do not know, there is reason to be confi-
dent of the following:

1. Human motives, including those of athletes, are deeply personal
   and sometimes involve unidentified attitudes, beliefs, and values.

2. Reasons for engaging in sport are complicated as well as multiple.

3. Prior experiences in competitive situations and the individuals and
   occurrences that make up such experiences tend to influence
   decisions about subsequent achievement-oriented activities.

4. To date, no specific link has been established between adult
   women's level of skilled performance and identifiable motivational
   factors.

5. An athlete's perception of her personal responsibility for the outcome of a sport event and chance phenomena affecting the results
   of competition are inextricably tied to her motivational tendencies.

6. The stability of motives for sport involvement over a period of
   time is an unstudied parameter. Whereas change occurs in sport
   from game to game, season to season, and year to year, and numerous physical characteristics of participating athletes are also
   acknowledged to be somewhat variable, fluctuations in sport
   motivation have not been investigated.

7. The competitive sport experience is not necessarily unique in
   contributing to the satisfaction of human needs which help create
   self-actualizing individuals.

8. Both self-reports and projective techniques as means of measuring
   sport motivation place a heavy burden of interpretation upon
   researchers.

9. It is not possible to catch an elephant with a butterfly net. Uni- and
   bi-variate studies, simple questionnaires, and inferences made about
   sport behavior from general motivation inventories will not reveal
   insights into the intricacies of why some women make a commitment to competitive sport in spite of societal expectations and
   standards, demands made for personal sacrifices, and conflicting
   needs and/or goals.

Hopefully, the current increase in popularity of women's sport
programs and modifications in some sex-role standards will alter the

present state of knowledge. School- and college-sponsored athletics for females that are more equitable with male opportunities, new emphases on training women coaches and administrators to provide inspiring and capable leadership to girls and women in sport, more readily available research technologies, and better qualified individuals to pursue sport psychology studies suggest that the discussion of this topic be concluded on a note of optimism.

# Chapter 11

# Other Psychological Considerations

Regrettably, numerous aspects of the psychology of women athletes are omitted from discussion in this chapter, i.e., group identification, conformity and intragroup processes, communication and interaction, leadership and power, just to mention a few. No apology is made for not discussing these for there are simply insufficient data about these sociopsychological processes as they derive from, and/or relate to, the sportswoman to permit more than superficial generalizing. Nonetheless, the centrality of these phenomena to the attainment of in-depth under-standings of female sport competitors is herewith acknowledged. Furthermore, the writer is optimistic that data are forthcoming which will permit thoughtful analyses of these behaviors as they occur in sport. Current expansion of opportunities for women in competitive physical activities with attendant improvement and intensification in programs of recruitment and training will, hopefully, provide larger populations for fact gathering. The emergence and growth of sport psychology as a field of inquiry, with its focus on research and recog-nition of qualified women within its member ranks, leads to the expec-tation that there soon will be personnel capable of designing, conduct-ing, and interpreting studies about female athletes.

What follows in rounding out this description of the behaviors of sportswomen is not necessarily based on importance to the state of our knowledge. Who would judge this? Rather, inclusion or exclusion has been determined in accord with that which is more fundamental—the matter of evidence. Serious contemplation of the evidence—qualitatively and quantitatively—that underlies what we know about human behavior in general and, more specifically, about women's behavior in particular, is worthy of a few passing comments. Such recognition is awarded because evidence, either newly acquired or appropriately reordered, is critical to the garnering of meanings.

Two characteristics of psychological evidence are especially relevant to the study of women athletes. One has to do with the early focus of scientific psychology and schools of thought which were formulated from systematic investigations of human beings. Most behavior of so-called normal individuals was interpreted from studying atypical persons. Secondly, that which came to be known and/or accepted about female behavior was largely inferred from investigations about males. Schaeffer (1971), for example, points out that Havelock Ellis, whose name is rarely, if ever, seen in today's "going" psychology books, pioneered in the study of sex differences relating to intelligence. Ellis postulated a theory that generally men and women were equal in all characteristics, but that males were more variable. He based his ideas on two facts: (1) that although half of the people in the world were female, only a small fraction of famous people were female, and (2) a far larger number of inmates in mental institutions were male than female. It was Leta Hollingworth* according to Schaeffer (1971) who, within two decades, and based on her intense work with the mentally ill, proposed a theory of social learning; in effect, she claimed that the lower stature of females was due to societal expectations and prohibitions and was not merely the result of an accident of birth or marriage. Freud's explanations for differences between the sexes provides another example of clinical origins and inferences about the female psyche from the viewpoint and biases of the male.

Illustrations about the study of women for the purpose of establishing a psychology of the female are difficult to cite. Bardwick (1971) indicates that her book, an extension of her doctoral research, was conceived in rebellion against the psychoanalytic belief that "anatomy is destiny." She states that "we tend to ignore the similarities between men and women and focus on differences as if they were absolutes" (p. 3). Bardwick also points out, "I sometimes have the feeling that the psychological data on human beings bear little resemblance to the people we know" (p. 3).

If one accepts Lawther's (1972, p. 1) explanation of what sport

---

* Leta Hollingworth, wife of noted psychologist H.L. Hollingworth, would perhaps now be more acclaimed for having introduced Carl Rogers to clinical psychology.

psychology is all about, namely, the application of psychological facts and principles to sport, it follows that there is barely sufficient substantive evidence—about women—to provide bases for comparison of female athletes with other female populations. We are, then, at a point of origin in identifying the psychological meanings and understandings of women athletes' behaviors. Present students of women in sport, readers of this book, would do well to bear in mind the role of evidence in shaping the strategies for data collection, analyses, and interpretations of much-needed research about female athletes.

Consideration of the nature of available evidence, particularly its focus and depth, led to the delineation of the "other" psychological issues which are considered in this chapter. Four major categories, arbitrarily selected, provide the organization for the material that follows. The first group of studies is about attitudes. Then, two unrelated concepts are identified. Eustress is a relatively new term applied to an aspect of human behavior about which we have long been intrigued; superstition is, no doubt, as old as humankind, but very little attempt has been made to relate it to the study of behavior in sport. Third, the fascinating subject of aggression is briefly reviewed. A much larger section of the chapter is devoted to the perceptions of self and others. To conclude, the entire consideration of THE WOMAN ATHLETE, a theme the writer most desires to emphasize, is discussed: The need to remain ever aware of the individuality of the sportswoman. Two strategies for approaching the study of the person are then offered as closing thoughts.

## ATTITUDES

It is pointed out by Bem (1970) that the foundations of human beliefs and attitudes reside in four activities: thinking, feeling, behaving, and interacting with others. It would be impossible to do justice to a discussion of prevailing attitudes of and toward the female athlete within each of the above realms. Only a few carefully selected commentaries and research reports, most of which are current and related to the changing sport scene for women, are described. The intent is more heuristic than information-sharing though, hopefully, the findings will be of interest to the reader.

## About the Woman Athlete

One of the really innovative investigations about attitudes toward women athletes was reported by Brown (1965). She used a semantic differential to assess perceptions of the "feminine girl," the girl athlete, cheerleader, sexy girl, twirler, tennis player, swimmer, basketball player, track athlete, and girl with high grades. The responses of college men and women revealed that clear stereotypes of each of these roles do exist. Cheerleaders were closest to an ideal standard. Tennis players and swimmers were closest to the feminine image except on those scale items (evaluative) that would be considered to be preferred. In fact, none of the sport roles were seen to be consistent with perceptions of "the feminine girl." Differences between the sexes in the role perceptions were also found by Brown.

Using the same technique, assessment of stereotypic roles by the semantic differential, P.S. Griffin (1972) compared women's roles and female sport involvement. Roles investigated were: ideal woman, girlfriend, mother, housewife, woman professor, woman athlete. Griffin found the profile of the woman athlete to be somewhat neutral. Although all six roles closely fit the female stereotype, girlfriend, mother and housewife were more highly evaluated than either woman professor or woman athlete by the undergraduate college students who served as subjects in the survey. Her finding that males appear to be more favorable toward the role of the woman athlete than females led her to suggest that the study of sex-role expectations be pursued.

## About Competitive Sport
## Involvement of Women

In the days before the pill, and long hair, and notions like those of Edwards (1972) about desegregating sexist sport, McGee (1956), utilizing an instrument indicative of the times in psychological measurement (a combined Thurstone and Likert scale), studied attitudes held by administrators, teachers, and parents toward intensive competition for high school girls. She drew her subjects from two groups of Iowa residents: (1) those associated with schools which promoted intensive competiton which she referred to as Member Schools, and (2) those associated with schools which did not promote such programs, or Nonmember Schools. She also included subjects from Illinois where there was no intensive competition for high school girls.

McGee found slightly more favorable attitudes among groups where intensive competition was promoted. Parents were found to be favorably inclined toward a more vigorous program of active competition regardless of which group they represented. Coaches and boys' physical education teachers had higher attitude scores than teachers of girls' physical education and a group of mathematics teachers from Iowa Member Schools. In general, parents and coaches from all groups were significantly more in favor of intensive competition for girls than administrators and other categories of school personnel (pp. 68, 69).

A decade later, Harres (1966) investigated attitudes of men and women college students toward the desirability of intensive competition in athletics for women. In addition to an attitude scale of 38 statements organized in four categories  social-cultural, mental-emotional, physical, and personality items  Harres had subjects rank six sports according to judgment as to their desirability, and complete a background questionnaire that sought to reveal influences on respondents' attitude formation. Harres' conclusions were

1.  Participation in athletic competition did have a part in the formation of a more favorable attitude toward the desirability of athletic competition for girls and women.

2.  The observation of girls and women in athletic competition, both including and excluding television, did not affect the attitudes of the respondents toward the desirability of athletic competition for girls and women.

3.  The population for this study was favorable, though not highly favorable, in attitude toward the desirability of athletic competition for girls and women.

4.  Although the population was favorable in attitude, the range of scores indicated that considerable differences of opinion existed concerning the desirability of athletic competition for girls and women.

5.  There was no significant difference between the attitudes of men and women concerning the desirability of athletic competition for girls and women.*

---

* Fron B. Harres, "Attitudes of Students toward Women's Athletic Competition," *Research Quarterly*, 39 (May, 1968), p. 283, 284. Reprinted by permission.

Sherriff (1969) studied the status of female athletes as viewed by selected peers and parents. High school students served as the focus of her inquiry. They represented rural and urban samples. Both an attitude inventory and background questionnaire were used as data-gathering tools. Twenty-two parents (11 fathers and 11 mothers) and 175 students (81 males and 94 females) comprised the urban group; 14 parents (8 fathers and 6 mothers) and 78 students (41 males and 37 females) participated as members of the rural group. Sherriff's first conclusion was somewhat of a surprise. She reported that 66% of the total sample were undecided about female athletic competition. However, 95% indicated that girls and women should have the opportunity to engage in competition. Parents and teenage girls had even more favorable attitudes, but, like teenage boys, they indicated such activity was more appropriate to males' physical make-up. Approximately half of the girls who served as subjects indicated that they associate intensive competition with masculine manners and attitudes. The majority thought that undesirable qualities are brought out by intensely competitive sports. (The stereotype is obviously fixed by high school age!)

Boys who served as subjects were equally divided about the following: (1) whether girl athletes are socially accepted by their peers, (2) whether the competitive drive essential for successful sport participation is, in fact, unfeminine, and (3) whether or not there are advantages to being a girl and identifying with an athletic team. Curiously, high school boys' criticism of female athletes was not shared by older men, the fathers, who took part in the research.

Analysis of Sherriff's background questionnaire data revealed that 86% of the males and only 43% of the females had participated in competitive athletics. However, in response to the question as to whether or not they had observed female athletic competition, only 7 subjects reported that they had not. Sports most frequently observed on TV included swimming, roller derby, gymnastics, track and field, and tennis.

Finally, Sherriff (1969) reported activities considered to be most and least desirable. Table 21 presents her data arranged according to subject category and sex.

Concern about attitudes toward softball players led Garman (1969) to investigate opinions of female athletes as they are held by players (*N*=61), spectators (*N*=150), and the general public (*N*=116). She also obtained rankings of appropriateness of activities for womens' competition and judgments of eight adjective pairs describing female competi-

TABLE 21

Rank Order of Sports Believed to be the Most and Least Desirable for Female
Competitors*

| Most desirable | | Least desirable | |
|---|---|---|---|
| Male | Female | Male | Female |
| *Parents* (N=36) | | | |
| Swimming | Swimming | Soccer | Field hockey |
| Tennis | Tennis | Field hockey | Soccer |
| Gymnastics | Gymnastics | Track and field | Basketball |
| Bowling | Golf | Fencing | Track and field |
| Golf | Bowling | Bowling | Fencing |
| Softball | Diving | Basketball | Field games |
| | | | Gymnastics |
| | | | Archery |
| | | | Softball |
| *Peers* (N=175) | | | |
| Swimming | Swimming | Soccer | Field hockey |
| Gymnastics | Gymnastics | Basketball | Soccer |
| Tennis | Tennis | Field hockey | Track and field |
| Diving | Diving | Fencing | Fencing |
| Bowling | Badminton | Track and field | Basketball |
| Volleyball | Volleyball | Softball | Softball |

* From Marie Christine Sherriff, "The Status of Female Athletes as Viewed by
Selected Peers and Parents in Certain High Schools of Central California," M.A.
thesis, Chico, California State College, 1969. Reprinted by permission.

tors in each of six sports. In summary, Garman found that all groups
had favorable attitudes toward competition—players and spectators
were slightly more favorable than the general public. Individual sports
were designated as being more appropriate for womens' competition
than team sports. Her sample described gymnasts as the most feminine
female athletes; softball players were identified as least feminine. In
comparing what Garman referred to as player characteristics with those
characteristics specifically associated with softball players, she found
lower means assigned to the player characteristic category.

DeBacy, Spaeth, and Busch (1970) attempted to answer the
question, "What do men really think about athletic competition for
women?" They devised a Likert-type instrument to obtain their measurement of attitude. College students, both physical education majors and

nonmajors, served as subjects of the investigation. In general, responses of the college students indicated a positive but moderate attitude toward female sport competition. Consistent with the findings of Sherriff, male preference for individual sport involvement of women athletes was also determined.

Given the passage of a few years since the above studies were completed and the popularization of competitive sport for women that has occurred since then, it would appear to be timely to determine, "What do women really think about athletic competition for women?" Persons knowledgeable about the results of Goldberg's (1968) inquiry into women's prejudice against women might find such research to be most revealing particularly in the light of attempts to verify Goldberg's conclusion that women devalue female work for no reason other than its association with a female. Three hypotheses tested by Pheterson, Kiesler, and Goldberg (1971) that have implications for the acceptance of women athletes by women were: (1) women place higher value on male attempts to achieve, (2) women evaluate female accomplishments as equal to, or better than, male accomplishments, and (3) women place higher value on the accomplishments of individuals with greater odds against them in their performance. College students believing they were evaluating eight paintings—with manipulated artists' profiles containing facts of their personal backgrounds—viewed slides of the works and then responded to a series of specific questions. The first two hypotheses stated above were supported; the third was not. If one were to interpret the discussion of the study offered by the investigators in the light of women who participate in sports, it would suggest that unbiased evaluations of sportswomen cannot be anticipated until as athletes they demonstrate their skills and competencies. Meanwhile, the anti-female sport voices are more likely prejudiced *against the ideas* underlying female competition than they are against the actual success that is achieved by some women in sport. Pheterson, Kiesler, and Goldberg's hypotheses seem to merit testing in the sport context.

A comment about more popular sources of evidence that reflect attitude seems to be in order. Numerous opinions and beliefs are revealed, directly and indirectly, in the May-June 1973 *Sports Illustrated* series by Gilbert and Williamson about women and sport. One might argue that these selections probably reveal, more accurately and more timely, the prevailing attitude about women and sport than the scholarly inquiries described above. Such a possibility is duly acknowledged.

## EUSTRESS AND SUPERSTITION

Problem-solving, reasoning, and information processing are among the cognitive processes used by human beings to make decisions about their behaviors. But not all behavior is based on rational thinking. A good deal of what we know and do derives from tradition. Sometimes people act out of whim or fancy, fear, patriotism, or commitment to an idea. One explanation for interest in sports that have an element of thrill, risk, and excitement is eustress.

Bernard (1968) gave us the term eustress. She explained carefully the distinction between being turned on in relation to thrilling and exhilarating types of experiences in contrast to being turned on by tensions, anxieties, and frustrations which build up in the coping, re-acting, surviving behaviors of human beings. Bernard (1968) expressed the point of view that "There is, then, no reason to believe that women are naturally any less stress-seeking than men, or even, perhaps, less violent" (p. 39).

Harris (1972) picked up Bernard's ideas and provided a thorough discourse on opportunities within the realm of sport for satisfying stress-seeking needs. Her explanations of such concepts as risk-seeking, counterphobic pleasure, vicarious eustress, and pleasurable risk, to name but a few, would have no need to be sex-specified. Among sports cited by Harris to which individuals seeking eustress are attracted are sky-diving, mountain climbing, automobile racing, and bull fighting. It seems logical that many women attracted to water skiing, scuba diving, downhill skiing, and similar activities wish to experience either a bit more or a different type of stress than occurs from the chance and skill combination of events in a competitive game of tennis, basketball, or hockey.

We have hardly investigated the phenomenon of eustress. Its relationship, if any, to other motivational factors might help us to understand better the individual stress-seekers and the activities which have special appeal to them. Does the well-known symbolic formula of achievement need, e.g., resultant motivation = $f$ (expectancy x motive x incentive), accommodate eustress (Atkinson and Feather, 1966, p. 36)? Are fear and eustress the opposite sides of the same coin? Wyrick (1971) in her discussion of fear in human motor performance spoke about the agony of being afraid and the exhilaration experienced after fear is overcome. She never hinted at any pleasurable sensations

Completed 11-woman star at 5,000 feet. [Photo by Ray Cottingham.]

that might be a concomitant of the aroused anxious-state we generally associate with being afraid. When, if ever, are stress-seekers afraid? Progen (1972) discussing high-risk sports which take place in the natural setting suggests that mountaineers, for example, are not afraid. She pointed out that risk (and stress) are, after all, inextricably related to skill and the belief one has in his/her ability to control the environment. Thus, the well-trained and adventuresome climber finds pleasure and satisfaction in what others might interpret as dangerous. Progen cited *control* as the critical element in distinguishing the difficult from the dangerous.

Is there some special effect of eustress when one is responsible to a group of people? It was on April 8, 1972 that a group of female parachutists formed an eleven-girl star at 5000 feet! (Bahen, 1972) Risk and sport: what meanings can be found in the association of these human experiences?

Superstition seems almost to be as much a part of sport as the game plan! In fact, some of the pre-game ritual-like routines we observe athletes to follow have the entertainment value of the "main event." Gregory and Petrie (1973) studied the responses of Canadian athletes to an open-ended questionnaire designed to determine the prevalence of general superstitions and those superstitions related to sport. They obtained the same responses from a group of nonathletes. Black cats, walking under ladders, breaking mirrors, touching wood, rabbits feet, and sixty other items were identified among general superstitions. Athletes identified fewer superstitions of a general nature than nonathletes. Females in both groups identified a larger number of superstitions than males. Among sport-related superstitions were routines practiced on the day of the game, the order of putting on one's clothes and personal equipment, foods eaten, and repetitive actions such as touching first base after each inning.

A greater number of superstitious beliefs related to personal appearance and socially related functions were identified by female athletes. Female nonathletes' superstitions were associated with charms, hair, and team cheers. The authors concluded that "emotions motivate superstitious behavior and the environment suppresses some and enlarges upon others" (p. 22).

## AGGRESSION

One of the most relevant psychological constructs to behavior in sport is aggression. It would appear that the study of this phenomenon would contribute much more to our understanding of human beings than investigations, for example, of athletes' personality traits. There is, as a part of many game structures, a built-in offensive and defensive strategy with accompanying specific skills. And when all is said and done, in sport, the winning team is the one that piles up the most points!

## Theoretical Explanations

For some reason, systematic investigations of aggression in sport have not captured the interests, imaginations, or abilities of researchers. Most of the relationships that have been espoused between aggression and sport have been largely of a theoretical nature. Explanations of aggression have been associated with the consequences of frustration, release of pent-up energies, a method of controlling violence, and vicarious expression. Lorenz (1966) said

> The value of sport, however, is much greater than that of a simple outlet of aggression in its coarser and more individualistic behavior patterns, such as pummeling a punch-ball. It educates man to a conscious and responsible control of his own fighting behavior (p. 27).

Berkowitz (1969), Layman (1970a, 1970b), and Scott (1970) have outlined factors influencing aggression behavior, hereditary bases of behavior, and characteristics inherent in the sport situation which figure in the study of aggression. Each of these individuals has expressed concerns for the control of human aggression. Layman, in particular, distinguished carefully between controlled and uncontrolled aggression and reactive aggression as compared to instrumental aggression. She emphasized the perception of "the enemy" and anger in the former and pointed out that in instrumental aggression the goal is not to injure the enemy but, rather, to achieve some form of reward. None of the authorities on the subject consider the sportswoman separately from male athletes. But Smith (1972) indicated:

> Although there is little evidence of genetically determined temperamental differences between the sexes (males appear to be predisposed toward "activity" and females to "passivity") which may affect the expression of aggression, there is no doubt that cultural standards interact with and probably override differences in temperament (p. 103).

He also pointed out that there are cultural considerations to be associated with sex differences which complicate the problem somewhat.

Of particular interest to women athletes and coaches is Smith's prediction for the future of female sport. Considering current expansions of girls' and women's programs of athletic competition and increased varieties of activities in which females may participate (e.g., race-car driving, horse racing, football), Smith suggested female sport might well be moving toward the male model. He predicted

> As sex-roles blur, as sport for women continues to expand—including a move toward greater participation in body contact activities —and as winning assumes greater importance, women's sport seems bound to become more characterized by violence (p. 106).

Some women sport leaders would like to disagree with Smith no doubt, but for the present, the possibility of his prediction becoming reality must be acknowledged as likely.

Harris (1972a), declaring that there could hardly be a more aggressive sport model for women than the roller derby, considered this activity to be the exception rather than the rule. She reported a variety of data about aggressive behavior in relation to educational settings, specific cultures, and measures of masculinity and femininity. Harris generalized that ". . . female athletes exhibit higher levels of aggression than their non-athletic counterparts" (p. 425). She explained this in two ways. First she cited the use of male behavior standards. And sport is, of course, regarded as a male activity. Second, she alleged that expectations have a great deal to do with resultant behavior.

> . . . as long as we continue to associate competitive sports with masculinity and with aggressive behavior, we will continue to expect females to enjoy these activities, to be more masculine . . . (p. 425).

Smith and Harris, like most of us, come by their points of view out of specifically-derived knowledges and experiences. But the thought occurs to the writer that we may be losing some meanings inherent in their ideas because of semantics. Words like violence, hostility, and assaultiveness are affect-linked words which connote different meanings within and external to the sport environment. Are there some fine distinctions warranted in our discussions of the subject?

## Research-derived Data

Bird (1972) undertook an extensive review and evaluation of aggression as a measured personality trait among female athletes. From her stated bias that neither level of competition nor sport type, per se, are necessarily factors in the extent of aggression associated with female athletes, her research uncovered many more methodological problems pertaining to the study of personality than it yielded data about the subject under investigation. Her ultimate conclusion was that "It cannot be said, however, that women athletes are aggressive or not aggressive until a variety of interdisciplinary studies have been undertaken and consistent findings reported and cross-validated" (p. 362).

An examination of sex differences as they pertain to self-reported feelings about some 51 sports, games, and other activities arranged on an aggressiveness-competitiveness scale was described by Radford and Gowan (1970). Eighty-five males and 113 females, college physical education majors, served as subjects for the investigation. Participants in the survey reported: (1) feelings of enjoyment, (2) desire to continue with the activity at some time in the future, and (3) feelings of proficiency in relation to sex-appropriate listings of the activities. (Boxing, for example, was eliminated from the female list.) Radford and Gowan were primarily concerned with activities at the extremes of the scale, first and fourth quartiles, in relation to the above response options. The research concluded that "both males and females have more negative feelings about activities that require, encourage, or reward overt aggressiveness and highly competitive behavior than about activities that are low in aggressiveness/competitiveness" (p. 21). The tendency was also identified, on the part of women, to feel more negatively toward aggressive activities and more positively toward nonaggressive activities than males.

In what the writer considers to be a "model study" for those who desire to carry on research in the *real* sport situation, Wyrick's (1972) investigation of interpersonal aggression in foil fencers in relation to personality correlates is cited. The study was conceptualized on sound theoretical bases; it demonstrates careful data collection, thorough and appropriate analysis, and meaningful interpretation. Wyrick logically reasoned, in designing the inquiry, that the fencer's lunge is the culmination of the attack and represents an unquestioned aggressive move. This is fundamental to the research and is not necessarily related to whether or not the lunge results in a touch. Devising a complicated but very realistic "system" for quantifying her observations of lunging within the fencing act, she was able to test three hypotheses: (1) that her behavioral measure of interpersonal aggression would not correlate significantly with the aggression/ascendance factor (E) of the Cattell 16PF, (2) that the behavioral measures of aggression would not dis-

Olympic fencing bout, 1964. [Courtesy USOC.]

criminate successful performance, and (3) that fencers who are "excessive attackers" are releasing hostile aggression.

The data-gathering part of the design involved 73 intercollegiate fencers, 26 of whom were female. Measures of behavioral aggression were collected during two successive years of state-level tournaments. In her thorough analysis, Wyrick correlated personality factor data with aggression scores, univariately and in terms of the total personality score. She also examined success and aggression by analyzing the interpersonal behavior measure of fencers who reached the final pools. In addition, the data were studied according to the subjects' sex. Wyrick's findings revealed that for women, only two of Cattell's 16 factors were significantly related to the aggression scores—intelligence (A) and radicalism (Q1). For males, six of the personality factors were significantly correlated, though low, to behavioral aggression: surgency (F), superego strength (conscientiousness) (G), suspiciousness (L), radicalism (Q1), control, willpower (Q3) and tense-excitable (Q4). Consideration of total personality, not separate Cattell factors, of females turned up no differences between aggression scores and personality. Nor were there any differences when success of women's aggressive behavior was analyzed; means of finalists were almost identical with means obtained for those participating in the preliminary pools.

Wyrick reported some interesting sex differences though she cautioned that the sample was small and the results not necessarily generalizable. It was noted, however, that Cattell's Q1 factor, radicalism, correlated—.42 with behavioral aggression for males and .00 for females. In her summary, the researcher confirming that the expected correlations between personality and attacking behavior of women in fencing were obtained, wittingly stated "it continues to be socially unacceptable for ladies to physically attack other ladies" (p. 555) in spite of women's lib. Given Smith's predictions about the future of women and sport and continuously changing sex-role standards in our society, one cannot help but wonder for how long such social unacceptability will prevail.

## PERCEPTIONS OF SELF AND OTHERS

### Self-Concept

Self-concept is a vital psychological construct. It is purported to have been the subject of well more than 2000 publications in psychology and sociology alone. Like scholarly inquiry into personality and motivation,

research about self-concept has been plagued with problems of measurement and semantics. For example, in her 1961 book, *The Self Concept,*
Wylie identified more than 75 instruments—questionnaires, adjective
checklists, and rating scales for indexing self-regard. At that time, the
"era of self theories" had not yet quite come into its own. Presently,
the number of such paper and pencil "tests" is astonishing! Needless to
say, few, if any, of these tools of inquiry are especially suited to assessment of the female athlete.

Gordon and Gergen (1968) reminded the readers of their text of
four orienting issues around which the inconsistencies, ambiguities,
dilemmas, and problems of self-concept theory can be organized. They
identify (1) self as fact in contrast to self as construct, (2) self as subject versus self as object, (3) self as structure compared to self as process, and (4) self as a single entity or self considered to be multiple in
character. The very nature of the subject, its relationships to "consciousness," "awareness," "experiencing," "perceiving," and such other
conceptualizations makes it a most perplexing and difficult phenomenon
to study. For purposes of considering the self-concept in relation to the
female athlete, it may be helpful to examine Syngg and Combs' (1949)
idea that although the concept of self (as a dynamic dimension of the
conscious individual) to a large degree modifies and/or influences the
role one is called upon to play, these roles are a function of need
satisfaction.

> So long as the role we perceive to be required leads to maintenance
> or enhancement of self, it will be retained. Whenever it becomes
> clear to us that our roles do not lead to satisfaction or are incon-
> sistent with our way of regarding ourselves, we will change them to
> others more likely to produce results more consistent with our
> phenomenal selves (pp. 97-98).

According to Syngg and Combs, then, as long as being a "female jock"
contributes positively to an athletes' concept of self, she will pursue the
role—regardless of traditional sex-role standards. The individual athlete's
own interpretation of herself as an athlete as well as the interpretation
by those significant others in her life who influence her self-concept
seems to be a critical consideration in the ultimate growth of female
participation and involvement in sport.

Recently, Allen (1972) reported her extensive survey of the literature pertaining to self-concept and the female sport participant. Although
she stated that it was impossible to synthesize the knowledge about the

subject, she did cull from some 25 studies a few general observations. These were based on data which were collected in physical education class situations, used subjects ranging from junior high school through college, and employed a dozen different assessment techniques. Only one study was concerned specifically with female athletes. The epitome of Allen's findings about self-concept and females who engage in some form of physical activity is that (1) "there is an interdependence of self, body and movement concepts within the individual" (p. 41), (2) cause-effect relationships between specific activity experiences and self-concept cannot be investigated with current research strategies, and (3) the intuitively derived notion that body-oriented activities, such as sports participation, influence one's conceptualization of self is highly worthy of systematically designed study.

Two studies conducted within the last year were not included in Allen's review. They bear comment because of some similarities. Both utilized a Q sort to assess self-concept. Both involved female basketball players. Both used as subjects college women who would be generally considered to be in the higher skill level of performers. Evans' (1971) subjects were members of the varsity team of her institution. Her attempt to discern changes in self-concept that might be associated with the season of competition and participation was not realized. The focus of Warren's (1971) investigation with physical education professional students was much more pointed. She found that general self-concept measures were not related to basketball skill test scores. She also reported that neither experience in basketball nor a composite score of skill tests was an adequate predictor of self-concept. And the finding that relationships between experience and skill are higher than those between self-concept and skill was also indicated by Warren.

According to Fisher and Cleveland (1958), body image

> . . . refers to the body as a psychological experience, and focuses on the individual's feelings and attitudes toward his own body. It is concerned with the individual's subjective experiences with his body and the manner in which he has organized these . . . (p. x).

Although one would presume the topic to be of great interest to individuals concerned with skilled movement, it was noted by the writer that through the May 1970 cumulative index of the *Research Quarterly,* primary vehicle of physical educators for disseminating reports of scholarly studies, the term *body image* does not appear. Definitive research about this concept in relation to physical activity has been directed largely toward studies with kindergarten and elementary school children, toward required college physical education class members' estimates of body sizes, proportions and contours, and, recently, toward studies involving male athletes. Limited data are available about relationships of body image to specific subject characteristics; i.e., low and/or high fitness levels, motor ability, and so forth. The most recent trend in body image research seems to be to compare body image boundary, as it is represented in Barrier scores (derived from projective measures) and developmental factors, personality correlates, and utilization of space. It appears, too, that the use of the Secord and Jourard (1953) Body Cathexis Test is somewhat on the wane.

Thirty women athletes and 30 nonathletes were studied by Strati (1972) in regard to their estimation of five body dimensions: arm span, extended height and standing height, hip width, and shoulder span. Athletes were reported to have significantly underestimated their arm span and both height measures. No underestimations were found in the nonathlete group. Comparison of underestimations between groups yielded no statistically significant differences. Strati cautiously speculated the possibility that athletic involvement might be either a cause or an effect of her findings.

Numerous individuals, many knowledgeable about human movement phenomena of both a theoretical and practical nature, are totally convinced of the centrality of body image in the development of high level skills of sport and dance. According to Hunt (1964), for example, perceptual processes culminate in the body image concept. She reiterated Schilder's idea that the attitude and orientation of the body are absolutely essential to perception.

Nelson (1967) ambitiously attempted to gain some insights into relationships between three self-concept dimensions: self-actualization, body and self-cathexis, and bodily concern as they relate to motor creativity and movement concepts. In her investigation of these phenomena in college women, one group of physical education majors, presumed by their career-intentions to possess interest and skill in physical activity, served as subjects. Nelson's findings were supportive, to a large degree, of the statements associated with Hunt, above. She found that feelings of satisfaction with one's body and its functions and the self and one's movement all vary in the same direction and to a similar extent. She also concluded that "there is a tendency for the abilities to be inner-directed, spontaneous, self-accepting, and self-regarding to vary in the same direction as the satisfaction with the body and its functions" (p. 79). Similarly, self-regard varies directionally with both the satisfaction with which self is cathected and the confidence with which one regards her movement. There are strong implications in these conclusions for those who would point out the contributions of movement experiences, sport, to one's entire sense of being.

Nelson's subsequent work, in which she collaborated with Allen (Nelson and Allen, 1970) to develop a scale for the appraisal of movement satisfaction, seems to be an extension of the research reported above. The existence of such an instrument to assess one's attitude toward her ability to move or to study this self-perception in relation to other variables may not be well known among coaches, teachers of physical education, dancers, psychologists, and others interested in self concept—particularly its physical parameters. Nelson and Allen's 50-item movement satisfaction scale was developed for use with 14-21 year old males and females. In the development of the instrument, sex differences were found to exist in 16 of the 50 items. Men have a higher degree of satisfaction and women are pleased with items pertaining to rhythm and grace. Nelson and Allen also found that satisfaction with ability to move tended to lessen with age.

Although they might be viewed from a somewhat different perspective if one were engaging in philosophical analysis, the ridiculous comments by Weiss (1969) seem appropriate to this discussion of body concept. Unfortunately, as long as the remarks remain in print, they may well be read and accepted by naive or otherwise uninformed readers. Weiss, as if he has all the knowledge in the world upon which to base his conviction, pointed to

> . . . the fact that a young woman's body does not challenge her in a way in which a young man's body challenges him. She does not have to face it as something to be conquered, since she has already conquered it in the course of her coming of age (pp. 216, 217).

And from the depths of his experience, Weiss also made two other comments that bear upon female athletes' body conceptions. He stated that a woman ". . . masters her body more effortlessly and surely" (p. 217) than a man masters his. (How does he know?) Furthermore, alleged Weiss, "a woman is less abstract than a man because her mind is persistently ordered toward bodily problems" (p. 217).

All of the above remarks are offered by Weiss as explanations for why comparatively few women commit themselves to athletics over a period of time. It is astonishing that he disregards, totally, the limited opportunities and incentives for women in athletics, the outright discrimination against women in competitive sports, the social inhibitors to female athletic success, the lack of early identification of talent and training, and a raft of other plausible factors.

Smith and Clifton (1962) investigated sex differences in relation to males' concepts of themselves in the execution of a series of gross motor skills and female self-perceptions of the same skills. Walking, running, catching, throwing, and jumping made up the movement battery. Their expectation that females have less favorable concepts of themselves in performance was upheld by the research. As a follow-up investigation (Clifton and Smith, 1963) involving highly skilled performers—as identified by motor ability tests—the hypothesis that there would be no difference in the self-ratings of males and females was supported in all but one of the skills. Females rate themselves less favorably than males on the standing broad jump. Although these studies used relatively small samples and were limited to college-age students, the findings provoke several questions for research. To what extent do self-perceptions of skill level compare to standard motor ability test results *and* self-concept? Are there any more or less common gross movement tasks, like those used by Smith and Clifton, in which males tend to rate themselves unfavorably? To what extent, if at all, do differences show up between individuals with poor physical skills, middle-of-the-road performers, and highly skilled individuals? At what age does one's movement self-rating take on consistency and accuracy? Is there place to incorporate in movement self-rating measures a satisfaction index such as the one developed by Nelson and Allen? What would this tell us? About males? About females?

## Stereotypic Perceptions

Within recent years, there seems to have been a surge of interest in ascertaining female athletes' perceptions of themselves with special regard for their roles as sportswomen. Numerous reasons could explain the popularity of this subject. Obviously, the mood created by the women's liberation movement and the affiliation of many women sport leaders with its rationale and purposes had somewhat of an effect on such studies. Some female sport psychologists were curious as to whether or not a current stereotype of the woman athlete, as it might be compared to others, was, in fact, identifiable. Present-day desires to attract talented athletes to competition suggests still another reason for finding out about the woman athlete; that is, what is she really like?

Hall (1972) presented female participants in sport and nonparticipants with semantic differential scales for purposes of determining the perceptions of each group of the two concepts: feminine woman and athletic woman. Her work was carried on in England and provides data for comparing our own college students and athletes with those having different national backgrounds. The athlete sample involved participants in the All England Netball Trials; the nonathlete subjects were students enrolled at the University of Birmingham. Results of the investigation supported Hall's original hypothesis.

> . . . For female participants in sport, the concepts 'feminine woman' and 'athletic woman' are significantly less dissonant and more congruent than they are for female non-participants. In other words, the non-participant considers the athletic woman to be much less feminine than does her sports-minded counterpart. Possibly this comparison is made not only on the basis of culturally sanctioned traits and characteristics, but is also an aspect of internal mediational activity which goes on in everyone's mind, much of it unconscious. It is interesting that when subjective comments were elicited from the non-participating group concerning the femininity of the athletic woman, many denied that they considered her less feminine than other women. However, as a group they show quite clearly that they view the feminine woman more favourably than they do the athletic woman.*

As might be expected, Hall also determined that the attitude of the sport participant subjects was more favorable toward the athletic woman than the attitude of nonparticipants. Hall alludes to the notion that the challenge to make sports more attractive to women is represented in the differences between these two perceptions.

Attempting to determine similar information, Berlin (1973c) investigated college students' perceptions of "the ideal woman" and "the woman athlete." Her subjects added another dimension to that of Hall's. Four groups were a part of the Berlin survey: female athletes and nonathletes and male athletes and nonathletes. The Activity Vector Analysis, an adjective checklist, was used as the data gathering tool. The AVA

---

* From M.A. Hall, "A 'Feminine Woman' and an 'Athletic Woman' as Viewed by Female Participants and Nonparticipants in Sport," *British Journal of Physical Education* (November, 1972), p. xliii. Reprinted by permission.

measures four unipolar factors: aggressiveness, sociability, emotional control, and social adaptability and integrates them in a personality profile (Clarke, 1956). Findings revealed that "the ideal woman" perception was highly concentrated around the AVA Perfect Person Profile. Such adjectives as sociable, kind, interesting, open-minded, friendly, considerate, and good-natured describe the image. "The woman athlete" is perceived almost identically by males and females regardless of their athletic involvements. Words most commonly considered as descriptive of the woman athlete included: determined, aggressive, enthusiastic, high-spirited, persistent, and go-getter. No relationship at all between the two stereotypes was perceived by male nonathletes and by female athletes. Male athletes, however, view the ideal woman and the woman athlete as having a low positive relationship (+.27). In contrast, female nonathletes' perceptions yielded a low negative relationship (-.23) between the two images. The study raised some questions about sex-role standards as they are held and invoked by both sexes and by distinct types of interest groups. McKee and Sherriff's (1957) comments have some relevance to the perceptions distinguished in this study.

> . . . the content of self-conceptions of men and women will very likely reflect the differences in esteem with which the two sexes are regarded. And further, the sex difference in the discrepancy between what one believes one is and what one would like to be will also reflect this differential esteem (p. 371).

A cluster of four master's level studies (Kennicke, 1972; Meiser, 1971; Rector, 1971; and Ziegler, 1972) all completed at The Pennsylvania State University were concerned with a comparison of perceptions. All four of the studies used the Gough Adjective Check List (1965). Two of the investigations involved varsity athletes; two were directed toward the high school level competitor.

Kennicke compared two perceptions, social profile and participant profile, of high school athletes who engaged in what she referred to as structured sport; i.e., tennis, badminton, softball, volleyball, and speed swimming. She also investigated the two perceptions of those engaged in creative activities, namely, modern dance and synchronized swimming. Kennicke found few differences in self-profiles, both the social and the participant, between the two groups. She did, however, find differences within group profiles that were quite marked. Structured sportswomen scored higher on achievement and aggression scales and lower on nurturance, affiliation, heterosexuality, change, and deference.

Creative activity participants scored higher on scales of unfavorability, succorance and aggression; they were lower on favorability, self-confidence, self-control, nurturance, affiliation, heterosexuality, change, and deference. The investigator made the point that individuals perceive themselves to be different in different situations.

Meiser's variation of the same test-retest design sought to determine distinctions between perceptions of self as a function of a season of intercollegiate competition in field hockey. Levels of competition were also a variable inasmuch as Meiser categorized her intercollegiate hockey players in three groups: A was comprised of first and second team members; B was made up of third and fourth team players, and Group C accommodated those players who were either cut from the squad or voluntarily dropped out of competition. At the termination of the season, changes in self-perceptions were identified for all three groups including those who were in the cuts/dropout category. Level of competition was not considered to be a determinant in producing the changes.

Rector studied two perceptions in order to ascertain if college female athletes participating in individual sports describe themselves differently in social as contrasted to competitive situations.* The first responses to the ACL were made describing the social self; on the retest, the athlete responded to the self in the competitive situation. Findings of the social self-perception responses revealed that the sportswomen considered themselves to be quite like their peers. However their perceptions of themselves as competitors yielded higher scores on achievement, endurance, aggression, and dominance and lower scores were identified for change, affiliation, abasement, deference, and heterosexuality. Rector concluded that there is a distinct athletic personality that seems to be "turned on" in the competitive situation.

Ziegler's study involving four rural high school basketball teams used still another design for data gathering with the Gough Adjective Check List. She administered the ACL three times. On the first response, players checked those adjectives that applied to them socially—as they perceived themselves with their peers. On the second administration, they responded in terms of their perceptions of themselves as basket-

---

* Data collected by Rector apparently served as the basis for a paper entitled "The Social Self and Competitive Self of the Female Athlete" presented at the Third International Symposium on the Sociology of Sport, University of Waterloo, Waterloo, Ontario, August 1971, by Dorothy V. Harris.

ball players. Then, on a third administration, adjectives descriptive of their coaches were checked. Coaches on three administrations considered a social self-perception, a coaching self-perception, and a perception of the way they considered the team to view them. Analyses were made of the three responses and also took into account league winners and losers, regular players, and substitutes. Ziegler's findings revealed differences between pre- and post-season social and basketball images. The data on the coaches was somewhat confused.

What are the meanings of these four studies? Harris (1971) perhaps summarizes it best.

> . . . there is indeed a Dr. Jekyll - Mr. Hyde-type personality operating among females who also happen to be involved in competitive athletic endeavors. It appears that the athletic female must assume the role of chameleon; she must be feminine or assume the socially acceptable role for the female in social situations. At the same time, if she desires to be successful in athletic competition, she must become more aggressive, dominant, achievement oriented and demonstrate more tough-mindedness and endurance and be less afraid to take risks (Harris, 1971, p. 5).

Harris and her students have made their point. One very important characteristic, though, ever present in the successful athlete does not show up on the Gough ACL, Edwards Personal Preference Schedule, and all other paper and pencil tests. The successful female athlete is skilled—she uses her body well, has quick reactions, strengths, stamina, and other specific competencies that contribute to her high-quality performance. In the midst of this discussion about the sportswoman's self-concept, it seems wise to keep this skill factor in mind.

Using Griffin's semantic differential scales (refer to p. 360), Buhrer (1973) investigated the perceptions of "the woman athlete" and "the woman coach." One-hundred twelve female collegiate athletes and 48 coaches responded to the two stereotypes. Profile analyses showed the perceptions to be very similar. When D models were plotted, however, four distinct perceptions with no overlapping were located in semantic space. According to Buhrer, "woman athlete" as perceived by women coaches and "woman coach" as perceived by women athletes have the greatest distance from each other. There are some implications here for leadership, communication, and interpersonal relations between coaches and their players. Possibly this will emerge as an area of study as women and sport programs mature. Buhrer inferred that the stereotype of "the woman coach" might not be well conceptualized for relatively inexperienced athletes.

As a second part of her investigation, Buhrer sought information relative to the "real" person who comes to mind when contemplating the percept "woman coach." A majority of the responses designated a former coach or the athletes' present coaches. Buhrer commented that in some young sportswomen's lives, the coach may fill the role of "significant other."

All of these investigations of stereotypic perceptions leave little doubt that women who participate in sport do have firm concepts of self. At the same time, they are aware that their manner of behaving as a competitor is contrary to the traditional feminine stereotype. As stated by Gerber (1973),

> One can't compete in sport and be non-competitive; one can't shoot for goals and be non-aggressive; one can't practice for two physically demanding hours a day and be physically weak; one can't put one's skill on the line against an opponent and be too afraid to take risks; one can't come out on the court or field or pool against opponents who have demonstrated their superiority and be wanting in courage; one can't give up many hours a week to train for competition and not have self-discipline; one can't accept the results of the contest as proof of who's best for the moment and be unobjective; one can't strive to win, win, win and not be achievement-oriented (p. 5).

The foregoing discussion about self-concept has suggested to the writer the sensitivity and wisdom in de Beauvoir's comment that "evidently it is not reality that dictates to society *or* to individuals their choice between two opposed basic categories; in every period, in each case, society *and* the individual decide in accordance with their needs" (1961, p. 239, italics added).

## THE CONCEPT OF INDIVIDUALITY AND THE WOMAN ATHLETE

It is possible to regard females who engage in competitive sport as unique. A case could be made for their standing apart, as a class or a category in our society, from other groups of women. We have data that permit us to generalize about their characteristics because we have invoked nomothetic research strategies in our studies, thus far, of sportswomen. Most of the reports presented in this section of the book are illustrative of the nomothetic tradition. Obviously, this has been the predominant strategy of the field of psychology.

But there are other ways of studying human beings. More than 35 years ago, Allport (1937) delineating his "Psychology of the Individual" distinguished between common and individual personality traits. Yet he allowed that because no two people could possibly be exactly the same, all traits were, in a sense, unique and applicable to but one person. Allport's emphasis, although respected, did little to deter psychologists from searching for general laws that could describe behavior. More recently, Allport (1955) said that

> Man talks, laughs, feels bored, develops a culture, prays, has a foreknowledge of death, studies theology, and strives for the improvement of his own personality. . . . For this reason we should exercise great caution when we extrapolate the assumptions, methods and concepts of natural and biological science to our subject matter. In particular we should refuse to carry over the indifference of other sciences to the problem of individuality (p. 22).

There are many valid arguments to consider in support of idiographic approaches to the study of human beings. Consider Nash's statement:

> Not only is the individual unique within himself, but he also interacts with an environment that is unique to him. In the psychological domain, part of this uniqueness of the environment arises from the fact . . . that the individual *perceives* the environment differently even when the physical attributes are uniform. But each individual in his social environment interacts with others who are also unique. Hence one becomes far removed from the physicist's world of uniform matter operating in standard systems (Nash, 1970, p. 12).

It was pointed out in the opening remarks of this chapter that we are "at origin" in our systematic study of women athletes. It seems to be most timely, then, to seriously consider the potentials of a commitment to invoke idiographic research strategies *as well as* those in the nomothetic tradition. It would appear that systematic study of women athletes idiographically might lead toward answers to such questions as:

1.  What is the *function,* if any, of the specific attributes, feeling states, perceptions, and cognitions that distinguish a female ath-

lete's individuality? Do these unique aspects of the person serve an integrative role within the psychological structure of her make-up? Do such distinctive features facilitate interaction between athlete and sport situation and vice versa?

2.  Do extended investigations into the privacy of athletes' sport experiences provide insights into the meanings of sport involvement? Can the identification of such deeper meanings serve to elevate the quality of the sport experience (Gerber, 1972)?

3.  Do the behaviors of female athletes and the underlying beliefs and values which they in fact represent, contribute to one's sense of personhood?

4.  What do female athletes perceive as the distinctly humanizing aspects of sport competition? How are these valued in relation to other parameters of the experience? By what means are such values developed in relation to sport?

5.  Does the female athlete come to know herself better through her sport experience? How are psychological limits identified? In what ways does the sportswoman perceive them as relating to her physiological limits?

6.  In summation, who is the American woman in sport? How does she herself identify, then cultivate, and ultimately come to excel in skills and dispositions necessary for successful performance? Why and at what expense, if any, does she so behave?

Possibly it is unrealistic to expect one day to be able to know answers to such questions. But it is 1973. We send human beings to the moon and bring them back. We also seed hurricanes.

# Bibliography

Acampora, B., "A Comparison of Personality Traits Among Three Levels of Female Field Hockey Competitors," Master's thesis, San Jose State College, San Jose, Calif., 1971.

Allen, D.J., "Self Concept and the Female Participant," *Women and Sport: a National Research Conference*, Ed. by D.J. Harris, University Park, Pennsylvania: The Pennsylvania State University, 1972.

Allport, G. W., "The Trend in Motivational Theory," *The American Journal of Orthopsychiatry*, 23 (January, 1953), 107-119.

——————, *Becoming*, New Haven, Conn.: Yale University Press, 1955.

——————, *The Nature of Prejudice*, Reading, Mass.: Addison-Wesley, 1954.

——————, *Pattern and Growth in Personality*, New York: Holt, Rinehart & Winston, 1961.

——————, *The Person in Psychology*, Boston: The Beacon Press, 1968.

——————, *Personality: a Psychological Interpretation*, New York: Holt, Rinehart & Winston, 1937.

Anderson, B.J., "The Effect of Videotape Replay on the Movement Self-Concept of College Women Badminton Players," Master's thesis, The Pennsylvania State University, University Park, Pa., 1971.

Angrist, S., "The Study of Sex Roles," *Journal of Social Issues*, 25 (January, 1969), 215-232.

Angyal, A., *Foundations for a Science of Personality*, Commonwealth Fund, 1941.

Atkinson, J.W., *An Introduction to Motivation*, Princeton, N.J.: D. Van Nostrand, 1964.

——————, Ed., *Motives in Fantasy, Action, and Society*, Princeton, N.J.: D. Van Nostrand Company, 1958.

——————, and Feather, N.T., Eds., *A Theory of Achievement Motivation*, New York: John Wiley & Sons, 1966.

Bahen, D., "Pie in the Sky," *Parachutist*, 13 (July, 1972), 18-20.

Baitsch, H., Bock, H., Bolte, M., Bokler, W., Group, O., Heidland, H., and Lotz, F., *The Scientific View of Sport Perspectives, Aspects, Issues,* Berlin-Heidelberg-New York: Springer-Verlag, 1972.

Bardwick, J., *Psychology of Women: a Study of Biocultural Conflicts,* New York: Harper & Row, 1971.

——————— , Douvan, E., Horner, M.S., and Gutmann, D., *Feminine Personality and Conflict,* Belmont, Calif.: Brooks/Cole, 1970.

Barry, H., III, Bacon, M.K., and Child, I.L., "A Cross-cultural Survey of Some Sex Differences in Socialization," *Research in Personality,* Ed. by M.T. Mednick and S.A. Mednick, New York: Holt, Rinehart & Winston, 1964.

Beck, B.A., "A Comparative Study of the Feminine Role Concept of Undergraduate and Graduate Women Majoring in the Department of Physical Education and the School of Home Economics at The University of North Carolina at Greensboro," Master's thesis, The University of North Carolina at Greensboro, 1971.

Beisser, A.R., *The Madness in Sports,* New York: Appleton-Century-Crofts, 1967.

Bem, D.J., *Beliefs, Attitudes, and Human Affairs,* Belmont, Calif.: Brooks/Cole, 1970.

Bem, S.L., and Bem, D.J., "Training the Woman to Know Her Place: the Power of a Nonconscious Ideology," *Roles Women Play: Readings Toward Women's Liberation,* Ed. by M.H. Garskof, Belmont, Calif.: Brooks/Cole, 1971, 84-96.

Berkowitz, L., Ed., *Roots of Aggression,* New York: Atherton Press, 1969.

——————— , "Sports, Competition, and Aggression," *Proceedings of the Fourth Canadian Symposium on Psycho-Motor Learning and Sports Psychology,* Waterloo, Ontario, Canada, October, 1972, 321-326.

Berlin, P., "Motivational Dispositions of Collegiate Women Athletes: A Tentative Theoretical Structure," Paper presented at the Conference on Women and Sport, Western Illinois University, Macomb, Ill., June, 1973a.

——————— , "Need to Achieve in Selected Collegiate Tennis Players," Unpublished paper, 1973b.

——————— , " 'The Ideal Woman' and 'The Woman Athlete' as Perceived by Selected College Students," paper presented at The First Canadian Congress for the Multi-Disciplinary Study of Sport and Physical Activity, Montreal, Quebec, October, 1973c.

——————— , "The Media: Perceptual 'Double-Agents'," paper presented at The 15th Canadian-American Seminar, "Sport or Athletics: A North American Dilemma," Windsor, Ontario, November, 1973d.

——————— , "Women's Sport Motivations," Paper presented at the Scientific Congress, "Sport in the Modern World—Prospects and Problems," Munich, Germany, August, 1972.

——————— , "A Theoretical Explanation of the Motives of Collegiate Women Athletes: an Exploratory Study," Paper presented at The Third Canadian Psycho-Motor Learning and Sports Psychology Symposium, Vancouver, British Columbia, Canada, October, 1971.

_____ , "Prologemena to the Study of Personality by Physical Educators," *Quest,* 8 (January, 1970), 54-62.

Berlyne, D.E., *Conflict, Arousal and Curiosity,* New York: McGraw-Hill, 1960.

Bernard, J., "The Eudaemonists," in *Why Man Takes Chances,* Ed. by S.Z. Klausner, Garden City, New York: Anchor Books, 1968, 6-47.

Bird, A.M., "A Comparative Study of Personality Characteristics of College Women Participating in Basketball and Modern Dance," Master's thesis, University of Maryland, College Park, Md., 1965.

Bird, E.I., "Personality Structure of Canadian Intercollegiate Women Ice Hockey Players," *Contemporary Psychology of Sport,* Ed. by G.S. Kenyon, Chicago: The Athletic Institute, 1970.

_____ , "A Review and Evaluation of the Assessment of Aggression Among Women Athletes as Measured by Personality Inventories," *Proceedings of the Fourth Canadian Symposium on Psycho-Motor Learning and Sports Psychology,* Waterloo, Ontario, Canada, October, 1972, 353-364.

Birrell, S., "The Influence of Selected Family Factors on Choice of Sport Mode Among College Women," Unpublished paper, 1972.

Blum, G.S., *Psychodynamics: the Science of Unconscious Mental Forces,* Belmont, Calif.: Brooks/Cole, 1968.

Bott, M.M., "The M-F Scale: Yesterday and Today," *Measurement and Evaluation in Guidance,* 3 (Summer, 1970), 92-96.

Bouet, M.A., *Les Motivations des Sportifs (The Motivation of Sportsmen,)* Paris: Editions Universitaires, 1969.

Broverman, I.K., Vogel, S.R., Broverman, D.M., Clarkson, F.E., and Rosenkrantz, P.S., "Sex-role Stereotypes: a Current Appraisal," *Journal of Social Issues,* 28 (Spring, 1972), 59-78.

Brown, Ruth, "A Use of the Semantic Differential to Study the Feminine Image of Girls Who Participate in Competitive Sports and Certain Other School Related Activities," Ph.D. dissertation, Florida State University, Tallahassee, Fla., 1965.

Bühler, C., and Massarik, F., Eds., *The Course of Human Life,* New York: Springer, 1968.

Buhrer, N.E., "Perceptions of 'the Woman Athlete' and 'the Woman Coach,' " Master's thesis, The University of North Carolina at Greensboro, 1973.

Burton, E.C., "State and Trait Anxiety, Achievement Motivation and Skill Attainment in College Women," *Research Quarterly,* 42 (May, 1971), 139-144.

Butt, D.S., "Aggression, Neuroticism and Competence: Theoretical Models for the Study of Sports Motivation," Paper presented at The Third Canadian Psycho-Motor Skills and Sports Psychology Symposium, University of British Columbia, Vancouver, Canada, October, 1971.

Carlson, R., "Understanding Women: Implications for Personality Theory and Research," *Journal of Social Issues,* 28 (Spring, 1972), 17-32.

_____ , "Where is the Person in Personality Research?" *Psychological Bulletin,* 75 (March, 1971), 203-219.

Carter, F.H., "Selected Kinesthetic and Psychological Differences Between the Highly Skilled in Dance and in Sports," Ph.D. dissertation, University of Iowa, Iowa City, Iowa, 1965.

Cattell, R.B., Eber, H.W., and Tatsuoka, M.M., *Handbook for the Sixteen Personality Factor Questionnaire (16 PF)*, Champaign, Ill.: Institute for Personality and Ability Testing, 1970.

Chesler, P., "Men Drive Women Crazy," *Psychology Today* (July, 1971), 18, 22, 26-27, 97.

Cirlot, J.E., *A Dictionary of Symbols*, Trans. by J. Sage, New York: Philosophical Library, 1962.

Clarke, W.V., "The Construction of an Industrial Selection Personality Test," *Journal of Psychology*, 41 (April, 1956), 379-394.

Clifton, M.A., and Smith, H.M., "A Comparison of Expressed Self-Concepts of Highly Skilled Males and Females Concerning Motor Performance," *Perceptual and Motor Skills*, 16 (February, 1963), 199-201.

Cofer, C.N., *Motivation and Emotion*, Glenview, Ill.: Scott, Foresman, 1972.

——————— , and Appley, M.H., *Motivation: Theory and Research*, New York: John Wiley, 1964.

Cogan, M., "Motives for Participation in Physical Education," Paper presented at the annual meeting of the National College Physical Education Association for Men, Houston, Texas, January, 1968.

Cohen, A.R., *Attitude Change and Social Influence*, New York: Basic Books, 1964.

Cooper, L., "Athletics, Activity and Personality," *Research Quarterly*, 40 (March, 1969), 17-22.

Costello, C.G., "Two Scales to Measure Achievement Motivation," *Journal of Psychology*, 66 (July, 1967), 231-235.

Coutts, C.A., "Freedom in Sport," *Quest*, 10 (May, 1968), 68-71.

Cross, K.P., "College Women: a Research Description," *Journal of the National Association of Women's Deans and Counselors*, 32 (Fall, 1968), 12-21.

Crowne, D.P., and Marlowe, D., *The Approval Motive*, New York: John Wiley, 1964.

Daly, M., "Althea Gibson: A Long Hard Road to Where?" *The Sportswoman*, 1 (Spring, 1973), 11.

Daugert, P.J., "The Relationships of Anxiety and the Need for Achievement to the Learning of Swimming," Ph.D. dissertation, University of Michigan, Ann Arbor, Mich., 1966.

Dayries, J.L., and Grimm, R.L., "Personality Traits of Women Athletes as Measured by the Edwards Personal Preference Schedule," *Perceptual and Motor Skills*, 30 (February, 1970), 229-230.

De Beauvoir, S., *The Second Sex*, New York: Bantam Books, 1961.

De Charms, R., *Personal Causation* (The Internal Affective Determinants of Behavior), New York: Academic Press, 1968.

_____ , and Prafulachandra, N.D., "Hope of Success, Fear of Failure, Subjective Probability, and Risk-Taking Behavior," *Journal of Personality and Social Psychology*, 1 (June, 1965), 558-568.

DeBacy, D.L., Spaeth, R., and Busch, R., "What Do Men Really Think About Athletic Competition for Women?," *Journal of Health, Physical Education, and Recreation*, 41 (November-December, 1970), 28-29.

Dember, I., "My Word: Women in the Casino Locker Room?," *Yankee*, August, 1972, 70-73, 152-155, 158, 159, 163.

Doudlah, A.M., "The Relationship Between the Self-Concept, the Body-Image and the Movement-Concept of College Freshmen Women with Low and Average Motor Ability," Master's thesis, Women's College of the University of North Carolina, Greensboro, N.C., 1962.

Edwards, H., "Desegregating Sexist Sport," *Intellectual Digest*, 3 (November, 1972), 82-83.

_____ , *Sociology of Sport*, Homewood, Ill.: The Dorsey Press, 1973.

Epuran, M., and Horghidan, V., "Report: Motivation Factors in Sport," *Contemporary Psychology of Sport*, Ed. by G.S. Kenyon, Chicago: The Athletic Institute, 1970.

Erikson, E.H., "Inner and Outer Space: Reflections on Womanhood," *The Woman in America*, Ed. by R.J. Lifton, Boston: The Beacon Press, 1967.

Evans, B., "An Investigation of Changes in the Self-Concepts of Women Participants on an Intercollegiate Basketball Team During a Competitive Season," Master's thesis, The Pennsylvania State University, University Park, Pa., 1971.

Eysenck, H.J., "The Measurement of Motivation," *Scientific American*, 208 (May, 1963), 130-140.

Fabun, D., Ed., "Motivation," *Kaiser Aluminum News*, 26, 1968 (entire issue).

Feather, N.T., "Valence of Success and Failure in Relation to Task Difficulty: Past Research and Recent Progress," *Australian Journal of Psychology*, 20 (1968), 111-122.

Fisher, S., and Cleveland, S.E., *Body Image and Personality*, Princeton, N.J.: Van Nostrand, 1958.

Fitts, W.H., *Tennessee Self-Concept Scale*, Nashville, Tenn.: Counseling Recordings and Tests, 1965.

Flemming, E.G., "Personality and the Athletic Girl," *School and Society*, 39 (February, 1934), 166-169.

Flora, C.B., "The Passive Female, Her Comparative Image by Class and Culture in Women's Magazine Fiction," *Journal of Marriage and the Family*, 33 (August, 1971), 435-444.

French, E.G., and Lesser, G.S., "Some Characteristics of the Achievement Motive in Women," *Journal of Abnormal and Social Psychology*, 68 (February, 1964), 119-128.

Frost, R.B., "Motivation for Peak Performance," Paper presented at the Second Canadian Symposium on Psycho-Motor Learning and Sports Psychology, Windsor, Ontario, Canada, October, 1970.

Garman, J.F., "A Study of Attitudes Toward Softball Competition for Women," Master's thesis, University of California, Santa Barbara, Calif., 1969.

Gerber, E.W., Ed., *Sport and The Body: A Philosophical Symposium*, Philadelphia: Lea & Febiger, 1972.

_____ , "Little Ms. Muffett Has Left Her Tuffet," Paper presented at the 35th Annual Conference of the New York Association for Health, Physical Education and Recreation, Kiamesha Lake, N.Y., January, 1973.

Gibson, A., *I Always Wanted to be Somebody*, Ed. by E. Fitzgerald, New York: Pyramid Publications, 1958.

Goldberg, P., "Are Women Prejudiced Against Other Women?," *Transaction*, 5 (April, 1968), 28-30.

Goldstein, K., *The Organism*, New York: American Book Company, 1939.

Gordon, C., and Gergen, K. J., Eds., *The Self in Social Interaction*, New York: John Wiley & Sons, Inc., 1968.

Gorsuch, H.H., "The Competitive Athlete and the Achievement Motive as Measured by a Projective Test," Master's thesis, The Pennsylvania State University, University Park, Pa., 1968.

Gough, H.G., and Heilbrun, A.B., *The Adjective Check List Manual*, Palo Alto, Calif.: Consulting Psychologists Press, 1965.

Grebow, H., "The Relationship of Some Parental Variables to Achievement and Values in College Women," *The Journal of Educational Research*,66 (January, 1973), 203-209.

Griffin, M.R., "An Analysis of State and Trait Anxiety Experienced in Sports Competition by Women at Different Age Levels," *The Foil* (Spring, 1972), 58-64.

Griffin, P.S., "Perceptions of Women's Roles and Female Sport Involvement Among a Selected Sample of College Students," Master's thesis, University of Massachusetts, Amherst, Mass., 1972.

_____ , "What's A Nice Girl Like You Doing in a Profession Like This?" *Quest*, 19 (January, 1973), 96-101.

Haber, R.N., Ed., *Current Research in Motivation*, New York: Holt, Rinehart and Winston, 1966.

Hall, C.S., and Lindzey, G., *Theories of Personality*, New York: John Wiley, 1957.

Hall, M.A., "A 'Feminine Woman' and an 'Athletic Woman' as Viewed by Female Participants and Non-participants in Sport," *British Journal of Physical Education*, (November, 1972), xliii-xlvi.

_____ , "Women and Physical Recreation: A Cross-Cultural Analysis of Two Societies," Lecture presented at Coventry College of Education, England, March, 1972.

Hancock, J.G., and Teevan, R.C., "Fear of Failure and Risk-taking Behavior," *Journal of Personality*, 32 (June, 1964), 200-209.

Harbeson, G., *Choice and Challenge for the American Woman*, Cambridge, Mass.: Schenkman, 1967.

Harres, B., "Attitudes of Students toward Women's Athletic Competition," *Research Quarterly*, 39 (May, 1968), 278-284.

Harris, D.V., Ed., *DGWS Research Reports: Women in Sports*, Washington, D.C.: AAHPER, 1971.

_____ , "Female Aggression and Sport Involvement," *Proceedings of the Fourth Canadian Symposium on Psycho-Motor Learning and Sports Psychology*, Waterloo, Ontario, Canada, October, 1972, 422-426.

_____ , Ed., *Proceedings from the National Research Conference, Women and Sport*, The Pennsylvania State University, University Park, Pa., August, 1972.

_____ , "The Social Self and Competitive Self of the Female Athlete," Paper presented at the Third International Symposium on the Sociology of Sport, University of Waterloo, Ontario, Canada, 1971.

Hart, M.M., "On Being Female in Sport," *Sport in the Socio-cultural Process*, Ed. by M.M. Hart, Dubuque, Iowa: Wm. C. Brown, 1972.

"Hat Trick for Kathy," *Golf Digest* (February, 1971), 24.

Heckhausen, H., *The Anatomy of Achievement Motivation*, New York: Academic Press, Inc., 1967.

Heldman, G.M., "Recipe for WITF Circuit," *Lob*, April, 1973, 43-44.

Helson, R., "The Changing Image of the Career Woman," *Journal of Social Issues*, 28 (Spring, 1972), 33-46.

Henderson, E.B., *The Black Athlete*, New York: Publishers Company, 1968.

Heuser, I., "The Adolescents of Today": *Report of the Fifth International Congress of the International Association of Physical Education and Sports for Girls and Women*, Deutsche Sporthochschule, Köln, Germany, August, 1965.

Hill, A.H., "Autobiographical Correlates of Achievement Motivation in Men and Women," *Psychological Reports*, 18 (June, 1966), 811-817.

Hisey, C.N., "A Comparison of Selected Physical Performance and Emotional Characteristics of Two Groups of Former High School Athletes in Girls' Basketball," Master's thesis, Women's College of the University of North Carolina, 1957.

Holbrook, L., "Women's Participation in American Sport," *Athletics in America*, Ed. by A. Flath, Corballis, Oregon: Oregon State University Press, 1972.

Horner, M.S., "Femininity and Successful Achievement: A Basic Inconsistency," *Feminine Personality and Conflict*, J.M. Bardwick, E. Douvan, M.S. Horner, and D. Guttmann, Belmont, Calif.: Brooks/Cole, 1970.

"How the Lady Pros Relax," *Golf Digest* (July, 1971), 44.

Huelster, L., "The Role of Sports in the Culture of Girls," *Proceedings of the Second National Institute on Girls' Sports*, Washington, D.C., 1966.

Hunt, V., "Movement Behavior: A Model for Action," *Quest*, 2 (April, 1964), 69-91.

Husman, B.F., "Sport and Personality Dynamics," *Proceedings of the Annual*

*Meeting of the National College Physical Education Association for Men*, Durham, North Carolina, 1969.

Ibrahim, H., "Comparison of Temperament Traits Among Intercollegiate Athletes and Physical Education Majors," *Research Quarterly*, 38 (December, 1967), 615-622.

Institufe for the Study of Athletic Motivation, Publicity Communication, n.d.

International Swimming Hall of Fame, Inc., *Fifth Anniversary Yearbook 1965-1970*, Ft. Lauderdale, Fla.: International Swimming Hall of Fame, Inc., 1971.

Jameison, A., "Why Kathy Whitworth Is So Good," *The Sportswoman*, 1 (Summer, 1973), 10-12.

James, D., "Micki King Talks," *The Sportswoman*, I (Summer, 1973), 10-12.

Jersild, A.J., *In Search of Self*, New York: Teachers College, Columbia University, 1960.

Johnson, P.A., "A Comparison of Personality Traits of Superior Skilled Women Athletes in Basketball, Bowling, Field Hockey and Golf," *Research Quarterly*, 43 (December, 1972), 409-415.

Johnson, W., "The Go-Go Girls of Saporo," *Sports Illustrated*, February 21, 1972, 10-13.

_____ , "Ice-cold Games and a Solid-gold Girl," *Sports Illustrated*, January 31, 1972, 30-43.

Jones, M.R., Ed., *Human Motivation: A Symposium*, Lincoln, Neb.: University of Nebraska Press, 1965.

Kaatz, D.M., "Psychological Anxiety of Members of Selected Intercollegiate Athletic Teams," Master's thesis, The University of North Carolina at Greensboro, 1973.

Kane, J.E., "Motivation and Performance," *Women and Sport: A National Research Conference*, Ed. by D.V. Harris, University Park, Pa.: The Pennsylvania State University, 1972.

_____ , "Psychology of Sport With Special Reference to the Female Athlete," *Women and Sport: A National Research Conference*, Ed. by D.V. Harris, University Park, Pa.: The Pennsylvania State University, 1972.

Kane, M., "Scorecard," *Sports Illustrated*, January 18, 1971, 8-9.

Kelley, S.L., "Personality Characteristics of Female High School Athletes and Non-participants in Athletics," Master's thesis, University of Iowa, Iowa City, Iowa, 1969.

Kennicke, L., "Masks of Identity," *Woman and Sport: A National Research Conference*, University Park, Pa.: Pennsylvania State University, 1972.

_____ , "Self Profiles of High Skilled Female Athletes Participating in Two Types of Activities: Structured and Creative," Master's thesis, The Pennsylvania State University, University Park, Pa., 1972a.

Klafs, C.E., and Lyon, M.J., *The Female Athlete*, St. Louis, Mo.: C.V. Mosby, 1973.

Kogan, N., and Wallach, M.A., *Risk Taking: A Study in Cognition and Personality*, New York: Holt, Rinehart, and Winston, 1964.

Kroll, W., "Current Strategies and Problems in Personality Assessment of Athletes,"

*Psychology of Motor Learning*, Ed. by L.E. Smith, Chicago, Ill.: The Athletic Institute, 1970.

**Ladies Professional Golf Association,** *1972 Guide*, Atlanta, Georgia: Ladies Professional Golf Association.

**Landers, D.M.,** "Psychological Femininity and the Prospective Female Physical Educator," *Research Quarterly,* **41** (May, 1970a), 164-170.

——————— , "Siblings, Sex, Status, and Ordinal Position Effects on Female's Sport Participation and Interests," *Journal of Social Psychology,* (April, 1970b), 247-248.

——————— , **and Lüschen, G.,** "Report: Sibling Sex-status and Ordinal Position Effects on the Sport Participation of Females," *Contemporary Psychology of Sport,* Ed. by G.S. Kenyon, Chicago, Ill.: Athletic Institute, 1970.

**Lawther, J.D.,** *Sport Psychology,* Englewood Cliffs, N.J.: Prentice-Hall, Inc., 1972.

**Layman, E.M.,** "Reaction: Aggression in Relation to Play and Sports," in *Contemporary Psychology of Sport,* Ed. by G.S. Kenyon, Chicago, Ill.: Athletic Institute, 1970a, 25-34.

——————— , "Theories and Research on Aggression in Relation to Motor Learning and Sports Performance," in *Psychology of Motor Learning,* Ed. by L.E. Smith, Chicago, Ill.: The Athletic Institute, 1970b.

**Lefcourt, H.M.,** "Internal Versus External Control of Reinforcement: A Review," *Psychological Bulletin,* **65** (April, 1966), 206-220.

**Lenk, H., and Lueschen, G.,** "The Problem of Explanation in Social Psychology and the Personality and Social System Levels," Paper presented at the Allerton Park Conference of the North American Society for Psychology of Sport and Physical Activity, Allerton Park, Ill., 1973.

**Lesser, G.S., and Krawitz, R.,** "Experimental Arousal of Achievement Motivation in Adolescent Girls," *Journal of Abnormal and Social Psychology,* **66** (January, 1963), 59-66.

**Lewis, E.C.,** *Developing Woman's Potential,* Ames, Iowa: Iowa State University Press, 1968.

**Lorenz, K.,** *On Aggression,* New York: Bantam Books, 1966.

**Loy, J.W., Jr.,** "Socio-psychological Attributes Associated with the Early Adoption of a Sport Innovation," *The Journal of Psychology,* **70** (November, 1968), 141-147.

**Lynn, Richard,** "An Achievement Motivation Questionnaire," *British Journal of Psychology,* **60** (November, 1969), 529-534.

**McClelland, D.C.,** *The Achievement Motive,* New York: Appleton-Century-Crofts, 1953.

——————— , *The Achieving Society,* Princeton, N.J.: D. Van Nostrand, 1961.

——————— , *Studies in Motivation,* New York: Appleton-Century-Crofts, 1955.

——————— , "Wanted: A New Self-image for Women," *The Woman in America,* Ed. by R.J. Lifton, Boston: The Beacon Press, 1967.

_____ , Atkinson, J.W., Clark, R.A., and Lowell, E.L., *The Achievement Motive*, New York: Appleton-Century-Crofts, 1953.

Maccoby, E.E., "Feminine Intellect and the Demands of Science," *Impact of Science in Society*, 20 (January-March, 1970), 13-28.

McFadden, Strauss, Eddy and Irwin, Public Relations Firm, 903 Third Avenue, New York, (Typewritten Public Relations Biography), 1968.

McGee, R., "Comparison of Attitudes Toward Intensified Competition for High School Girls," *Research Quarterly*, 27 (March, 1956), 60-73.

McKee, J., "Men's and Women's Beliefs, Ideas, and Self Concepts," *American Journal of Sociology*, 64 (January, 1959), 356-363.

_____ , and Sheriffs, A., "The Differential Evaluation of Males and Females," *Journal of Personality*, 25 (March, 1957), 356-371.

Madsen, K.B., *Theories of Motivation*, Cleveland, Ohio: Howard Allen, 1964.

Maehr, M.L., "Toward a Framework for the Cross-Cultural Study of Achievement Motivation," Paper presented at the Allerton Park Conference of the North American Society for Psychology of Sport and Physical Activity, Allerton Park, Ill., 1973.

_____ , and Sjogren, D., "Atkinson's Theory of Achievement Motivation: First Step Toward a Theory of Academic Achievement Motivation?," *Review of Educational Research*, 41 (April, 1971), 143-161.

Malumphy, T.M., "The College Woman Athlete—Questions and Tentative Answers," *Quest*, 14 (June, 1970), 18-27.

_____ , "Personality of Women Athletes in Intercollegiate Competition," *Research Quarterly*, 39 (October, 1968), 610-620.

Maslow, A.H., *Motivation and Personality*, Second ed., New York: Harper & Row, 1970.

Mathes, S., "Social Stereotyping of Body Image and Movement Orientation," Doctoral dissertation, Purdue University, Lafayette, Ind., 1972.

Mead, G.H., *Mind, Self, and Society*, Chicago, Ill.: University of Chicago Press, 1934.

Meiser, P.H., "The Self-Perception of Intercollegiate Field Hockey Players at the Beginning and End of a Season of Competition," Master's thesis, The Pennsylvania State University, University Park, Pa., 1971.

Metheny, E., *Connotations of Movement in Sport and Dance*, Dubuque, Iowa: Wm. C. Brown, 1965.

"Micki King, Air Force Officer Who Flies Without Wings," *Women's Sports Reporter* (March/April, 1970), 9, 30.

Mischel, W., "Continuity and Change in Personality," *American Psychologist*, 24 (February, 1969), 1012-1018.

Mitchell, J.V., "An Analysis of the Factorial Dimensions of The Achievement Motivation Construct," *Journal of Educational Psychology*, 52 (August, 1962), 179-187.

Moe, D.A., "The Personality Factors of University Women Participating in Creative Dance, Speed Swimming or Synchronized Swimming," Master's thesis, University of Washington, Seattle, Wash., 1971.

Morgan, W.P., "Sports Psychology," *Psychomotor Domain: Movement Behaviors*, Ed. by R. Singer, Philadelphia, Pa.: Lea & Febiger, 1972.

Morris, B.J., "College Women Swimmers' Attitudes toward Training and Competing," Master's thesis, University of Illinois, Urbana-Champaign, Ill., 1972.

Moss, H.A., and Kagan, J., "Stability of Achievement and Recognition-seeking Behaviors from Early Childhood Through Adulthood," *Journal of Abnormal and Social Psychology*, 62 (May, 1961), 504-513.

"Motivation," *Theory Into Practice*, February, 1970 (whole issue).

Mulvoy, M., "Mis Avis Against Miss Hertz," *Sports Illustrated*, November 27, 1967, 62-63.

Mushier, C.L., "Personality and Selected Women Athletes: A Cross Sectional Study," *International Journal of Sport Psychology*, 3 (Spring, 1972), 25-31.

Nash, J., *Developmental Psychology: A Psychobiological Approach*, Englewood Cliffs, N.J.: Prentice-Hall, 1970.

Neal, P., "Personality Traits of US Women Athletes Who Participated in the 1959 Pan-American Games as Measured by EPPS," Master's thesis, University of Utah, Salt Lake City, Utah, 1963.

Nelson, B.A., "The Relationships Between Selected Aspects of Self-Actualization, Body and Self Cathexis, and Two Movement Factors," Doctoral dissertation, The University of Michigan, Ann Arbor, Mich., 1967.

_____ , and Allen, D.J., "Scale for the Appraisal of Movement Satisfaction," *Perceptual and Motor Skills*, 31 (December, 1970), 795-800.

Niblock, M.W., "Personality Traits and Intelligence Level of Female Athletes and Nonparticipants from McNally High School," Master's thesis, University of Washington, Seattle, Wash., 1967.

Ogilvie, B.C., "Psychological Consistencies within the Personality of High-level Competitors," *Journal of the American Medical Association*, 205 (September 9, 1968), 780-786.

_____ , "The Unconscious Fear of Success," *Quest*, 10 (May, 1968), 35-39.

_____ , and Tutko, T.A., "The Unanswered Question: Competition, Its Effect upon Femininity," Paper presented to the Olympic Development Committee, Santa Barbara, Calif., June, 1967.

_____ , and Tutko, T.A., *Problem Athletes and How to Handle Them*, London: Pelham Books, 1966.

Orr, J., *The Black Athlete: His Story in American History*, New York: Pyramid Publications, 1970.

Osgood, C., Suci, G., and Tannenbaum, P., *The Measurement of Meaning*, Urbana, Ill.: University of Illinois Press, 1957.

Owens, N.D., "A Descriptive Study of the Personality of Selected Amateur Golfers," Master's thesis, The University of North Carolina at Greensboro, 1970.

Peterson, S., Weber, J., and Trousdale, W., "Personality Traits of Women in Team Sports vs. Women in Individual Sports," *Research Quarterly*, 38 (December, 1967), 686-690.

Petrie, B.M., "Physical Activity, Games and Sport: A System of Classification and an Investigation of Social Influences among Students of Michigan State University," Ph.D. dissertation, Michigan State University, 1970.

Pheterson, G.I., Kiesler, S.B., and Goldberg, P.A., "Evaluation of the Performance of Women as a Function of Their Sex, Achievement and Personal History," *Journal of Personality and Social Psychology*, 19 (July, 1971), 114-118.

Phillips, M., "Sociological Considerations of the Female Participant," *Women and Sport: A National Research Conference*, Ed. by D.V. Harris, University Park, Pa.: The Pennsylvania State University, 1972.

"Player Profiles," *Lob*, April, 1973, 32-36.

Plummer, P.J., "A Q-sort Study of the Achievement Motivation of Selected Athletes," Master's thesis, University of Massachusetts, Amherst, Mass., 1969.

Progen, J., "Man, Nature and Sport," *Sport and The Body: A Philosophical Symposium*, Ed. by E.W. Gerber, Philadelphia: Lea & Febiger, 1972, 197-202.

Radford, P., and Gowan, G., "Sex Differences in Self-Reported Feelings about Activities at the Extremes of the Aggressiveness/Competitiveness Scale," Paper presented at the Second Canadian Symposium of Psycho-Motor Learning and Sports Psychology, Windsor, Ontario, Canada, October, 1970.

Ramsey, L.M., "A Comparison of the Personality Variables and Attitudes toward Physical Education Between Highly Skilled Girls Participating in Varsity Programs and in Girls' Athletic Association Programs," Master's thesis, Women's College of the University of North Carolina, Greensboro, N.C., 1962.

Raynor, J.O., and Smith, C.P., "Achievement-Related Motives and Risk-Taking in Games of Skill and Chance," *Journal of Personality*, 34 (June, 1966), 176-198.

Rector, J., "Self Perception of the Female Athlete in Social and Competitive Situations," Master's thesis, The Pennsylvania State University, University Park, Pa., 1972.

Renneckar, C.A., "Personality Traits of Selected Women Intercollegiate Athletes," Master's thesis, Illinois State University, Normal, Ill., 1970.

Rogers, C., *On Becoming a Person*, Boston, Mass.: Houghton Mifflin, 1961.

Rohaly, K.A., "The Relationships between Movement Participation, Movement Satisfaction, Self-Actualization, and Trait Anxiety in Selected College Freshmen Women," Doctoral dissertation, The Ohio State University, Columbus, Ohio, 1971.

Rosen, B.C., "Family Structure and Achievement Motivation," *American Sociological Review*, 26 (August, 1961), 574-585.

_____ , "Race, Ethnicity, and the Achievement Syndrome," *American Sociological Review*, 24 (February, 1959), 47-60.

_____ , and D'Andrade, R.C., "The Psychosocial Origins of Achievement Motivation," *Sociometry,* 22 (September, 1959), 185-218.

Rosenfeld, H.M., and Franklin, S.S., "Arousal of Need for Affiliation in Women," *Journal of Personality and Social Psychology,* 3 (February, 1966), 245-248.

Rosenthal, R., and Rosnow, R.L., *Artifact in Behavioral Research,* New York: Academic Press, 1969.

Rotter, J.B., "Generalized Expectancies for Internal versus External Control of Reinforcement," *Psychological Monographs,* 80 (Whole No. 609, 1966), 1-28.

Rushall, B.S., "Report: An Evaluation of the Relationship between Personality and Physical Performance Categories," *Contemporary Psychology of Sport,* Ed. by G.S. Kenyon, Chicago, Ill., The Athletic Institute, 1970a, 157-165.

_____ , "Report: Some Practical Application of Personality Information to Athletics," *Contemporary Psychology of Sport,* Ed. by G.S. Kenyon, Chicago, Ill., The Athletic Institute, 1970b, 167-173.

_____ , "The Status of Personality Research and Application in Sports and Physical Education," Paper presented at the Physical Education Forum, Dalhousie University, Nova Scotia, Canada, January, 1972.

Sakers, A., "The Relationship between a Selected Measure of Motor Ability and the Actual-Ideal Self Concept, Body Image and Movement Concept of the Adolescent Girl," Master's thesis, University of Maryland, College Park, Md., 1968.

Sanford, N., Ed., *The American College,* New York: John Wiley, 1962.

Schachter, S., *The Psychology of Affiliation,* Stanford, Calif.: Stanford University Press, 1959.

Schaeffer, D.L., *Sex Differences in Personality: Readings,* Belmont, Calif.: Brooks/Cole, 1971.

Schilder, P., *The Image and Appearance of the Human Body,* New York: John Wiley & Sons, Inc., Science Editions, 1964 (originally published in 1935).

Schreckengaust, V.J., "Comparison of Selected Personality Variables between Women Athletes in Individual Sports and Women Athletes in Team Sports," Master's thesis, The Pennsylvania State University, 1968.

Scott, J.P., "Sport and Aggression," *Contemporary Psychology of Sport,* Ed. by G.S. Kenyon, Chicago, Ill.: The Athletic Institute, 1970.

Secord, B., and Jourard, S.M., "The Appraisal of Body Cathexis: Body Cathexis and the Self," *Journal of Consulting Psychology,* 17 (October, 1953), 343-347.

Shafor, L.K., "Personality Trait Differences between High School Female Athletes in Team and Individual Sports," Master's thesis, Long Beach State College, Long Beach, Calif., 1971.

Sherif, C.W., "Females in the Competitive Process," in *Women and Sport: A National Research Conference,* Ed. by D.V. Harris, University Park, Pa.: The Pennsylvania State University, 1972.

_____ , "The Social Context of Competition," Paper presented at the

Conference on Sport and Social Deviancy, State University College at Brockport, Brockport, N.Y., December, 1971.

**Sherif, M., and Cantril, H.,** *The Psychology of Ego-Involvements,* New York: John Wiley, 1947.

**Sherriff, M.C.,** "The Status of Female Athletes as Viewed by Selected Peers and Parents in Certain High Schools of Central California," Master's thesis, Chico State College, 1969.

**Shontz, F.C.,** *Perceptual and Cognitive Aspects of Body Experience,* New York: Academic Press, 1969.

**Siedentop, D.,** "Motivation Management," Presentation to the First DGWS-OHSAA Sports Institute, Ashland, Ohio, January, 1973.

**Slaughter, M.,** "An Analysis of the Relationship between Somatotype and Personality Traits of College Women," *Research Quarterly,* **41** (December, 1970), 569-575.

**Slovenko, R., and Knight, J.A.,** Eds., *Motivations in Play, Games and Sports,* Springfield, Ill.: Charles C Thomas, Publisher, 1967.

**Small, C.,** "The Motives of Selected College Women to Participate in Sports-oriented Activity," Unpublished paper, 1970.

**Smith, G.,** "A Factor Analysis of the Motivation of Women Collegiate Athletes," Master's thesis-in-progress, The University of North Carolina at Greensboro.

**Smith, H.M., and Clifton, M.A.,** "A Comparison of the Expressed Self Concepts of Athletes and Non-athletes in Their Performance of Movement Patterns," *Perceptual and Motor Skills,* **16** (February, 1963), 199-201.

_____ , and Clifton, M.A., "Sex Differences in Expressed Self Concepts Concerning the Performance of Selected Motor Skills," *Perceptual and Motor Skills,* **14** (February, 1962), 71-73.

**Smith, L.E.,** "Personality and Performance Research—New Theories and Directions Required," *Quest,* **13** (January, 1970), 74-83.

**Smith, M.D.,** "Aggression and the Female Athlete," *Women and Sport: A National Research Conference,* University Park, Pa.: The Pennsylvania State University, 1972.

**Snygg, D., and Combs, A.W.,** *Individual Behavior,* New York: Harper and Brothers, 1949.

**Steinmann, A.,** "A Study of the Concept of the Feminine Role of 51 Middle-class American Families," *Genetic Psychology Monographs,* **66** (May, 1963), 275-352.

_____ , Levi, J., and Fox, D., "Self-concept of College Women Compared with Their Concept of Ideal Woman and Men's Ideal Woman," *Journal of Counseling Psychology,* **11** (Winter, 1964), 370-374.

**Stephenson, W.,** *The Study of Behavior,* Chicago, Ill.: The University of Chicago Press, 1953.

**Strati, J.,** "Body Image and Performance," *Women and Sport: A National Research Conference,* Ed. by D.V. Harris, University Park, Pa.: The Pennsylvania State University, 1972.

Sutton-Smith, B., and Rosenberg, B.G., *The Sibling*, New York: Holt, Rinehart and Winston, 1970.

Teger, A.I., and Pruit, D.G., "Components of Risk Taking," *Journal of Experimental Social Psychology*, 3 (April, 1967), 189-205.

Thomas, B., *Donna de Varona Gold Medal Swimmer*, Garden City, N.Y.: Doubleday, 1968.

United States (roster) *Women's World Softball Championship Osaka 1970*.

"U.S. Women Dedicate Victory to Smith, Carlos," *The New York Times*, October 21, 1968, 60.

Vincent, V., "Personality Factors of Competitors and Non-competitors in Athletic Activities," Master's thesis, Lamar State College. Beaumont, Texas, 1969.

Walterscheid, T.E., "A Study of the Effects of Competition upon the Personality Adjustment of High School Girls," Master's thesis, North Texas State University, Denton, Texas, 1968.

Warren, B.J., "The Relationship between Self-Concept and Performance on Tests of Skill in Basketball," Master's thesis, Southern Illinois University, Carbondale, Ill., 1971.

Webber, J.C., II, "A Comparison of Social Desirability and Achievement Motivation as Measured by Q-technique," Master's thesis, University of Massachusetts, Amherst, Mass., 1970.

Weiss, P., *Sport: A Philosophic Inquiry*, Carbondale, Ill.: Southern Illinois University Press, 1969.

Weisstein, N., "Psychology Constructs the Female," *Woman in Sexist Society*, Ed. by V. Gornick and B.K. Moran, New York: New American Library, A Signet Book, 1971.

——————— , "Woman as Nigger," *Psychology Today*, October, 1969, 20, 22, 58.

Werner, A.C., and Gottheil, E., "Personality Development and Participation in College Athletics," *Research Quarterly*, 37 (March, 1966), 126-131.

Wherry, R.J., Sr., and Waters, L.K., "Motivational Constructs: A Factor Analysis of Feelings," *Educational and Psychological Measurement*, 28 (Winter, 1968), 1035-1046.

White, R.W., "Motivation Reconsidered: The Concept of Competence," *Psychological Review*, 66 (September, 1959), 297-333.

Williams, J.M., Hoepner, B.J., Moody, D.L., and Ogilvie, B.D., "Personality Traits of Champion Level Female Fencers," *Research Quarterly*, 41 (October, 1970), 446-453.

Willis, J.D., "Achievement Motivation, Success, and Competitiveness in College Wrestling," Ph.D. dissertation, The Ohio State University, Columbus, Ohio, 1968.

Wright, B., and Tuska, S., "The Nature of Origin of Feeling Feminine," *British Journal of Social and Clinical Psychology*, 5 (January, 1966), 140-149.

Wylie, R.C., *The Self-Concept*, Lincoln, Neb.: University of Nebraska Press, 1961.

Wyrick, W., "Aggression in Foil Fencers and Personality Correlates," *Proceedings of the Fourth Canadian Symposium on Psycho-Motor Learning and Sports Psychology,* Waterloo, Ontario, October, 1972, 545-555.

_____ , "Fear in Human Motor Performance," *Proceedings of the Annual Conference of the Southern Association for Physical Education of College Women,* Biloxi, Miss., October, 1971.

Ziegler, S.G., "Changes in Self Perception of High School Girls towards Themselves and Their Coaches during a Basketball Season," Master's thesis, The Pennsylvania State University, University Park, Pa., 1972.

_____ , "Self-Perception of Athletes and Coaches," *Women and Sport: A National Research Conference,* Ed. by D.V. Harris, University Park, Pennsylvania: The Pennsylvania State University, 1972.

Zion, L.C., "Body Concept as it Relates to Self Concept," *Research Quarterly,* 36 (December, 1965), 490-495.

Zoble, J.E., "Femininity and Achievement in Sports," *Women and Sport: A National Research Conference,* Ed. by D.V. Harris, University Park, Pa., The Pennsylvania State University, 1972.

# Part 4
# BIOPHYSICAL PERSPECTIVES

Waneen Wyrick

# Chapter 12
# Physical Performance

Biologically and physically, the sportswoman is different from her nonactive counterpart in many respects. She has, if generalization is permitted for the moment, a stronger body, more endurance, a slightly different body composition, and a superior physiological support system. In many sports, the woman finds herself participating in activities which demand muscular power and speed and which have traditionally been the arena of the male athlete. Since sport is a game of records and statistics, she finds her own performances compared to those of men and discussed as a function of biophysical sex differences. Finally, she has the special functions of menstruation and pregnancy, both of which may affect and be affected by strenuous physical performance.

   Although much has been said about the characteristics of the sportswoman, not much is really known—in the scientific sense—about her. The physical performances of women are a matter of public record and are available for study and interpretation. The records themselves, and the particular features that characterize the women who set them, are subjects which are little understood. Theoretically, neuromuscular control mechanisms, anthropometrics, body composition, and the physiological support systems are areas which should influence physical performance and which would therefore be of interest in the understanding of the sportswoman. Although a considerable amount of information is available concerning the sportsman, little valid research has been produced in which the sportswoman was the subject of investigation. The few investigators who have reported data on women have been so heavily quoted and their results so frequently dragged about as cannonade in defense of one or another issue, that one can only cross one's fingers and pray that their every procedure was meticulously completed and their interpretations were blessed with clarity and reason.

The paucity of data on sportswomen is, of course, not without cause. Special problems exist in the measurement of biophysical aspects of women in general, and sportswomen in particular. Within the framework of the special problems discussed below, it may be understandable why some controversies seem unresolved, and some questions inadequately answered.

Historically, the sex of the preponderance of researchers has been male, and our culture has evolved well-defined taboos relating to the interaction of males and females, even when one is a subject and the other an experimenter. The need to pinch a fold of abdominal fat to measure in fat-calipers, to photograph a subject in the nude for somatotyping, or to place electrodes above and below the left breast in order to record heart rate have in the past posed special problems to researchers other than medical doctors. Male subjects simply don't present these problems. Perhaps the male researchers didn't feel that the questions relating to characteristics of women were pressing enough to overcome the experimental difficulties. At any rate, these problems are no longer relevant, in that the cultural taboos are disintegrating, and the number of female investigators has impressively increased over the past few years.

Another problem in the collection of female biophysical data has been the cultural expectations of the work capacities of women. Researchers complain that women will not produce the "all-out" physical effort that is required in some physiological testing. It is difficult for some women to attempt great feats of muscular exertion or overwhelming displays of power, when they have never been culturally rewarded for that type of activity. The problem can be appreciated better by imagining the difficulty one would have in finding a sample of women who would be willing to run cross-country for four hours while carrying plastic bottles on their belts, stopping each hour to obtain a urine sample. Similarly, how easy would it be to find a sample of women who would be willing, with an inserted rectal thermometer, to run on a treadmill under high temperature conditions until they crash to their knees from fatigue?

Finally, the pool of sportswomen from which samples might have been drawn, is a very small pool indeed. Whereas most colleges and universities have fielded male athletic teams in many sports, few have supported women's teams of equivalent size and quality. Most collegiate sportswomen have really been only slightly better than average at their sport, making the definitions of sportswoman and female athlete quite ambiguous. There simply haven't been many sportswomen in the "varsity" sense of the word; so that a female athlete in the past was not usually the analog of the male athlete. For this reason, much of the information reported herein was gleaned from Olympic athletes. Because information was not plentiful, research on European athletes has also been included. Since intercollegiate female competition in this country has only recently become fashionable, sportswomen in any substantial quantity are just beginning to become available as subjects of investigation.

Despite the obstacles in the measurement of various parameters of women, some questions have been generated, and some answers proposed. It is within the context of these limitations of research evidence, that the biophysical characteristics of the sportswoman will be described and compared, in terms of her physical performance, physique, physiological support system, and conditions of menstruation and pregnancy.

## SPORTS SKILL PERFORMANCES

Women participate in almost every sport currently played in America today. For the most part they compete against other women, and the records of other women. Each sport in which females participate has task demands that are unique to that sport; the demands include psychological control, intellectual analysis, neuromuscular integration, and physiological excellence. These demands play differential roles in varying sports; hence the level of physiological excellence is not as important to the archer and golfer as it is to the swimmer and runner and the level of explosive power is not as critical for the tennis player as it is for the long jumper.

Biophysical factors are of primary concern to those women who participate in the sports that require the ultimate physical function of the human body as a machine. Several provocative questions might well be raised. What are the potential physical performance levels that the female physical machine is capable of achieving? How do these performance levels compare to those of women who are not participants in competitive sports? How do ultimate physical performances of women compare with those of men?

Currently these questions of physical potential and biological limitation in women in sports competition comprise a controversial

issue, for the answers have enormous sociological and economical implications. Females are demanding equal benefits in collegiate, amateur,
and professional sports. On the collegiate level they are claiming equal
opportunity for scholarships and financial support. On the amateur
and professional level they are claiming the right to equal publicity and
financial reward. In their zeal to attain equal status, some feminists have
argued that women are biologically and physically equal to men, that
statistically there is much more overlap in male and female performance
than there is difference, and that their physical performance over the
years has been depressed due to cultural restrictions rather than physical
inadequacies. These arguments have led to the preposterous recommendations by some that if female athletes desire equal status they
should compete against males for scholarships, or that they should
perform as well as males if they expect equal financial rewards.

Generally, these factors have been rather emotionally argued, but
objective assessment of the performance potential of women in comparison to women of earlier decades and in comparison to performances
of men has not been undertaken. Rational decisions regarding the role
of women in sport cannot be made, however, until knowledge is gained
regarding the potential physical performance of females, the interactions
that occur between task demands in various sports and the female biological system, and the comparative performances of males and females.

## Sports Performance of Olympic Female Athletes

The Olympic competitions provide records that represent a majority of
the highest levels of attainment in sport. In addition the Olympics
represent a fairly homogeneous environment, in that many countries
are always represented, the events are generally known well in advance,
and the atmosphere is always charged with as great an excitement as is
ever generated by an athletic event. In examining the physical capacities
of women, it is necessary to select sports that fully tax the competitor;
that is, sports that require not only psychological control but also
optimum capacity in terms of neuromuscular integration and physiological excellence. For these reasons, two sports that are represented in
the Olympics that should be quite edifying, in terms of examining the
performances of women, are track and field and swimming. These events
require maximum muscular power and endurance in basic movements
of the body: running, jumping, throwing, and swimming. In addition,
the performances are measured on the objective ratio scales of time
and distance, rather than on subjective assessment such as occurs in

**TABLE 22**
**Comparison of Male and Female Track and Field Improvement**

| Event | Female | | | Male | | | Sex difference* (%) |
|---|---|---|---|---|---|---|---|
| | First available record | Best record | Improvement (%) | First available record | Best record | Improvement (%) | |
| 100m | 12.2 | 11.0 | 10 | 12.0 | 9.9 | 17 | 10 |
| 200m | 24.4 | 22.4 | 8 | 22.2 | 19.8 | 11 | 11 |
| Long jump | 18'8¼" | 22'4½" | 23 | 20'10" | 29'2½" | 14 | 23 |
| High jump | 5'2 5/8" | 6'3½" | 11 | 5'11¼" | 7'4½" | 13 | 13 |
| Shot put | 45½" | 69'0" | 43 | 36'9¾" | 69'6" | 20 | 43† |
| Discus | 129'11¾" | 218'7" | 40 | 95'7¾" | 212'6½" | 55 | 48† |
| Javelin | 143'4" | 209'7" | 35 | 179'10½" | 296'10" | 28 | 50† |

* Percent of difference between male and female best performances.
† Calculated as above, except that weight difference in implements used is held relatively constant.

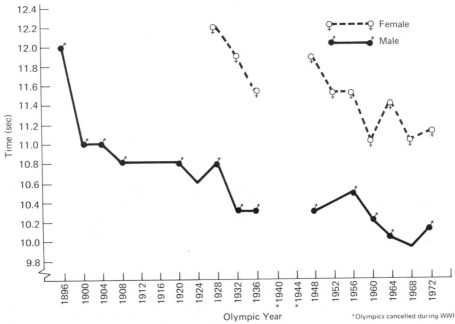

*Fig. 7*   *Records of Olympic performance in the 100-m running event.*

gymnastics and fencing. Finally, the Olympic events of track and field and swimming include some events that are exactly the same for both males and females, so that the objective records may be compared between sexes and over time.

**Running, jumping, and throwing performances.** From an observation of Fig. 7, it may be seen that the fastest woman in the world can run 100 meters (m) in 11.0 seconds, which means generating a velocity of approximately 20.4 miles per hour. An inspection of Table 22 reveals that this is a 10% improvement from the 1928 Olympic performance, or an improvement of 10% in 40 years. Moreover, she can maintain this velocity (which is underestimated as a result of omitting acceleration in the calculation) over a 200-m distance, inasmuch as it takes her almost exactly twice as long to run twice the distance (Fig. 8). Since its inception, more or less steady improvement has been made by women in the 200-m event, and it appears that women have not yet reached their potential in this event.

The highest jump by a woman was made in 1972 at Munich by a 16-year-old West German "Fosbury flopper" who jumped 6 feet 3½

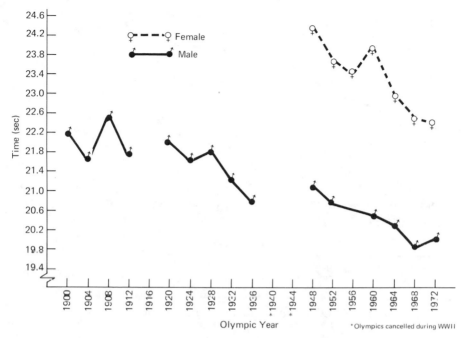

*Fig. 8*    *Records of Olympic performance in the 200-m running event.*

inches to equal the world record and established a new Olympic record (Fig. 9). Whereas 5 feet 10¾ inches used to be cleared by a very select few world competitors, just prior to the 1972 Games there were as many as 40 jumpers who were clearing that height. More than five consistent 6 feet jumpers were omitted from the 1972 Games due to the fact that there simply was an excess of good high jumpers in their country.

The longest distance recorded in a long jump for a woman was 22 feet 4½ inches, made at Mexico City. Long jump performances over the past eight years appear to have leveled off (Fig. 10). The shot put performance by a Russian woman set both a new world and Olympic record. She put the shot 69 feet, and only one other woman in the world has cleared 65.6 feet. The Pentathlon Tables for women equate a 21.03 meter shot put to a 10.6 sec 100-m dash, a 21.5 sec 200-m dash, and a high jump of 6 feet 6 inches; so it is apparent that this shot put performance was one of the great female athletic performances in history. In addition, the steep slope of the regression line of distance over Olympic years indicates the phenomenal improvement that has occurred in this event since 1948 (Fig. 11).

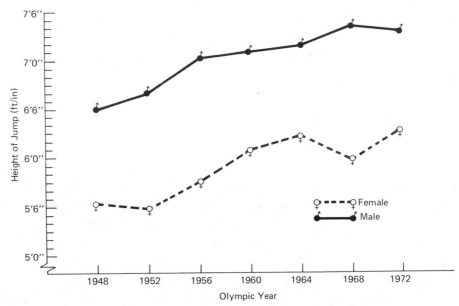

*Fig. 9     Records of Olympic performance in the high jump.*

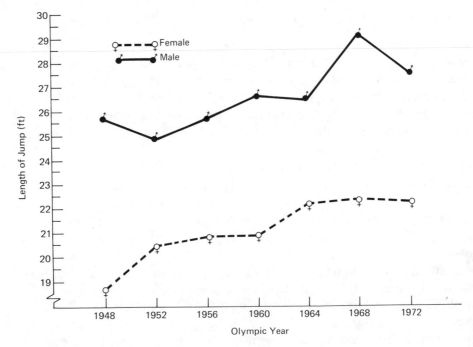

*Fig. 10     Records of Olympic performance in the long jump.*

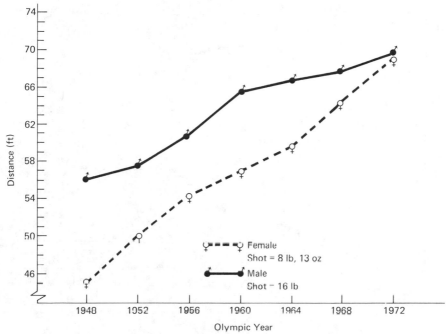

Fig. 11    *Records of Olympic performance in the shot put.*

Just as female performance in the javelin throw appeared to have peaked, the Olympic record was broken at Munich with a 209'7", set by a 5'6½", 143-pound medical student from Jena (Fig. 12). Earlier she had set the world record at 213'5". Discus throwing has also improved remarkably with each Olympic Games (Fig. 13). The champion in Mexico City threw farther than she did for her gold medal in 1968, and didn't even qualify for one of the eight positions in the finals. The longest discus throw ever recorded by a woman was that of 218'9" by a Russian.

As evidenced in Table 22, greater improvement has been made in the field events than in the running events. This may be partially due to the fact that each successive generation of women has increased in size, and size correlates relatively well with strength and field event performance. In addition, the throwing events of discus, shot, and javelin have probably had more masculine connotations than the running and jumping events. Only recently has the cultural acceptance in this country for field events improved. Greater cultural acceptance in a sport generally yields a greater number of competitors which, in turn, raises the performance levels in competition. Understanding of female

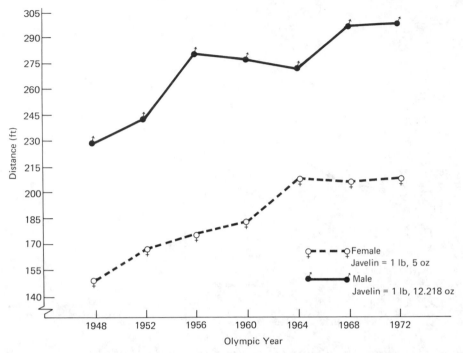

*Fig. 12    Records of Olympic performances in the javelin throw.*

biomechanics has also improved over the years. Finally, more and more coaches are taking a greater interest in women's athletics, so that women are benefiting from improved techniques.

### Male and Female Olympic Record Comparisons

Only the most casual observation of Figs. 7 through 14 is necessary to become convinced that, even though the female physical machine can become quite efficient, it is inferior in the production of muscular force and speed when compared to that of the male. Several sex-differentiated factors—such as comparative body size, body composition, skeletal differences, muscle strength and mass, and cardiorespiratory function-ing—have been cited as reasons why these performance differences are as great as they are. A discussion of these factors is included in the remaining sections.

**Track and field performances.** Many persons maintain that the reason male and female performances are so different is that women have been culturally repressed over the years, and have consequently not been

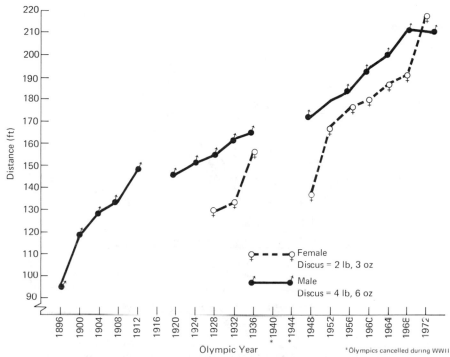

*Fig. 13    Records of Olympic performance in the discus throw.*

trained and coached as well as men. Some have made the observation, perhaps expressed in more detail by Frucht and Jokl (1964), that recent interest and acceptability in women's sport has resulted in the development of sportswomen who have improved their physical performances to the point that they are superior to some of the male competitors of early years. The point is made that all of the female competitors in the 100-m race from 1932 to current times would have defeated the male winner in 1896 (Fig. 7). This is a rather whimsical comparison, however, when the small magnitude of the differences between early male and recent female performances is noted or when the comparison is made from 1900, rather than 1896. Such comparisons are also of dubious value when the myriad of technical changes that have occurred in the running surfaces and timing devices are considered. The overall shape of the regression lines of performance over Olympic years is ample evidence that male and female physical performance in events of running, throwing, jumping, and swimming are in different performance classifications.

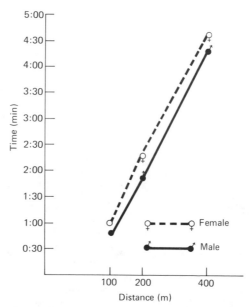

*Fig. 14    Records of Olympic performance in freestyle swimming events.*

A wide gap exists between male and female performances on all track and field events. In shot putting and discus throwing, male performances are superior in spite of the heavier shot (16 lb) and discus (4 lb, 6 oz) used by men as compared to the 8 lb, 13 oz shot and 2 lb, 3 oz discus used by women. The fact that the women's distances with lighter implements are approaching those of men may indicate that women are beginning to reach a relative level of potential that is similar to that reached by men. The javelins, though heavier for the men, are not as different for the two sexes, and once again considerable differences between male and female performances occur.

Another comparison that might be made between male and female performances is that of their endurance performances. In Figs. 14 and 15, swimming and running distance performances are plotted. Note that distance swimming is not available to females except at the 400-m distance, and that the performances of females relative to males are very similar through the range of distances. The females may derive an increasing advantage from their superior buoyancy as the length of the race increases.

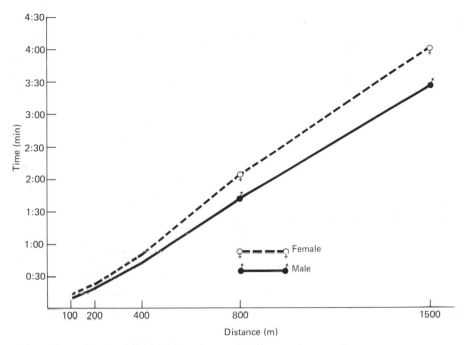

*Fig. 15    Records of Olympic performance in running events.*

In running events, however, the female performance relative to
male performance is worse with increasing distances up to 400m, then
levels off at the distances of 800m and 1500m. Although the difference
between male and female times appears to be greater at 800-m and
1500-m distances, the proportion of these differences to the total times
run by each sex is not as great as it is at shorter distances. The production of power is less a factor at distances greater than 400m; and although
females have lower aerobic capacity than males, the sex difference in
aerobic capacity appears to contribute less to sex differences than the
difference in power production. At any rate, the substantial differences
in performances at the 400, 800, and 1500m distances is ample evidence
that cumulative effects of structural and physiological factors working
to the disadvantage of the female are operating at greater distances.

    A final comparison that might be made between male and female
performances is the opportunities provided for competition. Women's
track and field is representative of most women's sports which have
only been available in the competitive world since World War II. Men's

TABLE 23
Comparison of Male and Female Olympic Swimming Improvement

| Event | Female | | | Male | | | Sex difference |
|---|---|---|---|---|---|---|---|
| | First available record | Best available | Improve-ment (%) | First available record | Best available | Improve-ment (%) | |
| 100-m freestyle | 1:22.2 (1912) | 58.6 | 29 | 1:22.2 (1896) | 51.2 | 38 | Males 13¹ faster |
| 400-m freestyle | 6:02.2 (1924) | 4:19.0 | 28 | 6:16.2 (1904) | 4:00.3 | 36 | Males 7% faster |
| 100-m backstroke | 1:23.2 (1924) | 1:05.8 | 21 | 1:24.6 (1908) | 56.6 | 33 | Males 14¹ faster |

track and field was an important part of the Olympic Games 22 years before the first female event—the 100-m run—was provided in 1928. Most of the women's events were post-war, initiated in London in 1948. Women athletes have only been seriously competing for 24 years, compared to 44 years of male competition. Distance events for women have only recently been acceptable. The 400-m race was initiated in 1964, while the 1500-m distance was run for the first time in the 1972 Olympics.

**Swimming performances.** A statistical analysis of Olympic swimming records reveals that females are probably far from recognizing their peak potential in speed, strength, and stamina in swimming (Hodgkins and Skubic, 1968). Swimming techniques and training processes are improving yearly. Åstrand et al. (1963) pointed out that intense training is most effective in increasing aerobic capacity if it occurs in early adolescence. It is not surprising, then, to find in a sport that makes large demands on the oxygen transport system, that the age of successful swimmers is quite young. The 1964 U.S. Olympic team's average age, for example, was 15.8 years.

Swimming performances mirror those of track and field, in that the males are superior (Table 23) and the performances of both sexes have been improving (Figs. 16 to 18). Female performances are closer to those of males in the 400-m freestyle than in any other swimming or track and field event (Table 23, Fig. 18). Several explanations are plausible. Buoyancy is greater in females and the additional energy expended

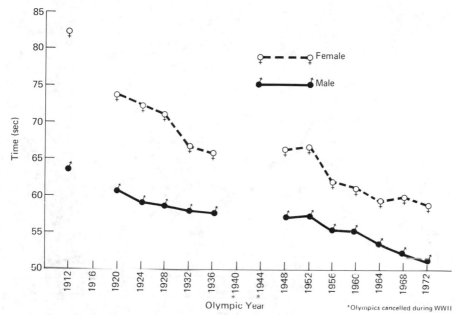

Fig. 16    Records of Olympic performance in the 100-m freestyle
event.

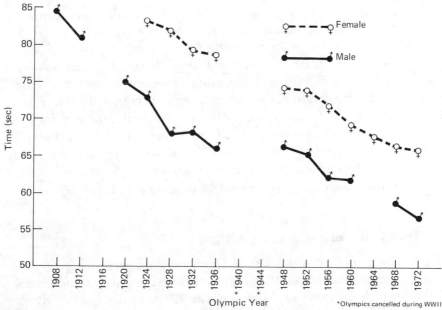

Fig. 17    Records of Olympic performance in the 100-m back stroke
event.

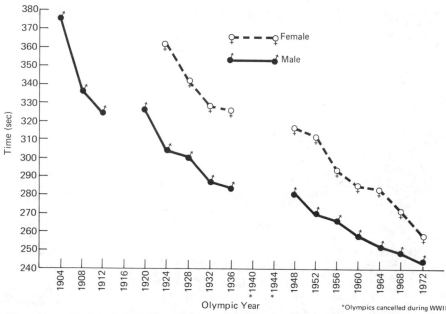

**Fig. 18    Records of Olympic performance in the 400-m freestyle event.**

by males to keep the body afloat over longer distances, such as the 400-m freestyle, may be cumulative. It is also possible that female swimmers train harder and participate in weight training programs more than female athletes in track and field. Swimming programs for young children are more prevalent and more organized than track and field programs for children; thus women swimmers may be closer to their potential than female track participants. Finally, the cooling factor of water dissipates body heat in swimming and is not present in track and field. As will be shown later, females experience greater heat stress sooner than males; so that in an event where a body coolant is provided, the disadvantage of greater heat stress may be overcome.

## Sex Tests in International Competition

Male performance in world-class competitions has been so superior to that of women that within the sporting context females are no competition for males. From approximately the 1930s to the Tokyo Olympics in 1964, rumors were circulated that several of the outstanding performances that had occurred in women's track and field competitions were contributed, not by females, but by males. A few documented cases were published of purported female athletes who were really males, and of athletes who were pseudohermaphrodites. Apparently some of the middle European countries, in their zeal to have winning teams, either actively recruited these types of individuals, or at the least, didn't discourage their participation.

The female world high jump record of 5 feet 7 inches was set in 1938 at the European championships by a German who later revealed that he was completely male. He stated that he had been forced to grow long hair and pose as a female in order to compete "for the sake of the honor and the glory of the Third Reich." Several other cases have been reported of individuals in which there was a confusion of their sex.

Sexual anomalies, or intersex problems, often result in ambiguous genitalia which results in a misdiagnosis of sex at birth. The child is reared as one sex until the time of puberty, at which time the development of secondary sex abnormality occurs. Sexual anomalies can occur as a result of chromosomal abnormalities or endocrine dysfunction. A hermaphrodite is an individual in which both male and female gonads are present, whereas pseudohermaphroditism refers to an individual who has gonads of one sex and external genitalia of the other. Male pseudo-hermaphrodites are genetic males in whom the testes are nonfunctional. They generally do not develop female secondary sex characteristics, and usually do not menstruate. Their somatotype and body composition is typically feminine, and when their transformation into males has been attempted, it has not been very successful in eradicating feminine behavior. Female pseudohermaphrodites have a hereditary metabolic disorder of the adrenal gland, in which the individual has an excess of androgens—the male sex hormones. In mild cases the clitoris is hyper-trophied and the labia slightly fused, but there are distinct urethral and vaginal openings. In severe cases there is a phallus with a penile urethra opening at its tip and complete scrotal fusion. Although these individuals have the external genitalia of a male, internally they are female, with ovaries, fallopian tubes, and the upper part of a vagina (Hutt, 1972).

Several cases of varying degrees of pseudohermaphroditism in athletes have been reported. In the world games in London in 1934 a Czech set the 800-m world record with a time of 2:12.8. This individual had both a masculine somatic androgyny and sexual deviation. Following the individual's termination of her racing career, medical evidence revealed relatively well-developed male genitals, with the omission of testicles (Tachezy, 1969). Remedial surgery was performed and was successful to the extent that the former female athlete became a male, able to achieve coital ejaculation, but not able to produce sperm. He later married his housekeeper and apparently had a successful marriage.

In 1946 at the Oslo European Championships two French competitors placed third in the 100-m and 200-m races, but both have since been transformed through surgery into men. One of them is a father. Two other "suspected" athletes were a 6-foot-2-inch Russian who held the world record in high jump and pentathlon, and a Korean who holds the current world record of 51.9 sec in the 400-m race (Bank, 1967).

The instances of participation by intersexed individuals in the female events initiated a clamor for some type of test in which the sex of the female could be validated. In the Tokyo Olympics, physical examinations were made mandatory for all female track and field competitors. In the Mexico City Olympics, a five-step test was used, as follows:

1. study of the reproductive organs and pelvic region,
2. study of the male and female hormones,
3. determination of the sex of the chromosomes,
4. determination of the sex of the nuclei,
5. study of the sexual characteristics of the individual.

Chromosomal sex (step 3 above) is determined by examining white blood cells in a blood sample. Determination of the sex of the nuclei (step 4 above) is determined by searching for the presence of Barr-bodies, a darkly staining body that is present only in the nuclei of female cells. Barr-bodies are examined in slides prepared from a buccal smear, a sample obtained by lightly scraping the inside of the cheek.

Recently, the sex tests have been made much less embarrassing and inconvenient. Rather than suffer through all of the tests as described above, athletes simply provide a hair from their head, and the cell constituents can be determined from it. In addition, rather than submitting to the sex tests prior to each competition, athletes are now provided with a certificate validating their female identification and exempting them from future tests.

These tests have served the purpose of ensuring female competition for females only, for several noted world-class "female" competitors have dropped out of competition. In 1966 a Polish co-world record holder in the 100-m race was determined to be ineligible for future competition. The winner of the downhill skiing championship in 1966 withdrew from the 1968 Olympics because of difficulty in proving her sex. She has since undergone surgery and is now a male. Several eastern European champions no longer compete outside their country.

Women's track and field should now be free of those individuals who have glandular differences that enable them, through heavy training, to achieve strength levels that normal healthy women cannot achieve. In addition, the sex test eliminates potential psychological damage that can occur to individuals of questionable sex when they are publicly accused.

## Physical Performances of Sportswomen Compared to Other Women

The American sportswoman is far superior in physical performance to her nonathletic counterpart. She is much farther from the average population of nonathletic women in running performance than the male athlete is from his respective nonathletic population. Direct comparisons of female athletes with nonsportswomen are difficult, because the nonathletes don't participate in many comparable events. However, it is interesting to analyze the difference between the average college female's physical performance and the trained female athlete's performance in order to determine the distance from average to ultimate in female performance.

In Fig. 19, the Olympic female track and field performances are compared to record performances from college intramural track and field tournaments. Some of the values of the intramural records were interpolated for the Olympic distances, since intramural meets don't generally include the same distances that are run in the Olympics. The difference between the trained female athlete and the nontrained intramural champions is dramatic. The longer the distance to be run, the greater the difference between the athlete and nonathlete. The enormous difference between the trained athlete's shot put and the college woman's probably represents the accumulation of differences in coaching techniques, training methods, and strength development programs. These differences between trained and untrained performers are even greater in actuality than they would seem to be because the records of intramural meets represent the *very best* of a tremendously heterogeneous group. If average performance of running speed in the

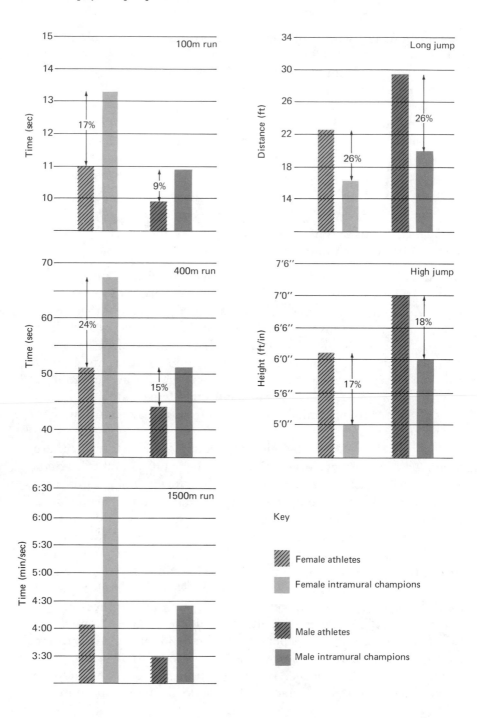

100-m event were obtained, the times for nonathletic females would be substantially slower. In summary, the female athlete finds herself widely divergent in ability from her ordinary peer's average performance.

In Fig. 19 male Olympic records compared to male intramural records are also included. Several observations are noteworthy. First, male athletes are not as superior to intramural record holders as are female athletes. Second, the performances of male intramural champions, who represent the best of average males, are very close but not better than female athletes. In other words, female athletes are better physical performers than the best of average men. Third, while male and female athletes and male intramural record holders are clustered around similar performance levels, the female intramural performance is clearly quite inferior.

## NEUROMUSCULAR CHARACTERISTICS
## OF SPORTSWOMEN

The complexity of the neuromotor communication, the profusion of discriminations made, and the efficient retrieval of specific templates from motor memory stores that occur in the wink of an eyelash during the execution of a sports skill is mind-boggling. So mind-boggling is human motor control, in fact, that it has been seriously neglected by those who seek to understand sport performance.

Components such as balance, agility, flexibility, and coordination have been named and studied, but so little standardization, validity, and reliability has been achieved in investigations of these components that the synthesized results are largely uninformative. A vast chasm yawns between scientific information about basic mechanisms of neuromotor control and a scholarly understanding of the integrative processes that occur during a world-record-shattering performance. Nevertheless, a few neuromuscular characteristics of sportswomen have been investigated with some standardization. These are reaction time,

◀ *Fig. 19    Comparison of Olympic female athlete performances with average "record" performances. (Average "record" performances of women are averages of values published in the* National Intramural Newsletter, *1972. Intramural records for men are performances averaged from the records published in 15 major university Intramural Handbooks.)*

movement time, discrimination reaction time, muscular strength, and muscular endurance. Although these components, in addition to those mentioned earlier, have—when isolated—correlated very poorly with specific sports abilities, the cumulative effects should not be discounted.

### Reaction Time, Movement Time, and Discrimination Reaction Time

Reaction time is the length of time it takes an individual to perceive a stimulus and initiate a response to it. It is typically measured by having a person take her hand off a telegraph key or some other switch as soon as she either sees a light, hears a buzzer, or feels some contact with her hand.

The reaction times of the sportswomen who have been measured are faster than nonsportswomen. Tennis players were the subjects of investigation in three of the four studies, and in all instances were faster in reaction time than the nonathletic women with whom they were compared. The tennis players, when combined with fencers, swimmers, and hockey players, were much faster than the nonathletes (Younger, 1959). Their reaction time mean to a visual stimulus was 248 milliseconds (msec) compared to 273 msec for the nonathletes. The difference of 25 milliseconds, although it seems to be a very short time, is an enormous difference in terms of expected reaction times. Both 248 and 273 msec averages are very slow compared to commonly reported simple reaction time means, but the explanation probably lies in the fact that the reaction times were followed by a movement. When the organism has to follow a simple reaction with a movement, the reaction time is slowed (Henry, 1960).

Tennis players were also quicker reactors with both their arms and legs than archers and golfers (Beise and Peaseley, 1937). All three sports groups were faster than nonsportswomen, but the tennis players surpassed all groups. Hagerman (1972) measured the total body reaction time (the length of time it takes an individual to move her entire body in response to a stimulus) of 89% of the ranked tennis players in the state of Texas. A peripheral aspect of her study included an analysis of the reaction times of the winners of the Texas Open and Southwest Championship Tournaments when compared to the losers. In addition, she considered the length of the match. An interesting trend was that those who won in short matches (i.e., those who defeated their opponents with little difficulty) had the fastest reaction times of the four groups. Those who lost were the slowest reactors.

Forty-one Regional High School Volleyball champions were measured and compared to 10 nonathletic girls of similar ages (Wyrick, 1972). The volleyball team players' simple reaction times were obtained immediately before and immediately after one of their tournament games. Their times over 8 blocks of 25 trials were impressively faster than the controls with whom they were compared, and much faster than reported reaction times of other females. Their average reaction time to a visual stimulus was 166 msec, which, when compared to the times of average females of comparable age reported by Hodgkins (1963), is very fast. The most obvious explanation is that the volleyball girls were in a high state of arousal as well as being in a competitive psychological "set" at the time they were measured; nevertheless, the reaction times obtained reveal that sportswomen can achieve extremely fast reaction times.

Movement time refers to the speed with which an individual can move a limb with body through space, irrespective of reaction time. Movement time is usually measured by having an individual move her hand, arm, or leg from one location to another as quickly as possible. Movement time is often combined with reaction time measures, by requiring the person to lift her hand off a switch as soon as she sees a stimulus, and to move her arm to another location as soon as possible.

Movement time of 47 varsity intercollegiate athletes was significantly faster than 75 women who were not athletes (Younger, 1959). Within the sports groups, the swimmers were reported to be significantly slower movers than the tennis, fencing, and hockey competitors. The statistical technique used to detect that difference between the swimmers and other sportswomen was not an appropriate one, however, and it is very probable that the significant difference was obtained by a chance occurrence.

Two groups of physically active and fit women, one in their middle forties and the other group averaging twenty years of age, were compared in discriminatory reaction time to two similar groups who were not physically active or fit. Their discriminatory reaction times displayed the typical age function, but there also was a decided trend for the fit groups to have a faster discriminatory reaction time than the unfit groups (Scarborough, 1973).

Comparison of the reaction and movement times of sportswomen to sportsmen have not been made, but reaction times of nonsportsmen and nonsportswomen have been. In almost all studies, the reaction and movement times of men have been faster than those of the women (Ellis, 1929). Hodgkins (1963) found, in 1930 subjects aging from 5 to 84 years of age, that males were significantly faster than females in all age groups except the first graders and the groups from 55 to 84 years. The greatest difference between the sexes was at age 20, where the simple reaction times of males averaged 168 msec and the times of females averaged 210 msec. Henry (1960) also found a statistically significant difference between the reaction times of males and females, but he speculated that the real difference was so small that it might be of no practical importance. He did find that males were dramatically faster in movement time than females. When females train, their reaction times decrease in about the same way that males' do (Zimkin, 1956).

An appropriate question to be raised is, "Why are males faster than females in reaction time and movement time, and of what significance is it to sports performance?" Men may be faster in reacting due to cultural expectations and higher motivation levels. Men are expected to be performers in our society, whereas women have been expected to be functional or decorative. Men may be more competitive than women, and may interpret a reaction time test as more of a challenge than do women. Men do have superior visual acuity and spatial ability (Hutt, 1972; pp. 83 and 92), both of which may contribute to reaction time. In addition, there is some evidence that men are more bilateral in their cerebral organization, a characteristic that promotes more efficient control in nonverbal functions (Buffery and Gray, 1972). The faster movement speeds of men may be explained by their higher percentage of muscle and greater strength (Henry, 1960).

## Muscular Strength and Endurance

Muscular strength contributes enormously to many sports performances and serves as the final limiting factor in some athletes' agonizing struggles to reach their sport potential. It is common knowledge that when the muscles are pressed into overload work against resistance, they hypertrophy. Thus it is not surprising to find that women who demand heavy work from their muscles grow stronger. Women who are physical education majors, and thus are active in many sports daily, are generally stronger than the average college woman (Mynatt, 1960). When Conger and Macnab (1967) compared 40 intercollegiate sportswomen to 40 nonsportswomen, they found that the sportswomen were stronger in nine strength measures, including flexion and extension of upper and lower limbs and hips. Conger and Wessel (1968) found that when they grouped women according to their physical activity levels, the physically active women were stronger in trunk extension than the nonactive women. It is possible that women who are genetically endowed with a greater number of muscle fibers have early success in strength events and thus "select themselves" into physical education or into competitive sport. Whatever the reasons, evidence of the superior strength of women who participate in strength-demanding sports is abundant, and to recite evidence endlessly would belabor the point.

Although sportswomen are stronger than nonsportswomen, they are certainly no match for sportsmen. Nöcker (1955) stated bluntly that sex determines strength and power. The superior size and strength of sportsmen, in addition to their greater quantity of lean body mass, explain to a large extent the superior physical performances of men over women in sports that require explosive power; e.g., javelin throw, discus throw, shot put, and sprints.

The amount of muscle mass in the female is only about half the amount in men. Shaffer (1964) clearly articulated the well-established fact that this additional muscle mass develops in men after childhood, during the additional growth spurt which boys experience between the ages of 12½ and 15 years. The strength that women generate has been estimated to be anywhere from 75-80% (Ufland, 1933), 60% (Hettinger, 1953) to 50% (Shaffer, 1964; Kroll, 1971) that of men. Asmussen (1973) indicates that an average estimate from all studies might be that an adult woman can produce about 65% of the strength that an average man can produce. Åstrand (1956) reported strength of women in flexors to be about 20-25% less, in extensors to be 40% less, in flexors and extensors of leg muscles, 30%, and in muscles of the hand, 40% less than men.

Some of the strength difference between men and women can be attributed to the superior size of the male. Since strength is proportional to the transverse sectional area of muscle, isometric strength theoretically varies to the second power with the individual's height, providing the body shapes are geometrically similar (Åstrand and Rodahl, 1970). A male six feet tall is taller than a five foot female by a factor of 1.2, therefore the strength increase from size alone would be by a factor of $1.2^2$, or 1.44. In addition, when strength is measured as torque, the distance over which the muscle can shorten is proportional to height and is greater in the taller male. In the previous example, the torque increase would be by a factor of $1.2^3$, or 1.73.

Even when size is held constant, however, females are only 80% as strong as males. The superiority of male strength is attributed to the quantitative increase in muscle mass that occurs in men at puberty. Prior to puberty, when muscle strength is plotted in relation to body height on a double logarithmic scale, male superiority is not so dramatic. At puberty, there is a sudden increase in the slope of this line for boys, but not for girls. In addition, at puberty creatinine excretion (an indicator of muscle mass) increases significantly in males but not in females. Both of these changes, attributable to hormonal changes, are indications that muscle mass increases significantly in males at puberty. At puberty, boys experience an increase in the production of androgens, hormones which influence the development of muscle mass. Testosterone causes nitrogen retention, which in turn facilitates protein synthesis. Square centimeter for centimeter, however, the muscle strength of males and females is not significantly different (Ikai and Fukunaga, 1968).

Hettinger has stated that in particular the muscles of the back, stomach, and perineum are less developed in the female than in the male. Even when females had similar training programs, males improved 50% whereas females only improved 24% (Zimkin, 1955).

Very little study has been made of muscle fatigue in women, but Kroll (1971) reported that, just as in men, women's level of strength is directly related to the pattern of their fatigue. Female fatigue patterns in repeated wrist flexor trials were similar to those of men, though they were only half as strong. The weakest women's fatigue patterns were significantly different from the moderate and strong women's fatigue patterns.

Laboratory or field tests of women's strength have revealed the fact that in this country females seem to reach their peak performances at about the age of 12½, or one year before menarche (Shaffer, 1973; Asmussen, 1973; Fleishman, 1965). The development of strength seems to level off or even decrease in the average girl as she progresses through puberty. Asmussen (1973) has speculated that, since the average age of menarche has decreased from age 17 one hundred years ago to age 13 in current times, perhaps sports events demanding great strength and aerobic capacity will be won by younger and younger females. Asmussen's prediction is somewhat verified by Åstrand's (1963) documentation of the decreasing age of female champion swimmers.

No doubt exists that men are stronger than women, but the actual strength of women, particularly in this country, has been underestimated. The potent social stigma that is attached to the attainment of strength by females is a powerful influence that certainly must affect the amount of force produced by females on strength tests. Women have been conditioned throughout their lives to avoid displays of strength, and they are not likely to ignore these social expectations and produce maximum strength on experimental tests. A compounding factor is that many strength tests are administered to females in groups, or worse, in the presence of males. Finally, almost all experimenters who have measured the strength of females are males. Adolescent females are loathe to display strength under any circumstances, but particularly in the presence of a male. In summary, women are certainly not as strong as men, but they may not be as weak as they have been credited to be. More specifically, the age of 12½ as the age of maximum strength may be an artifact of the adolescent society.

## PERFORMANCE SIMILARITY OR SPORTS EQUALITY?

The preceding information has been presented as a representation of the physical capacity of females in selected sports, competing as individuals against other women and against athletic records. Their performances were compared to those of men, because the relationship of the female athlete to the male athlete has important sociological and economic implications. Repeatedly, the female's performance has suffered in the comparison, yet the foregoing discussions in this chapter should not be interpreted as a panegyric for the superiority of men, but rather as an objective assessment of the physical similarities of sportswomen to other women and to men. The simple truth is that as physical performers, sportswomen are far superior to nonsportswomen, but are inferior to sportsmen. Those who would claim sports *equality* as synonymous to sports *similarity* by emphasizing the overlap in male and female performance in the population are confusing training, age, and motivational differences with sex differences. The more highly trained and specialized the female and male athlete population, the less variance shared between their distributions.

The essential fact is that the superior physical performance of the male is to be accepted as a performance dissimilarity, but it must not be used as a basis for sport inequality. Saying that a man is a "better" athlete than a woman because he can defeat her is tantamount to saying that a heavyweight wrestler is a "better" wrestler because he can easily defeat a lightweight wrestler. No one suggests that the heavyweight athlete receive a more golden medal at the Olympics than the lightweight athlete, but some are suggesting that women should receive less award for their professional championships. Some large and prestigious universities are claiming to provide equal opportunity, but are requiring females to compete against men for athletic scholarships. At least 11 states have regulations that girls must be permitted to try out for boys' high school teams. Such situations do not provide equal opportunity for the vast majority of potential sportswomen.

The sportswoman is a beautiful creature. She is a sun-browned girl filled with vigor and robustness. She is strong and healthy, a symphony of neuromuscular timing and gracefulness, and a glorious half of the human species. Her performances have been magnificent within her capabilities, and her zenith is as yet undreamed. When she runs her 100-m dash in 11.0 seconds, she should receive the accolades that he receives; she should be crowned with the winner's garland that is settled upon his head. Although her performance is dissimilar, in every aspect of the agonistic essence of sport, she is equal to him. She has struggled and suffered to prepare her body to its fullest potential, she has studied and drilled in unending repetitions of her skills, she has battled within the framework of the competition, she has asked no advantage from her opponent, and she has marshaled every ounce of her psychological and physiological capabilities together for the moment of physical commitment. In the fullest sense, although she breaks her own tape a few yards behind him, she is his equal in sport.

# Chapter 13
# Physique*

The study of body conformation and structure is of critical interest to those who seek to define the determinants of physical performance. As the body attempts to meet the task demands of a sports skill, it may be thought of as a mass with a center of gravity which is subject to the basic laws of inertia, acceleration, and counterforce. The body segments in motion are subject to principles of leverage, and when the body is projected into space it becomes subject to the laws governing projectiles and application of force. Thus the height, weight, shape, and relative proportions of the body segments are to some extent determinants of an individual's capacity to meet the demands of physical tasks.

Physique has been variously described by anthropometrics (measures of the structure of the body), body composition, and somatotyping rating techniques. Anthropometric records include: linear measures of height, sitting height, lower leg length, and biacromial (shoulder) width; girth measures such as calf, arm, and chest; and measures of weight, total body and/or segmental weight. Body composition determinations include estimates of the percent of fat, bone, muscle, water, or mineral that comprise the total body weight. Somatotyping is a somewhat arbitrary system of describing the body shape of an individual basically in terms of two dimensions: muscularity, and a continuum progressing from fatness to leanness.

Eminent physical anthropologists have been curious about the physique of sportsmen and sportswomen, because a clear relationship appears to exist between structure and function in sports performance.

* Gratitude is expressed to Dr. Robert Malina, Department of Anthropology and Department of Health, Physical Education, and Recreation at The University of Texas at Austin, for his valuable guidance and knowledgeable suggestions in the preparation of this manuscript.

Additionally, in sporting competition clearly defined levels of competency are apparent. In the sporting world, competency levels range from neophyte to local, regional, national, and, finally, world or Olympic championship levels. Within each competency level are further defined levels of success, such as consistency in first, second, or third place finishing. Several questions naturally surface. Is the morphology of a group of individuals who participate in the same sport similar? Is structure a limiting factor in sports success, and if so, at what level of performance? Are sportswomen who participate in different sports homogeneous in physique, or is a specific physique identifiable for each sport? How different is the physique of the sportswoman from that of the sportsman, and to what extent do these differences contribute to the differences in their performances?

Spectators, through casual observation, have identified homogeneity in the body conformations of participants in various sports, for example, the tall basketball player, the small, light-framed jockey, and the lanky cross-country runner. Body weight, for instance, is so well known to affect success in boxing and wrestling that classifications based on weight have been developed within which individuals must compete. It should be remembered, of course, that sports performance is a highly complex behavior. Many factors—psychological, physiological, and sociological—interact with the morphological attributes of an athlete in the performance process. To attempt to attribute athletic success only to physique is indeed simplistic. At the ultimate levels of physical performance, i.e., the exquisite moment when human beings surpass barriers previously thought unattainable, all of the factors contributing to the performance must be operating at maximum levels. This implies that high-level physical performance requires a physical machine that is structured in such a way that it will provide all the biomechanical advantages possible. Physique should be considered as a limiting and contributing factor rather than as a predictive factor in physical performance.

To determine the extent to which body structure contributes to sports performance, attention must be directed to those individuals who have attained great physical accomplishments, or at least to those for whom sports skills of one type or another constitute a lifestyle, i.e., the female athlete.

The quantification of body shape and structure has produced some generalizations about athletes. Athletes do, as a group, tend to have somatotypes that are different from the general population (Cureton, 1951; Carter, 1970; Tanner, 1964; Malina, 1971). For example, Tanner (1964) found that over half of the somatotypes that are present in the general population are not present in the 1960 sample of Olympic athletes at Rome. Certain athletic groups are different from each other, and competitors within specific athletic events tend to be homogeneous within each level of competency. These generalizations are based primarily on anthropometric observations for male athletes, but as reports of studies investigating sportswomen are becoming available, the physiques of sportswomen appear to be following a trend that is similar to that of males.

As is true with any generalization, some precautions are necessary. First, some factors involving physique are very much influenced by age. When comparisons are made across samples, age must be considered as a possible alternative. Second, as will be noted from the following discussion, much of the available data on sportswomen are from European populations. Third, most of the available data are derived from very small samples, making statistical inferences at times questionable. Small samples are somewhat understandable and forgivable when the size of the population of sportswomen relative to the size of the female population as a whole is considered.

## HEIGHT AND WEIGHT

Sportswomen as a group have tended to be taller and heavier than non-sportswomen, but this is partially a function of the sport samples by researchers. Sportswomen competing in certain sports tend to be significantly larger than sportswomen in other activities. Although these sports are predominant in the sporting arena, there are some sports for which a small size is an advantage. Consequently, smaller sportswomen in these events influence the average values found among sportswomen as a group. For instance, in Hirata's (1966) report, the low height of the gymnasts, swimmers, and distance runners (when combined with the tallness of other Olympic competitors) resulted in an average height that was not significantly different from the nonsportswoman. Yet, the distribution of the two groups is substantially different. A normal distribution is evident for stature of the nonsportswoman population, whereas a bimodal distribution may best describe Olympic female athletes as a group. (See Fig. 20.) The weight of sportswomen tends to be greater than that of nonsportswomen, probably due to the greater muscularity of sportswomen. Reported heights and weights of female

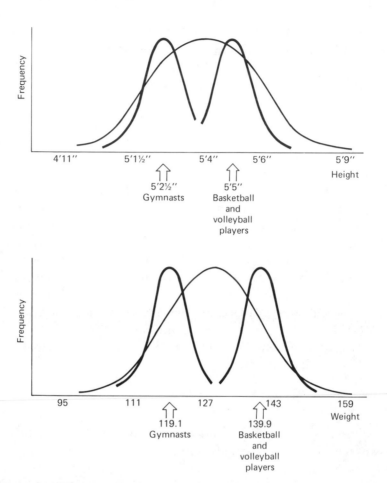

*Fig. 20    Distributions of height and weight of two extreme athletic groups compared to the normal distribution of height and weight in the population.*

athletes are presented in Table 24. (Refer to p. 284 for other data on this subject.)

Basketball and volleyball team members appear to be, with little question, taller and/or heavier (McArdle, 1971; Carter, 1970; Conger and Macnab, 1967). Medved (1968), to the contrary, reported that volleyball and basketball players in his study sample were no taller than average. He speculated that this was so because the small number of sportswomen in his sample made the authenticity of their membership in a sportswoman classification questionable.

Another group of female athletes that are consistently taller and heavier are those women excelling in the field events of track and field: shot putting, discus throwing, javelin throwing, long and high jumping. Carter (1970) found the track and field throwers to be among the tallest and heaviest of his sample, and in Medved's (1968) study, the track and field specialists were one of the few groups of sportswomen who were taller and heavier. The female high jumpers in the Tokyo Olympics were the tallest and leanest females in the competition (Hirata, 1966). All of the track and field athletes except distance runners were taller and heavier than their nonathletic controls in the report of Malina et al. (1971). Throwers, jumpers, and sprinters were taller, in that order, than distance runners and nonathletes. In terms of weight, the groups from heaviest to lightest were shot putters, discus/javelin throwers, jumpers, sprinters, nonathletes, and distance runners. Malina et al.'s (1971) results paralleled with lower values those of Eiben (1969), who measured 125 women athletes competing in the 1966 European championships in track and field held at Budapest. The shot putters in this competition averaged 5 feet 6 inches in height and 178 pounds in weight. At least one of the shot putters was 6 feet tall and weighed 198 pounds. The discus throwers averaged 176 pounds and 5 feet 6 inches in height. Javelin competitors were somewhat smaller, averaging 158.4 pounds and 5 feet 4 inches in height. As can be readily seen from these values, the track and field throwers of world class caliber are relatively enormous women. Their mean weights are off the scale shown in Fig. 20. Although no data are available regarding their percent body fat, it is probably safe to assume that a substantial percentage of their weight is muscle. These descriptions of champion athletes certainly underscore the fact that in events where total body strength and muscular power are requisite to superior levels of performance, one finds tall, heavy, long-limbed competitors. In addition, body size becomes more and more a determinant as the level of competition increases, from college competition to world-class competitive events.

Female gymnasts are a more homogeneous group of athletes, and data on their heights and weights are more consistent than any other sports group reported. The average weight of gymnasts reported in four investigations was 53.52 kilograms (kg), whereas the average college populations reported have been approximately 57.6 kg (Carter, 1970; Pool et al., 1969; Sinning and Lindberg, 1968; Sprynarova and Parizkova, 1969). The average height of the gymnasts sampled by those same investigators, in addition to the heights reported by Medved (1966), was 159.34 cm, as compared to 165.6 cm for the nonsports-

**TABLE 24**
**Published Heights and Weights of Female Athletes**

| Sports type | No. | Country | Height (cm) | Height (ft/in) | Weight (kg) | Weight (lb) | Age | Source |
|---|---|---|---|---|---|---|---|---|
| Basketball | 14 | USA | 169.1 | 5′5 | 62.0 | 136.4 | 19.1 | Sinning, 1973 |
| Basketball | 15 | USA | 165.3 | 5′4½ | 65.2 | 143.4 | 19.3 | Lundgren, 1968 |
| Basketball | 6 | USA | 165.3 | 5′4 | 61.5 | 135.3 | Col. age | McArdle, *et al.*, 1971 |
| Basketball | 17 | USA | 167.0 | 5′4⅔ | 63.9 | 140.6 | 19.4 | Conger & Macnab, 1967 |
| Basketball | 10 | USA | 173.0 | 5′6 | 71.4 | 157.1 | —* | Carter, 1970 |
| Basketball | 7 | USA | 166.4 | 5′4½ | 61.3 | 134.9 | 20.3 | Sinning & Adrian, 1968 |
| Volleyball | 10 | USA | 166.0 | 5′4½ | 59.8 | 131.6 | 19.4 | Conger & Macnab, 1967 |
| Hockey | 12 | USA | 165.1 | 5′4 | 63.5 | 139.7 | 18.7 | Lundgren, 1968 |
| Track and field | 61 | USA | 167.1 | 5′4⅔ | 56.8 | 125.0 | 17.2 | Carter, 1970 |
| Track and field | 53 | Yugoslavia | 164.7 | 5′4 | — | — | 20.4 | Medved, 1966 |
| Track and field | 125 | Europe | 168.3 | 5′5 | 63.5 | 139.6 | 23.0 | Eiben, 1969 |
| Track and field (sprinters) | 22 | Europe | 165.0 | 5′4 | 56.0 | 123.2 | 22.0 | Eiben, 1969 |
| Track and field (sprinters) | 8 | USA | 161.0 | 5′2¾ | 53.9 | 118.6 | 14.9 | Raven *et al.*, 1972 |
| Track and field (sprinters) | 24 | USA | 164.5 | 5′3¾ | 57.2 | 125.8 | 20.1 | Malina, 1971 |
| Track and field (jumpers) | 11 | USA | 165.3 | 5′4 | 58.8 | 129.4 | 20.3 | Malina, 1971 |
| Track and field | 22 | Europe | 172.0 | 5′6 | 63.4 | 139.5 | 21.0 | Eiben, 1969 |
| Track and field (distance runners) | 13 | USA | 161.2 | 5′2¾ | 50.9 | 112.0 | 15.0 | Raven *et al.*, 1972 |
| Track and field (distance runners) | 12 | USA | 161.2 | 5′2¾ | 53.0 | 116.6 | 19.9 | Malina, 1971 |
| Track and field (distance runners) | 26 | Europe | 165.0 | 5′4 | 55.0 | 121.0 | 23.0 | Eiben, 1969 |
| Track and field (discus/javelin) | 10 | USA | 167.1 | 5′4¾ | 71.0 | 156.2 | 21.1 | Malina, 1971 |
| Track and field | 16 | Europe | 173.0 | 5′6¾ | 76.5 | 168.3 | 24.0 | Eiben, 1969 |
| Track and field (shot putters) | 9 | USA | 166.6 | 5′4½ | 77.8 | 171.2 | 21.5 | Malina, 1971 |
| Track and field (shot putters) | 11 | Europe | 171.0 | 5′6 | 80.0 | 176.0 | 25.0 | Eiben, 1969 |

| | N | | | | | | | |
|---|---|---|---|---|---|---|---|---|
| Swimming | 10 | Czechoslovakia | 166.2 | 5'4½ | 63.9 | 140.5 | 19.5 | Sprynarova & Parizkova, 1969 |
| Swimming | 20 | Yugoslavia | 163.4 | 5'3½ | — | — | 19.1 | Medved, 1966 |
| Swimming | 9 | USA | 168.0 | 5'5 | 63.8 | 140.6 | 19.4 | Conger & Macnab, 1967 |
| Golf (amateur) | 26 | USA | 164.8 | 5'4 | 62.9 | 138.4 | 40.5 | Carter, 1970 |
| Golf (pro) | 26 | USA | 167.6 | 5'4¾ | 62.4 | 137.3 | 27.8 | Carter, 1970 |
| Gymnastics | 14 | USA | 158.5 | 5'2 | 51.1 | 112.4 | | Sinning & Lindberg, 1968 |
| Gymnastics | 67 | Yugoslavia | 160.5 | 5'2½ | — | | 20.1 | Medved, 1966 |
| Gymnastics | 5 | USSR | 157.0 | 5'1½ | 53.9 | 118.6 | — | Carter, 1970 |
| Gymnastics | 4 | USSR | 163.0 | 5'3½ | 57.9 | 127.4 | | Conger & Macnab, 1967 |
| Gymnastics | 38 | Europe | 158.4 | 5'1¾ | 52.6 | 115.7 | 20.5 | Pool & Binkhorst, 1969 |
| Gymnastics | 16 | World Champions | 158.7 | 5'1¾ | 53.5 | 117.7 | 22.9 | Pool & Binkhorst, 1969 |
| Gymnastics | 10 | Czechoslovakia | 162.3 | 5'3 | 56.5 | 124.3 | 17.2 | Sprynarova & Parizkova, 1969 |
| Gymnastics | 7 | Czechoslovakia | — | — | 55.4 | 121.9 | 23.0 | Parizkova & Poupa, 1963 |
| Gymnastics | | USSR | 160.3 | 5'2½ | 55.3 | 121.7 | | Kukushkin, 1964 |
| Gymnastics | 13 | Holland | 156.3 | 5'1 | 51.0 | 112.2 | 19.0 | Pool & Binkhorst, 1969 |
| Tokyo Olympic participants | 722 | International | 166.8 | 5'4¾ | 60.0 | 132.0 | 22.8 | Hirata, 1966 |
| Physically active | | USA | — | — | 64.6 | 142.0 | 18-22 | Conger & Wessel, 1968 |
| Physical Education majors | 39 | USA | 165.1 | 5'4 | 58.8 | 129.4 | 22.4 | Carter, 1965 |
| Physical Education majors | 61 | New Zealand | 164.3 | 5'4 | 60.0 | 132.0 | 19.4 | Carter, 1965 |
| Average Female | 31 | USA | 165.6 | 5'4 | 57.6 | 126.7 | 19.0 | Carter, 1965 |
| Average Female | 61 | USA | 165.2 | 5'4 | 57.7 | 127.0 | — | Heath, 1961 |
| Average Female | 30 | USA | 161.3 | 5'2¾ | 55.8 | 122.8 | 20.1 | Malina, 1971 |

* Data not available.

woman population. Gymnasts were, as a group, more like gymnasts of other countries than they were like females of their own country (Pool et al.).

The height-weight description of swimmers is not so clear. Sprynarova and Parizkova (1969) found their swimmers to be about average height, but heavier than nonsportswomen, whereas Åstrand (1964) found 30 female swimmers between the ages of 12 to 16 to be taller than nonathletes of that age.

Conger and Macnab (1967) combined the heights and weights of four intercollegiate teams—swimming, basketball, volleyball, and gymnastics—and found that as a group they were heavier and taller than nonathletes. Their mean height was 166.3 cm and their mean weight was 62 kg. Although this average height might represent a taller group than their comparative sample, it is not much greater than the height of the average college female. It is surprising that the average weight of this group, even with their gymnastics team members included, was so much greater (approximately 4½ kg) than the average college female weight.

The heights and weights of sportswomen take on impressive significance given the fact that many sports events are height-weight biased in favor of the taller and heavier athlete. Height-weight bias is particularly true in the Olympic events, and within these events the champion athletes naturally tend to be taller and heavier. Khosla (1971, 1968) has published two impressive arguments for the addition of weight-height classifications in several sports in the Olympics. He has statistically analyzed the heights and weights of male medal winners as well as participants in the 1960, 1964, and 1968 Olympics, and found impressive evidence that medal winners are taller than nonmedal winners, and nonmedal winners are taller than the non-Olympic population. Even in weight-classification events, the winner's average weight is usually at the upper limit of the weight class and is greater than that of nonwinners. His evidence is in terms of male athletes, but he states that the same weight-height bias is also inherent in many sports events for women.

It is not unexpected that in many events tall athletes have advantages over short athletes. Longer strides may be taken by a taller athlete, so that a shorter competitor must increase the number of strides taken to surpass the tall athlete. Increasing the number of strides increases the effort necessary, which in turn has a debilitating effect upon endurance. Taller athletes have greater lung volume, so that a man 72 inches tall has 35% more lung volume than one of 62 inches (Lowe et al., 1968).

The longer limbs of the taller athlete provide her with a longer lever which in turn represents a longer force arm. Since the linear speed of a point in rotation is directly proportional to the distance of that point from the axis of rotation, a discus released from a longer arm would have developed a greater moment of force at the time of release; that is, given an identical trajectory, it will travel farther than one released from a lesser moment of force. In addition, if the discus is released from a higher point above the ground, as it would be by a taller athlete, it will travel farther.

The result of the height-weight bias in many sporting events is that when strength, power, or speed are requisite to becoming champion, the winners tend to be taller and heavier than their nonsporting counterparts. Only in a sport such as gymnastics, where small limb levers favor quick, rotary movements, are the smaller and lighter female athletes found. In sports where the premium is placed on precision, strategy, and psychological control—such as badminton, tennis, or fencing—the height-weight bias is not apparent and the competitors tend to be of average size.

## Skeletal Measures

Height, weight, and age data have been obtained from competition records and applications, but skeletal data are not so easily obtained. Consequently, few investigators have obtained skeletal measures from sportswomen. Most research reported in terms of female skeletal structure has been with regard to the similarities and dissimilarities of the female skeleton to that of the male, and the possible consequence of such differences in terms of athletic performance. Presumably, the more like the male skeletal structure the female structure is, the greater advantage accrued. These studies will be discussed later.

A few investigators have reported skeletal comparisons of athletes. Malina et al. (1971) found that track and field competitors classified as throwers had larger shoulder and hip widths. The distance runners and jumpers and hurdlers were long-legged, while the sprinters were short-legged. Sinning and Adrian (1968) found that female gymnasts had smaller trunk and lower limb skeletal structures, but their upper limb structure was comparable to other college females. Parizkova (1961) found athletes delayed in skeletal age, with relatively shorter legs and narrower hips.

The issue of the size and shape of the female athlete's pelvis in comparison to that of the nonathletic female and to men is far from being settled. Some speculations have been advanced that heavy training regimes, particularly prior to puberty, might influence the structural development of the pelvis. The bony structure might, for instance, grow heavier as the result of greater and more constant pull of musculature on the bony attachments. If this were true, the pelvis of athletes might be expected to be slightly different from that of the nonathlete, perhaps resembling some of the characteristics of the male pelvis. When Ivata and Kadsua (1971) compared the pelvic measurements of 253 athletes with 3,000 nonathletes, however, they found no significant difference. Duntzer and Kustner (1930) speculated that vigorous participation in sports during adolescence may have an unfavorable effect on the development of the pelvis, but they did not present substantial evidence for their proposition and it remains untested. Whether the female athlete's pelvis differs from that of the nonathlete will have to await systematic and longitudinal roentgenographic and autopsy study.

### Body Composition

As bioinstrumentation has become more sophisticated within recent years, attention has turned to the composition of the body. Height, weight, and skeletal measures, although interesting and informative, certainly provide little information regarding the relative proportion of the basic components of the body: fat, water, protein, and mineral; or, more grossly: fat, muscle, and bone. An excellent review of the purpose and methods of measurement of these three basic components of body composition is provided by Malina (1969b). The relative proportions of these three components would obviously have an effect upon physical performance. Furthermore, regular physical activity influences body composition especially in the leanness-fatness continuum (Behnke, 1963; Sloan, 1961). One might easily predict that the relative proportions of each basic component might be specifically different in sportswomen when compared to women who do not train. Both fat and muscle proportions in the body are affected by chronic physical activity, fat more so than muscle (Malina, 1969b; Parizkova, 1968).

As Malina (1969) clearly indicates, the percentage of body fat has been far more carefully studied and methods of measurement more validly contrived than similar efforts in the study of muscle and bone. Body fat has been of concern to those in several biological professions who recognize the relationship between fat accumulation, disease, and mortality. Also, the substantial influence that nutrition and physical activity have on body fat has made it a source of interest to investigators.

The accumulation of fat is regulated by estrogen, the ovarian hormone, and is distributed principally to the pelvic girdle, buttocks, thighs, shoulders, and breasts in women (Shaffer, 1972). This distribution is the general pattern of distribution to be found in normal females. Several estimates of the percent body fat in average college females have been provided: 23.7% (Garn, 1957), 25.6% (Conger and Macnab, 1967), 24.9% (Young, 1961), and 23% (Parizkova, 1973). Little is known regarding the distribution of fat in sportswomen. In terms of gross percent body fat, Sloan, Burt, and Blyth (1962) found gymnasts to have a very small amount (15.5%) of body fat. Even lower values of 10.1, 12.8, and 13.3% have been reported by Pool et al. (1969), Vos in Pool and Binkhorst (1969), and Parizkova and Poupa (1963). Gymnasts also had the lower body fat estimates (23.8%) of the women in three other sports teams (Conger and Macnab, 1967). These fat percentages of gymnasts are remarkably low when compared to the average 20-25% total body fat in women.

The percent body fat of women in track and field competition appears to be predicted by the type of event in which they specialize. Runners, distance runners, and jumpers have been measured as having 19.1%, 19.4%, and 20.7%, respectively. Throwers, on the other hand, have higher percent body fat than average, with 25.1% and 27.9%, respectively (Malina et al., 1971).

The swimmers, basketball players, and volleyball players in Conger and Macnab's (1967) study fell within average body fat estimates, 26.3%, 26.9%, and 25.3%, respectively. Conger and Wessel (1968) measured the percent body fat of college women who were "active" women by virtue of their participation in many different sports, but who would not be classified as highly trained competitors. These active women were found to have average values of percent body fat, but they were also heavier in total body weight. From this, the investigators concluded that the weight differential was a function of other components of the body, presumably muscle.

If the pattern of percent body fat of the few women athletes studied is observed, and if the fact that exercise is a contributor to weight control is considered, it appears that women who train and frequently approach states of physical exhaustion have a lower than aver-

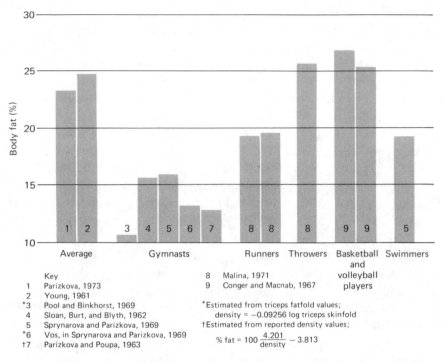

*Fig. 21    Percent fat of total body weight found in athletes from various studies.*

age amount of body fat. It is difficult to compare the percent fat values obtained from women who compete in one sport with those who compete in another, due to the fact that many different techniques of body fat estimation are used. Some of these techniques systematically provide higher estimates than others (Malina, 1969). Nevertheless, those sportswomen who consistently place prolonged physical demands upon their bodies may be predicted to have lower percentages of body fat (Fig. 21).

The percentage of muscle and bone component in the body has received very little attention. No information could be found relative to the muscle or bone percentage of female athletes. Urinary creatinine excretion has been used for some time to estimate the muscular component of the body, since creatinine is partially a biproduct of muscle metabolism and is considered to be a measure of total muscle mass. Trained boys have been shown to have higher creatinine excretion than untrained boys (Novak, 1963, 1966). Young (1963) has reported the estimated muscle mass (from creatinine measures) of women to be 23.5 kilograms, or 39.9 percent of their body weight.

The creatinine output of women before and after a physical conditioning program was measured and found to be greater following the program (Richardson et al., 1968). These results somewhat support the findings for men that creatinine excretion is greater in men who have more muscle mass, and greater following a conditioning program designed to increase muscle mass. No information pertaining to the muscular proportion of body weight is available for sportswomen, but one might expect a higher creatinine excretion level indicating greater muscle mass would be found.

## Somatotypes

A very popular assessment of body characteristics of athletes, both male and female, has been the determination of the somatotypes, or overall body shapes, of athletes. Although many attempts were made to describe body shapes, Sheldon et al. (1940) were the first to classify total body form on a continuous quantitative scale. Sheldon described somatotyping as ". . . a quantification of the three primary components determining the morphological structure of an individual expressed as a series of three numerals, the first referring to endomorphy, the second to mesomorphy, and the third to ectomorphy" (Sheldon et al., 1940). Endomorphy is characterized by relative predominance of digestive or visceral tissue, mesomorphy by a relative predominance of muscle tissue, and ectomorphy by a predominance of skin, its appendages, and the nervous system. A scale of seven was used to express the preponderance of a component. Thus a predominantly endomorphic individual would have a somatotype of 6-2-2, while a predominantly ectomorphic person might have a somatotype of 1-3-7. Sheldon's entire somatotyping system is based upon the premise that an individual's somatotype does not change, even with age, nutritional variations, or physical exercise. Sheldon's system had several problems, specifically: (a) somatotypes have been shown to change; (b) somatotyping is not entirely objective; (c) only two primary components exist in the system, not three; and (d) somatotyping omits the factor of size. An additional problem in using this system to somatotype sportswomen is that his system was developed on the basis of the morphology of men. For these reasons and others, several other approaches have been devised: Parnell's (1954), which uses only anthropometric dimensions to derive a *phenotype;* and the Heath-Carter method (1963), which provided an improved rating scale. Sheldon has also revised his system to meet some of the objections (1965). In spite of the problems of Sheldon's system, it did reveal the need to assess physique in addition to height and weight, and his somatotyping scheme probably strongly influenced the field of body composition analysis.

Carter (1970) has provided an excellent review of studies in which the somatotypes of sportswomen are reported. Somatotypes reported by Carter and others are shown in Table 25. It should be remembered throughout the discussion of somatotypes of sportswomen, that somatotypes are basically quantitative descriptions of women who participate in specific types of sports. Although somatotypes of champion women in a sport are similar and appear to be more similar the higher the skill level, it cannot be assumed that a woman with the somatotype similar to those of championship level performers will become a champion. Many abilities and learned skill patterns are requisite to the development of championship levels of performance. Somatotype does appear to be a limiting factor, however, since some somatotypes are not found in groups of champion athletes.

The somatotype patterns found among women athletes in various sports are not as specific as those exhibited by men; that is, more overlapping of somatotypes from sport to sport are found in female competitors. A general finding is that sportswomen have a higher muscular component than nonsportswomen (Morris, 1960); but among themselves, only the gymnasts and track and field jumpers and throwers have a specifically different somatotype from other female athletes (Carter, 1970). From an observation of Table 25, it can be seen that when compared to nonsportswomen, who have a general mesomorphic rating of 3.0, the sportswomen have a substantially higher (3.5-6.0) value on the muscularity scale. Similarly, nonsportswomen are more endomorphic than sportswomen. This finding compares well with the earlier discussion regarding the greater percent body fat in nonsportswomen.

Track and field sportswomen have specifically different somatotypes, not only from nonsportswomen, but also from female athletes of other sports. Even within the track and field competitors it is important to specify event specialties, since attempts at describing all track and field competitors with one somatotype are misleading. Distance runners, for instance, are short (Carter, 1970; Hirata, 1966; Malina et al., 1971), and long-legged (Malina et al., 1971). Distance runners are less linear

TABLE 25
Reported Somatotypes for Various Athletic Groups

| Sport type | No. | Country | Source | Somatotype system | Age | Endo-morph | Meso-morph | Ecto-morph |
|---|---|---|---|---|---|---|---|---|
| Track and field | 61 | USA | Westlake, 1967 | Heath-Carter | 17.2 | 3.5 | 3.6 | 3.6 |
| Basketball | 10 | USSR | Carter, 1970 | Heath | — | 4.3 | 4.5 | 3.0 |
| Gymnastics | 5 | USSR | Carter, 1970 | Heath | — | 3.8 | 5.2 | 1.6 |
| Gymnastics | | Europe | Brandova, 1968 | Sheldon | | 2.0 | 6.0 | 2.0 |
| Swimming and diving | 11 | USA | Cureton, 1947 | | | 4.0 | 5.0 | 4.0 |
| Golf (pro) | 26 | USA | Carter, 1970 | Parnell | 27.8 | 4.1 | 4.0 | 2.7 |
| Golf (amateur) | 26 | USA | Carter, 1970 | Heath-Carter | 40.5 | 4.9 | 4.6 | 2.1 |
| Athletes (mixed) | 150 | USA | Morris, 1960 | Sheldon | | 4.5 | 4.0 | 3.0 |
| Sportswomen | 225 | Europe | Brandova, 1968 | Sheldon | | 3.0 | 5.0 | 2.0 |
| Physical Education teachers | 61 | New Zealand | Carter, 1965 | Parnell | 19.4 | 4.5 | 4.0 | 2.5 |
| Physical Education majors | 112 | England | Carter, 1965 | Parnell | | 4.5 | 4.5 | 2.5 |
| Physical Education majors | 57 | England | Carter, 1965 | Parnell | | 4.0 | 4.0 | 3.5 |
| Physical Education majors | 136 | England | Heath, 1961 | Parnell | | 4.5 | 3.5 | 3.5 |
| Physical Education majors | 93 | USA | Perbix, 1954 | Parnell | | 4.5 | 3.5 | 3.0 |
| Average college women | | New Zealand | | Parnell | 19.4 | 4.5 | 3.0 | 3.5 |
| Average college women | 54 | USA | Perbix, 1954 | Parnell | | 5.0 | 3.0 | 3.0 |
| Average college women | 2,434 | USA | Heath, 1961 | | | 4.5 | 3.0 | 3.5 |
| Average college women | | USA | Huelster, 1966 | | | 5.0 | 3.0 | 3.0 |

than sprinters and jumpers. Jumpers and sprinters are similar in that they are lean (Hirata, 1966), but are longer-legged and more muscular than distance runners. The throwers in track and field are the heaviest and most endomorphic, and they are more mesomorphic than other sportswomen. They have broad shoulders and hips, large muscles, more muscles in the upper arms, and more body fat (Malina et al., 1971).

Gymnasts, in all studies, have been small, light, and mostly mesomorphic (Carter, 1970). Brandova (1968), for instance, found his gymnasts to be rated 2-6-2 on the Sheldon scale. Hirata (1966) reported the Tokyo Olympic gymnasts to be small, light, and compact.

The somatotypes of physical education major students have been studied on the basis that they represent a group of women who have a keen interest in one or more sports. Although they may not train to the extremes that female athletes do, they are usually consistent participators in at least one, and sometimes many, sports. Since a relationship exists between consistent physical activity and body composition (Behnke, 1963; Sloan, Burt, and Blyth, 1962; vonDobelin, 1956), it is logical to hypothesize that the somatotypes of physical education majors as representative sportswomen would exemplify a relatively homogeneous sample of unique somatotypes.

In the studies of physical education majors shown in Table 25 it is apparent that, in all samples across three countries, physical education majors are higher in the muscular component than non-physical education majors. The nonmajors are slightly higher on the endomorphic and ectomorphic components. A striking observation from Table 25 is that all cross-national samples of physical education majors are quite homogeneous with respect to predominant somatotype. Of course all samples are from countries largely Anglo-Saxon in composition.

## Comparisons of Male and Female Physique

Both theoretically and empirically, sexual dimorphism in adult physique accounts for many of the discrepancies between the physical performances of males and females. Somatic androgyny ratings are used to classify an individual's physique on a masculinity-femininity scale, irrespective of genitalia classification. Wide shoulders, narrow hips, heavy musculature, and a preponderance of body hair are examples of physique characteristics of a person classified as hypermasculine.

Bayley (1951) has shown that strength performance is at least in part a function of somatic androgyny. In Fig. 22 it may be noted that

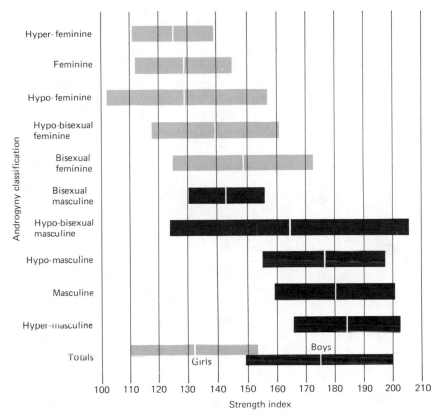

*Fig. 22     Strength index scores according to somatic androgyny classification (strength scores: sum of right and left grip, pull and thrust).* [*From N. Bayley, "Some Psychological Correlates of Somatic Androgyny,"* Child Development *22 (March, 1951), p. 51. Reprinted by permission.*]

somatic androgyny ratings correlate fairly well with genitally classified individuals' strength performance. An interesting comparison is that between the total male-female strength scores, and those of the males and females classified as bisexual. The bisexual females' best performance approached 82% of the best strength performance of males, whereas if just the totals are examined, girls only approached 74% of male force production. It should also be pointed out that a large percentage of girls in the bisexual feminine group were stronger than all the boys in the bisexual masculine group. In almost all groups, wide variation in strength is apparent. Thus even though the means of

**TABLE 26**
**Summary of Adult Male and Female Physique Comparisons Relevant to Physical Performance**

| Physique characteristic | Male | Favors | Female | Favors | Source |
|---|---|---|---|---|---|
| Height | taller | greater lung volume, speed, power | shorter | quick rotary movements | Lowe, 1968 |
| Weight | 20–25% heavier | throwing power | lighter | | |
| Muscle mass of total body weight (%) | 51.5% (greater) | power, speed, strength | less (39.9%) | | Shaffer, 1973 Young, 1961 Norris, 1963 |
| Body fat of total body weight (%) | | | greater (23.7–31.0%) | buoyancy | Garn, 1957 Parizkova, 1973 |
| Bone mass | larger bones, more massive | | smaller, less massive | | Bradbury and Edwards, 1949 |
| Center of gravity | .6% higher | rotary movement | .6% lower | balance | Cotton, 1933 |

| | | | | | |
|---|---|---|---|---|---|
| Pelvis | shallower, narrower, heavier | running speed | ½" wider, rounder | lateral sway in running, injury production | Adrian, 1972 Zaharieva, 1961 |
| Bi-iliac diameter (hips) | narrower | power production | wider | stability, child birth | Simmons, 1944 |
| Biacromial diameter (shoulders) | wider | weight support production | narrower | flexibility | Simmons, 1944 |
| Chest girth | greater | thoracic cavity, ventilation capacity | smaller | | |
| Trunk length | relatively shorter | | relatively longer | lower center of gravity | |
| Leg length | relatively longer | acceleration, speed, power, greater kicking velocity | relatively shorter | agility | |
| Elbow joint (?) | arms parallel from shoulders | leverage in throwing, supporting weight | arms form an "x" from shoulder | | Mateef, 1958 |

androgyny classifications are disparate, great overlap occurs between the sexes of adjacent classifications.

Tanner (1951) has proposed a discriminant-function androgyny scale, in which individuals are normally distributed throughout the distribution. A very large number of individuals, who are classified as male or female by genitalia, have similar physiques. At the extremes are found extremely feminine physiques, almost all of whom are women, and extremely masculine physiques, almost all of whom are men. The physiques that appear most in men seem to favor physical performance. A corollary of this would be that champion sportswomen tend toward those physiques that favor physical performance; that is, towards physiques that are more commonly found in men. It should be readily recognized that the possession of characteristics such as small hips, broad shoulders, and a predominance of lean body mass over total body fat—characteristics more commonly found in men than women— is quite independent from social interpretation of masculinity or femininity. Social interpretations of masculinity and feminity are based primarily on behavior rather than physique. Whether society expects certain behaviors from different physiques, even when children are very young, is a matter that is far from being resolved.

In the normal population, if means are examined, sexual dimorphism is common. Many differences exist between the physiques of the "average" male and female, as are shown in Table 26. However, it should be remembered that variation in each sex on each parameter is quite great, so that considerable overlap exists. Nevertheless, when means are examined, adult males are heavier (by 20-25%) than females. Their chest girth is greater, allowing for a greater thoracic cavity. Males have larger and more massive bones. A simplistic explanation for this is that the larger bones are partially due to a longer ossification period, a slower calcium metabolic rate during adolescence, greater retention of calcium during growth periods, and greater pull on the bones caused by the stronger muscular development (Bradbury and Edwards, 1949). Interestingly, the adolescent male who excels in strength and performance is more advanced in skeletal maturity than the poor performer, while superior performing girls tend to be slightly delayed in menarche and skeletal age compared to poor performers (Malina et al., 1973).

Ulrich, in an early synthesis of studies relating to sex differences, stated that the knee joint of females is wider and thus more stable (1960). No recent writer has confirmed this observation, however, and no experimenters have seriously studied the matter. Controversy exists regarding the angle of the female upper arm with regard to the lower arm. Some researchers have stated that when the female elbow joint is hyperextended and the arms drawn out in a supine position, the elbows are much closer to each other than in males, and the female arms form an "X," whereas the male arms form parallel lines extending from the shoulders (Mateef, 1958; Rasch and Bruke, 1967, Ulrich, 1960). Mateef goes on to speculate that this angular displacement of the female forearm on the upper arm, comparatively considered, would result in poorer performances in the discus and javelin events, and be a handicap in sports requiring maximum leverage, such as rowing, tennis, and gymnastics. Adrian (1972), however, takes exception to this presumed sex difference, noting that an eminent anatomist does not mention any differences with regard to the elbow joint. Adrian suggests that any sex differences to be found in elbow joints may be functionally developed.

The angle of the femur with the pelvis is, however, sexually different. The female pelvis is one-half inch wider and is rounder than the male's. From the slightly wider pelvis the femurs extend at a greater angle. The addition of fat pads on the female thighs make the inter-thigh space a differentiating item in androgyny scales. It has been speculated that the X-shaped leg tendencies, the joint distensions, and the softer joints and ligaments in the pelvic girdle of females would be disadvantageous in running and jumping events, but there is little evidence to support such a statement (Zaharieva, 1961).

The shoulders of the female are narrower and the hips are broader (Simmons, 1944; Ulrich, 1960). This relationship, bi-iliac diameter/biacromial diameter, is significantly different enough to have been used for years as a rough measure of sexual androgyny. Tanner (1951) has improved upon the measure with his proposal that it be substituted with the following relationship: 2 biacromial + .53 subischia - 1.25 bi-iliac - 81 = 0.

In terms of body composition, females have less bone mass, less muscle component, but more fat than males. Males average approximately 36.5 kilograms of muscle or 51.5% of their total body weight is muscle (Young, 1961). Females average about 23.5 kilograms of muscle, or 39.9% of their total body weight (Norris, 1963). The combination of more fat and less muscle per unit volume has a deleterious effect upon physical performances requiring strength, speed, and power. In addition, females accumulate fat on the waist, arms, and thighs, whereas males accumulate fat primarily on the back, chest, and abdomen (Skerlj, 1953; Wessel, Ufer, Von Huss, and Cederquist, 1963). This differential distribution has implications for movement efficiency, as is discussed later.

Some differentiation occurs in the responses of each of the sexes to consistent physical activity, at least at the time of puberty. Parizkova (1973) is a researcher of immense authority in the area of body composition and factors that affect it. She has completed many studies investigating both short-term and long-term effects of physical activity on body composition. For example, she has analyzed (1968) changes in body composition in several longitudinal studies of young boys and one of girls who differed in the amount of their involvement in physical activity. When boys were divided into four groups differing from little activity to great activity, she found that changes in the different groups were nonsignificant in most skeletal measures and in skeletal age. The group of boys who participated in the least activity were significantly fatter than the boys in the high exercise group. The largest amounts of lean body mass were found in the group that exercised the most.

The relative amount of lean body mass in boy and girl competitive swimmers, age 12 and 13, was not significantly different. Both groups were significantly higher in lean body mass than noncompetitive swimmers. But at age 14, the boys were still greater in lean body mass, while the females were no longer different from their noncompetitive female counterparts. Apparently the heavy swimming training regimen did not inhibit the increase in body fat that normally occurs with puberty (Parizkova, 1961, 1963; Parizkova and Poupa, 1963).

Sex differences in somatotypes are reflected in the differences already mentioned in skeletal measures and body composition. Thus females tend to be higher in the endomorphy and lower in the mesomorphy components. However, sportswomen differ from the general female population less than sportsmen differ from the general male population (Carter, 1970). Females have a relatively longer trunk and shorter legs, with the weight distributed lower than it is in the males. The abdominal space of females is larger (Ulrich, 1960), and greater weight resides in the pelvis and thighs. Thus the female center of gravity is .6% lower than that of the males (Cotton, 1933). As Adrian (1973) observes, the greater weight in the thigh in proportion to the muscle mass provides the female lower limbs with more inertia and more resistance to rotary movement than the lower limbs of the males.

Accordingly, on a proportional muscular force basis the speed of movement in females is necessarily slower.

From a biomechanical point of view, the longer the female limbs,
and the less fat in proportion to muscle mass, the greater the rotary
speed that may be produced. When Malina (1971) compared the limb
proportions of the 1969 intercollegiate female track and field competitors, he found them to be in similar proportions to Tanner's (1969)
male Olympic competitors in track and field. In other words, the sizes
and body proportions of competitors are consistent for each event in
both sexes. One exception to this was the distance runners. In Malina's
sample, the female distance runners were relatively long-legged, whereas
Tanner's distance runners were short-legged. This exception might have
been the result of the difference in distances of the male and female
events. The males, for instance, run distances of 1500, 5,000, 10,000
meters, and the marathon, whereas the longest distance of the females of
Malina's study was the 800-m run. Malina's data clearly support the
notion that size, skeletal, and somatotype characteristics exist that favor
superior performance in athletes, regardless of sex, and those performers
who most exemplify these characteristics experience greater success at
high levels of competition.

## Implications

Although physique is known to be quite variable, female athletes in a
variety of sports have been shown to be a relatively homogeneous group
with respect to body structure. Since the homogeneity increases with
increasing levels of expertise within sports, some measures of physique
are likely contributory components in a sport-success equation. One
might envision, for instance, that future generations of coaches would
insert measures of height, weight, lean body mass, percent body fat,
and somatotype—along with several other variables—into an equation
that would predict with a reasonable degree of accuracy the success
level as well as the most compatible sport for an athlete. Certainly
knowledge about physique should provide data for a coach in her
counseling of girls with regard to their athletic ambitions. A 5-foot, 2-
inch girl would, for example, be discouraged from high level competition in the high jump.

The questions raised regarding the contribution of height and
weight to success in some sports are also valid enough to merit consideration. Perhaps some competitive classifications should be created,

in the interest of the Greek agonistic ideas, for varying heights and weights. It would be innovative and enlightening to provide a track meet in which categories based on height, weight, and oxygen consumption (see Chapter 15) were generated. The results would indicate which competitor most nearly achieved her potential for that given day. Although Olympic or intercollegiate competition officials are unlikely to entertain the idea, high school and college intramural directors would do well to give it serious consideration.

Although hard training and heavy exercise change somatotypes very little, it seems clear that they may alter body composition substantially. With intensive training, lean body mass increases and percent body fat decreases. Both of these changes are conducive to good health.

Comparisons of the physiques of male and female athletes reveal that males have specific physical advantages that should preclude their competing with females. Much has been made by some writers of the great overlap between the sexes in such measures as height, weight, and lean body mass. Some have even stated that there are more similarities than differences in the physiques of males and females. Perhaps so, but it should also be remembered that in sports favoring height, weight, and lean body mass, the females of the upper limits of these variables are matched against males of their own upper limits, not the males in lower limits to whom the female competitors would be more equitably comparable.

A worthy contribution would be for researchers to compare, by similar techniques and within the same study, the physiques of high level male and female athletes. Champion athletes regardless of sex may be much more similar in physique than are the average male and female. This is primarily a question of theoretical interest, however. For even if considerable similarities were discovered between male and female athletes' height, weight, and lean body mass, ample evidence of other differential variables exists.

# Chapter 14
# The Physiological Support System

Moderate to high intensities of physical work in large muscle groups extended over lengthy time periods are requisite for success in several sports: for example, distance running, cross country skiing, canoeing, competitive ice skating, and distance swimming. In other sport skills, such as sprinting, throwing the discus/javelin, or executing a gymnastic routine, short bursts of high-intensity muscle contraction are required. In both of these types of work physiological changes occur as a result of the physical activity. The body must provide the energy for muscular contraction either aerobically as in the distance events in which oxygen is provided in amounts as demanded, or anaerobically, as in sprinting in which short periods of gross muscle contraction are made in excess of available oxygen. It has been theorized for years that, in the latter case, lactic acid, a waste product of muscle metabolism, is accumulated and an oxygen debt is incurred. The oxygen debt theory, however, has recently been seriously questioned.

The physiological mechanisms that determine both aerobic and anaerobic work, and consequently the physiological support for sports performance, have been discussed by Tulloh (1969) and are summarized in Table 27. By Tulloh's admission, these factors may seem oversimplified to physiology purists, but the list may serve as an heuristic paradigm for the systematic study of human performance by exercise scientists. In any event, the outline emphasizes the enormous complexity of the physiological functioning of the human being during physical work. The factors in Table 27 were initially suggested as limitations for runners of varying distances; but, they would seem to apply to all sports where continuous gross body movement is required for time periods and intensities equivalent to those associated with various running events.

**TABLE 27**
**Factors Limiting Running Performance\***

| | | |
|---|---|---|
| ‡† | 1. | Size and number of muscle fibers in the muscles involved |
| ‡† | 2. | Nerve-muscle response: number of fibers responding, transmission of nervous impulses under fatigue conditions |
| ‡† | 3. | Flexibility/elasticity of the joints and antagonistic muscles |
| §‡† | 4. | Level of energy-producing phosphates in the muscle fiber |
| § | 5. | Level of blood sugar |
| §‡ | 6. | Muscle glycogen supply |
| ‡ | 7. | Efficiency of the oxygen absorption system: maximum ventilation of the lungs, speed of diffusion of gases across the alveolar membrane, speed of removal of oxygen from the blood at the sites of oxidative reactions |
| ‡ | 8. | Efficiency of the oxygen transport system: red blood corpuscle count and hemoglobin content; development of the blood supply to the muscles; size, strength, and endurance of the heart muscle |
| ‡† | 9. | Ability of the body to tolerate accumulated fatigue products |
| ‡ | 10. | Efficiency of the cell chemistry in carrying out the respiration reactions, particularly in the presence of fatigue products |
| §‡† | 11. | The supply of adrenalin |
| §‡† | 12. | The powers of endurance of the nervous system in general |
| §‡† | 13. | Efficiency of heat regulatory mechanisms: amount of heat generated at any given speed, efficiency of the individual in losing heat, ability to tolerate a high internal temperature |

\*  Modified from Tulloh, 1969.
†  Important to the sprinter.
‡  Important to the middle distance runner.
§  Important to the distance runner.

Several of the factors listed in Table 27, although speculated to affect physical performance, have been studied primarily in animals, and less frequently in man. Rarely have they been examined throughout a training program, and they probably never have been measured within the context of a competitive environment. Other factors have been measured infrequently, and primarily in male, rather than female, athletes. The principal scientific study of the physiological support system has focused on the efficiency of the oxygen absorption system, efficiency of the oxygen transport system, and the ability of the body to tolerate accumulated fatigue products (Items 7, 8, and 9 in Table 27).

Because circulatory and respiratory capacities are the cardinal limiting factors in many sports performances, and since it is possible to increase the capacities of both, the characteristics of these two systems in athletes and the techniques by which capacities might be increased have been of intense interest to exercise physiologists for many years. Cardiorespiratory endurance is the term that is used to indicate the level of efficiency of the two systems to adapt to physical activity demands.

## CARDIORESPIRATORY CHARACTERISTICS OF THE SPORTSWOMAN

Data regarding the cardiorespiratory characteristics of sportswomen have been almost nonexistent until fairly recently, probably due to a lack of interest in female sports performance on the part of male exercise physiologists, the small population of sportswomen from which to sample, and the rigorous physical demands of exercise physiology tests. Most of the cardiorespiratory research conducted with women as subjects prior to the last decade was in regard to comparing cardiorespiratory characteristics of women with men or to the changing cardiovascular characteristics of women as a function of age. Only relatively recently, with the proliferation of women into the areas of athletic competition, coaching, and exercise physiology, have data about the woman athlete begun to appear in the scientific journals.

Before proceeding, a note of caution should be extended to those who would widely generalize on the basis of available information concerning the physiological characteristics of sportswomen. First, results about sportswomen from exercise physiologists using valid experimental designs and reliable, sophisticated equipment are few and have been accumulated only over the past 10 years. Much of what has been written is in the form of medical opinion or speculated inference based on male athletes' performances. Second, the types of measurement and techniques reported have not been standardized; thus comparisons of the results of several studies are very difficult. For instance, some investigators report aerobic capacity as the total amount of oxygen consumed in one minute; whereas others report it as the ratio of oxygen used to total body weight. These measures are not comparable. Third, the age ranges of sportswomen studied have been quite varied, a factor which limits the generalizability of the total information pool. Fourth, exercise physiologists are notorious for ignoring within-individual differences that exist and have systematically failed to analyze the temporal reliability of measures used. The majority of the studies have involved only a few subjects. Perhaps due to the historical development of a clinical approach, studies in exercise physiology have suffered from sampling, design, and statistical problems. Finally, the cultural climate for the development of female athletes in this country, although drastically changing, has not been highly favorable. Women are probably far from their athletic and physiological potential, and current physiological understandings of them are only descriptions of the emerging female athlete.

A futile attitude, however, is not very beneficial to the understanding of a phenomenon, so with the appropriate amount of caution based upon the admonishments just presented, some generalizations regarding women in sport must be made. The primary physiological functions that have been studied in sportswomen are cardiovascular characteristics, pulmonary function, aerobic capacity, hematocrit, and hemoglobin content of the blood.

## Cardiovascular Characteristics

Roughly speaking, heart rate increases linearly with work load until maximal aerobic power is attained, at which time the heart rate of women is between 184 to 198 beats/minute (Åstrand, 1960; Darwick, 1964; Metheny, 1942; Raven et al., 1972; Sinning and Adrian, 1968). In young girls ages 7 to 13, higher maximum heart rates of 196 to 211 have been reported (Wilmore and Sigerseth, 1967). When McArdle (1971) telemetered the heart rates of female basketball players during a competitive game situation, he found that heart rates in guards rose to levels of 154 beats/min., whereas the heart rates of the players who played the full court (rovers) rose to levels as high as 195 beats/min. Skubic and Hodgkins (1967) monitored the heart rates of two college sportswomen as they played eleven different sports. Although the equality of the girls' competence in all eleven sports was not assessed, the highest average heart rates (180 beats/min.) occurred in the rover basketball players. These high rates were the average for a 50 to 60 minute time period, and according to Skubic and Hodgkins are much higher averages than most physiologists have said are possible for females. Either basketball is a game that provides frequent intermittent rest pauses between high work intensities and the high averages are not representative of the actual heart rate throughout the time period, or women are physiologically capable of meeting far greater energy requirements than is generally assumed. Perhaps both factors are operative.

Training lowers the resting heart rate, so that the conditioned sportswoman has a resting heart rate that is lower than nonsportswomen. Whereas the average 20- to 30-year-old woman has a resting rate of 70±, a rate of 42 beats/min. in a heavily trained distance runner was reported by Knowlton and Weber (1968). True resting heart rates are very difficult to obtain, either in laboratory or field conditions, due to the high levels of excitation elicited by the experimental protocol or competition. For these reasons, the relatively meaningless resting heart rates that are obtained under experimental conditions are rarely reported. Heart rates at submaximal work loads are lower, however, in trained women.

Since the resting cardiac output doesn't change with training, it is logical to assume that the decrease in heart rate resulting in women who consistently participate in endurance type sport must indicate an increase in stroke volume of the heart; or, the amount of blood forced from the heart for each beat. Very little information is available about the maximal cardiac output of female athletes. Raven et al. (1972) reported cardiac outputs of 20.94 liters/minute (l/min) for distance runners and 16.66 l/min for sprinters after 5 minutes of sustained strenuous exercise. Resting values of approximately 5 l/min are reported for nonathletes, rising to approximately 12 l/min after 5 minutes of sustained maximum exercise.

## Pulmonary Function

Vital capacity (VC) and pulmonary ventilation ($\dot{V}_E$) are two measures of pulmonary function that are frequently assessed as components of cardiorespiratory function. Vital capacity is the maximal volume of air that can be expelled from the lungs following a maximal inspiration, while $\dot{V}_E$ is the maximum volume of air that can be expelled in a specified time period (one minute) during a test of aerobic capacity. Vital capacity is greatly dependent upon body size, but can be increased through training. VC in 12- and 13-year-old track runners was reported to be 2.82 l/min (Brown et al., 1972). In those same young runners, $\dot{V}_E$ was 78.5 l/min after 5 minutes of strenuous exercise, as compared to 70.1 l/min for the nonathletic girls of similar age in Wilmore and

Sigerseth's (1967) study. This difference may not be a significant one, as Brown et al. speculated that the difference could have been attributed to an instrumentation artifact in their study.

## Aerobic Capacity

Aerobic capacity is an indication of the ability of an individual to continue delivering the required amount of oxygen demanded by the working muscles under varying work loads. It is generally expressed as oxygen uptake, ($\dot{V}O_2$), which is defined as the volume of oxygen [corrected to $0°$ C, 760 mm Hg, dry (STPD)] that can be extracted from the inspired air. Maximum oxygen uptake ($\dot{V}O_2$max) is the maximum amount of oxygen that can be extracted while performing heavy work loads and is expressed as liters per minute (l/min). After an individual reaches her maximum oxygen uptake level, further increases in work will not increase the $\dot{V}O_2$ maximum; however, the work may be continued using nonoxidative energy sources until the build-up of waste products forces a cessation of work.

$\dot{V}O_2$ is dependent to some extent on the amount of active tissue in the body, so that the larger an individual is, the greater her $\dot{V}O_2$. For this reason a more meaningful expression of $\dot{V}O_2$ is in terms of total body weight, or milliliters of oxygen per kilogram of body weight per minute (ml/kg-min). Working muscle tissue consumes more oxygen than other body tissues; hence the greater the muscle mass that is contracting, the higher the $\dot{V}O_2$ values will be. Similarly, the more muscle an individual has relative to her adipose tissue, the higher the $\dot{V}O_2$ values will be when compared to an individual of similar body weight but of more adipose tissue. This is partly why adults have higher $\dot{V}O_2$ than children, and why sportswomen have higher $\dot{V}O_2$ than nonsportswomen (Drinkwater, 1973). Because of the relationship between $\dot{V}O_2$ and muscle mass, $\dot{V}O_2$ has sometimes been described in terms of the amount of lean body mass per minute (ml/kg-min LBM). It has already been shown in Fig. 21 (Chapter 13) that average women, with a few exceptions, have more adipose tissue than sportswomen. It has also been well established that women have more adipose tissue than men. Part of the explanation of lower $\dot{V}O_2$ values in the average woman, then, lies in the percent of relatively inert body fat that these women must support through physical activity. Not only must they support this weight, but it is of no value! The superiority of the sportswoman's $\dot{V}O_2$, however, is certainly not entirely attributable to differences in body composition. Much of their superiority can be attributed to a trained oxygen transport system.

From the few studies of highly trained sportswomen that are available, it is apparent that women can reach rather high levels of aerobic capacity. In Table 28, $\dot{V}O_2$ values are presented from several studies, but comparisons should be made rather cautiously in view of the variations in measurement and training techniques. With the exception of the first three studies shown, all values are $\dot{V}O_2$ of women who were post-pubescent. The effects of potential body composition differences across nationalities on the $\dot{V}O_2$ in females is not known, but they are probably of little consequence.

The average untrained young adult female in America has a $\dot{V}O_2$ of approximately 31.9, compared to the considerably higher $\dot{V}O_2$ (38.0 ml/kg-min) of European women. Although average European women have higher aerobic capabilities than average American women, the difference doesn't seem to exist among the sportswomen. For example, if the $\dot{V}O_2$ values reported from European sportswomen are compared to the $\dot{V}O_2$ values from American sportswomen, they compare very favorably—50.6 to 50.8 ml/kg-min, respectively.

Fairly active women achieve $\dot{V}O_2$ levels of from 37 to 39 ml/kg-min (Hermansen, 1965; Maksud, 1970; Goodhartz, 1969; and Wilmore, 1969), while highly trained women average from 46 to 55 ml/kg-min (Åstrand, 1960; Hermansen and Anderson, 1965; Maksud, 1970). Until recently the highest $\dot{V}O_2$ ever recorded for a woman was 68.4 ml/kg-min (Hermansen and Anderson, 1965); however, Brown et al. (1972) reported a $\dot{V}O_2$ of 78.3 ml/kg-min in a 12- or 13-year-old girl who had trained for six weeks at cross-country running. The members of this athlete's team were measured prior to their training season, and after six and twelve weeks of training. Her pre-training $\dot{V}O_2$ max was extraordinarily high—56.8 ml/kg-min, so she was either genetically blessed with a high $\dot{V}O_2$ max or was in a semi-trained condition at the beginning of the experiment. The final post-training measure that was taken by the experimenters was not reported for this girl, which is unfortunate since it would have been very satisfying to have had a validating measure for a reported $\dot{V}O_2$max that high.

The difference between $\dot{V}O_2$ in trained and untrained women is significant, and has been reported to be as high as 40% (Matsui, 1970). The difference between the $\dot{V}O_2$ of women classified as "active" as opposed to "nonactive" in ages 20 to 69 is also significant (Profant

**TABLE 28**
Oxygen Uptake Values in Sportswomen of Varying Sports*

| Sport type | Number of subjects | Country | $\dot{V}O_2$ max (ml/kg·min) | Age | Source |
|---|---|---|---|---|---|
| Track | 5 | USA | 56.1 | 10–11 | Brown et al., 1972 |
| Track | 5 | USA | 55.4 | 12–13 | Brown et al., 1972 |
| Track | | Canada | 52.5 | 12.7 | (Wells) Drinkwater, 1973 |
| Track | 7 | USA | 48.5 | 14–15 | Drinkwater & Horvath, 1971 |
| Track, runners | 13 | USA | 49.4 | 13–18 | Raven et al., 1972 |
| Track, sprinters | 8 | USA | 44.2 | 14–17 | Raven et al., 1972 |
| Track | 7 | USA | 47.8 | 13–17 | Drinkwater & Horvath, 1972 |
| Swimming | 13 | Japan | 49.3 | 16–18 | Miyashita et al., 1970 |
| Swimming | 4 | Japan | 54.0 | | Miyashita et al., 1970 |
| Swimming | 10 | Czechoslovakia | 46.0 | 19.5 | Sprynarova & Parizkova, 1969 |
| Swimming | 27 | Sweden | 51.2 | 12–16 | Åstrand et al., 1963 |
| Swimming | | USA | 49.5 | 14–15 | Kramer & Lurie, 1967 |
| Swimming | | Japan | 49.6 | 13–18 | Matsui, 1971 |
| Skiing | 12 | Norway | 55.0 | 25.1 | Hermansen, 1965 |
| Skiing | | Canada | 50.2 | 16.5 | (Wells) Drinkwater, 1973 |
| Gymnastics | 10 | Czechoslovakia | 42.5 | 17.2 | Sprynarova & Parizkova, 1969 |
| Figure skating | | Canada | 47.9 | 19.0 | Gordon, 1969 |
| Speed skating | 13 | | 46.1 | | Maksud, 1970 |

| | | | | | |
|---|---|---|---|---|---|
| Basketball | 14 | USA | 43.0 | 19.1 | Sinning, 1973 |
| Basketball | 7 | USA | 38.8 | 19–21 | Sinning & Adrian, 1968 |
| Basketball | 6 | USA | 35.8 | 20.0 | McArdle et al., 1971 |
| Physical education majors | 20 | USA | 41.3 | College age | Higgs, 1973 |
| Physical education majors | 24 | USA | 39.1 | 18.7 | Macnab, 1969 |
| Active, untrained | 10 | Sweden | 39.9 | | Åstrand, I, 1960 |
| Active, untrained | | USA | 37.3 | | Goodhartz, 1969 |
| Active | | | 28.1 | | Profant, 1972 |
| Active | 3 | USA | 41.2 | | Skubic & Hodgkins, 1967 |
| General (highly trained) | | Sweden | 48.4 | | Åstrand, 1969 |
| Mixed sports | 40 | USA | 40.7[†] | College age | Conger & Macnab, 1967 |
| Mixed sports | 3 | USA | 41.2 | College age | Skubic & Hodgkins, 1967 |
| Nonathletes | 12 | Europe | 38.0 | | Hermansen & Anderson, 1965 |
| Nonathletes | 30 | USA | 29.8 | | Michael & Horvath, 1965 |
| Nonathletes | 8 | USA | 34.1 | College age | Sinning & Adrian, 1968 |

* Note: Comparisons of the absolute values of means in this table may be questionable, for several reasons: (1) The general level of competition for females is lower than that of males and a larger percentage of moderately talented girls might depress the mean values. Relatively severe selective pressures among males remove all but the very talented and very motivated from their samples, making comparisons across male samples more valid. It is possible, for a highly motivated but talentless girl—through hard work—to be included in a sample of "female athletes," and therefore lower the group mean. (2) Experimental protocol is very important when wide ranges of athletic types and untrained females are compared. (3) Athletes present a smaller motivation problem which allows use of a more severe test (Taylor type). The more severe test yields approximately 5% higher values for the same subject than the easier Balke protocol so often used with the untrained. The values shown for nonathletes, for instance, may not really represent their maximum values.

† Estimated $\dot{V}O_2$ max

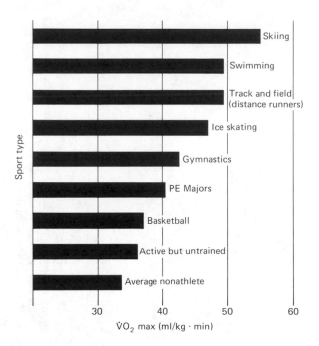

*Fig. 23    Average $\dot{V}O_2$ max for sportswomen across several countries in varying activities. (A slight statistical problem may confound the above comparisons. Competition is more intense in some of the sports shown above on international levels; thus competitors in these events have to compete under more rigorous selective processes. Other sports make lesser selective demands. In effect, the values above are due not only to demands of the sport and training, but sport sample selectivity. Due to sociological differences, these three factors may be operating differentially across the data included.)*

et al., 1972; Wessel and VanHuss, 1969). In terms of cardiorespiratory endurance, it seems clear that the female who trains, either for more efficient sports performance or for other reasons, is superior to her sedentary counterpart.

As previously mentioned, different sports tax the aerobic capacity of individuals to varying degrees. Sports such as diving, golf, and archery require little of the participant in the way of cardiorespiratory efficiency. Athletes with high $\dot{V}O_2$ are found in any sport that places heavy demands on the aerobic power of an athlete. The work load demands that a particular sport places on an athlete may be determined by examining the aerobic capacity of the athletes who excel in the sport. In Fig. 23 it may be seen that cross-country female skiers have the highest $\dot{V}O_2$ values, followed fairly closely by swimmers and track runners. Figure 23 should be interpreted as a matter of interest rather than fact when attempting across-sport comparisons, since it was derived from data obtained from a small number of studies using small samples from several different countries. These values do, however, compare well with those Swedish female values reported by Saltin and Åstrand (1967), who found the following $\dot{V}O_2$ in descending order: cross-country skiing, swimming, running (800m), speed skating, alpine skiing, table tennis, fencing, and archery. All of these Swedish sportswomen had higher values than Swedish housewives. The Swedish $\dot{V}O_2$ values for different sports are in the same rank order as those shown in Fig. 23, except that in all cases the $\dot{V}O_2$ values are greater for the Swedish sample. The magnitudes of the Swedish values are especially impressive when it is noted that Swedish investigators generally use a bicycle ergometer in aerobic tests rather than a treadmill, and bicycle ergometers consistently yield a lower $\dot{V}O_2$max.

The physical education majors that have been sampled have revealed $\dot{V}O_2$ higher than those females who play competitive basketball. Several explanations for this finding immediately present themselves. First, physical education majors are generally a group of girls who enjoy activity and consistently engage in many sports. While they are not systematically training for a single sport as a group, they may be active in similar intensities to, and for similar time periods as, the varsity competitors in specific sports. Second, although it is considered an endurance activity for males, varsity basketball for girls generally has not reached the pressured stage that it has in male varsity competition, so that female practice sessions are not as intensive or extensive as those of male teams. Third, the half-court rules limit the amount of running required of female basketball players. Both Skubic and Hodgkins (1967) and McArdle (1971) found substantially different cardiac responses of the rovers in basketball from the other players. Full-court basketball with only five players is now being played by females, and may influence the $\dot{V}O_2$ max values obtained from future female basketball players. Sinning (1973), however, found no immediate changes in $\dot{V}O_2$ max in basketball players who had been playing the five-player game for three years. Fourth, the only values available for basketball players, those of 43.0, 38.8, and 35.8 ml/kg-min, were obtained from college basketball teams. It is probable that world-class basketball teams—for instance, those of the Russian or Czech teams—have a higher $\dot{V}O_2$.

A direct comparison of the $\dot{V}O_2$ of gymnasts and swimmers was made by Sprynarova and Parizkova (1969). The swimmers produced higher $\dot{V}O_2$ values (46.5 ml/kg-min), both totally and when lean body mass was considered, than the gymnasts (42.5 ml/kg-min). The gymnasts had less lean body mass as well as adipose tissue than the swimmers. Both groups were well above average values of nonsportswomen.

An interesting comparison was that made of the distance runners and the sprinters of a girls' track and field team (Raven et al., 1972). The $\dot{V}O_2$ values of eight sprinters, who were defined as girls who trained for and competed in the 100-m and 220-m running events, were 44.15 ml/kg-min. The distance runners, defined as girls running the 440-m, 880-m, and one-mile events, evidenced a $\dot{V}O_2$ of 49.41 ml/kg-min. This difference of 5.26 ml/kg-min was significant, and the authors interpreted this as evidence that the distance runners had a slightly greater aerobic capacity than the sprinters. The sprinters were also heavier by 3.9 kg, and the increased weight was probably muscle. If true, the difference in $\dot{V}O_2$max of 5.26 was probably not indicative of a superior $\dot{V}O_2$max in the runners.

## Hematocrit and Hemoglobin

Hematocrit is the proportion of red blood cell volume to the plasma volume (liquid portion of the volume). If plasma volume is determined, then the total red blood cell volume can be determined. The hematocrit for women is about 42%, and for men about 47% (Åstrand and Rodahl, 1972). The red blood cells in the hematocrit have a protein pigment, called hemoglobin, which gives them their red color. The pigment aspect of hemoglobin has an affinity for oxygen; therefore hemoglobin via the red blood cells is the oxygen-carrying vehicle in the circulating blood. The amount of hemoglobin affects the amount of oxygen available, and is an important aspect of the oxygen transport system. Women average 13.9 grams per 100 milliliters of blood (13.9 g/100 ml), while men average 15.8 g/100 ml of blood (Åstrand and Rodahl, 1972).

Hemoglobin concentration represents a significant resting measure of physical fitness (Åstrand, P., 1956), and correlates .81 with $\dot{V}O_2$max (Åstrand et al., 1963). The hemoglobin concentrations shown in Table 29 for female runners are average or below. The two most highly trained women, those in Åstrand's (1956) and Knowlton and Weber's (1968) study, were the lowest. Åstrand's swimmers represent the most sub-

**TABLE 29**
Hemoglobin Content in Female Athletes

| Athletes | Number | Hemoglobin content* (g/100 ml) | Source |
|---|---|---|---|
| Runners | 13 | 14.4 | Raven et al., 1972 |
| Sprinters | 8 | 14.0 | Raven et al., 1972 |
| Runner | 1 | 12.0 | Knowlton & Weber, 1968 |
| Endurance runner | 1 | 11.2 | Åstrand, 1956 |
| Swimmers | 30 | 12.8 | Åstrand et al., 1963 |
| Basketball players | 7 | 13.0 | Sinning & Adrian, 1968 |
| Average women | | 13.9 | Åstrand & Rodahl, 1972 |
| Average women, English | 20 | 13.3 | Cotes et al., 1969 |

* It should be noted that the standard deviation is 2.25 (Åstrand & Rodahl, 1972); thus values from 11.5–16.0 g/100ml are within normal range.

stantial number of subjects tested, and their hemoglobin level is quite low compared to normal levels.

When hematological variables of field hockey players were compared to moderately active sedentary women, the trained and moderately active females had lower hemoglobin concentration than the sedentary (Haymes et al., 1972). A linear relationship was found between the hemoglobin concentration and $\dot{V}O_2$max in both trained and active groups, indicating a relationship between hemoglobin levels and training. More importantly, approximately 25% of the trained group and 32% of the active group were iron deficient. Only 8% of the sedentary group were low in iron. Since iron concentration/100 cc blood may be used to estimate hemoglobin concentration, it can be assumed that the women in these groups were substantially low in hemoglobin concentration. Research is obviously needed to determine whether trained female athletes are indeed low in hemoglobin, or whether the average of 13.9 is not an average but a desired normal value.

## EFFECTS OF TRAINING AND DETRAINING

Relatively little is known about the effects of training and detraining on the physiological support system of women. At the present time, coaches are utilizing the physiological principles that are effective with male athletes, while presuming that the female organism responds similarly. Questions relating to the effect of hard training on the menstrual cycle, or the effect of various phases of the menstrual cycle on training, remain unanswered. The effects of heavy training on prepubescent girls, or upon menarche, are largely a matter of educated speculation. Whether severe training is beneficial or detrimental is not fully understood. In short, very little information of a definite nature is available for women to use as a basis for developing training and detraining techniques.

Several obstacles have hindered the collection of dependable data. The few scientists studying women who train have measured girls or women who were, at the time of measurement, members of track teams. The girls' interest in track competition probably had motivated them to train intermittently for a considerable period of their lives before they were brought in for the "initial" test. The consequence of this is that subjects in the various investigations are initially tested at many different points in their training regime. When an investigator reports a pre-training heart rate of 58 beats/min and a pre-training $\dot{V}O_2$ of 42 ml/kg-min, it is obvious, since these are well above average, that the values are not really "pre-training" values. The investigator doesn't know whether the training effects that he is measuring are those of early training where substantial gains are to be made, or those of late training, where less dramatic results may be expected. The problem of comparing results from different studies is exaggerated under these conditions.

Another problem that has plagued those studying training effects is the nature of the training. Although the exercise physiologist can control the testing periods, he usually can do little in the way of controlling the independent variable. In most instances, he has little control over the training schedule. Competitors are not likely to change their training regimen if they believe it to be the most effective device by which they can become the winners of their event. The exercise physiologist then is left with accepting the training program as it is, taking the personal observations of the subject as evidence of the type of training that occurred, and being satisfied with obtaining post-training measures as best he can. The training regimen can be controlled by having all training occur on a treadmill in a laboratory, but of course the use of this technique precludes the generalization of training effects to field training methods and also fails to account for the special motivational and environmental influences that are a part of field training.

A final problem in the collection of training data is that the oxygen uptake test which provides the most valid evidence of training effects requires maximum physical performance. If the tests are administered at different phases of the menstrual cycle, then repeated measures of the same woman or of different women are likely to produce differential results. Very little is known about the effects of the different phases of the menstrual cycle on $\dot{V}O_2$ max measures.

In spite of all these difficulties, a few studies have been completed, and they must serve as evidence until higher quantity and quality of information is provided.

## Effects of Training

Heart rate in men is noticeably affected by systematic training, and the results reveal that a similar effect occurs in women. When women work to exhaustive levels, their maximum heart rate, whether they are trained or untrained, reaches similar levels. The difference is that trained women can perform more physical work under similar submaximal as well as maximal heart rates than nontrained women. Trained women also take longer to arrive at the higher levels of heart rate. At a recent sports conference in Europe, a study was reported where trained and untrained women worked on a bicycle ergometer until they reached heart rates of 170 beats/min (LaCava, 1967). The trained women had considerably higher physical working capacities than the untrained, some reaching values characteristic for the average male. They reported that the sports that seemed to have the greatest influence on physical work capacity were swimming, running, and cross country skiing. Basketball and tennis influenced work capacity to a lesser extent.

Brown et al. (1972) measured young girls after they had trained in running for 11 or 12 weeks, and they found that the girls, when performing the same work loads required by the pre-training tests, had heart rates 7.4 beats/min slower. Their submaximal heart rates consistently declined throughout the training period. The training had also decreased their maximum heart rates. In a case study of a female who trained vigorously for 17 months, the contractile force of the heart was shown to be much greater in addition to the decreased heart rate (Knowlton and Weber, 1968). Consistent with this was the finding that heavy training in sportswomen has been shown to cause hypertrophy in both heart ventricles. A drop in heart rate during recovery from similar work loads also accelerates as training progresses.

Two female basketball teams were studied prior to and immediately after a basketball season in an attempt to ascertain training effects resulting from basketball practice sessions and game participation (Sinning and Adrian, 1972; McArdle, 1971). In both instances, no training effects were found regarding heart rate characteristics. Maximum heart rates didn't decrease nor was more submaximal work performed with lower heart rates. The $\dot{V}O_2$ values obtained in both samples were easily within the expected range of average untrained females. In these two samples, players did not undergo preseason training and basketball activity per se did not have much effect upon their physical fitness level in terms of oxygen uptake.

According to Åstrand, resting cardiac output should be relatively unaffected by training, because the heart rate decreases but the stroke volume increases. The net result is little change in resting cardiac output. The study of Raven et al. (1972) on young female runners, however, showed that higher cardiac outputs and stroke volumes resulted from training. The difference in the runners' cardiac outputs, which were higher than the sprinters', was attributed primarily to the increase of 22 ml/beat in the stroke volume of the runners. These findings are consistent with Raven's contention that cardiac output increases as a result of an increase in stroke volume and oxygen extraction from the blood. He cites eight studies which support this thesis.

The effects of systematic training on oxygen uptake in women appear to be quite substantial. The classic study was that by Åstrand (1963) of young female swimmers between the ages of 12 and 16. Other training effects, such as higher heart volume, greater blood volume, and expanded lung volume also accompanied the great increases in aerobic capacity. The female swimmers' $\dot{V}O_2$max values averaged 3.8 l/min which is higher than the 3.5 l/min value that is the average for males of college age levels. Åstrand theorized that the intense training during adolescence combines the benefits of normal body development with the effects of training and produces the highest capacities for aerobic process.

The young female track runners in the study of Brown et al. (1972) experienced dramatic increases in $\dot{V}O_2$ following their intense training program. The young girls increased their $\dot{V}O_2$max an average of 18.5% at the end of six weeks of training, and 26.2% at the end of 12 weeks of running. The majority of the improvement in $\dot{V}O_2$ occurred in the first six weeks. The results of this study indicate that the physiological support system of the preadolescent female is as capable of responding to training as is the adolescent's or adult's. The relatively high lean body mass of the prepubertal girls probably contributed in some degree to their high $\dot{V}O_2$ values, but Brown concluded by corroborating Åstrand's comments that maximal training effects and high levels of $\dot{V}O_2$ may occur more in preadolescents than in adults.

The difference between the $\dot{V}O_2$ mean for the distance runners and the sprinters previously mentioned (Raven, 1972), was attributed to a training effect. As was discussed earlier, however, this difference may have been a function of body weight differences rather than training. The two basketball samples previously mentioned changed little in terms of oxygen uptake. One group of basketball players' $\dot{V}O_2$ did increase 4.1 ml/kg-min, but their $\dot{V}O_2$ values were below average even after training (Sinning and Adrian, 1972). Their post-training $\dot{V}O_2$ was only 38.7 ml/kg-min, which indicates that the players did not reach very high levels of fitness. There were also no differences in their $\dot{V}O_2$ at submaximal levels of 300 kpm/min work load. The other group (McArdle, 1971) of basketball players experienced no changes in $\dot{V}O_2$ at all. Their pre-season $\dot{V}O_2$ was 35.51 ml/kg-min and their post-season $\dot{V}O_2$ was 35.75 ml/kg-min. The authors suggested that the subjects may have already been in a highly trained state for the pre-season test and therefore changes couldn't be expected; however, their $\dot{V}O_2$ of 35.75 argues against the speculation that they were in a highly trained state.

Although training increases the total blood volume, and consequently the total hemoglobin, Åstrand (1956) maintains that it has no effect in hemoglobin concentration. Two other researchers have, however, cited changes in the hemoglobin content of women following training. Raven et al. (1972) calculated the oxygen-carrying capacity of the runners in his study, and found it to be 6 ml of oxygen per liter of blood greater than that of the sprinters. This was attributed to a training effect. The female runner who trained for 17 months also increased the hemoglobin concentration from 12.0 gm/100 cc on pre-training tests to 13.3 gm/100 cc on the ninth test, with 12.5 gm/100 cc being the recorded value on the tenth and last test. The investigators proposed that these values could represent real increases in hemoglobin concentration, or they could simply represent test artifact due to the use of more vigorous tests on those test periods. These values, although perhaps tending toward an increase with training, are still lower than the mean of 13.9 for the average woman. With only one subject, as in the latter study, and only 21 subjects in the former study, it is difficult to conclude anything about training effects on hemoglobin. Sinning and Adrian (1968) found that the change in hemoglobin concentration from 12.7 to 13.0 following the basketball season was insignificant, but the basketball activities in that study have already been described as being of inadequate intensity to expect any training effects.

## A Case Study

The case study of Knowlton and Britt (1968) of a female runner in training is worth examining closer. It represents several contributions to the understanding of sportswomen that have not been made by other investigators. The woman that was the subject of investigation was a high-caliber runner, being able to run the 880-yard event in 2:20 on a very poor indoor track. This was the only time provided, but the authors implied that she could run the 220 much faster on a good track surface.

In addition to being a high-caliber runner, she trained much more strenuously than does the average woman in track. For instance, in the early part of her training she was running approximately 5 miles daily, followed by six 120-yard sprints, and four 60-yard sprints. By the end of her training period, she was running 10 miles daily, 5 miles track and 5 miles cross-country. The ten tests to which she was subjected produced a much greater physical stress than most women can endure. Each of the ten work tests were all-out treadmill runs. Each was continuous and progressive as follows:

| | |
|---|---|
| 15 min | 2% grade, 7 mph |
| 5 min | 4% grade, 7 mph |
| 5 min | 6% grade, 7 mph |
| 5 min | 7% grade, 8 mph |

Finally, she was studied for 17 months, a much longer period of time than is commonly reported. In Fig. 24 a few of the measures obtained from her study are presented. The heavy regression line represents actual measures, while the light line eliminates the small fluctuations of variation and represents a line of best fit which is more representative of the general trend of the response. These responses appear to be classic responses to training: slight decrease in body weight, dramatic decrease in resting heart rate, no change in systolic or diastolic blood pressure, and a decrease in basal oxygen consumption. The increase in hemoglobin concentration may or may not be a real increase, yet the investigators suggested that the mechanism which permits an augmentation of concentration with exertion seemed to become more

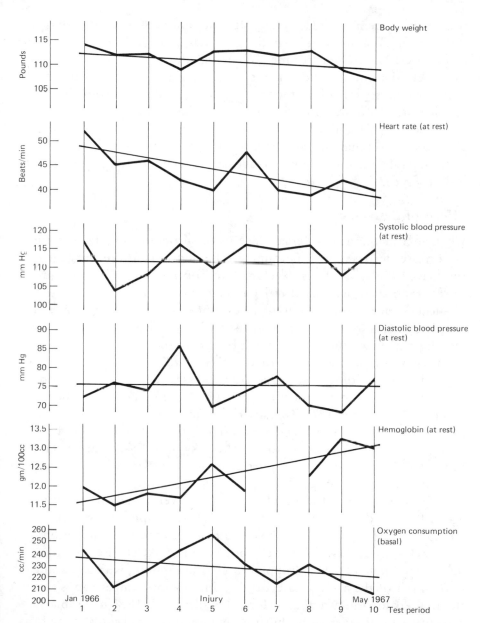

*Fig. 24    Cardiorespiratory measures of a female runner during 15 months of training.*

responsive to demands placed upon it. The results of Knowlton and Weber parallel findings from studies of males undergoing similar training procedures. The training regimen of the female in their case study was extremely rigorous when compared to general training procedures of female runners, yet, at no time were there signs or indications that the physical stress was inappropriate for the subject. Upon analysis of their work-recovery data, the researchers concluded that the runner's tolerance to both submaximal and maximal exertion tests was vastly improved, while a definite ability to accelerate recuperative processes was observed.

### Effects of Detraining

When an athlete, male or female, begins to curtail his training activities, he regresses into a state of detraining. The physiological mechanisms that have been so carefully developed into optimum efficiency begin to return to average levels of efficiency. The entire pattern of physiological change during detraining is less understood, in either males and females, than is the pattern of increased physiological efficiency. Few investigators have studied detraining responses to work tests, and their efforts have simply been concerned with measuring the athletes following an interval of time to see what fitness losses have occurred. Periodic measurement of sportswomen following heavy training has not been recorded by anyone. The $\dot{V}O_2$ max of Åstrand's female swimmers was measured five years after they had ceased to train, and was found to have decreased 19%, from 52 to 37 ml $O_2$/kg-min (Erickson, 1971). In other words, these females dropped from the excellent to the average category of aerobic power.

Drinkwater and Horvath (1972) tested seven female track runners, ages 14 to 17, three months after the girls had completed a rather strenuous training season. At the conclusion of their training period, their $\dot{V}O_2$ was 47.8, which is well above average. After three months of detraining, their $\dot{V}O_2$ had dropped to 40.4 ml/kg-min, which is at the upper limit of the average category. An interesting comparison is that the runners in Drinkwater and Horvath's study lost 18% in aerobic capacity after three months, but the swimmers in Erickson's study lost only 19% efficiency after five years.

Drinkwater and Horvath cited the results of a thesis that corroborated their findings. Ten weeks after the cessation of training in young girls, recovery pulse rate and blood pressure following a step test had returned to pre-training levels. Apparently detraining effects occur rather suddenly following the cessation of training, but stabilize at average levels. The high levels of physiological efficiency that are attained through rigorous physical conditioning can be maintained only through consistent and dedicated training programs.

## COMPARISON OF FEMALE AND MALE SUPPORT SYSTEMS

In an effort to explain the superior physical performances of male athletes in endurance events, researchers turned to a comparison of the physiological support system of females and males. In fact, this comparison has been a strong motivational force in the generation of research relating to the physiological responses of sportswomen to the grueling demands of competitive athletics. Although male and female athletes have rarely been compared by the same investigator, average male work performances have been compared to those of females. It has been theorized on the basis of these results, that the differences between male athletes and female athletes are probably about the same as the differences between males and females in the average population, but their overall values are different. These assumptions are, however, untested. The physiological efficiency of the sportswoman compared to the sportsman may not be analogous to the comparison between the average woman and man. The female athlete may be more similar to the male athlete than the average female is similar to the average male; however, the reverse may also be true.

Before puberty, boys and girls are quite similar in most rest and exercise measures of physiological functions. But puberty ushers in several significant differences in the male and female physiological functioning, most of which render the female at a disadvantage if she is to be compared to the male in endurance performance. The differences that are important in terms of physical performance are chiefly cardiovascular characteristics, aerobic capacity, blood characteristics, and heat tolerance.

### Cardiovascular Characteristics

Physically, the female heart and lungs are smaller than those of the male. Not only are they smaller, but the relative weight of the female heart and lungs to her total body weight is less. The smaller female heart and lungs produce lower stroke volumes (130 ml) and vital capacities (4.25 l) (Åstrand and Rodahl, 1970) than those of men (138 ml and 5.70 l respectively) (Ellis, 1929; Zimkin, 1955). The resting heart rate of females is approximately 5 to 8 beats/min faster than that of males, both at rest and at all levels of exercise (Åstrand, 1956; Åstrand et al., 1964; Brouha and Harrington, 1954; Metheney, 1942; Zoethout, 1952).

The larger heart and the slower resting heart rate of males, if cardiac output is held constant, are conducive to greater stroke volumes. The stroke volume of well-conditioned females during exercise has been shown by Åstrand et al. (1964) to increase from a resting value of 68 ml to 100 ml, while in the well-conditioned male, stroke volume increased from 88 ml to 134 ml per stroke. They also found that both sexes increased their stroke volume about the same amount, but the male overall volume per stroke was greater. Their findings corroborated the conclusions of eight other studies. Moreover, they report that the heart rate of females during maximum exercise increased to rates of 189, 194 beats/min, while the male heart rates only increased to 185, 186 beats/min. The consequence of increased heart rate and stroke volume is an increase in cardiac output, and in males the cardiac output is greater than in females. For instance, the cardiac output in one group of males was 24.1 l/min, whereas in the females it was 18.5 l/min. In addition, adult females of all ages have to produce a relatively higher cardiac output—approximately 10%—for a given $\dot{V}O_2$ value than do males (Åstrand, 1956; Bar-Or, 1971; Becklake, 1965).

The oxygen content in arterial blood is higher in men, due to higher hemoglobin values, than in women, but the oxygen content of the mixed venous blood is not significantly different. Therefore, the arteriovenous oxygen difference in men is greater than it is in women. The variations of oxygen content of arterial blood that occur during exercise are met by compensatory modifications in cardiac output. Since maximal cardiac output is limited by heart dimension, the female cannot compensate for the lower content of oxygen in the arterial blood; therefore, the maximum oxygen that can be consumed is lower in females than in males.

Although sexual differences may exist in blood pressure, they are small and are probably inconsequential in terms of sports performance determinants. Practically no difference exists in male and female diastolic blood pressure, except that the female diastolic pressure is slightly lower from ages 15 to 38 and slightly higher from ages 38 to 65. The systolic blood pressure of females is notably lower from ages 17 to 45, but is also notably higher starting at the age of 46 (Morris, 1960). These differences are partially a function of estrogen in the female, which increases at menarche and decreases dramatically at menopause.

The maximum ventilation rate per liter of oxygen of females during similar work loads has to be greater than those of males, since the female has lower arterial oxyhemoglobin, as shall be discussed later. The ventilation rate per liter of oxygen in females is about 10% greater in submaximal work, and about 20% greater in maximal work, than males (Metheney, 1942). When the overall $\dot{V}_E$ of 350 females and males was compared after a five-minute work load that brought the $\dot{V}O_2$ of all subjects to maximum, the females' $\dot{V}_E$ was 82 l/min compared to the males' 148 l/min. Well-trained females averaged 91 l/min compared to well-trained males at 121 l/min (Brown et al., 1972).

## Aerobic Capacity

In a maximum oxygen uptake test, a measure considered to be the best single criterion of cardiovascular endurance, men clearly are superior to women. More evidence has been accumulated in support of this finding than of findings regarding other sex differences in physiological functioning during exercise. The reports of the Åstrands (1952, 1960) have been most frequently cited, for they revealed $\dot{V}O_2$ max values for women as 36.0 ml/kg-min compared to 51.0 ml/kg-min for men. As early as 1942, however, Metheny compared females aged 20 to 29 years to males of equivalent ages and found the female $\dot{V}O_2$ max to be 40 ml/kg-min as compared to 51 ml/kg-min for the males. These values were obtained from partially conditioned subjects, as the values are considered to be higher for average males. Åstrand (1952) has estimated that the female $\dot{V}O_2$ capacity is about 17% less than the males, while Zimkin (1955) suggested an even greater difference of 20 to 30% in the male and female $\dot{V}O_2$ max.

VonDöbeln (1956) has suggested that the determination of the value in units of ml/kg-min does not adequately represent the differences in male and female aerobic capacity, since the larger males have a relatively larger mass of active tissue which will produce higher $\dot{V}O_2$ max values. He found that when he compared male and female aerobic capacity by considering the oxygen uptake in relation to lean body mass, no sex differences emerged. Macnab et al. (1969) also compared males' and females' $\dot{V}O_2$ max in three ways: (a) l/min, (b) ml/kg-min, and (c) ml-kg/min, LBM. He found the male values to be 50, 23, and 11% higher, respectively, than females. They concluded that males are superior in oxygen uptake, whether it is expressed as a ratio of total body weight or as a ratio of lean body mass. A resolution of the conflict of results of these two studies was offered by Drinkwater (1972), who pointed out that the relative fitness levels of the men and women in the two studies were different. The men in vonDöbeln's and Macnab's studies were fairly similar in $\dot{V}O_2$, but the women in Macnab's study, at 39.06 ml/kg-min, were 25% less fit than those in vonDöbeln's study (49.35 ml/kg-min). It was suggested that the women were so low in $\dot{V}O_2$ that they would have been inferior to the men no matter how $\dot{V}O_2$ was expressed. However, rather than the females of Macnab's study being low in fitness, it seems to be more a case of the women in von-Döbeln's study being at exceptionally high levels of fitness; that is, they were closer to their potential than were his men.

The other interesting point brought out by Drinkwater was that whether male and female $\dot{V}O_2$ max values differ when computed as a ratio of lean body mass is more a subject for intellectual dialogue than for predicting differences in male and female physical performance. Females carry their total body weight—adipose tissue and lean body mass—through all physical activity, so the most predictive measure is one that relates oxygen uptake to total body weight, or, $\dot{V}O_2$ = ml/kg-min. The exception to this would be in the comparison of some female world-class runners who may have the same or lower percent body fat than the men. Unfortunately, under these circumstances the athletes are so homogeneous that the prediction value of $\dot{V}O_2$ max isn't very high anyway. When the ratio ml/kg-min is used, males have from 15 to 20% higher $\dot{V}O_2$ values than females (Åstrand, 1952; Coates, 1969; Hermansen and Anderson, 1965; Knuttgen, 1967; Macnab et al., 1969; Shepherd, 1966; Shepherd et al., 1969).

At this juncture it should be emphasized that these data do not support the contention that all average males have higher aerobic capacity than all average females. Quite the contrary is true. In Fig. 25 some frequency distributions of $\dot{V}O_2$ of average and athletic males and females are shown. The interesting aspect of this figure is the great overlap in the $\dot{V}O_2$ of average females and males. Note that 76% of the females fall in the same $\dot{V}O_2$ range as 46% of the males. Not many of

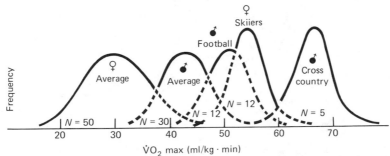

*Fig. 25    Distributions of $\dot{V}O_2$ max in the normal and athletic populations. Note the magnitude of overlap in male and female distributions compared to the magnitude of overlap in athletic distributions.*

the $\dot{V}O_2$ max values of the female athletes are comparable to those of the male athletes, but they are almost all superior to the $\dot{V}O_2$ of average males. No overlap at all exists between the average females and the male athletes. Apparently genetic differences account for a large proportion of the overlap in the average population, but when the environmental influence of training intervenes so that both sexes achieve their potential, little overlap is evident between the sexes.

The $\dot{V}O_2$ max of male and female athletes have seldom been compared by the same investigator, but an examination of independent studies reporting $\dot{V}O_2$ max values of male athletes and $\dot{V}O_2$ max values of female athletes shows that values for male athletes are decidedly higher than for female athletes. The male athlete has a 20 to 25% higher $\dot{V}O_2$ than the female athlete (Drinkwater, 1972), which is an even greater difference than the 15 to 20% difference apparent in the average population. An exception to this is Miyashita's (1970) study whose results reveal that male swimmers had only 16% greater $\dot{V}O_2$ than female swimmers.

Female athletes, in spite of being inferior in $\dot{V}O_2$ to male athletes, are relatively higher in $\dot{V}O_2$ max than males when compared to their respective average populations. Female swimmers were 40% greater in oxygen uptake when compared to average women, while male swimmers were only 15% greater than their nontrained counterparts (Matsui, 1970). Average young adult males are apparently more active than average females, and when a female athlete trains, she enjoys a decided advantage in cardiorespiratory endurance over her average female peers. The trained female athlete is also superior to the average male in oxygen consumption.

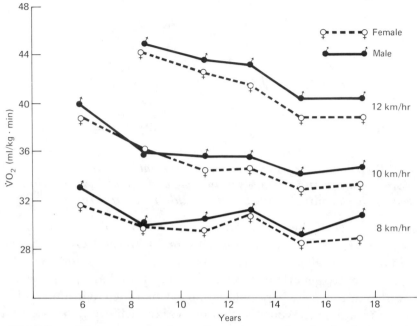

*Fig. 26    The average values of net oxygen intake for boys and girls while running at speeds of 8, 10, and 12 km per hour. The numbers in each age group average approximately 10. [From P.O. Astrand, Experimental Studies of Working Capacity in Relation to Sex and Age, Copenhagen: Munksgaard, p. 132. Copyright © 1952 by Munksgaard and reprinted by permission.]*

Similar differences exist between the sexes for submaximal oxygen consumption. From Fig. 26 it is apparent that the $\dot{V}O_2$ of adolescent males is higher than that of females. At lower work loads such at 8 km per hour, little difference exists between the $\dot{V}O_2$ values of boys and girls. However, as adolescence begins and the work load increases, $\dot{V}O_2$ differences between the sexes increase.

### Blood Characteristics

As can be seen in Table 30, males have a higher percentage of red blood cells, the oxygen-carrying component in the body. The increase in number of red blood cells occurs at puberty and is due to the action of androgens (Hutt, 1972). They also have 30% greater amount of total body hemoglobin, due to their greater body size. Although males have greater body hemoglobin and a higher average hemoglobin content in the blood, the maximal uptake capacity per unit of hemoglobin is the same in both sexes.

The lower average hemoglobin content of arterial blood in females has been posited as a principal explanation for the lower aerobic capacity of women. When the amount of hemoglobin is related to $\dot{V}O_2$max, the differences between males and females become insignificant (Åstrand and Rhodahl, 1970). During heavy exercise women must increase cardiac output in order to compensate for lower arterial oxyhemoglobin. Under demanding and exhaustive physical exertion, women have to step up heart rate since stroke volume and performance is limited by total blood volume. Thus for a given submaximal work load women are always operating at closer to their maximum than men, and will reach exhaustion sooner.

## Heat Tolerance

Heat is a limiting factor in athletics, so that both male and female athletes must develop methods of coping with increases in temperature. Metabolic heat consists of higher internal body temperatures, and is generated by the athlete's vigorous physical activity. Ambient heat is the environmental temperature, and interacts with humidity to produce thermal stresses on the body. Little investigation has been made of athletes' ability to perform under high temperature conditions. What research has been completed has been primarily in regard to sexual differentiation in the ability to perform under varying climatic conditions.

It is known that females have a higher body temperature at rest than men (Lofstedt, 1966). Women also have fewer sweat glands, lower, sweat production, and they start to sweat at higher temperatures ($\cong 4°$ F) than do men. Their greater adipose tissue serves as insulation and inhibits heat dissipation. This sex difference has important implications for sports performance. The evaporation of sweat is the mechanism by which the skin is cooled. Dilated surface capillaries underlying the cooling skin allow the blood to discharge the deep internal body heat. Ample sweat production, therefore, provides protection against heat stress, and an increase in sweat production is an indication of heat acclimatization. It is not surprising that even though the female body temperature at maximum endurance work is similar to that of men, their heat tolerance is less (Lofstedt, 1966). The greater the heat stress, the greater the sex difference in heat tolerance (Morimoto et al., 1967). However, Weinman et al. (1967) have suggested that once women have

**TABLE 30**
Comparison of Female and Male Physiological Support Systems

| Component | Subjects | Unit of measure | Female | Male | Difference (%) | Source |
|---|---|---|---|---|---|---|
| Heart volume | | ml | 640 | 880 | 27.0 | Åstrand & Rodahl, 1972 |
| Red blood cells | | No./cubic min | 4,500,000 | 5,000,000 | 8.0 | Ellis, 1929 |
| Hemoglobin | Average | gm/100 cc | 13.9 | 15.8 | 13.2 | Åstrand, 1956 |
| | Average | | | greater | 14.3 | Holmgren, 1967 |
| | | | | greater | 10.9 | vonDöbeln, 1956 |
| | Average, College | | 13.9 | 14.8 | 10.0 | Cotes et al., 1969 |
| Oxygen content of blood | | ml $O_2$/100 ml | 16.7 | 19.2 | 13.0 | Åstrand & Rodahl, 1972 |
| Hemoglobin (total body) | | gm | | greater | 30.0 | Åstrand, 1956 |
| | | | 510 | 776 | 34.0 | Cotes et al., 1969 |
| Vital capacity | College age | | | greater | 30.0 | Metheny, 1942 |
| | Adults | $l$ | 3.66 | 5.66 | 35.0 | Cotes et al., 1969 |
| | Well-trained | $l$ | 4.25 | 5.70 | 25.0 | Åstrand & Rodahl, 1972 |
| Ventilation after 5 min load | Average | $l$/min. | 82 | 148 | 44.0 | Brown et al., 1972 |
| | Well-trained | | 91 | 121 | 25.0 | Brown et al., 1972 |
| | Average | $V/lO_2$ | greater in max; | | 10.0 | Metheny, 1942 |
| | | | greater in sub-maximal | | 20.0 | Metheny, 1942 |

| Measure | Category | Units | | | | Reference |
|---|---|---|---|---|---|---|
| Diffusing capacity of alveolar membrane | Average | ml min$^{-1}$ Torr$^{-1}$ | 37.0 | 47.6 | 22.0 | Cotes et al., 1969 |
| Volume of bolld in alveolar caps | Average | ml | 55.2 | 63.0 | 13.0 | Cotes et al., 1969 |
| Cardiac output | | Q necessary to carry 1 $l$/min. at maximum work | 7 | 5 | 14.0 | Åstrand & Rodahl, 1972 |
| Heart rate in max tests | | beats/min. | 185.6 | | | Raven et al., 1972 |
| | | | 186.9 | | | Sinning & Adrian, 1968 |
| | | | 187 | | | Åstrand, I., 1960 |
| | | | 189 | | | Darwick, 1964 |
| | | | 198 | | | Metheny, 1942 |
| | | | 193 | 190 | 2.0 | Cotes et al., 1969 |
| | | | 189 | 185 | 2.0 | Åstrand et al., 1964 |
| | | | 194 | 186 | 4.0 | Åstrand et al., 1964 |
| $\dot{V}O_2$ max | College | ml/kg-min | 36.0 | 51.0 | 30.0 | Åstrand, 1956 |
| | Swimmers | | 40.0 | 51.0 | 22.0 | Metheny, 1942 |
| | | | 51.65 | 61.86 | 22.0 | Mijashita, 1970 |
| | | | 36.4 | 55.6 | 35.0 | Matsui, 1970 |
| | | | 39.2 | 48.5 | 19.0 | Cotes et al., 1969 |

become acclimated to a certain temperature level they may have a more efficient thermoregulatory mechanism because they maintain the same body temperature that men do at the same level but with less water loss. Of course, the female motivation for working under high temperature conditions should not be entirely discounted. Women may just be more unwilling than men to tolerate heavy work under heat stress. Simonson (1971) cites seven studies which corroborate the fact that women are more subject to heat stress than are men. Under heat conditions and at low levels of work, the female heart rate is 10 to 12 beats/min faster than that of males. At high levels of work the female heart rate is 20 to 30 beats/min faster. Thus under hot climatic conditions, the female has to work relatively harder than the male to achieve similar work loads.

### Summary and Implications

The implications of sex differences in physiological support systems (Table 30) for competitive sports programs should be obvious. It is apparent that men have larger hearts, greater stroke volume, greater cardiac output, greater lung capacity, faster return from exercise to resting levels, greater hemoglobin content and, consequently, a higher aerobic capacity. Males have a greater potential for endurance that cannot be matched by females, and at submaximal work levels, females have to work much harder to produce similar work capacities of males. If athletic competition is to be controlled so that at the outset competitors have relatively equal opportunities to win, then it seems quite evident that women should not compete against men in endurance events for any extrinsic reward, be it team membership, trophies, or athletic scholarships.

# Chapter 15

# Menstruation and Pregnancy

The special female functions of menstruation and pregnancy substantially differentiate the female from the male athlete. Although many sportswomen notice no physical change in their feelings or performances at varying phases of their menstrual cycle, other women seem to be more subject to hormonal fluctuations and their concomitant physiological and psychological cyclic variations. Certainly all women experience physical changes and interruptions of their sports performances in the event of a pregnancy.

Fluctuations of hormones associated with the menstrual cycle have been blamed for criminal behavior (Dalton, 1961), suicide (Mandell and Mandell, 1967; Tonks, Rack, and Rose, 1968), accident rate increase (Dalton, 1960), and decline in intellectual test performance (Dalton, 1960). Dalton (1972) has claimed that women in the premenstrual phase of their cycle have a slower reaction time which makes them more susceptible to accidents in that phase. In this age of scientific technology and increased understanding of natural phenomena, myths and superstition still abound regarding the subject of menstruation and performance. Although little evidence is available, a general belief pervades our society that somehow, in some way, menstruation affects a woman's ability to function—both physically and mentally. This particular belief is of concern to the athlete who wants to function at optimal capacity at completion, as well as during certain phases, of the training program.

The intricacies of menstruation and pregnancy are such that it is not adequate simply to modify male athletes' training schedules and competitive guidelines for use by sportswomen. Much has been written about the supposed ill effects of intensive training on the periodicity of the menstrual cycle. Athletic participation has been credited with both detrimental and ameliorative effects upon childbirth. In an age when athletic competition is both accepted and popular for women, coaches are finding they have a carte-blanche approval from the public and from the athletes to develop the strongest, finest, and most enduring female athlete that science and technology will assist them in developing. But at this point in time, no one is quite sure exactly how the variables of menstruation and pregnancy should be handled in a scientifically developed training schedule.

The basic questions, some of them asked as long as 60 years ago, still remain. What effect does menstruation have upon (a) the general predisposition toward physical activity, (b) the physical performance levels of average women, and (c) the performances of world-class female athletes? How does heavy, intensive physical training affect the periodicity of the menstrual cycle or the characteristics of menses? Does exhaustive and systematic physical training in young girls delay or hasten the age of menarche? Are there basic physiological cyclic changes which occur that affect physical performance? What are the implications of oral contraceptive control of the menstrual cycle? Finally, how do pregnancy and childbirth interact with performance?

Little systematic attention has been given to these questions by American doctors or physiologists. European sports doctors have shown some interest in gynecological issues and have provided rather widely publicized opinions. As will be seen below in the review of what has been published with regard to such questions, the available reports fall short of what is needed to form a comprehensive understanding of the interaction between sport and gynecological considerations. Nevertheless, the information is presented in this chapter along with some comment regarding its validity as a theoretical substrate from which decisions regarding women in sport are to be made.

## MENSTRUATION

### The Menstrual Cycle

From puberty until menopause, the female's physiological behavior is somewhat influenced by the cyclical changes and interaction of the gonadotropic and gonadal hormones. The changes in gonadotropic hormones (GTH) evoke corresponding changes in the sexual organs themselves. It is also highly probable that psychological interpretations of the environment influence the activity of the GTH. Just below the

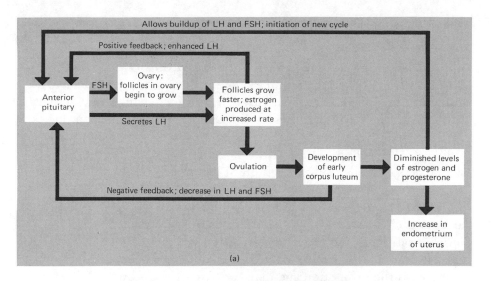

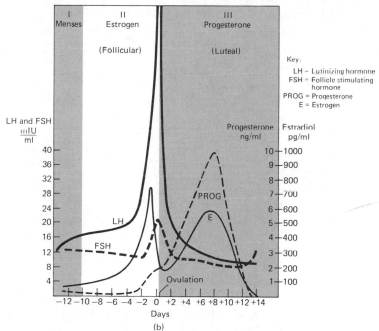

Fig. 27    (a) Interaction between gonadotropin and gonadal steroid
activity.  (b) Plasma levels of gonadotropins and gonadal steroids
during the human menstrual cycle. The cycle is centered on Day 0,
the day of the mid-cycle LH peak. [From L. Speroff and R.L. Vande
Wiele, "Regulation of the Human Menstrual Cycle," American Journal
of Obstetrics and Gynecology 109 (January, 1971), p. 234. Copyright
© 1971 by the American Journal of Obstetrics and Gynecology and
reprinted by permission.]

hypothalamus, a very small area at the base of the brain, lies the pituitary gland. The anterior portion of the pituitary gland secretes two gonadotropic hormones that are known to effect changes and activity in the ovaries. The first of these is the follicle-stimulating hormone (FSH), which causes the ovaries to begin developing ovum-encased follicles. The second of the hormones is the luteinizing hormone (LH), which acts synergistically with the FSH to greatly facilitate follicular secretion and growth.

After an ovarian follicle erupts and produces an ovum, the tissue around it changes in structure and begins to secrete the gonadal hormones: estrogens and progesterone. Although there are several estrogen-type hormones, the principle one is estradiol. The primary function of estrogen is the promotion and maintenance of the growth of sexual organs and secondary sex characteristics. Progesterone prepares the uterus for pregnancy and the breasts for lactation, should the need arise. Both estrogen and progesterone interact with FSH and LH, serving as a feedback device to alter levels secreted by the gonadotrophic hormones. The feedback mechanism is shown in the top part of Fig. 27. In the bottom portion of Fig. 27, the levels of the pertinent hormones throughout the cycle are shown.

The periodicity of the influence of these hormones is primarily due to the changes in estrogen level. From Fig. 27 it may be seen that estrogen level increases sharply just prior to ovulation, decreases dramatically just after ovulation, and peaks again about eight days before menses. The menstrual cycle is generally described as having three phases: (I) the period of menses, or dismantling phase; (II) the estrogen, or follicular phase, and (III) the progesterone, or luteal phase.

**Effects of estrogen and progesterone.**  Estrogen has the very important role of initiating changes in the secondary sex characteristics at puberty; for example, developing the sexual organs and breasts, causing early uniting of the epiphyses with the shafts of the long bones, initiating pubic hair growth, and causing the deposition of adipose tissue. Progesterone has as its central purpose the preparation of the endometrium of the uterus and the development of the breasts, should pregnancy occur. The pubertal changes that are caused by these two hormones are not as pertinent to this discussion, however, as are the cyclic effects of blood estrogen and progesterone in the active adult female.

The cyclic changes of estrogen and progesterone levels influence many other functions of the body, some of which may be important to physical performance. For instance, blood pressure, blood volume, vascular tone, body temperature, and electrolyte and water exchange are all variables influenced by gonadal hormone levels. Red blood cell count and blood platelet count rise sharply when estrogen is injected into the bloodstream. A similar rise is seen at ovulation. At peak levels of estrogen, arterial blood has a high saturation of oxygen (Garlick, 1968). The implication is that at the end of the estrogen phase and the middle of the progesterone phase of the cycle, hemoglobin content is higher. At the onset of menses, the lowest hemoglobin levels are found.

Estrogen also facilitates weight gain, usually through the retention of sodium and chloride which, in turn, causes a retention of water. Cyclical weight changes have been clearly documented (Robinson and Watson, 1965; Watson and Robinson, 1965). Weight increases during the premenstrual phase reach a maximum value on the second day of menstruation, and then follow a clear downward trend until the eighth day after the onset of menstruation. Since the water retention is greatest at onset of menses, the hematocrit and hemoglobin levels are also low.

Subtle changes in capillary permeability, diffusion shifts, dilation, and osmotic pressure occur with higher levels of estrogen (Garlick, 1968). The effects of these subtle changes on sports performance are not known at this time. Body temperature and metabolism are slightly increased with increased levels of estrogen.

Gonadal hormones have a differential effect on metabolizing drugs; that is, the male hormones metabolize drugs faster than female hormones do. If barbiturates are administered, females sleep longer than males (Hutt, 1972). The differential metabolizing effects of gonadal hormones is reason enough for cautiousness in prescribing drugs, in the same form and quantity as are prescribed for males, to female athletes.

An interesting finding that may have some influence upon high levels of performance is that estrogen alone lowers the arousal threshold (Vogel, Broverman, and Klaiber, 1971), while estrogen and progesterone together raise the arousal threshold. The central adrenergic functioning accompanying high arousal is enhanced during high cyclic levels of estrogen, so that sympathetic tone is enhanced resulting in: dilated eye pupils, increased heart rate, increased cardiac contractile force, dilated lungs, increased glucose release from liver, decreased kidney output, and constricted muscle and skin blood vessels. During the progesterone phase, when both progesterone and estrogen levels are high, the reverse might be expected.

High arousal levels, if not excessive, are conducive to keener sensory perception. Subtle differences in the female athlete's ability to detect and respond to environmental stimuli may exist among the different phases of the cycle. Although to date intracycle differences have not been found in the simple reaction time of females, more sophisticated measures of reaction time or reflex latency in athletes may reveal differences. Reflex latencies, which have been shown to be dramatically affected by different levels of arousal, may very well differ by several milliseconds in various phases of the menstrual cycle. High-level sports performance may many times be a matter of milliseconds and reflexes. Whether these differences are great enough to substantially affect the outcome of sports performance must be answered by future scientists.

## Menstruation and Physical Performance

Over the past twenty years, the study of hormones has grown more and more sophisticated, so that knowledge regarding the influence of hormones on human behavior has become increasingly comprehensive. It has become quite clear that hormones exert a powerful influence over many human behaviors, both in quantity and quality. Several studies have been conducted in which the influence of the varying phases of the menstrual cycle upon voluntary physical activity level, reaction time, movement time, running and bicycling performances, hand steadiness, standardized motor tests, strength performances, and sports performances has been investigated.

**Effects of menstruation on voluntary physical activity level.**  Results from animal research, in which female rodents have been observed to voluntarily run on treadmills more during estrus than at other times, suggested that women may be more active during the peak levels of estrogen, that is, at ovulation, than at other times during their cycle. Billings (1934) found a similar relationship between hip movement activity and the differential phases of the menstrual cycle of women. However, his subjects were psychiatric patients, and his instrument's reliability was questionable. Recently, Morris and Udry (1970) connected pedometers to 34 women, most of whom wore them daily through three or more menstrual cycles. By the use of pedometer records and daily entries into diaries regarding the extent of their activity and the occurrences of menstruation, the researchers were able to determine the normal amount of daily activity for the women. Their hypothesis was confirmed: the women of their sample were more active around the time of ovulation. Their discovery is consistent with findings of animal researchers who have found that animal activity increases during estrus.

In both the studies of Billings and of Morris and Udrey, the onset of ovulation was not carefully determined; thus, the relationship between estrogen level and activity was not validly established. In a study of 7 females over 17 menstrual cycles, the daily body temperature was taken in an effort to better specify the period of ovulation (Stenn and Klinge, 1972). Only those cycles for which ovulation could be determined were used. Actometers, devices that measured activity of the arm, were used to estimate amount of daily physical activity. In no subject did "activity peaks" occur in the five days following flow onset. Both day and night activity peaks were more likely to occur in the second half of the cycle. They concluded that a small but positive relationship existed between bodily activity and changes in basal body temperature throughout the menstrual cycle. They did not find, when all subjects were taken as a group, significant relationships of bodily activity and different phases of the cycle. When subjects were analyzed individually, however, they found that in two subjects physical activity level varied cyclically with the phases of the menstrual cycle.

The evidence produced by researchers concerned with the relationship between physical activity level and cycle phases is meager and insufficiently replicated. One must also be skeptical of the test instruments, in terms of validity and reliability. Conclusions regarding intrasubject variability, such as those of Stenn and Klinge, are not warranted on the basis of a sample of two subjects. Despite procedural difficulties, the evidence from studies of variability does seem to be tending to move in the direction of substantiating a relationship between activity and cycle phase. If physical activity is more spontaneously generated by the female during the time of ovulation, the implications for training schedules and competition selection are obvious. For instance, training might be intensified for the female in the follicular phase of the cycle. In addition, if a limited number of competitions is to be selected in lieu of competing in all available competitions, some attention might be given to the potential coincidence of the tournament with regard to probable times of ovulation. Training schedules in females, rather than being planned for the team as a whole, might better be planned for individuals on the basis of their cycles. On the other hand, the changes in basal levels of physical activity that have been attributed to hormonal fluctuation may have very little impact on the generation of the high intensities of activity that the female athlete must produce. Increased spontaneous activity may not necessarily result in the best performance. The biological propensity toward activity may prove to be only a small contributory factor in temporarily increasing the athlete's motivation for the day's training regimen. Another implication is that the voluntary sports participation of the "nonvarsity" sportswoman might peak cyclicly with regard to her period.

**Effects of menstruation on levels of physical performance.** Effects of menstruation phases upon simple reaction time have been investigated by several researchers, but the results are inconclusive. Smith and Kime (1971) reported a slower reaction time from female subjects just prior to their menstrual period. Two other investigators failed to corroborate these results. Pierson and Lockhart (1963) measured simple reaction and arm movement time to a light stimulus as a function of menstrual phase. They found no differences in simple reaction time, but unfortunately they only investigated one phase of the cycle—that of the menses. In addition, they assumed that all subjects experienced 28-day cycles and that all cycles were regular.

Phillips (1971) tested the simple reaction time of female members of varsity athletic teams, before and after (1) an academic test, (2) a varsity game, and (3) a typical class period. These pre- and posttests were obtained in three phases of the cycle: preflow, flow, and resting. Simple reaction time was unaffected by cycle phase. Hand steadiness was also included as a dependent variable, the assumption being that it would fluctuate as a function of cycle phase. Hand steadiness decreased just prior to menstrual flow, particularly prior to an athletic varsity game that occurred during the premenstrual phase of the cycle.

Results seem conclusive regarding the effect of the menstrual cycle phase on running and bicycling performance in the case of the assessment of average women under test conditions. Beginning with the early investigations of Scott and Tuttle (1932) and Hellebrandt (1939), no effect of menstruation on cardiovascular efficiency or on treadmill performance was found. Doolittle and Lipson (1971) analyzed female performance in the 1½-mile run-walk, by obtaining performance records 9 to 12 times during a 35-day period. Performances were grouped into

**TABLE 31**
**Sports Performance of Female Athletes During Menses**

| Better performance during menses (%) | Similar performance during menses (%) | Worse performance during menses (%) | Source |
|---|---|---|---|
| | 36.9 | 17.0 | Zaharieva, 1965 |
| 13.0–15.0 | 42.0–48.0 | 30.7 | Erdelyi, 1962 |
| 15.0 | 46.5 | 38.5 | Duntzer & Hellandall, 1929 |
| | 42.0 | 48.0 | Antoine, 1941 |
| 13.0 | 48.2 | 30.0 | *Kiss, Erdelyi & Haraszthy, 1957 |

* Cited in Erdelyi, 1965.

those that occurred: (1) 24 hours after onset of menses, (2) the day of ovulation, (3) during the mid-follicular phase, and (4) during the mid-luteal phase. Again, no performance differences were found among the four phases.

In other standardized motor tests, no cyclic effect was recorded with regard to skill, speed, or accuracy of motion (Bilhuber, 1927). The only study in which some cyclic effect was reported is that of Moore and Barker (1923) in which strength was observed to decrease just prior to menses.

The evidence seems conclusive that when average women are tested, the phase of the menstrual cycle has little effect upon their physical performance. From results such as those discussed above, statements have been made that "the female machine is as fit to perform physically at menstruation as any other time of the cycle" (Doolittle, 1971; Helle-brandt, 1939). Certainly it appears that for average performances in commonly found lifestyles physical performance is not depreciated at the time of menses. But what of the physical performance of the female athlete throughout the various phases of the menstrual cycle? Her performances require infinitely greater energy levels, considerably more refined motor integration, and greater psychological control. Are her performances—as has been theorized—lessened at the time of menses, and enhanced at the onset of ovulation?

In Table 31 patterns of sports performance as a function of menses are shown. By far the majority of athletes performed about the same during menses, but a substantial percentage also performed below their usual standards. The conclusion of the investigators represented in Table 31 was that the best performances probably occurred in the post-menses period. Good performances also occurred in the inter-menses period, but the poorest performances came during the pre-menses and first two days of the menses. Perhaps more importantly, 46% of Zaharieva's athletes expressed, on a self-report inventory, that they felt no differently at menses than at any other time. Thirty-two percent indicated that they felt somewhat weaker during menses.

Optimum skill and strength in post-menses was also reported by Noack (Erdelyi, 1962), and optimum muscle tone by Dorn (Erdelyi, 1962). These results support Kliment's (LaCava, 1969) suggestion that the most intensive training should be in the post-menses period; from the 15th day of the cycle training intensity should decrease.

It has been pointed out by many writers in popular magazines that Olympic medals have been won by women who were in all phases of the menstrual cycle at the time of their victory. Although medals have been won by menstruating females, no one has computed the probable number of menstruating females to be found in an Olympic sample and compared it to the probability of the individual competitors winning a medal. A better analysis of the effect of menses on Olympic performance would be to predict, over several Olympic years, the probable winners. The predicted performance, and eventual performance, should be entered into the analysis along with data specifying the menstrual phase of each competitor. The accuracy of predicted wins of those who were not menstruating compared to those predicted winners who were menstruating might be more elucidating than simply pointing out that some athletes win their medals during menses. Since some female athletes do not perform as well during menses, how does one account for the performances of those who seem improved or unaffected by menses? A woman might, due to her knowledge that she was menstruating, generate higher levels of motivation which would compensate for biological disadvantages. The reports shown in Table 31 of athletic performances during menses seem to support the concept that menstruation does affect the competitive performances of a substantial number of high-level female athletes; however, the lack of systematic and statistical analyses of these performances is reason enough to postpone a final commitment to the idea that performance is affected by menstruation.

## Effects of Exercise, Training, or Sports Participation on the Menstrual Cycle

Questions concerning the effects of strenuous activity on the periodicity and characteristics of the menstrual cycle are far from being resolved and are very difficult to answer experimentally, due to the extreme variability of subjects' menstrual phases. Under such diverse conditions, it is very difficult to control activity level as an independent variable. In addition, in order to answer the question, subjects must be studied over several months of sports participation; and careful records must be kept regarding type of activity, illness, and cycle fluctuation. These experimental design problems are discouraging to many conscientious researchers.

Much of the available information regarding menstrual cycle changes as a function of strenuous exercise is medical opinion. All of the research conclusions have been based on data obtained by self-report inventories or questionnaires, in which the subject is asked to recall, sometimes many years past, symptoms and feelings related to her menstrual flow. However, the reliability of these inventories has never been validated. Experimenter bias and the Hawthorne effect* may have exerted a considerable influence on the outcome of these studies. Nevertheless, they have been extensively reported and heavily relied upon by those concerned about the influence of sports on menstruation; they represent, in effect, all that is available in lieu of opinion.

Phillips, Fox, and Young (1959) surveyed the opinions of a large number of women doctors and gynecologists regarding sports activities for girls. They sampled women doctors because they felt that the doctors were not only knowledgeable but also had the empathy necessary to appreciate the emotional aspect of the problem. The majority of doctors expressed the opinion that sports activity has little effect on menstruation and that no restriction should be placed on the physical activity of average girls at any phase of their cycle. Those few physicians who suggested restrictions recommended that activity be somewhat curtailed during the first half of menses only. They emphasized that menstruation is a normal phenomenon and in most cases, that pain and

---

* The Hawthorne effect in experimental research is the confounding that occurs when experimenters fail to realize that the fact that subjects are in an investigation affects their performance and changes their perceptions of their performance.

stress are caused by the individual's psychogenic reaction to the onset of menses or to the particular connotations that menstruation holds for her.

Gendel (1971) stated that heavy exercise is, rather than detrimental to the periodicity of the menstrual cycle, ameliorative. In her survey of 67 college students who had only been exposed to 1.3 years of physical education in high school, the most common complaint was menstrual difficulty. Gendel attributed the lack of a systematic physical education program as a significant factor in menstrual pain. She even expressed the fact that the literature on menstruation indicated that routine strenuous activity on a systematic basis decreases chronic dysmenorrhea, except where pelvic pathology is involved.

Light exercise, on a systematic basis, also appears to have beneficial effects in the prevention of premenstrual pain. Junior high school girls, who exercised lightly but constantly, were tested over a period of three years, from their 7th to 9th grades. They had less dysmenorrhea and premenstrual tension than their equivalent control group. It is surprising that differences in the exercising girls occurred, since the activities used in this study were primarily stretching exercises that included very little strength-developing or cardiovascular endurance activity. Inasmuch as the subjects of the study completed, at the conclusion of each semester, two questionnaires related to menstrual pain, it is probable that they associated the questionnaires with their activities of exercise. An alternative hypothesis to the ameliorative effect of exercise on menstrual pain, then, is that the girls expected the exercises to prevent pain and they therefore responded on the questionnaires in the manner in which they were expected to respond. Their questionnaire responses were probably affected as much by the tests as by the exercise treatment. For these reasons, it is difficult to believe that the dramatic decreases in dysmenorrhea reported by Golub et al. were a function of exercise. They might rather have been a function of a changed mental attitude regarding the onset of menstruation.

Timonen and Procope (1971) studied the effect of sports participation on premenstrual syndrome in 748 female university students. The subjects of their investigation were physical education students who were in above-average physical condition. They participated in cross-country track, skiing, swimming, gymnastics, or athletics. Decreased constipation, and consequently decreased rectal pressure pain, were prevalent in the endurance sports participants. The most significant finding was that premenstrual headache, a secondary symptom of premenstrual tension, was much less frequent in the endurance sport groups than in the gymnastics group. Why might headaches occur infrequently in the endurance sport participants? Timonen and Procope speculated that premenstrual tension can be explained as a state of mental stress. In the initial stages of mental stress, catecholamine is released, causing vasoconstriction and an increased circulatory resistance to the brain. The result is premenstrual headache. Exercise increases the total capacity of the cardiac pulmonary pump and also therefore stabilizes circulation in the brain. If a greater circulation capacity is required for adequate perfusion of the brain due to the increased peripheral resistance caused by edema, then sports provides this additional capacity. As a result of the increased supply of oxygenated blood, the cerebral circulation can compensate for the increased peripheral resistance. On the basis of this theory, the girls who participated in gymnastics did not derive the increased circulatory capacity from their participation that the girls who ran, swam, or participated in other athletics derived.

**Effects of high-level competition on the menstrual cycle.** The rigors of training and high-level competition, which are totally different from the sports participation of the average girl, have been suspected of having detrimental effects on the periodicity of the cycle. Additionally, dysmenorrhea has been attributed to hard training and competition by Bausenwein (1954), Duntzer (1930), and Motiljanszleaja et al., Schroder, and Westman (cited in Erdelyi, 1962). On the other hand, several doctors have found sports to be ameliorative for dysmenorrhea—Aresin, Burger, Golum, Vegh (cited in Erdelyi, 1962).

The data collected by Zaharieva (1965) in his study of 66 female athletes at the Tokyo Olympics were derived from personal interviews with the athletes and with their accompanying physicians. His subjects were record holders from 10 countries in the sports of track and field, swimming, gymnastics, and volleyball. They had led active sporting careers for between 6 to 8 years, with over 12 years of training and competition being prevalent in the track and field athletes. On the whole, the athletes' cycles were rhythmic (for 92.4% of the athletes) and normal in interval length (86% experienced intervals from 21 to 30 days). The loss of blood in this group was moderate for all sports except swimming. Swimmers were slightly below average in terms of loss of blood. The swimmers were also the youngest group, which probably accounts for the less-than-average blood loss. The duration of their menses was also normal, from 3 to 6 days.

Irregularity of menstrual cycle was present in only 6.1% of the Olympic athletes and in these cases the girls were young enough to be quite irregular anyway, regardless of athletic activity. Fifty percent of the females reported no change in their cycle that they interpreted as being a result of their training and competition. Forty-one percent reported some disturbance, while 7.7% reported an improvement in the menstrual cycle as a result of training for Olympic competition. When disturbances did occur, the next cycle was normal in 81.6% of the cases. These results were corroborated by Erdelyi, Kiss, and Havaszthy (cited in Erdelyi, 1962) and Stammer (cited in Erdelyi, 1962), who found high percentages of Hungarian athletes (70.5 and 85.1%) whose menstrual cycle was unaffected by their training and competition. Erdelyi found that 467 (83.8%) of the Hungarian females noticed no change in their cycle throughout training and competition. Twenty-eight (5%) noticed a favorable change and 62 (11%) noticed an unfavorable change. Bausenwein (1954), however, noticed unfavorable changes in females who started their intensive training prior to menarche. Kral (LaCava, 1967), after 5 years of controlled study, also found irregularity in track runners, but emphasized that running seemed to have no influence on morphological development of female organs. When comparing gymnasts and controls, Vaclavinkova' and Druckmuller (LaCava, 1967) found more menstrual disorders in the gymnasts.

Åstrand (1963) failed to corroborate these negative findings and reported no more irregularity or dysmenorrhea in his young girl swimmers than were present in nonathletic Swedish populations. Zaharieva concluded that training and competition at high levels of skill do not essentially affect the course of the menstrual cycle. He did note, however, that when changes in the normal course of menstruation were reported, they seemed to be more prevalent in the top sportswomen. Erdelyi concurred and also observed more menstrual disorders and irregularities in the sportswomen who participated in sports requiring tremendous physical effort and endurance. In rowing particularly, he found a number of women whose menstrual disorders cleared up in the off-season.

Erdelyi also found, along with five other investigators, that female competitors in swimming and water sports may have more dysmenorrhea. He stated that due to humidity and thermal factors, a greater possibility of vaginal inflammation also existed for swimmers, divers, ice skaters, and skiers.

If strenuous activity were to have a detrimental effect on the menstrual cycle, it should certainly be revealed in such studies as those of Zaharieva and Erdelyi. The women of these samples probably trained harder and more consistently than women at any other level of competition. They rarely interrupted their training during their menses, but did sometimes change the type and intensity of training. Sixty to eighty percent of them continued training during menstruation, and only 4 to 5% never trained during menses. In addition, the Olympic athletes reported that they always took part in competitions of importance, whether they occurred during menses or not. The swimmers were the most reluctant group to train during menses, with 33% of them reporting that they interrupted training during the early phase of menses.

A question that remains is, "Should women be encouraged or permitted to compete during their menstrual period?" Quite a controversy surrounds this question with several European sports doctors taking the view that all sports should be prohibited during menses, and other doctors supporting the prohibition of only the most vigorous sports, such as skiing, gymnastics, tennis, and rowing. Soykova (in LaCava, 1969) reported that he is of the opinion that girls with normal menses may do any physical exercise or compete in tournaments without fear of physical damage. Girls with evidence of pathological abnormality probably should not strain themselves physically during their menses.

Swimming during menstruation, either in training or in competition, seems to be an unresolved question. Most of the sports doctors unanimously affirmed that swimming should be prohibited during menses (Erdelyi, 1962). Their opinion is based on the fact that physiological conditions of the female during menstruation favor the growth and transmission of bacteria. At menstruation, the cervical canal is open to the uterine cavity, in which the encosa of the endometrium is an extremely good environment for the growth of bacteria. In addition, the pH changes that occur during menstruation favor bacterial growth. Prolonged exposure to cold water, together with the intensive physical exertion that might lower the body's resistance to bacteria, are factors conducive to inflammation. Åstrand (1963) failed to find any pathology that was directly attributed to swimming training, but he also did not rule out intensive training in swimming as a possible cause of some gynecological disorders. The risk, however, seems very slight. From the point of view of potential inflammation, many medical doctors advise against swimming during menstruation. Training and competing during menstruation, however, have not been shown to have any long-range gynecological implications.

It should be emphasized once again that an enormous difference exists between the competitive girl swimmer who spends six hours a day at exhausting training sessions, and the average female who might swim for a forty-five minute period for recreation or for instructional purposes. Swimming in the latter case is certainly not exhausting nor chilling and would probably not be contraindicated except in certain exceptional cases.

### Menarche in Sportswomen

Vigorous athletic participation on the part of young girls has been suspect for some time as a possible influence on menarche. Authorities through the years have suggested that female organs may be damaged by jumping, landing, and running. Pros (1962) has said, for instance, that girls should not take jumps in horseback riding the first day before menstruation and the first day of menstruation, since the jarring landing of the horse might damage the female organs. In addition, young girls should not jump horses for fear that it would affect the menarche. This is of course largely speculation and is unsupported by evidence.

The American researchers who have studied age of menarche in young girls who participate in sports have found that menarche is significantly later in athletes. In an early study (Espenschade, 1940) young girls who were not athletes but who were superior physical performers in motor tests were also late maturers, both in terms of skeletal age and menarche. The tests that were used in Espenschade's study included several items that were related to track and field, i.e., 50-yard dash, standing broad jump, softball throw, etc. Malina et al. (1973) also found the age of menarche to be older in girls who were track and field athletes. These girls were 66 college track and field competitors at the National Intercollegiate Competition for Women Track and Field Meet held in the spring of 1969. In Table 32 the chronological and menarcheal age of these athletes is shown. The mean menarcheal age of the nonathletes of the Malina et al. sample is quite consistent with many other menarcheal ages reported by many other investigators.

TABLE 32
Age at Time of Reporting and Age at Menarche in Athletes and Nonathletes

|  | Chronological age | | | Age at menarche | | |
|---|---|---|---|---|---|---|
|  | n | X̄ | s.d. | X̄ | ±s.e. | s.d. |
| Nonathletes | 30 | 20.1 | 1.5 | 12.23 | .30 | 1.65 |
| Shot putters | 9 | 21.5 | 1.7 | 13.44 | .56 | 1.67 |
| Sprinters | 24 | 20.1 | 1.3 | 13.54 | .26 | 1.28 |
| Distance runners | 12 | 19.9 | 1.1 | 13.58 | .29 | 1.00 |
| Discus and javelin | 10 | 21.1 | 1.1 | 13.60 | .48 | 1.51 |
| Jumpers and hurdlers | 11 | 20.3 | 1.1 | 13.73 | .38 | 1.27 |
| All athletes | 66 | 20.4 |  | 13.58 | .16 | 1.29 |

* From Malina, R. M., "Age at Menarche in Athletes and Nonathletes," *Medicine and Science in Sports,* 5 (1973), 11–13. Reprinted by permission.

In this same study, for instance, the ages of eight other samples reported by other investigators ranged from 12.2 to 12.8. The athletes' menarcheal age on the other hand was 13.58. An interesting observation, as pointed out by Malina et al., is that if female athletes are indeed late maturers, this is a maturity-performance relationship that is opposite to that of males. When male athletes are sampled during the years of active growth, the good performers are generally found to be early maturers. It could be speculated that girls who are late maturers are more successful in sports, due to a body composition that was conducive to success, and therefore stayed in sports activities. A young girl who at the age of 12 and 13 still had very low percentage of body fat and undeveloped breasts might, for instance, enjoy success over those who mature early. Her success might encourage her to continue in sports competition. In addition, the late-maturing are probably more likely to maintain their interest in sports in lieu of pursuing heterosexual activities. Since athletics is very attractive to men, boys who are early to mature acquire, at puberty, increased lean body mass as well as a social incentive to be superior in athletics. Early-maturing girls, on the other hand, are socially encouraged toward heterosexual activities. Although there is no evidence with regard to the effect of strenuous training on menarche, it is possible that consistent vigorous physical activity over several years has some effect in delaying menarche.

The age of menarche in European athletic samples has not been significantly later than the average age of menarche of European females. In a Hungarian sample of 729 female athletes who participated in many different sports events, the age of menarche was 13.6. The age is almost identical to that reported by Malina et al. (1972) but in the Hungarian sample the athlete's menarcheal age was not significantly different from the average Hungarian girl's (Erdelyi, 1962). It was Erdelyi's opinion, after analysis of his data, that participation in sports competition does not affect age of menarche. Åstrand (1963), on the other hand, reported that menarche in his 30 girl swimmers was 12.88, which was slightly earlier than the average Swedish girl. Åstrand did observe, however, that his comparative norm was determined one decade earlier, so that it might be reflective of a generation change. In addition, other sources of error might have affected the age of menarche reported by Åstrand. Similarly, Bugyi and Kaush (1970) reported that the eight "best Hungarian swimmers" were significantly accelerated in skeletal age relative to chronological age.

No clear-cut generalization can be made concerning athletic participation and menarcheal age. If the values may be considered to be accurate and representative of the populations in question, the contradiction between the American data and the European data suggests several alternative hypotheses. One possibility is that sports participation has no effect, nor is it related, to age of menarche. Thus the significantly late maturers in the Espenschade (1940) and the Malina et al. (1973) studies and the significantly early maturers in Åstrand's (1963) study have to be interpreted as chance occurrences; or, alpha errors of experimental design. A second possibility is that differential nutritional and physical activity patterns exist between the two countries, so that the relationship of athletic to average samples is different in the two countries. A third possibility is that the performance-maturation relationship may be different in different sports. Although the underlying causative mechanisms are at this time unclear, it may be possible that female swimmers are early maturers and female track and field participants are late maturers. This is a particularly appealing hypothesis when one considers that Erdelyi's (1962) sample was a mixture of many different sports, including swimming and track, and menarcheal age in that sample was not significantly different from average.

## Cyclic Fluctuations of the Support System

Efficient functioning of the physiological support system of the athlete is critical, especially during competitive events in certain types of sports. Any influence that the menstrual cycle might have upon the functioning of the support system would have implications for training procedures and competitive practices. Questions regarding the influence that the different phases of the cycle might have upon heart rate, blood pressure, and hemoglobin/hematocrit were generated as early as 1842. Scant information seems to be available regarding cycle phases and aerobic power.

**Cycle phase and heart rate.** The theoretical rationale for expecting an increased resting heart rate just prior to ovulation and a decreased heart rate just prior to menses is quite clear. As discussed earlier, the autonomic nervous system sympathetic tone is enhanced during high cyclic levels of estrogen, so that resting heart rates might be somewhat higher during the latter part of the follicular phase of the cycle, and lower during the latter part of the luteal phase of the cycle. Unfortunately, theoretical expectations are not so easily shown empirically. Some researchers have found a slightly lower heart rate during menstruation, but almost as many have found no cyclic effect at all on resting heart rate.

As early as 1912, Viville (1912) followed the pulse rate of 46 females during 47 menstrual cycles, and reported no characteristic pattern. In a less persevering study, Schmotkin (1912) made daily observations of the pulse rate of 8 females for three months and found no patterned change at any phase of the cycle. Grollman (1931) took extra precautions to establish careful baseline conditions, and made rigorous attempts to distinguish the phases of the cycle. Nevertheless, he failed to find any characteristically consistent patterns of heart rate in the one female that he measured over a lengthy period. Even when heart rate was measured periodically after allowing it to stabilize for 30 minutes, no cyclic pattern was noted (Blunt and Dye, 1921).

In two studies, the resting heart rate was found to be lower during menses and highest during the follicular phase, but in both cases the differences were not statistically significant (Moore and Cooper, 1923; Scott and Tuttle, 1932). Cullis (1922) was the only researcher to report a low heart rate during flow with a rapid postmenstrual rise. He observed "several subjects" over "several" months.

In several studies, the results were opposite to theoretical expectations. In 1842, Brierre De Boismont reported the heart rate to be highest during the menstrual period. In a much more recent investigation, MacKinnon (1954) measured the pulse rate of 9 subjects for one cycle and the pulse rate of one subject for 13 cycles; each time the average pulse rate during the follicular phase was lower than during the luteal phase of the cycle. King (1914), too, found the pulse rate to be highest just before flow phase and lowest just a few days following menses, but his results were not statistically significant.

A synthesis of these studies of heart rate and cycle phase appears to support a generalization that resting heart rate is not substantially affected by menstrual cycle phases. Most of the studies were plagued by experimental design problems, which might partially explain the contradictions, but the overwhelming majority of the results regarding cycle phase and heart rate were nonsignificant. At any rate, the question seems to have been exhausted, as can be seen from observing the early dates of the majority of the research reports.

**Cycle phase and blood pressure.**  Information regarding the effects of cycle phase on blood pressure are inconclusive and conflicting. Several investigators have found a rise in blood pressure during the high estrogen and progesterone levels of the luteal phase and the lowest blood pressure level immediately following menses (Amos, 1922; Jacobi, 1877; King, 1914; Moore and Cooper, 1923; Truesdell and Croxford, 1922). In most cases, however, the differences were very small and not statistically significant. Truesdell and Croxford (1922) also found a rise above average during the late follicular phase. No variability in blood pressure that could be attributed to the cycle was reported by Grollman (1931), and King (1914), and Cullis and Oppenheimer (1922).

Approximately as many investigators have found blood pressure to be higher on the first two days of the cycle (Bogdonovics, 1914; Eggleson, 1924; Giles, 1914; Griffith, 1929; Truesdell and Croxford, 1922) as those who have found it to be lower on the first two days of menses (Amos, 1922; Hitchcock, 1929; Moore and Cooper, 1923; Mosher, 1901).

**Cycle phase and hematocrit/hemoglobin levels.**  The number of red blood cells reaches its lowest count during menses (Novak, 1966; Sinclair, 1937). Similarly, blood viscosity peaks at the third and fourth week of the menstrual cycle and rapidly decreases at menses (Dintenfass, 1966). The red blood cell concentration, or hematocrit, is the major factor affecting blood viscosity. It is not surprising to find hematocrit lower during menses, with 37.5% red blood cells as compared to 38.5% and 39% on the fourteenth day of the cycle (Garlick, 1968). Hemoglobin was also found by Garlick to be lower during menses (12.6 g/100 ml) than on the fourteenth day of the cycle (13.1 and 13.2 g/100 ml).

**Cycle phase and support system adjustments to exercise.** The question regarding the ability of the support system to cope with exercise stress during the different phases of the menstrual cycle is a much more important question to answer for the sportswoman than the question regarding cyclic changes in baseline measures of the support system. Yet few studies have been reported in which the cardiorespiratory system of the sportswoman has been studied during and immediately following strenuous exercise.

Garlick (1968) studied the heart rate, blood pressure, and hemoglobin/hematocrit content values of 18 females from 19 to 25 years old, on the first and fourteenth day of the cycle, in response to resting and exercise conditions. He found that heart rate was significantly lower during menstruation, but found no difference in heart rate during exercise between the first and fourteenth day of the cycle. Since the heart rate was lower at rest during menses, however, the increase in heart rate from resting to strenuous exercise was greater during menstruation. The exercise increment at menses was approximately 95 beats/min, while the increment at the fourteenth day was approximately 88 or 90 beats/min. Some of the differences that were reported by Garlick might have been chance differences, since the statistical technique used to detect them was one which increases the probability of significant differences occurring by chance. Garlick did conclude that, although vascular changes in the cycle seem to be apparent at rest, they are masked during exercise.

A common flaw in studies of menstrual cycle effects on different variables is that the investigators fail to sample enough days of the cycle, so that a pattern is presumed on the basis of two data points. Truesdell and Croxford, for instance, measured pulse rate after a standard exercise, and found circulatory efficiency to be highest during the flow phase and lowest between periods (1926). They only made two measurements, however. Phillips (1968), however, measured 24 females, from the age of 17 to 22, during four phases of the cycle: preflow, flow, postflow, and resting. In addition, Phillips strengthened her study by dividing the subjects into four groups and measuring each group in a different test order for each phase. Her subjects rested for 15 minutes, after which measures of heart rate and blood pressure were obtained. They then took a one-minute step test at a cadence of 90

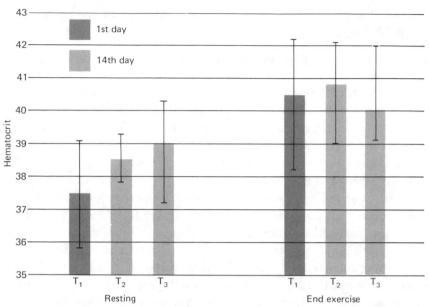

*Fig. 28    Variations in baseline hematocrit values pre- and post-exercise during different phases of the menstrual cycle. [From M.A. Garlick and E.M. Bernauer, "Exercise during the Menstrual Cycle: Variations in Physiological Baselines," Research Quarterly 39 (October, 1968), p. 537. Copyright © 1968 by Research Quarterly and reprinted by permission.]*

steps/min. Heart rate and blood pressure were again obtained. Phillips concluded that menstrual cycle did not have an effect on pulse rate or blood pressure, before or after exercise, and that periodic fluctuations of these variables were the result of factors other than menstruation.

Exercise during different phases of the cycle seems to mask the cyclic effects on both hematocrit and hemoglobin (Fig. 28). A 2.75% incremental rise in hematocrit from resting levels after exercise was found during the menses phase of the cycle, and incremental rises of 1.9% and 1.5% after exercise were found on the fourteenth day of the cycle (Garlick, 1968). It is difficult to interpret Garlick and Bernauer's findings due to the cumbersome statistical analysis used, but it seems probable that their conclusions, since they tend toward the conservative, are plausible. Cyclic changes in vascular resistance and blood pressure may reflexively affect the heart rate during resting conditions. But the responses to exercise are of a level great enough that cyclic influences are masked and are not relevant to exercise response.

Although it might be speculated that, due to possible changes in hematocrit and hemoglobin during the cycle phases, the oxygen-carrying capacity of the blood would be affected, only one investigator seems to have studied aerobic power during different phases of the cycle. Grollman (1931) failed to find a cyclic influence on $\dot{V}O_2$.

## Control of the Menstrual Cycle

Within the past few years, the use of oral contraceptives has become quite common as a means of birth control. Oral contraceptives are pills which contain a combination of estrogen and progesterone in a quantity sufficient to prevent ovulation. The contraceptive is administered daily from the fifth day of the cycle until the twenty-seventh day. At that time, menstruation occurs for five days, and the administration of the pill is continued for another three weeks. Besides serving the purpose of preventing conception, the pill completely regulates the cycle so that every cycle is exactly 28 days. Approximately two days after ceasing to take the pill, menstruation begins. Some women claim that their cycles are so regular under these conditions that they can predict the very hour at which menses will occur.

Just as the use of the pill can regularize the cycle, the pill may be used to control the length of the cycle. In most women as long as the pill is administered, no menstrual period occurs. As soon as the pill is stopped, menstruation occurs within a few days. Thus the pill can be used to delay the menstrual flow or to initiate it at a time prior to its regular onset. It would be completely unrealistic to suppose that women would not quickly take advantage of this characteristic of the pill and regulate their menstrual flow so that it occurs at convenient times. In the case of the athlete, it would be advantageous for some to control the onset of menstrual flow so that their competition would occur during the advantageous postmenstrual phase. Evoking the onset early so that the menses will be completed by the time of the competition is preferable, but more difficult to do. Postponing the onset of menses, which is relatively simple, is useless as it leaves the athlete in the least advantageous premenstrual period.

Controversy rages concerning the long-range physiological implications of tampering with the periodicity of the menstrual cycle. Whether risks may occur in addition to those known risks that are associated with the use of oral contraceptives is not known. Rather strong negative statements have been made concerning the use of the pill for control of the cycle, but they are based on opinion or clinical observation rather than on research evidence. For instance, Kiss (1961) suggested, upon the basis of his clinical observations, that the postponement of menses has led to many menstrual displacements. One physician's opinion was that "the displacement of ovulation or its suppression represents such far-reaching interventions in the female organism that it will lead to irrevocable damage over time" (Klaus, 1964). Although no valid evidence seems to be available regarding the repeated and deliberate displacement of menses by female athletes, most physicians propose a cautious approach to the problem and discourage the use of the pill in this manner. They suggest that, although hormonal therapy and control of the cycle has been used for years, the female athlete should not prescribe dosages for herself nor should her physician encourage her to tamper with her cycle except in exceptional cases under unusual circumstances (LaCava, 1969).

As has been historically common with controversial ideas, the physiological implications of menstrual cycle control are entangled with ethical and moral ramifications. Some have been concerned that the use of the pill to control the cycle might be considered a form of "doping," which is specifically forbidden in athletic competitions. Others have pointed out that the pill is not a form of doping since it does not enhance the original capability of the female, but only places her in her most advantageous condition (Erdelyi, 1962). Others have violently disagreed, and declared that control of the cycle for athletic events is unethical and immoral (Dalton, 1972; Klaus, 1964). The moral argument of Dalton's is particularly obscure, if not amusing. Dalton argues that hormonal therapy has been frequently used to alter or to stop the menstrual cycles of women who are paraplegics, hemiplegics, or seriously handicapped. She suggests that alteration of the cycle is appropriate when a woman is in a plaster cast for a broken bone and would find menstruation inconvenient. She even suggests that certain times exist in a woman's life, such as her wedding night, or an important examination, or even an annual vacation, when she might wish to control her cycle and have it at a more convenient time. Then Dalton makes this statement:

> It must be added that alteration of menstrual patterns is not permitted in respect of athletic events. This is because the male hormone, testosterone, has been known to be used. Testosterone has the effect not only of suppressing the feminine function of men-

struation, but also of developing the masculine features of increased physical strength and endurance (Dalton, 1972, p. 90).

Why the female athlete is doomed to testosterone therapy in lieu of the same hormonal control that is suggested for those who would postpone their vacations was not explained. It is obvious that Dalton recommends hormonal therapy in some circumstances with little fear of injurious consequences. It appears that the contradiction represents a pervasive philosophy that "something is not quite right about controlling and changing something as fundamental as menstruation just to compete in an athletic event"—even though little evidence is available to support such a belief.

# PREGNANCY

## Pregnancy in Physically Active Women

From the moment the fertilized ovum implants itself in the endometrium of the uterus to begin its development from ovum to fetus to embryo, a substantial change begins to occur in the physiological functioning of the female. Many hormonal changes are initiated; for example, by the fourth month of pregnancy the placenta becomes an appreciable hormone production center. Just before birth it is producing 100 times more progesterone than the normal woman produces (Dalton, 1972). It is no wonder that some questions might arise concerning the effects that pregnancy might have on physical performance. Conversely, what are the effects of a lifestyle of vigorous activity or heavy training on the term of pregnancy and upon birth itself?

Statements are made that no evidence exists to the effect that sports participation has adverse effects on childbearing, but the truth is that little evidence exists to support the concept that sports training does not have adverse effects. The unfortunate state of affairs is that most of what is in the literature regarding pregnancy and sports training is in the form of medical opinion which is supported by clinical observation rather than experimental evidence. A great deal of public attention has been given to two gynecological surveys of top female athletes (Erdelyi, 1962; Zaharieva, 1965), perhaps because organized information of this sort is rare. These two studies do represent a substantial contribution to the area in question because they were surveys of women who were world-class athletes. Their subjects probably represent the highest levels of physical training and body stress that women anywhere endure. Their findings, therefore, would represent the most serious implications that strenuous exercise might have for pregnancy. The studies of Erdelyi and Zaharieva have been quoted repeatedly in popular magazines by those who support the cause of women in athletics. Unfortunately quotations have been taken out of context in some cases. Because the studies have been cited extensively, and because they do represent a considerable amount of information regarding the topic of pregnancy and sports participation, they will be discussed at length. Much of the following information is derived from these studies.

Erdelyi, a medical doctor, surveyed 729 Hungarian female athletes. Questionnaires, personal interviews, menstrual charts, and pelvic and rectal examinations were used as information-gathering devices. Zaharieva studied 13 of the sportswomen at the Tokyo Olympics. His survey covered women from 10 different countries, competing in track and field, swimming, gymnastics, and volleyball. All of the women in this study were top athletes: former and present Olympic champions, world and national record holders. They were between the ages of 16 and 33 years, with the greatest majority of them being about 25 years old. Most of the women had active sporting careers extending over 6 and 8 years. Twelve years of competitive training was common in the track and field women.

**Effects of pregnancy on sports performance.**  Top class athletes don't permit pregnancy to serve as much of an interruption in their training and competing schedules. Two-thirds of the women athletes surveyed continued training and competing up until the third month of pregnancy with no deterioration of performance noted (Erdelyi, 1962; Kiss, 1957). A few athletes (50%) in one study engaged in sports up until the sixth month of pregnancy (Casper, 1928). The development of performance deterioration at about the end of the third month generally was the motivation for the athlete's cessation of training.

Some women don't even experience significant performance deterioration at the third and fourth months of pregnancy. Some fairly startling performances have been recorded by pregnant women. For instance, during the 1952 Olympics a diver, pregnant 3½ months, received the bronze medal. One pregnant female performed very well in the 1956 Olympic discus event. Zaharieva and Sigler (1963) combined their efforts to survey 207 well-trained athletes from Hungary and Spain. All these athletes had from 1 to 4 children, and 70% of them reported that they continued their training up until the sixth month. Of 26 of their athletes who competed in the Melbourne Olympics, 10 were pregnant. A rower in the sample had won the national championship in the individual rowing class when she was three months pregnant. A discus thrower produced her very best performance in a national competition when she was 4½ months pregnant. Perhaps most spectacular of all, one of the divers of the sample won a national championship while 6 months pregnant.

In the Olympic sample, 46% of the women bettered their results by the end of the first year after childbirth, and 30.8% of the women between their first and second year following childbirth. The mothers in that sample even stated that they felt stronger, had greater stamina, and were better balanced in every way after the birth of their child. Childbirth, apparently, is not a barrier to top level performance providing the training schedule following birth is reasonable. It was suggested by Pros (cited in LaCava, 1969) that two months after birth a moderate training program should begin. Intensive training may begin at four months following pregnancy and top form should be reached by the sixth month after pregnancy.

**Effects of training and competition on pregnancy.** Heavy training and competition has been questioned by some as having detrimental effects upon the nine-month gestation period, as well as on the act of childbirth. The studies of both Erdelyi and Zaharieva refuted this statement. Erdelyi found less toxemia and no more abortions and premature deliveries in the Hungarian athletes than in the nonathletic sample. Similarly, Zaharieva reported no abortions that were caused by sport participation. In another study of 50 athletes, only one had even a premature birth (Casper, 1928).

Two theories have been proposed concerning the effects of vigorous activity as a lifestyle and its consequences upon childbirth. One of these theories states that intensive sports activity makes the muscles of the pelvic floor and perineum more rigid; consequently, childbirth is much more difficult in women who participate in athletics (Sellheim; Kustner; Westman; cited in Erdelyi, 1962). The second theory is that sports performance has a favorable effect of strengthening the abdominal musculature, thus making the second stage of labor a much more efficient and shorter function (Antoine, 1941; Friedrich, 1942; Kiss, 1961; Knoll, 1939; Pfeiffer, 1951; Tietze, 1939). The entire process of childbirth should be easier due to the superior body of the female athlete, the heavier musculature, and the efficiency of the nervous system. The athletes' reports in both the Hungarian and the Olympic sample overwhelmingly support the second theory. In the Olympic sample, 87.2% of the athletes delivered their babies faster than the established average. The second stage of labor for them was one-half the time of average. There were also 50% fewer Caesarean sections in the athletic sample than in normal populations. These figures were true for the very top-class athletes as well as the second-class athletes that were present in Tokyo. Zaharieva also reported normal deliveries among the Hungarian athletes. In another study, females who played competitive baseball were reported to have suffered no harm regarding childbirth (Niemuneva, 1953).

Turning for a moment from the world-class athlete, some consideration should be given to the average female and physical activity. Gendel (1971) studied 100 of her female patients who were between the ages of 18 and 23, who had low backaches and chronic fatigue following pregnancy. After eliminating the pathologies of her sample, she discovered 35 patients who had several factors in common. They lacked regular physical activity since early childhood, and they had very poorly developed anterior abdominal musculature. She prescribed physical activity and found that in all their cases their condition was improved.

## MENSTRUATION AND PREGNANCY IN PERSPECTIVE

The preceding discussion of menstruation and pregnancy with regard to physical activity and athletics makes it abundantly clear that little has been done in this country in the way of systematically studying the problem. The menstrual cycle seems to be affected by many variables other than sport, such as lifestyle, nutritional patterns, and mental stress. The cycle has even been shown to be influenced by social groups; for instance, the menses of mothers, daughters, "best friends," or dormitory roommates who have lived in very close contact have been shown to grow closer together in terms of onset (McClintock, 1971). Considered within the perspective of all the factors that influence the menstrual cycle, sports participation may be one of the least important variables. The preponderance of information that is available comes from European sports doctors, who are affiliated with athletic teams and who

work with females throughout the training and competitive season.
Very few American medical personnel parallel the functioning of the
European sports doctor, and very little concern has been given to the
female athlete's unique problems. The information available then has
been obtained from clinical observations, and many of their reports
are steeped in opinion. Statements supporting or rejecting female athletics have been taken out of context from the few available studies
of menstruation and pregnancy. Trainers, coaches, and athletes are still
more or less blundering along with educated guesses as the basis for
their decisions regarding performance and menstruation. Hopefully the
1970s will be a decade of intensive and formalized study of the female
in competition. Until more valid information is available, however,
some generalizations must be made.

Menstruation is a normal biological function and in most women
physical performances are not dramatically changed in a cyclic manner.
Although there are some phases of the cycle which seem to put the
female in a condition more conducive to efficient performance, the
differences are so slight in average daily performance that they are not
noticeable in field tests. In other words, average physical tasks performed
by average women are probably unaffected by varying phases of the
cycle. This may not be the case in high-level performances by a small
but substantial percentage of highly trained women athletes. While
many female athletes may never need to consider the varying phases of
the cycle in their training program and selection of competitive events,
other athletes may.

Vigorous exercise in a woman's lifestyle and even during menses
seems to be highly indicated and conducive to good health. Most female
athletes find no problems with menstrual disorders or irregularity that
might be attributed to sports activities. Conversely, it should be emphasized that some athletes have reported dysmenorrhea and irregularity
that accompanies and seems to be a function of unusual, intensive
training. In the modern woman's zeal to obliterate old superstitions
that women can't physically perform during or because of menses, she
should not leap to the extreme point of view that any amount of intensive training is acceptable for all women. The final decisions should
probably rest with the individual athlete in counsel with her trainer
and coach. Criteria that should be used to make decisions regarding
training and competing at various phases of the cycle should include:
(a) menstrual cycle characteristics and changes, (b) physical performance

characteristics at various phases of the cycle, and (c) the athlete's attitude toward her performance as a function of the menstrual cycle. If the athlete appears to have no changes, no pain, and no cyclical performance deterioration throughout her training program, her training schedule can probably be planned with little regard for menstruation. In the event of pain, amenorrhea, dysmenorrhea, or reduction in the level of performance during menses, the athlete should reevaluate her training schedule with regard to her cycle. No athlete should be forced by her coach or trainer to compete during menses if she requests not to.

Although at this time it is on the basis of medical opinion rather than research evidence, it seems wise to discourage frequent and repeated displacement of the menses period by hormonal treatment. Information about such practice simply does not at this time preclude long-range deleterious effects.

Finally, girls who contemplate an athletic career should not fear possible implications for pregnancy and childbirth. Medical evidence seems to point in the direction of beneficial effects on pregnancy and childbirth rather than detrimental ones. Pregnancy produces no substantial alterations in ability to ventilate or in aerobic capacity (Guzman, 1970; Ueland, 1973). There should not be, on any identifiable physiological grounds, any limitation on exercise except very late in pregnancy (Bruser, 1968). Pregnant women can perform quite adequately up to 36 weeks of pregnancy, providing they can cope with the handicaps of changes in balance and center of gravity. This particularly is true in nonweight-bearing activities. Female animals of all species are quite vigorously active during pregnancy, for they must pursue their food and also flee from predators up until the moment of birth. Why should the female homo sapiens be dramatically different?

Two situations exist in which exercise should be modified: when bumping and compressing activities are involved, and when changes occur in the symphysis pubis. Any activity which causes physical contact or compression of the abdomen is highly discouraged. Also, in some women the symphysis pubis during pregnancy becomes softened and the bones may separate very slightly so that bone movement can occur. This movement is sometimes painful and can be debilitating. Naturally, exercise is contraindicated in these situations.

Currently, female athletes of this country marry at about an average age, although it is possible that their first births are delayed somewhat beyond average. On the whole, female athletes can look forward to a normal, vigorous and robust life, for the most part free of menstrual disorders and complications with marriage, pregnancy, and childbirth.

# Bibliography

Adrian, M., "Sex Differences in Biomechanics," in *Women and Sport: A National Research Conference,* The Pennsylvania State University HPER Series No. 2, 1972.

Amos, S.E., and Lord, L.R., "Note on Variations on Blood Pressure during Menstruation," *Lancet,* 203 (1922), 956-957.

Anderson, K.L., "Physical Fitness—Studies of Healthy Men and Women in Norway," *International Research in Sport and Physical Education,* Ed. E. Jokl and E. Simon, Springfield, Ill.: Charles C. Thomas, 1964.

"Anthropometric Studies in the World University Summer Games in Sofia, 1961," *Bulletin d'information Comite Olympique Bulgare,* 7 (1962), 22.

Antoine, *Deutsche Arzteblatt,* (1941), 85-89.

Asmussen, E., "Growth and Athletic Performance," *Proceedings of International Congress of Sport Sciences,* Ed. by Kitsuo Kato, The Japanese Union of Sport Sciences, 1966.

—————— , "Growth in Muscular Strength and Power," *Physical Activity: Growth and Development,* Ed. by G.L. Rarick, New York: Academic Press, 1973.

Åstrand, I., "Aerobic Work Capacity in Men and Women with Special Reference to Age," *Acta Physiologica Scandinavia,* 49 (Supplementum 169, 1960), 11.

—————— , "Exercise Electrocardiograms Recorded Twice with an 8-Year Interval in a Group of 204 Women and Men 48-63 Years Old," *Acta Medica Scandinavia,* 178 (1965), 27.

Åstrand, P.O., *Experimental Studies of Physical Working Capacity in Relation to Sex and Age,* Munksgaard, Copenhagen, 1952.

—————— , "Human Physical Fitness with Special Reference to Sex and Age," *Physiological Reviews,* 36 (May, 1956), 307.

—————— , Cuddy, T.E., Saltin, B., and Stenberg, J., "Cardiac Output during Submaximal and Maximal Work," *Journal of Applied Physiology,* 19 (1964), 268-274.

—————— , Engstrom, L., Erikson, B., Karlberg, P., Nylander, I., Saltin, B., and Thoren, C., "Girl Swimmers," *Acta Paediabrica, Supplement,* 147 (1963), 1-75.

_____ , and Rodahl, K., *Textbook of Work Physiology*, New York: McGraw-Hill Book Co., 1970.

Bank, D., "Dick Bank Discusses the Sex Test: Its History and Why it is Needed," *Women's Track and Field World*, 1 (November, 1967), 12-13.

Bar-Or, O., Shephard, R.J., and Allen, C.L., "Cardiac Output of 10- to 13-year-old Boys and Girls During Submaximal Exercise," *Journal of Applied Physiology*, 30 (1971), 219-223.

Bausenwein, I., "Zur Frage Sport und Menstruation," *Deutsche Med Wschr.*, 79 (1954), 1526.

Bayer, L., and Bayley, N., *Growth Diagnosis*, Chicago: The University of Chicago Press, 1959.

Bayley, N., "Some Psychological Correlates of Somatic Androgyny," *Child Development*, 22 (March, 1951), 47-60.

Becklake, M.R., Frank, H., Dagenais, C.R., Ostiguy, G.L., and Guzman, C.A., "Influence of Age and Sex on Exercise Cardiac Output," *Journal of Applied Physiology*, 20 (1965), 938-947.

Behnke, A.R., "Anthropometric Evaluation of Body Composition through Life," *Annals of the New York Academy of Science*, 110 (1963), 450.

Beise, D., and Peaseley, V., "Relation of Reaction Time, Speed, and Agility of Big Muscle Groups to Certain Sports Skills," *Research Quarterly*, 8 (1937), 133-142.

Benedict, F.G., and Emmes, L.E., "A Comparison of the Basal Metabolism of Normal Men and Women," *Journal of Biological Chemistry*, 20 (1915), 253-262.

_____ , and Parmenter, H.S., "The Energy Metabolism of Women while Ascending or Descending Stairs," *American Journal of Physiology*, 84 (1928), 675.

Bilhuber, G., "Functional Periodicity and Motor Ability in Sports," *American Physical Education Review*, 32 (1927), 22-25.

Billings, E.G., "The Occurrence of Cyclic Variations in Motor Activity in Relation to the Menstrual Cycle in the Human Female," *Johns Hopkins Hospital Bulletin*, 54 (1934), 440-454.

Blunt, K., and Dye, M., "Basal Metabolism of Normal Women," *Journal of Biological Chemistry*, 47 (1921), 69-87.

Bodganovics, O., *Zentralbl. für gynak*, 34 (1910), 994, from King, J., "Concerning the Periodic Cardiovascular and Temperature Variations in Women," *American Journal of Physiology*, 34 (1914), 203-218.

Boogens, J., and Keatings, W.R., "The Expenditure of Energy by Men and Women Walking," *Journal of Physiology*, 138 (1957), 165.

Bradbury, C.E., *Anatomy and Construction of the Human Figure*, New York: McGraw-Hill, 1949.

Brandova, A., "Somatotypes of Women and Their Efficiency," *Teor. Prax. tel Vych.*, 16(1) (1968), 26-32.

Brierre, De B., A.J.F., *De la Menstruation, Considerée dans ses Rapports Physiologiques*, Paris: Germer Bailliere, 1842.

Brouha, L., and Harrington, M.E., "Heart Rate and Blood Pressure Reactions of Men and Women During and After Muscular Exercise," *Lancet,* 77 (1957), 79-80.

Brown, C.H., Harrower, J.R., and Deeter, M.F., "The Effects of Cross Country Running on Pre-adolescent Girls," *Medicine and Science of Sports,* 41 (1972), 1-5.

Bruser, M., "Sporting Activities during Pregnancy," *Obstetrics and Gynecology,* 32 (November, 1968), 721-725.

Buffery, A.W.H., and Gray, J.A., "Sex Differences in the Development of Perceptual and Linguistic Skills," *Gender Differences: Their Ontogeny and Significance,* Ed. by C. Ounsted and D.C. Taylor, Churchill, 1972.

Bugyi, B., and Kausz, I., "Radiographic Determination of the Skeletal Age of the Young Swimmers," *Journal of Sports Medicine and Physical Fitness,* 10 (1970), 303-308.

Carter, J.E.L., "The Physiques of Female Physical Education Teachers in Training," *Physical Education* (British), 57 (March, 1965), 6-16.

_____ , "The Somatotypes of Athletes—A Review," *Human Biology,* 42 (1970), 535-569.

Casper, H., *Deutsch. Med. Wochenschr,* 54 (1928), 25.

Conger, P.A., and Macnab, R.B.J., "Strength, Body Composition, and Work Capacity of Participants and Nonparticipants in Women's Intercollegiate Sports," *Research Quarterly,* 38 (May, 1967), 184-192.

Conger, P.A., and Wessel, J., "Physical Performance and Body Form as Related to Physical Activity of College Women," *Research Quarterly,* 39 (Dec., 1968), 908-914.

Cotes, J.E., Davis, C.T.M., Edholm, O.G., Healy, M.J.R., and Tanner, J.M., "Factors Relating to the Aerobic Capacity of 46 Healthy British Males and Females, Ages 18 to 28 Years," *Proceedings of the Royal Society of London,* 174 (1969), 91-114.

Cotton, F.S., "Center of Gravity in Man," *American Journal of Physical Anthropology,* 18 (1933), 401-405.

Cullis, W.C., Oppenmeimer, E., and Ross-Johnson, M., "Observations on Temperature and Other Changes in Women during the Menstrual Cycle," *Lancet,* 203 (1922), 945-956.

Cureton, T.K., *Physical Fitness of Champion Athletes,* University of Illinois Press, Urbana, 1951.

Dalton, K., "Effect of Menstruation on Schoolgirls' Weekly Work," *British Medical Journal,* 1 (1960), 326-328.

_____ , "Menstruation and Accidents," *British Medical Journal,* 5210 (1960), 1425.

_____ , "Menstruation and Crime," *British Medical Journal,* 2 (1961), 1752-1753.

_____ , *The Menstrual Cycle,* New York: Warner Paperback Library, 1972.

Darwick, D., "Maximal Work Capacity as Related to Strength, Body Composition, and Physical Activity in Young Women," Unpublished Master's thesis, Michigan State University, East Lansing, Mich., 1964.

Dintenfass, L., et al., "Viscosity of Blood in Healthy Young Women and the Effect on the Menstrual Cycle," *Lancet,* 1 (1966), 234-235.

Doolittle, T.L., and Lipson, L., "Performance Variations Associated with the Menstrual Cycle," Paper presented at the 87th meeting of the AAHPER, Detroit, Michigan, 1971.

Drinkwater, B., "Maximal Oxygen Uptake of Females," *Women and Sport: A National Research Conference,* Ed. by D. Harris, The Pennsylvania State University, University Park, Pa., 1973.

_____ , and Horvath, S.M., "Responses of Young Female Track Athletes and Exercise," *Medicine and Science of Sports,* 3 (1971), 56-62.

_____ , and Horvath, S.M., "Detraining Effects on Young Women," *Medicine and Science of Sports,* 4 (Summer, 1972), 91-95.

Duntzer, E., "Amount of Athletic Exercises that Can Be Safely Indulged in during Menstruation," *Zentraebl. für Gynakologie,* 54 (1930), 29-35.

_____ , and Hellendall, *Muchener Medizenesche Wochenschrift,* 1835 (1929).

Eggleson, M., "Periodic Changes in Blood Pressure, Muscle Coordination, and Mental Efficiency in Women," Unpublished Ph.D. dissertation, Johns Hopkins University, Baltimore, Md., 1924.

Eiben, O., "Konstitutionsbiologische Untersuchangen an europäischen Hochleistungssportlerinnen," *Wissenschaftliche Zeitschrift der Humboldt-Universität zu Berlin, Math.-Nat. R.,* 18 (May, 1969), 941-946.

Ellis, H., *Man and Woman,* Boston: Houghton-Mifflin, 1929.

Erdelyi, G.J., "Gynecological Survey of Female Athletes," *Journal of Sports Medicine and Physical Fitness,* 2-3 (1962), 174-179.

Eriksson, B.O., Engström, I., Karlberg, P., Saltin, B., and Thoren, C., "A Physiological Analysis of Former Girl Swimmers," *Pediatric Work Physiology,* Ed. by C. Thoren, *Acta Paediat* (Suppl. 217), 68-71, 1971.

Espenschade, A., "Motor Performance in Adolescence," *Monograph of Social Research in Child Development,* Serial Number 24, 1940.

_____ , "Development of Motor Coordination in Boys and Girls," *Research Quarterly,* 18 (1947), 30.

Fleishman, E., *The Structure and Measurement of Physical Fitness,* Englewood Cliffs, N.J., 1965.

Fox, R.H., Lofstedt, B.E., Woodward, P.M., Eriksson, E., and Werkstrom, B., "Comparison of Thermoregulatory Function in Men and Women," *Journal of Applied Physiology,* 26 (1969), 444-453.

Friedrich, *Sport und korper,* Munchen, 1942.

Frucht, A.H., and Jokl, E., "The Future of Athletic Records," *International Research in Sport and Physical Education,* Ed. by E. Jokl, E. Simon, Springfield, Ill.: Charles C. Thomas Co., 1964.

Garlick, M.A., and Bernauer, E.M., "Exercise during the Menstrual Cycle: Variations in Physiological Baselines," *Research Quarterly,* 39 (1968), 533-542.

Garn, S.M., "Fat Weight and Fat Placement in the Female," *Science*, 125 (1957), 1091-1092.

Gendel, E.S., "Pregnancy, Fitness, and Sports," *Journal of the American Medical Association*, (Sept., 1967), 751-754.

—————— , "Fitness and Fatigue in the Female," *Journal of Health, Physical Education, and Recreation*, 42 (October, 1971), 53-58.

Giles, H., *Trans. Obstet. Soc. London*, 39 (1897) 115, from King, J., "Concerning the Periodic Cardiovascular and Temperature Variations in Women," *American Journal of Physiology*, 34 (1914), 203-218.

Golob, L.J., Menduke, H., and Lang, W.R., "Exercise and Dysmenorrhea in Young Teenagers: A 3-Year Study," *Obstetrics and Gynecology*, 32 (Oct., 1968), 508-511.

Goodhartz, N., "The Place of Women as Subjects of Scientific Investigation," Paper presented at the 85th meeting of the American Association for Health, Physical Education, and Recreation, Boston, Mass., April, 1969.

Gordon, T.I., Bannister, E.W., and Gordon, B.P., "The Caloric Cost of Competitive Figure Skating," *Journal of Sports Medicine*, 9 (1969), 98-103.

Griffith, F.R., et al., "Studies in Human Physiology: Pulse Rate and Blood Pressure," *American Journal of Physiology*, 88 (1929), 295-311.

Grollman, A., "The Effect of the Menstrual Cycle on the Cardiac Output, Pulse-Rate, Blood Pressure, and Oxygen Consumption of a Normal Woman," *American Journal of Physiology*, 96 (1931), 1-7.

Guzman, C.R., "Cardiorespiratory Response to Exercise During Pregnancy," *American Journal of Obstetrics and Gynecology*, 108 (October, 1970), 600-605.

Hagerman, B., "Effects of Age and Success on Arousal Levels of Advanced Female Tennis Competitors before and after Tournament Competition," Unpublished Master's thesis, The University of Texas, Austin, Texas, 1972.

Haymes, E.M., Harris, D.M., Beldon, M.D., Loomis, J.L., and Nicholass, W.C., "The Effect of the Physical Activity Level in Selected Hematological Variables in Adult Women," Paper presented at the 88th Meeting of the AAHPER, Houston, Texas, 1972.

Heath, B.H., "Need for Modification of Somatotyping Methodology," *American Journal of Physical Anthropology*, 21 (1963), 227-233.

Heath, B.H., Hopkins, C.E., and Miller, C.D., "Physiques of Hawaii-born Young Men and Women of Japanese Ancestry, Compared with College Men and Women of the United States and England," *American Journal of Physical Anthropology*, 19 (1961), 173-184.

Hellebrandt, F., and Meyer, M., "Physiological Data Significant to Participation by Women in Physical Activities," *Research Quarterly*, 10 (1939), 19-26.

Henry, F.M., "Increased Response Latency for Complicated Movements and A Memory Drum Theory of Neuromotor Reaction," *Research Quarterly*, 31 (October, 1960), 459-468.

Henry, F.M., "Factorial Structure of Speed and Static Strength in a Lateral Arm Movement," *Research Quarterly*, 31 (October, 1960), 440-447.

Hermansen, L., and Anderson, K.L., "Aerobic Work Capacity in Young Norwegian Men and Women," *Journal of Applied Physiology*, 20 (1965), 425-431.

Hettinger, Th., "Muskelkraft und Muskeltraining bei Frauen und Männern," *Arbeitphysiology*, 15 (1953), 201-206.

Higgs, S., "Maximal Oxygen Intake and Maximal Work Performance of Active College Women," *Research Quarterly*, 44 (May, 1973), 125-131.

Hirata, K., "Physique and Age of Tokyo Olympic Champions," *Sports Medicine and Physical Fitness*, 6 (December, 1966), 207-222.

Hitchcock, F., and Wardell, R., "Cyclic Variations in Basal Metabolic Rate of Women," *Journal of Nutrition*, 2 (1929), 203-215.

Hodgkins, J., "Influence of Age on the Speed of Reaction and Movement in Females," *Journal of Gerontology*, 17 (1962), 385-389.

_____ , "Reaction Time and Speed of Movement in Males and Females of Various Ages," *Research Quarterly*, 34 (1963), 335-343.

_____ , and Skubic, V., "Women's Swimming Records: Analysis and Predictions," *Journal of Sports Medicine and Physical Fitness*, 8 (June, 1968), 96-102.

Holmgren, A., "Cardiorespiratory Determinants of Cardiovascular Fitness," *Canadian Medical Journal*, 96 (1967), 697-702.

Holmgren, A., Mossfeldt, F., Sjostrand, T., and Strom, G., "Effect of Training on Work Capacity, Total Hemoglobin, Blood Volume, Heart Volume, and Pulse Rate in Recumbant and Upright Positions," *International Research in Sport and Physical Education*, Ed. by E. Jokl and E. Simon, Springfield, Ill.: Charles C Thomas Co., 1964.

Huelster, L.J., "The Role of Sports in the Culture of Girls," *Proceedings: Second National Institute on Girls' Sports*, Washington, D.C.: AAHPER, 1966.

Humphrey, D.L., and Falls, H.B., "Assessment of the Aerobic Capacity of Young Active Female American Physical Education Majors," Paper presented at the 88th meeting of the American Association for Health, Physical Education, and Recreation, Minneapolis, Minnesota, April, 1973.

Hutt, C., *Males and Females*, Baltimore, Md.: Penguin Books, Inc., 1972.

Ikai, M., and Fukunaga, T., "Calculation of Muscle Strength per Unit Cross-Sectional Area of Human Muscle by Means of Ultrasonic Measurement," *Internationale Zeitschrift für Angewandte Physiologie einschliesslich Arbeitsphysiologie*, 26 (1968), 26.

Ingman, O., "Menstruation in Finnish Sports Women," *Sports Medicine*, Ed. by M.J. Karvoren, Helsinki, 1953.

Ivata and Kadsua: cited in Erdelyi, G.J., "Pregnancy," *Encyclopedia of Sport Sciences and Medicine*, I[A] 38, Ed. by L. Larson, New York: The Macmillan Company, p. 67.

Jacobi, M.P., *The Question of Rest for Women during Menstruation*, New York: G.P. Putnam's Sons, 1877.

Jellinek, "Leibesabungen und Menstruation," *Sportmedizin*, (1958), 96.

Jokl, E., and Simon, E., *International Research in Sport and Physical Education*, Springfield, Ill.: Charles C Thomas Company, 1964.

Katch, F.I., Michael, E.D., Jr., and Jones, E.M., "Effects of Physical Training on the Body Composition and Diet of Females," *Research Quarterly*, **40** (1969), 99-108.

Khosla, T., "Unfairness of Certain Events in the Olympic Games," *British Medical Journal*, **4** (October, 1968), 111-113.

————————, "The Community and Sport Participation," *British Journal of Preventive and Social Medicine*, **25** (May, 1971), 114-118.

King, J.L., "Concerning the Periodic Cardio-vascular and Temperature Variations in Women," *American Journal of Physiology*, **34** (1914), 203-219.

Kiss, L., Frauensport, Menstruation und Gerbert, in Bausenwein-Plank: *Jugend-sport-Frauensport*, Der geschädigte Mensch in der Rehabilitation, Vortr. 19., Dtsch. Sportärztekongresses, Banaschewski, München-Gräfelfing, 1961.

————————, et al., "Deliveries of Sport Athletes," *Orvosi Hetilap*, **7-8** (1957), 153-158.

Klaus, E.J., "The Athletic Status of Women," *International Research in Sport and Physical Education*, Ed. by E. Jokl and E. Simon, Springfield, Ill.: Charles C Thomas, 1964.

Kleitman, N., and Ramsaroop, A., "Periodicity in Body Temperature and Heart Rate," *Endocrinology*, **43** (1948), 7-11.

Knoll, *Medizenische Klinik Wochenschrift* **1** (1939), 845.

Knowlton, R.G., and Weber, H., "A Case Study of Training Responses in a Female Endurance Runner," *Sports Medicine and Physical Fitness*, **8** (1968), 228-235.

Knuttgen, H.G., "Aerobic Capacity of Adolescents," *Journal of Applied Physiology*, **22** (1967), 655-658.

Kramer, J.D., and Lurie, P.R., "Maximal Exercise Tests in Children," *American Journal of Diseases of Children*, **108** (1967), 283-297.

Kroll, W., "Isometric Strength Fatigue Patterns in Female Subjects," *Research Quarterly*, **42** (October, 1971), 286-298.

Kudzma, D.J., Bradley, E.M., and Goldzieher, J.W., "A Metabolic Balance Study of the Effects of an Oral Steroid Contraceptive on Weight and Body Composition," *Contraception*, **5** (January, 1972), 31-37.

LaCava, G., Ed., "Top Sport in Women," in *Journal of Sports Medicine and Physical Fitness*, **9** (March, 1969), 62-63.

Lofstedt, B., *Human Heat Tolerance*, Lund, Department of Hygiene, Universtiee of Lund, Sweden, 1966.

Lowe, C.R., Pelmear, P.L., Campbell, H., Hitchens, R.A.N., Khosla, T., and King, T.C., *British Journal of Preventive and Social Medicine*, **22** (1968), 1.

Lundgren, H.M., "Changes in Skinfold and Girth Measures of Women Varsity Basketball and Field Hockey Players," *Research Quarterly*, **39** (December, 1968), 1020-1024.

McArdle, W.D., Katch, F.I., Rechar, G.S., Jacobson, L., and Ruck, S., "Reliability and Interrelationships between Maximum Oxygen Intake, Work Capacity, and Step-Test Scores in College Women," *Medicine and Science in Sports*, 4 (Winter, 1972), 182.

_____ , Magel, J.R., and Kyrallos, L., "Aerobic Capacity, Heart Rate, and Estimated Energy Cost During Women's Competitive Basketball," *Research Quarterly*, 42 (May, 1971), 178-186.

McClintoch, M.K., "Menstrual Synchrony and Suppression," *Nature*, 229 (January, 1971), 244-245.

Mackennion, I.L., "Observations on the Pulse Rate During the Human Menstrual Cycle," *Journal of Obstetrics and Gynaecology of British Empire*, 61 (1954), 109-117.

Macnab, R.B., Conger, R.P., and Taylor, P.S., "Differences in Maximal and Submaximal Work Capacity in Men and Women," *Journal of Applied Physiology*, 47 (November, 1969), 644-648.

Maksud, M.G., Wiley, R.L., Hamilton, L.H., and Lockhart, B., "Maximal VO$_2$, Ventilation and Heart Rate of Olympic Speed Skating Candidates," *Journal of Applied Physiology*, 29 (1970), 186-190.

Malina, R.M., "Quantification of Fat, Muscle, and Bone in Man," *Clinical Orthopaedics*, 65 (1969), 9-38.

_____ , "Exercise as an Influence upon Growth," *Clinical Pediatrics*, 9 (1969b), 273-287.

_____ , "Adolescent Changes in Size, Build, Composition, and Performance," Unpublished manuscript, 1973.

_____ , Harper, A.B., Avent, H., and Campbell, D.F., "Physique of Female Track and Field Athletes," *Medicine and Science in Sports*, 3 (1971), 32-38.

_____ , Harper, A., Avent, H., and Campbell, D., "Age at Menarche in Athletes and Non-athletes," *Medicine and Science in Sports*, 5 (1973), 11-13.

Mandell, A., and Mandell, M., "Suicide and the Menstrual Cycle," *Journal of the American Medical Association*, 200 (1967), 792.

Mateef, D., "Age Morphology and Physiology of Man," *Sofia: Medizina i Fizkultura*, 1958.

Matsui, H., et al., "Aerobic Work Capacity of Japanese Adolescents," *Journal of Sports Medicine and Physical Fitness*, (1970).

_____ , Miyashita, M., Miura, M., Amano, K., Mizutani, S., Hoshikawa, T., Toyoshima, S., and Kamei, S., "Aerobic Work Capacity of Japanese Adolescents," *Journal of Sports Medicine*, 11 (1971), 28-35.

Medved, R., "Body Height and Predisposition for Certain Sports," *Journal of Sports Medicine and Physical Fitness*, 6 (June, 1966), 89-91.

Metheny, E.L., Brouha, L., Johnson, R.E., and Forbes, W.H., "Some Physiologic Responses of Women and Men to Moderate and Strenuous Exercise: A Competitive Study," *American Journal of Physiology*, 137 (1942), 318-326.

Michael, E.D., and Horvath, S.M., "Physical Work Capacity of College Women," *Journal of Applied Physiology,* **20** (1965), 263-266.

Miyashita, M., Hayashi, Y., and Furuhashi, H., "Maximum Oxygen Intake of Japanese Top Swimmers," *Journal of Sports Medicine and Physical Fitness,* **10** (Dec., 1970), 211-216.

Moore, L.M., and Cooper, C., "Monthly Variations in Cardiovascular Activities and Respiratory Rates in Women," *American Journal of Physiology,* **64** (1923), 416-423.

_____ , and Barker, L., "Monthly Variations in Muscle Efficiency in Women," *American Journal of Physiology,* **64** (1923), 405-415.

Morimoto, T., Slabochova, Z., Naman, R.K., and Sargent, S., II, "Sex Differences in Physiological Reactions to Thermal Stress," *Journal of Applied Physiology,* **22** (1967), 526-532.

Morris, N.M., and Udry, J.R., "Variations in Pedometer Activity during the Menstrual Cycle," *Obstetrics and Gynecology,* **35** (1970), 199-201.

Morris, P.C., "A Comparative Study of Physical Measures of Women Athletes and Unselected College Women," Unpublished Ph.D. thesis, Temple University, 1960.

Mosher, C., "Normal Menstruation and Some of the Factors Modifying It," *Johns Hopkins Hospital Bulletin,* **12** (1901), 178-179.

Mynatt, C.V., "A Study of Differences in Selected Physical Performance Test Scores of Women in Tennessee Colleges," *Research Quarterly,* **31** (1960), 60-65.

*National Intramural Association Newsletter,* February 1972.

Niemineva, K., "Course of Delivery of Finnish Baseball Players and Swimmers," *Sports Medicine,* Ed. by M.J. Karvonen, Helsinki, 1953.

Nöcker, I., "Gründrisse der Biologie der Körperubüngen," *Berlin: Sportverlag,* (155), 399-410.

Norris, A.H., Lundy, T., and Shock, N.W., "Trends in Selected Indices of Body Composition in Men Between the Ages 30 and 80 Years," *Annals of the New York Academy of Sciences,* **110** (1963), 623.

Novak, L., "Age and Sex Differences in Body Density and Creatinine Excretion of High School Children," *Annals of the New York Academy of Sciences,* **110** (1963), 545.

_____ , "Physical Activity and Body Composition of Adolescent Boys," *Journal of the American Medical Association,* **197** (1966), 169.

Parizkova, J., "Total Body Fat and Skinfold Thickness in Children," *Metabolism & Clinical Experiments,* **10** (1961), 794-802.

_____, "Impact of Age, Diet, and Exercise on Man's Body Composition," *Annals of the New York Academy of Science,* **110** (1963), 661-674.

_____ , "Body Composition and Physical Fitness," *Current Anthropology,* **9** (1968), 273-287.

_____ , "Longitudinal Study of the Development of Body Composition and Body Build in Boys of Various Physique and Activity," *Human Biology,* **40** (1968, 1968b), 212-225.

_____ , "Body Composition and Exercise during Growth and Development," in *Physical Activity: Human Growth and Development*, New York: Academic Press, 1973.

Parizkova, J., and Poupa, O., "Some Metabolic Consequences of Adaptation to Muscular Work," *British Journal of Nutrition*, 17 (1963), 341-345.

Parnell, R.W., "Somatotyping by Physical Anthropometry," *American Journal of Physical Anthropology*, 12 (1954), 209-239.

Perbix, J., "Relationships between Somatotype and Motor Fitness in Women," *Research Quarterly*, 25 (1954), 84-90.

Pfeiffer, *Zenbralblatt für Gynaekologie* (1951), 17.

Phillips, M., "The Effect of the Menstrual Cycle on Heart Rate during and following Strenuous Exercise," Paper presented at the 80th meeting of the AAHPER, Minneapolis, Minnesota, 1963.

_____ , "The Effect of the Menstrual Cycle on Task Performance under Different Stressful Conditions," Paper presented at the 87th meeting of the AAHPER, Detroit, Michigan, 1971.

_____ , Fox, K., and Young, O., "Recommendations from Women Doctors and Gynecologists about Sports Activity for Girls," *Journal of Health, Physical Education, and Recreation*, 30 (December, 1959), 23-27.

Pierson, W.R., and Lockhart, A., "Effect of Menstruation on Simple Reaction and Movement Time," *British Medical Journal*, 1 (1963), 796-797.

Pool, J., Binkhorst, R.A., and Vos, J.A., "Some Anthropometric and Physiological Data in Relation to Performance of Top Female Gymnasts," *International Z. Angew. Physiol.*, 27 (1969), 329-338.

Profant, G.R., Early, R.G., Nilson, K.L., Kusumi, F., Hofer, V., and Bruce, R.A., "Responses to Maximal Exercise in Healthy Middle-aged Women," *Journal of Applied Physiology*, 33 (November, 1972), 595-599.

Pros, J.R., "A Gynecologist's Remarks on Women's Competitive Swimming," Teorie a praxe Tel. Vych (Prasha, USSR), No. 9, 1961. Abstract in *Journal of Sports Medicine and Physical Fitness*, 2 (1962), 122.

_____ , "Equestrian Dressage," *Encyclopedia of Sport Sciences and Medicine*, II[A] 32, Ed. by L. Larson, New York: The Macmillan Company, 1971.

Rasch, P.J., and Burke, R.K., *Kinesiology and Applied Anatomy*, Philadelphia: Lea & Febiger, 1967.

Raven, P.B., Drinkwater, B.L., and Horvath, S.M., "Cardiovascular Responses of Young Female Track Athletes during Exercise," *Medicine and Science in Sports*, 4 (1972), 205-209.

Richardson, R.J., Hupp, E.W., and Amos, R., "Changes in Creatinine Output and the Physical Condition of College Women Enrolled in a Program of Conditioning Exercises," *Sports Medicine and Physical Fitness*, 3 (Dec., 1968), 191-197.

Robinson, M.F., and Watson, P.E., "Day-to-day Variations in Body Weight of Young Women," *British Journal of Nutrition*, 19 (1965), 225-235.

Roskamm, H., "Optimum Patterns of Exercise for Healthy Adults," *Canadian Medical Association Journal*, **96** (1967), 167-169.

Saltin, B., and Astrand, P.O., "Maximal Oxygen Uptake in Athletes," *Journal of Applied Physiology*, **23** (1967), 353.

Scarbrough, K.L., "Central Processing of Adult Females of Divergent Age and Activity Levels," Unpublished Ph.D. dissertation, The University of Texas, 1973.

Schmotkin, *Archives of Gynakologie*, **97** (1912), 495. Referred to by I.L. Mackennan, "Observations on the Pulse Rate during the Human Menstrual Cycle," *Journal of Obstetrics and Gynocologie of the British Empire*, **61** (1954), 109-117.

Scott, G., and Tuttle, W., "Periodic Fluctuation in Physical Efficiency during the Menstrual Cycle," *Research Quarterly*, **3** (1932), 137-144.

Shaffer, T.E., "Principles of Growth and Development as Related to Girls Participating in Track and Field and Gymnastics," *Proceedings: First National Institute on Girls' Sports*, Washington, D.C.: AAHPER, 1964.

_____ , "Physiological Considerations of the Female Participant," in *Women in Sport: A National Research Conference*, University Park, Pa.: Pennsylvania State University, 1973.

Sheldon, W.H., "A Brief Communication on Somatotyping, Psychiatyping and other Sheldonian Delinquencies," Paper read at the Royal Society of Medicine, London, May 13, 1965.

_____ , Stevens, S.S., and Tucker, W.B., *The Varieties of Human Physique*, New York: Harper and Brothers, 1940.

Shepherd, R.J., "World Standards of Cardiovascular Performance," *Archives of Environmental Health*, **13** (1966), 664-672.

_____ , Allen, C., Bar-Or, O., Davies, C.T., Degre, S., Hedman, R., Ishii, I., Kaneko, M., LaCour, J.R., di Prampero, P.E., and Seliger, V., "The Working Capacity of Toronto Schoolchildren, Part I," *Canadian Medical Association Journal*, **100** (1969), 165-172.

Simmons, K., "The Brush Foundation Study of Child Growth and Development, II. Physical Growth and Development," *Monograph of Social Research in Child Development*, **9** (1944), Ser. No. 37, N.I.

Simonson, E., *Physiology of Work Capacity and Fatigue*, Springfield, Ill.: Charles C. Thomas, 1971.

Sinclair, C., "An Abstract of a Study of the Effects of Varying Degrees of Physical Activity during the Menstrual Cycle," *Research Quarterly*, **8** (1937), 32-37.

Singh, M., and Karpovich, P.V., "Strength of Forearm Flexors and Extensors in Men and Women," *Journal of Applied Physiology*, **25** (August, 1968), 177-180.

Sinning, W.E., "Body Composition, Cardiorespiratory Function, and Rule Changes in Women's Basketball," *Research Quarterly*, **44** (October, 1973), 313-321.

_____ , and Adrian, M.J., "Cardiorespiratory Changes in College Women due to a Season of Competitive Basketball," *Journal of Applied Physiology*, **25** (1968), 720-724.

_____ , and Lindberg, G.D., "Physical Characteristics of College Age Women Gymnasts," *Research Quarterly*, 43 (1972), 226-234.

Skerlj, B., Brozek, J., and Hunt, E.E., Jr., "Subcutaneous and Age Changes in Body Build and Body Form in Women," *American Journal of Physical Anthropology*, 11 (1953), 11.

Skubic, V., and Hodgkins, J., "Cardiac Response to Participation in Selected Individual and Dual Sports as Determined by Telemetry," *Research Quarterly*, 36 (October, 1965), 316-326.

_____ , and Hodgkins, J., "Relative Strenuousness of Selected Sports as Performed by Women," *Research Quarterly*, 38 (May, 1967), 305-316.

Sloan, A.W., "Effect of Training on Physical Fitness of Women Students," *Journal of Applied Physiology*, 16 (1961), 167-169.

_____ , Burt, J.J., and Blyth, C.S., "Estimation of Body Fat in Young Women," *Journal of Applied Physiology*, 17 (1962), 967.

Smith, W.E., and Kime, R.E., "Family," *Encyclopedia of Sports Sciences and Medicine*, III[c] 5, Ed. by L. Larson, New York: The Macmillan Company, 1971.

Sommer, B., "Menstrual Cycle Changes and Intellectual Performance," *Psychosomatic Medicine*, 34 (June, 1972), 263-269.

Southam, A.L., and Gonzaga, F.P., "Systematic Changes During the Menstrual Cycle," *American Journal of Obstetrics*, 91 (1965), 142-165.

Speroff, L., and Vandeweile, R.L., "Regulation of the Human Menstrual Cycle," *American Journal of Obstetrics and Gynecology*, 109 (January, 1971), 234-247.

Sprynarova, S., and Parizkova, J., "Comparison of the Functional, Circulatory and Respiratory Capacity in Girl Gymnasts and Swimmers," *Journal of Sports Medicine and Physical Fitness*, 9 (September, 1969), 165-171.

Stenn, P.G., and Klinge, V., "Relationship between the Menstrual Cycle and Bodily Activity in Humans," *Hormones and Behavior*, 3 (December, 1972), 297-305.

Stiles, M.H., "Olympic Doctors Face Controversial Problems: Sex Testing and Drug Use by Athletes," *Modern Medicine*, 36 (September, 1968), 60-64.

Tachezy, R., "Pseudohermaphroditism and Physical Efficiency," *Sports Medicine and Physical Fitness*, 9 (June, 1969), 119-122.

Tanner, J.M., "Current Advances in the Study of Physique," *The Lancet*, 260 (March, 1951), 574-579.

_____ , *Growth at Adolescence*, 2nd Edition, Oxford: Blackwell, 1962.

_____ , *The Physique of the Olympic Athlete*, London: George Allen & Unwin, 1964.

Tietze, *Medizinesche Welt*, 1606 (1939).

Timonen, J., and Procope, B., "Premenstrual Syndrome and Physical Exercise," *Acta Obstetriks Gynecologie Scandanavia*, 50 (1971), 331-337.

Tonks, C.M., Rack, P.H., and Rose, M.J., "Attempted Suicide and the Menstrual Cycle," *Journal of Psychosomatic Research*, 11 (1968), 319-323.

Truesdell, D., and Croxford, G., "Periodic Variations in Blood Pressure, Pulse, and the Physical Efficiency Test," *American Journal of Physiology,* 79 (1926), 112-118.

Tulloh, B., "The Physiologist and the Athlete," *Journal of Sports Medicine and Physical Fitness,* 9 (March, 1969), 54-55.

Tuttle, W.W., and Frey, H., "Study of the Physical Efficiency of College Women as Indicated by the Pulse-Ratio Test," *Research Quarterly,* 1 (1930), 17-25.

Ueland, K., Novy, M.J., and Metchalfe, J., "Cardiorespiratory Responses to Pregnancy and Exercise in Normal Women and Patients with Heart Disease," *American Journal of Obstetrics and Gynecology,* 115 (January, 1973), 4-10.

Ufland, J.M., Einfluss des Lebensalters, Geschlechts, der Konstitution und des Berufs auf die Kraft verschiedener Muskelgruppen; über die dynamometrischen Werte bei Mannern und bei-Frauen," *Arbeitsphysiology,* 7 (1933), 251-258.

Uflyand, U.M., *Physiology of Man's Motor System,* Leningrad: Medizina, 1965.

Ulrich, C., "Women and Sport," *Science and Medicine of Exercise and Sports,* Ed. by W.R. Johnson, New York: Harper & Bros., 1960.

Viville, G., *Archives of Gynakologie,* 97 (1912), 511. Referred to by I.L. MacKennon, "Observations on the Pulse Rate during the Human Menstrual Cycle," *Journal of Obstetrics and Gynaecology of the British Empire,* 61 (1954), 109-117, 1954.

Vogel, W., Broverman, D.M., and Klaiber, E.L., "EEG Responses in Regularly Menstruating Women and in Amenorrheic Women Treated with Ovarian Hormones," *Science,* 172 (1971), 388-391.

vonDobeln, W., "Human Standard and Maximal Rate in Relation to Fat-free Body Mass," *Acta Physiologica Scandinavian Supplement,* 126 (1956), 1.

Watson, P.E., and Robinson, M.F., "Variations in Body-Weight of Young Women During the Menstrual Cycle," *British Journal of Nutrition,* 19 (1965), 237-248.

Weinman, K.P., Slabochova, Z., Bernauer, E.M., Morimoto, T., and Sargent, F., II, "Reactions of Men and Women to Repeated Exposure to Humid Heat," *Journal of Applied Physiology,* 22 (1967), 533-538, 1967.

Well, J.B., Jokl, E., and Bohranen, J., "The Effect of Intensive Physical Training upon Body Composition of Adolescent Girls," *Journal of the Association of Physical and Mental Rehabilitation,* 17 (1963), 68-72.

Wessel, J., Ufer, A., VanHuss, W.D., and Cederquist, D., "Age Trends of Various Components of Body Composition and Functional Characteristics in Women Aged 20-69 Years," *Annals of the New York Academy of Science,* 110 (September, 1963), 608-622.

Wessel, J., and VanHuss, W.D., "The Influence of Physical Activity and Age on Exercise Adaptation of Women, 20-69 Years," *Sports Medicine and Physical Fitness,* 9 (1969), 173-180.

Westlake, D.J., "The Somatotypes of Female Track and Field Competitors," M.A. thesis, San Diego State College, San Diego, Calif., 1967.

Wilmore, J., "Maximal $O_2$ Intake and Its Relationship to Endurance Capacity on a Bicycle Ergometer," *Research Quarterly,* 40 (March, 1969), 203-210.

_____ , and **Sigerseth, P.O.**, "Physical Work Capacity of Young Girls, 7-13 Years of Age," *Journal of Applied Physiology*, **22** (1967), 923-928.

**Wyrick, W.**, "Effects of Exercise, Championship Level Competition, and Winning or Losing on Simple Reaction Time," Unpublished Research Report, 1972.

**Young, C., et al.,** "Body Composition of Young Women," *Journal of American Dietary Association*, **38** (1961), 332-340.

**Young, C.M., Blondin, J., Tensuan, R., and Fryer, J.H.**, "Body Composition Studies of 'Older' Women, Thirty to Seventy Years of Age," *Annals of the New York Academy of Sciences*, **110** (1963), 589.

**Younger, L.**, "A Comparison of Reaction and Movement Times of Women Athletes and Non-athletes," *Research Quarterly*, **30** (October, 1959), 349-355.

**Zaharieva, E.**, *Physical Culture and Women*, Sofia: Medizina i Fizkultura, 1961.

_____ , "Survey of Sportswomen at the Tokyo Olympics," *Journal of Sports Medicine and Physical Fitness*, **5** (December, 1965), 215-219.

_____ , "Olympic Participation by Women. Effects on Pregnancy and Childbirth," *Journal of the American Medical Association*, **221** (August, 1972), 992-995.

_____ , and **Sigler, J.J.G.**, "Maternidad y deporte," *Tokoginec Pract.*, (1963), 144-149.

**Zanta, L.**, *Arch. für gynak.* 78 (1966) 106, from King, J., "Concerning the Periodic Cardiovascular and Temperature Variations in Women," *American Journal of Physiology*, **34** (1914), 203-218.

**Zhovnavataya, O.D.**, "The Pulse, Arterial Pressure and Breathing in Women-Sportsmen in Various Phases of the Ovarian-Menstrual Cycle," *Theory and Practice of Physical Culture*, **9** (1962), 29-32. Trans. by Michael Yessis in *Index and Abstracts of Foreign Physical Education Literature*, **9** (1964), 70.

**Zimkin, N.V.**, *Physiological Characteristics of Strength, Speed, and Endurance*, Moskow: Fizkultura i Sport, 1956.

_____ , *Physiological Basis of Physical Culture and Sports*, Moscow: Fizkultura i Sport, 1955.

**Zoethout, D., and Tuttle, W.W.**, *Textbook of Physiology*, St. Louis: Mosby, 1952.

# Toward
# the Future

# Toward
# the Future

This final chapter of *The American Woman in Sport* is intended to be both a summary of the book and a "going beyond." The poet T.S. Eliot wrote: "Time present and time past/Are both perhaps present in time future." As sport for women moves toward new shapes in the future, its direction depends, in part, on where it has been and where it is. As with all things, it is continually changing shape.

The contemporary era is marked as a point in time in which there is intellectual acceptance of the American woman in sport. After a century of accomplishment, women in sport are finally an integral part of the American scene. As a result, a quantitative and qualitative increase in sport opportunities for women is beginning to take place. Success begets success!

Consonant with that acceptance is a liberalization of attitudes about the intensity with which women should compete and the kind of sports in which they can appropriately participate. The serious competitor is no longer considered unusual. Americans now care that women win Olympic medals, set records, beat the Russians in track, and win fame on the courts and fields, and in the pools of the world. Feminists, families, and even physical educators are beginning to understand the role that sport can play in forging the new woman.

More and more barriers to free choice of activities are falling as sportswomen win sympathy for their choices by demonstrating with their actions and skill that women are able to do and risk much more than anyone ever believed. The contemporary sport era has made it possible for the sportswoman to really extend herself. She has taken up the challenge and mastered new levels of skill and new heights of physical conditioning.

Time past and time present are shaping a direction for the future. But the substantive gains are insufficient. They do not yet satisfy even the current needs of women nor provide a situation that has the characteristic of simple justice. Despite the growth, the need for increased opportunities for girls and women at any age remains paramount. Schools, colleges, municipal recreation programs, industries, agencies, private clubs, national sport organizations—any place where sport is sponsored—will have to make an all-out effort for sportswomen if they wish to fulfill their declared responsibilities. Not one varsity team in a college is needed, but three, five, even ten may be appropriate for a popular sport. Scheduled national and international events for women should be doubled, tripled, quadrupled. The 4-to-1 ratio of athletes, men to women, on our Olympic teams needs equalizing. Every town and city with a recreation program should have a full range of women's sport competitions.

Generations of active sportswomen have proved that, given the opportunity, women find sport a meaningful element in their lives. There is no longer any excuse (if there ever was) for failing to provide half of the events, facilities, budgets, and leadership for half of the population. The financing of sport in large measure comes from public funds. It is patently illegal to discriminate in the use of facilities built with such financing. If a tax-supported or tax-exempt facility—such as a college arena—is used primarily by one sex to the exclusion of the other, illegal discrimination is taking place. If a town opens its fields and recreation centers to a group that practices discrimination, whether of race or sex—as does the Little League organization—the law is being broken. When tax-exempt organizations—such as churches—use part of their funds to sponsor men's teams and offer no comparable opportunities to women, they not only violate constitutional statutes, but appear to ignore their own moral precepts. When institutions which receive federal funds—as do virtually all colleges—award scholarships to take part in the educational endeavor called  sport to one sex and not the other, they are in conflict with the law and their stated purposes. In sum, in most situations, the decision to finance full sport programs for women, in *every way* comparable to those provided for men, is an action *required* by law and the ethical tradition which asserts that equal opportunity for *all* is the basis of American democracy.

In addition to more opportunities for participation, the sportswoman's needs in the future will be satisfied only if all restrictions are removed from her choice of activities. The women of the past and present have testified by their performance that they have the strength, endurance, and resiliency to take part in any kind of sport contest. The bones and organs and faces of young women are no more susceptible than those of young men to injury or disfigurement—and they are just as easily protected.

The past and the present make it clear that the future must hold opportunities for women to choose to experience body contact and/or high-risk sports. The denial of the exciting and challenging activities is unjust. Women want and must have the chance to feel their bodies competing against those of others, to demonstrate their courage in situations which risk life and limb, to know the pleasurable stress that is associated with the attempt to control one's personal fate through one's own abilities in a dangerous situation.

The needs of women in the future will not be satisfied unless a wide variety of roles in sport become widely available to them. Women must be given the responsibilies of coaches, officials, trainers, and administrators of sport programs. If necessary, opportunities must be made by regulation to compensate for a century of partial exclusion from these vital roles. The need and precedent for this have been amply set by other groups which have suffered discrimination.

Unquestionably, women's sport in the future must be more directly in the control of women. Sport organizations have shamefully ignored women's abilities to plan and organize competitions. The past and the present have demonstrated that the absence of women in roles of decision-making power has meant the unfair disbursement of funds to women, unequal conditions for performance, few opportunities, and a general lack of cognizance of women in sport. Boards of national organizations can and should give voting seats to women—and not just in a token manner.

Sports publications, television, newspapers, magazines have thus far failed to notice women in sport. By being unaware, they have deprecated the effort. In the future, sport for women must be brought out of the shadow of Victorian modesty into the openness of the late twentieth century. The past and the present have shown that women athletes, like their male counterparts, work to develop skill and take pride in their accomplishments. The measure of a sportswoman in the future should be her performance and not her appearance or personality.

Finally, to complete the prescription in good academic fashion, the future must tell us what the past and the present have not. Our lack of knowledge about women in sport must be dispelled by imaginative

Practicing to be the first woman to run the steeple chase. [Courtesy *Massachusetts Daily Collegian.*]

research. The sportswoman should no longer be ignored by scholars who study sport and athletes. Women and their sport must become the focus of inquiry for researchers if their potential in sport is ever to be realized. Priorities for studying the sportswoman should be set and proper conditions and procedures generated. A fair portion of the financing offered by governments, foundations, and educational institutions will have to be set aside for this effort if the needs of women in sport are to be met. Though each researcher will have her/his own conceptions of what is relevant and important to know, some immediate questions come to our minds:

- What are the effects on various psychological states of women's commitment to sport over a period of time?
- What are the potentials of the sport experience for influencing the quality of women's lives?
- What barriers inhibit the sportswoman from developing to her full potential as an athlete?
- What are the biophysical limitations on women as athletes?
- How can the positive aspects of the sport experience be maximized for women?
- How can institutions and organizations maximize their contribution to sport for women?
- What are appropriate sport relationships between men and women?
- What actions from the past provide models potentially good for the future of women in sport?

With this pointing toward the future our efforts are completed insofar as this book is concerned. The past and the present of women in sport have been described to the best of our abilities. The future is in the hands of teachers, parents, coaches, administrators, school boards, sportswriters, agencies, organizations, the general public, and the sportswoman herself. What happens to women in sport will depend on the willingness of all those who have an interest in and concern for the American sportswoman to join in a unified, cooperative, intense effort on her behalf.

# Index

# Index